MW00810824

EVERYMAN,
I WILL GO WITH THEE,
AND BE THY GUIDE,
IN THY MOST NEED
TO GO BY THY SIDE

LORD BYRON

BYRON'S TRAVELS

POEMS, LETTERS, AND JOURNALS

SELECTED AND INTRODUCED
BY FIONA STAFFORD

EVERYMAN'S LIBRARY

Alfred A. Knopf New York London Toronto

419

THIS IS A BORZOI BOOK
PUBLISHED BY ALFRED A. KNOPF

First included in Everyman's Library, 2024
Introduction copyright © 2024 by Fiona Stafford
Selection, Bibliography, Chronology and other editorial material
copyright © 2024 by Everyman's Library

All rights reserved. Published in the United States by Alfred A. Knopf,
a division of Penguin Random House LLC, New York, and in Canada by
Penguin Random House Canada Limited, Toronto. Distributed by
Penguin Random House LLC, New York. Published in the United
Kingdom by Everyman's Library, 50 Albemarle Street, London
W1S 4BD and distributed by Penguin Random House UK,
20 Vauxhall Bridge Road, London SW1V 2SA.

everymanslibrary.com
www.everymanslibrary.co.uk

ISBN: 978-1-101-90842-6 (US)
978-1-84159-419-4 (UK)

A CIP catalogue reference for this book is available from the
British Library

Typography by Peter B. Willberg
Book design by Barbara de Wilde and Carol Devine Carson
Typeset in the UK by Input Data Services Ltd, Bridgwater, Somerset
Printed and bound in Germany by GGP Media GmbH, Pössneck

Contents

Introduction   xv
Note on the Text   xxvi
Select Bibliography   xxviii
Chronology   xxxii
Byron's Correspondents   xlv

SCOTLAND

Don Juan X, 17–19   3
Lachin Y Gair   5
Song ("When I rov'd, a young Highlander")   7
Stanzas ("I would I were a careless child")   9
Letter to John Murray, October 16th, 1820   11

HARROW

Don Juan I, 40–42   13
Inscriptions in *Homeri Ilias* (1804)   15
Letters to Mrs Catherine Gordon Byron, June 23rd–30th, 1803;
    September 15th?, 1803; May 1st–10th, 1804?   16
Letters to Augusta Byron, March 22nd, 1804; November 2nd,
    1804; November 11th, 1804   18
Lines Written Beneath an Elm, in the Churchyard of Harrow
    on the Hill   24

SOUTHWELL, NOTTINGHAMSHIRE

Epitaph on John Adams of Southwell, A Carrier who died of
    Drunkenness   27
Letters to Augusta Byron, April 23rd, 1805; July 2nd, 1805;
    August 10th, 1805   29
Letter to Charles David Gordon, August 4th, 1805   32
Letter to Edward Noel Long, August 9th, 1806   33
Letter to the Earl of Clare, November 4th, 1806   34
Letters to Edward Noel Long, April 16th, 1807; May 1st, 1807   35

CAMBRIDGE

Don Juan I, 52–53   39
Reading List (1807)   41
Letters to Elizabeth Bridget Pigot, June 30th, 1807;
    July 5th, 1807; October 26th, 1807   48
To Thyrza   53
Letter to John Cam Hobhouse, October 22nd, 1811   55

NEWSTEAD ABBEY

Don Juan XVI, 16–18   57
To an Oak in the Garden of Newstead Abbey, planted by
    the Author in the 9th Year of his age   59
Letter to Francis Hodgson, November 18th, 1808   61
Inscription on the Monument of a Newfoundland Dog   62
Letter to the Hon. Augusta Leigh, December 14th, 1808   63
Don Juan XIII, 55–72   64
Letter to John Murray, November 19th, 1820 (with
    reminiscence of Newstead, May 1809)   70
Letter to Scrope Berdmore Davies, August 7th, 1811   75
Letter to John Cam Hobhouse, August 10th, 1811   75
Letter to Francis Hodgson, September 25th, 1811   77

FALMOUTH, CORNWALL

from Verse Letter to Francis Hodgson, June 30th, 1809   79
Letter to Mrs. Catherine Gordon Byron, June 22nd, 1809   81
Letter to Charles Skinner Matthews, June 22nd, 1809   82
Letter to Edward Ellice, June 25th, 1809   82
Letter to Francis Hodgson, June 25th, 1809   83
Childe Harold's Pilgrimage I, 6–13 (including "Harold's
    Good Night")   85

SPAIN AND PORTUGAL

Childe Harold's Pilgrimage I, 14, 16   91
Letters to Francis Hodgson, July 16th, 1809;
    August 6th, 1809   93
Childe Harold's Pilgrimage I, 71–80   95

Letter to Mrs. Catherine Gordon Byron, August 11th, 1809   99
Don Juan I, 90–187   103

THE MEDITERRANEAN

Childe Harold's Pilgrimage I, 20   131
Letter to Mrs. Catherine Gordon Byron,
   September 15th, 1809   133
Don Juan II, 26–114   134

ALBANIA

Childe Harold's Pilgrimage II, 42   159
Letter to John Hanson, September 29th, 1809   161
Letter to Mrs. Catherine Gordon Byron,
   November 12th, 1809   161

TURKEY

from Verse Letter to Francis Hodgson, June 30th, 1809   169
Don Juan IV, 76–78   171
Letters to Mrs. Catherine Gordon Byron, March 19th, 1810;
   April 10th, 1810; April 17th 1810   172
Letter to Henry Drury, May 3rd, 1810   174
Letter to Francis Hodgson, May 5th, 1810   177
Written After Swimming from Sestos to Abydos,
   May 9th, 1810   180
Childe Harold's Pilgrimage II, 79–81   181
Letters to Mrs. Catherine Gordon Byron, May 18th, 1810;
   May 24th, 1810; June 28th, 1810   182
Letter to Robert Adair, July 4th, 1810   186

GREECE

Childe Harold's Pilgrimage II, 73, 85–86   189
Don Juan II, 177–194   191
Letters to Mrs. Catherine Gordon Byron, July 20th, 1810;
   July 30th, 1810   197
Letters to John Cam Hobhouse, August 16th, 1810;
   August 23rd, 1810; September 25th, 1810   201

Letter to Mrs. Catherine Gordon Byron, October 2nd, 1810   205
Letter to Francis Hodgson, November 14th, 1810   206
Don Juan III, 84–89 (including "The Isles of Greece")   208
Letter to Francis Hodgson, January 20th, 1811   214
Letters to Mrs. Catherine Gordon Byron, January 14th, 1811;
    February 28th, 1811   216

THE VOYAGE HOME

Don Juan X, 64, 66   219
Letter to Francis Hodgson, June 29th, 1811   221
Letter to John Cam Hobhouse, July 2nd, 1811   222
Letter to Henry Drury, July 7th, 1811   223
Letter to John M. B. Pigot, August 2nd, 1811   225

LONDON

Don Juan X, 82   227
Letters to Elizabeth Bridget Pigot, August 2nd, 1807;
    August 11th, 1807   229
Letters to John Cam Hobhouse, February 29th, 1808;
    March 14th, 1808   232
Letter to Francis Hodgson, February 16th, 1812   234
Letter to Lord Holland, February 25th, 1812   235
Letters to Lady Caroline Lamb, April, 1812?; May 19th, 1812?   237
Letter to Thomas Moore, May 20th, 1812   238

CHELTENHAM AND EYWOOD

Don Juan XI, 33   241
Letters to Lady Melbourne, September 13th, 1812;
    October 30th, 1812   243
Letters to Lady Caroline Lamb, November 1812?   247
Letter to Lady Melbourne, March 18th, 1813   247

LONDON ONCE MORE

Don Juan XI, 65–67   249
Letters to Lady Melbourne, August 20th, 1813;
    August 23rd, 1813   251

Letters to Annabella Milbanke, September 6th, 1813;
    September 26th, 1813; November 29th, 1813 — 253
Letter to Lady Melbourne, November 25th, 1813 — 260
from Journal, November 14th 1813–April 19th, 1814 — 263
Letters to Thomas Moore, April 9th, 1814;
    April 20th, 1814 — 303
She Walks in Beauty, like the Night — 307
Letter to Leigh Hunt, October 30th, 1815 — 308

ENGLISH TRAVELS

Don Juan X, 28 — 311
Letter to Thomas Moore, August 3rd, 1814 — 313
Letter to Lady Melbourne, September 18th, 1814 — 315
Letters to Annabella Milbanke, September 18th, 1814;
    September 19th, 1814; September 20th, 1814;
    December 25th, 1814 — 315
Letter to Lady Melbourne, January 3rd, 1815 — 319
Letter to Thomas Moore, January 10th, 1815 — 320

OFF TO THE CONTINENT

Don Juan II, 12–13 — 321
Letters to Lady Byron, February 3rd, 1816; February 5th, 1816;
    February 15th, 1816; April 14th, 1816 — 323
Childe Harold's Pilgrimage III, 1–9 — 327
Letter to Augusta Leigh, April 24th?, 1816 — 330
Letter to John Cam Hobhouse, May 1st, 1816 — 330
Letter to Augusta Leigh, May 1st, 1816 — 332
Childe Harold's Pilgrimage III, 17–18, 21–28 — 334

SWITZERLAND

Childe Harold's Pilgrimage III, 61 — 339
Sonnet on Chillon — 341
Darkness — 342
Stanzas to Augusta — 345
Childe Harold's Pilgrimage III, 68–75, 85–90, 92–97 — 347
Letter to John Cam Hobhouse, June 23rd, 1816 — 354

Letters to John Murray, June 27th, 1816; August 28th, 1816;
    September 30th, 1816   355
Letters to Augusta Leigh, September 8th, 1816;
    September 17th, 1816   358
Alpine Journal, September 18th, 1816   362
Manfred I, ii   373

ITALY

Childe Harold's Pilgrimage IV, 26   377
Beppo, 41–46   379

MILAN

Don Juan II, 209–210   381
Letters to Augusta Leigh, October 13th, 1816;
    October 15th, 1816   383
Letter to John Murray, November 1st, 1816   384
Letter to Thomas Moore, November 6th, 1816   385

VENICE

Venice: An Ode, 1–4   389
Childe Harold's Pilgrimage IV, 1–4, 18–19   391
Letter to Thomas Moore, November 17th, 1816   393
Letter to Augusta Leigh, December 19th, 1816   395
Letter to John Murray, December 27th, 1816   397
Letter to Douglas Kinnaird, January 20th, 1817   399
Beppo, 10–20   403
Letters to Thomas Moore, February 28th, 1817 (including
    "So we'll go no more a roving"); April 11th, 1817   407

FOLIGNO, UMBRIA

Don Juan V, 52   411
Letter to John Murray, April 26th, 1817   413

VENICE AGAIN

Don Juan I, 61–63   415
Letters to John Murray, June 4th, 1817; October 12th, 1817;
    August 1st, 1819   417
Letter to Thomas Moore, February 2nd, 1818   429
Letter to Richard Belgrave Hoppner, February 28th, 1818   430
from Letter to Thomas Moore, June 1st, 1818   431
Letter to John Murray, June 18th, 1818   432
Letter to James Wedderburn Webster, September 8th, 1818   433
Letter to Augusta Leigh, September 21st, 1818   435
Letter to John Cam Hobhouse, April 6th, 1819   437
Letter to John Murray, April 6th, 1819   439
Letter, in translation, to Countess Teresa Guiccioli,
    April 22nd, 1819   440
Letter to Douglas Kinnaird, April 24th, 1819   443
Letter to John Murray, May 15th, 1819   444
Letter to Augusta Leigh, May 17th, 1819   447
Letter to John Cam Hobhouse, October 3rd, 1819   448
Letters to Douglas Kinnaird, October 26th, 1819;
    November 16th, 1819   451
Letter to John Cam Hobhouse, November 20th, 1819   455
Letter to Augusta Leigh, November 28th, 1819   458
Letter to John Murray, December 10th, 1819   460

BOLOGNA

Childe Harold's Pilgrimage IV, 42   463
Letter to Richard Belgrave Hoppner, June 6th, 1819   465
To the Po. June 2nd 1819   468
Letters to John Murray, August 12th, 1819;
    August 29th, 1819   470

RAVENNA

Beppo, 88–90   477
Letter to John Murray, June 29th, 1819   479
Letter to Augusta Leigh, July 26th, 1819   480
Letter to Thomas Moore, January 2nd, 1820   482

Letters to John Murray, February 21st, 1820;
    March 14th, 1820   485
Letter to Harriette Wilson, March 30th, 1820   489
Letters to John Murray, April 16th, 1820; April 23rd, 1820   490
Letter to Thomas Moore, July 13th, 1820   494
Letter, in translation, to Countess Teresa Giuccioli,
    September 9th, 1820   497
Letter to Richard Belgrave Hoppner, September 10th, 1820   498
Letter to Augusta Leigh, October 18th?, 1820   498
Letter to Thomas Moore, December 9th, 1820   500
Ravenna Journal, January 4th–February 27th, 1821   504
Letter to John Murray, February 21st, 1821   545
Letter to Percy Bysshe Shelley, April 26th 1821   548
Letter to Richard Belgrave Hoppner, May 11th, 1821   550
Letters to John Murray, May 19th, 1821; July 22nd, 1821   551
Letter, in translation, to Countess Teresa Guiccioli,
    August [16th], 1821   555
Letter to Douglas Kinnaird, August 31st, 1821   556
Letter to Augusta Leigh, September 13th, 1821   556
Letter to Lady Byron, September 14th, 1821   557
Letter to Thomas Moore, September 19th, 1821   558
Letter to John Murray, September 24th, 1821   561
Letter to Thomas Moore, October 1st, 1821   564
Letter to Augusta Leigh, October 5th, 1821   565

PISA

When Coldness Wraps this Suffering Clay, 1–4   569
from Detached Thoughts, October 15th, 1821–
    May 18th, 1822   571
Letters to John Murray, December 4th, 1821;
    April 22nd, 1822   593
Letter to Percy Bysshe Shelley, April 23rd, 1822   595
Letter to Sir Walter Scott, May 4th 1822   595
Letter to John Murray, May 26th, 1822   597
Letter to Captain Daniel Roberts, July 14th, 1822   598
Letter to Edward J. Dawkins, July 15th, 1822   598
Letter to Douglas Kinnaird, July 19th, 1822   598

Letter to John Murray, August 3rd, 1822   599
Letters to Thomas Moore, August 8th, 1822;
    August 27th, 1822   600

GENOA AND LIVORNO

Don Juan X, 4   605
Letters to Augusta Leigh, October 20th, 1822;
    November 7th, 1822   607
Letter to Mary Shelley, [November 16th?], 1822   609
Letter to John Murray, December 25th, 1822   610
Letter to Edward Le Mesurier, R.N., May 5th, 1823   613
Letter to John Bowring, May 12th, 1823   613
Letter to Henri Beyle (Stendhal), May 29th, 1823   617
Letter to Edward John Trelawny, June 15th, 1823   618
Letter to Countess Teresa Guiccioli, July 22nd, 1823   618
Letter to Johann Wolfgang von Goethe, July 22nd, 1823   619

CEPHALONIA

Don Juan VII, 79–81   621
Letter to Countess Teresa Guiccioli, September 11th, 1823   623
Letter to John Cam Hobhouse, September 11th, 1823   623
Journal in Cephalonia, June 19th, 1823   628
Letter to Countess Teresa Guiccioli, October 7th, 1823   636
Letter to Charles F. Barry, October 9th, 1823   636
Letter to Colonel John Duffie, October 9th, 1823   636
Letter to Augusta Leigh, October 12th, 1823   637
Letter, in translation, to Prince Alexander Mavrocordatos,
    December 2nd, 1823   641

MISSALONGHI

Don Juan XV, 99   643
Letter to Lord Sydney Osborne, January 7th, 1824   645
Letter to Charles Hancock, January 13th, 1824   646
Letter, in translation, to Andreas Londos,
    January 30th, 1824   648
Letter to Charles Hancock, February 5th, 1824   649

Journal, February 15th, 1824   654
Letter to Mr. Mayer, February 21st, 1824?   656
Letter to Augusta Leigh, February 23rd, 1824   656
Letter to Countess Teresa Guiccioli, February 24th, 1824   658
Letter to John Murray, February 25th, 1824   658
Letter to John Bowring, March 30th, 1824   660
Letter to the Earl of Clare, March 31st, 1824   662

On this day I complete my thirty sixth year,
    January 22nd, 1824   664

Introduction

Unsettled and unsettling. The life, works and times of George Noel Gordon, Lord Byron, were both. Born in January 1788, the year before the French Revolution, coming of age while the Napoleonic Wars were raging, and dying in 1824, in the midst of the Greek War of Independence, Byron's life spanned one of the most turbulent eras of European history. As the most famous poet of the age, loved, resented, admired, celebrated, vilified and, ultimately, lamented across the Western world, Byron gave voice to the endlessly shifting experience of a generation, while remaining unique and irreplaceable. A peer who stood up for workers, a lover of women and men, a British aristocrat and a cosmopolitan, a poet who excelled in prose, a satirist and songwriter, a gregarious outsider, a man of action and cool observer, Byron embodied many of the tensions of his day, while negotiating the peculiar challenges of his own circumstances. From his earliest years, Byron was conscious of the past: pride in his own lineage was amplified by a fascination with history. Among the many attractions of Lord Delawarr, a younger boy at Harrow, as he explained to his beloved half-sister Augusta, was that "one of our forefathers in Charles the 1st's time married into their family".[1] At the same time, he was always making plans for the future, both immediate and longer term. As a schoolboy at Harrow, he wrote to his mother, "the way to *riches*, to *Greatness* lies before me. I can, I will cut myself a path through the world or perish in the attempt."[2] Both elegiac and prophetic by nature, Byron also revelled in first-hand experience. Irrespective of whatever might be discovered through reading and learning, he knew that the world was out there to be seen, heard, felt, and enjoyed. The quintessential Romantic traveller, Byron was forever on the move, forever torn by ties and tomorrows.

Where did Byron come from? Although he made much of his Scottish heritage ("half a Scot by birth, and bred /A whole one", as he put it in *Don Juan*), he was born and baptized in London.[3] His mother, Catherine Gordon, was a Scottish heiress, whose family inheritance disappeared rapidly after her marriage to a wayward English widower, John ("Jack") Byron in 1785.[4] Their only son was still a toddler when his parents moved to Aberdeen, where they lived together for a few weeks, before taking separate residences in the same street. Within a year, Jack, once more on the run from creditors, headed for Revolutionary France, leaving his wife and child behind in Aberdeen. He died of tuberculosis in 1791 at the age of thirty-six. Little George grew up with Catherine's unmanageable burden of grief, loss, anger and anxiety, as well as her intense maternal devotion and ambition. He also had to cope with a club foot and the unkind reactions provoked by his lameness. When he was six, the death of his second cousin William, in Corsica, made the young boy heir apparent to the title and estates of the Byron family. He was at school when he learned, four years later, that his great uncle, the 5th Baron Byron of Rochdale, was dead. George was now Lord Byron, and at the start of a highly individual journey to becoming "Lord Byron".

Catherine set off for Nottinghamshire with her son in the summer of 1798 to visit the Byrons' ancestral home, the somewhat dilapidated Newstead Abbey in Sherwood Forest. As the family seat, Newstead was now the official centre of his life, but still Byron found himself being packed off to Nottingham to have his foot treated before going south to school, first in Dulwich and then at Harrow. During vacations from school, and later Cambridge, he spent most of his time in London or Burgage Manor, the handsome house occupied by his mother in the small cathedral town of Southwell, in Nottinghamshire. Newstead Abbey, though close at hand, was rented out to Lord Grey until Byron came of age. It was not until 1808 that Byron finally took full possession of his ancestral seat and set about renovation on a grand scale. But within months, he was setting off with his Cambridge friend, John Cam Hobhouse, on a two-year voyage that would take him to Portugal and Spain, across the Mediterranean via Sardinia, Malta and Sicily to Albania, Turkey and Greece. By now a published poet, he wanted to see the world – his estates would still be there when he got back. When he did finally return to Newstead in the summer of 1811, he arrived too late to see his mother before she died.

Throughout his teens, Byron's life had been divided geographically and emotionally. In London or Nottinghamshire, living with his mother and an abusive nurse, he was the only child. At school and university, bereft of female influence, he was one among many. If being the sole focus of his mother's attention was oppressive, the experience of being no one's sole focus was equally difficult. He wanted to stand out from the crowd, but on his own terms, as his carefully cultivated personal image, elaborate costumes, heroic gestures and menagerie of unusual pets make obvious. The young man who took a tame bear to Cambridge because of a College prohibition on pet dogs, who would go on to swim the Hellespont, address the House of Lords, pose for his portrait in Albanian dress, race up the Grand Canal in Venice and join the fight for Greek Independence was not a man for the shadows. Byron needed attention and he knew how to get it. His acute awareness of an attentive audience also intensified a conflicting impulse towards silence, secrecy and escape. For all the drinking binges, society soirées and riotous parties, there were many days of soda-water, near starvation and solitude. Excess and self-denial acted like centripetal and centrifugal forces on his being.

Although he knew from the beginning that "Lord Byron" was born to command centre stage, the arena always seemed to be slipping off into the distance. Wherever he was, whatever he was doing, the present was everything and yet never quite enough. Driven to excellence and experience, Byron remained unsatisfied. The poet Thomas Moore, who met Byron on his return from the Eastern Mediterranean, was immediately struck by "a mind too inquisitive and excursive to be imprisoned".[5] Byron was constantly on the move, mentally and physically, making "travel" an essential aspect of his character. When Moore came to write his friend's biography, he emphasized Byron's restless intelligence and related demand for independence, recognizing "the powers and movements of a mind like Byron's, which might well be allowed to take a privileged direction of its own".[6] Never inclined to take a standard route, Byron preferred to make his own way through life and the world, leaving rich written trails for others to follow.

Rarely resident in any one place for more than a few consecutive months – often no longer than a few weeks or days – Byron was always making plans for future travels or travelling mentally into places he had known. His early poems look back wistfully on the young Highlander roaming free through Scottish mountains and

lochs or elegize his favourite haunts at Harrow. The ruined cloisters of Newstead Abbey inspired thoughts of medieval ancestors,
whose fame would sustain their young descendant as he left them
far behind. Byron is a poet of departures: from his earliest poems
to Childe Harold's famous "Good Night", from the melancholy,
morning-after lyric sent from the Venetian carnival, "So we'll go
no more a roving", to his late reflection "On this day I complete
my thirty-sixth year", he anticipated the aftermath almost before
enjoying the experience. Though he set off on horse, by carriage or
sailing ship often enough, embarkation rarely brought unalloyed
hope: all too often regret, unease and even dread were hovering
nearby. The bleak dream of universal destruction in "Darkness"
was a magnified version of perennial anxieties, which seep into his
writings, bringing the brighter moments into relief.

The need to be on the move meant a succession of temporary
residences and brief sojourns, with ties being both severed and
secured as he went on his way. Many of his letters and journals are
attempts to re-create through words what he had left behind – and
to emphasize what he retained. His Alpine Journal, written after
leaving England, his wife Annabella and their baby daughter amid
rumours of insanity and incest in 1816, was at once a vivid record
of a mountain excursion and an affirmation of love for Augusta.
Notes on the weather, the different peaks, the glaciers, the state
of the bed sheets or the tourists ("on our return met an English
party in a carriage—a lady in it fast asleep!—fast asleep in the most
anti-narcotic spot in the world—excellent") are punctuated by the
most tender addresses to "dearest Augusta".[7]

Writing was a way of arresting and sharing experience, of resist-
ing time's destructive tendency and collapsing painful distances.
When he was composing *Don Juan* three years later, Byron acknowledged the power of the written word to create links through
time and space:

> But words are things, and a small drop of ink,
>   Falling like dew, upon a thought, produces
> That which makes thousands, perhaps millions, think;
>   'Tis strange, the shortest letter which man uses
> Instead of speech, may form a lasting link
>   Of ages; to what straits old Time reduces

Frail man, when paper—even a rag like this,
Survives himself, his tomb, and all that's his.

(*Don Juan*, canto III, 88)

Letters could last longer than people and so offered a means to preserve feelings and thoughts, however fleeting. Despite the self-mockery of the preceding stanza, with its witty dismissal of poets as "liars", who "take all colours—like the hands of dyers", Byron was celebrating the redemptive power of words. A skilfully handled pen could not only arrest the endless flow of experience, but also create connections to distant readers, while acting as a catalyst for new ideas. Such faith in writing, though persistently undercut by jokes, was borne out by his own voluminous outpourings.

Given what his writings reveal of his experiences between the ages of eighteen and thirty-six, it is remarkable that Byron had time to write so much. While long hours at sea afforded plenty of time for composition, most of his life seems to have been very fully occupied. The creative genius who dashed off poem after poem, letter after letter, between riding, swimming, partying, dining, conversing, arguing, laughing, loving, hating, talking and travelling must have very much enjoyed writing. The sheer quantity of poems, letters, journals and other jottings suggest that it was as important to him as anything in his life – and may well have been the central enduring passion.

Compulsive travelling meant compulsive composition – and vice versa. Words poured out of Byron – wherever he was, he was writing. As he confessed, or boasted, to Moore, *The Bride of Abydos* was "written in four, and the Corsair in ten days".[8] For Byron, writing was inseparable from the physical world, as evident in his reference to poetry as "the lava of the imagination whose eruption prevents an earth-quake".[9] It's a fiery, violent version of Wordsworth's definition of poetry as "the spontaneous overflow of powerful feelings".[10] Byron's eruptions were much more explosive. Although he later dismissed such volcanic imagery as "a tired metaphor", he still strove to unite the concrete and abstract – "words are things".[11] In Venice, where he revelled in a physical culture unlike anything encountered before, Byron realized the direct connection between his actions and his art. In a memorable letter to his old friend Douglas Kinnaird, he defended his controversial new poem:

As to "Don Juan"—confess—confess—you dog—and be candid—that it is the sublime of *that there* sort of writing—it may be bawdy—but is it not good English?—it may be profligate—but is it not *life*, is it not *the thing*?—Could any man have written it—who has not lived in the world?[12]

Byron's insatiable appetite for immediate experience, for living to the full regardless of the consequences, was being immortalized in ink – but the same impulses that powered *Don Juan* are to be found in his travel letters, too. The story of Margharita Cogni, as recounted to John Murray from Ravenna, has all the melodrama, colour and comic timing of Byron's greatest poetry.[13]

If his poetry demonstrates a natural creative talent and mastery of language and form, his letters convey a powerful impulse to share experience and entertain friends. The difference in tone, style and content from correspondent to correspondent reveals not only his understanding of how to engage a reader, but also a deep sensitivity to the individuals he addressed. He knew what interested different friends, and what kind of an impression he made. A letter to his Southwell friend Eliza Pigot offers a comic self-portrait of the undergraduate:

I get awkward in my academic habiliments, for want of practice, got up in a Window to hear the Oratorio at St. Mary's, popped down in the middle of the *Messiah*, tore a *woeful rent* in the Back of my best black Silk gown, & damaged an *egregious pair* of Breeches, mem.—never tumble from a church window, during Service.[14]

A letter to Lady Melbourne dramatizes an internal monologue from a deserted London:

Town is empty but not the worse for that—it is a delight of a place now there's no one in it—I am totally & unutterably possessed by the ineffable power of Indolence—I see no one—I say nothing—I do nothing—and I wish for noth—oh yes—I wish to see you—& next to that—to hear from you.[15]

Such thoughtful fluency reveals an irresistible combination of affection, mental agility, and sense of humour.

The surviving letters sent from his first major expedition – the voyage from Falmouth to the Eastern Mediterranean – show a travel writer in the making, sending lively accounts of cities, land-scapes, incidents and memorable encounters. From an opera box in Spain to the Ionian bay where the Battle of Actium took place, from the women of Cadiz to an audience with Ali Pasha in his mountain refuge in Albania, Byron was observing attitudes, man-ners, architecture, dress, while soaking up the atmosphere of each distinctive place. What he selected to share with correspondents depended not just on what he had seen, but also what he thought the recipient might like to see. As he waited in Falmouth for a favourable wind, he told his mother about the German servant he had hired, his solicitor about where business letters should be sent, his friend Edward Ellice about the claret and Quakers, and his Cambridge crony Matthews about the "Hyacinths & other flowers" of this "delectable region".[16]

Since most of the voyage letters were written for his mother, Byron's records of his first Mediterranean travels are tailored ac-cordingly. While this may have led to a certain restraint, it also allows glimpses of a very human writer – for instance when he tells her how Ali Pasha's ten-year-old grandson asked him "how I came to travel about so *young*, without any body to take care of me".[17] Byron's letters show a young man far from home, often relishing the freedom, sometimes in need of reassurance. The correspond-ence also embodies the difficulty of exchanging letters between different ports in wartime Europe, as increasingly anxious letters sent in the absence of any replies demonstrate both the enormity of his expedition and the importance of emotional lifelines.

A highlight of the trip was swimming across the Dardanelles – or, as Byron referred to it, the Hellespont. The strait was familiar to every nineteenth-century schoolboy because of Troy's situation at its confluence with the Aegean and its other crucial role in the story of Hero and Leander. For a strong, fearless, classically educated swimmer, the opportunity to equal Leander's legendary feat was not to be missed, even though, as Byron admitted to his mother, "I had no *Hero* to receive me on the other shore".[18] Understand-ably proud of his success (not least because the first attempt had been thwarted by adverse winds and tides), Byron recounted his achievement to his friends Francis Hodgson, Henry Drury, John Hanson, Edward Ellice and Robert Dallas, as well as including the tale in three separate letters to his mother. While Hodgson, Hanson and Ellice received only offhand references to Byron's crossing, Drury was given details of the conditions, the distance and the effort required, while to Dallas the feat was presented as Byron's "only remarkable personal achievement".[19] Throughout his travels in Turkey and Greece, Byron was reminded of his classical education and testing the tales against what he found to be the facts. Swimming the treacherous Hellespont was a feat to equal the ancient heroes, and yet he was conscious that it might provoke ridicule from friends such as Dallas. His poem "Written After Swimming from Sestos to Abydos" pre-empts any mockery by puncturing his attempt to match Leander with comic bathos and a rhyme worthy of *Don Juan*:

> 'Twere hard to say who fared the best:
>   Sad mortals! thus the Gods still plague you!
> He lost his labour, I my jest:
>   For he was drown'd, and I've the ague.[20]

Byron's desire to try himself mentally and physically constantly collided with his awareness that life would always intervene to trip up the would-be hero. The greatest plans so often ended in frustration – and laughter. Though driven to action in spite of the odds, Byron's ability to observe himself through others' eyes gave him a rare comic brilliance, which developed in his travel letters before finding perfect poetic form in *Don Juan*.

The multi-faceted character of Byron's travel writing is even more obvious in his Alpine sojourn than in the earlier voyage to the Levant. The variety of the Alpine Journal offers a very different perspective from the melancholy poems published in 1816, which saw self-exiled Harold setting out once more and the prisoner of Chillon chained in solitary confinement. The many layers and shifting tone of the travel writings reappear in *Don Juan* through the dual perspectives of the hapless protagonist and worldly narrator. As young Juan travels from country to country, beginning in Spain, washed ashore in Greece, sold as a slave into a Turkish harem, escaping into the Russian army, before finally landing in England, Byron was able to return imaginatively to his earlier experiences, while maintaining a cool distance in the telling.

Casting himself as the grand Napoleon of rhyme, now toppled by newer poets and a fickle readership, Byron reflected wryly on his perennial lust for new lands to conquer and the concomitant disappointments. The mock-heroic impulse and the urge to compose travelogues were very closely aligned: the writer who was driven on and on to fresh starts and discoveries, to repeated reminders of the world's absurdities, excelled in both.

W. H. Auden, commissioned to write a travel book about Iceland in 1936, was on a cross-country bus when it struck him that Byron was the perfect role model for his own project. His chatty verse "Letter to Lord Byron" would have "very little to do with Iceland" – instead it would be "a description of an effect of travelling in distant places which is to make one reflect on one's past and one's culture from the outside".[21] He had been reading *Don Juan* when he realized that the most congenial travel writing was not the dutiful description found in guide books, but something more dynamic, personal and, above all, amusing. Local history and physical terrain had their place, but the best travel writing had as much to do with the writer, his opinions, interactions and interest in his readers. When well-managed, it was (as Laurence Sterne also knew), another name for conversation:

> Art, if it doesn't start there, at least ends,
> Whether aesthetics like the thought or not,
> In an attempt to entertain our friends[22]

This is as good an insight into Byron's travel writings as into Auden and MacNeice's *Letters from Iceland*. To read the travelling Byron is to be entertained and addressed as a friend.

As we accompany Byron through letters, poems and places, we begin to see how he found himself through his awareness of others. Whether friends or rivals, his audience was never out of mind. To follow so mercurial a figure was at once enticing and impossible for his contemporaries, and the challenge has not become easier with the passage of time. Despite the superbly edited texts, well-researched biographies and illuminating critical works that have appeared over the two centuries since his death, Byron remains elusive. This is why his own words continue to intrigue, surprise, provoke and delight.

The selection that follows offers Byron's own writings in and about many of the places he visited. Sometimes he wrote immediately about his latest encounters, at other times years might pass before he drew on his experience. While *Beppo* burst from his internal magma field soon after he landed in Venice, almost a decade elapsed between his visit to Constantinople and the Turkish cantos of *Don Juan*. He had dashed off his popular Turkish tales in the interim, but still the travels of 1810 were there to inform his comic epic. Although this book follows Byron from place to place, his reflections vary with the years and with his audience, making every response to society, every observation somehow provisional. Byron's "Newstead" is complicated by retrospect, whether in a poem written on site but recalling a tree-planting a few years before, or in later reminiscences sent to Murray from Ravenna, or in the light of more recent developments which have turned the Abbey into a tourist attraction, wedding venue and conference centre.[23]

Byron's travels make mental travellers of us all: whether or not the places he passed through are familiar from first-hand or virtual experience, from reading, viewing or listening, from maps and itineraries or memory and imagination, they can never be quite the same again once Byron has entered the scene. Though provisional and shifting his travel writing may be, it still makes a mark. The opening line of *Childe Harold* IV, "I stood in Venice, on the Bridge of Sighs", is apt to surface at the Doge's Palace, while each passing gondola seems to promise the ghost of Byron, his inamorata, or his friends and faithful dogs. Seville will always be known to his readers as "a pleasant city, /Famous for oranges and women", while the memorable rhymes of "Cadiz" and "graceful ladies", or of "Ancona" and "bella donna" invite a smile from Byronically minded visitors to either city.

Byron's legacy, however, lies not in words alone. Beyond the poems and letters, the quotations and stories, there have been prints, portraits, cartoons, figurines, novels, films, plays, postage stamps and dinner plates inspired by Byron's memory. He is still to be found across Europe – in statues, plaques and street names. The places he visited, which are revisited in these pages, are still marked by his presence. In Missalonghi and Athens, statues of

Byron stand high above the formal gardens in celebration of the hero of Independence. In London, he is situated in Park Lane, at the centre of high society. At Aberdeen Grammar School, a bronze Byron towers above the front courtyard on a tall, granite plinth. At Trinity College, Cambridge, in the Villa Borghese Gardens in Rome, and the Thorvaldsen Museum in Copenhagen the distinctive figure sits enrobed in white marble, book on his knee, foot on a broken column, staring into space. Finally at rest in these tranquil works of art, Byron manages to be in many places at the same time, while his words continue to speak to readers around the world.

Fiona Stafford

1. To Augusta Byron, November 2, 1804, *Byron's Travels*, 21.
2. To Catherine Gordon Byron, May 1–10, 1804, *Byron's Travels*, 17.
3. *Don Juan*, X, 17, *Byron's Travels*, 3.
4. For biographical information, I am variously indebted to Thomas Moore, *Letters and Journals of Lord Byron, with Notices of his Life*, 2 vols (Paris, 1833); L. A. Marchand, *Byron: A Portrait*, new edn (London: Cresset Library, 1987); Benita Eisler, *Byron: Child of Passion, Fool of Fame* (London and New York: Vintage, 2000) and Fiona MacCarthy, *Byron, Life and Legend* (London: John Murray, 2002). Jerome McGann's scholarly edition of *The Complete Poetical Works of Byron*, 7 vols (Oxford: Clarendon, 1988–) and L. A. Marchand's edition of *Byron's Letter's and Journals*, 13 vols (London: John Murray, 1973–94) (*BLJ*) have also proved invaluable.
5. Moore, *Letters and Journals of Lord Byron*, I, 51.
6. Ibid.
7. *Byron's Travels*, 364.
8. To Moore, March 4, 1814, *BLJ*, 77.
9. To Annabella Milbanke, November 29, 1813, *Byron's Travels*, 259.
10. William Wordsworth, Preface, *Lyrical Ballads*, ed. Fiona Stafford (Oxford: Oxford University Press, 2013), 111.
11. *Don Juan*, XIII, 36; III, 88.
12. To Kinnaird, October 26, 1819, *Byron's Travels*, 451.
13. To Murray, August 1, 1819, *Byron's Travels*, 422.
14. To Elizabeth Pigot, July 5, 1807, *BLJ*, I, 123–4.
15. To Lady Melbourne, August 20, 1813, *Byron's Travels*, 251.
16. To Charles Skinner Matthews, June 22, 1809, *Byron's Travels*, 82.
17. To Catherine Gordon Byron, June 28, 1810, *Byron's Travels*, 184.
18. To Catherine Gordon Byron, May 24, 1810, *Byron's Travels*, 182.
19. To Robert Dallas, June 23, 1810, *BLJ*, I, 248.
20. *Byron's Travels*, 180.
21. W. H. Auden, "W. H. A. to E. M. A. No. 2", W. H. Auden and Louis MacNeice, *Letters from Iceland*, new edn (London: Faber, 1967), 139.
22. W. H. Auden, "Letter to Lord Byron. Part III", *Letters from Iceland*, 101.
23. "To an Oak in the Garden of Newstead Abbey", "To John Murray, October 19, 1820", *Byron's Travels*, 59.

Note on the Text

Since this selection follows Byron from place to place throughout his life, it is arranged geographically and chronologically, though the chronology is guided by his travels rather than by the dates of composition. It begins in Scotland, because that is where Byron spent his early boyhood, even though no writing survives from this period. Although most of his letters reflected the places where he was staying when he dashed them off, some of these also look back on earlier periods and are placed accordingly (for example a reminiscence about a party with his Cambridge friends at Newstead Abbey, which was recalled for the benefit of John Murray some thirteen years later, when Byron was staying in Ravenna). His poetry often draws on memories of earlier events or places he had visited long before he immortalized them in verse, and so many of the poems selected for *Byron's Travels* are grouped with prose composed in response to the same place. Both of his most celebrated longer poems, *Childe Harold* and *Don Juan*, draw inspiration from the long voyage around the Mediterranean that he undertook in 1809–11, and so passages from each appear in sections representing Byron's travels in Spain or Greece. Although excerpts may at times be frustrating for those who wish to settle down to read a long poem in its entirety, this arrangement is designed to enable readers to travel *with* Byron and to see his poems afresh in the light of where he went. (There are many good editions of the complete poems, to which this selection is, of course, indebted, and it is hoped that readers who are encountering Byron's long poems for the first time in *Byron's Travels* may go on to read these poems in full.) Byron remains the most illuminating companion for readers of his poetry, as his letters and journals offer incomparable insights into his experiences of the places where his poems are set. As a travel writer, he is second to none, so this selection also celebrates Byron as a great prose writer as well as a Romantic poet.

The texts of the poems are collated from early complete editions rather than the first editions of individual poems (the first edition of *Don Juan*, for example, was heavily 'edited' by Byron's publisher John Murray, with many stanzas and sections suppressed for fear of the offence the poem might cause in 1819). The texts of the *Letters and Journals* are from Leslie Marchand's definitive edition, published by John Murray and Harvard University Press between 1973 and 1994.

FIONA STAFFORD is Professor of English Language and Literature at the University of Oxford. She specializes in literature of the Romantic period; place and nature writing; Scottish and Irish literature.

Select Bibliography

EDITIONS OF BYRON'S WORKS

MARCHAND, LESLIE A. (ed.), *Byron's Letters and Journals*, 13 vols (London: John Murray, 1973–94).

MCGANN, JEROME J. (ed.), *Lord Byron: The Complete Poetical Works*, 7 vols (Oxford: Clarendon Press, 1980–93).

THOMAS MOORE, *Letters and Journals of Lord Byron, with Notices of his Life*, 2 vols (London: John Murray, 1830).

NICHOLSON, ANDREW (ed.), *Lord Byron: The Complete Miscellaneous Prose* (Oxford: Clarendon Press, 1991).

PROTHERO, ROWLAND E. (ed.), *The Works of Lord Byron: A New, Revised and Enlarged Edition, with Illustrations. Letters and Journals*, 6 vols (London: John Murray, 1898–1901).

STEFFAN, T. G., and PRATT, W. W. (eds), *Byron's Don Juan*, 4 vols (Austin: University of Texas Press, 1957).

STEFFAN, T. G. and PRATT, W. W. (eds), *Lord Byron: Don Juan*, rev. edn (Harmondsworth: Penguin, 1996).

BIOGRAPHY

EISLER, BENITA, *Byron, Child of Passion, Fool of Fame* (London: Hamish Hamilton, 1999; Vintage, 2000).

FRANKLIN, CAROLINE, *Byron: A Literary Life* (London: Macmillan, 2000).

HAY, DAISY, *Young Romantics: The Shelleys, Byron and Other Tangled Lives* (London: Bloomsbury, 2010).

MACCARTHY, FIONA, *Byron: Life and Legend* (London: Faber, 2003).

MARCHAND, LESLIE A., *Byron: A Biography*, 3 vols (London: John Murray, 1957).

CRITICISM

BAINBRIDGE, SIMON, *Napoleon and English Romanticism* (Cambridge: Cambridge University Press, 1995).

BARTON, ANNE, *Byron: Don Juan* (Cambridge: Cambridge University Press, 1992).

BEATON, RODERICK, *Byron's War: Romantic Rebellion, Greek Revolution* (Cambridge: Cambridge University Press, 2013).

BEATTY, BERNARD, *Byron's Don Juan* (Totowa, NJ: Barnes & Noble, 1985).

BEATTY, BERNARD, *Reading Byron* (Liverpool: Liverpool University Press, 2023).

BEATTY, BERNARD, and NEWEY, VINCENT (eds), *Byron and the Limits of Fiction* (Liverpool: Liverpool University Press, 1988).

BEATY, FREDERICK L., *Byron the Satirist* (DeKalb: Northern Illinois University Press, 1985).

BONE, DRUMMOND (ed.), *The Cambridge Companion to Byron* (Cambridge: Cambridge University Press, 2004).

CHEEKE, STEPHEN, *Byron and Place: History, Translation, Nostalgia*, Basingstoke: Palgrave Macmillan, 2003).

CROMPTON, LOUIS, *Byron and Greek Love: Homophobia in 19th-century England*, Berkeley: University of California Press, 1985).

CRONIN, RICHARD, *Byron's Don Juan: The Liberal Epic of the Nineteenth Century* (Cambridge: Cambridge University Press, 2023).

ELIOT, T. S., "Byron", in *On Poetry and Poets* (London: Faber, 1957).

FRANKLIN, CAROLINE, *Byron's Heroines* (Oxford: Oxford University Press, 1992).

GLECKNER, ROBERT F., *Byron and the Ruins of Paradise* (Baltimore: Johns Hopkins Press, 1967).

HASLETT, MOYRA, *Byron's Don Juan and the Don Juan Legend* (Oxford: Oxford University Press, 1997).

LENNARD, JOHN, *But I Digress* (Oxford: Oxford University Press, 1991).

KELSALL, MALCOLM, *Byron's Politics* (Brighton: Harvester, 1987).

MCGANN, JEROME J., *Fiery Dust* (Chicago: University of Chicago Press, 1968).

MCGANN, JEROME J., *"Don Juan" in Context* (Chicago: University of Chicago Press, 1976).

RAWES, ALAN, *Byron's Poetic Experimentation* (Aldershot: Ashgate, 2000).

RAWES, ALAN, and SAGLIA, DIEGO (eds), *Byron and Italy* (Manchester: Manchester University Press, 2017).

RUTHERFORD, A. (ed.), *Byron: The Critical Heritage* (London: Routledge, 1970).

STABLER, JANE (ed.), *Byron* (Harlow: Longman, 1998).

STABLER, JANE, *Byron, Poetics and History* (Cambridge: Cambridge University Press, 2002).

TUITE, CLARA, *Byron and Scandalous Celebrity* (Cambridge: Cambridge University Press, 2014).

VASSALLO, PETER, *Byron: The Italian Literary Influence* (New York: St Martin's Press, 1984).

WOLFSON, SUSAN J., " 'Their She-Condition': Cross-Dressing and the Politics of Gender in *Don Juan*", *ELH* 54 (1987), 598–612.

WOOD, NIGEL (ed.), *Don Juan* (Theory in Practice series) (Buckingham: Open University Press, 1993).

OTHER USEFUL RESOURCES

The Byron Society website http://www.thebyronsociety.com/
The Byron Journal
Peter Cochran's Website https://petercochran.wordpress.com/byron-2

Chronology

DATE	AUTHOR'S LIFE	LITERARY CONTEXT
1788	Birth of Byron, 22 January, London.	
1789	Catherine Gordon Byron, Byron's mother, moves to Aberdeen, where she is joined by his father, John Byron.	William Blake: *Songs of Innocence.* Richard Price: *A Discourse on the Love of Our Country.*
1790	John Byron goes to France, leaving his wife and son in Aberdeen.	Edmund Burke: *Reflections on the Revolution in France.* Mary Wollstonecraft: *A Vindication of the Rights of Men.* Helen Maria Williams: *Letters written in France.* Johann Wolfgang von Goethe: *Faust. A Fragment.*
1791	Byron's father dies in France.	James Boswell: *Life of Samuel Johnson.* Robert Burns: *Tam O'Shanter.* Thomas Paine: *Rights of Man.* Ann Radcliffe: *The Romance of the Forest.* Death of Wolfgang Amadeus Mozart.
1792		Birth of Percy Bysshe Shelley. Mary Wollstonecraft: *A Vindication of the Rights of Woman.* Charlotte Smith: *Desmond.* Paine: *Rights of Man, Part 2.* Death of Joshua Reynolds.
1793		Birth of John Clare. Birth of Felicia Hemans. William Godwin: *An Enquiry concerning Political Justice.* Hannah More: *Village Politics.* Blake: *Visions of the Daughters of Albion.* William Wordsworth: *An Evening Walk; Descriptive Sketches.*

National Assembly established in France in June; Storming of the Bastille in Paris, 14 July. Start of the French Revolution.
In London, Richard Price, celebrating the centenary of the Glorious Revolution of 1688–9, delivers a political sermon, hailing the French Revolution as the successor of the American Revolution.

Mirabeau elected President of the National Constituent Assembly in France.
Joseph Priestley's house and laboratory sacked during anti-radical Birmingham Riots.

Paine charged with seditious libel, escapes to France and is elected to the National Convention.
Storming of the Tuileries Palace; Louis XVI overthrown; National Convention takes control and abolishes the French monarchy. September Massacres in Paris.

Britain at war with France. Executions of Louis XVI and Marie Antoinette. Fall of the Girondins. Arrest and execution of Madame Roland. Jean-Paul Marat assassinated; Charlotte Corday executed for his murder. Revolutionary Tribunal established in Paris. Reign of Terror begins. Paine arrested and only narrowly escapes execution.

DATE	AUTHOR'S LIFE	LITERARY CONTEXT
1794	Byron, heir to the Byron title and estates following the death of the 5th Baron Byron's grandson, enters Aberdeen Grammar School.	Blake: *Songs of Experience*. Radcliffe: *The Mysteries of Udolpho*.
1795		Birth of John Keats. Goethe: *Wilhelm Meister's Years of Apprenticeship*.
1796	Byron falls in love with his distant relation Mary Duff.	Death of Robert Burns. Death of James Macpherson. Matthew Lewis: *The Monk*.
1797	A bout of scarlet fever prompts Catherine to take her son to recover in the Scottish Highlands, where he rides among the mountains.	Samuel Taylor Coleridge: *Poems*. Birth of Franz Schubert. Birth of Mary Shelley. Death of Mary Wollstonecraft.
1798	On the death of his grandfather in May, Byron becomes 6th Baron Byron of Rochdale. He and his mother visit Newstead Abbey, his ancestral home, in August.	Friedrich Schiller: *Wallenstein*. Wordsworth and Coleridge: *Lyrical Ballads*. Thomas Malthus: *Essay on the Principle of Population*.
1799	Living in Nottingham, Byron is abused by his nurse, May Gray. Enters school in Dulwich in September and spends Christmas in London with the Hanson family.	Richard Brinsley Sheridan: *Pizarro*.
1800	Summer visit to Newstead Abbey.	Wordsworth and Coleridge: enlarged 2nd volume of *Lyrical Ballads*. Burns: *Works*, ed. James Currie. Maria Edgeworth: *Castle Rackrent*. Death of Mary Robinson. Death of William Cowper.
1801	Byron enters Harrow. Start of lifelong friendship with Edward Noel Long, who arrives at the same time. In the summer, visits Cheltenham and the Malverns with his mother. Meets his half-sister, Augusta, in London during the Christmas holidays.	Ludwig van Beethoven: *Moonlight Sonata*.

HISTORICAL EVENTS

Priestley leaves for America. Treason Trials. Pitt suspends Habeas Corpus (to 1795).
Thermidor Coup in Paris overturns Jacobin rule. Execution of Robespierre.

Seditious Meetings Act in Britain.
Louis XVII dies in captivity.

Napoleon Bonaparte's victorious campaign against Austria in Northern Italy (to 1797).

United Irishmen uprising and defeat.
French conquest of Malta and campaign to take Egypt. Nelson victorious at the Battle
of the Nile, in Aboukir Bay.
French invasion of Switzerland leads to the establishment of the Helvetic Republic.

Napoleon Bonaparte elected First Consul under new constitution.

Act of Union between Great Britain and Ireland.
France defeats Austria at the Battle of Marengo, in Piedmont.

DATE	AUTHOR'S LIFE	LITERARY CONTEXT
1802	Christmas in Bath.	Foundation of the *Edinburgh Review*.
1803	Catherine Byron moves into Burgage Manor in Southwell, but fraught relations prompt Byron to move into the Gatehouse at Newstead Abbey. Byron falls in love with Mary Chaworth.	Beethoven: *Eroica Symphony*.
1804	Byron becomes friendly with the Pigots in Southwell during school vacations.	
1805	Byron goes up to Cambridge and is admitted at Trinity College.	Sir Walter Scott: *The Lay of the Last Minstrel*. Wordsworth: *The Prelude* (unpublished until 1850).
1806	Private printing of Byron's first poetry collection, *Fugitive Pieces*, rapidly withdrawn. Attachment to John Edleston, Trinity College choirboy.	Death of Charlotte Smith.
1807	*Poems on Various Occasions* privately printed and then published as *Hours of Idleness*. Friendships with John Cam Hobhouse, Charles Skinner Matthews, Scrope Davies and Francis Hodgson.	Wordsworth: *Poems, in Two Volumes*. Smith: *Beachy Head and Other Poems*. George Crabbe: *Poems*. Mme de Staël: *Corinne, ou l'Italie*.
1808	Byron graduates from Cambridge. *Poems Original and Translated* published. Moves into Newstead Abbey and begins renovations. Negative review of *Hours of Idleness* appears in the *Edinburgh Review*.	Scott: *Marmion*. *The Examiner* founded by John and Leigh Hunt.
1809	*English Bards and Scotch Reviewers* published. Death of Edward Long. Lucy, maidservant at Newstead, gives birth to Byron's illegitimate child. In June Byron leaves for his voyage to Portugal and the Mediterranean with John Cam Hobhouse.	Birth of Felix Mendelssohn. Birth of Alfred Tennyson. John Murray founds the *Quarterly Review*.
1810	Travels in Greece and Turkey with Hobhouse. Swims the Hellespont.	Beethoven: *25 Irish Songs* (to 1812). Scott: *The Lady of the Lake*.

Treaty of Amiens brings an end to the French Revolutionary Wars and allows movement between Britain and the Continent once again.

Britain, alarmed by Napoleon Bonaparte's policies in Europe, declares war on France, ending the brief peace. Fear of French invasion grips Britain.
Robert Emmet's Rebellion in Ireland ends in defeat.

Napoleon Bonaparte is crowned Emperor Napoleon I by Pope Pius VII in Paris.
In Wales, Richard Trevithick's steam locomotive makes its first journey.

Napoleon crowned King of Italy in Milan in May.
French victories at Ulm and Austerlitz.
Nelson's victory – and death – at Trafalgar in October.

Death of William Pitt. Death of Charles James Fox.
End of Holy Roman Empire.
Napoleon defeats the Prussians and occupies Berlin.

Act for the Abolition of the Slave Trade.
France and Spain invade Portugal, triggering the Peninsular War.

France turns against Spain: Napoleon's brother Joseph is installed as King of Spain;
Charles IV and his son Ferdinand VII forced to abdicate.
Arthur Wellesley (later Duke of Wellington) arrives in Portugal with an army to fight the French invaders. The Convention of Cintra, allowing the evacuation of French troops, ends the occupation of Portugal, but not the Peninsular War.
Wars of independence in Latin America begin (to 1826).

Napoleon enters Vienna. Austrian army defeated at Wagram.
Peninsular War continues to rage in Spain.
Death of Thomas Paine in New York.

The newly elected Cortes of Cadiz declares itself the legitimate representative of royal sovereignty in the Spanish Empire. Siege of Cadiz by French army begins.

DATE	AUTHOR'S LIFE	LITERARY CONTEXT
1811	"The Curse of Minerva" begun. Byron returns from Greece in July. His mother dies in August before seeing Byron. Death of Cambridge friend, Matthews, and schoolfriend from Harrow, John Wingfield.	Jane Austen: *Sense and Sensibility*. Beethoven: *The Ruins of Athens*.
1812	*Childe Harold I and II* published, making Byron famous. Byron gives his maiden speech in the House of Lords, arguing against the Frame-Breaking Bill. Affairs with Lady Oxford and Lady Caroline Lamb. Friendship with Caroline's mother-in-law Lady Melbourne develops as relationship with Caroline becomes explosive.	Birth of Charles Dickens.
1813	*The Giaour* and *The Bride of Abydos* published. Passionate attachment to Augusta Leigh. Flirtation with Frances Wedderburn Webster.	Austen: *Pride and Prejudice*. Robert Southey: *Life of Nelson*. De Staël: *De l'Allemagne*. Shelley: *Queen Mab*.
1814	*The Corsair* and *Lara* published. Augusta Leigh gives birth to Medora, almost certainly Byron's daughter.	Austen: *Mansfield Park*. Frances Burney: *The Wanderer*. Scott: *Waverley*. Wordsworth: *The Excursion*. Schubert sets text from Goethe's *Faust* as "Gretchen am Spinnrade".
1815	Byron marries Annabella Milbanke on 2 January. Their daughter Ada is born in December. Byron on the Management Committee for the Theatre Royal, Drury Lane. *Hebrew Melodies* published.	Austen: *Emma* (pub. December, 1816 on title-page). Scott: *Guy Mannering*. Wordsworth: *Poems*.
1816	Annabella leaves Byron in January. Byron leaves England in April. He travels through Belgium, visits Waterloo, arrives in Switzerland and takes the Villa Diodati for the summer. He spends time with Percy Bysshe Shelley, Mary Godwin and Claire Clairmont, who is expecting Byron's child. *The Siege of Corinth, Parasina, The Prisoner of Chillon and Other Poems* and *Childe Harold III* published.	Coleridge: *Christabel, Kubla Khan*. Benjamin Constant: *Adolphe*. Goethe: *Italian Journey*. Gioachino Rossini: *Il barbiere di Siviglia*.

Regency begins in England, when George III is declared insane.
Luddite movement begins in Nottingham.

Napoleon's Russian campaign; retreat from Moscow.
Siege of Cadiz ends after Allies' victory at Salamanca. Cortes of Cadiz drafts a liberal
constitution (revoked by Ferdinand VII on his return in 1814).
Assassination of British Prime Minister, Spencer Perceval. Lord Liverpool Prime
Minister (to 1827); Lord Castlereagh Foreign Secretary (to 1822).
The United States declares war on Britain.

Austria becomes part of the Quadruple Alliance against France.
Abdication of Napoleon's brother Joseph Bonaparte from Spanish throne.
Wellington's army enters France. Napoleon's defeat by Coalition armies at the Battle
of Leipzig.
The Hunt brothers imprisoned for libel on the Prince Regent in *The Examiner*.

Allies enter Paris. Napoleon abdicates. Treaty of Paris signed in May between France
and the Allies (Britain, Russia, Austria, Prussia, Sweden and Portugal), ending the
Napoleonic Wars. Napoleon exiled to Elba.
Congress of Vienna begins.
Treaty of Ghent in December ends war between America and Britain.

Napoleon escapes from Elba, returns to France; The Hundred Days; Allies mobilize
against Napoleon, who is finally defeated at the Battle of Waterloo in July. Restoration
of Louis XVIII.
Final Act of Congress of Vienna (June) settles map of Europe.
Holy Alliance between Austria, Russia and Prussia formed to act against liberalism
and secularism in Europe.

Parthenon or "Elgin" Marbles purchased from Lord Elgin by British government and
put on display in the British Museum.
"Dark Summer", where extreme weather and crop failures across Europe are triggered
by the eruption of Mount Tambora in Indonesia, though the cause is unknown at the
time.
Spa Field Riots.

DATE	AUTHOR'S LIFE	LITERARY CONTEXT
1817	*Manfred* published. Claire Clairmont gives birth to Allegra, Byron's daughter. Byron travels to Italy and settles in Venice, where he has an affair with Margarita Cogni and casual relationships with many other Venetians. Newstead Abbey sold.	Death of Jane Austen. *Northanger Abbey, Persuasion* published posthumously. Coleridge: *Biographia Literaria*. Keats: *Poems*. Thomas Moore: *Lalla Rookh*. Scott: *Rob Roy*. *Blackwood's Magazine* founded.
1818	*Beppo, Childe Harold IV* published. Begins *Don Juan*. Allegra is brought to Venice. The Shelleys visit Byron.	Beethoven: *12 Scottish Songs*. Keats: *Endymion*. Scott: *The Heart of Midlothian*. Mary Shelley: *Frankenstein*. Thomas Love Peacock: *Nightmare Abbey*.
1819	*Mazeppa* and *Don Juan*, cantos I and II published. Byron falls for Countess Teresa Guiccioli and later in the year follows her to Ravenna. Byron entrusts his Memoirs to Thomas Moore.	Scott: *Ivanhoe*. Shelley writes *The Masque of Anarchy*.
1820	In Ravenna, living in Count Guiccioli's palace until relations become too fraught, Byron becomes involved with revolutionary activities through Teresa's family, the Gambas.	Keats: *Lamia, Isabella, The Eve of St Agnes and Other Poems*. Shelley: *Prometheus Unbound*. Wordsworth: *The River Duddon*. Alphonse de Lamartine: *Méditations poétiques*.
1821	*Marino Faliero, The Prophecy of Dante, Don Juan*, cantos III–V, *Sardanapalus, The Two Foscari* and *Cain* published. Byron leaves Ravenna to join the Shelleys in Pisa. Teresa follows.	Death of John Keats in Rome. De Quincey: *Confessions of an English Opium-Eater*. Clare: *The Village Minstrel and Other Poems*. Goethe: *Wilhelm Meister's Journeyman Years*.
1822	Byron's daughter, Allegra, dies in April. Disagreement with John Murray over *Don Juan* leads to agreement with John Hunt to publish the rest of the poem. *The Vision of Judgement* published in the Hunts' new journal, *The Liberal*, leading to the prosecution of John Hunt. *Werner* published.	Percy Bysshe Shelley drowns in the Bay of Lerici, Italy.

Suspension of Habeas Corpus.
Trial and acquittal of the political satirist William Hone.

Habeas Corpus restored.

Peterloo Massacre. Six Acts passed.
Metternich instigates repressive Carlsbad Decrees in the German Confederation.
Bolívar's march across the Andes into New Granada, defeating the Spanish at the
Battle of Boyacá and taking the capital, Bogota.

George III dies on 29 January. Prince Regent becomes George IV.
Trial of Queen Caroline.
Cato Street Conspiracy – a failed plot to murder the Prime Minister and the Cabinet.
Liberal Revolutions in Spain, where Ferdinand VII is forced to adopt the Constitution
of 1810, and Portugal.
Liberal Revolution in Naples and Sicily organized by the Carbonari and other secret
societies.

Greek War of Independence begins.
Ferdinand I calls in Austrian assistance to overthrow newly established constitutional
governments in Naples and Sicily.
Napoleon's death on St Helena.

Suicide of Castlereagh.
Massacre of Chios.

DATE	AUTHOR'S LIFE	LITERARY CONTEXT
1823	*Heaven and Earth, The Age of Bronze, Don Juan*, cantos VI–XIV published. Byron sails for Greece and offers £4,000 in support of the Greek cause.	Beethoven: *Ninth Symphony*.
1824	Byron travels to Missolonghi where he dies of a fever on 19 April. Body returned to England and buried in Hucknall Torkard Church, near Newstead Abbey.	Hogg: *The Private Memoirs and Confessions of a Justified Sinner*. Scott: *Redgauntlet*.

HISTORICAL EVENTS

Louis XVIII, sanctioned by the Congress of Verona (1822), invades Spain and restores absolutism there.

Repeal of Combination Acts of 1799–1800 allows workers to form unions.
Bolívar liberates Peru from Spanish control.

Byron's Correspondents

ROBERT ADAIR (1763–1855)
Whig politician, British diplomat, Ambassador to Constantinople in 1809–10.

CHARLES F. BARRY (1790–1832)
Banker, business agent, friend. After meeting Byron in Genoa, Barry, who lived in the Italian port city, assisted with preparations for the final voyage, securing a ship for Byron and looking after numerous manuscripts, papers, books and effects.

HENRI BEYLE (STENDHAL) (1783–1842)
French writer and novelist. After the defeat of Napoleon, in whose campaigns he was a serving officer, Beyle moved to Italy. His book *Rome, Naples et Florence* was published in 1817 under the pseudonym M. de Stendhal, by which he is generally known. Although Byron did not meet Stendhal, his longstanding interest in Napoleon enhanced the interest of this highly accomplished writer, former cavalry officer and restless exile.

JOHN BOWRING (1792–1872)
Politician, writer, Honorary Secretary to the London Greek Society which was committed to supporting Greek Independence. Byron was elected as a member in May 1823.

MRS. CATHERINE GORDON BYRON (1765–1811)
Byron's mother. Catherine was the daughter of a Scottish laird, George Gordon of Gight. In 1785, she married the widower John Byron, who changed his name to Gordon in order to inherit her family estate in Aberdeenshire. Once he had squandered much of her fortune, he abandoned Catherine and their small son, the future poet, dying in France in 1791. Catherine's son was at school in Aberdeen when he learned of his paternal grandfather's death and his own elevation in 1798. The young Lord Byron, 6th Baron Byron of Rochdale, was heir to Newstead Abbey, so his mother took her son south to Nottinghamshire, but lived for a few years at Burgage Manor in Southwell, while Newstead Abbey was let out. From 1808 until her death in 1811, she lived at Newstead Abbey.

Byron had a volatile relationship with his mother, but despite teenage embarrassment, wrote to her regularly during his Mediterranean travels in 1809 to 1811 and was profoundly affected by her unexpected death.

EARL OF CLARE (1792–1851)
John Fitzgibbon, 2nd Earl of Clare, Anglo-Irish statesman and schoolfriend of Byron.

SCROPE BERDMORE DAVIES (1782–1852)
Wit, dandy, friend. Byron saw Davies frequently in London before his departure for the Continent in 1816, when Davies and Hobhouse accompanied him to Dover. Byron dedicated his poem *Parisina* (1816) to Davies.

EDWARD J. DAWKINS (1792–1865)
British diplomat. Byron requested assistance from Dawkins, the British Chargé d'Affaires, over an affray involving two of his servants in Pisa in March 1822.

HENRY DRURY (1778–1841)
Scholar and schoolmaster at Harrow, lifelong friend.

JOHN DUFFIE [DUFFY] (d. 1854)
British army officer, friend during the final months in Greece.

EDWARD ELLICE (1783–1863)
Whig politician, friend of Hobhouse.

JOHANN WOLFGANG VON GOETHE (1749–1832)
German writer, poet and scientist. Byron greatly admired the "illustrious patriarch of European letters" and dedicated his tragedy *Sardanapalus* to Goethe.

COUNTESS TERESA GUICCIOLI (1800–1873)
Venetian countess and lover. Byron met Teresa in Venice, in January 1818, three days after her marriage to the powerful Italian nobleman, Count Alessandro Guiccioli. At eighteen, Teresa, Guiccioli's third wife, was not very taken with her much older husband. When Byron met her again in April 1819, they began a passionate affair. Byron followed Teresa to Ravenna, Bologna, back to Venice and to Ravenna again. As Teresa's *cavalier servente*, Byron became

friendly with her father and brother, Count Ruggiero and Pietro Gamba, who were leaders of the Carbonari, a revolutionary group committed to independence from the Austrian Empire and the unification of Italy. When the Pope granted the Guicciolis a decree of separation, Teresa was free to rejoin her family, though they were exiled from Ravenna for political reasons. Byron left Ravenna in 1821, and moved into a villa in Pisa which Shelley had secured for him. The Gambas moved to Pisa very soon afterwards, enabling Teresa and Byron to reunite. After Byron's death, Teresa returned briefly to Count Guiccioli and later married the French Count de Boissy in Paris. She treasured mementos of Byron throughout her life, eventually composing her own tributes in *Lord Byron, Jugée par les Témoins de sa Vie*, and *Vie de Lord Byron en Italie.*

CHARLES HANCOCK (1793–1858)
British merchant based in Argostoli, who looked after Byron's financial affairs after their meeting in Cephalonia in 1823.

CHARLES HANSON (1791–1845)
Son of Byron's solicitor, John Hanson, and childhood friend. Visited Byron in Venice in November 1818 to address legal and financial matters. Co-executor, with John Cam Hobhouse, of Byron's Will

JOHN HANSON (1755–1841)
Family friend, business adviser and solicitor. Hanson looked after Byron's business interests after he became 6th Baron Byron at the age of ten. His family welcomed Byron into their home for school holidays and maintained their friendship after Byron's final departure for Europe in 1816, though by then Douglas Kinnaird was looking after most of Byron's financial affairs. Hanson oversaw the sale of Newstead Abbey in 1818.

JOHN CAM HOBHOUSE (1786–1869)
Whig politician, reformer, writer, close friend from Byron's under-graduate days in Cambridge to the end of his life. Hobhouse was Byron's travelling companion during the two-year tour of the Mediterranean in 1809–11, the best man at his wedding in 1815, visitor at the Villa Diodati in 1816, Venice in 1817 and Pisa in 1822. He published his own *Journey through Albania* in 1813 and, in

1818, *Historical Illustrations to the Fourth Canto of Childe Harold's Pilgrimage*, which Byron had dedicated to Hobhouse. As Byron's executor, Hobhouse oversaw the destruction of the unpublished Memoirs at Murray's office in 1824. Though devastated by Byron's death, Hobhouse continued to pursue a distinguished political career, becoming a member of the Cabinet and then 1st Baron Broughton in 1851.

FRANCIS HODGSON (1781–1852)

Scholar, tutor, friend. Byron met Hodgson at Cambridge, where he was a classics tutor, and remained on friendly terms. Hodgson later became Provost of Eton.

LORD HOLLAND (HENRY RICHARD FOX, 3RD BARON HOLLAND) (1773–1840)

Whig leader, friend. During his time in London from 1812 to 1816 Byron was a frequent visitor to Holland House, where Lord and Lady Holland presided over frequent gatherings of Whig aristocrats, politicians, writers and intellectuals.

RICHARD BELGRAVE HOPPNER (1786–1872)

British diplomat, artist and friend. Byron met Hoppner in Venice in 1817, where Hoppner was the British Consul. They often went riding together and the Hoppners looked after Byron's daughter Allegra. Byron described Hoppner as "a thoroughly good man".

JAMES HENRY LEIGH HUNT (1784–1859)

Poet, political writer, critic, journalist. Byron made several visits to the Surrey County Gaol in 1813–14, to see Leigh Hunt during his imprisonment after libelling the Prince Regent. He admired Hunt's long poem, *The Story of Rimini*, and later assisted Hunt in launching a new periodical *The Liberal*, and the related visit to Italy in 1822. Hunt arrived shortly before Shelley's death and published his own recollections of the poets in *Lord Byron and Some of his Contemporaries* in 1828.

DOUGLAS KINNAIRD (1788–1830)

Banker, Whig politician, wit, friend. Byron met Kinnaird in Cambridge, became better acquainted in London and remained a close friend to the end. Kinnaird worked with Byron on the Drury Lane

Theatre committee and visited him in Venice in 1817. He looked after Byron's financial affairs. Byron dedicated his drama, *Marino Faliero*, to Kinnaird.

LADY CAROLINE LAMB (1785–1828)

Novelist, society lady, lover. After meeting Caroline Lamb, wife of the future Prime Minister George Lamb, Lord Melbourne, in London in 1812, Byron plunged into an intense, volatile and well-publicized affair. Caroline was distressed and angered by the break-up of their relationship, and modelled the protagonist of her 1816 Gothic novel *Glenarvon* on Byron, who was unimpressed.

AUGUSTA LEIGH (NÉE BYRON) (1783–1851)

Half-sister, friend, lover. Augusta Byron, five years older than Byron, was the only surviving daughter of his father's first marriage to Amelia d'Arcy, who died in 1784. Byron corresponded with Augusta during his schooldays, but the step siblings only became close in 1813, after seeing each other at society events in London. By then Augusta was married to George Leigh, but the attraction was powerful and mutual. Augusta's baby, Elizabeth Medora, born in 1814, was probably Byron's daughter. Although Byron married Annabella Milbanke the following January, rumours of incest led to the breakdown of the marriage and Byron's departure for Europe. He continued to write poems and deeply affectionate letters to Augusta until his death.

EDWARD LE MESURIER (1795–1855)

British naval officer who moved to Italy after leaving the navy in 1817. When Byron was in Genoa preparing to embark for Greece, Le Mesurier gave him a Newfoundland dog, reminiscent of his beloved Boatswain, as a companion for the voyage.

ANDREAS LONDOS (1786–1846)

Military leader in the Greek War of Independence from the initial declaration in March 1821 onwards. Byron had stayed with him during his Mediterranean tour in 1809, when Londos was the Governor of Vostitsa, under Turkish rule. Londos was among the first to rally to the revolutionary cause of liberating Greece from the Ottoman Empire.

EDWARD NOEL LONG (1788–1809)
Byron's schoolfriend from Harrow, who died at sea during the Peninsular War.

CHARLES SKINNER MATTHEWS (1785–1811)
Friend at Cambridge, who later drowned when swimming in the Cam. Byron heard about his death on his return from the Mediterranean in 1811.

PRINCE ALEXANDROS MAVROCORDATOS (1791–1865)
Greek statesman and later Prime Minister, who became a close associate of the Shelleys during his years of exile in Pisa. In 1821, when the Greek War of Independence began, he returned to join the fight, commanding forces in western Greece. Byron supported his campaign with a loan of £4,000, before joining the Greek army at Missalonghi in January 1824.

MR. MAYER (WILLIAM MEYER) (1778–1869)
British Consul at Prevesa from 1819 to 1835. After the downfall of Ali Pasha in 1822, Meyer's influence over western Greece was of great importance during the War of Independence.

LADY MELBOURNE (ELIZABETH LAMB, NÉE MILBANKE, VISCOUNTESS MELBOURNE) (1751–1818)
Society lady, political hostess, close friend, confidante, adviser. Byron met Lady Melbourne in 1812 through the Holland House circle. Mother of nine children, including the future Prime Minister William Lamb, she and Byron bonded over Byron's tumultuous and scandalous affair with her daughter-in-law, Caroline. Byron's interest in Annabella Milbanke was also mediated by Lady Melbourne, Annabella's aunt. Byron was deeply saddened by Lady Melbourne's death in 1818, "the best & kindest & ablest female I ever knew".

ANNABELLA MILBANKE (ANNA ISABELLA BYRON, NÉE MILBANKE, BARONESS BYRON) (1792–1860)
Heiress and spouse. Byron met Annabella in London in 1812 and proposed marriage to her a few months later, through her aunt Lady Melbourne. Unlike most of his recent amours, Annabella was an unmarried, religious, serious young woman with a spotless

reputation. Although she refused, they continued to correspond and his later proposal in 1814 was successful. They were married on January 2, 1815, at Annabella's family home in County Durham, but separated a year later, following the scandalous rumours about Byron's relationship with Augusta Leigh. Annabella and Byron's daughter, Augusta Ada, born in December 1815 but sent away with her mother five weeks later, would become famous in her own right as Ada Lovelace, pioneer of computer science. Although Byron never saw his daughter after the first weeks of her life, he dedicated *Childe Harold* III to Ada and continued to take a keen interest in her welfare, as evident in his letters to Annabella and Augusta Leigh.

THOMAS MOORE (1779–1852)
Irish poet, friend and biographer. Since the fashionable poet, Thomas Moore, was seriously offended by the satirical jibes in *English Bards and Scotch Reviewers*, he was keen to meet Byron on his return from the Mediterranean in 1811. The dispute was settled quickly and amicably and led to a lifelong friendship. When Moore visited Byron in Venice in 1819, he was given Byron's Memoirs for safekeeping, but subsequently passed them on to John Murray. Moore's own biography of Byron, *Letters and Journals of Lord Byron: With Notices of His Life*, published in 1830, contained a wealth of letters, stories and personal reminiscences and remains an invaluable resource.

JOHN MURRAY (1778–1843)
Publisher and friend. After inheriting a thriving book business from his father and namesake, John Murray became the foremost literary publisher of the Regency period, with a list that included not just Byron but Scott, Austen, Moore, Crabbe, Irving and the *Quarterly Review*. Murray's influence in literary London was unparalleled, his publishing house in Albemarle Street a hub of literary talent. Byron's relationship with Murray was close, if sometimes fraught: the poet objected to his publisher's objections to the more shocking content of *Don Juan*. After Byron's death, his Memoirs were destroyed in Albemarle Street in order to protect various reputations.

LORD SYDNEY [SIDNEY] OSBORNE (1789–1861)
Secretary to the Government of the Ionian islands, connected to
Augusta Leigh through his father, the Duke of Leeds, whose first
wife Amelia d'Arcy had run away with Byron's father. He visited
Byron in Venice in 1818 and in Cephalonia in 1823, when Byron
found him "Clever and insouciant as ever".

ELIZABETH BRIDGET PIGOT (1783–1866)
Friend from Southwell, where Byron lived at Burgage Manor with
his mother in between school and university terms, from 1803 to
1808. When Moore was working on his biography of Byron, Elizabeth Pigot was able to supply information and letters from Byron's
teenage and undergraduate years.

JOHN PIGOT (1785–1871)
Boyhood friend from Southwell. Younger brother of Elizabeth.

CAPTAIN DANIEL ROBERTS (1780–1869)
Naval officer, boat builder, friend of Trelawny. Daniel Roberts,
who had left the navy in 1817, was introduced to Byron and
the Shelleys in Pisa by Trelawny, and commissioned to design a
yacht for Byron, the *Bolivar*, and a schooner for Shelley, the *Don
Juan*. After Shelley's death and Byron's departure for Greece,
Roberts repaired the *Don Juan* for his own use and also bought
the *Bolivar*.

SIR WALTER SCOTT (1770–1832)
Poet, novelist, lawyer, sheriff, tree-planter. Byron greatly admired
the writings of Sir Walter Scott, regarding him as the finest poet of
the age. They met in 1815 in Murray's parlour in Albemarle Street
and continued to exchange occasional letters. After he left Britain
in 1816, Byron requested copies of Scott's novels as they appeared
and dedicated his heavenly drama, *Cain,* to Scott.

MARY WOLLSTONECRAFT SHELLEY (1797–1851)
Writer, novelist and friend. Mary, daughter of writers Mary Woll-
stonecraft and William Godwin, became the wife of Percy Bysshe
Shelley, after the suicide of his first wife, Harriet. In 1816, Mary
and Shelley travelled to Switzerland with her half-sister, Claire
Clairmont, who was pregnant with Byron's daughter, Allegra.

They rented a house on Lake Geneva close to the Villa Diodati, where Byron was staying for the summer. Often confined by bad weather during the "dark summer" of 1816, they spent many days in Byron's company, including the evening of ghost-story-writing, which gave Mary Shelley the inspiration for *Frankenstein*. After the Shelleys moved to Italy in 1818, they visited Byron in Venice and he lived near them in Pisa in 1822. After Shelley's death, Byron gave Mary financial, practical and moral support. She often acted as an amanuensis for him, prior to his departure for Greece.

PERCY BYSSHE SHELLEY (1792–1822)
Poet and friend. Shelley was the husband of Mary Wollstonecraft Shelley and met Byron in Switzerland in 1816 (see above). Shelley continued his friendship with Byron and acted as a mediator between Byron and Claire Clairmont. His visit to Venice in 1818 inspired the portrait of Byron in *Julian and Maddalo*. Shelley visited Byron in Ravenna and invited him to move to Pisa, where the Shelleys had taken up residence. In July 1822, Shelley's sailing trip in a boat called the *Don Juan* ended in tragedy. After Shelley's body was recovered from the sea, Byron attended the cremation on the beach at Viareggio.

EDWARD JOHN TRELAWNY (1792–1881)
Writer, adventurer, friend. Trelawny became friendly with Byron and the Shelleys in Pisa in 1822 and was responsible for the cremation of Shelley's body on the seashore at Viareggio. Trelawny accompanied Byron to Greece, where he joined the Greek warlord, Odysseus Androutzos, enemy to Mavracordatos, in his mountain stronghold on Mount Parnassus. When Byron died, Trelawny travelled to Missalonghi to organize the safe return of Byron's body and papers to England. After further adventures in Greece, including serious wounds in action, a second marriage and divorce, Trelawny returned to Britain. His proposals to Mary Shelley were rejected, but his experiences with her circle were eventually published in his *Recollections of the Last Days of Shelley and Byron* in 1858 (revised and enlarged in 1878, as *Records of Shelley, Byron, and the Author*).

JOHN WEDDERBURN WEBSTER (LATER JAMES WEBSTER WEDDERBURN) (1788–1840)

Army officer, dandy, friend. Webster joined Hobhouse, Matthews and Davies for Byron's house party at Newstead in 1809 and remained a friend. Byron had a very close relationship with Webster's wife, Frances, whom he met in London in 1811, soon after her marriage to James.

HARRIETTE WILSON (1786–1845)

Memoirist and courtesan. Byron declined an overture from her in 1814, but a few years later sent £50 when she asked him for help from financial straits. In her celebrated *Memoir*, published in 1825, Harriette Wilson included an account of her encounter with Byron at a London party and claimed to have received many letters from him, though all but the two relating to her 1820 request for money had been mislaid.

BYRON'S
TRAVELS

The world is all before me—or behind;
    For I have seen a portion of that same,
And quite enough for me to keep in mind;—
    Of passions, too, I have proved enough to blame,
To the great pleasure of our friends, mankind,
    Who like to mix some slight alloy with fame;
For I was rather famous in my time,
Until I fairly knocked it up with rhyme.

I have brought this world about my ears, and eke
    The other; that's to say, the clergy, who
Upon my head have bid their thunders break
    In pious libels by no means a few.
And yet I can't help scribbling once a week,
    Tiring old readers, nor discovering new.
In youth I wrote because my mind was full,
And now because I feel it growing dull.

But "why then publish?"—There are no rewards
    Of fame or profit when the world grows weary.
I ask in turn,—Why do you play at cards?
    Why drink? Why read?—To make some hour less
        dreary.
It occupies me to turn back regards
    On what I've seen or pondered, sad or cheery;
And what I write I cast upon the stream,
To swim or sink—I have had at least my dream.

DON JUAN XIV, 9–11

SCOTLAND

And when I use the phrase of "Auld Lang Syne!"
    'Tis not addressed to you—the more 's the pity
For me, for I would rather take my wine
    With you, than aught (save Scott) in your proud city.
But somehow,—it may seem a schoolboy's whine,
    And yet I seek not to be grand nor witty,
But I am half a Scot by birth, and bred
A whole one, and my heart flies to my head,—

As "Auld Lang Syne" brings Scotland, one and all,
    Scotch plaids, Scotch snoods, the blue hills, and
        clear streams,
The Dee, the Don, Balgounie's brig's black wall,
    All my boy feelings, all my gentler dreams
Of what I then dreamt, clothed in their own pall,
    Like Banquo's offspring; floating past me seems
My childhood in this childishness of mine:
I care not—'tis a glimpse of "Auld Lang Syne."

And though, as you remember, in a fit
    Of wrath and rhyme, when juvenile and curly,
I railed at Scots to show my wrath and wit,
    Which must be owned was sensitive and surly,
Yet 'tis in vain such sallies to permit,
    They cannot quench young feelings fresh and early:
I "scotched not killed" the Scotchman in my blood,
And love the land of "mountain and of flood."

DON JUAN X, 17–19

Lachin Y Gair

LACHIN Y GAIR, or as it is pronounced in the Erse, LOCH NA GARR, towers proudly pre-eminent in the Northern Highlands, near Invercauld. One of our modern Tourists mentions it as the highest mountain perhaps in GREAT BRITAIN; be this as it may, it is certainly one of the most sublime, and picturesque, amongst our "Caledonian Alps." Its appearance is of a dusky hue, but the summit is the seat of eternal snows; near Lachin y Gair, I spent some of the early part of my life, the recollection of which, has given birth to the following Stanzas.

Away, ye gay landscapes! ye gardens of roses!
    In you let the minions of luxury rove;
Restore me the rocks, where the snow-flake reposes,
    Though still they are sacred to freedom and love:
Yet, Caledonia! belov'd are thy mountains,
    Round their white summits though elements war,
Though cataracts foam, 'stead of smooth flowing
      fountains,
    I sigh, for the valley of dark Loch na Garr.

Ah! there my young footsteps, in infancy, wander'd,
    My cap was the bonnet, my cloak was the plaid;
On chieftains, long perish'd, my memory ponder'd,
    As daily I strode through the pine-cover'd glade;
I sought not my home, till the day's dying glory
    Gave place to the rays of the bright polar star;
For Fancy was cheer'd, by traditional story,
    Disclos'd by the natives of dark Loch na Garr.

"Shades of the dead! have I not heard your voices
    Rise on the night-rolling breath of the gale?"
Surely the soul of the hero rejoices,
    And rides on the wind, o'er his own Highland vale:

Round Loch na Garr, while the stormy mist gathers,
    Winter presides in his cold icy car;
Clouds, there, encircle the forms of my Fathers,
    They dwell in the tempests of dark Loch na Garr:

"Ill starred, though brave, did no visions foreboding,
    Tell you that Fate had forsaken your cause?"
Ah! were you destin'd to die at Culloden,
    Victory crown'd not your fall with applause;
Still were you happy in death's earthy slumber,
    You rest with your clan, in the caves of Braemar,
The Pibroch resounds, to the piper's loud number,
    Your deeds, on the echoes of dark Loch na Garr.

Years have roll'd on, Loch na Garr, since I left you,
    Years must elapse, e'er I tread you again;
Nature of verdure and flowers has bereft you,
    Yet still are you dearer than Albion's plain:
England! thy beauties are tame and domestic,
    To one, who has rov'd on the mountains afar;
Oh! for the crags that are wild and majestic,
    The steep, frowning glories of dark Loch na Garr.

[1807]

Song

When I rov'd, a young Highlander, o'er the dark heath,
    And climb'd thy steep summit, oh Morven of Snow,
To gaze on the torrent, that thunder'd beneath,
    Or the mist of the tempest that gather'd below;
Untutor'd by science, a stranger to fear,
    And rude as the rocks, where my infancy grew,
No feeling, save one, to my bosom was dear,
    Need I say, my sweet Mary, 'twas centred in you?

Yet, it could not be Love, for I knew not the name,
    What passion can dwell in the heart of a child?
But still I perceive an emotion the same
    As I felt, when a boy, on the crag-cover'd wild:
One image, alone, on my bosom imprest,
    I lov'd my bleak regions, nor panted for new,
And few were my wants, for my wishes were blest,
    And pure were my thoughts, for my soul was
            with you.

I arose with the dawn, with my dog as my guide,
    From mountain to mountain I bounded along,
I breasted the billows of *Dee's* rushing tide,
    And heard, at a distance, the Highlander's song:
At eve, on my heath-cover'd couch of repose,
    No dreams, save of Mary, were spread to my view,
And warm to the skies my devotions arose,
    For the first of my prayers was a blessing on you.

I left my bleak home, and my visions are gone,
    The mountains are vanish'd, my youth is no more;
As the last of my race, I must wither alone,
    And delight but in days, I have witness'd before;
Ah! splendour has rais'd, but embitter'd my lot,
    More dear were the scenes, which my infancy knew;
Though my hopes may have fail'd, yet they are not forgot,
    Tho' cold is my heart, still it lingers with you.

When I see some dark hill point its crest to the sky,
    I think of the rocks, that o'ershadow Colbleen;
When I see the soft blue of a love-speaking eye,
    I think of those eyes that endear'd the rude scene;
When, haply, some light-waving locks I behold,
    That faintly resemble my Mary's in hue,
I think on the long flowing ringlets of gold,
    The locks that were sacred to beauty, and you.

Yet, the day may arrive, when the mountains, once more,
    Shall rise to my sight, in their mantles of snow:
But, while these soar above me, unchang'd as before,
    Will Mary be there to receive me? ah, no!
Adieu! then, ye hills, where my childhood was bred,
    Thou sweet flowing Dee, to thy waters adieu!
No home in the forest shall shelter my head,
    Ah! Mary, what home could be mine, but with you?

[1807 or 1808]

Stanzas

I would I were a careless child,
    Still dwelling in my Highland cave,
Or roaming through the dusky wild,
    Or bounding o'er the dark blue wave;
The cumbrous pomp of Saxon pride,
    Accords not with the freeborn soul,
Which loves the mountain's craggy side,
    And seeks the rocks where billows roll.

Fortune! take back these cultur'd lands,
    Take back this name of splendid sound!
I hate the touch of servile hands,
    I hate the slaves that cringe around:
Place me along the rocks I love,
    Which sound to Ocean's wildest roar,
I ask but this—again to rove
    Through scenes my youth hath known before.

Few are my years, and, yet, I feel
    The World was ne'er design'd for me,
Ah! why do dark'ning shades conceal
    The hour when man must cease to be?
Once I beheld a splendid dream,
    A visionary scene of bliss;
Truth!—wherefore did thy hated beam
    Awake me to a world like this?

I lov'd—but those I lov'd, are gone,
    Had friends—my early friends are fled,
How cheerless feels the heart alone,
    When all its former hopes are dead!

Though gay companions, o'er the bowl,
    Dispel awhile the sense of ill,
Though Pleasure stirs the maddening soul,
    The heart—the heart is lonely still.

How dull! to hear the voice of those
    Whom Rank, or Chance, whom Wealth, or Power,
Have made; though neither Friends or Foes,
    Associates of the festive hour;
Give me again, a faithful few,
    In years and feelings still the same,
And I will fly the midnight crew,
    Where boist'rous Joy is but a name.

And Woman! lovely Woman, thou!
    My hope, my comforter, my all!
How cold must be my bosom now,
    When e'en thy smiles begin to pall.
Without a sigh would I resign
    This busy scene of splendid Woe;
To make that calm Contentment mine,
    Which Virtue knows, or seems to know.

Fain would I fly the haunts of men,
    I seek to shun, not hate mankind,
My breast requires the sullen glen,
    Whose gloom may suit a darken'd mind;
Oh! that to me the wings were given,
    Which bear the Turtle to her nest!
Then would I cleave the vault of Heaven,
    To flee away, and be at rest.

[1807 or 1808]

Ravenna, 8bre 16th, 1820

Dear Moray,—*The Abbot* has just arrived: many thanks; as also for the *Monastery—when you send it* !!!

The Abbot will have more than ordinary interest for me; for an ancestor of mine by the mother's side, Sir J. Gordon of Gight, the handsomest of his day, died on a Scaffold at Aberdeen for his loyalty to Mary, of whom he was an imputed paramour as well as her relation. His fate was much commented on in the Chronicles of the times. If I mistake not, he had something to do with her escape from Loch Leven, or with her captivity there. But this you will know better than I.

I recollect Loch Leven as it were but yesterday. I saw it in my way to England in 1798, being then ten years of age. My Mother, who was as haughty as Lucifer with her descent from the Stuarts, and her right line, from the *old Gordons, not the Seyton Gordons,* as she disdainfully termed the Ducal branch, told me the story, always reminding me how superior *her* Gordons were to the southern Byrons,—notwithstanding our Norman, and always masculine descent, which has never lapsed into a female, as my mother's Gordons had done in her own person.

I have written to you so often lately, that the brevity of this will be welcome.

Yours ever and truly,

BYRON

HARROW

The languages, especially the dead,
    The sciences, and most of all the abstruse,
The arts, at least all such as could be said
    To be the most remote from common use,
In all these he was much and deeply read;
    But not a page of any thing that's loose,
Or hints continuation of the species,
Was ever suffered, lest he should grow vicious.

His classic studies made a little puzzle,
    Because of filthy loves of gods and goddesses,
Who in the earlier ages raised a bustle,
    But never put on pantaloons or bodices;
His reverend tutors had at times a tussle,
    And for their Aeneids, Iliads, and Odysseys,
Were forced to make an odd sort of apology,
For Donna Inez dreaded the Mythology.

Ovid's a rake, as half his verses show him,
    Anacreon's morals are a still worse sample,
Catullus scarcely has a decent poem,
    I don't think Sappho's Ode a good example,
Although Longinus tells us there is no hymn
    Where the sublime soars forth on wings more ample:
But Virgil's songs are pure, except that horrid one
Beginning with "Formosum Pastor Corydon."

DON JUAN I, 40–42

Inscriptions in *Homeri Ilias* (1804)

Byrone. October 23ᵈ 1804
Monday Dʳ Drury's *Museum*
Harrow on the Hill
Middlesex
England
Europe
the world
the universe.

TO MRS. CATHERINE GORDON BYRON   *Harrow on the Hill*
                                   June 23rd. 6th. 8th. 30th. 1803

My dear Mother—I am much obliged to you for the money you sent me, I have already wrote to you several *times* about writing to Sheldrake. I have wrote myself to not [any] Purpose, I wish you would write to him or Mr. Hanson to call on him, to tell him to make an instrument for my leg immediately, as I want one, rather, I have been placed in a higher form in this School to day and Dr. Drury and I go on very well, write Soon My Dear Mother

I remain your affectionate Son
BYRON

TO MRS. CATHERINE GORDON BYRON   *Sept. 15? 1803*

My Dear Mother,—I have sent Mealey to Day to you, before William Came, but now I shall write myself, *I promise* you upon my *honour* I will come over *tomorrow* in the *afternoon*, I was not wishing to resist your *Commands*, and really seriously intended, Coming over tomorrow, ever since I received your Last letter, you know as well as I do that it is not your Company I dislike, but the place you reside in. I know it is time to go to Harrow, It will make me *unhappy*, but I will *obey*; I only *desire*, *entreat*, this one day, and on my *honour* I will be over tomorrow, in the evening or afternoon. I am Sorry you disapprove my Companions, who however are the first this county affords, and my equals in most respects, but I will be permitted to Chuse for myself, I shall never interfere in yours and I desire you will not molest me in mine; if you Grant me this favour, and allow me this one day unmolested you will eternally oblige your

unhappy Son
BYRON

I shall attempt to offer no excuse as you do not desire one. I only entreat you as Governor, not as a Mother, to allow me this one day. Those that I most Love live in this county, therefore in the name of Mercy I entreat this one day to take leave, and then I will

Join you again at Southwell to prepare to go to a place where—I will write no more it would only incense you, adieu, Tomorrow I come.

TO MRS. CATHERINE GORDON BYRON *Harrow-on-the-Hill,*
May 1–10, 1804?

My Dear Mother—I received your letter and was very Glad to hear that you are well, I am very comfortable here as far as relates to my Comrades, but, I have got into two or three scrapes with Drury and the other Masters, which are not very convenient, the other day as he was reprimanding me, (perhaps very properly) for my misdeeds he uttered the following words, "it is not probable that from your age and situation in the School your Friends will permit you to remain longer than Summer, but because you are about to leave Harrow, it is no reason you are to make the house a scene of riot and Confusion." this and much more said the Doctor, and I am informed From creditable authority that Dr. Drury, Mr. Evans and Mark Drury said I was a *Blackguard*, that Mark Drury said so I *know*, but I am inclined to doubt the authenticity of the report as to the rest, perhaps it is true perhaps not, but thank God they may call me a Blackguard, but they can never make me one, if Dr. Drury can bring one boy or any one else to say that I have committed a dishonourable action, and to prove it, I am content, but otherwise I am stigmatized without a cause, and I disdain and despise the malicious efforts of him and his Brother. His Brother Mark not Henry Drury (whom I will do the Justice to say has never since last year interfered with me) is continually reproaching me with the narrowness of my fortune, to what end I know not[;] his intentions may be Good, but his manner is disagreeable, I see no reason why I am to be reproached with it. I have as much money, as many Clothes, and in every respect of appearance am equal if not superior to most of my schoolfellows, and if my fortune is narrow, it is my misfortune not my fault.

But however the way to *riches* to *Greatness* lies before me, I can, I will cut myself a path through the world or perish in the attempt. others have begun life with nothing and ended Greatly.

And shall I who have a competent if not a large fortune, remain idle, No, I will carve myself the passage to Grandeur, but never with Dishonour. These Madam are my intentions, but why this upstart Son of a Button maker is to reproach me about an estate which however, is far superior to his own, I know not, but that he should call me a Blackguard, is far worse, on account of the former I can blame only Hanson (and that officious Friend Lord Grey de Ruthyn, whom I shall ever consider my most inveterate enemy), it is a mere trifle, but the latter I cannot bear, I have not deserved it, and I will not be insulted with impunity. Mr. Mark Drury rides out with his Son, sees me at a distance on a poney which I hired to go to the bathing place which is too far for me to walk, he calls out, tells his son I am a Blackguard, This son, who is no friend of mine comes home relates the story to his companions, possibly with a few exaggerations, but however the Greatest part was true, and I am to be considered as such a person by my comrades, it shall not be, I will say no more, I only hope you will take this into your consideration and remove me at Summer from a place where I am goaded with insults by those from whom I little deserved it.

I remain your affectionate Son,

BYRON

TO AUGUSTA BYRON   *Burgage Manor, March 22d. 1804*

Although, My ever Dear Augusta, I have hitherto appeared remiss in replying to your kind and affectionate letters; yet I hope you will not attribute my neglect to a want of affection, but rather to a shyness naturally inherent to my Disposition. I will now endeavour as amply as lies in my power to repay your kindness, and for the Future I hope you will consider me not only as *a Brother* but as your warmest and most affectionate *Friend*, and if ever Circumstances should require it as your *protector*. Recollect, My Dearest Sister, that you are *the nearest relation* I have in *the world both by the ties of Blood* and *Affection*, If there is anything in which I can serve you; you have only to mention it; Trust to your Brother, and be assured he will never betray your confidence. When You see my Cousin and future Brother George Leigh, tell him that I already consider him as my Friend, for whoever is beloved by you, my amiable Sister, will always be equally Dear to me.—I arrived here today at 2 o'Clock after a fatiguing Journey, I found my Mother perfectly well, She desires to be kindly remembered to you; as She is just now Gone out to an assembly, I have taken the first opportunity to write to you, I hope she will not return immediately; for if she was to take it into her head to peruse my epistle, there is one part of it which would produce from her a panegyric on *a friend of yours* not at all agreeable to me, and I fancy, *not particularly delightful to you*. If you see Lord Sidney Osborne I beg you will remember me to him, I fancy he has almost forgot me by this time, for it is rather more than a year Since I had the pleasure of Seeing him.—Also remember me to poor old Murray, tell him we will see that something is to be done for him, for *while I live he shall never be abandoned In his old Age*. Write to me Soon, my Dear Augusta, And do not forget to love me, In the mean time I remain more than words [can] express, your ever sincere, affectionate

Brother and Friend

BYRON

P.S.—Do not forget to Knit the purse you promised me, Adieu my beloved Sister.—

TO AUGUSTA BYRON *Friday November 2d. 1804*

This morning my dear Augusta I received your affectionate letter, and it reached me at a time when I wanted consolation, not however of your kind for I am not old enough or Goose enough to be in love, no, my sorrows are of a different nature though more calculated to provoke risibility than excite compassion. You must know Sister of mine, that I am the most unlucky wight in Harrow perhaps in Christendom, and am no sooner out of one scrape than into another. And today, this very morning I had a thundering Jobation from our Good Doctor, which deranged my *nervous system* for at least five minutes. But notwithstanding He and I now and then disagree, yet upon the whole we are very good friends, for there is so much of the Gentleman, so much mildness, and nothing of pedantry in his character, that I cannot help liking him and will remember his instructions with gratitude as long as I live. He leaves Harrow soon, apropos, so do I. His quitting will be a considerable loss to the school. He is the best master we ever had, and at the same time respected and feared, greatly will he be regretted by all who know him. You tell me you don't know my friend Ld. Delawarr he is considerably younger than me, but the most good tempered, amiable, clever fellow in the universe. To all which he adds the quality (a good one in the eyes of women) of being remarkably handsome, almost too much so for a boy. He is at present very low in the school, not owing to his want of ability, but to his years, I am nearly at the top of it, by the rules of our Seminary he is under my power but he is too goodnatured ever to offend me, and I like him too well ever to exert my authority over him. If you should ever meet, and chance to know him, take notice of him on my account.

You say that you shall write to the Dowager Soon her address is at Southwell, *that* I need hardly inform you. Now Augusta I am going to tell you a secret, perhaps I shall appear undutiful to you, but believe [me] my affection for you is founded on a more firm basis. My mother has lately behaved to me in such an eccentric manner, that so far from feeling the affection of a Son, it is with difficulty I can restrain my dislike. Not that I can complain of want of liberality, no, She always supplies me with as much money, as I can spend, amd more than most boys hope for or desire. But with all this she is so hasty, so impatient, that I dread the approach of the holidays, more than most boys do their return from them. In former days she spoilt me, now she is altered to the contrary, for the most trifling thing, she upbraids me in a most outrageous manner, and all our disputes have been lately heightened by my one with that object of my cordial, deliberate detestation, Lord Grey de Ruthyn. She wishes me to explain my reasons for disliking him, which I will never do, would I do it to any one, be assured you my dear Augusta would be the first who would know them. She also insists on my being reconciled to him, and once she let drop such an odd expression that I was half inclined to believe the dowager was in love with him. But I hope not for he is the most disagreeable person (in my opinion) that exists. He called once during my last vacation, she threatened, stormed, begged, me to make it up, he himself loved me, and wished it, but my reason was so excellent that neither had effect, nor would I speak or stay in the same room, till he took his departure. No doubt this appears odd but was my reason known, which it never will be if I can help it, I should be justified in my conduct. Now if I am to be tormented with her and him in this style I cannot submit to it. You Augusta are the only relation I have who treats me as a friend, <Impart this to> if you too desert me, I have nobody I can love but Delawarr. If it was not for his sake, Harrow would be a desert, and I should dislike staying at it. You desire me to burn your epistles, indeed I cannot do that, but I will take care that They shall be invisible. If you burn any of mine, I shall be *monstrous angry* take care of them till we meet. [Two lines referring to Delawarr crosssed out.] Delawarr and myself are in a manner connected, for one of our forefathers in Charles the 1st's time married into their family. Hartington, whom you enquire after, is on very good terms with me, nothing more, he is of a soft milky disposition, and of a happy apathy of temper which defies the softer emotions, and is insensible of ill treatment—so much for him. Don't betray me to the Dowager, I should like to know your Lady Gertrude, as you and her are so great Friends Adieu my pretty Sister, write Soon.

TO AUGUSTA BYRON   *Harrow Saturday 11th. Novr. 1804*

I thought my dear Augusta that your opinion of my *meek mamma* would coincide with mine; Her temper is so so variable, and when inflamed, so furious, that I dread our meeting, not but I dare say, that I am troublesome enough, but I always endeavour to be as dutiful as possible. She is so very strenuous, and so tormenting in her entreaties and commands, with regard to my reconciliation, with that detestable Lord G[rey] that I suppose she has a penchant for his Lordship, but I am confident that he does not return it, for he rather dislikes her, than otherwise, at least as far as I can judge. But she has an excellent opinion of her personal attractions, sinks her age a good six years, avers that when I was born she was only eighteen, when you my dear Sister as well as I know that she was of age when she married my father, and that I was not born for three years afterwards, but vanity is the weakness of *your sex*, and these are mere foibles that I have related to you, and provided she never molested me I should look upon them as follies very excusable in a woman. But I am now coming to what must shock you, as much as it does me, when she has occasion to lecture me (not very seldom you will think no doubt) she does not do it in a manner that commands respect, and in an impressive style. no. did she do that I should amend my faults with pleasure, and dread to offend a kind though just mother. But she flies into a fit of phrenzy upbraids me as if I was the most undutiful wretch in existence, rakes up the ashes of of my *father*, abuses him, says I shall be a true Byrrone, which is the worst epithet she can invent. Am I to call this woman mother? Because by natures law she has authority over me, am I to be trampled upon in this manner? Am I to be goaded with insult, loaded with obloquy, and suffer my feelings to be outraged on the most trivial occasions? I owe her respect as a Son, But I renounce her as a Friend. What an example does she shew me? I hope in God I shall never follow it. I have not told you all nor can I, I respect you as a female, nor although I ought to confide in you as a Sister, will I shock you with the repetition of Scenes, which you may judge of by the Sample I have given you, and which to all but you are buried in oblivion. Would they were so in my mind. I am afraid they never will. And can I, my dear Sister, look up to this mother, with that respect, that affection I ought. Am I to be eternally subjected to her caprice! I hope not, indeed a few short years will emancipate me from the Shackles I now wear, and then perhaps she will govern her passion better than at present. You mistake me, if you think I dislike Lord Carlisle, I respect him, and might like him did I know him better. For him too my mother has an antipathy, why I know not. I am afraid he could be but of little use to me, in separating me from her, which she would oppose with all her might, but I dare say he would assist me if he could, so I take the will for the Deed and am obliged to him exactly the [sic] in the same manner, as if he succeeded in his efforts. I am in great hopes, that at Christmas I shall be with Mr. Hanson during the vacation, I shall do all I can to avoid a visit to my mother wherever she is. It is the first duty of a parent, to impress precepts of obedience in their children, but her method is so violent, so capricious, that the patience of Job, the versatility of a member of the House of Commons could not support it. I revere Dr. Drury much more than I do her, yet he is never violent, never outrageous, I dread offending him, not however through fear, but the respect I bear him, makes me unhappy when I am under his displeasure. My mother's precepts, never convey instruction, never fix upon my mind, to be sure they are calculated, to inculcate obedience, so are chains, and tortures, but though they may restrain for a time the mind revolts from such treatment. Not that Mrs. Byron ever injures my *sacred* person. I am rather too old for that, but her words are of that rough texture, which offend more than personal ill usage. "A talkative woman is like an Adder's tongue," so says one of the prophets, but which I can't tell, and very likely you don't wish to know, but he was a true one whoever he was. The postage of your letters My dear Augusta don't fall upon me, but if they did it would make no difference, for I am Generally in cash, and should think the trifle I paid for your epistles the best laid out I ever spent in my life. Write Soon. Remember me to Lord Carlisle, and believe me I ever am your affectionate Brother and Friend

BYRON

Lines Written Beneath an Elm, in the Churchyard of Harrow on the Hill

September 2d, 1807

Spot of my youth! whose hoary branches sigh,
Swept by the breeze that fans thy cloudless sky,
Where now alone, I muse, who oft have trod,
With those I lov'd, thy soft and verdent sod;
With those, who scatter'd far, perchance, deplore,
Like me the happy scenes they knew before;
Oh! as I trace again thy winding hill,
Mine eyes admire, my heart adores thee still,
Thou drooping Elm! beneath whose boughs I lay,
And frequent mus'd the twilight hours away;
Where, as they once were wont, my limbs recline,
But, ah! without the thoughts, which, then, were mine;
How do thy branches, moaning to the blast,
Invite the bosom to recall the past,
And seem to whisper, as they gently swell,
'Take, while thou canst, a ling'ring, last farewell!'

When Fate shall chill at length this fever'd breast,
And calm its cares and passions into rest;
Oft, have I thought, 'twould soothe my dying hour,
If aught may soothe, when Life resigns her power;
To know, some humbler grave, some narrow cell,
Would hide my bosom, where it lov'd to dwell;
With this fond dream, methinks 'twere sweet to die,
And here it linger'd, here my heart might lie.
Here might I sleep, where all my hopes arose,
Scene of my youth, and couch of my repose;
Forever stretch'd beneath this mantling shade,
Prest by the turf, where once my childhood play'd;
Wrapt by the soil, that veils the spot I lov'd,

Mix'd with the earth, o'er which my footsteps mov'd;
Blest by the tongues, that charm'd my youthful ear,
Mourn'd by the few, my soul acknowledg'd here;
Deplor'd by those, in early days allied,
And unremember'd by the world beside.

[1807]

SOUTHWELL

NOTTINGHAMSHIRE

Epitaph on John Adams of Southwell,
A Carrier who died of Drunkenness

John Adams lies here, of the parish of Southwell,
A *Carrier* who carried his can to his mouth well;
He *carried* so much, and he *carried* so fast,
He could *carry* no more—so was *carried* at last;
For the liquor he drank, being too much for one,
He could not *carry off*,—so he's now *carri-on*.

September 1807

Burgage Manor April 23d. 1805

My dearest Augusta.—I presume by this time, that you are safely arrived at the Earls, at least I *hope* so; nor shall I feel myself perfectly easy, till I have the pleasure of hearing from yourself of your safety. I myself shall set out for town this day (Tuesday) week, and intend waiting upon you on Thursday at farthest; in the mean time I must console myself as well as I can; and I am sure, no unhappy mortal ever required much more consolation than I do at present.—You as well as myself know the *sweet* and *amiable* temper of a certain personage to whom I am nearly related; of *course*, the pleasure I have enjoyed during my vacation, (although it has been greater than I expected) yet has not been so *superabundant* as to make me wish to stay a day longer than I can avoid. However, notwithstanding the dullness of the place, and certain *unpleasant things* that occur In a family not a hundred miles distant from Southwell, I contrived to pass my time in peace, till to day, when unhappily, In a most inadvertent manner, I said that Southwell was not *peculiarly* to my taste, but however, I merely expressed this in common conversation, without speaking disrespectfully of the *sweet town*; (which between you and I; I wish was swallowed up by an Earthquake, provided my *Eloquent mother* was not in it) No sooner had the unlucky Sentence, which I believe was prompted by my evil Genius, escaped my lips, than I was treated with an Oration in the *ancient style*, which I have often so *pathetically* described to you, unequalled by any thing of *modern* or *antique* date; nay the Philippics against Ld. Melville were nothing to it, one would really Imagine to have heard the *Good Lady*, that I was a most *treasonable Culprit*, but thank St. Peter, after undergoing this *Purgatory* for the last hour, it is at length blown over, & I have sat down under these *pleasing impressions* to address you, so that I am afraid my epistle will not be the most entertaining. I assure you upon my *honour*, jesting apart, I have never been so *scurrilously* and *violently* abused by any person, as by that woman, whom I think, I am to call mother, by that being who gave me birth, to whom I ought to look up with veneration and respect, but whom I am sorry I cannot love or admire. Within one little hour, I have not only [heard] myself, but have heard my *whole family* by the fathers side, *stigmatized* in terms that the *blackest malevolence* would [per-haps] shrink from, and that too in words [you] would be shocked to hear. Such, Augusta, such is my mother; *my mother*. I disclaim her from this time, and although I cannot help treating her with respect, I cannot reverence as I ought to do, that parent who by her outrageous conduct forfeits all title to filial affection. To you Augusta, I must look up, as my nearest relation, to you I must confide what I cannot mention to others, and I am sure you will pity me, but I entreat you to keep this a secret, nor expose that unhappy failing of this woman, which I must bear with patience. I would be very sorry to have it discovered, as I have only one week more, for the present. In the mean time you may write to me with the greatest safety, as she would not open any of my letters, even from you. I entreat then that you will favour me with an answer to this. I hope however to have the pleasure of seeing you on the day appointed, but If you could contrive any way that I may avoid being asked to dinner by Ld. C[arlisle] I would be obliged to you, as I hate strangers. Adieu, my Beloved Sister,

> I remain ever yours,
> BYRON

TO AUGUSTA BYRON   *Tuesday July 2d. 1805*

My dearest Augusta.—I am just returned from Cambridge, where I have been to enter myself at Trinity College.—Thursday is our Speechday at Harrow, and as I forgot to remind you of its ap-proach, previous to our first declamation. I have given you *timely* notice this time. If you intend doing me the *honour* of attending, I would recommend you not to come without a Gentleman, as I shall be too much engaged all the morning to take care of you, and I should not imagine you would admire *stalking* about by yourself. You had better be there by 12 o'clock as we begin at 1, and I should like to procure you a good place; Harrow is 11 miles from town, it will just make a *comfortable* morning's drive for you. I don't know how you are to come, but for *Godsake* bring as few women with you as possible, I would wish you to Write me an answer immediately, that I may know on Thursday morning, whether you will drive over or not, and I will arrange my other engagements accordingly. I *beg Madam* you may make your appearance in one of his Lordships most *dashing* carriages, as our Harrow *etiquette*, admits of nothing but the most *superb* vehicles, on our Grand *Festivals*. In the mean time believe me dearest Augusta your affectionate Brother,

BYRON

TO AUGUSTA BYRON   *Burgage Manor August 10th. 1805*

I have at last succeeded, my dearest Augusta, in pacifying the dowager, and mollifying that *piece* of *flint* which the good Lady denominates her heart. She now has condescended to send you her *love*, although with many comments on the occasion, and many compliments to herself. But to me she still continues to be a torment, and I doubt not would continue so till the end of my life. However this is the last time she ever will have an opportunity, as, when I go to college, I shall employ my vacations either in town; or during the summer I intend making a tour through the Highlands, and to visit the Hebrides with a party of my friends, whom I have engaged for the purpose. This my old preceptor Drury recommended as the most improving way of employing my summer vacation, and I have now an additional reason for following his advice, as I by that means will avoid the society of this woman, whose detestable temper destroys every Idea of domestic comfort. It is a happy thing that she is my mother and not my wife, so that I can rid myself of her when I please, and indeed if she goes on in the style that she has done for this last week that I have been with her, I shall quit her before the month, (I am to drag out in her company) is expired, and place myself any where, rather than remain with such a vixen. As I am to have a very handsome allowance, which does not deprive her of a sixpence, since there is an addition made from my fortune by the Chancellor for the purpose, I shall be perfectly independent of her, and as she has long since trampled upon, and [harrowed] up every affectionate tie, It is my [serious] determination never again to visit, or be upon any friendly terms with her. This I owe to myself, and to my own comfort, as well as Justice to the memory of my nearest relations, who have been most shamefully libelled by this female Tisiphone, a name which your *Ladyship* will recollect to have belonged to one of the Furies.——— You need not take the precaution of speaking in so enigmatical a style, in your next, as bad as the woman is, she would not dare to open any letter addressed to me from you, whenever you can find time to write believe me your epistle will be productive of the greatest pleasure, to your

affectionate Brother
BYRON

TO CHARLES DAVID GORDON   *Burgage Manor Southwell*
                                 Notts. August 4th. 1805

Although I am greatly afraid, *my* Dearest Gordon, that you will not receive this Epistle till your return from *Abergeldie*, (as your letter states that you leave Ledbury on Thursday next) yet, that it may not be my fault, I have not deferred answering yours a Moment, and, as I have just now concluded my Journey, my first, and, I trust you will believe me when I say, most pleasing occupation will be to write to you. We have played the Eton and were most confoundedly beat, however it was some comfort to me that I got 11 notches the 1st Innings and 7 the 2d. which was more than any of our side, except Brockman and Ipswich, could contrive to hit. After the match we dined [together, and were] extremely friendly, not a single [discordant word] was uttered by either party. To be sure, we were most of us *rather* drunk, and went together to the Haymarket Theatre where we kicked up a row, as you may suppose when so many *Harrovians* and *Etonians* met at one place, I was one of seven in a single Hackney Coach, 4 Eton and 3 Harrow fellows, we all got into the same box, the consequence was that such a devil of a noise arose that none of our neighbours could hear a word of the drama, at which, not being *highly delighted*, they began to quarrel with us, and we nearly came to a *battle royal.* How I got home after the play God knows. I hardly recollect, as my brain was so much confused by the heat, the row, and the wine I drank, that I could not remember in the morning how the deuce I found my way to bed. The rain was so incessant in the evening that we could [hardly get our] Jarveys, which was the cause of so many [being stowed into] one. I saw young Twilt, your brother at the match, and saw also an old schoolfellow of mine whom I had not beheld for six years, but, he was not the one whom you were so good as to enquire after for Me, and for which I return you my sincere thanks. I set off last night at eight o'clock for my mothers and am just arrived this afternoon and have not delayed a second in thanking you for so soon fulfilling my request that you would correspond with me. My address at Cambridge will be Trinity College but I shall not go [there] till the 20th of October[;] you may [continue] to direct your letters here; when I go to Hampshire which will not be till you have returned to Harrow, I will send my address previous to my departure from my mothers. I agree with you in the hope that we shall continue our correspondence for a long time. I trust *my* dearest Friend that it will only be interrupted by our being some time or other again in the same place or under the same roof, as when I have finished my *Classical labours* and my minority is expired, I shall expect you to be a frequent visitor to Newstead Abbey, my seat in this county, which lies about 12 miles from my mothers house where I now am; There I can show you plenty of hunting, shooting, and fishing, and be assured no one ever will be a more welcome Guest than yourself Nor is there any one whose correspondence can give me more pleasure, or whose friendship yield me greater delight than yours. Such, dearest Charles, Believe me, will always be the sentiments of

> yours most affectionately,
>
> BYRON

TO EDWARD NOEL LONG   *16 Piccadilly August 9th. 1806*

My dear Long,—You will probably *marvel*, at the Date of this Epistle, conceiving me still at Burgage, with my *agreeable* Relative.—To explain this Revolution, it is necessary to relate that finding *Gam*, worse instead of Better, I took the Liberty of departing in my Carriage & four, without "*Beat of Drum*" in the "Dead of the Night" but as you will possibly imagine, without "*singing out three Times*" to inform the Inhabitants, of my Retreat.—I shall remain in Town, about a week, till renovated with "*Suskins*" & then proceed to the Sea, but what part is indifferent to me, if you will therefore in your answer, mention the Place where you at present *sojourn*, & the Best Hotel, I will join you speedily.—I have some Idea if I find it convenient, of visiting Cambridge for a couple of Days, to pay my Bills, Should I execute this plan, & you feel an Inclination to review our ancient Residence, I shall be happy in your Society, & we will afterwards proceed to the Ocean together.—In my next, you will learn what I have determined, but in the Interim, I shall expect some Intelligence from your prolific pen. I decamped from Notts. in such a Devil of a hurry that my poem's are left in the hands of the printer, and *Gam* [was?] so suspicious of my Intents [that?] my [pistols?] were left behind, and my Clothes brought off in Bundles.—I wait with some Impatience your Answer, doubtless full of Amazement, at my sudden March, of which you shall hear the Detail at length on our Meeting. Adieu believe me

yours & &

BYRON

THE EARL OF CLARE   *Southwell. Novr. 4th. 1806*

My dearest Clare,—The Date of my Letter will seem rather extraordinary, when in my last, some Months since, I requested you to address your Answer to Cambridge.—I now shall commence with the same Request, as I am about to visit College, after having protracted my Residence here, much longer than was my original Intention.—I have been principally detained by some private Theatricals, in which I sustained the first parts, of these I have given a long Account to Wingfield, who has probably mentioned it, therefore my Recapitulation will be unnecessary.—I am truly sorry your Situation at Harrow is so uncomfortable, but the prospect of a speedy Liberation, will reconcile you to it for the present.—

TO EDWARD NOEL LONG   *Southwell, Ap. 16th, 1807*

Your Epistle, my dear *Standard Bearer*, augurs not much in
favour of your new life, particularly the latter part, where you say
your happiest Days are over. I most sincerely hope not. The past has
certainly in some parts been pleasant, but I trust will be equalled, if
not exceeded by the future. "You hope it is not so with me."

To be plain with Regard to myself. Nature stampt me in the
Die of *Indifference*. I consider myself as destined never to be happy,
although in some instances fortunate. I am an isolated Being on
the Earth, without a Tie to attach me to life, except a few Schoolfellows, and a *score of females*. Let me but "hear my fame on the
winds" and the song of the Bards in my Norman house, I ask no
more and don't expect so much. Of Religion I know nothing,
at least in its *favour*. We have *fools* in all sects and Impostors in
most; why should I believe mysteries no one understands, because
written by men who chose to mistake madness for Inspiration,
and style themselves *Evangelicals*? However enough on this subject.
Your *piety* will be *aghast*, and I wish for no proselytes. This much
I will venture to affirm, that all the virtues and pious *Deeds* performed on Earth can never entitle a man to Everlasting happiness
in a future State; nor on the other hand can such a Scene as a Seat
of eternal punishment exist, it is incompatible with the benign
attributes of a Deity to suppose so; I am surrounded here by parsons & Methodists, but, as you will perceive not infected with the
Mania, I have lived a *Deist*, what I shall die I know not—however
come what may, "*ridens moriar*".—Nothing detains me here, but
the publication, which will not be complete till June, about 20
of the present pieces, will be cut out, & a number of new things
added, amongst them a complete Episode of Nisus & Euryalus
from Virgil, some Odes from Anacreon, & several original Odes,
the whole will cover 170 pages, my last production has been a
poem in Imitation of Ossian, which I shall not publish, having
enough without it. Many of the present poems are enlarged and
altered, in short you will behold an "Old friend with a new face."
Were I to publish all I have written in Rhyme, I should fill a decent
Quarto; however, half is quite enough at present. You shall have *all*
when we meet.

I grow thin daily; since the commencement of my System I have lost 23 lbs. in my weight (*i.e.*) 1 st. and 9 lbs. When I began I weighed 14 st. 6 lbs., and on Tuesday I found myself reduced to 12 st. 11 lb. What sayest thou, Ned? do you not envy? I shall still proceed till I arrive at 12 st. and then stop, at least if I am not too fat, but shall always live temperately and take much exercise.

If there is a possibility we shall meet in June. I shall be in Town, before I proceed to Granta, and if the "mountain will not come to Mahomet, Mahomet will go to the mountain." I don't mean, by comparing you to the mountain, to insinuate anything on the Subject of your Size. Xerxes, it is said, formed Mount Athos into the Shape of a Woman; had he lived now, and taken a peep at Chatham, he would have spared himself the trouble and made it unnecessary by finding a *Hill* ready cut to his wishes.

Adieu, dear Mont Blanc, or rather *Mont Rouge*; don't, for Heaven's sake, turn Volcanic, at least roll the Lava of your indignation in any other Channel, and not consume

Your's ever,
BYRON

Write Immediately.

TO EDWARD NOEL LONG   *Southwell May 1st. 1807*

My dear Long—I am happy my Epistle in Rhyme pleased you, it was sent with all it's imperfections, rough from the Imagination, without the polish of Correction, or the merit of Labour.—I am truly sorry the duties of your profession call you to combat, for what? can you tell me? the ambition of Despotism, or the caprice of men placed by chance in the Situation of Governors, & probably inferior to yourself & many more of their victims in every Respect.—You know, at least I *think* you know I am no *coward*, nor would I shrink from Danger on a proper occasion, indeed Life has too little valuable for me, to make Death horrible; I am not insensible to Glory, & even hope before I am at *Rest*, to see some service in a military Capacity, yet I cannot conquer my repugnance to a Life absolutely & exclusively devoted to Carnage, or bestow any appellation in my Idea applicable to a *mercenary* Soldier, but

the *Slave* of *Blood*. You will excuse the freedom of my Remarks &
smile again at Sentiments to which you are no Stranger; as you
have heard me declare them before, to *very little* purpose; you have
entered into a profession with all the ardour hope &c.&c. of *19*
excusable enough at our age, I sincerely hope some one may hear
your opinion on the Subject at *50*.— —However with all my detestation of *licensed Murder* you will probably be surprised to hear
me say, that I seriously intend on the expiration of my minority,
(if we are still at war) to raise a corps of Cavalry, & if possible, to
volunteer for foreign Service.—Such however is my Intention, but
Heaven forbid, my whole existence should be devoted to Slaughter, or that I should commence professional "*Helmet Breaker*" no,
no, in peace I would *strike* the *Lyre* however unskilfully for my
own amusement.—If the war is concluded when I *commence man*,
I shall travel not over France & Italy the common *Turnpike* of
coxcombs & *virtuosos*, but into Greece & Turkey in Europe, Russia
& at which parts of our Globe, I have a singular propensity to in-
vestigate.—I know nothing of the Harrow [race?], I saw something
in the paper, about the "*young Gentlemen* of the *Boarding School*",
& the ["]*Inhabitants*", but of what nature I am ignorant—I had
a dozen correspondents at Ida half a year ago, but have dropped
them *all* by degrees, I am become rather *misanthropias* & no longer
feel the same romantic attachment to Harrow & my *Theban Band*,
which formerly swayed my nature, my last Letter to you (in verse)
was it's dying Effusion, the *final Spark* of enchanted Romance &
boyish (Fancy) Enthusiasm.—I shall not visit the Speeches, without *you*, they would be dull indeed, I did hope we should have trod
our former paths together.—I have done with *Hope*— —When
you return from the *field*, bring me the *Scalp* of *Massena*, or the
chine of *Bonaparte*, write from *Warsaw*, or *Calabria*, know you
which is your Destination? I grow thin, have lost 2 Stone & 1 LB.
so am much diminished.— —Answer this before you embark, of
my Regret at your departure, I shall say nothing, it is unavailing,
if ever you return, believe me there is no one, who will greet your
arrival with more unfeigned Satisfaction than

yours ever most sincerely

BYRON

2 in the morning, May 2nd 1807.

CAMBRIDGE

For my part I say nothing—nothing—but
 This I will say—my reasons are my own—
That if I had an only son to put
 To school (as God be praised that I have none),
'Tis not with Donna Inez I would shut
 Him up to learn his catechism alone,
No—no—I'd send him out betimes to college,
For there it was I picked up my own knowledge.

For there one learns—'tis not for me to boast,
 Though I acquired—but I pass over that,
As well as all the Greek I since have lost:
 I say that there's the place—but "Verbum sat."
I think I picked up too, as well as most,
 Knowledge of matters—but no matter what—
I never married—but, I think, I know
That sons should not be educated so.

DON JUAN I, 52–53

Reading List
(1807)

List of the different poets, Dramatic or otherwise, who have distinguished their respective languages by their productions.—

England–
: Milton, Dryden, Spenser, Pope Shakespeare, Massinger, Ben Johnson Beaumont & Fletcher. &^c–

Scotland.-
: Ossian or Macpherson, Burns, Ramsay, Walter Scott, Macneill Home Author of Douglas.–

Ireland–
: Swift, a Hist[ory] in himself.

Wales– – –
: Taliessin and the Bards.

France– – –
: Voltaire, Chaulieu, Boileau, Moliere, Corneille, Racine, DeLille esteemed the greatest of living Poets certainly the most successfull.–

Spain– – –
: Lope de Vega, Cervantes author of Galatea a Poem in 6 books but more renowned as the writer of Don Quixote.

Portugal– –
: Camoens Author of the Lusiad, a dull poem, but prized by his countrymen as their only epic effort.

Germany– –
: Klopstock, Wieland Goethe, Gesner, Kleist, Lessing Schiller, Kotzebue

Italy
: Tasso, Ariosto, Petrarch, Dante, Bembo, Metastasio.

Arabia,
: Mahomet, whose Koran contains most sublime poetical passages far surpassing European Poetry

Persia–
: Ferdausi, author of the Shah Nameh the Persian Iliad, Sadi, and Hafiz, the immortal Hafiz the oriental Anacreon, the last is reverenced beyond any Bard of ancient or modern times by the

Persians, who resort to his tomb near Schiraz
to celebrate his memory, a splendid copy of his
works is chained to his Monument.–

Greece–	Homer, Hesiod, Anacreon, Sappho Alcæus, Apollonius Rhodius, Callimachus Menander, Aristophanes, Sophocles, Euripides, Æschylus, Pindar.
Latin	Virgil, Lucan, Horace, Claudian, Statius, Ovid, Catullus, Tibullus, Propertius, Ennius Plautus, Terentius, Seneca
America,	an epic Poet has already appeared in that Hemisphere, Barlow, author of the Columbiad, but not to be compared with the work of more polished nations.–

Iceland, Denmark, Norway, were famous for their Skalds among
these Lodbrog, was one of the most distinguished, his death Song
breathes ferocious sentiments, but a glorious and impassioned
Strain of Poetry.–

Hindostan, is undistinguished by any great Bard at least the San-
scrit is so imperfectly known to Europeans, we know not what
poetical Relics may exist.– – – –

The Birman Empire,	Here the natives are passionately fond of Poetry, but their Bards are unknown
China– – –	I never heard of any Chinese Poet but the *Emperor Kien Long*, and his ode to *Tea*, what a pity their Philosopher Confucius did not write Poetry with his precepts of morality.–
Africa– – – –	In Africa, some of the native melodies are plaintive, & the words simple and affecting, but whether these rude strains of nature, can be classed with Poetry, as the songs of the Bards, the Skalds of Europe &c. I know not –

This brief list of Poets, I have written down from memory, without any Book of Reference, consequently some errors may occur, but I think if any very trivial, the works of the European & some of the Asiatic, I have perused either in the original, or Translations, in my list of English, I have merely mentioned the greatest, to enumerate the minor poets would be useless, as well as tedious, perhaps Gray, Goldsmith, and Collins, or Thomson might have been added as worthy of mention in a *Cosmopolite* account, but as for the others from Chaucer down to Churchill they are "voces & præterea nihil" sometimes spoken of, rarely read, & never with advantage.—Chaucer notwithstanding the praises bestowed on him, I think obscene, and contemptible, he owes his celebrity, merely to his antiquity, which he does not deserve so well as Pierce Plowman, or Thomas of Ercildoune, English living poets I have avoided mentioning, we have none who will not survive their productions. Taste is over with us, & another century, will sweep our Empire, our literature, & our name from all, but a place in the annals of mankind.– – – – –

Byron Nov.ʳ 30.ᵗʰ. *1807*

List of Historical Writers whose Works I have perused in different languages.

Hume, Gibbon, Robertson, Orme, Voltaire, Rollin, Rapin, Smollet, Henry, Knolles Cantemir, Paul Rycaut, Vertot, Livy, Tacitus, Eutropius, Arrian, Thucydides, Xenophon Herodotus, with several others whom I shall enumerate under their respective heads.

History of England– –	Hume, Rapin, Henry Smollet, Tindal, Belsham, Bisset Adolphus, Holinshed, Froissart's Chronicles belonging properly to France.– – – – –
Scotland,	Buchanan, Hector Boethius, both in the Latin,
Ireland,	by, Gordon
Rome,– –	Hooke, Decline and fall by Gibbon, Ancient History by Rollin, including an Account of the Carthaginians &ᶜ. &ᶜ. besides Livy, Tacitus, Eutropius, Cornelius Nepos, Julius Caesar, Arrian Sallust,

Greece,	Mitford's Greece, Lelands Philip, Plutarch, Potters Antiquities, Xenophon Thucydides, Herodotus.
France– – –	Mezeray, Voltaire.
Spain– – –	I Chiefly derived my Knowledge of old Spanish History from a Book called the Atlas, now obsolete, the modern history from the intrigues of Alberoni down to the Prince of Peace I learned from their connection with European Politics.–
Portugal– –	From Vertot, as also his account of the Siege of Rhodes, though the last is his own Invention, the real facts being totally different, – so much for his Knights of Malta.–
Turkey,	I have read Knolles, Sir Paul Rycaut, and Prince Cantemir, besides a more modern History, anonymous, of the Ottoman History I know every event, from Tangralopix, and afterwards Othman 1st. to the peace of Passarowitz, in 1718. – the Battle of Crotzka in 1739 & the treaty between Russia & Turkey in 1790.
Russia,	Tookes, Life of Catherine 2^d.Voltaires Czar Peter.
Sweden,	Voltaires Charles 12th. also Norberg's Charles 12th. in my opinion the best of the two, a Translation of Schiller's thirty years war contains the exploits and Death of Gustavus Adolphus, besides Harte's Life of the same Prince,– – – – – I have somewhere read an account of Gustavus Vasa, the Deliverer of Sweden, but do not remember the author's name.
Prussia,	I have seen at least twenty Lives of Frederick the 2^d. the only Prince worth recording in Prussian annals. Gillies, His own works, and Thiebault, none very amusing, the last is paltry, but circumstantial.–

Denmark,	I know little of, of Norway I understand the natural History, but not the Chronological.–
Germany,	I have read long Histories of the Houses of Swabia, Wenceslaus and at length Rudolph of Hapsburg & his *thick lipped* Austrian Descendants.
Switzerland,	Ah! William Tell and the Battle of Morgarten, where Burgundy was slain.–
Italy,	Davila, Guiccadini, The Guelphs, & Gibellines, the Battle of Pavia, Massaniello, the Revolutions of Naples &^{c} &^{c}
Hindostan– –	Orme, & Cambridge.
America, – –	Robertson, Andrews American War.
Africa– –	merely from Travels as Mungo Parke, Bruce.
Biography– –	Robertson's Charles 5th. Caesar, Sallust, Catiline, & Jugurtha, Lives of Marlborough & Eugene, Tekeli Bonneval, Buonaparte, all the British Poets, both by Johnson & Anderson, Rousseau's Confessions, LIfe of Cromwell, British Plutarch British Nepos, Campbell's lives of the Admirals, Charles 12th. Czar Peter, Catherine 2^d, Henry L^d. Kames, Marmontel, Teignmouth's Sir William Jones, Life of Newton, Belisaire, with thousands not to be detailed.
Law,	Blackstone, Montesquieu.
Philosophy,	Paley, Locke, Bacon, Hume, Berkeley, Drummond Beattie, and Bolingbroke, Hobbes I detest.–
Geography,	Strabo, Cellarius, Adams, Pinkerton, and Guthrie.
Poetry, –	all the British Classic's as before detailed, with most of the living Poets Scott, Southey &c. some

French in the original of which the Cid is my
favourite, a little Italian, Greek & Latin without
number, these last I shall give up in future, I
have translated a good deal from Both languages,
verse as well as prose.– –

Eloquence,   Demosthenes, Cicero, Quintilian Sheridan,
Austin's Chironomia, and Parliamentary
Debates from the Revolution to the year
1742.– –

Elocution,   Enfield's Speaker.–

Divinity,   Blair, Porteus, Tillotson, Hooker all very
tiresome,– –
I abhor Religion, though I reverence & love
my God, without the blasphemous notions of
Sectaries, or a belief in their absurd & damnable
Heresies, mysteries, & thirty nine articles.

Miscellanies   turn over

Miscellanies,–   Spectator, Rambler, World &c &c novels by
the thousand.– – –

All the Books here enumerated, I have taken down from memory, I
recollect reading them, & can quote passages from any mentioned,
I have of course omitted several, in my catalogue, but the greater
part of the above I perused before the age of fifteen, but since I left
Harrow I have become idle, & conceited, from scribbling rhyme,
& making love to Women–

B. Novr. 30th. *1807*

I have also read (to my regret at present) above four thousand
novels including the Works of Cervantes, Fielding, Smollett
Richardson Mackenzie, Sterne, Rabelais & Rousseau, &^{c} &^{c} – The
Book in my opinion most useful to a man, who wishes to acquire
the reputation of being well read, with the least trouble, is "Burton's Anatomy of Melancholy" the most amusing & instructive
medley, of quotations & Classical anecdotes I ever perused.– –But
a superficial Reader must take care, or his intricacies will bewilder

him, if however he has patience to go through his volumes, he will be more improved for literary conversation, than by the perusal of any twenty other works with which I am acquainted at least in the English Language.–

Cambridge. June 30th. 1807

My dear *Elizabeth*,—"Better late than never Pal" is a saying of which you know the origin, & as it is applicable on the present occasion, you will excuse its conspicuous place in the front of my Epistle. I am almost *superannuated* here, my old friends (with the exception of a very few) *all* departed, & I am preparing to follow them, but remain till monday to be present at *3 Oratorios*, 2 Concerts, a *fair*, a *boxing match*, & a Ball.—I find I am not only *thinner*, but *taller* by an Inch since my last visit, I was obliged to tell every body my *name*, nobody having the least recollection of my *visage*, or person.—Even the *Hero* of my *Cornelian* (Who is now sitting *vis a vis*, reading a volume of my *poetics*) passed me in Trinity walks without recognizing me in the least, & was thunderstruck at the alteration, which had taken place in my Countenance &c. &c.—Some say I look *better*, others *worse*, but all agree I am *thinner*, more I do not require.—I have lost 2 LB in my weight since I left your *cursed*, *detestable* & *abhorred* abode of *Scandal*, *antiquated virginity*, & universal *Infamy*, where excepting yourself & John Becher, I care not if the whole Race were consigned to the *Pit* of *Acheron*, which I would visit in person, rather than contaminate my *sandals* with the polluted Dust of *Southwell*.—*Seriously* (unless obliged by the *emptiness* of my purse to revisit Mr. B) you will see me no more, on monday I depart for London, & quit Cambridge forever, with little regret, because our *Set* are *vanished*, & my *musical protegé* above mentioned, has left the Choir, & is to be stationed in a mercantile house of considerable eminence in the Metropolis. You may have heard me observe he is exactly to an hour, 2 years younger than myself, I found him grown considerably, & as you will suppose, very glad to see his former *patron*.—He is nearly my height, very thin, very fair complexion, dark eyes, & light locks, my opinion of his mind, you already know, I hope I shall never have reason to change it.—Every Body here conceives me to be an *Invalid*, the University at present is very gay from the *fêtes* of divers kinds, I supped out last night, but *eat* (or ate) nothing, sipped a bottle of Claret, went to bed at 2, & rose at 8. I have commenced early rising, & find it agrees with me, the master & the *fellows* all very *polite*, but look a little *askance*, dont much admire *lampoons*, truth always disagreeable.—Write & tell me how the Inhabitants of your *menagerie go on*, & if my publication *goes off* well, do the *Quadrupeds growl*, apropos how is *Boatswain* & *Bran*, alas! my Bulldog is deceased, *"Flesh both of cur & man is grass"*——Address your answer to Cambridge, if I am gone it will be forwarded, sad news just arrived, Russians beat, a bad set, eat nothing but oil, consequently must melt before a *hard fire*.—I get awkward in my academic habiliments, for want of practice, got up in a Window to hear the Oratorio at St. Mary's, popped down in the middle of the *Messiah*, tore a *woeful rent* in the Back of my best black Silk gown, & damaged an *egregious pair* of Breeches, mem.—never tumble from a church window, during Service.—Adieu, dear Bess, do not remember me to any one, to *forget*, & be forgotten by the people of S.—is all I *aspire* to, too contemptible for hatred, & totally insignificant I leave them to their fate, & think of the tedious *dream* I past there, as a *Blank* in my life, when men without religion are priests, & women without principle, are compelled to drag on a weary form of *involuntary chastity*, what *can* be said? *nothing*—so here ends my *chapter*.—

[Signature torn out]

TO ELIZABETH BRIDGET PIGOT   *Trin. Coll. Camb.*
                                              July 5th. 1807

My dear *Eliza*,—Since my last letter I have determined to reside *another year* at *Granta* as my Rooms &c. &c. are finished in *great Style*, several old friends *come up* again, & many *new* acquaintances made, consequently my Inclination leads me *forward*, & I shall return to College in October if still *alive*. My life here has been one continued *routine* of Dissipation, out at different places every day, engaged to more *dinners* &c. &c. than my *stay* would permit me to *fulfil*, at this moment I write with a *bottle* of *Claret* in my *Head*, & *tears* in my *eyes*, for I have just parted from "my *Corneilan*" who spent the evening with me; as it was our last Interview, I postponed my engagements to devote the hours of the *Sabbath* to friendship, Edleston & I have separated for the present, & my mind is a *Chaos* of *hope & Sorrow*.—Tomorrow I set out for London, you will address your answer to *"Gordon's Hotel" Albemarle Street*, where I *sojourn*, during my visit to the *Metropolis*.—I rejoice to hear you are interested in my "protegè", he has been my *almost constant* associate since October 1805, when I entered Trinity College; his *voice* first attracted my notice, his *countenance* fixed it, & his *manners* attached me to him forever, he departs for a *mercantile house* in *Town*, in October, & we shall probably not meet, till the expiration of my minority, when I shall leave to his *decision*, either *entering* as a *Partner* through my Interest, or residing with me altogether. Of course he *would* in his present *frame* of mind prefer the *latter*, but he may alter his opinion previous to that period, however he shall have his choice, I certainly *love* him more than any human being, & neither *time* or Distance have had the least effect on my (in general) changeable Disposition.—In short, We shall put *Lady E. Butler*, & Miss *Ponsonby* to the *Blush*, *Pylades* & *Orestes* out of countenance, & want nothing but a *Catastrophe* like *Nisus* & *Euryalus*, to give *Jonathan* & *David* the *"go by"*.—He certainly is perhaps more *attached* to *me*, than even I am in *return*, during the whole of my residence at *Cambridge*, we met every day summer & Winter, without passing *one tiresome moment*, & separated *each time* with increasing Reluctance. I hope you will *one day* see *us* together, he is the only *being* I *esteem*, though I *like many*.—The Marquis of *Tavistock* was down the other day, I supped with him at his *Tutor's*, entirely a *whig party*, the opposition *muster* very *strong* here, & Lord Hartington, the Duke of Leinster, &c. &c. are to join us in October, so every thing will be *splendid*.—The *Music* is all over at present, met with another *"accidency"*, upset a *Butter Boat* in the *lap* of a *lady*, looked very *blue*, *spectators* grinned, *"curse em"* apropos, sorry to say, been *drunk* every day, & not quite *sober yet*, however touch no meat, nothing but fish, soup & vegetables, consequently does me no harm, sad dogs all the *Cantabs*, mem, *we mean* to reform next January.—This place is a *Monotony* of *endless variety*, *like it*, hate Southwell, full of old maids, how is Anne Becher? wants a husband, *men scarce*, wont *bite*, mem—tell Anne to fish more cautiously or the *Gudgeons* will be off; catch nothing but *Roach* & *Dace*.—Write soon, has Ridge sold well or do the Ancients demur? what Ladies have bought? all disappointed I dare say nothing *indecent* in the present publication, <sorry for it> *bad*

set at Southwell, no *faces* & dont ever "*mean* well".—Saw a Girl at
St. Mary's the Image of Anne Houson, thought it was her, all in the
wrong, the Lady stared, so did I, I blushed, so did *not* the Lady, sad
thing, wish women, had *more modesty.*—Talking of women brings
my *terrier Fanny* into my head[;] how is she? very well I thank
you.—Got a Headach, must go to bed, up early in the morning to
travel, my "protegé" breakfasts with me, parting spoils my appetite,
excepting from Southwell, mem—*I hate Southwell,*

yours ever

BYRON

TO ELIZABETH BRIDGET PIGOT *Trinity College Cambridge*
October 26th. 1807

My dear Elizabeth,—Fatigued with sitting up till four in the
morning for these last two days at Hazard, I take up my pen to
enquire how your Highness, & the rest of my female acquaintance at the seat of Archiepiscopal Grandeur *Southwell,* go on.—I
know I deserve a scolding for my negligence in not writing more
frequently, but racing up & down the Country for these last three
months, how was it possible to fulfil the Duties of a Correspondent?—Fixed at last for 6 weeks, I write, as *thin* as ever (not having
gained an ounce since my Reduction) & rather in better humour,
for after all, *Southwell* was a detestable residence; thank St. Dom-
inic I have done with it, I have been twice within 8 miles of it,
but could not prevail on myself to *suffocate* in its heavy atmosphere.—This place is wretched enough, a villainous Chaos of Dice
and Drunkenness, nothing but Hazard and Burgundy, Hunting,
Mathematics and Newmarket, Riot and Racing, yet it is a Paradise
compared with the eternal dullness of Southwell, oh! the misery of
doing nothing, but make *Love, enemies,* and *Verses.*—Next January
(but this is *entre nous* only, and pray let it be so, or my maternal
persecutor will be throwing her Tomahawk at any of my curious
projects) I am going to *Sea* for four of [or?] five months, with my
Cousin Capt. Bettesworth, who commands the Tartar the finest
frigate in the navy. I have seen most scenes, and wish to look at a
naval life.—We are going probably to the Mediterranean, or to the

West Indies, or to the Devil, and if there is a possibility of taking me to the Latter, Bettesworth will do it, for he has received four and twenty wounds in different places, and at this moment possesses a Letter from the late Ld. Nelson, stating Bettesworth as the only officer of the navy who had more wounds than himself.— — —I have got a new friend, the finest in the world, a *tame Bear*, when I brought him here, they asked me what I meant to do with him, and my reply was "he should *sit* for *a Fellowship*."—*Sherard* will explain the meaning of the sentence if it is ambiguous.—This answer delighted them not,—we have eternal parties here, and this evening a large assortment of *Jockies*, Gamblers, *Boxers*, *Authors*, *parsons*, and *poets*, sup with me.—A precious Mixture, but they go on well together, and for me, I am a *spice* of every thing except a Jockey, by the bye, I was dismounted again the other day.— —Thank your Brother in my name, for his Treatise. I have written 214 pages of a novel, one poem of 380 Lines, to be published (without my name) in a few weeks, with notes, 560 Lines of Bosworth Field, and 250 Lines of another poem in rhyme, besides half a dozen smaller pieces, the poem to be published is a Satire, apropos, I have been praised to the Skies in the Critical Review, and abused equally in another publication, so much the Better, they tell me, for the sale of the Book, it keeps up controversy, and prevents it from being forgotten, besides the first men of all ages have had their share, nor do the humblest escape, so I bear it like a philosopher, it is odd enough the two opposite Critiques came out on the same day, and out of five pages of abuse, [my?] Censor only quotes *two lines*, from different poems, in support of his opinion, now the proper way to *cut* up, is to quote long passages, and make them appear absurd, because simple allegation is no proof.—on the other hand, there are seven pages of praise, and more than *my modesty* will allow, said on the subject.—Adieu yours truly

BYRON

P.S.—Write, Write, Write!!!

To Thyrza

Without a stone to mark the spot,
    And say, what Truth might well have said,
By all, save one, perchance forgot,
    Ah, wherefore art thou lowly laid?
By many a shore and many a sea
    Divided, yet belov'd in vain;
The past, the future fled to thee
    To bid us meet—no—ne'er again!
Could this have been—a word—a look
    That softly said, "We part in peace",
Had taught my bosom how to brook,
    With fainter sighs, thy soul's release.
And didst thou not, since Death for thee
    Prepar'd a light and pangless dart,
Once long for him thou ne'er shalt see,
    Who held, and holds thee in his heart?
Oh! who like him had watch'd thee here?
    Or sadly mark'd thy glazing eye,
In that dread hour ere death appear,
    When silent Sorrow fears to sigh,
Till all was past? But when no more
    'Twas thine to reck of human woe,
Affection's heart-drops, gushing o'er,
    Had flow'd as fast—as now they flow.
Shall they not flow, when many a day
    In these, to me, deserted towers,
Ere call'd but for a time away,
    Affection's mingling tears were ours?
Ours too the glance none saw beside;
    The smile none else might understand;
The whisper'd thought of hearts allied,
    The pressure of the thrilling hand;
The kiss so guiltless and refin'd
    That Love each warmer wish forbore;
Those eyes proclaim'd so pure a mind,

Ev'n passion blush'd to plead for more.
The tone, that taught me to rejoice,
   When prone, unlike thee, to repine
The song, celestial from thy voice,
   But sweet to me from none but thine;
The pledge we wore—I wear it still,
   But where is thine?—ah, where art thou?
Oft have I borne the weight of ill,
   But never bent beneath till now!
Well hast thou left in life's best bloom
   The cup of woe for me to drain.
If rest alone be in the tomb,
   I would not wish thee here again;
But if in worlds more blest than this
   Thy virtues seek a fitter sphere,
Impart some portion of thy bliss,
   To wean me from mine anguish here.
Teach me—too early taught by thee!—
   To bear, forgiving and forgiv'n:
On earth thy love was such to me,
   It fain would form my hope in heav'n!

King's Coll: C[ambridg]e
Octr. 22d. 1811

My dear Hobhouse,—I write from Scrope's rooms, whom I have just assisted to put to bed in a state of *outrageous* intoxication.—I think I never saw him so bad before.—We dined at Mr. Caldwell's of Jesus Coll: where we met Dr. Clarke & others of the Gown, & Scrope finished himself as usual.—He has been in a similar state every evening since my arrival here a few days ago.—We are to dine at Dr. Clarke's on Thursday.—I find he knows little of Romaic, so we shall have *that department* entirely to ourselves, I tell you this that you need not fear any competition, particularly so formidable a one as Dr. Clarke would probably have been.—I like him much, though Scrope says *we* talked so bitterly that he (the Said Scrope) lost his listeners.—I proceed hence to town, where I shall enquire after your work which I am sorry to say stands still for "*want of Copy*" to talk in Technicals.—I am very low-spirited on many accounts, & wine, which however I do not quaff as formerly, has lost it's power over me.—We all wish you here, & well wherever you are, but surely better with us.—If you don't soon return, Scrope & I mean to visit you in quarters.—The event I mentioned in my last has had an effect on me, I am ashamed to think of, but there is no arguing on these points. I could "have better spared a better being."—Wherever I turn, particularly in this place, the idea goes with me, I say all this at the risk of incurring your contempt, but you cannot despise me more than I do myself.—I am indeed very wretched, & like all complaining persons I can't help telling you so.— —The Marquis Sligo is in a great scrape, about his kidnapping the seamen. I, who know him, do not think him so culpable as the Navy are determined to make him.—He is a good man.—I have been in Lancs. Notts. but all places are alike, I cannot live under my present feelings, I have lost my appetite, my rest, & can neither read write or act in comfort.—Every body here is very polite & hospitable, my friend Scrope particularly. I wish to God he would grow sober, as I much fear no constitution can long support his excesses.—If I lose him & you, what am I?— — Hodgson is not here but expected soon.—Newstead is my regular address.—Demetrius is here much pleased with ye. place. Ld. Sligo is about to send back his Arnaouts.—Excuse this dirty paper, it is of Scrope's best.—Good night'

ever yrs.
BYRON

NEWSTEAD ABBEY

A lamp burned high, while he leant from a niche,
　　Where many a Gothic ornament remained,
In chiselled stone and painted glass, and all
That time has left our fathers of their hall.

Then, as the night was clear though cold, he threw
　　His chamber door wide open—and went forth
Into a gallery, of a sombre hue,
　　Long, furnished with old pictures of great worth,
Of knights and dames heroic and chaste too,
　　As doubtless should be people of high birth.
But by dim lights the portraits of the dead
Have something ghastly, desolate, and dread.

The forms of the grim knight and pictured saint
　　Look living in the moon; and as you turn
Backward and forward to the echoes faint
　　Of your own footsteps—voices from the urn
Appear to wake, and shadows wild and quaint
　　Start from the frames which fence their aspects stern,
As if to ask how you can dare to keep
A vigil there, where all but death should sleep.

DON JUAN XVI, 16–18

To an Oak in the Garden of Newstead Abbey, planted by the Author in the 9th Year of his age; this tree at his last visit was in a state of decay, though perhaps not irrecoverable.—15th March 1807

[1]

Young Oak! when I planted thee deep in the ground,
　　I hoped that thy days would be longer than mine;
That thy dark-waving branches would flourish around,
　　And ivy thy trunk with her mantle entwine.
Such, such was my hope, when, in infancy's years,
　　On the land of my fathers I viewed thee with pride:
They are past, and I water thy stem with my tears,—
　　Thy decay not the weeds that surround thee can hide.

2

I left thee, my Oak, and, since that fatal hour,
　　A stranger has dwelt in the hall of my sire;
Till manhood shall crown me, not mine is the power,
　　But his, whose neglect may have bade thee expire.
Oh! hardy thou wert—even now little care
　　Might revive thy young head, and thy wounds
　　　　gently heal:
But thou wert not fated affection to share—
　　For who could suppose that a Stranger would feel?

3

Ah, droop not, my Oak! lift thy head for a while;
　　Ere twice round yon Glory, this planet shall run,
The hand of thy Master will teach thee to smile,
　　When Infancy's years of probation are done.
Oh, live then, my Oak! tower aloft from the weeds,
　　That clog thy young growth, and assist thy decay,
For still in thy bosom are life's early seeds,
　　And still may thy branches their beauty display.

4

Oh! yet, if maturity's years may be thine,
 Though *I* shall lie low in the cavern of death,
On thy leaves yet the day-beam for ages may shine,
 Uninjured by time, or the rude winter's breath.
For centuries still may thy boughs lightly wave
 O'er the corse of thy lord, in the canopy laid;
While the branches thus gratefully shelter his grave,
 The chief who survives may recline in thy shade.

5

And as he, with his boys, shall revisit the spot,
 He will tell them in whispers more softly to tread.
Ah! surely, by these I shall ne'er be forgot:
 Remembrance still hallows the dust of the dead.
And here, will they say, when in life's glowing prime,
 Perhaps he has pour'd forth his young simple lay,
And here must he sleep, till the moments of time
 Are lost in the hours of Eternity's day.

15 Mar. 1807

TO FRANCIS HODGSON *Newstead Abbey Notts. Novr. 18th. 1808*

My dear Hodgson,—Boatswain is dead! he expired in a state of madness on the 10th. after suffering much, yet retaining all the gentleness of his nature to the last, never attempting to do the least injury to any one near him.—I have lost every thing except Old Murray.— —I sent some game to Drury lately, which I hope escaped the scrutiny of the mutineers, I trust the letter to Claridge was equally fortunate (after being put in the post by you at London) as it contained some cash, which my correspondent notwithstanding the patriotic fervour of the moment, might not chuse to submit to the inspection of the William Tells, and Gracchi of the day.—If my songs have produced the *glorious* effects you mention, I shall be a complete Tyrtaeus, though I am sorry to say, I resemble that interesting Harper, more in his person than Poesy.— —I only lament that Drury's conjecture should be more facetious than well founded, nothing would give me greater glee than to suppose, it was perfectly correct.—It is singular enough, that Wingfield and [Kemmis?] were both my fags at Harrow, and they have now obtained that honour to which their master aspired in vain.—I have written to Government for letters &c.—wont you come and broach a farewell batch at Xmas? cant you "tice Drury into the woods and afterwards dewour him" this day twelvemonth, Deo favente, I shall be crossing Mount Causasus.—Is your information of Jefferies's proposal to Southey well authenticated, if so, pray favour both with a few couplets in your satire.—I should be too happy to think Gifford had troubled [one line cut from MS.] could discover if he really wrote the "expose" in your possession. —My Rhymes on the Bards are forthcoming,—tell Drury he must purchase a copy, I cant afford to give away.—Hobhouse & myself nearly suffocated a person in the Bath yesterday, by way of ascertaining the soundings, I was obliged to jump in, and extricate the Drownee.—Drury will find a letter from me at Harrow, which I hope he will answer, if still at Cambridge, greet him with an embrace, Hobhouse presents all sorts of remembrances to both. But in the words of Gaffer Thumb, "I can no more" believe me dear H. yours

[Signature missing]

Inscription on the Monument of a Newfoundland Dog

When some proud son of man returns to earth,
Unknown to glory, but upheld by birth,
The sculptor's art exhausts the pomp of woe,
And storied urns record who rests below;
When all is done, upon the tomb is seen,
Not what he was, but what he should have been:
But the poor dog, in life the firmest friend,
The first to welcome, foremost to defend,
Whose honest heart is still his master's own,
Who labours, fights, lives, breathes for him alone,
Unhonoured falls, unnoticed all his worth,
Denied in heaven the soul he held on earth:
While man, vain insect! hopes to be forgiven,
And claims himself a sole exclusive heaven.
Oh man! thou feeble tenant of an hour,
Debased by slavery, or corrupt by power,
Who knows thee well must quit thee with disgust,
Degraded mass of animated dust!
Thy love is lust, thy friendship all a cheat,
Thy smiles hypocrisy, thy words deceit!
By nature vile, ennobled but by name,
Each kindred brute might bid thee blush for shame.
Ye! who perchance behold this simple urn,
Pass on—it honours none you wish to mourn:
To mark a friend's remains these stones arise,
I never knew but one, and here he lies.

1808

TO THE HON. AUGUSTA LEIGH   *Newstead Abbey. Notts.—*
                                        Decr. 14th. 1808

My dearest Augusta,—When I stated in my last, that my intercourse with the world had hardened my heart, I did not mean
from any matrimonial disappointment, no, I have been guilty
of many absurdities but I hope in God I shall always escape that
worst of evils, Marriage.—I have no doubt there are exceptions,
and of course include you amongst them, but you will recollect,
that "*exceptions only prove the Rule*."—I live here much in my own
manner, that is, *alone*, for I could not bear the company of my
best friend, above a month; there is such a sameness in mankind
upon the whole, and they grow so much more disgusting every
day, there were it not for a portion of Ambition, and a conviction
that in times like the present, we ought to perform our respective
duties, I should live here all my life, in unvaried Solitude.—I have
been visited by all our Nobility & Gentry, but I return no visits.—
Joseph Murray is at the head of my household, poor honest fellow!
I should be a great Brute, if I had not provided for him in the
manner most congenial to his own feelings, and to mine.—I have
several horses, and a considerable establishment, but I am not addicted to hunting or shooting, I hate all field sports, though a few
years since, I was a tolerable adept in the *polite* arts of Foxhunting,
Hawking, Boxing &c. &c.—My library is rather extensive, (and as
you perhaps know) I am a mighty Scribbler; I flatter myself I have
made some improvements in Newstead, and as I am independent,
I am happy, as far as any person unfortunately enough to be born
into this world, can be said to be so.—I shall be glad to hear from
you when convenient, and beg you to believe me very sincerely
yours

BYRON

Don Juan XIII, 55–72

[Juan, after long travels, arrives in England and visits a Norman Abbey]

55

To Norman Abbey whirled the noble pair,—
     An old, old monastery once, and now
Still older mansion of a rich and rare
     Mixed Gothic, such as artists all allow
Few specimens yet left us can compare
     Withal. It lies perhaps a little low,
Because the monks preferred a hill behind,
To shelter their devotion from the wind.

56

It stood embosomed in a happy valley,
     Crowned by high woodlands, where the Druid oak
Stood like Caractacus in act to rally
     His host, with broad arms 'gainst the thunderstroke.
And from beneath his boughs were seen to sally
     The dappled foresters; as day awoke,
The branching stag swept down with all his herd
To quaff a brook, which murmured like a bird.

57

Before the mansion lay a lucid lake,
     Broad as transparent, deep, and freshly fed
By a river, which its softened way did take
     In currents through the calmer water spread
Around. The wildfowl nestled in the brake
     And sedges, brooding in their liquid bed.
The woods sloped downwards to its brink, and stood
With their green faces fixed upon the flood.

58

Its outlet dashed into a deep cascade,
    Sparkling with foam, until again subsiding,
Its shriller echoes, like an infant made
    Quiet, sank into softer ripples, gliding
Into a rivulet; and thus allayed,
    Pursued its course, now gleaming and now hiding
Its windings through the woods, now clear, now blue,
According as the skies their shadows threw.

59

A glorious remnant of the Gothic pile
    (While yet the church was Rome's) stood half apart
In a grand arch, which once screened many an aisle.
    These last had disappeared—a loss to art:
The first yet frowned superbly o'er the soil,
    And kindled feelings in the roughest heart,
Which mourned the power of time's or tempest's march,
In gazing on that venerable arch.

60

Within a niche, nigh to its pinnacle,
    Twelve saints had once stood sanctified in stone;
But these had fallen, not when the friars fell,
    But in the war which struck Charles from his throne,
When each house was a fortalice, as tell
    The annals of full many a line undone,
The gallant Cavaliers, who fought in vain
For those who knew not to resign or reign.

61

But in a higher niche, alone, but crowned,
    The Virgin Mother of the God-born Child,
With her Son in her blessed arms, looked round,
    Spared by some chance when all beside was spoiled;
She made the earth below seem holy ground.
    This may be superstition, weak or wild,

But even the faintest relics of a shrine
Of any worship wake some thoughts divine.

62

A mighty window, hollow in the centre,
    Shorn of its glass of thousand colourings,
Through which the deepened glories once could enter,
    Streaming from off the sun like seraph's wings,
Now yawns all desolate: now loud, now fainter,
    The gale sweeps through its fretwork, and oft sings
The owl his anthem, where the silenced quire
Lie with their hallelujahs quenched like fire.

63

But in the noontide of the moon, and when
    The wind is winged from one point of heaven,
There moans a strange unearthly sound, which then
    Is musical, a dying accent driven
Through the huge arch, which soars and sinks again.
    Some deem it but the distant echo given
Back to the night wind by the waterfall,
And harmonised by the old choral wall:

64

Others, that some original shape, or form
    Shaped by decay perchance, hath given the power
(Though less than that of Memnon's statue, warm
    In Egypt's rays, to harp at a fixed hour)
To this grey ruin, with a voice to charm.
    Sad, but serene, it sweeps o'er tree or tower;
The cause I know not, nor can solve; but such
The fact;—I've heard it—once perhaps too much.

65

Amidst the court a Gothic fountain played,
    Symmetrical, but decked with carvings quaint—
Strange faces like to men in masquerade,
    And here perhaps a monster, there a saint:

The spring gushed through grim mouths of granite made,
    And sparkled into basins, where it spent
Its little torrent in a thousand bubbles,
Like man's vain glory and his vainer troubles.

66

The mansion's self was vast and venerable,
    With more of the monastic than has been
Elsewhere preserved. The cloisters still were stable,
    The cells too and refectory, I ween:
An exquisite small chapel had been able,
    Still unimpaired, to decorate the scene;
The rest had been reformed, replaced, or sunk,
And spoke more of the baron than the monk.

67

Huge halls, long galleries, spacious chambers, joined
    By no quite lawful marriage of the arts,
Might shock a connoisseur, but when combined,
    Formed a whole which, irregular in parts,
Yet left a grand impression on the mind,
    At least of those whose eyes are in their hearts.
We gaze upon a giant for his stature,
Nor judge at first if all be true to nature.

68

Steel barons, molten the next generation
    To silken rows of gay and gartered earls,
Glanced from the walls in goodly preservation.
    And Lady Marys blooming into girls
With fair long locks had also kept their station,
    And countesses mature in robes and pearls,
Also some beauties of Sir Peter Lely,
Whose drapery hints we may admire them freely.

69

Judges in very formidable ermine
    Were there, with brows that did not much invite
The accused to think their lordships would determine
    His cause by leaning much from might to right;
Bishops, who had not left a single sermon;
    Attorney Generals, awful to the sight,
As hinting more (unless our judgments warp us)
Of the Star Chamber than of habeas corpus.

70

Generals, some all in armour, of the old
    And iron time, ere lead had ta'en the lead,
Others in wigs of Marlborough's martial fold,
    Huger than twelve of our degenerate breed;
Lordlings, with staves of white or keys of gold:
    Nimrods, whose canvas scarce contained the steed;
And here and there some stern high patriot stood,
Who could not get the place for which he sued.

71

But ever and anon, to soothe your vision,
    Fatigued with these hereditary glories,
There rose a Carlo Dolce or a Titian,
    Or wilder group of savage Salvatore's.
Here danced Albano's boys, and here the sea shone
    In Vernet's ocean lights; and there the stories
Of martyrs awed, as Spagnoletto tainted
His brush with all the blood of all the sainted.

72

Here sweetly spread a landscape of Lorraine;
    There Rembrandt made his darkness equal light,
Or gloomy Caravaggio's gloomier stain
    Bronzed o'er some lean and stoic anchorite.
But, lo! a Teniers woos, and not in vain,
    Your eyes to revel in a livelier sight:
His bell-mouthed goblet makes me feel quite Danish
Or Dutch with thirst—What, ho! a flask of Rhenish.

Dear Murray,—What you said of the late Charles Skinner Matthews has set me to my recollections; but I have not been able to turn up anything which would do for the purposed Memoir of his brother,—even if he had previously done enough during his life to sanction the introduction of anecdotes so merely personal. He was, however, a very extraordinary man, and would have been a great one. No one ever succeeded in a more surpassing degree than he did as far as he went. He was indolent, too; but whenever he stripped, he overthrew all antagonists. His conquests will be found registered at Cambridge, particularly his *Downing* one, which was hotly and highly contested, and yet easily *won*. Hobhouse was his most intimate friend, and can tell you more of him than any man. William Bankes also a great deal. I myself recollect more of his oddities than of his academical qualities, for we lived most together at a very idle period of *my* life. When I went up to Trinity, in 1805, at the age of seventeen and a half, I was miserable and untoward to a degree. I was wretched at leaving Harrow, to which I had become attached during the two last years of my stay there; wretched at going to Cambridge instead of Oxford (there were no rooms vacant at Christchurch); wretched from some private domestic circumstances of different kinds, and consequently about as unsocial as a wolf taken from the troop. So that, although I knew Matthews, and met him often *then* at Bankes's (who was my collegiate pastor, and master, and patron,) and at Rhode's, Milnes's, Price's, Dick's, Macnamara's, Farrell's, Gally Knight's, and others of that *set* of contemporaries, yet I was neither intimate with him nor with any one else, except my old schoolfellow Edward Long (with whom I used to pass the day in riding and swimming), and William Bankes, who was good-naturedly tolerant of my ferocities.

It was not till 1807, after I had been upwards of a year away from Cambridge, to which I had returned again to *reside* for my degree, that I became one of Matthew's familiars, by means of Hobhouse, who, after hating me for two years, because I wore a *white hat*, and a *grey* coat, and rode a *grey* horse (as he says himself), took me into his good graces because I had written some poetry. I had always lived a good deal, and got drunk occasionally,

in their company—but now we became really friends in a morning. Matthews, however, was not at this period resident in College.
I met *him* chiefly in London, and at uncertain periods at Cambridge. Hobhouse, in the mean time, did great things: he founded
the Cambridge "Whig Club" (which he seems to have forgotten),
and the "Amicable Society," which was dissolved in consequence of
the members constantly quarrelling, and made himself very popular with "us youth," and no less formidable to all tutors, professors,
and heads of Colleges. William Bankes was gone; while he stayed,
he ruled the roast—or rather the *roasting*—and was father of all
mischiefs.

Matthews and I, meeting in London, and elsewhere, became
great cronies. He was not good tempered—nor am I—but with
a little tact his temper was manageable, and I thought him so
superior a man, that I was willing to sacrifice something to his
humours, which were often, at the same time, amusing and provoking. What became of his *papers* (and he certainly had many),
at the time of his death, was never known. I mention this by the
way, fearing to skip it over, and *as* he *wrote* remarkably well, both
in Latin and English. We went down to Newstead together, where
I had got a famous cellar, and *Monks'* dresses from a masquerade
warehouse. We were a company of some seven or eight, with an occasional neighbour or so for visiters, and used to sit up late in our
friars' dresses, drinking burgundy, claret, champagne, and what
not, out of the *skull-cup*, and all sorts of glasses, and buffooning all
around the house, in our conventual garments. Matthews always
denominated me "the Abbot," and never called me by any other
name in his good humours, to the day of his death. The harmony
of these our symposia was somewhat interrupted, a few days after
our assembling, by Matthews's threatening to throw Hobhouse
out of a *window*, in consequence of I know not what commerce
of jokes ending in this epigram. Hobhouse came to me and said,
that "his respect and regard for me as host would not permit him
to call out any of my guests, and that he should go to town next
morning." He did. It was in vain that I represented to him that the
window was not high, and that the turf under it was particularly
soft. Away he went.

Matthews and myself had travelled down from London

together, talking all the way incessantly upon one single topic. When we got to Loughborough, I know not what chasm had made us diverge for a moment to some other subject, at which he was indignant. "Come," said he, "don't let us break through—let us go on as we began to our journey's end;" and so he continued, and was as entertaining as ever to the very end. He had previously occupied, during my year's absence from Cambridge, my rooms in Trinity, with the furniture; and Jones, the tutor, in his odd way, had said, on putting him in, "Mr. Matthews, I recommend to your attention not to damage any of the moveables, for Lord Byron, Sir, is a young man of *tumultuous passions*." Matthews was delighted with this; and whenever anybody came to visit him, begged them to handle the very door with caution; and used to repeat Jones's admonition in his tone and manner. There was a large mirror in the room, on which he remarked, "that he thought his friends were grown uncommonly assiduous in coming to *see him*, but he soon discovered that they only came to *see themselves*." Jones's phrase of "*tumultuous passions*," and the whole scene, had put him into such good humour, that I verily believe that I owed to it a portion of his good graces.

When at Newstead, somebody by accident rubbed against one of his white silk stockings, one day before dinner; of course the gentleman apologised. "Sir," answered Matthews, "it may be all very well for you, who have a great many silk stockings, to dirty other people's; but to me, who have only this *one pair*, which I have put on in honour of the Abbot here, no apology can compensate for such carelessness; besides, the expense of washing." He had the same sort of droll sardonic way about every thing. A wild Irishman, named Farrell, one evening began to say something at a large supper at Cambridge, Matthews roared out "Silence!" and then, pointing to Farrell, cried out, in the words of the oracle, "*Orson is endowed with reason*." You may easily suppose that Orson lost what reason he had acquired, on hearing this compliment. When Hobhouse published his volume of poems, the *Miscellany* (which Matthews *would* call the "*Miss-sell-any*"), all that could be drawn from him was, that the preface was "extremely like *Walsh*." Hobhouse thought this at first a compliment; but we never could make out what it was, for all we know of *Walsh* is his Ode to

King William, and Pope's epithet of "*knowing Walsh*." When the
Newstead party broke up for London, Hobhouse and Matthews,
who were the greatest friends possible, agreed, for a whim, to *walk
together* to town. They quarrelled by the way, and actually walked
the latter half of the journey, occasionally passing and repassing,
without speaking. When Matthews had got to Highgate, he had
spent all his money but three-pence half-penny, and determined
to spend that also in a pint of beer, which I believe he was drinking before a public-house, as Hobhouse passed him (still without
speaking) for the last time on their route. They were reconciled in
London again.

One of Matthew's passions was "the fancy;" and he sparred
uncommonly well. But he always got beaten in rows, or combats
with the bare fist. In swimming, too, he swam well; but with *effort*
and *labour*, and *too high* out of the water; so that Scrope Davies
and myself, of whom he was therein somewhat emulous, always
told him that he would be drowned if ever he came to a difficult
pass in the water. He was so; but surely Scrope and myself would
have been most heartily glad that

> "the Dean had lived,
> And our prediction proved a lie."

His head was uncommonly handsome, very like what *Pope's* was
in his youth.

His voice, and laugh, and features, are strongly resembled by his
brother Henry's, if Henry be *he* of *King's College*. His passion for
boxing was so great, that he actually wanted me to match him with
Dogherty (whom I had backed and made the match for against
Tom Belcher), and I saw them spar together at my own lodgings
with the gloves on. As he was bent upon it, I would have backed
Dogherty to please him, but the match went off. It was of course
to have been a private fight, in a private room.

On one occasion, being too late to go home and dress, he was
equipped by a friend (Mr. Baillie, I believe,) in a magnificently
fashionable and somewhat exaggerated shirt and neckcloth.
He proceeded to the Opera, and took his station in Fop's Alley.
During the interval between the opera and the ballet, an acquaintance took his station by him and saluted him: "Come round,"

said Matthews, "come round."—"Why should I come round?" said the other; "you have only to turn your head—I am close by you."—"That is exactly what I cannot do," said Matthews; "don't you see the state I am in?" pointing to his buckram shirt collar and inflexible cravat,—and there he stood with his head always in the same perpendicular position during the whole spectacle.

One evening, after dining together, as we were going to the Opera, I happened to have a spare Opera ticket (as subscriber to a box), and presented it to Matthews. "Now, sir," said he to Hobhouse afterwards, "this I call *courteous* in the Abbot—another man would never have thought that I might do better with half a guinea than throw it to a door-keeper;—but here is a man not only asks me to dinner, but gives me a ticket for the theatre." These were only his oddities, for no man was more liberal, or more honourable in all his doings and dealings, than Matthews. He gave Hobhouse and me, before we set out for Constantinople, a most splendid entertainment, to which we did ample justice. One of his fancies was dining at all sorts of out-of-the-way places. Somebody popped upon him in I know not what coffee-house in the Strand—and what do you think was the attraction? Why, that he paid a shilling (I think) to *dine with his hat on*. This he called his "*hat* house," and used to boast of the comfort of being covered at meal times.

When Sir Henry Smith was expelled from Cambridge for a row with a tradesman named "Hiron," Matthews solaced himself with shouting under Hiron's windows every evening

> "Ah me! what perils do environ
> The man who meddles with *hot Hiron*."

He was also of that band of profane scoffers who, under the auspices of * * * *, used to rouse Lort Mansel (late Bishop of Bristol) from his slumbers in the lodge of Trinity; and when he appeared at the window foaming with wrath, and crying out, "I know you, gentlemen, I know you!" were wont to reply, "We beseech thee to hear us, good *Lort*!"—"Good *Lort* deliver us!" (Lort was his Christian name.) As he was very free in his speculations upon all kinds of subjects, although by no means either dissolute or intemperate in his conduct, and as I was no less independent, our conversation and correspondence used to alarm our friend Hobhouse to a considerable degree.

You must be almost tired of my packets, which will have cost a mint of postage.

Salute Gifford and all my friends.

Yours,
B

TO SCROPE BERDMORE DAVIES *Newstead Abbey, August 7, 1811*

My dearest Davies,—Some curse hangs over me and mine. My mother lies a corpse in this house: one of my best friends is drowned in a ditch. What can I say, or think, or do? I received a letter from him the day before yesterday. My dear Scrope, if you can spare a moment, do come down to me, I want a friend. Matthews's last letter was written on *Friday*,—on Saturday he was not. In ability, who was like Matthews? How did we all shrink before him? You do me but justice in saying, I would have risked my paltry existence to have preserved his. This very evening did I mean to write, inviting him, as I invite you, my very dear friend, to visit me. God forgive * * * for his apathy! What will our poor Hobhouse feel! His letters breathe but of Matthews. Come to me, Scrope, I am almost desolate—left almost alone in the world—I had but you and H[obhouse] and M[atthews] and let me enjoy the survivors whilst I can. Poor M. in his letter of Friday, speaks of his intended contest for Cambridge, and a speedy journey to London. Write or come, but come if you can, or one or both. Yours ever.

TO JOHN CAM HOBHOUSE *Newstead Abbey. August 10th. 1811*

My dear Hobhouse,—From Davies I had already received the death of Matthews, & from M. a *letter* dated the *day* before his *death*,—In that letter he mentions you, & as it was perhaps the last he ever wrote, you will derive a poor consolation from hearing that he spoke of you with that affectionate familiarity, so much more pleasing from those we love, than the highest encomiums of the World.— —My dwelling, you already know, is the House of Mourning, & I am really so much bewildered with the different shocks I have sustained, that I can hardly reduce myself to reason by the most frivolous occupations.—My poor friend J. Wingfield, my Mother, & your best friend, & (surely not the worst of mine) C[harles] S[kinner] M[atthews] have disappeared in one little month since *my return*, & without my seeing *either*, though I have *heard* from *All.*—There is to me something so incomprehensible in death, that I can neither speak or think on the subject.—Indeed when I looked on the Mass of Corruption, which was the being from whence I sprang, I doubted within myself whether I *was*, or She *was not.*—I have lost her who gave me being, & some of those who made that Being a blessing.—I have neither hopes nor fears beyond the Grave, yet if there is within us a "spark of that Celestial Fire" M[atthews] has already "mingled with the Gods".— —In the room where I now write (flanked by the *Skulls* you have seen so often) did you & M. & myself pass some joyous unprofitable evenings, & here we will drink to his Memory, which though it cannot reach the dead, will soothe the Survivors, & to them only death can be an Evil.—I can neither receive or administer Consolation, Time will do it for us, in the Interim let me see or hear from you, if possible both.—I am very lonely, & should think myself miserable, were it not for a kind of hysterical merriment, which I can neither account for, or conquer, but, strange as it is, I do laugh & heartily, wondering at myself while I sustain it.—I have tried reading & boxing, & swimming, & writing, & rising early & sitting late, & water, & wine, with a number of ineffectual remedies, & here I am, wretched, but not "melancholy or gentle-manlike."—My dear "*Cam of the Cornish*" (M's *last* expression!!) may Man or God give you the happiness, which I wish rather than expect you may attain; believe me none living are more sincerely yours than

BYRON

Newstead Abbey, Sept. 25, 1811

My dear Hodgson,—I fear that before the latest of October or the first of November, I shall hardly be able to make Cambridge. My everlasting agent puts off his coming like the accomplishment of a prophecy. However, finding me growing serious he hath promised to be here on Thursday, and about Monday we shall remove to Rochdale. I have only to give discharges to the tenantry here (it seems the poor creatures must be raised, though I wish it was not necessary), and arrange the receipt of sums, and the liquidation of some debts, and I shall be ready to enter upon new subjects of vexation. I intend to visit you in Granta, and hope to prevail on you to accompany me here or there or anywhere.

I am plucking up my spirits, and have begun to gather my little sensual comforts together. Lucy is extracted from Warwickshire; some very bad faces have been warned off the premises, and more promising substituted in their stead; the partridges are plentiful, hares fairish, pheasants not quite so good, and Girls on the Manor * * * * Just as I had formed a tolerable establishment my travels commenced, and on my return I find all to do over again; my former flock were all scattered; some married, not before it was needful. As I am a great disciplinarian, I have just issued an edict for the abolition of caps; no hair to be cut on any pretext; stays permitted, but not too low before; full uniform always in the evening; Lucinda to be commander—*vice* the present, about to be wedded (*mem*. she is 35 with a flat face and a squeaking voice), of all the makers and unmakers of beds in the household.

My tortoises (all Athenians), my hedgehog, my mastiff and the other live Greek, are all purely. The tortoises lay eggs, and I have hired a hen to hatch them. I am writing notes for *my* quarto (Murray would have it a *quarto*), and Hobhouse is writing text for *his* quarto; if you call on Murray or Cawthorn you will hear news of either. I have attacked De Pauw, Thornton, Lord Elgin, Spain, Portugal, the *Edinburgh Review*, travellers, Painters, Antiquarians, and others, so you see what a dish of Sour Crout Controversy I shall prepare for myself. It would not answer for me to give way, now; as I was forced into bitterness at the beginning, I will go through to the last. *Væ Victis!* If I fall, I shall fall gloriously, fighting against a host.

Felicissima Notte a Voss. Signoria,

BRYON

FALMOUTH

CORNWALL

Now our boatmen quit their mooring,
    And all hands must ply the oar;
Baggage from the quay is lowering,
    We're impatient—push from shore.
"Have a care! that case holds liquor—"
    "Stop the boat—I'm sick—oh Lord!"
"Sick, ma'am, damme, you'll be sicker,
    Ere you've been an hour on board."
        Thus are screaming
        Men & women,
    Gemmen, ladies, servants, Jacks;
        Here entangling,
        All are wrangling,
    Stuck together close as wax.—
Such the genial noise and racket,
Ere we reach the Lisbon Packet.

from Verse Letter to Francis Hodgson, June 30th, 1809

Dear Mother,—I am about to sail in a few days, probably before this reaches you; Fletcher begged so hard that I have continued him in my service, if he does not behave well abroad, I will send him back in a *transport.*—I have a German servant who has been with Mr. Wilbraham in Persia before, and was strongly recommended to me by Dr. Butler of Harrow, Robert, and William, they constitute my whole suite.—I have letters in plenty.—You shall hear from me at different ports I touch upon, but you must not be alarmed if my letters miscarry.—The Continent is in a fine state! an Insurrection has broken out at Paris, and the Austrians are beating Buonaparte, the Tyrolese have risen.—There is a picture of me in oil to be sent down to Newstead soon, I wish the Miss Parkyns's had something better to do than carry my miniature to Nottingham to copy.— —Now they have done it, you may ask them to copy the others, which are greater favourites than my own.— — —As to money matters I am ruined, at least till Rochdale is sold, & if that does not turn out well I shall enter the Austrian or Russian service, perhaps the Turkish, if I like their manners, the world is all before me, and I leave England without regret, and without a wish to revisit any thing it contains, except *yourself*, and your present residence.— — — —

Believe me yours ever sincerely
BYRON

P.S.—Pray tell Mr. Rushton his son is well, and *doing* well, so is Murray, indeed better than I ever saw him, he will be back in about a month, I ought to add leaving Murray to my few regrets, as his age perhaps will prevent my seeing him again; Robert I take with me, I like him, because like myself he seems to be a friendless animal.—

TO CHARLES SKINNER MATTHEWS   *Falmouth June 22 [1809]*

My dear Mathieu,—I take up the pen which our friend has for a moment laid down merely to express a vain wish that you were with us in this delectable region, as I do not think Georgia itself can emulate in capabilities or incitements to the "Plen. and optabil.—Coit." the port of Falmouth & parts adjacent.— —We are surrounded by Hyacinths & other flowers of the most fragrant [na]ture, & I have some intention of culling a handsome Bouquet to compare with the exotics we expect to meet in Asia.—One specimen I shall certainly carry off, but of this hereafter.—Adieu Mathieu!— —

TO EDWARD ELLICE   *Falmouth June 25 1809*

Dear Ellice,—You will think me a very sad dog for not having written a long acknowledgement of what I really feel, viz, a sincere sense of the many favours I have received at your hands concerning my coming Tour.—But if you knew the hurry I have been in & the natural laziness of my disposition, you would excuse an omission which cannot be attributed to neglect, or ingratitude.—I beg you will now accept my very hearty thanks for the divers troubles you have had on my account, which I am sure no person but yourself would have taken for so worthless an animal, I am afraid I shall never have any opportunity of repaying them, except by a promise that they shall not be repeated.—We are waiting here for a wind & other necessaries, nothing of moment has occurred in the town save castigation of one of the fair sex at a Cart's tail yesterday morn, whose hands had been guilty of "picking & stealing" and whose tongue of "evil speaking" for she stole a Cock, and *damned* the corporation; she was much whipped but exceeding impenitent.—I shall say nothing of Falmouth because I know it, & you dont, a very good reason for being silent as I can say nothing in it's favour, or you hear any thing that would be agreeable.—The Inhabitants both female & male, at least the young ones, are remarkably handsome, and how the devil they came to be so, is the marvel! for the place is apparently not favourable to Beauty.— — —The Claret is good, and Quakers plentiful, so are Herrings salt & fresh,

there is a fort called St. Mawes off the harbour, which we were
nearly taken up on suspicion of having carried by storm, it is well
defended by one able-bodied man of eighty years old, six ancient
demi-culverins; that would exceedingly annoy anybody—except
an enemy;—and parapet walls which would withstand at least half
a dozen kicks of any given grenadier in the kingdom of France.—
Adieu believe me

your obliged & sincere

BYRON

TO FRANCIS HODGSON   *Falmouth June 25th. 1809*

My dear Hodgson,—Before this reaches you, Hobhouse, two
officers' wives, three children two waiting maids, ditto subalterns
for the troops, three Portuguese esquires, and domestics, in all
nineteen souls will have sailed in the Lisbon packet with the noble
Capt. Kidd, a gallant commander as ever smuggled an anker of
right Nantz.— —We are going to Lisbon first, because the Malta
Packet has sailed d'ye see? from Lisbon to Gibraltar, Malta, Constantinople and "all that," as Orator Henley said when he put the
Church and "all that" in danger.   This town of Falmouth as you
will partly conjecture is no great ways from the sea, it is defended
on the seaside by tway castles St. Mawes, & Pendennis, extremely
well calculated for annoying every body except an enemy, St.
Mawes is garrisoned by an able bodied person of fourscore, a
widower, he has the whole command and sole management of six
most unmanageable pieces of ordnance admirably adapted for the
destruction of Pendennis a like tower of strength on the opposite
side of the Channel, we have seen St. Mawes, but Pendennis they
will not let us behold, save at a distance, because Hobhouse & I
are suspected of having already taken St. Mawes by a Coup de
Main.— —The Town contains many Quakers and salt-fish, the
oysters have a taste of copper owing to the soil of a mining country,
the women (blessed be the Corporation therefore!) are flogged at
the cart's tail when they pick and steal, as happened to one of the
fair sex yesterday noon, she was pertinacious in her behaviour, and
damned the Mayor.—This is all I know of Falmouth, nothing of

note occurred in our way down, except that on Hartford Bridge
we changed horses at an Inn where the great Apostle of Paeder-
asty Beckford! sojourned for the night, we tried in vain to see the
Martyr of prejudice, but could not; what we thought singular,
though you perhaps will not, was that Ld. Courtney travelled the
same night on the *same road* only one stage *behind* him.— — —
— —Hodgson! remember me to the Drury, and remember me to
yourself when drunk;—I am not worth a sober thought.—Look
to my satire at Cawthorn's Cockspur Street, and look to the Miscellany of the Hobhouse[;] it has pleased Providence to interfere in
behalf of a suffering Public by giving him a sprained wrist so that
he cannot write, and there is a cessation of inkshed.— —I don't
know when I can write again, because it depends on that experienced navigator Capt. Kidd, and the "stormy winds that—(dont)
blow" at this season.— —I leave England without regret, I shall
return to it without pleasure.— —I am like Adam the first convict
sentenced to transportation, but I have no Eve, and have eaten no
apple but what was sour as a crab and thus ends my first Chapter.

Adieu yrs ever
BYRON

Childe Harold's Pilgrimage I, 6–13

6

And now Childe Harold was sore sick at heart,
And from his fellow bacchanals would flee;
'Tis said, at times the sullen tear would start,
But Pride congeal'd the drop within his ee:
Apart he stalk'd in joyless reverie,
And from his native land resolv'd to go,
And visit scorching climes beyond the sea;
With pleasure drugg'd he almost long'd for woe,
And e'en for change of scene would seek the shades below.

7

The Childe departed from his father's hall:
It was a vast and venerable pile;
So old, it seemed only not to fall,
Yet strength was pillar'd in each massy aisle.
Monastic dome! condemn'd to uses vile!
Where Superstition once had made her den
Now Paphian girls were known to sing and smile;
And monks might deem their time was come agen,
If ancient tales say true, nor wrong these holy men.

8

Yet oft-times in his maddest mirthful mood
Strange pangs would flash along Childe Harold's
      brow,
As if the memory of some deadly feud
Or disappointed passion lurk'd below:
But this none knew, nor haply car'd to know;
For his was not that open, artless soul
That feels relief by bidding sorrow flow,
Nor sought he friend to counsel or condole,
Whate'er his grief mote be, which he could not control.

9

And none did love him—though to hall and bower
He gather'd revellers from far and near,
He knew them flatt'rers of the festal hour;
The heartless parasites of present cheer.
Yea! none did love him—not his lemans dear—
But pomp and power alone are woman's care,
And where these are light Eros finds a feere;
Maidens, like moths, are ever caught by glare,
And Mammon wins his way where Seraphs might despair.

10

Childe Harold had a mother—not forgot,
Though parting from that mother he did shun;
A sister whom he lov'd, but saw her not
Before his weary pilgrimage begun:5
If friends he had, he bade adieu to none.
Yet deem not thence his breast a breast of steel;
Ye, who have known what 'tis to doat upon
A few dear objects, will in sadness feel
Such partings break the heart they fondly hope to heal.

11

His house, his home, his heritage, his lands,
The laughing dames in whom he did delight,
Whose large blue eyes, fair locks, and snowy hands
Might shake the saintship of an anchorite,
And long had fed his youthful appetite;
His goblets brimm'd with every costly wine,
And all that mote to luxury invite,
Without a sigh he left, to cross the brine,
And traverse Paynim shores, and pass Earth's central line.

12

The sails were fill'd, and fair the light winds blew,
As glad to waft him from his native home;
And fast the white rocks faded from his view,
And soon were lost in circumambient foam:
And then, it may be, of his wish to roam
Repented he, but in his bosom slept
The silent thought, nor from his lips did come
One word of wail, whilst others sate and wept,
And to the reckless gales unmanly moaning kept.

13

But when the sun was sinking in the sea
He seiz'd his harp, which he at times could string,
And strike, albeit with untaught melody,
When deem'd he no strange ear was listening:
And now his fingers o'er it he did fling,
And tun'd his farewell in the dim twilight.
While flew the vessel on her snowy wing,
And fleeting shores receded from his sight,
Thus to the elements he pour'd his last "Good night".

1

"Adieu, adieu! my native shore
    Fades o'er the waters blue;
The Night-winds sigh, the breakers roar,
    And shrieks the wild seamew.
Yon Sun that sets upon the sea
    We follow in his flight;
Farewell awhile to him and thee,
    My native Land—Good Night.

2

"A few short hours and He will rise
    To give the Morrow birth;
And I shall hail the main and skies,
    But not my mother Earth.

Deserted is my own good hall,
    Its hearth is desolate;
Wild weeds are gathering on the wall;
    My dog howls at the gate.

3
"Come hither, hither, my little page!
    Why dost thou weep and wail?
Or dost thou dread the billows' rage,
    Or tremble at the gale?
But dash the tear-drop from thine eye;
    Our ship is swift and strong:
Our fleetest falcon scarce can fly
    More merrily along."

4
"Let winds be shrill, let waves roll high,
    I fear not wave nor wind;
Yet marvel not, Sir Childe, that I
    Am sorrowful in mind;
For I have from my father gone,
    A mother whom I love,
And have no friend, save these alone,
    But thee—and one above.

5
"My father bless'd me fervently,
    Yet did not much complain;
But sorely will my mother sigh
    Till I come back again."—
"Enough, enough, my little lad!
    Such tears become thine eye;
If I thy guileless bosom had
    Mine own would not be dry.

6

"Come hither, hither, my staunch yeoman,
　　Why dost thou look so pale?
Or dost thou dread a French foeman?
　　Or shiver at the gale?"—
"Deem'st thou I tremble for my life?
　　Sir Childe, I'm not so weak;
But thinking on an absent wife
　　Will blanch a faithful cheek.

7

"My spouse and boys dwell near thy hall,
　　Along the bordering lake,
And when they on their father call,
　　What answer shall she make?"—
"Enough, enough, my yeoman good,
　　Thy grief let none gainsay;
But I, who am of lighter mood,
　　Will laugh to flee away.

8

"For who would trust the seeming sighs
　　Of wife or paramour?
Fresh feres will dry the bright blue eyes
　　We late saw streaming o'er.
For pleasures past I do not grieve,
　　Nor perils gathering near;
My greatest grief is that I leave
　　No thing that claims a tear.

9

"And now I'm in the world alone,
　　Upon the wide, wide sea:
But why should I for others groan,
　　When none will sigh for me?
Perchance my dog will whine in vain,
　　Till fed by stranger hands;

But long ere I come back again,
    He'd tear me where he stands.

10
"With thee, my bark, I'll swiftly go
    Athwart the foaming brine;
Nor care what land thou bear'st me to,
    So not again to mine.
Welcome, welcome, ye dark-blue waves!
    And when you fail my sight,
Welcome, ye deserts, and ye caves!
    My native Land—Good Night!"

SPAIN and PORTUGAL

On, on the vessel flies, the land is gone,
And winds are rude in Biscay's sleepless bay.
Four days are sped, but with the fifth, anon,
New shores descried make every bosom gay;
And Cintra's mountain greets them on their way,
And Tagus dashing onward to the deep,
His fabled golden tribute bent to pay;
And soon on board Lusian pilots leap,
And steer 'twixt fertile shores where yet few rustics reap.

What beauties doth Lisboa first unfold!
Her image floating on that noble tide,
Which poets vainly pave with sands of gold,
But now whereon a thousand keels did ride
Of mighty strength, since Albion was allied,
And to the Lusians did her aid afford:
A nation swoln with ignorance and pride,
Who lick yet loath the hand that waves the sword
To save them from the wrath of Gaul's unsparing lord.

CHILDE HAROLD'S PILGRIMAGE I, 14, 16

Thus far have we pursued our route, and seen all sorts of marvellous sights, palaces, convents, &c.—which, being to be heard in my friend Hobhouse's forthcoming Book of Travels, I shall not anticipate by smuggling any account whatsoever to you in a private and clandestine manner. I must just observe that the village of Cintra in Estramadura is the most beautiful, perhaps in the world. * * *

I am very happy here, because I loves oranges, and talk bad Latin to the monks, who understand it, as it is like their own,—and I goes into society (with my pocket-pistols), and I swims in the Tagus all across at once, and I rides on an ass or a mule, and swears Portuguese, and have got a diarrhœa and bites from the mosquitoes. But what of that? Comfort must not be expected by folks that go a pleasuring. * * *

When the Portuguese are pertinacious, I say, "Carracho!"—the great oath of the grandees, that very well supplies the place of "Damme,"—and, when dissatisfied with my neighbor, I pronounce him "Ambra di merdo." With these two phrases, and a third, "Avra Bouro," which signifieth "Get an ass," I am universally understood to be a person of degree and a master of languages. How merrily we lives that travellers be!—if we had food and raiment. But, in sober sadness, any thing is better than England, and I am infinitely amused with my pilgrimage as far as it has gone.

To-morrow we start to ride post near 400 miles as far as Gibraltar, where we embark for Melita [Malta?] and Byzantium. A letter to Malta will find me, or to be forwarded, if I am absent. Pray embrace the Drury and Dwyer and all the Ephesians you encounter. I am writing with Butler's donative pencil, which makes my bad hand worse. Excuse illegibility. * * *

Hodgson! send me the news, and the deaths and defeats and capital crimes and the misfortunes of one's friends; and let us hear of literary matters, and the controversies and the criticisms. All this will be pleasant—"Suave mari magno," &c. Talking of that, I have been seasick, and sick of the sea. Adieu. Yours faithfully, &c.

TO FRANCIS HODGSON   *Gibraltar, August 6, 1809*

I have just arrived at this place after a journey through Portugal, and a part of Spain, of nearly 500 miles. We left Lisbon and travelled on horseback to Seville and Cadiz, and thence in the Hyperion frigate to Gibraltar. The horses are excellent—we rode seventy miles a day. Eggs and wine and hard beds are all the accommodation we found, and, in such torrid weather, quite enough. My health is better than in England. * * *

Seville is a fine town, and the Sierra Morena, part of which we crossed, a very sufficient mountain,—but damn description, it is always disgusting. Cadiz, sweet Cadiz!—it is the first spot in the creation. * * * The beauty of its streets and mansions is only excelled by the loveliness of its inhabitants. For, with all national prejudice, I must confess the women of Cadiz are as far superior to the English women in beauty as the Spaniards are inferior to the English in every quality that dignifies the name of man. * * * Just as I began to know the principal persons of the city, I was obliged to sail.

You will not expect a long letter after my riding so far "on hollow pampered jades of Asia." Talking of Asia puts me in mind of Africa, which is within five miles of my present residence. I am going over before I go on to Constantinople.

* * * Cadiz is a complete Cythera. Many of the grandees who have left Madrid during the troubles reside there, and I do believe it is the prettiest and cleanest town in Europe. London is filthy in the comparison. * * * The Spanish women are all alike, their education the same. The wife of a duke is, in information, as the wife of a peasant,—the wife of a peasant, in manner, equal to a duchess. Certainly, they are fascinating; but their minds have only one idea, and the business of their lives is intrigue. * * *

I have seen Sir John Carr at Seville and Cadiz, and, like Swift's barber, have been down on my knees to beg he would not put me into black and white. Pray remember me to the Drurys and the Davies, and all of that stamp who are yet extant. Send me a letter and news to Malta. My next epistle shall be from Mount Caucasus or Mount Sion. I shall return to Spain before I see England, for I am enamoured of the country. Adieu, and believe me, &c.

Childe Harold's Pilgrimage I, 71–80

71

All have their fooleries—not alike are thine,
Fair Cadiz, rising o'er the dark blue sea!
Soon as the matin bell proclaimeth nine,
Thy saint adorers count the rosary:
Much is the VIRGIN teaz'd to shrive them free
(Well do I ween the only virgin there)
From crimes as numerous as her beadsmen be;
Then to the crowded circus forth they fare,
Young, old, high, low, at once the same diversion share.

72

The lists are op'd, the spacious area clear'd,
Thousands on thousands pil'd are seated round;
Long ere the first loud trumpet's note is heard,
Ne vacant space for lated wight is found:
Here dons, grandees, but chiefly dames abound,
Skill'd in the ogle of a roguish eye,
Yet ever well inclin'd to heal the wound,
None through their cold disdain are doom'd to die,
As moon-struck bards complain, by Love's sad archery.

73

Hush'd is the din of tongues—on gallant steeds,
With milk-white crest, gold spur, and light-pois'd
        lance,
Four cavaliers prepare for venturous deeds,
And lowly bending to the lists advance;
Rich are their scarfs, their chargers featly prance:
If in the dangerous game they shine to-day,
The crowds loud shout and ladies lovely glance,
Best prize of better acts, they bear away,
And all that kings or chiefs e'er gain their toils repay.

74

In costly sheen and gaudy cloak array'd,
But all afoot, the light-limb'd Matadore
Stands in the centre, eager to invade
The lord of lowing herds; but not before
The ground, with cautious tread, is travers'd o'er,
Lest aught unseen should lurk to thwart his speed:
His arms a dart, he fights aloof, nor more
Can man achieve without the friendly steed,
Alas! too oft condemn'd for him to bear and bleed.

75

Thrice sounds the clarion; lo! the signal falls,
The den expands, and Expectation mute
Gapes round the silent Circle's peopled walls.
Bounds with one lashing spring the mighty brute,
And, wildly staring, spurns, with sounding foot,
The sand, nor blindly rushes on his foe:
Here, there, he points his threatening front, to suit
His first attack, wide waving to and fro
His angry tail; red rolls his eye's dilated glow.

76

Sudden he stops; his eye is fix'd: away,
Away, thou heedless boy! prepare the spear:
Now is thy time, to perish, or display
The skill that yet may check his mad career.
With well-tim'd croupe the nimble coursers veer;
On foams the bull, but not unscath'd he goes;
Streams from his flank the crimson torrent clear:
He flies, he wheels, distracted with his throes;
Dart follows dart; lance, lance; loud bellowings speak
     his woes.

77

Again he comes; nor dart nor lance avail,
Nor the wild plunging of the tortur'd horse;
Though man and man's avenging arms assail,
Vain are his weapons, vainer is his force.
One gallant steed is stretch'd a mangled corse;
Another, hideous sight! unseam'd appears,
His gory chest unveils life's panting source,
Tho' death-struck still his feeble frame he rears,
Staggering, but stemming all, his lord unharm'd he bears.

78

Foil'd, bleeding, breathless, furious to the last,
Full in the centre stands the bull at bay,
Mid wounds, and clinging darts, and lances brast,
And foes disabled in the brutal fray:
And now the Matadores around him play,
Shake the red cloak, and poise the ready brand:
Once more through all he burst his thundering way—
Vain rage! the mantle quits the conynge hand,
Wraps his fierce eye—'tis past—he sinks upon the sand!

79

Where his vast neck just mingles with the spine,
Sheath'd in his form the deadly weapon lies.
He stops—he starts—disdaining to decline:
Slowly he falls, amidst triumphant cries,
Without a groan, without a struggle dies.
The decorated car appears—on high
The corse is pil'd—sweet sight for vulgar eyes—
Four steeds that spurn the rein, as swift as shy,
Hurl the dark bulk along, scarce seen in dashing by.

80
Such the ungentle sport that oft invites
The Spanish maid, and cheers the Spanish swain.
Nurtur'd in blood betimes, his heart delights
In vengeance, gloating on another's pain. . . .

Dear Mother,—I have been so much occupied since my departure from England that till I could address you a little at length, I have forborn writing altogether.—As I have now passed through Portugal & a considerable part of Spain, & have leisure at this place I shall endeavour to give you a short detail of my movements.—We sailed from Falmouth on the 2d. of July, reached Lisbon after a very favourable passage of four days and a half, and took up our abode for a time in that city.—It has been often described without being worthy of description, for, except the view from the Tagus which is beautiful, and some fine churches & convents it contains little but filthy streets & more filthy inhabitants.—To make amends for this the village of Cintra about fifteen miles from the capitol is perhaps in every respect the most delightful in Europe, it contains beauties of every description natural & artificial, Palaces and gardens rising in the midst of rocks, cataracts, and precipices, convents on stupendous heights a distant view of the sea and the Tagus, and besides (though that is a secondary consideration) is remarkable as the scene of Sir H[ew] D[alrymple]'s convention.—It unites in itself all the wildness of the Western Highlands with the verdure of the South of France. Near this place about 10 miles to the right is the palace of Mafra the boast of Portugal, as it might be of any country, in point of magnificence without elegance, there is a convent annexed, the monks who possess large revenues are courteous enough, & understand Latin, so that we had a long conversation, they have a large Library & asked [me?] if the *English* had *any books* in their country.— —I sent my baggage & part of the servants by sea to Gibraltar, and travelled on horseback from Aldea Gallega (the first stage from Lisbon which is only accessible by water) to Seville (one of the most famous cities in Spain where the Government called the Junta is now held) the distance to Seville is nearly four hundred miles & to Cadiz about 90 further towards the Coast.—I had orders from the Government & every possible accommodation on the road, as an English nobleman in an English uniform is a very respectable personage in Spain at present. The horses are remarkably good, and the roads (I assure you upon my honour for you will hardly believe it) very far superior to the best British roads, without the smallest toll or turnpike, you will suppose this when I rode post to Seville in four days, through this parching country in the midst of summer, without fatigue or annoyance.—

Seville is a beautiful town, though the streets are narrow they are clean, we lodged in the house of two Spanish unmarried ladies, who possess *six* houses in Seville, and gave me a curious specimen of Spanish manners.—They are women of character, and the eldest a fine woman, the youngest pretty but not so good a figure as Donna Josepha, the freedom of women which is general here astonished me not a little, and in the course of further observation I find that reserve is not the characteristic of the Spanish belles, who are in general very handsome, with large black eyes, and very fine forms.—The eldest honoured your *unworthy* son with very particular attention, embracing him with great tenderness at parting (I was there but 3 days) after cutting off a lock of his hair, & presenting him with one of her own about three feet in length, which I send, and beg you will retain till my return.—Her last words were "Adio tu hermoso! me gusto mucho" "Adieu, you pretty fellow you please me much."—She offered a share of her apartment which my *virtue* induced me to decline, she laughed and said I had some English "Amante," (lover) and added that she was going to be married to an officer in the Spanish army.—I left Seville and rode on to Cadiz! through a beautiful country, at Xeres where the Sherry we drink is made I met a great merchant a Mr. Gordon of Scotland, who was extremely polite and favoured me with the Inspection of his vaults & cellars, so that I quaffed at the Fountain head.—Cadiz, sweet Cadiz! is the most delightful town I ever beheld, very different from our English cities in every respect except cleanliness (and it is as clean as London) but still beautiful and full of the finest women in Spain, the Cadiz belles being the Lancashire witches of their land.—Just as I was introduced and began to like the grandees I was forced to leave it for this cursed place, but before I return to England I will visit it again.—The night before I left it, I sat in the box at the opera with Admiral Cordova's family, he is the commander whom Ld. St. Vincent defeated in 1797, and has an aged wife and a fine daughter.— — —Signorita

Cordova the girl is very pretty in the Spanish style, in my opinion by no means inferior to the English in charms, and certainly superior in fascination.—Long black hair, dark languishing eyes, *clear* olive complexions, and forms more graceful in motion than can be conceived by an Englishman used to the drowsy listless air of his countrywomen, added to the most becoming dress & at the same time the most decent in the world, render a Spanish beauty irresistible. I beg leave to observe that Intrigue here is the business of life, when a woman marries she throws off all restraint, but I believe their conduct is chaste enough before.—If you make a proposal which in England would bring a box on the ear from the meekest of virgins, to a Spanish girl, she thanks you for the honour you intend her, and replies "wait till I am married, & I shall be too happy."—This is literally & strictly true.—Miss C[ordova] & her little brother understood a little French, and after regretting my ignorance of the Spanish she proposed to become my preceptress in that language; I could only reply by a low bow, and express my regret that I quitted Cadiz too soon to permit me to make the progress which would doubtless attend my studies under so charming a directress; I was standing at the back of the box which resembles our opera boxes (the theatre is large and finely decorated, the music admirable) in the manner which Englishmen generally adopt for fear of incommoding the ladies in front, when this fair Spaniard dispossessed an old woman (an aunt or a duenna) of her chair, and commanded me to be seated next herself, at a tolerable distance from her mamma.—At the close of the performance I withdrew and was lounging with a party of men in the passage, when "en passant" the Lady turned round and called me, & I had the honour of attending her to the Admiral's mansion.—I have an invitation on my return to Cadiz which I shall accept, if I repass through the country on my way from Asia.—I have met Sir John Carr Knight errant at Seville & Cadiz, he is a pleasant man.—I like the Spaniards much, you have heard of the battle near Madrid, & in England they will call it a victory, a pretty victory! two hundred officers and 5000 men killed all English, and the French in as great force as ever.—I should have joined the army but we have no time to lose before we get up the Mediterranean & Archipelago,—I am going over to Africa tomorrow, it is only six miles from this

Fortress.—My next stage is Cagliari in Sardinia where I shall be presented to his S[ardinian] Majesty, I have a most superb uniform as a court dress, indispensable in travelling.—

August 18th

I have not yet been to Africa, the wind is contrary, but I dined yesterday at Algesiras with Lady Westmoreland [*sic*] where I met General Castanos the celebrated Spanish leader in the late & present war, today I dine with him, he has offered me letters to Tetuan in Barbary for the principal Moors, & I am to have the house for a few days of one of their great men, which was intended for Lady W[estmorland], whose health will not permit her to cross the Straits.—

August 15th

I could not dine with Castanos yesterday, but this afternoon I had that honour, he is pleasant, & for aught I know to the contrary, clever,—I cannot go to Barbary, the Malta packet sails tomorrow & myself in it, Admiral Purvis with whom I dined at Cadiz gave me a passage in a frigate to Gibraltar, but we have no ship of war destined for Malta at present, the Packets sail fast & have good accommodations, you shall hear from me on our route, Joe Murray delivers this, I have sent him & the boy back, pray shew the lad any kindness as he is my great favourite, I would have taken him on <but you *know boys* are not *safe* amongst the Turks.—> Say this to his father, who may otherwise think he has behaved ill.—[I hope] This will find you well, believe me yours ever sincerely—

BYRON

P.S.—So Ld. Grey is married to a rustic, well done! if I wed I will bring you home a sultana with half a score cities for a dowry, and reconcile you to an Ottoman daughter in law with a bushel of pearls not larger than ostrich eggs or smaller than Walnuts.— —

Don Juan I, 90–187

[*Juan, a Spanish teenager, feels a strange interest in his
mother's friend Donna Julia*]

90

Young Juan wandered by the glassy brooks
    Thinking unutterable things. He threw
Himself at length within the leafy nooks
    Where the wild branch of the cork forest grew.
There poets find materials for their books,
    And every now and then we read them through,
So that their plan and prosody are eligible,
Unless like Wordsworth they prove unintelligible.

91

He, Juan (and not Wordsworth), so pursued
    His self-communion with his own high soul
Until his mighty heart in its great mood
    Had mitigated part, though not the whole
Of its disease. He did the best he could
    With things not very subject to control
And turned, without perceiving his condition,
Like Coleridge into a metaphysician.

92

He thought about himself and the whole earth,
    Of man the wonderful and of the stars
And how the deuce they ever could have birth,
    And then he thought of earthquakes and of wars,
How many miles the moon might have in girth,
    Of air balloons and of the many bars
To perfect knowledge of the boundless skies.
And then he thought of Donna Julia's eyes.

93

In thoughts like these true wisdom may discern
    Longings sublime and aspirations high,
Which some are born with, but the most part learn
    To plague themselves withal, they know not why.
'Twas strange that one so young should thus concern
    His brain about the action of the sky.
If you think 'twas philosophy that this did,
I can't help thinking puberty assisted.

94

He pored upon the leaves and on the flowers
    And heard a voice in all the winds; and then
He thought of wood nymphs and immortal bowers,
    And how the goddesses came down to men.
He missed the pathway, he forgot the hours,
    And when he looked upon his watch again,
He found how much old Time had been a winner.
He also found that he had lost his dinner.

95

Sometimes he turned to gaze upon his book,
    Boscán or Garcilasso. By the wind
Even as the page is rustled while we look,
    So by the poesy of his own mind
Over the mystic leaf his soul was shook,
    As if 'twere one whereon magicians bind
Their spells and give them to the passing gale,
According to some good old woman's tale

96

Thus would he while his lonely hours away
    Dissatisfied, nor knowing what he wanted.
Nor glowing reverie nor poet's lay
    Could yield his spirit that for which it panted,
A bosom whereon he his head might lay
    And hear the heart beat with the love it granted,

With several other things, which I forget
Or which at least I need not mention yet.

97

Those lonely walks and lengthening reveries
    Could not escape the gentle Julia's eyes;
She saw that Juan was not at his ease.
    But that which chiefly may, and must surprise
Is that the Donna Inez did not tease
    Her only son with question or surmise;
Whether it was she did not see, or would not,
Or like all very clever people, could not.

98

This may seem strange, but yet 'tis very common;
    For instance, gentlemen, whose ladies take
Leave to o'erstep the written rights of woman
    And break the—which commandment is't they break?
I have forgot the number and think no man
    Should rashly quote for fear of a mistake.
I say, when these same gentlemen are jealous,
They make some blunder, which their ladies tell us.

99

A real husband always is suspicious,
    But still no less suspects in the wrong place,
Jealous of someone who had no such wishes,
    Or pandering blindly to his own disgrace
By harbouring some dear friend extremely vicious.
    The last indeed's infallibly the case,
And when the spouse and friend are gone off wholly,
He wonders at their vice, and not his folly.

100

Thus parents also are at times shortsighted.
    Though watchful as the lynx, they ne'er discover,
The while the wicked world beholds delighted,
    Young Hopeful's mistress or Miss Fanny's lover,

Till some confounded escapade has blighted
    The plan of twenty years, and all is over,
And then the mother cries, the father swears
And wonders why the devil he got heirs.

101

But Inez was so anxious and so clear
    Of sight that I must think on this occasion
She had some other motive much more near
    For leaving Juan to this new temptation.
But what that motive was I shan't say here;
    Perhaps to finish Juan's education,
Perhaps to open Don Alfonso's eyes
In case he thought his wife too great a prize.

102

It was upon a day, a summer's day—
    Summer's indeed a very dangerous season,
And so is spring about the end of May.
    The sun no doubt is the prevailing reason,
But whatsoe'er the cause is, one may say
    And stand convicted of more truth than treason
That there are months which Nature grows more merry in.
March has its hares, and May must have its heroine.

103

'Twas on a summer's day, the sixth of June—
    I like to be particular in dates,
Not only of the age and year, but moon.
    They are a sort of post-house, where the Fates
Change horses, making history change its tune,
    Then spur away o'er empires and o'er states,
Leaving at last not much besides chronology,
Excepting the post-obits of theology.

104

'Twas on the sixth of June about the hour
    Of half-past six, perhaps still nearer seven,

When Julia sate within as pretty a bower
 As e'er held houri in that heathenish heaven
Described by Mahomet and Anacreon Moore,
 To whom the lyre and laurels have been given
With all the trophies of triumphant song.
He won them well, and may he wear them long!

105

She sate, but not alone! I know not well
 How this same interview had taken place,
And even if I knew, I should not tell.
 People should hold their tongues in any case,
No matter how or why the thing befell.
 But there were she and Juan face to face.
When two such faces are so, 'twould be wise,
But very difficult, to shut their eyes.

106

How beautiful she looked! Her conscious heart
 Glowed in her cheek, and yet she felt no wrong.
Oh Love, how perfect is thy mystic art,
 Strengthening the weak and trampling on the strong.
How self-deceitful is the sagest part
 Of mortals whom thy lure hath led along.
The precipice she stood on was immense,
So was her creed in her own innocence.

107

She thought of her own strength and Juan's youth
 And of the folly of all prudish fears,
Victorious virtue and domestic truth,
 And then of Don Alfonso's fifty years.
I wish these last had not occurred in sooth,
 Because that number rarely much endears
And through all climes, the snowy and the sunny,
Sounds ill in love, whate'er it may in money.

108

When people say, "I've told you fifty times,"
    They mean to scold and very often do.
When poets say, "I've written fifty rhymes,"
    They make you dread that they'll recite them too.
In gangs of fifty, thieves commit their crimes.
    At fifty love for love is rare, 'tis true;
But then no doubt it equally as true is,
A good deal may be bought for fifty louis.

109

Julia had honour, virtue, truth, and love
    For Don Alfonso, and she inly swore
By all the vows below to powers above,
    She never would disgrace the ring she wore
Nor leave a wish which wisdom might reprove.
    And while she pondered this, besides much more,
One hand on Juan's carelessly was thrown,
Quite by mistake—she thought it was her own.

110

Unconsciously she leaned upon the other,
    Which played within the tangles of her hair.
And to contend with thoughts she could not smother,
    She seemed by the distraction of her air.
'Twas surely very wrong in Juan's mother
    To leave together this imprudent pair,
She who for many years had watched her son so.
I'm very certain mine would not have done so.

111

The hand which still held Juan's, by degrees
    Gently but palpably confirmed its grasp,
As if it said, "Detain me, if you please."
    Yet there's no doubt she only meant to clasp
His fingers with a pure Platonic squeeze.
    She would have shrunk as from a toad or asp,

Had she imagined such a thing could rouse
A feeling dangerous to a prudent spouse.

112

I cannot know what Juan thought of this,
    But what he did is much what you would do.
His young lip thanked it with a grateful kiss
    And then abashed at its own joy, withdrew
In deep despair, lest he had done amiss.
    Love is so very timid when 'tis new.
She blushed and frowned not, but she strove to speak
And held her tongue, her voice was grown so weak.

113

The sun set, and up rose the yellow moon.
    The devil's in the moon for mischief; they
Who called her chaste, methinks, began too soon
    Their nomenclature. There is not a day,
The longest, not the twenty-first of June,
    Sees half the business in a wicked way,
On which three single hours of moonshine smile,
And then she looks so modest all the while.

114

There is a dangerous silence in that hour,
    A stillness, which leaves room for the full soul
To open all itself, without the power
    Of calling wholly back its self-control.
The silver light which, hallowing tree and tower,
    Sheds beauty and deep softness o'er the whole,
Breathes also to the heart and o'er it throws
A loving languor, which is not repose.

115

And Julia sate with Juan, half embraced
    And half retiring from the glowing arm,
Which trembled like the bosom where 'twas placed.
    Yet still she must have thought there was no harm,

Or else 'twere easy to withdraw her waist.
　　But then the situation had its charm,
And then—God knows what next—I can't go on;
I'm almost sorry that I e'er begun.

116

Oh Plato, Plato, you have paved the way
　　With your confounded fantasies to more
Immoral conduct by the fancied sway
　　Your system feigns o'er the controlless core
Of human hearts than all the long array
　　Of poets and romancers. You're a bore,
A charlatan, a coxcomb, and have been
At best no better than a go-between.

117

And Julia's voice was lost, except in sighs,
　　Until too late for useful conversation.
The tears were gushing from her gentle eyes;
　　I wish indeed they had not had occasion,
But who, alas, can love and then be wise?
　　Not that remorse did not oppose temptation;
A little still she strove and much repented,
And whispering, "I will ne'er consent"—consented.

118

'Tis said that Xerxes offered a reward
　　To those who could invent him a new pleasure.
Methinks the requisition's rather hard
　　And must have cost His Majesty a treasure.
For my part I'm a moderate-minded bard,
　　Fond of a little love (which I call leisure);
I care not for new pleasures, as the old
Are quite enough for me, so they but hold.

119

Oh pleasure, you're indeed a pleasant thing,
    Although one must be damned for you no doubt.
I make a resolution every spring
    Of reformation, ere the year run out,
But somehow this my vestal vow takes wing;
    Yet still I trust it may be kept throughout.
I'm very sorry, very much ashamed,
And mean next winter to be quite reclaimed.

120

Here my chaste Muse a liberty must take.
    Start not, still chaster reader, she'll be nice hence-
Forward, and there is no great cause to quake.
    This liberty is a poetic licence,
Which some irregularity may make
    In the design, and as I have a high sense
Of Aristotle and the rules, 'tis fit
To beg his pardon when I err a bit.

121

This licence is to hope the reader will
    Suppose from June the sixth (the fatal day,
Without whose epoch my poetic skill
    For want of facts would all be thrown away),
But keeping Julia and Don Juan still
    In sight, that several months have passed. We'll say
'Twas in November, but I'm not so sure
About the day; the era's more obscure.

122

We'll talk of that anon. 'Tis sweet to hear
    At midnight on the blue and moonlit deep
The song and oar of Adria's gondolier,
    By distance mellowed, o'er the waters sweep.
'Tis sweet to see the evening star appear;
    'Tis sweet to listen as the nightwinds creep

From leaf to leaf. 'Tis sweet to view on high
The rainbow, based on ocean, span the sky.

123

'Tis sweet to hear the watchdog's honest bark
    Bay deep-mouthed welcome as we draw near home;
'Tis sweet to know there is an eye will mark
    Our coming and look brighter when we come.
'Tis sweet to be awakened by the lark
    Or lulled by falling waters; sweet the hum
Of bees, the voice of girls, the song of birds,
The lisp of children and their earliest words.

124

Sweet is the vintage, when the showering grapes
    In bacchanal profusion reel to earth,
Purple and gushing. Sweet are our escapes
    From civic revelry to rural mirth.
Sweet to the miser are his glittering heaps.
    Sweet to the father is his first-born's birth.
Sweet is revenge, especially to women,
Pillage to soldiers, prize money to seamen.

125

Sweet is a legacy, and passing sweet
    The unexpected death of some old lady
Or gentleman of seventy years complete,
    Who've made "us youth" wait too, too long already
For an estate or cash or country-seat,
    Still breaking, but with stamina so steady
That all the Israelites are fit to mob its
Next owner for their double-damned post-obits.

126

'Tis sweet to win, no matter how, one's laurels
    By blood or ink. 'Tis sweet to put an end
To strife; 'tis sometimes sweet to have our quarrels,
    Particularly with a tiresome friend.

Sweet is old wine in bottles, ale in barrels.
    Dear is the helpless creature we defend
Against the world; and dear the schoolboy spot
We ne'er forget, though there we are forgot.

127

But sweeter still than this, than these, than all
    Is first and passionate love. It stands alone,
Like Adam's recollection of his fall.
    The tree of knowledge has been plucked; all's known,
And life yields nothing further to recall
    Worthy of this ambrosial sin, so shown
No doubt in fable as the unforgiven
Fire which Prometheus filched for us from heaven.

128

Man's a strange animal and makes strange use
    Of his own nature and the various arts,
And likes particularly to produce
    Some new experiment to show his parts.
This is the age of oddities let loose,
    Where different talents find their different marts.
You'd best begin with truth, and when you've lost your
Labour, there's a sure market for imposture.

129

What opposite discoveries we have seen,
    Signs of true genius and of empty pockets!
One makes new noses, one a guillotine,
    One breaks your bones, one sets them in their sockets.
But vaccination certainly has been
    A kind antithesis to Congreve's rockets,
With which the Doctor paid off an old pox,
By borrowing a new one from an ox.

130

Bread has been made (indifferent) from potatoes;
　　And galvanism has set some corpses grinning,
But has not answered like the apparatus
　　Of the Humane Society's beginning,
By which men are unsuffocated gratis.
　　What wondrous new machines have late been spinning!
I said the smallpox has gone out of late;
Perhaps it may be followed by the great.

131

'Tis said the great came from America;
　　Perhaps it may set out on its return.
The population there so spreads, they say
　　'Tis grown high time to thin it in its turn
With war or plague or famine, any way,
　　So that civilization they may learn.
And which in ravage the more loathsome evil is—
Their real *lues* or our pseudo-syphilis?

132

This is the patent age of new inventions
　　For killing bodies and for saving souls,
All propagated with the best intentions.
　　Sir Humphry Davy's lantern, by which coals
Are safely mined for in the mode he mentions,
　　Timbuctoo travels, voyages to the poles
Are ways to benefit mankind, as true
Perhaps as shooting them at Waterloo.

133

Man's a phenomenon, one knows not what,
　　And wonderful beyond all wondrous measure.
'Tis pity though in this sublime world that
　　Pleasure's a sin and sometimes sin's a pleasure.

Few mortals know what end they would be at,
    But whether glory, power or love or treasure,
The path is through perplexing ways, and when
The goal is gained, we die you know—and then?

134

What then? I do not know, no more do you,
    And so good night. Return we to our story.
'Twas in November when fine days are few,
    And the far mountains wax a little hoary
And clap a white cape on their mantles blue,
    And the sea dashes round the promontory
And the loud breaker boils against the rock,
And sober suns must set at five o'clock.

135

'Twas, as the watchmen say, a cloudy night,
    No moon, no stars; the wind was low or loud
By gusts. And many a sparkling hearth was bright
    With the piled wood, round which the family crowd.
There's something cheerful in that sort of light,
    Even as a summer sky's without a cloud.
I'm fond of fire and crickets and all that,
A lobster salad and champagne and chat.

136

'Twas midnight, Donna Julia was in bed,
    Sleeping, most probably, when at her door
Arose a clatter might awake the dead,
    If they had never been awoke before,
And that they have been so we all have read,
    And are to be so, at the least, once more.
The door was fastened, but with voice and fist
First knocks were heard, then "Madam—Madam—hist!

137

"For God's sake, Madam—Madam—here's my master
  With more than half the city at his back.
Was ever heard of such a curst disaster!
  'Tis not my fault—I kept good watch—alack!
Do, pray undo the bolt a little faster.
  They're on the stair just now and in a crack
Will all be here. Perhaps he yet may fly.
Surely the window's not so very high!"

138

By this time Don Alfonso was arrived
  With torches, friends, and servants in great number.
The major part of them had long been wived
  And therefore paused not to disturb the slumber
Of any wicked woman, who contrived
  By stealth her husband's temples to encumber.
Examples of this kind are so contagious,
Were one not punished, all would be outrageous.

139

I can't tell how or why or what suspicion
  Could enter into Don Alfonso's head,
But for a cavalier of his condition
  It surely was exceedingly ill-bred,
Without a word of previous admonition,
  To hold a levee round his lady's bed
And summon lackeys, armed with fire and sword,
To prove himself the thing he most abhorred.

140

Poor Donna Julia, starting as from sleep
  (Mind—that I do not say she had not slept),
Began at once to scream and yawn and weep.
  Her maid Antonia, who was an adept,
Contrived to fling the bedclothes in a heap,
  As if she had just now from out them crept.

I can't tell why she should take all this trouble
To prove her mistress had been sleeping double.

141

But Julia mistress and Antonia maid
    Appeared like two poor harmless women, who
Of goblins, but still more of men afraid,
    Had thought one man might be deterred by two,
And therefore side by side were gently laid,
    Until the hours of absence should run through,
And truant husband should return and say,
"My dear, I was the first who came away."

142

Now Julia found at length a voice and cried,
    "In heaven's name, Don Alfonso, what d'ye mean?
Has madness seized you? Would that I had died
    Ere such a monster's victim I had been!
What may this midnight violence betide,
    A sudden fit of drunkenness or spleen?
Dare you suspect me, whom the thought would kill?
Search then the room!" Alfonso said, "I will."

143

He searched, they searched and rummaged everywhere,
    Closet and clothespress, chest and window seat,
And found much linen, lace, and several pair
    Of stockings, slippers, brushes, combs, complete
With other articles of ladies fair,
    To keep them beautiful or leave them neat.
Arras they pricked and curtains with their swords
And wounded several shutters and some boards.

144

Under the bed they searched and there they found—
    No matter what; it was not that they sought.
They opened windows, gazing if the ground
    Had signs or footmarks, but the earth said nought;

And then they stared each other's faces round.
    'Tis odd, not one of all these seekers thought,
And seems to me almost a sort of blunder,
Of looking in the bed as well as under.

145

During this inquisition Julia's tongue
    Was not asleep. "Yes, search and search," she cried,
"Insult on insult heap, and wrong on wrong!
    It was for this that I became a bride!
For this in silence I have suffered long
    A husband like Alfonso at my side,
But now I'll bear no more nor here remain,
If there be law or lawyers in all Spain.

146

"Yes, Don Alfonso, husband now no more,
    If ever you indeed deserved the name,
Is't worthy of your years? You have threescore,
    Fifty or sixty—it is all the same.
Is't wise or fitting causeless to explore
    For facts against a virtuous woman's fame?
Ungrateful, perjured, barbarous Don Alfonso,
How dare you think your lady would go on so?

147

"Is it for this I have disdained to hold
    The common privileges of my sex?
That I have chosen a confessor so old
    And deaf that any other it would vex,
And never once he has had cause to scold,
    But found my very innocence perplex
So much, he always doubted I was married.
How sorry you will be when I've miscarried!

148

"Was it for this that no *cortejo* ere
    I yet have chosen from out the youth of Seville?
Is it for this I scarce went anywhere,
    Except to bullfights, mass, play, rout, and revel?
Is it for this, whate'er my suitors were,
    I favoured none—nay, was almost uncivil?
Is it for this that General Count O'Reilly,
Who took Algiers, declares I used him vilely?

149

"Did not the Italian *Musico* Cazzani
    Sing at my heart six months at least in vain?
Did not his countryman, Count Corniani,
    Call me the only virtuous wife in Spain?
Were there not also Russians, English, many?
    The Count Strongstroganoff I put in pain,
And Lord Mount Coffeehouse, the Irish peer,
Who killed himself for love (with wine) last year.

150

"Have I not had two bishops at my feet?
    The Duke of Ichar and Don Fernan Nunez,
And is it thus a faithful wife you treat?
    I wonder in what quarter now the moon is.
I praise your vast forbearance not to beat
    Me also, since the time so opportune is.
Oh valiant man, with sword drawn and cocked trigger,
Now tell me, don't you cut a pretty figure?

151

"Was it for this you took your sudden journey,
    Under pretence of business indispensable
With that sublime of rascals, your attorney,
    Whom I see standing there and looking sensible
Of having played the fool? Though both I spurn, he
    Deserves the worst, his conduct's less defensible,

Because no doubt 'twas for his dirty fee,
And not from any love to you nor me.

152

"If he comes here to take a deposition,
    By all means let the gentleman proceed.
You've made the apartment in a fit condition.
    There's pen and ink for you, sir, when you need.
Let everything be noted with precision;
    I would not you for nothing should be feed.
But as my maid's undrest, pray turn your spies out."
"Oh," sobbed Antonia, "I could tear their eyes out."

153

"There is the closet, there the toilet, there
    The antechamber, search them under, over.
There is the sofa, there the great armchair,
    The chimney, which would really hold a lover.
I wish to sleep and beg you will take care
    And make no further noise, till you discover
The secret cavern of this lurking treasure,
And when 'tis found, let me too have that pleasure.

154

"And now, Hidalgo, now that you have thrown
    Doubt upon me, confusion over all,
Pray have the courtesy to make it known
    Who is the man you search for? How d'ye call
Him? What's his lineage? Let him but be shown.
    I hope he's young and handsome. Is he tall?
Tell me, and be assured that since you stain
My honour thus, it shall not be in vain.

155

"At least perhaps he has not sixty years;
    At that age he would be too old for slaughter,
Or for so young a husband's jealous fears.
    Antonia, let me have a glass of water.

I am ashamed of having shed these tears;
 They are unworthy of my father's daughter.
My mother dreamed not in my natal hour
That I should fall into a monster's power.

156

"Perhaps 'tis of Antonia you are jealous;
 You saw that she was sleeping by my side
When you broke in upon us with your fellows.
 Look where you please; we've nothing, sir, to hide.
Only another time, I trust you'll tell us,
 Or for the sake of decency abide
A moment at the door that we may be
Drest to receive so much good company.

157

"And now, sir, I have done and say no more.
 The little I have said may serve to show
The guileless heart in silence may grieve o'er
 The wrongs to whose exposure it is slow.
I leave you to your conscience as before;
 'Twill one day ask you *why* you used me so?
God grant you feel not then the bitterest grief!
Antonia, where's my pocket-handkerchief?"

158

She ceased and turned upon her pillow. Pale
 She lay, her dark eyes flashing through their tears,
Like skies that rain and lighten. As a veil,
 Waved and o'ershading her wan cheek, appears
Her streaming hair. The black curls strive, but fail
 To hide the glossy shoulder, which uprears
Its snow through all. Her soft lips lie apart,
And louder than her breathing beats her heart.

159

The Señor Don Alfonso stood confused.
    Antonia bustled round the ransacked room
And turning up her nose, with looks abused
    Her master and his myrmidons, of whom
Not one, except the attorney, was amused.
    He, like Achates faithful to the tomb,
So there were quarrels, cared not for the cause,
Knowing they must be settled by the laws.

160

With prying snub-nose and small eyes, he stood,
    Following Antonia's motions here and there,
With much suspicion in his attitude.
    For reputations he had little care,
So that a suit or action were made good.
    Small pity had he for the young and fair
And ne'er believed in negatives, till these
Were proved by competent false witnesses.

161

But Don Alfonso stood with downcast looks,
    And truth to say he made a foolish figure.
When after searching in five hundred nooks
    And treating a young wife with so much rigour,
He gained no point, except some self-rebukes,
    Added to those his lady with such vigour
Had poured upon him for the last half-hour,
Quick, thick, and heavy as a thunder-shower.

162

At first he tried to hammer an excuse,
    To which the sole reply were tears and sobs
And indications of hysterics, whose
    Prologue is always certain throes and throbs,
Gasps and whatever else the owners choose.
    Alfonso saw his wife and thought of Job's.

He saw too in perspective her relations,
And then he tried to muster all his patience.

163

He stood in act to speak or rather stammer,
    But sage Antonia cut him short before
The anvil of his speech received the hammer,
    With "Pray sir, leave the room and say no more,
Or madam dies." Alfonso muttered, "Damn her,"
    But nothing else. The time of words was o'er.
He cast a rueful look or two and did,
He knew not wherefore, that which he was bid.

164

With him retired his *posse comitatus*,
    The attorney last, who lingered near the door
Reluctantly, still tarrying there as late as
    Antonia let him, not a little sore
At this most strange and unexplained hiatus
    In Don Alfonso's facts, which just now wore
An awkward look. As he revolved the case,
The door was fastened in his legal face.

165

No sooner was it bolted than—oh shame,
    Oh sin, oh sorrow, and oh womankind!
How can you do such things and keep your fame,
    Unless this world and t'other too be blind?
Nothing so dear as an unfilched good name.
    But to proceed, for there is more behind.
With much heartfelt reluctance be it said,
Young Juan slipped, half-smothered, from the bed.

166

He had been hid—I don't pretend to say
    How nor can I indeed describe the where.
Young, slender, and packed easily, he lay
    No doubt in little compass, round or square.

But pity him I neither must nor may
    His suffocation by that pretty pair;
'Twere better sure to die so than be shut
With maudlin Clarence in his malmsey butt.

167

And secondly, I pity not, because
    He had no business to commit a sin,
Forbid by heavenly, fined by human laws.
    At least 'twas rather early to begin,
But at sixteen the conscience rarely gnaws
    So much as when we call our old debts in
At sixty years and draw the accounts of evil
And find a deuced balance with the devil.

168

Of his position I can give no notion.
    'Tis written in the Hebrew chronicle
How the physicians, leaving pill and potion,
    Prescribed by way of blister a young belle,
When old King David's blood grew dull in motion,
    And that the medicine answered very well.
Perhaps 'twas in a different way applied,
For David lived, but Juan nearly died.

169

What's to be done? Alfonso will be back
    The moment he has sent his fools away.
Antonia's skill was put upon the rack,
    But no device could be brought into play.
And how to parry the renewed attack?
    Besides it wanted but few hours of day.
Antonia puzzled; Julia did not speak,
But pressed her bloodless lip to Juan's cheek.

170

He turned his lip to hers and with his hand
 Called back the tangles of her wandering hair.
Even then their love they could not all command
 And half forgot their danger and despair.
Antonia's patience now was at a stand;
 "Come, come, 'tis no time now for fooling there,"
She whispered in great wrath. "I must deposit
This pretty gentleman within the closet.

171

"Pray keep your nonsense for some luckier night.
 Who can have put my master in this mood?
What will become on't? I'm in such a fright,
 The devil's in the urchin, and no good.
Is this a time for giggling? This a plight?
 Why, don't you know that it may end in blood?
You'll lose your life, and I shall lose my place,
My mistress all, for that half-girlish face.

172

"Had it but been for a stout cavalier
 Of twenty-five or thirty (Come, make haste),
But for a child, what piece of work is here!
 I really, madam, wonder at your taste
(Come sir, get in). My master must be near.
 There for the present at the least he's fast,
And if we can but till the morning keep
Our counsel (Juan, mind, you must not sleep)."

173

Now Don Alfonso entering, but alone,
 Closed the oration of the trusty maid.
She loitered, and he told her to be gone,
 An order somewhat sullenly obeyed.
However, present remedy was none,
 And no great good seemed answered if she stayed.

Regarding both with slow and sidelong view,
She snuffed the candle, curtsied, and withdrew.

174

Alfonso paused a minute, then begun
　　Some strange excuses for his late proceeding.
He would not justify what he had done;
　　To say the best, it was extreme ill-breeding,
But there were ample reasons for it, none
　　Of which he specified in this his pleading.
His speech was a fine sample, on the whole,
Of rhetoric, which the learned call rigmarole.

175

Julia said nought, though all the while there rose
　　A ready answer, which at once enables
A matron who her husband's foible knows,
　　By a few timely words to turn the tables,
Which if it does not silence still must pose,
　　Even if it should comprise a pack of fables:
'Tis to retort with firmness and when he
Suspects with one, do you reproach with three.

176

Julia in fact had tolerable grounds;
　　Alfonso's loves with Inez were well known.
But whether 'twas that one's own guilt confounds,
　　But that can't be; as has been often shown,
A lady with apologies abounds.
　　It might be that her silence sprang alone
From delicacy to Don Juan's ear,
To whom she knew his mother's fame was dear.

177

There might be one more motive, which makes two;
　　Alfonso ne'er to Juan had alluded,
Mentioned his jealousy, but never who
　　Had been the happy lover, he concluded,

Concealed amongst his premises. 'Tis true,
   His mind the more o'er this its mystery brooded.
To speak of Inez now were, one may say,
Like throwing Juan in Alfonso's way.

178

A hint in tender cases is enough.
   Silence is best; besides there is a tact
(That modern phrase appears to me sad stuff,
   But it will serve to keep my verse compact)
Which keeps, when pushed by questions rather rough,
   A lady always distant from the fact.
The charming creatures lie with such a grace,
There's nothing so becoming to the face.

179

They blush, and we believe them; at least I
   Have always done so. 'Tis of no great use
In any case attempting a reply,
   For then their eloquence grows quite profuse,
And when at length they're out of breath, they sigh
   And cast their languid eyes down and let loose
A tear or two, and then we make it up,
And then—and then—and then—sit down and sup.

180

Alfonso closed his speech and begged her pardon,
   Which Julia half withheld and then half granted
And laid conditions, he thought, very hard on,
   Denying several little things he wanted.
He stood like Adam lingering near his garden,
   With useless penitence perplexed and haunted,
Beseeching she no further would refuse,
When lo! he stumbled o'er a pair of shoes.

181

A pair of shoes. What then? Not much, if they
    Are such as fit with ladies' feet, but these
(No one can tell how much I grieve to say)
    Were masculine. To see them and to seize
Was but a moment's act. Ah, well-a-day,
    My teeth begin to chatter, my veins freeze.
Alfonso first examined well their fashion
And then flew out into another passion.

182

He left the room for his relinquished sword,
    And Julia instant to the closet flew.
"Fly, Juan, fly! For heaven's sake, not a word!
    The door is open. You may yet slip through
The passage you so often have explored.
    Here is the garden key. Fly—fly—adieu!
Haste—haste! I hear Alfonso's hurrying feet.
Day has not broke, there's no one in the street."

183

None can say that this was not good advice;
    The only mischief was it came too late.
Of all experience 'tis the usual price,
    A sort of income tax laid on by fate.
Juan had reached the room door in a trice
    And might have done so by the garden gate,
But met Alfonso in his dressing gown,
Who threatened death—so Juan knocked him down.

184

Dire was the scuffle and out went the light.
    Antonia cried out "Rape!" and Julia "Fire!"
But not a servant stirred to aid the fight.
    Alfonso, pommelled to his heart's desire,
Swore lustily he'd be revenged this night;
    And Juan too blasphemed an octave higher.

His blood was up; though young, he was a Tartar
And not at all disposed to prove a martyr.

185

Alfonso's sword had dropped ere he could draw it,
    And they continued battling hand to hand,
For Juan very luckily ne'er saw it.
    His temper not being under great command,
If at that moment he had chanced to claw it,
    Alfonso's days had not been in the land
Much longer. Think of husbands', lovers' lives,
And how ye may be doubly widows—wives!

186

Alfonso grappled to detain the foe,
    And Juan throttled him to get away,
And blood ('twas from the nose) began to flow.
    At last as they more faintly wrestling lay,
Juan contrived to give an awkward blow,
    And then his only garment quite gave way.
He fled, like Joseph, leaving it, but there
I doubt, all likeness ends between the pair.

187

Lights came at length, and men and maids, who found
    An awkward spectacle their eyes before.
Antonia in hysterics, Julia swooned,
    Alfonso leaning breathless by the door,
Some half-torn drapery scattered on the ground,
    Some blood and several footsteps, but no more.
Juan the gate gained, turned the key about,
And liking not the inside, locked the out.

THE MEDITERRANEAN

Blow! Swiftly blow, thou keel-compelling gale!
Till the broad sun withdraws his lessening ray;
Then must the pennant-bearer slacken sail,
That lagging barks may make their lazy way.
Ah! Grievance sore, and listless dull delay,
To waste on sluggish hulks the sweetest breeze!
What leagues are lost before the dawn of day,
Thus loitering pensive on the willing seas,
The flapping sail hau'd down to halt for logs like these!

CHILDE HAROLD'S PILGRIMAGE I, 20

Dear Mother,—Though I have a very short time to spare, being to sail immediately for Greece, I cannot avoid taking an opportunity of telling you that I am well, I have been in Malta a short time & have found the inhabitants hospitable & pleasant.—This letter is committed to the charge of a very extraordinary woman whom you have doubtless heard of, Mrs. Spencer Smith, of whose escape the Marquis de Salvo published a narrative a few years ago, she has since been shipwrecked, and her life has been from its commencement so fertile in remarkable incidents, that in a romance they would appear improbable, She was born at Constantinople, where her father Baron Herbert was Austrian Ambassador, married unhappily yet has never been impeached in point of character, excited the vengeance of Buonaparte by a part in some conspiracy, several times risked her life, & is not yet twenty five.— —She is here on her way to England to join her husband, being obliged to leave Trieste where she was paying a visit to her mother by the approach of the French, & embarks soon in a ship of war, since my arrival here I have had scarcely any other companion, I have found her very pretty, very accomplished, and extremely eccentric.— — Bonaparte is even now so incensed against her that her life would be in some danger if she were taken prisoner a second time.—You have seen Murray and Robert by this time and received my letter, little has happened since that date, I have touched at Cagliari in Sardinia, and at Girgenti in Sicily, and embark tomorrow for Patras from whence I proceed to Yanina where Ali Pacha holds his court, so I shall soon be amongst the Mussulmen.—Adieu believe me with sincerity

yrs. ever
BYRON

Don Juan II, 26–114

[Juan, banished from his native Spain, is now at sea]

26

                              the wind
  Increased at night until it blew a gale;
And though 'twas not much to a naval mind,
  Some landsmen would have looked a little pale,
For sailors are in fact a different kind.
  At sunset they began to take in sail,
For the sky showed it would come on to blow
And carry away perhaps a mast or so.

27

At one o'clock the wind with sudden shift
  Threw the ship right into the trough of the sea,
Which struck her aft and made an awkward rift,
  Started the sternpost, also shattered the
Whole of her stern-frame, and ere she could lift
  Herself from out her present jeopardy
The rudder tore away. 'Twas time to sound
The pumps, and there were four feet water found.

28

One gang of people instantly was put
  Upon the pumps and the remainder set
To get up part of the cargo and what not,
  But they could not come at the leak as yet.
At last they did get at it really, but
  Still their salvation was an even bet.
The water rushed through in a way quite puzzling,
While they thrust sheets, shirts, jackets, bales of muslin

29

Into the opening, but all such ingredients
    Would have been vain, and they must have gone down,
Despite of all their efforts and expedients,
    But for the pumps. I'm glad to make them known
To all the brother tars who may have need hence,
    For fifty tons of water were upthrown
By them per hour, and they had all been undone
But for the maker, Mr. Mann, of London.

30

As day advanced the weather seemed to abate,
    And then the leak they reckoned to reduce
And keep the ship afloat, though three feet yet
    Kept two hand and one chain pump still in use.
The wind blew fresh again; as it grew late
    A squall came on, and while some guns broke loose,
A gust, which all descriptive power transcends,
Laid with one blast the ship on her beam ends.

31

There she lay, motionless, and seemed upset.
    The water left the hold and washed the decks
And made a scene men do not soon forget,
    For they remember battles, fires, and wrecks,
Or any other thing that brings regret
    Or breaks their hopes or hearts or heads or necks.
Thus drownings are much talked of by the divers
And swimmers who may chance to be survivors.

32

Immediately the masts were cut away,
    Both main and mizen. First the mizen went,
The mainmast followed, but the ship still lay
    Like a mere log and baffled our intent.
Foremast and bowsprit were cut down, and they
    Eased her at last (although we never meant

To part with all till every hope was blighted),
And then with violence the old ship righted.

33

It may be easily supposed, while this
    Was going on, some people were unquiet,
That passengers would find it much amiss
    To lose their lives as well as spoil their diet,
That even the able seaman, deeming his
    Days nearly o'er, might be disposed to riot,
As upon such occasions tars will ask
For grog and sometimes drink rum from the cask.

34

There's nought no doubt so much the spirit calms
    As rum and true religion; thus it was,
Some plundered, some drank spirits, some sung psalms.
    The high wind made the treble, and as bass
The hoarse harsh waves kept time. Fright cured the qualms
    Of all the luckless landsmen's seasick maws.
Strange sounds of wailing, blasphemy, devotion
Clamoured in chorus to the roaring ocean.

35

Perhaps more mischief had been done, but for
    Our Juan, who with sense beyond his years,
Got to the spirit-room and stood before
    It with a pair of pistols. And their fears,
As if Death were more dreadful by his door
    Of fire than water, spite of oaths and tears,
Kept still aloof the crew, who ere they sunk,
Thought it would be becoming to die drunk.

36

"Give us more grog," they cried, "for it will be
    All one an hour hence." Juan answered, "No!
'Tis true that death awaits both you and me,
    But let us die like men, not sink below

Like brutes." And thus his dangerous post kept he,
    And none liked to anticipate the blow,
And even Pedrillo, his most reverend tutor,
Was for some rum a disappointed suitor.

37

The good old gentleman was quite aghast
    And made a loud and pious lamentation,
Repented all his sins, and made a last
    Irrevocable vow of reformation:
Nothing should tempt him more (this peril past)
    To quit his academic occupation
In cloisters of the classic Salamanca,
To follow Juan's wake like Sancho Panca.

38

But now there came a flash of hope once more;
    Day broke, and the wind lulled. The masts were gone,
The leak increased, shoals round her, but no shore;
    The vessel swam, yet still she held her own.
They tried the pumps again, and though before
    Their desperate efforts seemed all useless grown,
A glimpse of sunshine set some hands to bale;
The stronger pumped, the weaker thrummed a sail.

39

Under the vessel's keel the sail was past,
    And for the moment it had some effect;
But with a leak and not a stick of mast
    Nor rag of canvas, what could they expect?
But still 'tis best to struggle to the last,
    'Tis never too late to be wholly wrecked.
And though 'tis true that man can only die once,
'Tis not so pleasant in the Gulf of Lyons.

40

There winds and waves had hurled them, and from thence
    Without their will they carried them away,

For they were forced with steering to dispense,
     And never had as yet a quiet day
On which they might repose, or even commence
     A jury mast or rudder, or could say
The ship would swim an hour, which by good luck
Still swam—though not exactly like a duck.

41

The wind in fact perhaps was rather less,
     But the ship laboured so, they scarce could hope
To weather out much longer. The distress
     Was also great with which they had to cope
For want of water, and their solid mess
     Was scant enough. In vain the telescope
Was used; nor sail nor shore appeared in sight,
Nought but the heavy sea and coming night.

42

Again the weather threatened, again blew
     A gale, and in the fore and after hold
Water appeared; yet though the people knew
     All this, the most were patient, and some bold,
Until the chains and leathers were worn through
     Of all our pumps. A wreck complete she rolled
At mercy of the waves, whose mercies are
Like human beings during civil war.

43

Then came the carpenter, at last, with tears
     In his rough eyes and told the captain he
Could do no more. He was a man in years
     And long had voyaged through many a stormy sea,
And if he wept at length, they were not fears
     That made his eyelids as a woman's be,
But he, poor fellow, had a wife and children,
Two things for dying people quite bewildering.

44

The ship was evidently settling now
    Fast by the head; and all distinction gone,
Some went to prayers again and made a vow
    Of candles to their saints, but there were none
To pay them with; and some looked o'er the bow;
    Some hoisted out the boats; and there was one
That begged Pedrillo for an absolution,
Who told him to be damned—in his confusion.

45

Some lashed them in their hammocks; some put on
    Their best clothes, as if going to a fair;
Some cursed the day on which they saw the sun
    And gnashed their teeth and howling tore their hair;
And others went on as they had begun,
    Getting the boats out, being well aware
That a tight boat will live in a rough sea,
Unless with breakers close beneath her lee.

46

The worst of all was that in their condition,
    Having been several days in great distress,
'Twas difficult to get out such provision
    As now might tender their long suffering less.
Men, even when dying, dislike inanition.
    Their stock was damaged by the weather's stress;
Two casks of biscuit and a keg of butter
Were all that could be thrown into the cutter.

47

But in the longboat they contrived to stow
    Some pounds of bread, though injured by the wet;
Water, a twenty gallon cask or so;
    Six flasks of wine. And they contrived to get
A portion of their beef up from below,
    And with a piece of pork moreover met,

But scarce enough to serve them for a luncheon;
Then there was rum, eight gallons in a puncheon.

48

The other boats, the yawl and pinnace, had
    Been stove in the beginning of the gale;
And the longboat's condition was but bad,
    As there were but two blankets for a sail
And one oar for a mast, which a young lad
    Threw in by good luck over the ship's rail.
And two boats could not hold, far less be stored,
To save one half the people then on board.

49

'Twas twilight and the sunless day went down
    Over the waste of waters. Like a veil,
Which if withdrawn would but disclose the frown
    Of one whose hate is masked but to assail,
Thus to their hopeless eyes the night was shown
    And grimly darkled o'er their faces pale
And the dim desolate deep. Twelve days had Fear
Been their familiar, and now Death was here.

50

Some trial had been making at a raft
    With little hope in such a rolling sea,
A sort of thing at which one would have laughed,
    If any laughter at such times could be,
Unless with people who too much have quaffed
    And have a kind of wild and horrid glee,
Half epileptical and half hysterical.
Their preservation would have been a miracle.

51

At half past eight o'clock, booms, hencoops, spars
    And all things for a chance had been cast loose,
That still could keep afloat the struggling tars,
    For yet they strove, although of no great use.

There was no light in heaven but a few stars,
    The boats put off o'ercrowded with their crews.
She gave a heel and then a lurch to port,
And going down head foremost—sunk, in short.

52

Then rose from sea to sky the wild farewell,
    Then shrieked the timid, and stood still the brave,
Then some leaped overboard with dreadful yell,
    As eager to anticipate their grave.
And the sea yawned around her like a hell,
    And down she sucked with her the whirling wave,
Like one who grapples with his enemy
And strives to strangle him before he die.

53

And first one universal shriek there rushed,
    Louder than the loud ocean, like a crash
Of echoing thunder, and then all was hushed,
    Save the wild wind and the remorseless dash
Of billows; but at intervals there gushed,
    Accompanied with a convulsive splash,
A solitary shriek, the bubbling cry
Of some strong swimmer in his agony.

54

The boats, as stated, had got off before,
    And in them crowded several of the crew.
And yet their present hope was hardly more
    Than what it had been, for so strong it blew
There was slight chance of reaching any shore.
    And then they were too many, though so few,
Nine in the cutter, thirty in the boat
Were counted in them when they got afloat.

55

All the rest perished; near two hundred souls
    Had left their bodies. And what's worse, alas,
When over Catholics the ocean rolls,
    They must wait several weeks before a mass
Takes off one peck of purgatorial coals,
    Because, till people know what's come to pass,
They won't lay out their money on the dead.
It costs three francs for every mass that's said.

56

Juan got into the longboat and there
    Contrived to help Pedrillo to a place.
It seemed as if they had exchanged their care,
    For Juan wore the magisterial face
Which courage gives, while poor Pedrillo's pair
    Of eyes were crying for their owner's case.
Battista, though (a name called shortly Tita),
Was lost by getting at some aqua vita.

57

Pedro, his valet, too he tried to save,
    But the same cause, conducive to his loss,
Left him so drunk he jumped into the wave
    As o'er the cutter's edge he tried to cross,
And so he found a wine-and-watery grave.
    They could not rescue him although so close,
Because the sea ran higher every minute,
And for the boat—the crew kept crowding in it.

58

A small old spaniel, which had been Don Jóse's,
    His father's, whom he loved as ye may think
(For on such things the memory reposes
    With tenderness), stood howling on the brink,
Knowing (dogs have such intellectual noses),
    No doubt the vessel was about to sink.

And Juan caught him up and ere he stepped
Off threw him in, then after him he leaped.

59

He also stuffed his money where he could
 About his person and Pedrillo's too,
Who let him do in fact whate'er he would,
 Not knowing what himself to say or do,
As every rising wave his dread renewed.
 But Juan, trusting they might still get through
And deeming there were remedies for any ill,
Thus re-embarked his tutor and his spaniel.

60

'Twas a rough night and blew so stiffly yet
 That the sail was becalmed between the seas,
Though on the wave's high top too much to set,
 They dared not take it in for all the breeze.
Each sea curled o'er the stern and kept them wet
 And made them bail without a moment's ease,
So that themselves as well as hopes were damped,
And the poor little cutter quickly swamped.

61

Nine souls more went in her. The longboat still
 Kept above water, with an oar for mast.
Two blankets stitched together, answering ill
 Instead of sail, were to the oar made fast.
Though every wave rolled menacing to fill,
 And present peril all before surpassed,
They grieved for those who perished with the cutter,
And also for the biscuit casks and butter.

62

The sun rose red and fiery, a sure sign
 Of the continuance of the gale. To run
Before the sea until it should grow fine
 Was all that for the present could be done.

A few teaspoonfuls of their rum and wine
    Were served out to the people, who begun
To faint, and damaged bread wet through the bags.
And most of them had little clothes but rags.

63

They counted thirty, crowded in a space
    Which left scarce room for motion or exertion.
They did their best to modify their case;
    One half sate up, though numbed with the immersion
While t'other half were laid down in their place,
    At watch and watch. Thus, shivering like the tertian
Ague in its cold fit, they filled their boat,
With nothing but the sky for a greatcoat.

64

'Tis very certain the desire of life
    Prolongs it; this is obvious to physicians,
When patients, neither plagued with friends nor wife,
    Survive through very desperate conditions,
Because they still can hope, nor shines the knife
    Nor shears of Atropos before their visions.
Despair of all recovery spoils longevity,
And makes men's miseries of alarming brevity.

65

'Tis said that persons living on annuities
    Are longer lived than others, God knows why,
Unless to plague the grantors; yet so true it is,
    That some, I really think, do never die.
Of any creditors the worst a Jew it is,
    And that's their mode of furnishing supply.
In my young days they lent me cash that way,
Which I found very troublesome to pay.

66

'Tis thus with people in an open boat;
    They live upon the love of life and bear
More than can be believed or even thought,
    And stand like rocks the tempest's wear and tear.
And hardship still has been the sailor's lot,
    Since Noah's ark went cruising here and there.
She had a curious crew as well as cargo,
Like the first old Greek privateer, the *Argo*.

67

But man is a carnivorous production
    And must have meals, at least one meal a day.
He cannot live like woodcocks upon suction,
    But like the shark and tiger must have prey.
Although his anatomical construction
    Bears vegetables in a grumbling way,
Your labouring people think beyond all question,
Beef, veal, and mutton better for digestion.

68

And thus it was with this our hapless crew,
    For on the third day there came on a calm,
And though at first their strength it might renew,
    And lying on their weariness like balm,
Lulled them like turtles sleeping on the blue
    Of ocean, when they woke they felt a qualm
And fell all ravenously on their provision,
Instead of hoarding it with due precision.

69

The consequence was easily foreseen:
    They ate up all they had and drank their wine
In spite of all remonstrances, and then
    On what in fact next day were they to dine?
They hoped the wind would rise, these foolish men,
    And carry them to shore. These hopes were fine,

But as they had but one oar, and that brittle,
It would have been more wise to save their victual.

70

The fourth day came, but not a breath of air,
    And ocean slumbered like an unweaned child.
The fifth day, and their boat lay floating there,
    The sea and sky were blue and clear and mild.
With their one oar (I wish they had had a pair)
    What could they do? And hunger's rage grew wild,
So Juan's spaniel, spite of his entreating,
Was killed and portioned out for present eating.

71

On the sixth day they fed upon his hide,
    And Juan, who had still refused, because
The creature was his father's dog that died,
    Now feeling all the vulture in his jaws,
With some remorse received (though first denied)
    As a great favour one of the forepaws,
Which he divided with Pedrillo, who
Devoured it, longing for the other too.

72

The seventh day and no wind. The burning sun
    Blistered and scorched, and stagnant on the sea
They lay like carcasses, and hope was none,
    Save in the breeze that came not. Savagely
They glared upon each other. All was done,
    Water and wine and food, and you might see
The longings of the cannibal arise
(Although they spoke not) in their wolfish eyes.

73

At length one whispered his companion, who
    Whispered another, and thus it went round,
And then into a hoarser murmur grew,
    An ominous and wild and desperate sound,

And when his comrade's thought each sufferer knew,
  'Twas but his own, suppressed till now, he found.
And out they spoke of lots for flesh and blood,
And who should die to be his fellow's food.

74

But ere they came to this, they that day shared
  Some leathern caps and what remained of shoes;
And then they looked around them and despaired,
  And none to be the sacrifice would choose.
At length the lots were torn up and prepared,
  But of materials that much shock the Muse.
Having no paper, for the want of better,
They took by force from Juan Julia's letter.

75

The lots were made and marked and mixed and handed
  In silent horror, and their distribution
Lulled even the savage hunger which demanded,
  Like the Promethean vulture, this pollution.
None in particular had sought or planned it;
  'Twas nature gnawed them to this resolution,
By which none were permitted to be neuter,
And the lot fell on Juan's luckless tutor.

76

He but requested to be bled to death.
  The surgeon had his instruments and bled
Pedrillo, and so gently ebbed his breath
  You hardly could perceive when he was dead.
He died as born, a Catholic in faith,
  Like most in the belief in which they're bred,
And first a little crucifix he kissed,
And then held out his jugular and wrist.

77

The surgeon, as there was no other fee,
 Had his first choice of morsels for his pains,
But being thirstiest at the moment, he
 Preferred a draught from the fast-flowing veins.
Part was divided, part thrown in the sea,
 And such things as the entrails and the brains
Regaled two sharks who followed o'er the billow.
The sailors ate the rest of poor Pedrillo.

78

The sailors ate him, all save three or four,
 Who were not quite so fond of animal food.
To these was added Juan, who, before
 Refusing his own spaniel, hardly could
Feel now his appetite increased much more.
 'Twas not to be expected that he should,
Even in extremity of their disaster,
Dine with them on his pastor and his master.

79

'Twas better that he did not, for in fact
 The consequence was awful in the extreme.
For they who were most ravenous in the act
 Went raging mad. Lord! how they did blaspheme
And foam and roll, with strange convulsions racked,
 Drinking salt water like a mountain stream,
Tearing and grinning, howling, screeching, swearing,
And with hyena laughter died despairing.

80

Their numbers were much thinned by this infliction,
 And all the rest were thin enough, heaven knows,
And some of them had lost their recollection,
 Happier than they who still perceived their woes,
But others pondered on a new dissection,
 As if not warned sufficiently by those

Who had already perished, suffering madly,
For having used their appetites so sadly.

81

And next they thought upon the master's mate
    As fattest, but he saved himself, because,
Besides being much averse from such a fate,
    There were some other reasons: the first was
He had been rather indisposed of late,
    And that which chiefly proved his saving clause
Was a small present made to him at Cadiz,
By general subscription of the ladies.

82

Of poor Pedrillo something still remained,
    But was used sparingly. Some were afraid,
And others still their appetites constrained,
    Or but at times a little supper made;
All except Juan, who throughout abstained,
    Chewing a piece of bamboo and some lead.
At length they caught two boobies and a noddy,
And then they left off eating the dead body.

83

And if Pedrillo's fate should shocking be,
    Remember Ugolino condescends
To eat the head of his archenemy,
    The moment after he politely ends
His tale. If foes be food in hell, at sea
    'Tis surely fair to dine upon our friends
When shipwreck's short allowance grows too scanty,
Without being much more horrible than Dante.

84

And the same night there fell a shower of rain,
    For which their mouths gaped like the cracks of earth
When dried to summer dust. Till taught by pain,
    Men really know not what good water's worth.

If you had been in Turkey or in Spain,
    Or with a famished boat's crew had your berth,
Or in the desert heard the camel's bell,
You'd wish yourself where truth is—in a well.

85

It poured down torrents, but they were no richer
    Until they found a ragged piece of sheet,
Which served them as a sort of spongy pitcher,
    And when they deemed its moisture was complete,
They wrung it out, and though a thirsty ditcher
    Might not have thought the scanty draught so sweet
As a full pot of porter, to their thinking
They ne'er till now had known the joys of drinking.

86

And their baked lips, with many a bloody crack,
    Sucked in the moisture, which like nectar streamed.
Their throats were ovens, their swoll'n tongues were
      black,
    As the rich man's in hell, who vainly screamed
To beg the beggar, who could not rain back
    A drop of dew, when every drop had seemed
To taste of heaven. If this be true, indeed
Some Christians have a comfortable creed.

87

There were two fathers in this ghastly crew
    And with them their two sons, of whom the one
Was more robust and hardy to the view,
    But he died early, and when he was gone,
His nearest messmate told his sire, who threw
    One glance on him and said, "Heaven's will be done!
I can do nothing," and he saw him thrown
Into the deep without a tear or groan.

88

The other father had a weaklier child,
    Of a soft cheek and aspect delicate,
But the boy bore up long and with a mild
    And patient spirit held aloof his fate.
Little he said and now and then he smiled,
    As if to win a part from off the weight
He saw increasing on his father's heart,
With the deep deadly thought that they must part.

89

And o'er him bent his sire and never raised
    His eyes from off his face, but wiped the foam
From his pale lips, and ever on him gazed,
    And when the wished-for shower at length was come,
And the boy's eyes, which the dull film half glazed,
    Brightened and for a moment seemed to roam,
He squeezed from out a rag some drops of rain
Into his dying child's mouth—but in vain.

90

The boy expired. The father held the clay
    And looked upon it long, and when at last
Death left no doubt, and the dead burden lay
    Stiff on his heart, and pulse and hope were past,
He watched it wistfully, until away
    'Twas borne by the rude wave wherein 'twas cast.
Then he himself sunk down all dumb and shivering,
And gave no sign of life, save his limbs quivering.

91

Now overhead a rainbow, bursting through
    The scattering clouds, shone, spanning the dark sea,
Resting its bright base on the quivering blue,
    And all within its arch appeared to be
Clearer than that without, and its wide hue
    Waxed broad and waving, like a banner free,

Then changed like to a bow that's bent, and then
Forsook the dim eyes of these shipwrecked men.

92

It changed of course—a heavenly chameleon,
    The airy child of vapour and the sun,
Brought forth in purple, cradled in vermilion,
    Baptized in molten gold and swathed in dun,
Glittering like crescents o'er a Turk's pavilion
    And blending every colour into one,
Just like a black eye in a recent scuffle
(For sometimes we must box without the muffle).

93

Our shipwrecked seamen thought it a good omen;
    It is as well to think so now and then.
'Twas an old custom of the Greek and Roman,
    And may become of great advantage when
Folks are discouraged; and most surely no men
    Had greater need to nerve themselves again
Than these, and so this rainbow looked like hope,
Quite a celestial kaleidoscope.

94

About this time a beautiful white bird,
    Webfooted, not unlike a dove in size
And plumage (probably it might have erred
    Upon its course), passed oft before their eyes
And tried to perch, although it saw and heard
    The men within the boat, and in their guise
It came and went and fluttered round them till
Night fell. This seemed a better omen still.

95

But in this case I also must remark,
    'Twas well this bird of promise did not perch,
Because the tackle of our shattered bark
    Was not so safe for roosting as a church,

And had it been the dove from Noah's ark,
 Returning there from her successful search,
Which in their way that moment chanced to fall,
They would have eat her, olive branch and all.

96

With twilight it again came on to blow,
 But not with violence. The stars shone out,
The boat made way; yet now they were so low
 They knew not where nor what they were about.
Some fancied they saw land, and some said, "No!"
 The frequent fog banks gave them cause to doubt.
Some swore that they heard breakers, others guns,
And all mistook about the latter once.

97

As morning broke the light wind died away,
 When he who had the watch sung out and swore,
If 'twas not land that rose with the sun's ray,
 He wished that land he never might see more.
And the rest rubbed their eyes and saw a bay
 Or thought they saw, and shaped their course for
   shore,
For shore it was and gradually grew
Distinct and high and palpable to view.

98

And then of these some part burst into tears,
 And others, looking with a stupid stare,
Could not yet separate their hopes from fears
 And seemed as if they had no further care,
While a few prayed (the first time for some years).
 And at the bottom of the boat three were
Asleep; they shook them by the hand and head
And tried to awaken them, but found them dead.

99

The day before, fast sleeping on the water,
　　They found a turtle of the hawksbill kind,
And by good fortune gliding softly, caught her,
　　Which yielded a day's life and to their mind
Proved even still a more nutritious matter,
　　Because it left encouragement behind.
They thought that in such perils more than chance
Had sent them this for their deliverance.

100

The land appeared a high and rocky coast,
　　And higher grew the mountains as they drew,
Set by a current, toward it. They were lost
　　In various conjectures, for none knew
To what part of the earth they had been tost,
　　So changeable had been the winds that blew.
Some thought it was Mount Etna, some the highlands
Of Candia, Cyprus, Rhodes, or other islands.

101

Meantime the current, with a rising gale,
　　Still set them onwards to the welcome shore,
Like Charon's bark of spectres, dull and pale.
　　Their living freight was now reduced to four,
And three dead, whom their strength could not avail
　　To heave into the deep with those before,
Though the two sharks still followed them and dashed
The spray into their faces as they splashed.

102

Famine, despair, cold, thirst, and heat had done
　　Their work on them by turns, and thinned them to
Such things a mother had not known her son
　　Amidst the skeletons of that gaunt crew.
By night chilled, by day scorched, thus one by one
　　They perished, until withered to these few,

But chiefly by a species of self-slaughter,
In washing down Pedrillo with salt water.

103

As they drew nigh the land, which now was seen
    Unequal in its aspect here and there,
They felt the freshness of its growing green,
    That waved in forest-tops and smoothed the air,
And fell upon their glazed eyes like a screen
    From glistening waves and skies so hot and bare.
Lovely seemed any object that should sweep
Away the vast, salt, dread, eternal deep.

104

The shore looked wild without a trace of man
    And girt by formidable waves; but they
Were mad for land, and thus their course they ran,
    Though right ahead the roaring breakers lay.
A reef between them also now began
    To show its boiling surf and bounding spray,
But finding no place for their landing better,
They ran the boat for shore and overset her.

105

But in his native stream, the Guadalquivir,
    Juan to lave his youthful limbs was wont,
And having learnt to swim in that sweet river,
    Had often turned the art to some account.
A better swimmer you could scarce see ever,
    He could perhaps have passed the Hellespont,
As once (a feat on which ourselves we prided)
Leander, Mr. Ekenhead, and I did.

106

So here, though faint, emaciated, and stark,
    He buoyed his boyish limbs and strove to ply
With the quick wave and gain, ere it was dark,
    The beach which lay before him, high and dry.

The greatest danger here was from a shark,
    That carried off his neighbour by the thigh.
As for the other two they could not swim,
So nobody arrived on shore but him.

107

Nor yet had he arrived but for the oar,
    Which providentially for him was washed
Just as his feeble arms could strike no more,
    And the hard wave o'erwhelmed him as 'twas dashed
Within his grasp. He clung to it, and sore
    The waters beat while he thereto was lashed.
At last with swimming, wading, scrambling, he
Rolled on the beach, half senseless, from the sea.

108

There breathless, with his digging nails he clung
    Fast to the sand, lest the returning wave,
From whose reluctant roar his life he wrung,
    Should suck him back to her insatiate grave.
And there he lay full length, where he was flung,
    Before the entrance of a cliff-worn cave,
With just enough of life to feel its pain
And deem that it was saved, perhaps in vain.

109

With slow and staggering effort he arose,
    But sunk again upon his bleeding knee
And quivering hand; and then he looked for those
    Who long had been his mates upon the sea,
But none of them appeared to share his woes,
    Save one, a corpse from out the famished three,
Who died two days before and now had found
An unknown barren beach for burial ground.

110

And as he gazed, his dizzy brain spun fast
    And down he sunk, and as he sunk, the sand
Swam round and round, and all his senses passed.
    He fell upon his side, and his stretched hand
Drooped dripping on the oar (their jury mast),
    And like a withered lily, on the land
His slender frame and pallid aspect lay,
As fair a thing as e'er was formed of clay.

111

How long in his damp trance young Juan lay
    He knew not, for the earth was gone for him,
And time had nothing more of night nor day
    For his congealing blood and senses dim.
And how this heavy faintness passed away
    He knew not, till each painful pulse and limb
And tingling vein seemed throbbing back to life,
For Death, though vanquished, still retired with strife.

112

His eyes he opened, shut, again unclosed,
    For all was doubt and dizziness. He thought
He still was in the boat and had but dozed,
    And felt again with his despair o'erwrought,
And wished it death in which he had reposed,
    And then once more his feelings back were brought,
And slowly by his swimming eyes was seen
A lovely female face of seventeen.

113

'Twas bending close o'er his, and the small mouth
    Seemed almost prying into his for breath.
And chafing him, the soft warm hand of youth
    Recalled his answering spirits back from death,
And bathing his chill temples tried to soothe
    Each pulse to animation, till beneath

Its gentle touch and trembling care, a sigh
To these kind efforts made a low reply.

114

Then was the cordial poured, and mantle flung
    Around his scarce-clad limbs; and the fair arm
Raised higher the faint head which o'er it hung.
    And her transparent cheek, all pure and warm,
Pillowed his death-like forehead. Then she wrung
    His dewy curls, long drenched by every storm,
And watched with eagerness each throb that drew
A sigh from his heaved bosom—and hers too.

ALBANIA

Morn dawns; and with it stern Albania's hills,
Dark Suli's rocks, and Pindus' inland peak,
Rob'd half in mist, bedew'd with snowy rills,
Array'd in many a dun and purple streak,
Arise; and, as the clouds along them break,
Disclose the dwelling of the mountaineer:
Here roams the wolf, the eagle whets his beak,
Birds, beasts of prey, and wilder men appear,
And gathering storms around convulse the closing year.

Now Harold felt himself at length alone,
And bade to Christian tongues a long adieu;
Now he adventur'd on a shore unknown,
Which all admire, but many dread to view

CHILDE HAROLD'S PILGRIMAGE II, 42–43

Sir,—I write merely on the old topic, to put you in mind in time to forward what remittances you can, through Hammersley to the same Bankers at Gibraltar, Malta, & Constantinople.—Address your own letters to the latter city to the care of Messrs Barbauld & Co. Bankers.—I am now in Greece where I shall travel some time, & so on to Constantinople.—I am going tomorrow to Yanina the court of Ali Pacha the Turkish Governor of this country.—I was well received at Malta by the Governor &c. who gave me a passage in a ship of war to this port.—We went from Cadiz to Gibraltar in a frigate, and thence to Sardinia, Sicily, & Malta.— —The Consul has gotten me a house here and when I have viewed the ruins of Nicopolis, I shall proceed to Ali Pacha up the interior.—The bay where we now lie was the scene of the famous battle of Actium.—I have seen Ithaca & touched in the Morea at Patras, where I found the Greeks polite & hospitable.—In a few weeks we shall be at Athens, cross the sea to Smyrna & thence to Constantinople is three days journey.—There I expect to hear from you, you are very *remiss*. Remember me to all your family, particularly to Mrs. Hanson, but do not expect to see me soon, I am now above three thousand miles from Chancery Lane —Above all, remember the remittances, & tell Mrs. Byron you have heard from me, you have doubtless seen Murray & the boy.—

yrs. truly
BYRON

P.S.—You should write two or three letters, *one* may miscarry, two have a better chance.

TO MRS. CATHERINE GORDON BYRON *Prevesa.*
Nov. 12th. 1809

My dear Mother,—I have now been some time in Turkey: this place is on the coast but I have traversed the interior of the province of Albania on a visit to the Pacha.—I left Malta in the Spider a brig of war on the 21st. of Septr. & arrived in eight days at Prevesa.—I thence have been about 150 miles as far as Tepaleen his highness's country palace where I staid three days.—The name of the Pacha is Ali, & he is considered a man of the first abilities, he governs the whole of Albania (the ancient Illyricum) Epirus, & part of Macedonia, his Son *Velly* Pacha to whom he has given me letters governs the Morea & he has great influence in Egypt, in short he is one of the most powerful men in the Ottoman empire.—When I reached Yanina the capital after a journey of three days over the mountains through a country of the most picturesque beauty, I found that Ali Pacha was with his army in Illyricum besieging Ibraham Pacha in the castle of Berat.—He had heard that an Englishman of rank was in his dominions & had left orders in Yanina with the Commandant to provide a house & supply me with every kind of necessary, *gratis*, & though I have been allowed to make presents to the slaves &c. I have not been permitted to pay for single article of household consumption.—I rode out on the viziers horses & saw the palaces of himself & grandsons, they are splendid but too much ornamented with silk & gold.—I then went over the mountains through Zitza a village with a Greek monastery (where I slept on my return) in the most beautiful Situation (always excepting Cintra in Portugal) I ever beheld.—In nine days I reached Tepaleen, our Journey was much prolonged by the torrents that had fallen from the mountains & intersected the roads. I shall never forget the singular scene on entering Tepaleen at five in the afternoon as the Sun was going down, it brought to my recollection (with some change of *dress* however) Scott's description of Branksome Castle in his lay, & the feudal system.—The Albanians in their dresses (the most magnificent in the world, consisting of a long *white kilt*, gold worked cloak, crimson velvet gold laced jacket & waistcoat, silver mounted pistols & daggers,) the Tartars with their high caps, the Turks in their vast pelises & turbans, the soldiers & black slaves with the horses, the former stretched in groupes in an immense open gallery in front of the palace, the latter placed in a kind of cloister below it, two hundred steeds ready caparisoned to move in a moment, couriers entering or passing out with dispatches, the kettle drums beating, boys calling the hour from the minaret of the mosque, altogether, with the singular appearance of the building itself, formed a new & delightful spectacle to a stranger.—I was conducted to a very handsome apartment & my health enquired after by the vizier's secretary "a la mode de Turque."—The next day I was introduced to Ali Pacha, I was dressed in a full suit of Staff uniform with a very magnificent sabre &c.— —The Vizier received me in a large room paved with marble, a fountain was playing in the centre, the apartment was surrounded by scarlet Ottomans, he received me *standing*, a wonderful compliment from a Mussulman, & made me sit down on his right hand.—I have a Greek interpreter for general use, but a Physician of Ali's named [Seculario?] who understands Latin acted for me on this occasion.—His first question was why at so early an age I left my country? (the Turks have no idea of travelling for amusement) he then said the English Minister Capt. Leake had told him I was of a great family, & desired his respects to my mother, which I now in the name of Ali Pacha present to you. He said he was certain I was a man of birth because I had small ears, curling hair, & little white hands, and expressed himself pleased with my appearance & garb.—He told me to consider him as a father whilst I was in Turkey, & said he looked on me as his son.—Indeed he treated me like a child, sending me almonds & sugared sherbet, fruit & sweetmeats 20 times a day.—He begged me to visit him often, and at night when he was more at leisure—I then after coffee & pipes retired for the first time. I saw him thrice afterwards.—It is singular that the Turks who have no heriditary dignities & few great families except the Sultan's pay so much respect to birth, for I found my pedigree more regarded than even my title.—His Highness is 60 years old, very fat & not tall, but with a fine face, light blue eyes & a white beard, his manner is very kind & at the same time he possesses that dignity which I find universal amongst the Turks.— —He has the appearance of any thing but his real character, for he is a remorseless tyrant, guilty of the most horrible cruelties, very brave & so good a general, that they call him the Mahometan Buonaparte.—Napoleon has twice offered to make him King of Epirus, but he prefers the English interest & abhors the French as he himself told me, he is of so much consequence that he is much courted by both, the Albanians being the most warlike subjects of the Sultan, though Ali is only nominally dependent on the Porte. He has been a mighty warrior, but is as barbarous as he is successful, roasting rebels &c.

&c.—Bonaparte sent him a snuffbox with his picture[;] he said the snuffbox was very well, but the picture he could excuse, as he neither liked *it* nor the *original.*—His ideas of judging of a man's birth from ears, hands &c. were curious enough.—To me he was indeed a father, giving me letters, guards, & every possible accommodation.—Our next conversations were of war & travelling, politics & England.—He called my Albanian soldier who attends me, and told him to protect me at all hazards.—His name is Viscillie & like all the Albanians he is brave, rigidly honest, & faithful, but they are cruel though not treacherous, & have several vices, but no meannesses.—They are perhaps the most beautiful race in point of countenance in the world, their women are sometimes handsome also, but they are treated like slaves, *beaten* & in short complete beasts of burthen, they plough, dig & sow, I found them carrying wood & actually repairing the highways, the men are all soldiers, & war & the chase their sole occupations, the women are the labourers, which after all is no great hardship in so delightful a climate, yesterday the 11th. Nov. I bathed in the sea, today It is so hot that I am writing in a shady room of the English Consul's with three doors wide open no fire or even *fireplace* in the house except for culinary purposes.—The Albanians [11 lines crossed out] Today I saw the remains of the town of *Actium* near which Anthony lost the world in a small bay where two frigates could hardly manouvre, a broken wall is the sole remnant.—On another part of the gulph stand the ruins of Nicopolis built by Augustus in honour of his victory.— — —Last night I was at a Greek marriage, but this & 1000 things more I have neither time or *space* to describe.—I am going tomorrow with a guard of fifty men to Patras in the Morea, & thence to Athens where I shall winter.—Two days ago I was nearly lost in a Turkish ship of war owing to the ignorance of the captain & crew though the storm was not violent.—Fletcher yelled after his wife, the Greeks called on all the Saints, the Mussulmen on Alla, the Captain burst into tears & ran below deck telling us to call on God, the sails were split, the mainyard shivered, the wind blowing fresh, the night setting in, & all our chance was to make Corfu which is in possession of the French, or (as Fletcher *pathetically* termed it) "a *watery* grave."—I did what I could to console Fletcher but finding him incorrigible wrapped myself up in my

Albanian capote (an immense cloak) & lay down on deck to wait the worst, I have learnt to philosophize on my travels, & if I had not, complaint was useless.—Luckily the wind abated & only drove us on the coast of Suli on the main land where we landed & proceeded by the help of the natives to Prevesa again; but I shall not trust Turkish Sailors in future, though the Pacha had ordered one of his own galleots to take me to Patras, I am therefore going as far as Missolonghi by land & there have only to cross a small gulph to get to Patras.—Fletcher's next epistle will be full of marvels, we were one night lost for *nine* hours in the mountains in a *thunder* storm, & since nearly wrecked, in both cases Fletcher was sorely bewildered, from apprehensions of famine & banditti in the first, & drowning in the second instance.—His eyes were a little hurt by the lightning or crying (I dont know which) but are now recovered.—When you write address to me at Mr. *Strané's* English Consul, Patras, Morea.— — —

I could tell you I know not how many incidents that I think would amuse you, but they crowd on my mind as much as would swell my paper, & I can neither arrange them in the one, or put them down on the other, except in the greatest confusion & in my usual horrible hand.—I like the Albanians much, they are not all Turks, some tribes are Christians, but their religion makes little difference in their manner or conduct; they are esteemed the best troops in the Turkish service.—I lived on my route two days at once, & three days again in a Barrack at Salora, & never found soldiers so tolerable, though I have been in the garrisons of Gibraltar & Malta & seen Spanish, French, Sicilian & British troops in abundance, I have had nothing stolen, & was always welcome to their provision & milk.—Not a week ago, an Albanian chief (every village has its chief who is called Primate) after helping us out of the Turkish Galley in her distress, feeding us & lodging my suite consisting of Fletcher, a Greek, Two Albanians, a Greek Priest and my companion Mr. Hobhouse, refused any compensation but a written paper stating that I was well received, & when I pressed him to accept a few sequins, "no, he replied, I wish you to love me, not to pay me." These were his words.—It is astonishing how far money goes in this country, while I was in the capital, I had nothing to pay by the vizier's order, but since, though I have generally had sixteen horses & generally 6 or 7 men, the expence has not been *half* as much as staying only 3 weeks in Malta, though Sir A. Ball the governor gave me a house for nothing, & I had only *one servant*.—By the bye I expect Hanson to remit regularly, for I am not about to stay in this province for ever, let him write to me at Mr. Strané's, English Consul, Patras.— —The fact is, the fertility of the plains are wonderful, & specie is scarce, which makes this remarkable cheapness.—I am now going to Athens to study modern Greek which differs much from the ancient though radically similar.—I have no desire to return to England, nor shall I unless compelled by absolute want & Hanson's neglect, but I shall not enter Asia for a year or two as I have much to see in Greece & I may perhaps cross into Africa at least the Ægyptian part.—Fletcher like all Englishmen is very much dissatisfied, though a little reconciled to the Turks by a present of 80 piastres from the vizier, which if you consider every thing & the value of specie here is nearly worth ten guineas English.—He has suffered nothing but from *cold*, heat, & vermin which those who lie in cottages & cross mountains in a wild country must undergo, & of which I have equally partaken with himself, but he is not valiant, & is afraid of robbers & tempests.—I have no one to be remembered to in England, & wish to hear nothing from it but that you are well, & a letter or two on business from Hanson, whom you may tell to write.— —I will write when I can, & beg you to believe me,

yr affect. Son

BYRON

P.S.—I have some very "magnifique" Albanian dresses the only expensive articles in this country they cost 50 guineas each & have so much gold they would cost in England two hundred.—I have been introduced to Hussein Bey, & Mahmout Pacha both little boys grandchildren of Ali at Yanina. They are totally unlike our lads, have painted complexions like rouged dowagers, large black eyes & features perfectly regular. They are the prettiest little animals I ever saw, & are broken into the court ceremonies already, the Turkish salute is a slight inclination of the head with the hand on the breast, intimates always kiss, Mahmout is ten years old &

hopes to see me again, we are friends without understanding each other, like many other folks, though from a different cause;—he has given me a letter to his father in the Morea, to whom I have also letters from Ali *Pacha*.—

TURKEY

Now at length we're off for Turkey,
    Lord knows when we shall come back!
Breezes foul and tempests murky
    May unship us in a crack.
But, since life at most a jest is,
    As philosophers allow,
Still to laugh by far the best is,
    Then laugh on—as I do now.
Laugh at all things,
Great and small things,
    Sick or well, at sea or shore;
While we're quaffing,
Let's have laughing—
    Who the devil cares for more?—

from Verse Letter to Francis Hodgson, June 30th, 1809

Don Juan IV, 76–78

[Juan, captive on a Greek vessel, is taken to Turkey to be sold as a slave]

76

There on the green and village-cotted hill is
    (Flanked by the Hellespont and by the sea)
Entombed the bravest of the brave, Achilles;
    They say so (Bryant says the contrary).
And further downward, tall and towering still, is
    The tumulus—of whom? Heaven knows; 't may be
Patroclus, Ajax, or Protesilaus,
All heroes who if living still would slay us.

77

High barrows without marble or a name,
    A vast, untilled, and mountain-skirted plain,
And Ida in the distance, still the same,
    And old Scamander (if 'tis he) remain.
The situation seems still formed for fame.
    A hundred thousand men might fight again
With ease; but where I sought for Ilion's walls,
The quiet sheep feeds, and the tortoise crawls,

78

Troops of untended horses, here and there
    Some little hamlets with new names uncouth,
Some shepherds (unlike Paris) led to stare
    A moment at the European youth,
Whom to the spot their schoolboy feelings bear,
    A Turk with beads in hand and pipe in mouth,
Extremely taken with his own religion,
Are what I found there—but the devil a Phrygian.

TO MRS. CATHERINE GORDON BYRON   *Smyrna.—*
                                     March 19th. 1810

Dear Mother,—I cannot write you a long letter, but as I know
you will not be sorry to receive any intelligence of my movements,
pray accept what I can give.—I have traversed the greatest part of
Greece besides Epirus &c. resided ten weeks at Athens, and am
now on the Asiatic side on my way to Constantinople.—I have
just returned from viewing the ruins of Ephesus a day's journey
from Smyrna.—I presume you have received a long letter I wrote
from Albania with an account of my reception by the Pashaw of
the Province.—When I arrive at Constantinople I shall determine whether to proceed into Persia, or return, which latter I do
not wish if I can avoid it.—But I have no intelligence from Mr.
Hanson, and but one letter from yourself.—I shall stand in need
of remittances whether I proceed or return.—I have written to him
repeatedly that he may not plead ignorance of my situation for neglect.—I can give you no account of any thing for I have not time
or opportunity, the frigate sailing immediately.—Indeed the farther I go the more my laziness increases, and my aversion to letter
writing becomes more confirmed. I have written to no one but
yourself and Mr. Hanson, and these are communications of duty
and business rather than of Inclination.—Fletcher is very much
disgusted with his fatigues, though he has undergone nothing that
I have not shared, he is a poor creature, indeed English servants
are detestable travellers.—I have besides him two Albanian soldiers and a Greek interpreter, all excellent in their way.—Greece,
particularly in the vicinity of Athens, is delightful, cloudless skies,
and lovely landscapes.— —But I must reserve all account of my
adventures till we meet, I keep no journal, but my friend Hobhouse scribbles incessantly.—Pray take care of Murray and Robert,
and tell the boy it is the most fortunate thing for him that he did
not accompany me to *Turkey*[.] Consider this as merely a notice of
my safety, and believe me

                                     yours &c. &c.
                                     BYRON

P.S.—If you address to Malta, your letters will be forwarded.—

TO MRS. CATHERINE GORDON BYRON *Smyrna.*
April 10th. 1810

Dear Mother,—Tomorrow, or this evening I sail for Constantinople in the Salsette 36 gun frigate, she returns to England with our Ambassador whom she is going up on purpose to receive.—I have written to you short letters from Athens, Smyrna, & a long one from Albania. I have not yet mustered courage for a second large epistle, and you must not be angry, since I take all opportunities of apprising you of my safety, but even that is an effort, writing is so irksome.—I have been traversing Greece, and Epirus, Illyria &c. &c. and you see by my date have got into Asia, I have made but one excursion lately, to the Ruins of Ephesus.—Malta is the rendezvous of my letters, so address to that Island.—Mr. Hanson has not written, though I wished to hear of the Norfolk sale, the Lancashire Lawsuit, &c. &c.—I am anxiously expecting fresh remittances. I believe you will like Nottinghamshire, at least my share of it.—Pray accept my good wishes in lieu of a long letter and believe me

yours sincerely & affectionately
BYRON

TO MRS. CATHERINE GORDON BYRON *Salsette Frigate*
off the Dardanelles April 17th. 1810

Dear Madam,—I write at anchor (on our way to Constantinople) off the Troad which I traversed two days ago, all the remains of Troy are the tombs of her destroyers, amongst which I see that of Antilochus from my cabin window.— —These are huge mounds of earth like the barrows of the Danes in your Island, the marble and granite have long perished.—There are several monuments about 12 miles distant of the Alexandrian Troas which I also examined, but by no means to be compared with the remnants of Athens & Ephesus.—This will be sent in a ship of war bound with dispatches for Malta; in a few days we shall be at Constantinople, barring accidents, I have also written from Smyrna, & shall from time to time transmit short accounts of my movements, but I feel totally unequal to long letters.—Believe me

yours very sincerely

BYRON

P.S.—No accounts from Hanson!!!—Do not complain of short letters, I write to nobody but yourself, and Mr. H.—

TO HENRY DRURY   *Salsette frigate. May 3d. 1810 in the Dardanelles off Abydos*

My dear Drury,—When I left England nearly a year ago you requested me to write to you.—I will do so.—I have crossed Portugal, traversed the South of Spain, visited Sardinia, Sicily, Malta, and thence passed into Turkey where I am still wandering.—I first landed in Albania the ancient Epirus where we penetrated as far as Mount Tomerit, excellently treated by the Chief Ali Pacha, and after journeying through Illyria, Chaonia, &ctr, crossed the Gulph of Actium with a guard of 50 Albanians and passed the Achelous in our route through Acarnania and Ætolia.—We stopped a short time in the Morea, crossed the gulph of Lepanto and landed at the foot of Parnassus, saw all that Delphi retains and so on to Thebes and Athens at which last we remained ten weeks.—His majesty's ship Pylades brought us to Smyrna but not before we had topographised Attica including of course Marathon, and the Sunian Promontory.—From Smyrna to the Troad which we visited when at anchor for a fortnight off the Tomb of Antilochus, was our next stage, and now we are in the Dardanelles waiting for a wind to proceed to Constantinople.—This morning I *swam* from *Sestos* to *Abydos*, the immediate distance is not above a mile but the current renders it hazardous, so much so, that I doubt whether Leander's conjugal powers must not have been exhausted in his passage to Paradise.—I attempted it a week ago and failed owing to the North wind and the wonderful rapidity of the tide, though I have been from my childhood a strong swimmer, but this morning being calmer I succeeded and crossed the "broad Hellespont" in an hour and ten minutes.— —Well, my dear Sir, I have left my home and seen part of Africa & Asia and a tolerable portion of Europe.—I have been with Generals, and Admirals, Princes and Pachas, Governors and Ungovernables, but I have not time or paper to expatiate. I wish to let you know that I live with a friendly remembrance of you and a hope to meet you again, and if I do this as shortly as possible, attribute it to any thing but forgetfulness.— Greece ancient and modern you know too well to require description. Albania indeed I have seen more of than any Englishman (but a Mr. Leake) for it is a country rarely visited from the savage character of the natives, though abounding in more natural beauties than the classical regions of Greece, which however are still eminently beautiful, particularly Delphi, and Cape Colonna in Attica.—Yet these are nothing to parts of Illyria, and Epirus, where places without a name, and rivers not laid down in maps, may one day when more known be justly esteemed superior subjects for the pencil, and the pen, than the dry ditch of the Ilissus, and the bogs of Bœotia.—The Troad is a fine field for conjecture and Snipe-shooting, and a good sportsman and an ingenious scholar may exercise their feet and faculties to great advantage upon the spot, or if they prefer riding lose their way (as I did) in a cursed quagmire of the Scamander who wriggles about as if the Dardan virgins still offered their wonted tribute. The only vestige of Troy, or her destroyers, are the barrows supposed to contain the carcases of Achilles[,] Antilochus, Ajax &c. but Mt. Ida is still in high feather, though the Shepherds are nowadays not much like Ganymede.—But why should I say more of these things? are they not written in the *Boke* of Gell? and has not Hobby got a journal? I keep none as I have renounced scribbling.—I see not much difference between ourselves & the Turks, save that we have foreskins and they none, that they have long dresses and we short, and that we talk much and they little.—In England the vices in fashion are whoring & drinking, in Turkey, Sodomy & smoking, we prefer a girl and a bottle, they a pipe and pathic.—They are sensible people, Ali Pacha told me he was sure I was a man of rank because I had *small ears* and hands and *curling hair*.—By the bye, I speak the Romaic or Modern Greek tolerably, it does not differ from the ancient dialects so much as you would conceive, but the pronunciation is diametrically opposite, of verse except in rhyme they have no idea.—I like the Greeks, who are plausible rascals, with all the Turkish vices without their courage.—However some are brave and all are beautiful, very much resembling the busts of Alcibiades, the women not quite so handsome.—I can swear in Turkish, but except one horrible oath, and "*pimp*" and "bread" and "water" I have got no great vocabulary in that language.—They are extremely polite to strangers of any rank properly protected, and as I have got 2 servants and two soldiers we get on with great eclât. We have been occasionally in danger of thieves & once of shipwreck but always escaped.—At Malta I fell in love with a married woman and challenged an aid du camp of Genl. Oakes (a rude fellow who grinned at something, I never rightly knew what,) but he explained and apologised, and the lady embarked for Cadiz, & so I escaped murder and adultery.—Of Spain I sent some account to our Hodgson, but I have subsequently written to no one save notes to relations and lawyers to keep them out of my premises.—I mean to give up all connection on my return with many of my best friends as I supposed them, and to snarl all my life, but I hope to have one good humoured laugh with you, and to embrace Dwyer and pledge Hodgson, before I commence Cynicism.—Tell Dr. Butler I am now writing with the gold pen he gave me before I left England, which is the reason my scrawl is more unentelligible [*sic*] than usual.—I have been at Athens and seen plenty of those reeds for scribbling, some of which he refused to bestow upon me because topographer Gell had brought them from Attica.— —But I will not describe, no, you must be satisfied with simple detail till my return, and then we will unfold the floodgates of Colloquoy.—I am in a 36 gun frigate going up to fetch Bob Adair from Constantinople, who will have the honour to carry this letter.—And so Hobby's *boke* is out, with some sentimental singsong of mine own to fill up, and how does it take? eh! and where the devil is the 2d Edition of my Satire with additions? and my name on the title page? and more lines tagged to the end with a new exordium and what not, hot from my anvil before I cleared the Channel?—The Mediterranean and the Atlantic roll between me and Criticism, and the thunders of the Hyberborean Review are deafened by the roar of the Hellespont.—Remember me to Claridge if not translated to College, and present to Hodgson assurances of my high consideration.—Now, you will ask, what shall I do next? and I answer I do not know, I may return in a few months, but I have intents and projects after visiting Constantinople, Hobhouse however will probably be back in September.—On the 2d. of July we have left Albion one year, "oblitus meorum, obliviscendus et illis," I was sick of my own country, and not much prepossessed in favour of any other, but I drag on "my chain" without "lengthening it at each remove".—I am like the jolly miller caring for nobody and not cared for. All countries are much the same in my eyes, I smoke and stare at mountains, and twirl my mustachios very independently, I miss no comforts, and the Musquïtoes that rack the morbid frame of Hobhouse, have luckily for me little effect on mine because I live more temperately.—I omitted Ephesus in my Catalogue, which I visited during my sojourn at Smyrna,—but the temple has almost perished, and St. Paul need not trouble himself to epistolize the present brood of Ephesians who have converted a large church built entirely of marble into a Mosque, and I dont know that the edifice looks the worse for it.—My paper is full and my ink ebbing, Good Afternoon!—If you address to me at Malta, the letter will be forwarded wherever I may be.—Hobhouse greets you, he pines for his poetry, at least some tidings of it.—I almost forgot to tell you that I am dying for love of three Greek Girls at Athens, sisters, two of whom have promised to accompany me to England, I lived in the same house, Teresa, Mariana, and Kattinka, are the names of these divinities all of them under 15.—your ταπεινοτατοσ δονλοσ

BYRON

TO FRANCIS HODGSON   *Salsette Frigate.—in the Dardanelles off Abydos. May 5th. 1810*

My dear Hodgson,—I am on my way to Constantinople after a turn through Greece, Epirus &c. and part of Asia minor, some particulars of which I have just communicated to our friend & Host H. Drury, with these then I shall not trouble you.—But as you will perhaps be pleased to hear that I am well &c. I take the opportunity of our Ambassador's return to forward the few lines I have

now time to dispatch.—We have undergone some inconveniences
and incurred partial perils, but no events worthy of commemora-
tion unless you will deem it one that two days ago I swam from
Sestos to Abydos.—This with a few alarms from robbers, and some
danger of shipwreck in a Turkish Galliot six months ago, a visit to
a Pacha, a passion for a married woman at Malta, a challenge to an
officer, an attachment to three Greek Girls at Athens, with a great
deal of buffoonery and fine prospects, form all that has distinguished my progress since my departure from Spain.—Hobhouse
rhymes and journalizes. I stare and do nothing, unless smoking
can be deemed an active amusement.—The Turks take too much
care of their women to permit them to be scrutinized, but I have
lived a good deal with the Greeks, whose modern dialect I can
converse in enough for my purposes.—With the Turks I have also
some male acquaintances, female society is out of the question.—I
have been very well treated by the Pachas and Governors, and have
no complaints to make of any kind. Hobhouse will one day inform
you of all our adventures, were I to attempt the recital, neither
my paper nor *your* patience would hold during the operation.—
Nobody, save yourself has written to me since I left England, but
indeed I did not request it, I except my relations who write quite
as often as I wish—Of Hobhouse's volume I know nothing except
that it is out, and of my 2d. Edition I do not even know *that*, and
certainly do not at this distance interest myself in the matter.—My
friend H. is naturally anxious on the head of his rhymes, which I
think will succeed or at least deserve success, but he has not yet
acquired the "calm indifference" (as Sir Fretful has it), of *us old*
Authors.—I hope you and Bland roll down the stream of Sale,
with rapidity, and that you have produced a new poem, and Mrs.
H. Drury a new child. Of my return I cannot positively speak,
but think it probable Hobhouse will precede me in that respect,
we have now been very nearly one year abroad.—I should wish to
gaze away another at least in these evergreen climates, but I fear
Business, Law business, the worst of employments, will recall me
previous to that period if not very quickly.—If so, you shall have
due notice, I hope you will find me an altered personage, I do not
mean in body, but in manner, for I begin to find out that nothing
but virtue will do in this damned world. I am tolerably sick of vice

which I have tried in its agreeable varieties, and mean on my return to cut all my dissolute acquaintance, leave off wine and "carnal company", and betake myself to politics and Decorum.—I am very serious and cynical, and a good deal disposed to moralize, but fortunately for you the coming homily is cut off by default of pen, and defection of paper. Good morrow! if you write, address to me at Malta, whence your letters will be forwarded. You need not remember me to anybody but believe me yours with all faith

BYRON

Written After Swimming from Sestos to Abydos

If in the month of dark December
　　Leander, who was nightly wont
(What maid will not the tale remember?)
　　To cross thy stream, broad Hellespont!

If when the wintry tempest roar'd
　　He sped to Hero, nothing loth,
And thus of old thy current pour'd,
　　Fair Venus! how I pity both!

For *me*, degenerate modern wretch,
　　Though in the genial month of May,
My dripping limbs I faintly stretch,
　　And think I've done a feat to-day.

But since he cross'd the rapid tide,
　　According to the doubtful story,
To woo,—and—Lord knows what beside,
　　And swam for Love, as I for Glory;

'Twere hard to say who fared the best:
　　Sad mortals! thus the Gods still plague you!
He lost his labour, I my jest:
　　For he was drown'd, and I've the ague.

MAY 9TH, 1810

Childe Harold's Pilgrimage II, 79–81

79

And whose more rife with merriment than thine,
Oh Stamboul! once the empress of their reign?
Though turbans now pollute Sophia's shrine,
And Greece her very altars eyes in vain:
(Alas! her woes will still pervade my strain!)
Gay were her minstrels once, for free her throng,
All felt the common joy they now must feign,
Nor oft I've seen such sight, nor heard such song,
As woo'd the eye, and thrill'd the Bosphorus along.

80

Loud was the lightsome tumult of the shore,
Oft Music chang'd, but never ceas'd her tone,
And timely echo'd back the measur'd oar,
And rippling waters made a pleasant moan:
The Queen of tides on high consenting shone,
And when a transient breeze swept o'er the wave,
'Twas, as if darting from her heavenly throne,
A brighter glance her form reflected gave,
Till sparkling billows seem'd to light the banks they lave.

81

Glanc'd many a light caique along the foam,
Danc'd on the shore the daughters of the land,
Ne thought had man or maid of rest or home,
While many a languid eye and thrilling hand
Exchang'd the look few bosoms may withstand,
Or gently prest, return'd the pressure still:
Oh Love! young Love! bound in thy rosy band,
Let sage or cynic prattle as he will,
These hours, and only these, redeem Life's years of ill!

TO MRS. CATHERINE GORDON BYRON   *Constantinople*
                                          May 18th. 1810

Dear Madam,—I arrived here in an English frigate from
Smyrna a few days ago without any events worth mentioning
except landing to view the plains of Troy, and afterwards when
we were at anchor in the *Dardanelles*, *swimming* from *Sestos* to
Abydos, in imitation of Monsieur Leander whose story you no
doubt know too well for me to add any thing on the subject except
that I crossed the Hellespont without so good a motive for the
undertaking.—As I am just going to visit the Captain Pacha you
will excuse the brevity of my letter, when Mr. Adair takes leave I
am to see the Sultan & the Mosques &c.

                                          Believe me yrs ever
                                              BYRON

TO MRS. CATHERINE GORDON BYRON   *Constantinople*
                                          May 24th. 1810

Dear Mother,—I wrote to you very shortly the other day on
my arrival here, and as another opportunity avails take up my
pen again that the frequency of my letters may atone for their
brevity.—Pray did you ever receive a picture of me in oil by
Sanders in *Vigo Lane* London? (a noted limner,) if not, write for
it immediately, it was paid for except the frame (if frame there
be) before I left England.—I believe I mentioned to you in my
last that my only notable exploit lately, has been swimming from
Sestos to Abydos on the 3d. of this month, in humble imitation of
Leander of amorous memory, though I had no *Hero* to receive me
on the other shore of the Hellespont.—Of Constantinople you
have of course read fifty descriptions by sundry travellers, which
are in general so correct that I have nothing to add on the Subject.—When our Ambassador takes his leave I shall accompany
him to see the Sultan, and afterwards probably return to Greece,
I have heard nothing of Mr. Hanson but one remittance without
any letter from that legal gentleman.—If you have occasion for
any pecuniary supply, pray use my funds as far as they *go* without

reserve, and lest this should not be enough, in my next to Mr. H. I will direct him to advance any sum you may want, leaving it to your discretion how much in the present state of my affairs you may think proper to require.—I have already seen the most interesting parts of Turkey in Europe and Asia Minor, but shall not proceed further till I hear from England, in the mean time I expect occasional supplies according to circumstances, and shall pass my summer amongst my friends the Greeks of the Morea.—You will direct to Malta, whence my letters are forwarded and believe me to be with great sincerity

yrs ever
BYRON

P.S.—Fletcher is well, pray take care of my boy Robert, and the old man Murray.—It is fortunate they returned, neither the youth of the one or age of the other, would have suited the changes of climate and fatigues of travelling.—

TO MRS. CATHERINE GORDON BYRON   *Constantinople*
                                          June 28th. 1810

My dear Mother,—I regret to perceive by your last letter, that several of mine have not arrived, particularly a very long one written in November last from Albania, when I was on a visit to the Pacha of that province.—Fletcher has also written to his spouse perpetually.—Mr. Hobhouse who will forward or deliver this and is on his return to England, can inform you of our different movements, but I am very uncertain as to my own return. He will probably be down in Notts some time or other, but Fletcher whom I send back as an Incumbrance, (English servants are sad travellers) will supply his place in the Interim, and describe our travels which have been tolerably extensive.—I have written twice briefly from this capital, from Smyrna, from Athens and other parts of Greece, from Albania, the Pacha of which province desired his respects to my mother, and said he was sure I was a man of high birth because I had "*small ears, curling hair,* and *white hands*"!!! He was very kind to me, begged me to consider him as a father, and gave me a guard of forty soldiers through the forests of Acarnania.—But of this and other circumstances I have written to you at large, and yet hope you will receive my letters.—I remember Mahmout Pacha, the grandson of Ali Pacha at Yanina, (a little fellow of ten years of age, with large black eyes which our ladies would purchase at any price, and those regular features which distinguish the Turks) asked me how I came to travel about so *young*, without any body to take care of me, this question was put by the little man with all the gravity of threescore.—I cannot now write copiously, I have only time to tell you that I have passed many a fatiguing but never a tedious moment, and that all I am afraid of *is*, that I shall contract a Gipsy-like wandering disposition, which will make home tiresome to me, this I am told is very common with men in the habit of peregrination, and indeed I feel it so.—On the third of May I swam from *Sestos* to Abydos, you know the story of Leander, but I had no *Hero* to receive me at landing,—I also passed a fortnight in the Troad, the tombs of Achilles and Æsietes [sic] &c. still exist in large barrows similar to those you have doubtless seen in the North.—The other day I was at Belgrade (a village in these environs) to see the house built on the same site as Lady Mary Wortley's, by the bye, her Ladyship, as far as I can judge, has lied, but not half so much as any other woman would have done in the same situation.—I have been in all the principal Mosques by virtue of a firman, this is a favour rarely permitted to infidels, but the Ambassador's departure obtained it for us. I have been up the Bosphorus into the Black Sea, round the walls of the city, and indeed I know more of it by sight than I do of London.—I hope to amaze you some winter's evening with the details but at present you must excuse me, I am not able to write long letters in *June*.—I return to spend my summer in Greece, I shall not proceed farther into Asia, as I have visited Smyrna, Ephesus, and the Troad.—I write often but you must not be alarmed when you do not receive my letters, consider we have no regular post farther than Malta where I beg you will in future send your letters, & not to this city.—Fletcher is a poor creature, and requires comforts that I can dispense with, he is very sick of his travels, but you must not believe his account of the country, he sighs for Ale, and Idleness, and a wife and the Devil knows what besides.—I have not been disappointed or disgusted, I have lived with the highest and the lowest, I have been for days in a Pacha's palace, and have passed many a night in a cowhouse, and I find the people inoffensive and kind, I have also passed some time with the principal Greeks in the Morea & Livadia, and though inferior to the Turks, they are better than the Spaniards, who in their turn excel the Portuguese. Of Constantinople you will find many correct descriptions in different travels, but Lady Wortley errs strangely when she says "St. Paul's would cut a poor figure by St. Sophia's". I have been in both, surveyed them inside & out attentively, St. Sophia's is undoubtedly the most interesting from its immense antiquity, and the circumstance of all the Greek Emperors from Justinian having been crowned there, and several murdered at the Altar, besides the Turkish Sultans who attend it regularly, but it is inferior in beauty & size to some of the other Mosques, particularly "Soleyman Etc" and not to be mentioned in the same page with St. P's (I speak like a *cockney*) however, I prefer the Gothic Cathedral of Seville to St. P's, St. Sophia's and any religious building I have ever seen.—The walls of the Seraglio are like the walls of Newstead Gardens only higher, and much in the same *order*, but the ride by the walls of the city on the land side is beautiful, imagine, four miles of immense triple battlements covered with *Ivy*, surmounted with 218 towers, and on the other side of the road Turkish burying grounds (the loveliest spots on earth) full of enormous cypresses, I have seen the ruins of Athens, of Ephesus, and Delphi, I have traversed great part of Turkey and many other parts of Europe and some of Asia, but I never beheld a work of Nature or Art, which yielded an impression like the prospect on each side, from the Seven Towers to the End of the Golden Horn.—Now for England, you have not received my friend Hobhouse's volume of Poesy, it has been published several months, you ought to read it.—I am glad to hear of the progress of E. Bards &c. of course you observed I have made great additions to the new Edition.—Have you received my picture from Sanders in Vigo lane London? it was finished and paid for long before I left England, pray send for it.—You seem to be a mighty reader of magazines, where do you pick up all this intelligence? quotations &c. &c.?—Though I was happy to obtain my seat without Ld. C[arlisle]'s assistance, I had no measures to keep with a man who declined interfering as my relation on that occasion, and I have done with him, though I regret distressing Mrs. Leigh, poor thing! I hope she is happy.—It is my opinion that Mr. Bowman ought to marry Miss Rushton, our first duty is not to do evil, but alas! that is impossible, our next is to repair it, if in our power, the girl is his equal, if she were his inferior a sum of money and provision for the child would be some, though a poor compensation, as it is, he should marry her. I will have no gay deceivers on my Estate, and I shall not allow my tenants a privilege I do not permit myself, viz—*that*, of debauching each other's daughters.—God knows, I have been guilty of many excesses, but as I have laid down a resolution to reform, and *lately* kept it, I expect this Lothario to follow the example, and begin by restoring this girl to society, or, by the Beard of my Father! he shall hear of it.—Pray, take some notice of Robert, who will miss his master, poor boy, he was very unwilling to return.—I trust you are well & happy, it will be a pleasure to hear from you, believe me

yours ever sincerely
BYRON

P.S.—How is Joe Murray?—

P.S.—July 6th. 1810

Dear M[othe]r,—I open my letter to tell you that Fletcher having petitioned [to] accompany me into the Morea, I have taken him with me contrary to the intention expressed in my letter.—

yours ever
BYRON

TO ROBERT ADAIR *Pera July 4th. 1810*

Sir,—I regret that your Excellency should have deemed me or my concerns of sufficient importance to give you a thought beyond the moment when they were forced (perhaps unreasonably) on your attention.—On all occasions of this kind one of the parties must be wrong, at present it has fallen to my lot, your authorities (particularly the *German*) are too many for me.—I shall therefore make what atonement I can by cheerfully following not only your excellency "but your servant or your maid your ox or your ass, or any thing that is yours."—I have to apologize for not availing myself of your Excellency['s] kind invitation and hospitable intentions in my favour, but the fact is, that I am never very well adapted for or very happy in society, and I happen at this time from some particular circumstances to be even less so than usual. Your excellency will I trust attribute my omissions to the *right* cause rather than disrespect in your

truly obliged & very obedient humble servant

BYRON

GREECE

Fair Greece! Sad relic of departed worth!
Immortal, though no more! Though fallen, great!
Who now shall lead thy scatter'd children forth,
And long accustom'd bondage uncreate?

. . .

And yet how lovely in thine age of woe,
Land of lost gods and godlike men! Art thou!
Thy vales of ever-green, thy hills of snow
Proclaim thee Nature's varied favourite now:
Thy fanes, thy temples to thy surface bow,
Commingling slowly with heroic earth,
Broke by the share of every rustic plough:
So perish monuments of mortal birth,
So perish all in turn, save well-recorded Worth,

Save where some solitary column mourns
Above its protrate brethren of the cave;
Save where Tritonia's airy shrine adorns
Colonna's cliff, and gleams along the wave;
Save o'er some warrior's half-forgotten grave,
Where the grey stones and unmolested grass
Ages, not oblivion, feebly brave,
While strangers only not regardless pass,
Lingering like me, perchance, to gaze, and sigh "Alas!"

CHILDE HAROLD'S PILGRIMAGE II, 73, 85–86

Don Juan II, 177–194

[Juan, after being washed ashore on a Greek island, is revived by Haidée]

177

It was a wild and breaker-beaten coast,
    With cliffs above and a broad sandy shore,
Guarded by shoals and rocks as by an host,
    With here and there a creek, whose aspect wore
A better welcome to the tempest-tost.
    And rarely ceased the haughty billow's roar,
Save on the dead long summer days, which make
The outstretched ocean glitter like a lake.

178

And the small ripple spilt upon the beach
    Scarcely o'erpassed the cream of your champagne,
When o'er the brim the sparkling bumpers reach,
    That spring-dew of the spirit, the heart's rain!
Few things surpass old wine; and they may preach
    Who please—the more because they preach in vain.
Let us have wine and woman, mirth and laughter,
Sermons and soda water the day after.

179

Man being reasonable must get drunk;
    The best of life is but intoxication.
Glory, the grape, love, gold, in these are sunk
    The hopes of all men and of every nation;
Without their sap, how branchless were the trunk
    Of life's strange tree, so fruitful on occasion.
But to return. Get very drunk, and when
You wake with headache, you shall see what then.

180

Ring for your valet, bid him quickly bring
    Some hock and soda water. Then you'll know

A pleasure worthy Xerxes, the great king;
    For not the blest sherbet, sublimed with snow,
Nor the first sparkle of the desert spring,
    Nor Burgundy in all its sunset glow,
After long travel, ennui, love, or slaughter,
Vie with that draught of hock and soda water.

181

The coast—I think it was the coast that I
    Was just describing—yes, it was the coast—
Lay at this period quiet as the sky,
    The sands untumbled, the blue waves untost,
And all was stillness, save the sea bird's cry
    And dolphin's leap and little billow crost
By some low rock or shelve, that made it fret
Against the boundary it scarcely wet.

182

And forth they wandered, her sire being gone,
    As I have said, upon an expedition.
And mother, brother, guardian, she had none,
    Save Zoe, who although with due precision
She waited on her lady with the sun,
    Thought daily service was her only mission,
Bringing warm water, wreathing her long tresses,
And asking now and then for cast-off dresses.

183

It was the cooling hour, just when the rounded
    Red sun sinks down behind the azure hill,
Which then seems as if the whole earth it bounded,
    Circling all nature, hushed and dim and still,
With the far mountain-crescent half surrounded
    On one side, and the deep sea calm and chill
Upon the other, and the rosy sky
With one star sparkling through it like an eye.

184

And thus they wandered forth, and hand in hand,
    Over the shining pebbles and the shells,
Glided along the smooth and hardened sand,
    And in the worn and wild receptacles
Worked by the storms, yet worked as it were planned,
    In hollow halls with sparry roofs and cells,
They turned to rest, and each clasped by an arm,
Yielded to the deep twilight's purple charm.

185

They looked up to the sky, whose floating glow
    Spread like a rosy ocean, vast and bright.
They gazed upon the glittering sea below,
    Whence the broad moon rose circling into sight.
They heard the wave's splash and the wind so low,
    And saw each other's dark eyes darting light
Into each other, and beholding this,
Their lips drew near and clung into a kiss,

186

A long, long kiss, a kiss of youth and love
    And beauty, all concentrating like rays
Into one focus, kindled from above;
    Such kisses as belong to early days,
Where heart and soul and sense in concert move,
    And the blood's lava, and the pulse a blaze,
Each kiss a heart-quake, for a kiss's strength,
I think, it must be reckoned by its length.

187

By length I mean duration; theirs endured
    Heaven knows how long; no doubt they never reckoned,
And if they had, they could not have secured
    The sum of their sensations to a second.

They had not spoken, but they felt allured,
    As if their souls and lips each other beckoned,
Which, being joined, like swarming bees they clung,
Their hearts the flowers from whence the honey sprung.

188

They were alone, but not alone as they
    Who shut in chambers think it loneliness.
The silent ocean and the starlight bay,
    The twilight glow, which momently grew less,
The voiceless sands and dropping caves, that lay
    Around them, made them to each other press,
As if there were no life beneath the sky
Save theirs, and that their life could never die.

189

They feared no eyes nor ears on that lone beach,
    They felt no terrors from the night, they were
All in all to each other. Though their speech
    Was broken words, they thought a language there,
And all the burning tongues the passions teach
    Found in one sigh the best interpreter
Of nature's oracle, first love, that all
Which Eve has left her daughters since her fall.

190

Haidée spoke not of scruples, asked no vows
    Nor offered any; she had never heard
Of plight and promises to be a spouse,
    Or perils by a loving maid incurred.
She was all which pure ignorance allows
    And flew to her young mate like a young bird,
And never having dreamt of falsehood, she
Had not one word to say of constancy.

191

She loved and was beloved, she adored
    And she was worshipped after nature's fashion.
Their intense souls, into each other poured,
    If souls could die, had perished in that passion,
But by degrees their senses were restored,
    Again to be o'ercome, again to dash on.
And beating 'gainst *his* bosom, Haidée's heart
Felt as if never more to beat apart.

192

Alas, they were so young, so beautiful,
    So lonely, loving, helpless, and the hour
Was that in which the heart is always full,
    And having o'er itself no further power,
Prompts deeds eternity cannot annul,
    But pays off moments in an endless shower
Of hell-fire, all prepared for people giving
Pleasure or pain to one another living.

193

Alas for Juan and Haidée! They were
    So loving and so lovely; till then never,
Excepting our first parents, such a pair
    Had run the risk of being damned forever.
And Haidée, being devout as well as fair,
    Had doubtless heard about the Stygian river
And hell and purgatory, but forgot
Just in the very crisis she should not.

194

They look upon each other, and their eyes
    Gleam in the moonlight, and her white arm clasps
Round Juan's head, and his around hers lies
    Half buried in the tresses which it grasps.

She sits upon his knee and drinks his sighs,
    He hers, until they end in broken gasps;
And thus they form a group that's quite antique,
Half naked, loving, natural, and Greek.

Dear Mother.—I have arrived here in four days from Constantinople which is considered as singularly quick particularly for the season of the year; *you Northern Gentry* can have no conception of a Greek Summer, which however is a perfect Frost compared with Malta, and Gibraltar, where I reposed myself in the *shade* last year after a gentle Gallop of four hundred miles without intermission through Portugal & Spain.—You see by my date that I am at Athens again, a place which I think I prefer upon the whole to any I have seen.—I left Constantinople with Adair at whose audience of leave I saw Sultan Mahmout, and obtained a firman to visit the Mosques of which I think I gave you some description in my last letter, now voyaging towards England in the Salsette frigate in which I visited the plains of Troy, and Constantinople.—My next movement is tomorrow into the Morea, where I shall probably remain a month or two, and then return to winter here if I do not change my plans, which however are very variable as you may suppose, but *none* of them verge to England.—The Marquis of Sligo my old fellow collegian is here, and wishes to accompany me into the Morea, we shall go together for that purpose, but I am already woefully sick of travelling companions after a years experience of Mr. Hobhouse who is on his way to Great Britain.—Ld. S[ligo] will afterwards pursue his way to the Capitol, and Ld. *B.* having seen all the wonders in that quarter, will let you know what he does next, of which at present he is not quite certain.—Malta is my perpetual post-office from which my letters are forwarded to all parts of the habitable Globe, by the bye, I have now been in Asia, Africa, and the East of Europe, and indeed made the most of my time, without hurrying over the most interesting scenes of the ancient world.—Fletcher, after having been toasted and roasted, and baked and grilled, and eaten by all sorts of creeping things begins to philosophise, is grown a refined as well as resigned character, and promises at his return to become an ornament to his own parish, and a very prominent person in the future family pedigree of the Fletchers whom I take to be Goths by their accomplishments, Greeks by their acuteness, and ancient Saxons by their appetite.—He (Fletcher) begs leave to send half a dozen sighs to Sally his spouse, and wonders (though I do not) that his ill written and worse spelt letters have never come to hand, as for that matter there is no great loss in either of our letters, saving and except, that I wish you to know we are well and warm enough at this present writing God knows.—You must not expect long letters at present for they are written with the sweat of my brow, I assure you.—It is rather singular that Mr. Hanson has not written a syllable since my departure, your letters I have mostly received, as well as others, from which I conjecture that the man of law is either angry or busy.—I trust you like Newstead and agree with your neighbours, but you know *you* are a *vixen*, is not that a dutiful appellation?—Pray take care of my Books, and several boxes of papers in the hands of Joseph, and pray leave me a few bottles of Champagne to drink for I am very thirsty, but I do not insist on the last article without you like it.—I suppose you have your house full of silly women, prating scandalous things;—have you ever received my picture in oil from Sanders London? it has been paid for these 16 months, why do you not get it?—My Suite consisting of two Turks, two Greeks, a Lutheran, and the non-descript Fletcher, are making so much noise that I am glad to sign myself yours &c.

BYRON

TO MRS. CATHERINE GORDON BYRON *Patras. July 30th. 1810*

Dear Madam,—In four days from Constantinople with a favourable wind I arrived in the frigate at the island of Zea, from whence I took a boat to Athens where I met my friend the Marquis of Sligo who expressed a wish to proceed with me as far as Corinth.—At Corinth we separated he for Tripolitza I for Patras where I had some business with the Consul Mr. Stranè in whose house I now write, he has rendered me every service in his power since I quitted Malta on my way to Constantinople, whence I have written to you twice or thrice.—In a few days I visit the Pacha at Tripolitza, make the tour of the Morea, and return again to Athens, which at present is my headquarters.—The heat is at present intense, in England if it reaches 98 you are all on fire, the other day in travelling between Athens and Megara the thermometer was at

125!!—Yet I feel no inconvenience, of course I am much bronzed, but I live temperately, and never enjoyed better health.—Before I left Constantinople I saw the Sultan (with Mr. Adair) and the interior of the Mosques, things which rarely happen to travellers.—Mr. Hobhouse is gone to England.—I am in no hurry to return, but have no particular communications for your country, except my surprise at Mr. Hanson's silence, and my desire that he will remit regularly.—I suppose some arrangement has been made with regard to Wymondham and Rochdale.—Mr. Hobhouse has letters for you from me.—Malta is my post office, or to Mr. Stranè Consul General Patras, Morea.—You complain of my silence, I have written twenty or thirty times within the last year, never less than twice a month, and often more. If my letters do not arrive you must not conclude that we are eaten, or that there is a war, or a pestilence, or famine, neither must you credit *silly* reports, which I dare say, you have in Notts as usual.—I am very well, and neither more or less happy than I usually am, except that I am very glad to be once more alone, for I was sick of my companion (not that he was a bad one) but because my nature leads me to solitude, and that every day adds to this disposition.—If I chose, here are many men who would wish to join me, one wants me to go to Egypt, another to Asia, of which I have seen enough, the greater part of Greece is already my own, so that I shall only go over my old ground, and look upon my old seas and mountains, the only acquaintances I ever found improve upon me.—I have a tolerable suite, a Tartar, two Albanians, and interpreter, besides Fletcher, but in this country, these are easily maintained.—Adair received me wonderfully well, and indeed I have no complaints against any one, hospitality here is necessary, for inns are not.—I have lived in the houses of Turks, Greeks, Italians, and English, today in a palace, tomorrow in a cowhouse, this day with the Pacha, and the next with a Shepherd.—I shall continue to write briefly but frequently, and am glad to hear from you, but you fill your letters with things from the papers, as if English papers were not found all over the world, I have at this moment a dozen before me.—Pray take care of my books, and believe me

my dear Mother yours very faithfully

BYRON

TO JOHN CAM HOBHOUSE   *Tripolitza. August 16th. 1810*

Dear Hobhouse,—I am on the rack of setting off for Argos amidst the usual creaking swearing loading and neighing of sixteen horses and as many men [serving us? servingers?] included.—You have probably received one letter dated Patras and I send this at a venture.—Velly Pacha received me even better than his Father did, though he is to join the Sultan, and the city is full of troops and confusion, which as he said, prevents him from paying proper attention.—He has given me a very pretty horse and a most par- ticular invitation to meet him at Larissa, which last is singular enough as he recommended a different route to Ld. Sligo who asked leave to accompany him to the Danube.—I asked no such thing, but on his enquiring where I meant to go, and receiving for answer that I was about to return to Albania for the purpose of penetrating higher up the country, he replied, "no you must not take that route, but go round by Larissa where I shall remain some time on my way. I will send to Athens, and you shall join me, we will eat and drink well, and go a hunting."—He said he wished all the old men (specifying under that epithet *North*, *Forresti*, and *Stranè*) to go to his father, but the young ones to come to him, to use his own expression "vecchio con vecchio, Giovane con Gio- vane."—He honored me with the appellations of his *friend* and *brother*, and hoped that we should be on good terms not for a few days but for Life.—All this is very well, but he has an awkward manner of throwing his arm round one's waist, and squeezing one's hand in *public*, which is a high compliment, but very much em- barrasses "*ingenuous youth*".—The first time I saw him he received me standing, accompanied me at my departure to the door of the audience chamber, and told me I was a παλικαρι and an εὔμορφω παιδι—He asked if I did not think it very proper that as *young* men (he has a *beard* down to his middle) we should live together, with a variety of other sayings, which made Stranè stare, and puzzled me in my replies.—He was very facetious with Andreas and Viscillie, and recommended that my Albanians' heads should be cut off if they behaved ill.—I shall write to you from Larissa, and inform you of our proceedings in that city.—In the mean time I sojourn at Athens.——

I have sent Eustathius back to his home, he plagued my soul out with his whims, and is besides subject to *epileptic* fits (tell *M*[atthews] this) which made him a perplexing companion, in *other* matters he was very tolerable, I mean as to his *learning*, being well versed in the Ellenics.—You remember Nicolo at Athens Lusieri's wife's brother.—Give my *compliments* to *Matthews* from whom I expect a congratulatory letter.——I have a thousand anecdotes for him and you, but at present Τι να καμω? I have neither time nor space, but in the words of Dawes, "I have things in store."—I have scribbled thus much, where shall I send it, why to Malta or Paternoster Row. Hobby you wretch how is the Miscellany? that damned and damnable work, "what has the learned world said to your paradoxes? I hope you did not forget the importance of Monogamy."—Stranè has just arrived with bags of piastres, so that I must conclude by the usual phrase of

yours &c. &c.

BYRON

P.S.—You knew young Bossari at Yanina, he is a piece of Ali Pacha's!! well did Horace write "Nil Admirari"

TO JOHN CAM HOBHOUSE *The Convent. Athens.*
August 23d. 1810

My dear Hobhouse,—Ld. Sligo's unmanageable Brig being remanded to Malta with a large quantity of vases amounting in value (according to the depreciation of Fauvel) to one hundred and fifty piastres, I cannot resist the temptation of assailing you in this third letter, which I trust will find you better than your deserts, and no worse than my wishes can make you.—I have girated the Morea, and was presented with a very fine horse (a stallion) and honoured with a number of squeezes and speeches by Velly Pacha, besides a most pressing invitation to visit him at Larissa in his way to the wars.—But of these things I have written already.—I returned to Athens by Argos where I found Ld. Sligo with a painter who has got a fever with sketching at mid day, and a dragoman who has actually lied himself into a lockjaw, I grieve to say the

Marchesa has done a number of young things, because I believe him to be a clever, and I am sure he is a good man.—I am most auspiciously settled in the Convent, which is more commodious than any tenement I have yet occupied, with room for my *suite*, and it is by no means solitary, seeing there is not only "il Padre Abbate" but his "schuola" consisting of six "Regatzi" all my most particular allies.—These Gentlemen being almost (saving Fauvel and Lusieri) my only associates it is but proper their character religion and morals should be described.—Of this goodly company three are Catholics and three are Greeks, which Schismatics I have already set a boxing to the great amusement of the Father who rejoices to see the Catholics conquer.—Their names are, Barthelemi, Giuseppe, *Nicolo*, Yani, and two anonymous at least in my memory.—Of these Barthelemi is a "simplice Fanciullo" according to the account of the Father, whose favourite is Giuseppe who sleeps in the lantern of Demosthenes.—We have nothing but riot from Noon till night.—The first time I mingled with these Sylphs, after about two minutes reconnoitering, the amiable Signor Barthelemi without any previous notice seated himself by me, and after observing by way of compliment, that my "Signoria" was the "pieu bello" of his English acquaintances saluted me on the left cheek, for which freedom being reproved by Giuseppe, who very properly informed him that I was "μεγαλοσ" he told him I was his "φιλοσ" and "by his beard," he would do so again, adding in reply to the question of "διατι ασπασετε?" you see he laughs, as in good truth I did very heartily.—But my friend as you may easily imagine is Nicolo, who by the bye, is my Italian master, and we are already very philosophical.—I am his "Padrone" and his "amico" and the Lord knows what besides, it is about two hours since that after informing me he was most desirous to follow *him* (that is me) over the world, he concluded by telling me it was proper for us not only to live but "morire insieme."—The latter I hope to avoid, as much of the former as he pleases.—I am awakened in the morning by these imps shouting "venite abasso" and the friar gravely observes it is "bisogno bastonare" every body before the studies can possibly commence.—Besides these lads, my suite, to which I have added a Tartar and a youth to look after my two new saddle horses, my suite I say; are very obstreperous and drink skinfuls of

Zean wine at 8 paras the oke daily.—Then we have several Albanian women washing in the "giardino" whose hours of relaxation
are spent in running pins into Fletcher's backside.—"*Damnata di
mi if I have seen such a spectaculo in my way from Viterbo.*"—In
short what with the *women*, and the *boys*, and the *suite*, we are very
disorderly.—But I am vastly happy and childish, and shall have a
world of anecdotes for you and the "Citoyen."—Intrigue flourishes, the old woman Teresa's mother was mad enough to imagine I
was going to marry the girl, but I have better amusement, Andreas
is fooling with Dudu as usual, and Mariana has made a conquest
of Dervise Tahiri, Viscillie Fletcher and Sullee my new Tartar have
each a mistress, "Vive l'Amour!"—I am learning Italian, and this
day translated an ode of Horace "Exegi monumentum" into that
language[.] I chatter with every body good or bad and tradute
prayers out of the Mass Ritual, but my lessons though very long
are sadly interrupted by scamperings and eating fruit and peltings
and playings and I am in fact at school again, and make as little
improvement now as I did then, my time being wasted in the same
way.—However it is too good to last, I am going to make a second
tour of Attica with Lusieri who is a new ally of mine, and Nicolo
goes with me at his own most pressing solicitation "per mare, per
terras"—"Forse" you may see us in Inghilterra, but "non so, come
&c."—For the present, Good even, Buona sera a vos signoria,
Bacio le mani.——August 24th. 1810.—I am about to take my
daily ride to the Piraeus where I swim for an hour despite of the
heat, here hath been an Englishman ycleped Watson, who died
and is buried in the Tempio of Theseus. I knew him not, but I am
told that the Surgeon of Ld. Sligo's brig slew him with an improper
potion and a cold bath.—Ld. Sligo's crew are sadly addicted to
liquor.—He is in some apprehension of a scrape with the Navy
concerning certain mariners of the King's ships.—He himself is
now at Argos with his hospital but intends to winter in Athens.
I think he will be sick of it, poor soul he has all the indecision of
your humble servant, without the relish for the ridiculous which
makes my life supportable.——I wish you were here to partake of
a number of waggeries which you can hardly find in the Gunroom
or in Grub-street, but then you are so very crabbed and disagreeable that when the laugh is over, I rejoice in your absence.—After

all I do love thee, Hobby, thou hast so many good qualities and so many bad ones it is impossible to live with or without thee.—
Nine in the Evening.—
I have as usual swum across the Piraeus, the Signore Nicolo also laved, but he makes as bad a hand in the water as L'Abbe Hyacinth at Falmouth, it is a curious thing that the Turks when they bathe wear their lower garments as your humble servant always doth, but the Greeks not, however questo Giovane e vergogno.—Ld. Sligo's surgeon has assisted very materially the malignant fever now fashionable here, another man *died* to day, two men a week like fighting Bob Acres in the country.—Fauvel says he is like the Surgeon whom the Venetians fitted out against the Turks with whom they were then at war.—I have been employed the greater part of today in conjugating the verb "ασπαζω" [ασπαζομαι] (which word being Ellenic as well as Romaic may find a place in the *Citoyen's* Lexicon) I assure you my progress is rapid, but like Caesar "nil actum reputans dum quid superesset agendum" I must arrive at the pl & opt C, and then I will write to ———[Matthews], I hope to escape the fever, at least till I finish this affair, and then it is welcome to try, I dont think without its friend the drunken Poticary it has any chance, take a quotation.— "Et Lycam *nigris* oculis, nigroque *Crine* decorum."—

yours & the *Sieur's* ever

B.

TO JOHN CAM HOBHOUSE   *Patras. Septr. 25th. 1810*

My Dear Hobhouse—I am at present in a very ridiculous situation, under the hands of Dr. Romanelli and a fever which hath confined me to my bed for these three days past, but by the blessing of God and two glysters, I am now able to sit up, but much debilitated.—I will describe my situation in a parody on Pope's lines on the Duke of Buckingham, the which I composed during an Interval for your edification.—

On a cold room's floor, within a bed
Of iron, with three coverlids like lead,

A coat and breeches dangling o'er a nook,
Where sits a doctor, and prescribes a puke,
Poor B-r-n sweats—alas! how changed from him
So plump in feature, and so round in limb,
Grinning and gay in Newstead's monkish fane
The scene of profanation and Champagne,
Or just as gay with scribblers in a ring
Of twenty hungry authors banqueting,
No whore to fondle left of half a score,
Yet one thing left him, which he values more,
Here victor of a fever and it's friends
Physicians and their art, his lordship *mends*.

I have been vomited and purged according to rule, and as my fever has almost subsided, I hope to weather this bout, which has been pretty tight I assure you.—Yet if I do fall by the Glyster pipe of Romanelli, recollect my injunction.

Odious! in boards, twould any Bard provoke,
(Were the last words that dying Byron spoke)
No let some charming cuts and frontispiece
Adorn my volume, and the sale increase,
One would not be unpublished when one's dead
And, Hobhouse, let my works be bound in *Red*.

TO MRS. CATHERINE GORDON BYRON   *Patras. October*
                                                  second. 1810

Dear Madam,—It is now several months since I have received any communication from you, but at this I am not surprised, nor indeed have I any complaint to make since you have written frequently, for which I thank you. But I very much condemn Mr. Hanson, who has not taken the smallest notice of my many letters, nor of my request before I left England, which I sailed from on this *very day* fifteen months ago.—Thus one year and a quarter have passed away, without my receiving the least intelligence on the state of my affairs, and they were not in a posture to admit of neglect, and I do conceive and declare that Mr. H. has acted negligently and culpably in not apprising me of his proceedings, I will also add uncivilly.—His letters were there any could not easily miscarry, the communications with the Levant are slow but tolerably secure, at least as far as Malta, and there I left proper directions which I know would be observed.—I have written to you several times from Constantinople and Smyrna, you will perceive by my date I am returned into the Morea, of which I have been making the tour and visiting the Pacha, who gave me a fine horse, and paid me all possible honours and attention.—I have now seen a good portion of Turkey in Europe and Asia Minor, and shall remain at Athens and in the vicinity till I hear from England.—I have punctually obeyed your injunctions of writing frequently, but I shall not pretend to describe countries which have been already amply treated of, I believe before this time Mr. Hobhouse will have arrived in England, and he brings letters from me written at Constantinople.— —In these I mention having seen the Sultan & the Mosques, and that I swam from Sestos to Abydos an exploit of which I take care to boast.— —I am here on business, at present, but Athens is my head quarters, where I am very pleasantly situated in a Franciscan convent.— —Believe me to be with great sincerity

yrs. very affectly.
BYRON

TO FRANCIS HODGSON   *Athens Novr. 14th. 1810*

My dear Hodgson,—This will arrive with an English servant whom I send homewards with some papers of consequence.—I have been journeying in different parts of Greece for these last four months, and you may expect me in England somewhere about April, but this is very dubious.—Hobhouse you have doubtless seen, he went home in August to look after his Miscellany, and to arrange materials for a tour he talks of publishing.—You will find him well and scribbling, that is scribbling if well, and well if scribbling.—I suppose you have a score of new works, all of which I hope to see flourishing, with a hecatomb of reviews.—*My* works are likely to have a powerful effect with a vengeance, as I hear of divers angry people, whom it is proper I should shoot at, by way of satisfaction.—Be it so, the same impulse which made "Otho a warrior," will make me one also.—My domestic affairs being moreover considerably deranged, my appetite for travelling pretty well satiated with my late peregrinations, my various hopes in this world almost extinct, and not very brilliant in the next, I trust I shall go through the process with a creditable "sang froid" and not disgrace a line of cut-throat ancestors.—I regret in one of your letters to hear you talk of domestic embarrassments, indeed I am at present very well calculated to sympathise with you on that point.—I suppose I must take to dram drinking as a succedaneum for philosophy, though as I am happily not married I have very little occasion for either just yet.—Talking of marriage puts me in mind of Drury, who I suppose has a dozen children by this time all fine fretful brats; I will never forgive Matrimony for having spoiled such an excellent Bachelor. If any body honours my name with an enquiry tell them of "my whereabouts" and write if you like it.—I am living alone in the Franciscan monastery with one Fri*ar* (a Capuchin of course) and one Fri*er* (a bandy legged Turkish Cook) two Albanian savages, a Tartar, and a Dragoman, my only Englishman departs with this and other letters.—The day before yesterday, the Waywode (or Governor of Athens) with the Mufti of Thebes (a sort of Mussulman Bishop) supped here and made themselves beastly with raw Rum, and the Padrè of the convent being as drunk as *we*, my *Attic* feast went off with great eclât.—I have had a present of a stallion from the Pacha of the Morea.—I caught a fever going to Olympia.—I was blown ashore on the Island of Salamis, in my way to Corinth through the gulph of Ægina.—I have kicked an Athenian postmaster, I have a friendship with the French Consul, and an Italian painter, and am on good terms with five Teutones & Cimbri, Danes and Germans, who are travelling for an Academy.—Vale!

yours ever,
μπαιρων

Don Juan III, 84–89

[*While Juan enjoys the Greek island, the narrator describes a poet*]

84

He had travelled amongst the Arabs, Turks and Franks
   And knew the self-loves of the different nations,
And having lived with people of all ranks,
   Had something ready upon most occasions,
Which got him a few presents and some thanks.
   He varied with some skill his adulations;
To "do at Rome as Romans do", a piece
Of conduct was which he observed in Greece.

85

Thus, usually, when he was asked to sing,
   He gave the different nations something national;
'Twas all the same to him—"God save the king"
   Or "*Ça ira*", according to the fashion all.
His Muse made increment of anything
   From the high lyric down to the low rational.
If Pindar sang horse races, what should hinder
Himself from being as pliable as Pindar?

86

In France, for instance, he would write a chanson;
   In England, a six canto quarto tale;
In Spain, he'd make a ballad or romance on
   The last war—much the same in Portugal;
In Germany, the Pegasus he'd prance on
   Would be old Goethe's (see what says de Staël);
In Italy, he'd ape the *Trecentisti*;
In Greece, he'd sing some sort of hymn like this t' ye:

1

The isles of Greece, the isles of Greece!
  Where burning Sappho loved and sung,
Where grew the arts of war and peace,
  Where Delos rose, and Phoebus sprung,
Eternal summer gilds them yet,
But all, except their sun, is set.

2

The Scian and the Teian Muse,
  The hero's harp, the lover's lute
Have found the fame your shores refuse.
  Their place of birth alone is mute
To sounds which echo further west
Than your sires' "Islands of the Blest".

3

The mountains look on Marathon,
  And Marathon looks on the sea.
And musing there an hour alone,
  I dreamed that Greece might still be free,
For standing on the Persian's grave,
I could not deem myself a slave.

4

A king sate on the rocky brow
  Which looks o'er sea-born Salamis;
And ships by thousands lay below,
  And men in nations—all were his!
He counted them at break of day,
And when the sun set where were they?

5

And where are they? And where art thou,
  My country? On thy voiceless shore
The heroic lay is tuneless now,
  The heroic bosom beats no more!

And must thy lyre, so long divine,
Degenerate into hands like mine?

6

'Tis something in the dearth of fame,
    Though linked among a fettered race,
To feel at least a patriot's shame,
    Even as I sing, suffuse my face.
For what is left the poet here?
For Greeks a blush, for Greece a tear.

7

Must we but weep o'er days more blest?
    Must we but blush? Our fathers bled.
Earth! Render back from out thy breast
    A remnant of our Spartan dead!
Of the three hundred grant but three,
To make a new Thermopylae!

8

What, silent still? And silent all?
    Ah no! The voices of the dead
Sound like a distant torrent's fall
    And answer, "Let one living head,
But one arise—we come, we come!"
'Tis but the living who are dumb.

9

In vain—in vain—strike other chords.
    Fill high the cup with Samian wine!
Leave battles to the Turkish hordes,
    And shed the blood of Scio's vine!
Hark, rising to the ignoble call,
How answers each bold bacchanal!

10

You have the Pyrrhic dance as yet,
    Where is the Pyrrhic phalanx gone?

Of two such lessons, why forget
*   The nobler and the manlier one?*
You have the letters Cadmus gave;
Think ye he meant them for a slave?

II

Fill high the bowl with Samian wine!
*   We will not think of themes like these.*
It made Anacreon's song divine;
*   He served, but served Polycrates,*
A tyrant; but our masters then
Were still at least our countrymen.

12

The tyrant of the Chersonese
*   Was freedom's best and bravest friend.*
That tyrant was Miltiades.
*   Oh that the present hour would lend*
Another despot of the kind!
Such chains as his were sure to bind.

13

Fill high the bowl with Samian wine!
*   On Suli's rock and Parga's shore,*
Exists the remnant of a line
*   Such as the Doric mothers bore.*
And there perhaps some seed is sown,
The Heracleidan blood might own.

14

Trust not for freedom to the Franks;
*   They have a king who buys and sells.*
In native swords and native ranks
*   The only hope of courage dwells,*
But Turkish force and Latin fraud
Would break your shield, however broad.

15

Fill high the bowl with Samian wine!
    Our virgins dance beneath the shade.
I see their glorious black eyes shine,
    But gazing on each glowing maid,
My own the burning teardrop laves,
To think such breasts must suckle slaves.

16

Place me on Sunium's marbled steep,
    Where nothing, save the waves and I,
May hear our mutual murmurs sweep;
    There, swan-like, let me sing and die.
A land of slaves shall ne'er be mine—
Dash down yon cup of Samian wine!

87

Thus sung or would or could or should have sung
    The modern Greek in tolerable verse.
If not like Orpheus quite, when Greece was young,
    Yet in these times he might have done much worse.
His strain displayed some feeling, right or wrong;
    And feeling in a poet is the source
Of others' feeling; but they are such liars
And take all colours—like the hands of dyers.

88

But words are things, and a small drop of ink,
    Falling like dew upon a thought, produces
That which makes thousands, perhaps millions, think.
    'Tis strange, the shortest letter which man uses
Instead of speech, may form a lasting link
    Of ages. To what straits old Time reduces
Frail man, when paper, even a rag like this,
Survives himself, his tomb, and all that's his.

89

And when his bones are dust, his grave a blank,
    His station, generation, even his nation
Become a thing, or nothing, save to rank
    In chronological commemoration,
Some dull MS, oblivion long has sank,
    Or graven stone found in a barrack's station
In digging the foundation of a closet,
May turn his name up as a rare deposit.

TO FRANCIS HODGSON   *Athens—January 20th. 1811*

My dear Hodgson,—In most of your letters, that is to say *two* the only ones I have received of yours, you complain of my silence, this complaint I presume to be removed by this time, as I have written frequently, but more particularly by H. who is of course long ago landed, and will amply gratify any further curiosity you may have beyond the limits of a letter.——I also wrote by the Black John, which however was taken off Algiers with the Capt. Moses Kennedy & several bags of long letters, but especially Hobhouse's intimates have to regret the capture of some enormous packets, which cost a world of pains at Constantinople in the Troad & elsewhere, as I can witness, & unless the French government publish them, I am afraid we have little chance of recovering these inestimable manuscripts.—But then to make amends to himself followed close on the heels of his letters (by the bye I fear *heels* of letters is a very incorrect metaphor) and will tell the world all how & about it, unless he also has been boarded & taken off Algiers.——Talking of taking, I was nearly taken myself six weeks ago by some Mainnote pirates (Lacedemonians & be damned to them) at Cape Colonna, but being well armed, & attended, the varlets were afraid, or they might have bagged us all with a little skirmishing.—I am still in Athens making little tours to Marathon, Sunium, the top of Hymettus, & the Morea occasionally to diversify the season.—My Grand Giro finished with Constantinople & I shall not (I think) go further Eastward, but I am sure of nothing so little as my own intentions, and if I receive cash & comfortable news from home I shant trouble your foggy Island for amusement.—I am studying modern Greek with a Master, and my current tongue is Levant Italian, which I gabble perforce, my late dragoman spoke bad Latin, but having dismissed him, I am left to my resources which consist in tolerably fluent Lingua Franca, middling Romaic (modern Greek) and some variety of Ottoman oaths of great service with a stumbling horse, or a stupid servant.—I lately sent to England my only remaining Englishman with some papers about money matters, and am left d'ye see all by myself in these outlandish parts, and I don't find it *never* the *worser* for friends and servants that is to say fellow countrymen in those capacities are troublesome fellow travellers.—I have a variety of acquaint-ance, French, Danes, Germans Greek Italian & Turkish, and have contracted an alliance with Dr. Bronstedt of Copenhagen a pretty philosopher as you'd wish to see.—Besides I am on good terms with some of my countrymen here, Messrs Grahame & Haygarth, & I have in pay a Bavarian Baron named "Lynch" (pronounce it Lyn*k*) who limns landscapes for the lucre of gain.—Here also are Messrs Fiott, Cockerell & Foster all of whom I know, and they are all vastly amiable & accomplished.—I am living in the Capuchin Convent, Hymettus before me, the Acropolis behind, the temple of Jove to my right, the Stadium in front, the town to the left, eh, Sir, there's a situation, there's your picturesque! nothing like that, Sir, in Lunnun, no not even the Mansion House. And I feed upon Woodcocks & red Mullet every day, & I have three horses (one a present from the Pacha of the Morea) and I ride to Piraeus, & Phalerum & Munychia, which however dont look quite so mag-nificent after the harbours of Cadiz, Lisbon, Constantinople & Gibralter not forgetting Malta. I wish to be sure I had a few books, one's own works for instance, any damned nonsense on a long Evening.—I had a straggling number of the E[dinburgh] Review given me by a compassionate Capt. of a frigate lately, it contains the reply to the Oxonian pamphlet, on the Strabonic controversy, the reviewer seems to be in a perilous passion & heaves out a deal of Slack-jaw as the Sailors call it.—You know to direct to Malta, whence my letters are or ought to be forwarded.—In two days I shall be twenty three, and on the 2d. above a year and a half out of England.—I suppose you & Drury sometimes drink one's health on a speechday, & I trust we shall meet merrily, and make a tour some summer to Wales or Scotland, it will be a great relaxation to me jaunting once more in a Chay.—I need not write at length as Hobby is brimful of remarks, and it would be cruel to curtail him of a syllable.—Tell him I have written to him frequently, as indeed I have to yourself and also to Drury & others, but this is a plaguy distance for a single sheet.—

yours always
BYRON—

TO MRS. CATHERINE GORDON BYRON   *Athens*
                                              January 14th. 1811

My dear Madam,—I seize an occasion to write to you as usual shortly but frequently, as the arrival of letters where there exists no regular communication is of course very precarious.—I have received at different intervals several of yours, but generally six months after date, some sooner, some later, and though lately tolerably stationary, the delays appear just the same.—I have lately made several small tours of some hundred or two miles about the Morea, Attica &c. as I have finished my grand Giro by the Troad Constantinople &c. and am returned down again to Athens.—I believe I have mentioned to you more than once that I swam (in imitation of Leander though without his lady) across the Hellespont from Sestos to Abydos. Of this and all other particulars Fletcher whom I have sent home with papers &c. will apprise you.—I cant find that he is any loss, being tolerably master of the Italian & modern Greek languages, which last I am also studying with a master, I can order and discourse more than enough for a reasonable man.—Besides the perpetual lamentations after beef & beer, the stupid bigotted contempt for every thing foreign, and insurmountable incapacity of acquiring even a few words of any language, rendered him like all other English servants, an incumbrance.—I do assure you the plague of speaking for him, the comforts he required (more than myself by far) the pilaws (a Turkish dish of rice & meat) which he could not eat, the wines which he could not drink, the beds where he could not sleep, & the long list of calamities such as stumbling horses, want of tea!!! &c. which assailed him, would have made a lasting source of laughter to a spectator, and of inconvenience to a Master.—After all the man is honest and in Christendom capable enough, but in Turkey—Lord forgive me, my Albanian soldiers, my Tartars & Janizary worked for him & us too as my friend Hobhouse can testify.——It is probable I may steer homewards in Spring, but to enable me to do that I must have remittances.—My own funds would have lasted me very well, but I was obliged to assist a friend, who I know will pay me, but in the meantime I am out of pocket.—At present I do not care to venture a winter's voyage, even if I were otherwise tired of travelling, but I am so convinced of the advantages of looking at mankind instead of reading about them, and of the bitter effects of staying at home with all the narrow prejudices of an Islander, that I think there should be a law amongst us to set our young men abroad for a term among the few allies our wars have left us.—Here I see and have conversed with French, Italians, Germans, Danes, Greeks, Turks, Armenians, &c. &c. &c. and without losing sight of my own, I can judge of the countries and manners of others.— Where I see the superiority of England (which by the bye we are a good deal mistaken about in many things) I am pleased, and where I find her inferior I am at least enlightened.—Now I might have staid smoked in your towns or fogged in your country a century without being sure of this, and without acquiring anything more useful or amusing at home.—I keep no journal, nor have I any intention of scribbling my travels.—I have done with authorship, and if in my last production I have convinced the critics or the world, I was something more than they took me for, I am satisfied, nor will I hazard *that reputation* by a future effort.—It is true I have some others in manuscript, but I leave them for those who come after me, and if deemed worth publishing, they may serve to prolong my memory, when I myself shall cease to remember.—I have a famous Bavarian Artist taking some views of Athens &c. &c. for me.—This will be better than scribbling, a disease I hope myself cured of.—I hope on my return to lead a quiet and recluse life, but God knows and does best for us all, at least so they say, and I have nothing to object, as on the whole I have no reason to complain of my lot.—I am convinced however that men do more harm to themselves than ever the Devil could do to them. I trust this will find you well and as happy as we can be, you will at least be pleased to hear that I am so &

yours ever

BYRON

TO MRS. CATHERINE GORDON BYRON *Athens.*
February 28th. 1811

Dear Madam,—As I have received a firman for Ægypt &c. I shall proceed to that quarter in the Spring, & I beg you will state to Mr. Hanson that it is necessary to [send] further remittances.—On the subject of Newstead I answer as before—*No.*—If it is necessary to sell, sell Rochdale.—Fletcher will have arrived by this time with my letters to that purport.—I will tell you fairly, I have in the first place no opinion of funded property.——If, by any particular circumstances I shall be led to adopt such a determination, I will at all events, pass my life abroad, as my only tie to England is Newstead, & that once gone neither interest or inclination lead me northward.—Competence in your country is ample Wealth in the East such is the difference in the value of money & the abundance of the necessaries of life, & I feel myself so much a citizen of the world, that the spot where I can enjoy a delicious climate, & every luxury at a less expense than a common college life in England, will always be a country to me, and such are in fact the shores of the Archipelago.—This then is the alternative, if I preserve Newstead, I return, if I sell it, I stay away.——I have had no letters since yours of June, but I have written several times, & shall continue as usual on the same plan, believe me

yrs. ever
BYRON

P.S.—I shall most likely see you in the course of the summer but of course at such a distance I cannot specify any particular month.—

THE VOYAGE HOME

Here he embarked, and with a flowing sail
    Went bounding for the island of the free,
Towards which the impatient wind blew half a gale;
    High dashed the spray, the bows dipped in the sea,
And sea-sick passengers turned somewhat pale;
    But Juan, seasoned, as he well might be,
By former voyages, stood to watch the skiffs
Which passed, or catch the first glimpse of the cliffs.

. . .

I've no great cause to love that spot of earth,
    Which holds what might have been the noblest
        nation;
But though I owe it little but my birth,
    I feel a mixed regret and veneration
For its decaying fame and former worth.

DON JUAN X, 64, 66

My dear Hodgson—In a week with a fair wind we shall be in Portsmouth, & on the 2d. July I shall have completed (to a day) two years of peregrination, from which I am returning with as little emotion as I set out.—I think, upon the whole, I was more grieved at leaving Greece, than England, which I am impatient to see, simply because I am tired of a long voyage.—Indeed my prospects are not very pleasant, embarrassed in my private affairs, indifferent to public, solitary without the wish to be social, with a body a little enfeebled by a succession of fevers, but a spirit I trust yet unbroken, I am returning *home*, without a hope, & almost without a desire.— —The first thing I shall have to encounter, will be a Lawyer, the next a Creditor, then Colliers, farmers, surveyors, & all the agreeable attachments to Estates out of repair, & Contested Coalpits.—In short I am sick, & sorry, & when I have a little repaired my irreparable affairs, away I shall march, either to campaign in Spain, or back again to the East, where I can at least have cloudless skies, & a cessation from impertinence.— —I trust to meet, or see you in town, or at Newstead whenever you can make it Convenient, I suppose you are in Love, & in Poetry, as usual. That husband H. Drury, has never written to me, albeit I have sent him more than one letter, but I dare say the poor man has a family, & of course all his cares are confined to his circle

> "For children fresh expences yet
> "And Dickey now for school is fit.
> > *Warton*

If you see him, tell him I have a letter for him from Tucker a regimental Chirurgeon & friend of his, who prescribed for me in a [two lines crossed out] & is a very worthy man, but too fond of hard words.— —I shall be too late for a speechday, or I should probably go down to Harrow.—Hobhouse is either abroad again, or in the Militia!!! so he writes, or perhaps at Cambridge, he has sent me a most humourous account of the failure of the Miscellany, which he attributes to Bawdry, but I always have said that if it fell, it must be owing to the preface, which Matthews swore was like Walsh. I regretted much in Greece, having omitted to carry

the Anthology with me.— —I mean Bland & Merival[e]'s.—I
trust something will weigh up H[obhouse]'s book again, I wish
he had only asked *seven* shillings, I thought he would split on
the odd three & sixpence.— —What has Sir Edgar done? & the
Imitations and Translations? where are they? I suppose you don't
mean to let the public off so easily, but charge them home with a
Quarto.—For me, I am "sick of Fops, & Poesy, & Prate" & shall
leave the "whole Castalian State" to Bufo or any body else, but
you are a Sentimental & Sensibilitous person, & will rhyme to the
end of the Chapter.—Howbeit I have written some 4000 lines of
one kind or another on my travels.—I need not repeat that I shall
be happy to see you, I shall be in town about the 8th. at Dorant's
Hotel in Albemarle St. & proceed in a few days to Notts, & thence
to Rochdale on business.—I am here, & there,

yrs. very sincerely

B.

TO JOHN CAM HOBHOUSE   *Volage Frigate—Bay of Biscay*
                                          July 2d. 1811

My dear Hobhouse,—This very day two years we sailed from
Inghilterra, so that I have completed the period I expected to be
absent, though my wishes were originally more extensive. When we
shall arrive, God knows! but till then I continue scribbling to you,
for lack of other Argument.—My Situation is one you have been
used to, so you will feel without further description, but I must
do Capt. Hornby the Justice to say, he is one of the best Marine
productions in my recollection. There is another Cabin passenger,
an elderly, prosing, pestiferous, Staff Surgeon, of Oakes's, who has
almost slain me with a thousand & one tales all about himself, &
"Genl. This," and "Lord That," and "says Hes" & "says Is,"—&
the worst of it is, I have no friend with me to laugh at the fellow,
though he is too common a character for mirth.—Damn him,—I
can make no more of him than a Hedgehog, he is too dull to be
ridiculous.— —We have been beating about with hazy weather
this last Fortnight, and today is foggy as the Isle of Man.— —I have
been thinking again & again of a literary project we have at times

started, to wit— —a periodical paper, something in the Spectator or Observer way. There certainly is no such thing at present.— Why not get one, Tuesdays & Saturdays.—You must be Editor, as you have more taste and diligence than either Matthews or myself (I beg M's pardon for lowering him to the same line with me) and I dont think we shall want other contributors if we set seriously about it.— —We must have for each day, one or two essays, miscellaneous, according to Circumstances, but now & then politics, and always a piece of poetry of one kind or other.—I give you these hints to digest the scheme at leisure,—it would be pleasant, and with success, in some degree profitable.—Above all we must be secret—at least at first.— —"Cosa pensate?" Perpend, pronounce, Respond?— —We can call it "La Bagatelle" (according to your idea) or Lillibulero, if you like it, the name wont matter so that the Contents are palatable.— —But I am writing & projecting without knowing where you are, in Country or College Quarters, though I hope you have abandoned your Militia Scheme. Matthews gave me hopes that Arms would give way to the Gown, as you had visions of returning to Granta.—God keep bad port out of your Carcase! you would certainly fall a victim to Messing the very first Campaign. I have brought your marbles, which I shall leave at Portsmouth till you can settle where to put them. I shall be in town a very short time, meaning to proceed to Notts, & thence to Rochdale. I am tolerably well in Health, that is to say, instead of an *Ague*, & a *Clap*, and the *Piles*, all at once, I have only the two last. I wrote to you from Malta, during my Fever, my Terzana, or rather Quotidiana, for it was called intermittent "a *Non* Intermittendo."—I am as I say well, but in bitter bad spirits, skies foggy, head muzzy, Capt. sulky, ship lazy.—The accursed Pharmacopole is at present on deck,—the only pleasure I have had these three weeks. But I hope to tell you in person how truly I am yrs

B.

TO HENRY DRURY   *Volage Frigate off Ushant. July 7th. 1811*

My dear Drury,—After two years absence (on the 2d.) & some odd days I am approaching your Country, the day of our arrival you will see by the outside date of my letter, at present we are becalmed comfortably close to Brest Harbour;—I have never been so near it since I left Duck Puddle.—The enclosed letter is from a friend of yours Surgeon Tucker whom I met with in Greece, & so on to Malta, where he administered to me for three complaints viz. a *Gonorrhea* a *Tertian fever*, & the *Hemorrhoides*, *all* of which I literally had at once, though he assured me the *morbid* action of only one of these distempers could act at a time, which was a great comfort, though they relieved one another as regularly as Sentinels, & very nearly sent me back to Acheron, my old acquaintance which I left fine & flowing in Albania.— —We left Malta 34 days ago, & (except the Gut of Gibraltar which we passed with an Easterly wind as easy as an oil Glyster) we have had a tedious passage on't.—You have never written, this comes of Matrimony, Hodgson has,—so you see the Balance of Friendship is on the Batchelor's side.—I am at present well, that is, I have only two out of the three aforesaid complaints, & these I hope to be cured of, as they say one's Native fogs are vastly salubrious.— — —You will either see or hear from or of me soon after the receipt of this, as I pass through town to repair my irreparable affairs, & thence I must go to Nott's & raise rents, & to Lanc's, & sell collieries, & back to London, & pay debts, for it seems I shall neither have coals or comfort till I go down to Rochdale in person. I have brought home some marbles for Hobhouse;—& for myself, "Four ancient Athenian Skulls["] dug out of Sarcophagi, a "phial of Attic Hemlock," ["]four live Tortoises" a Greyhound (died on the passage) two live Greek Servants one an *Athenian*, t'other a *Yaniote*, who can speak nothing but Romaic & Italian, & *myself*, as Moses in the "Vicar of Wakefield" says *slily*, & I may say it too for I have as little cause to boast of my expedition as he of his to the Fair.—I wrote to you from the Cyanean Rocks, to tell you I had swum from Sestos to Abydos, have you received my letter?— —Hobhouse went to England to fish up his Miscellany, which foundered (so he tells me) in the Gulph of Lethe, I dare say it capsized with the vile goods of his contributory friends, for his own share was very portable.— However I hope he will either weigh up or set sail with a fresh Cargo, & a luckier vessel. Hodgson I suppose is four deep by this time, what would he give? to have seen like me the *real Parnassus*, where I robbed the Bishop of Chrisso of a book of Geography, but this I only call plagiarism, as it was done within an hour's ride of Delphi.— —

Believe me yrs. ever
BYRON

TO JOHN M. B. PIGOT   *Newport Pagnell, August 2, 1811*

My dear Doctor,—My poor mother died yesterday! and I am on my way from town to attend her to the family vault. I heard *one* day of her illness, the *next* of her death.—Thank God her last moments were most tranquil. I am told she was in little pain, and not aware of her situation.—I now feel the truth of Mr. Gray's observation, "That we can only have *one* mother."—Peace be with her! I have to thank you for your expressions of regard, and as in six weeks I shall be in Lancashire on business, I may extend to Liverpool and Chester,—at least I shall endeavour.

If it will be any satisfaction, I have to inform you that in November next the Editor of the Scourge will be tried for two different libels on the late Mrs. B[yron] and myself (the decease of Mrs. B. makes no difference in the proceedings), and as he is guilty, by his very foolish and unfounded assertion, of a breach of privilege, he will be prosecuted with the utmost rigour.

I inform of this, as you seem interested in the affair, which is now in the hands of the attorney-general.

I shall remain at Newstead the greater part of this month, where I shall be happy to hear from you, after my two years' absence in the East.

I am, dear Pigot, yours very truly.
BYRON

LONDON

A mighty mass of brick, and smoke, and shipping,
  Dirty and dusky, but as wide as eye
Could reach, with here and there a sail just skipping
  In sight, then lost amidst the forestry
Of masts; a wilderness of steeples peeping
  On tiptoe through their sea-coal canopy;
A huge, dun cupola, like a foolscap crown
On a fool's head—and there is London Town!

DON JUAN X, 82

My dear Elizabeth—London begins to disgorge its contents, town is empty, consequently I can scribble at leisure, as my occupations are less numerous, in a fortnight I shall depart to fulfil a country engagement, but expect 2 Epistles from you previous to that period.—Ridge, you tell me, does not proceed rapidly in Notts, very possible, in Town things wear a most promising aspect, & a *Man* whose works are praised by *Reviewers*, admired by *Duchesses* & sold by every Bookseller of the Metropolis, does not dedicate much consideration to *rustic Readers.*—I have now a Review before me entitled, "Literary Recreations" where my *Bard-ship* is applauded far beyond my Deserts. I know nothing of the critic, but think *him* a very *discerning gentleman*, & *myself* a *devilish clever fellow*, his critique pleases me particularly because it is of great length, & a proper quantum of censure is administered, just to give an agreeable *relish* to the praise, you know I hate insipid, unqualified common-place compliments, if you would wish to see it, tell Ridge to order the 13th Number of "Literary Recreations" for the last Month. I assure you, I have not the most distant Idea, of the Writer of the article, it is printed in a periodical publication, & though I have written a paper (a Review of Wordsworth) which appears in the same work, I am ignorant of every other person concerned in it, even the Editor, whose name I have not heard.—My Cousin, Lord Alexander Gordon, who resided in the same Hotel, told me his Mother, her *Grace* of *Gordon*, requested he would introduce my *poetical* Lordship, to her *highness*, as she had bought my volume, admired it extremely, in common with the Rest of the fashionable world, & wished to claim her relationship with the Author.—I was unluckily engaged on an excursion for some days afterwards, & as the Duchess was on the eve of departing for Scotland, have postponed my Introduction till the Winter, when I shall favour this Lady, *whose Taste I shall not dispute*, with my *most sublime* & *edifying conversation.*—She is now in the Highlands, & Alexander, took his departure a few days ago, for the same *blessed* Seat, of "*dark-rolling Winds*".— Crosby my London publisher, has disposed of his second importation, & has sent to Ridge for a *third* (at least so he says) in every Bookseller's I see my *own name*, & *say nothing*, but enjoy my *fame* in *secret*.—My last Reviewer, kindly requests me to alter my determination of writing no more, and "*as a friend to the cause of Literature*" begs, I will *gratify* the *Public*, with some new *work* "at no very distant period".—Who would not be a Bard? *Elizabeth*, that is to say, if all critics would be so polite, however the others will pay me off I doubt not, for this *gentle* encouragement.—If so, have at 'em, By the Bye, I have written at my Intervals of leisure, after 2 in the *Morning*. 380 lines in *blank* verse, of "Bosworth Field," I have luckily procured Hutton's account, & shall extend the Poem to 8 or 10 Books, & shall have finished in a year, whether it will be published or not must depend on circumstances.—So much for *Egotism*, my *Laurels* have turned my Brain, but the *cooling acids* of forthcoming criticisms, will probably restore me to *Modesty*.— — — —Southwell, I agree with your Brother, is a *damned* place, I have done with it, & shall see it no more, (at least in all probability) excepting yourself, I esteem no one within its precincts, you were my only *rational* companion, & in plain truth I had more respect for you, than the whole *Bevy*, with whose foibles I *amused* myself in compliance with their *prevailing propensities*, you gave yourself more trouble with me & my *manuscripts*, than a thousand *dolls* would have done, believe me, I have not forgotten your good nature, in *this Circle* of *Sin*, & one day I trust shall be able to evince my gratitude.—As for the village "*Lass'es*" of *every description*, my *Gratitude* is also unbounded, to be equalled only by my *contempt*, I saw the *designs* of all *parties*, while they imagined me *every thing* to be *wished*, Adieu

> yours very truly
> BYRON

P.S.—Remembrance to *Dr. Pigot*.—

TO ELIZABETH BRIDGET PIGOT   *London, August 11th. 1807*

Dear Elizabeth,—On Sunday next I set off for the Highlands, a friend of mine accompanies me in my Carriege to Edinburgh, there we shall leave it, & proceed in a *Tandem* (a species of open Carriage) through the Western passes to Inverary, where we shall purchase *Shelties*, to enable us to view places inaccessible to *vehicular Conveyances*, on the Coast, we shall hire a vessel, & visit the most remarkable of the Hebrides, & if we have time & favourable weather mean to sail as far as Iceland only 300 miles from the Northern extremity of Caledonia, to peep at *Hecla*, this last Intention you will keep a secret, as my nice *Mamma* would imagine I was on a *voyage* of *Discovery*, & raise the accustomed *maternal* *"Warhoop."*—Last week I swam in the Thames from Lambeth through the 2 Bridges Westminster & Blackfriars, a distance including the different turns & tacks made on the way, of 3 miles!! you see I am in excellent training in case of a *squall* at Sea.—I mean to collect all the Erse traditions, poems, & & c. & translate, or expand the subjects, to fill a volume, which may appear next Spring, under the Denomination of "*the Highland Harp*" or some title equally *picturesque*. Of Bosworth Field, one Book is finished, another just begun, it will be a work of 3 or four years, & most probably never *concluded*.—What would you say to some Stanzas on Mount *Hecla*? they would be written at least with *Fire*.—How is the Immortal Bran? & the Phoenix of canine Quadrupeds, Boatswain? I have lately purchased a thoroug[h] bred Bulldog worthy to be the Coadjutor of the aforesaid celestials, his name is *Smut*! "bear it ye breezes! on your *balmy* wings".—Write to me before I set off, I conjure you by the 5th Rib of your Grandfather; you say, Ridge goes on well with the Book now, I thought that worthy *Phrygian*, had not done much in the Country, in Town they have been very very successful, Carpenter (Moore's publisher) told me a few days ago they sold all their's immediately, & had several enquiries made since, which from the Book being gone, they could not supply, the Duke of York, the Marchioness of Headfort, the Duchess of Gordon &c &c. were among the Purchasers, & Crosby says the circulation will be still more extensive in the Winter, the Summer Season being very bad for a sale, as most people are absent from London, however they have gone off extremely well altogether.—I shall pass very near you on my Journey, through Newark, but cannot approach, dont tell this to Mrs. B. who supposes I travel a different Road.—If you have any Letter, order it to be left at Ridge's shop, where I shall call, or the post office Newark, which you please, on Monday I shall change horses at Newark, about 6 or 8 in the Evening, if your Brother would ride over, I should be devilish glad to see him, he can return the same night, or sup with us, & go home the following Morning, the Kingston arms is my Inn.—Adieu,

yours ever

BYRON

P.S.—Lord Carlisle on receiving my poems, sent before he opened the Book, a tolerably handsome Letter, I have not heard of or from him since, his opinion I neither know nor care about, if he is the least insolent, I shall enroll him with "*Butler*" & the rest of the worthies, he is in Yorkshire poor man! very ill!—He said he had not had time to read the contents, but thought it necessary to acknowledge the Receipt of the volume immediately.—Perhaps the Earl "*bears no Brother near the Throne*" if so, I will make his *sceptre* totter in [his] *hands*.—Adieu!—

TO JOHN CAM HOBHOUSE   *Dorant's. February 29th. 1808*

Dear Hobhouse,—Upon my *honour* I do not recollect to have spoken of you and any friend of yours in the manner you state, and to the Club itself I am certain I never applied the epithets mentioned, or any terms of disrespect whatever.—As it is however possible I may have spoken of the very extraordinary state of Intoxication in which I have seen you and another, not conceiving it to be a secret as never having been looked upon to make a part of the *mysteries* of the meeting, I cannot altogether deny the charge, though I do deny and disclaim all malice in the statement.— Besides I do not exactly see, how "your sacrifice to the God of Wine" as you classically term it, can possibly involve the interests or reputation of the Club, or by what sophistry my mention of such a circumstance can be tortured into an "*attack* on the society as a Body."—I have never been in the habit of conversing much on the topic, I have never been entrusted with any particular confidence, consequently I can have betrayed no secret, but so far from treating the Club with disrespect, or joining any "*attack*" upon it as a "*Body*," I have more than once nearly endangered my own safety in it's defence.—As to any thing which passed between your-self and me, I have been cautious in avoiding the subject with all except Davies, I do not know who related it to Blackburne, I have never seen the latter since the event.—To conclude, I have still, and (though I do think there are circumstances which would justify me in a change of conduct) I ever have had a most sincere regard for the society of which I am a member, and if in a moment of Chagrin under the pressure of a *thousand* vexations I intimated an intention of withdrawing, it has constituted the *thousand* and *first* sensation of disquiet, that I have done so.—It is not very probable that I shall again appear at Cambridge till my degree is granted, and *that* is very problematical; my presence will never annoy you at your meetings, but if the continuance of my name upon your record displease the members, let them erase it, I do not wish to be the cause of discord, or spoil your conviviality "with most admired disorder."—Perhaps this is not enough, well! I am most willing to grant any species of satisfaction to any, or all the society, and he who shall avenge them successfully will do me a favour, for I am at present as miserable in mind and Body, as Literary abuse, pecuniary embarrassment, and total enervation can make me.—I have tried every kind of pleasure, and it is "Vanity."—

yours truly
BYRON

TO JOHN CAM HOBHOUSE   *Dorant's, March 14th. 1808*

My dear Hobhouse,—The Game is almost up, for these last five days I have been confined to my room, Laudanum is my sole support, and even Pearson wears a woeful visage as he prescribes, however I am now *better* and I trust my hour is not yet arrived.—I began to apprehend a complete Bankruptcy of Constitution, and on disclosing the mode of my Life for these last two years (of which my residence at Cambridge constituted the most sober part) my Chirugeon pronounced another quarter would have settled my earthly accounts, and left the worms but a scanty repast.—I have given up the Casta, but I hope to live and reestablish Medmenham Abbey, or some similar temple of Venus, of which I shall be Pontifex

Maximus.— — — —You have heard of one *nymph*. Rumour has
been kind in this respect, for alas! I must confess that *two* are my
property, one under my own immediate custody, as the other will
be also when I am recovered.—Scrope Davies has mounted a pye-
balled palfrey, and quitted London, he is a very profane Scoffer
and has but narrow ideas of Revelation; Sir Geoffrey I am happy
to hear has made you a Socinian, he hath also run up a long Bill
with Worgman the Jeweller who seems to have much faith, the
Baronet moreover is about to go to Ireland as he says by the way
of Sicily, a new half way house, and promises to be an ornament
to his profession, as soon as his Mustachios have attained their full
growth.—I am now in full contest with the fellows [concerning?]
my degree, they hesitate, [what can?] I do? not recede certainly
but [push on at?] all hazards.—Our personal squabbles have arisen
from the well meaning interference of Tattlers, if we lend our ears
to these Gentry, discontent will soon follow.—The Postman is
impatient, Adieu

yours very sincerely

BYRON

TO FRANCIS HODGSON   *8, St. James's Street, February 16, 1812*

Dear Hodgson,—I send you a proof. Last week I was very ill
and confined to bed with stone in the kidney, but I am now quite
recovered. The women are gone to their relatives, after many attempts to explain what was already too clear. If the stone had got
into my heart instead of my kidneys, it would have been all the
better. However, I have quite recovered *that* also, and only wonder
at my folly in excepting my own strumpets from the general corruption,—albeit a two months' weakness is better than ten years.
I have one request to make, which is, never to mention a woman
again in any letter to me, or even allude to the existence of the sex.
I won't even read a word of the feminine gender;—it must all be
propria quae maribus.

In the spring of 1813 I shall leave England for ever. Every thing
in my affairs tends to this, and my inclinations and health do not
discourage it. Neither my habits nor constitution are improved by

your customs or your climate. I shall find employment in making myself a good Oriental scholar. I shall retain a mansion in one of the fairest islands, and retrace, at intervals, the most interesting portions of the East. In the mean time, I am adjusting my concerns, which will (when arranged) leave me with wealth sufficient even for home, but enough for a principality in Turkey. At present they are involved, but I hope, by taking some necessary but unpleasant steps, to clear every thing. Hobhouse is expected daily in London: we shall be very glad to see him; and, perhaps, you will come up and "drink deep ere he depart," if not, "Mahomet must come to the mountain;"—but Cambridge will bring sad recollections to him, and worse to me, though for very different reasons. I believe the only human being, that ever loved me in truth and entirely, was of, or belonging to, Cambridge, and, in that, no change can now take place. There is one consolation in death—where he sets his seal, the impression can neither be melted nor broken, but endureth for ever.

Yours always,

B.

P.S.—I almost rejoice when one I love dies young, for I could never bear to see them old or altered.

TO LORD HOLLAND   *8 St. James's Street February 25th. 1812*

My Lord,—With my best thanks I have the honour to return the Notts letter to your Lordship.—I have read it with attention, but do not think I shall venture to avail myself of it's contents, as my view of the question differs in some measure from Mr. Coldham's.—I hope I do not wrong him, but *his* objections to ye. bill appear to me to be founded on certain apprehensions that he & his coadjutors might be mistaken for the "*original advisers*" (to quote him) of the measure.— —For my own part, I consider the manufacturers as a much injured body of men sacrificed to ye. views of certain individuals who have enriched themselves by those practices which have deprived the frame workers of employment.—For instance;—by the adoption of a certain kind of frame 1 man performs ye. work of 7—6 are thus thrown out of business.—But it is to be observed that ye. work thus done is far inferior in quality, hardly marketable at home, & hurried over with a view to exportation.—Surely, my Lord, however we may rejoice in any improvement in ye. arts which may be beneficial to mankind; we must not allow mankind to be sacrificed to improvements in Mechanism. The maintenance & well doing of ye. industrious poor is an object of greater consequence to ye. community than ye. enrichment of a few monopolists by any improvement in ye. implements of trade, which deprives ye. workman of his bread, & renders ye. labourer "unworthy of his hire."—My own motive for opposing ye. bill is founded on it's palpable injustice, & it's certain inefficacy.— —I have seen the state of these miserable men, & it is a disgrace to a civilized country.—Their excesses may be condemned, but cannot be subject of wonder.—The effect of ye. present bill would be to drive them into actual rebellion.—The few words I shall venture to offer on Thursday will be founded upon these opinions formed from my own observations on ye. spot.—By previous enquiry I am convinced these men would have been restored to employment & ye. country to tranquillity.—It is perhaps not yet too late & is surely worth the trial. It can never be too late to employ force in such circumstances.— —I believe your Lordship does not coincide with me entirely on this subject, & most cheerfully & sincerely shall I submit to your superior judgment & experience, & take some other line of argument against ye. bill, or be silent altogether, should you deem it more adviseable.— —Condemning, as every one must condemn the conduct of these wretches, I believe in ye. existence of grievances which call rather for pity than punishment.—I have ye. honour to be with great respect, my Lord, yr. Lordship's

most obedt. & obliged Servt.

BYRON

P.S.—I am a little apprehensive that your Lordship will think me too lenient towards these men, & *half* a *framebreaker myself.*

TO LADY CAROLINE LAMB *Sy. Even [April, 1812?]*

I never supposed you artful, we are *all* selfish, nature did that for us, but even when you attempt deceit occasionally, you cannot maintain it, which is all the better, want of success will curb the tendency.— — Every word you utter, every line you write proves you to be either *sincere* or a *fool*, now as I know you are not the one I must believe you the other. I never knew a woman with greater or more pleasing talents, *general* as in a woman they should be, something of every thing, & too much of nothing, but these are unfortunately coupled with a total want of common conduct.— For instance the *note* to your *page*, do you suppose I delivered it? or did you mean that I should? I did not of course.—Then your heart—my poor Caro, what a little volcano! that pours *lava* through your veins, & yet I cannot wish it a bit colder, to make a *marble slab* of, as you sometimes see (to understand my foolish metaphor) brought in vases tables &c. from Vesuvius when hardened after an eruption.—To drop my detestable tropes & figures you know I have always thought you the cleverest most agreeable, absurd, amiable, perplexing, dangerous fascinating little being that lives now or ought to have lived 2000 years ago.— —I wont talk to you of beauty, I am no judge, but our *beauties* cease to be so when near you, and therefore you have either some or something better. And now, Caro, this nonsense is the first & last compliment (if it be such) I ever paid you, you have often reproached me as wanting in that respect, but *others* will make up the deficiency.—Come to Ly. Grey's, at least do not let me keep you away.—All that you so often *say*, I *feel*, can more be said or felt?— —This same prudence is tiresome enough but one *must* maintain it, or what can we do to be saved?—Keep to it.—[written on cover]

If you write at all, write as usual—but do as you please, only as I never see you—Basta!

TO LADY CAROLINE LAMB *Tuesday [May 19, 1812?]*

You should answer the note for the writer seems unhappy.— And when we are so a slight is doubly felt.— —I shall go at 12, but you must send me a ticket which I shall religiously pay for. I shall not call because I do not see that we are at all improved by it, why did you send your boy? I was out, & am always so occupied in a morning that I could not have seen him as I wished had I been at home. I have seen Moore's wife, she is beautiful, with the darkest eyes, they have left town.—M[oore] is in great distress about us, & indeed people talk as if there were no other pair of absurdities in London.—It is hard to bear all this without cause, but worse to give cause for it.—Our folly has had the effect of a fault.—I conformed & could conform, if you would lend your aid, but I can't bear to see you look unhappy, & am always on the watch to observe if you are trying to make me so.—We must make an effort, this dream this delirium of two months must pass away, we in fact do not know one another, a month's absence would make us rational, you do not think so, I know it, we have both had 1000 previous fancies of the same kind, & shall get the better of this & be as ashamed of it according to the maxim of Rochefoucault.— But it is better that I should leave town than you, & I will make a tour, or go to Cambridge or Edinburgh.—Now dont abuse me, or think me altered, it is because I am not, cannot alter, that I shall do this, and cease to make fools talk, friends grieve, and the wise pity.—Ever most affectionately & sincerely yrs.

B.

TO THOMAS MOORE   *May 20th, 1812*

On Monday, after sitting up all night, I saw Bellingham launched into eternity, and at three the same day I saw * * * [Lady Caroline Lamb] launched into the country. * * * * * * *

I believe, in the beginning of June, I shall be down for a few days in Notts. If so, I shall beat you up "en passant" with Hobhouse, who is endeavouring, like you and every body else, to keep me out of scrapes.

I meant to have written you a long letter, but I find I cannot. If any thing remarkable occurs, you will hear it from me—if good; if *bad*, there are plenty to tell it. In the mean time, do you be happy.

Ever yours, &c.

P.S.—My best wishes and respects to Mrs. * * [Moore];—she is beautiful. I may say so even to you, for I never was more struck with a countenance.

CHELTENHAM and EYWOOD

Some rumour also of some strange adventures
  Had gone before him, and his wars and loves;
And as romantic heads are pretty painters,
  And, above all, an Englishwoman's roves
Into the excursive, breaking the indentures
  Of sober reason wheresoe'er it moves,
He found himself extremely in the fashion,
Which serves our thinking people for a passion.

DON JUAN XI, 33

My dear Lady M.—The end of Ly. B[essborough]'s letter shall be the beginning of mine "for Heaven's sake do not lose your hold on him" pray don't—*I* repeat,—& assure you it is a very firm one "but the yoke is easy & the burthen is light" to use one of my scriptural phrases.—So far from being ashamed of being governed like Lord Delacour or any *other Lord* or *master*, I am always but too happy to find one to regulate or misregulate me, & I am as docile as a Dromedary & can bear almost as much.—Will you undertake me? If you are sincere (which I still a little hesitate in believing) give me but time, let *hers* retain her in Ireland—the "*gayer*" the better, I want her just to be sufficiently gay that I may have enough to bear me out on my own part, grant me but till Decr. & if I do not disenchant the Dulcinea & Don *Quichotte* both,—then I must attack the Windmills, & leave the land in quest of adventures.—In the mean time I must & do write the greatest absurdities to keep her "gay" & the more so because ye. last epistle informed me that "8 guineas a mail & a packet *could* soon bring her to London" a threat which immediately called forth a letter worthy of the Grand Cyrus or the Duke of York, or any other hero of Madame Scudery or Mrs. Clarke.   Poor Ly. B[essborough]! with her hopes & her fears; in fact it is no jest for her—or indeed any of us; I must let you into one little secret, *her* folly half did this, at ye. commencement she piqued that "vanity" (which it would be the *vainest* thing on earth to deny) by telling me she was certain "I was not beloved," that "I was only led on for the sake of &c. &c." this raised a devil between us which now will only be laid I do really believe in the *Red* sea, I made no answer, but determined—not to *pursue*, for pursuit it was not—but to *sit* still, and in a week after I was convinced—not that———[Caroline] loved me—for I do not believe in the existence of what is called Love—but that any other man in my situation would have believed that he *was* loved.—Now my dear Ly. M. you are all out as to my real sentiments—I was, am, & shall be I fear attached to another, one to whom I have never said much, but have never lost sight of, & the whole of this interlude has been the result of circumstances which it may be too late to regret.— —Do you suppose that at my *time* of *life*, were I so very *far* gone, that I should not be in *Ireland* or at least have followed into Wales, as it was hinted was *expected*—now they have crossed the channel I feel anything but regret, I told you in my two last, that I did not "like any other &c. &c." I deceived you & myself in saying so, there was & is one whom I wished to marry, had not this affair intervened, or had not some occurrences rather discouraged me.—When our Drama was "rising" (I'll be d——d if it falls off I may say with Sir Fretful) in the 5th act, it was no time to hesitate, I had made up my mind, to bear ye. consequences of my own folly; honour pity, & a kind of affection all forbade me to shrink, but now if I can *honorably* be off, if *you* are not deceiving me, & if she does not take some accursed step to precipitate her own inevitable fall (if not with me, with some less lucky successor) if these impossibilities can be got over, all will be well.—If not,—she will travel.— — —As I have said so much I may as well say all—the woman I mean is Miss Milbank—I know nothing of her fortune, & I am told that her father is ruined, but my own will when my Rochdale arrangements are closed, be sufficient for both, my debts are not 25000 p[oun]ds & the deuce is in it, if with R[ochdale] & the surplus of N[ewstead] I could not contrive to be as independent as half the peerage.—But I know little of her, & have not the most distant reason to suppose that I am at all a favourite in that quarter, but I never saw a woman whom I *esteemed* so much.—But that chance is gone—and there's an end.—Now—my dear Ly. M. I am completely in your power, I have not deceived you; as to————[Caroline] I hope you will not deem it vanity—when I soberly say—that it would have been want of Gallantry—though the acme of virtue—if I had played the Scipio on this occasion.—If through your means, or any means, I can be free, or at least change my fetters, my regard & admiration would not be increased, but my gratitude would, in the mean time it is by no means unfelt for what you have already done.—To Ly. B[essborough] I could not say all this, for she would with the best intentions, make the most absurd use of it; what a miserable picture does her letter present of this daughter? she seems afraid to know her, & blind herself writes in such a manner as to open the eyes of all others.—I am still here, in Holland's house, quiet & alone without any wish to add to my acquaintances, your departure was

I assure you much more regretted than that of any of your lineals or collaterals, so do not you go to Ireland or I shall follow you oer "flood and fen" a complete Ignis fatuus—that is *I* the *epithet* will not apply to you, so we will divide the expression you would be the *light* & I the *fool*.—I send you back the letter, & this fearful ream of my own.—C[aroline] is suspicious about our counter plots, & I am obliged to be as treacherous as Tallyrand, but remember *that treachery* is *truth* to you; I write as rarely as I can, but when I do, I must lie like George Rose, your name I never mention when I can help it; & all my amatory tropes & figures are exhausted—I have a glimmering of hope, I *had* lost it, it is renewed—all depends on it, her worst enemy could not wish her such a fate as *now* to be thrown back upon me.—

yrs. ever most truly
[Byron]

P.S.—Dear Ly. M.—Dont think me careless, my correspondence since I was sixteen has not been of a nature to allow of any trust except to a Lock & key, & I have of late been doubly guarded—the few letters of yrs. & all others in case of the worst shall be sent back or burnt, surely after returning the one with Mr. *L[amb]'s message*, you will hardly suspect me of wishing to take any advantage, *that* was the only important one in behalf of my own interests;—think me bad if you please, but not *meanly* so. Ly. B[essborough]'s under another cover accompanies this.

TO LADY MELBOURNE *Eywood. Presteign.—Octr. 30th. 1812*

My dear Ly. M.—Though you have not written to me lately I can account for the *prudential* silence & do not blame you although one of your epistles *anywhere* is a great comfort.—Every thing stands as you could wish, & as I wished & nothing more need be said on that subject.— — —I have had an epistle from Ireland, short & full of resignation, so that I trust your cares are nearly wound up in that quarter; at least I must appeal to you if I have not done everything in my power to bring them to a conclusion, & now I have more reasons than ever for wishing them never to be renewed.— — — — —The Country round this place is wild & beautiful, consequently very delightful; I think altogether preferable even to Middleton (where the *beauties* certainly did not belong to the *landscape*) although the recollection of my visit there will always retain its "*proper*" preeminence— —I am at present however a little laid up, for a short time ago I received a blow with a stone thrown by accident by one of the children as I was viewing the remains of a Roman encampment.—It struck me—providentially—though near the eye—yet far enough to prevent the slightest injury to that very material organ, & though I was a little stunned & the stone being very sharp the wound bled rather profusely, I have now recovered all but a slight scar, which will remain I rather think for a considerable time.—It just missed an Artery, which at first from the blood's flowing in a little spout, was supposed to be cut, but this was a false alarm, indeed I believe it has done me good, for my headachs have since entirely ceased.—This is my old luck, always *near* something serious, & generally escaping as now with a *slight* accident.—An inch either way,—the temple—the eye—or eyelid—would have made this no jesting matter—as it is—I thank my good Genius that I have still two eyes left to admire you with, & a head (uncracked) which will derive great benefit from any thing which may spring from your own.— —I suppose you have left London, as I see by the papers Ld. & Ly. Cowper are returned to Herts.—If you hear anything that you think I ought to know, depend upon my seconding you to the utmost, but I believe you will coincide with me in opinion that there is little apprehension *now* of any scene from C[aroline] & still less occasion even to have recourse to A[nnabella] as your "forlorn hope" on that account.— —I leave it to you to deal with *Ly. B[essborough]* &c.—say of *me* what you please but do not let any *other name* be taken in vain—particularly to one whom you so well know as that *ingenious hyperbolist* Ly. B[essborough]. I am sick of scenes & have imbibed a taste for something like *quiet*.—Do not quite forget me—for *everywhere* I remember you.

ever dr. Ly. M. yr. most affectionate
[Byron]

P.S.—Why are you silent?—do you doubt me in the "bowers of Armida"?—I certainly am very much enchanted, but *your spells* will always retain their full force—try them.—

TO LADY CAROLINE LAMB (A) [*November 1812?*]

I am no longer your lover; and since you oblige me to confess it, by this truly unfeminine persecution,—learn, that I am attached to another; whose name it would of course be dishonourable to mention. I shall ever remember with gratitude the many instances I have received of the predilection you have shewn in my favour. I shall ever continue your friend, if your ladyship will permit me so to style myself; and, as a first proof of my regard, I offer you this advice, correct your vanity, which is ridiculous; exert your absurd caprices upon others; and leave me in peace.

Your most obedient servant,

TO LADY CAROLINE LAMB (B) [*November 1812?*]

Lady Caroline—our affections are not in our own power—mine are engaged. I love another—were I inclined to reproach you I might for 20 thousand things, but I will not. They really are not cause of my present conduct—my opinion of you is entirely alter'd, & if I had wanted anything to confirm me, your Levities your caprices & the mean subterfuges you have lately made use of while madly gay—of writing to me as if otherwise, would entirely have open'd my eyes. I am no longer yr. lover— I shall but never be less than your friend—it would be too dishonourable for me to name her to whom I am now entirely devoted & attached.

TO LADY MELBOURNE *Mh. 18th. 1813*

My dear Ly. M.—If I had gone to Mrs. Hope's I should have found the only "*novelty*" that would give me any pleasure in yourself—& lately I am sorry to say you have become quite a *rarity*—even more so than the subsidiary viands which you mention & which are not amiss in their way as additions to supper conversation.—But then I should have been checkmated by the Ly. Blarney who ranks next to a breast of Veal, an earwig, & her own offspring, amongst my antipathies.—"After all there is a charm in Novelty" is there indeed? it is very wicked in you to say so to a person who is so bigoted to the opposite system.— —I believe I leave town next week—in the meantime I am in the agonies of three different schemes—the first you know—the 2d. is Sligo's Persian plan—he wants me to wait till Septr. set off & winter at Athens (our old headquarters) & then in the Spring to Constantinople (as of old) & Bagdad & Tahiran.—This has its charms too & recalls one's predilections for gadding,—then there is Hobhouse with a Muscovite & Eastern proposal also—so that I am worse off than ever Ass was before to which bundle of hay I shall address myself.—However I am going somewhere though my agents want me to stay where I am—an additional reason for desiring to get away. I am hiring doctors, painters, and two or three stray Greeks, now here, and as tired of England as myself, and I have found a trusty vassal in one of Buonaparte's Mamaluke Guard, who will go with Sligo or myself. These I am measuring for uniforms, shoes, and inexpressibles without number, and quite overwhelmed with preparations of all sorts. As soon as I get me to the country, I shall cherish once more my dear mustachios—with whom I parted in tears—& trust they will now have the good manners to grow blacker than they did formerly—& assume the true Ottoman twist—of which your *hussars* are deplorably ignorant.— —I now recollect C[aroline]'s letter—let it come—if it will come—& let her stay which will be still better.—

ever dear Ly. M yrs.
[Byron]

LONDON ONCE MORE

His morns he passed in business—which, dissected,
    Was like all business a laborious nothing
That leads to lassitude, the most infected
    And Centaur Nessus garb of mortal clothing,
And on our sofas makes us lie dejected,
    And talk in tender horrors of our loathing
All kinds of toil, save for our country's good—
Which grows no better, though 'tis time it should.

His afternoons he passed in visits, luncheons,
    Lounging and boxing; and the twilight hour
In riding round those vegetable puncheons
    Called "Parks," where there is neither fruit nor flower
Enough to gratify a bee's slight munchings;
    But after all it is the only "bower"
(In Moore's phrase), where the fashionable fair
Can form a slight acquaintance with fresh air.

Then dress, then dinner, then awakes the world!
    Then glare the lamps, then whirl the wheels, then roar
Through street and square fast flashing chariots hurled
    Like harnessed meteors; then along the floor
Chalk mimics painting; then festoons are twirled;
    Then roll the brazen thunders of the door,
Which opens to the thousand happy few
An earthly paradise of Ormolu.

DON JUAN XI, 65–67

August 20th. 1813

My dear Ly. M[elbourn]e—When I don't write to you or
see you for some time you may be very certain I am about no
good,—& vice versa—I have sent you a long scrawl & here be
a second—which may convince you that I am not ashamed of
myself—or else I should keep out of the way of one for whom
I have so much regard.—C[aroline] has been a perfect Lake—a
mirror of quiet—& I have answered her last 2 letters.—I hope
they will neither ruffle the Lake nor crack the Mirror—but when
she really & truly has been behaving prettily—I could not write
ferociously—besides I happened just then to be in exquisite good
humour with myself and two or three other people.—

> "Perhaps Prosperity becalmed his breast—
> Perhaps the Wind just shifted from the East."

Everything in this life depends upon the weather & the state of
one's digestion—I have been eating & drinking—which I always
do when wretched for then I grow fat & don't show it—& now
that I am in very good plight & Spirits—I can't leave off the custom
though I have no further occasion for it—& shan't have till—the
next change of Weather—I suppose or some other atmospherical
reason.— —And now what are you doing? in this place we can
only say what we are not doing—Town is empty but not the worse
for that—it is a delight of a place now there's no one in it—I am
totally & unutterably possessed by the ineffable power of Indolence—I see no one—I say nothing—I do nothing—and I wish
for noth—oh yes—I wish to see you—& next to that—to hear
from you—I have great hopes of sailing soon—for Cadiz I believe
first—& thence wherever the Gods permit—I shan't be sorry to see
that best & whitest of Sea port towns again—but all this depends
upon the weather—or my own caprices which are much more
whimsical.— — —How is your sole companion the Countess of
Panshanger?—I have now been a retainer of your house one year &
sundry months & I know rather less of that illustrious Lady than
I did the first moment of my introduction—yet I have thought
as much about her as any of you—not the Gods know with any
but the most profound reverence—but she puzzled me—(which

is very easy) & furnished me with many an entertaining soliloquy upon a variety of topics—do you know I am an observer but my observations upon man—or rather womankind like deep metaphysical researches lead only to doubt—& then I leave them—or they me.—Is not this a laudable spirit of enquiry into things that don't concern myself? make my best respects—& don't be angry with me—which you will however—first for some things I have said—& then for others I have not said—you would not have me always talking *Egotism* though it is said to be allowable in a letter & only in a letter.—I am now going to dine—where I shall be obliged to drink more than is prudent—& I congratulate myself & you on having written this before dinner instead of after—though it is stupid enough to make you believe that I have anticipated my Claret—yours ever my dear Ly. M. in *sober sadness*—or as a winebibber ought to say—in *sad sobriety*—

B

TO LADY MELBOURNE   *August 23d. 1813*

My dear Ly. M[elbourn]e—Would that Luttrel had travelled —or that one could provide him with a mattress stuffed with peachstones to teach him more philosophy in such petty calamities —I remember my friend Hobhouse used to say in Turkey that I had no notion of comfort because I could sleep where none but a *brute* could—& certainly where *brutes did* for often have the *Cows* turned out of their apartment *butted* at the door all night extremely discomposed with the unaccountable ejectment.—Thus we lived—one day in the palace of the Pacha & the next perhaps in the most miserable hut of the Mountains—I confess I preferred the former but never quarrelled with the latter—& as to eating (by the bye I have lately stuffed like Count Staremberg) you know I am easily victualled.— — — —A pretty panegyric you have passed upon the Countess—"honourable & amiable"—God knows I have no reason to doubt either & never did—but methinks this is a marvellous insipid eulogium—"amiable" she must be because she reminds us very much of yourself—& "honourable" because she reminds one of nobody else—the fact is you love her better than anything in existence—& for that reason you don't know how to praise her properly—so you must confine yourself to abusing me in which if you don't succeed it is no fault of mine.— —You tell me I don't know women—did I ever pretend to be an unraveller of riddles?—& was there ever any one more easily deceived & led by anyone who will take the trouble than myself?—"Know them"—not I indeed—& I heartily hope I never may.—"Was my good humour from deceiving or being duped" the *last* of course—or how could I be so happy as you seem to think me.—My head is a little disturbed today—I have to write—first—a soothing letter to C[aroline] a sentimental one to X Y Z.—a sincere one to T. Moore—and one a mixture of all three to yourself with as much of the ludicrous as you like to find in it.—I ought to have said this in ye. beginning for now I must end it.—

Adieu ever yrs.

B

TO ANNABELLA MILBANKE   *Septr 6th 1813*

Agreed—I will write to you occasionally & you shall answer at your leisure & discretion.—You must have deemed me very vain & selfish to imagine that your candour could offend—I see nothing that "could hurt my feelings" in your correspondence—you told me you declined me as a lover but wished to retain me as a friend—now as one may meet with a good deal of what is called love in this best of all possible worlds—& very rarely with friendship I could not find fault—upon calculation at least.—I am afraid my first letter was written during some of those moments which have induced your belief in my *general despondency*—now in common I believe with most of mankind—I have in the course of a very useless & ill regulated life encountered events which have left a deep *impression*—perhaps something at the time recalled *this* so forcibly as to make it apparent in my answer—but I am not conscious of any habitual or at least long continued pressure on my spirits.—On the contrary—with the exception of an occasional spasm—I look upon myself as a very facetious personage—& may safely appeal to most of my acquaintance (Ly. M. for instance) in proof of my assertion.—Nobody laughs more—& though your friend Joanna Baillie says somewhere that "Laughter is the *child* of Misery" yet I don't believe her—(unless indeed in a hysteric)—though I think it is sometimes the *Parent*.—Nothing would do me more honour than the acquaintance of that Lady—who does not possess a more enthusiastic admirer than myself—she is our only dramatist since Otway & Southerne—I don't except Home—With all my presumed prejudice against your sex or rather the perversion of manners & principle in many which you admit in some circles —I think the worst woman that ever existed would have made a *man* of very passable reputation—they are all better than us—& their faults such as they are must originate with ourselves.—Your sweeping sentence "in the circles where we have met" amuses me much when I recollect some of those who constituted that society —after all bad as it is it has it's agremens.—The great object of life is Sensation—to feel that we exist—even though in pain—it is this "craving void" which drives us to Gaming—to Battle—to Travel— to intemperate but keenly felt pursuits of every description whose principal attraction is the agitation inseparable from their accomplishment.— —I am but an awkward dissembler—as my friend you will bear with my faults—I shall have the less constraint in what I say to you—firstly because I may derive some benefit from your observations—& next because I am very sure *you* can never be perverted by any paradoxes of mine.—You have said a good deal & very well too—on the subject of Benevolence *systematically* exerted—two lines of Pope will explain mine (if I have any) and that of half mankind—

> "Perhaps Prosperity becalmed his breast
> "Perhaps the Wind just shifted from ye. East.—

By the bye you are a *bard* also—have you quite given up that pursuit?—is your friend Pratt one of your critics?—or merely one of your "systematic benevolents?["] You were very kind to poor Blackett which he requited by falling in love rather presumptuously to be sure like Metastasio with the Empress Maria Theresa.— When you can spare an instant I shall of course be delighted to hear from or of you—but do not let me encroach a moment on better avocations—Adieu

ever yrs.

B

Septr. 26th. 1813

My dear friend—for such you will permit me to call you—on my return to town I find some consolation for having left a number of pleasant people—in your letter—the more so as I [had] begun to doubt if I should ever receive another.— —You ask me some questions—& as they are about myself—you must pardon ye. Egotism into which my answers must betray me.—I am glad that you know any "good deed" that I am supposed ever to have blundered upon—simply—because it proves that you have not heard me *invariably* ill spoken of—if true—I am sufficiently rewarded by a short step towards your good opinion.—You don't like my "restless" doctrines—I should be very sorry if *you* did—but *I* can't *stagnate* nevertheless—if I must sail let it be on the ocean no matter how stormy—anything but a dull cruise on a level lake without ever losing sight of the same insipid shores by which it is surrounded.— —"Gay" but not "content" very true.— —You say I never attempt to "justify" myself. you are right—at times I can't & occasionally I wont defend by explanations—life is not worth having on such terms—the only attempt I ever made at defence was in a poetical point of view—& what did it end in? not an exculpation of me but an attack on all other persons whatsoever—I should make a pretty scene indeed if I went on defending—besides by proving myself (supposing it possible) a good sort of quiet country gentleman—to how many people should I give more pain than pleasure?—do you think accusers like one the better for being confuted?— —You have detected a laughter "false to the heart"—allowed—yet I have been tolerably sincere with you—& I fear sometimes troublesome.—To the charge of Pride—I suspect I must plead guilty—because when a boy & a very young one it was the constant reproach of schoolfellows & tutors—since I grew up I have heard less about it—probably because I have

now neither schoolfellows nor Tutor—it was however originally
*def*ensive—for at that time my hand like Ishmael's was against
every one's & every one's against mine.—I now come to a subject
of your enquiry which you must have perceived I always hitherto
avoided—an awful one "Religion"— —I was bred in Scotland
among Calvinists in the first part of my life—which gave me a dislike to that persuasion—since that period I have visited the most
bigotted & credulous of countries—Spain—Greece—Turkey—as
a spectacle the Catholic is more fascinating than the Greek or ye.
Moslem—but the *last* is the only believer who practices the precepts of his Prophet to the last chapter of his creed.—My opinions
are quite undecided—I may say so sincerely—since when given
over at Patras in 1810—I rejected & ejected three Priest-loads of
spiritual consolation by threatening to turn Mussulman if they did
not leave me in quiet—I was in great pain & looked upon death
as in that respect a relief—without much regret of the past—&
few speculations on the future—indeed so indifferent was I to my
bodily situation—that though I was without any attendant but a
young Frenchman as ill as myself—two barbarous Arn[a]outs—
and a deaf & desperate Greek Quack—and my English servant (a
man now with me) within 2 days journey—I would not allow the
last to be sent for—worth all the rest as he would have been in at-
tendance at such a time because—I really don't know why—unless
it was an indifference to which I am certainly not subject when in
good health.—I believe doubtless in God—& should be happy to
be convinced of much more—if I do not at present place implicit
faith on tradition & revelation of any human creed I hope it is
not from a want of reverence for the Creator but the created—&
when I see a man publishing a pamphlet to prove that Mr. *Pitt*
is risen from the dead (as was done a week ago) perfectly positive in the truth of his assertion—I must be permitted to doubt
more miracles equally well attested—but the *moral* of Christianity
is perfectly beautiful—& the very sublime of Virtue—yet even
there we find some of its finer precepts in earlier axioms of the
Greeks.—particularly "do unto others as you would they should
do unto you."—the forgiveness of injuries—& more which I do
not remember.—Good Night—I have sent you a long prose—I
hope your answer will be equal in length—I am sure it will be

more amusing.—You write remarkably well—which you won't
like to hear so I shall say no more about it—

ever yrs. most sincerely
BYRON

P.S.—I shall post-scribble this half sheet.—When at Aston I
sent you a short note—for I began to feel a little nervous about the
reception of my last letter.—I shall be down there again next week
& merely left them to escape from ye Doncaster races—being very
ill-adapted for provincial festivities—but I shall rejoin ye party
when they are over.—This letter was written last night after a two
day's journey with little rest & no refreshment (eating on the road
throws me into a fever directly) you will therefore not wonder if it
is a meagre performance.—When you honour me with an answer
address to London—present my invariable respects to Sir R. &
Ly. Mil[bank]e & once more receive them for yourself—Good
Morning.—

TO ANNABELLA MILBANKE *Novr. 29th. 1813*

No one can *assume* or *presume* less than you do though very
few with whom I am acquainted possess half your claims to that
"Superiority" which you are so fearful of affecting—nor can I
recollect one expression since the commencement of our correspondence which has in any respect diminished my opinion of
your talents—my respect for your virtues.—My only reason for
avoiding the discussion of *sacred* topics—was the sense of my own
ignorance & the fear of saying something that might displease—
but I *have listened* & will listen to you with not merely patience
but pleasure.—When we meet—if we do meet—in Spring—you
will find me ready to acquiesce in all your notions upon the point
merely personal between ourselves—you will act according to
circumstances—it would be premature in us both to anticipate
reflections which may never be made—& if made at all—are certainly unfounded.—You wrong yourself very much in supposing
that "the charm" has been broken by our nearer acquaintance—on
ye. contrary—that very intercourse convinces me of the value of

what I have lost—or rather never found—but I will not deny that circumstances have occurred to render it more supportable.— — You will think me very capricious & apt at sudden fancies—it is true I could not exist without some object of attachment—but I have shewn that I am not quite a slave to impulse—no man of tolerable situation in life who was quite without self command could have reached the age of 26 (which I shall be—I grieve to speak it— in January) without marrying & in all probability foolishly.—But however weak—(it may merit a harsher term) in my disposition to attach myself—(and as society is now much the same in this as in all other European countries—it were difficult to avoid it) in my search for the "ideal" the being to whom I would commit the whole happiness of my future life—I have never yet seen but two approaching to the likeness—the first I was too young to have a prospect of obtaining—& subsequent events have proved that my expectations might not have been fulfilled had I ever proposed to & secured my early idol—the *second*—the *only* woman to whom I ever seriously pretended as a wife—had disposed of her heart already—and I think it too late to look for a third.—I shall take ye. world as I find it—& I have seen it much the same in most climates—(a little more fiery perhaps in Greece & Asia—for there they are a strange mixture of languid habits & stormy passions) but I have no confidence & look for no constancy in affections founded in caprice—& preserved (if preserved) by accident—& lucky conformity of disposition without any fixed principles.— How far this may be my case at present—I know not—& have not had time to ascertain—I can only say that I never was cured of loving any one but by the conduct—by the change—or the violence of the object herself—and till I see reason for distrust I shall flatter myself as heretofore—& perhaps with as little cause as ever.— — —I owe you some apology for this disquisition—but the singularity of *our* situation led me to dwell on this topic—& your friendship will excuse it.—I am anxious to be candid with you though I fear sometimes I am betrayed into impertinence.—They say that a man never *forgives* a woman who stands in the relation which you do towards me—but to *forgive*—we must first be offended—& I think I cannot recall—even a moment of pique at the past to my memory—I have but *2 friends* of your sex—yourself

& Ly. Melbourne—as different in years as in disposition—& yet I do not know which I prefer—believe me a better-*hearted* woman does not exist—and in talent I never saw her excelled & hardly equalled—her kindness to me has been uniform—and I fear severely & ungratefully tried at times on my part—but as it cannot be so again—at least in the same manner—I shall make what atonement I can—if a regard which my own inclination leads me to cultivate—can make any amends for my trespasses on her patience.— — —The word *patience* reminds me of ye. book I am to send you—it shall be ordered to Seaham tomorrow.—I shall be most happy to see any thing of your writing—of what I have already seen you once heard my favourable & sincere opinion.—I by no means rank poetry or poets high in the scale of intellect—this may look like Affectation—but it is my real opinion—it is the lava of the imagination whose eruption prevents an earth-quake—they say Poets never or rarely go *mad*—Cowper & Collins are instances to the contrary—(but Cowper was no poet)—it is however to be remarked that they rarely do—but are generally so near it—that I cannot help thinking rhyme is so far useful in anticipating & preventing the disorder.—I prefer the talents of *action*—of war—or the Senate—or even of Science—to all the speculations of these mere dreamers of another existence (I don't mean *religiously* but *fancifully*) and spectators of this.— —Apathy—disgust—& perhaps incapacity have rendered me now a mere spectator—but I have occasionally mixed in the active & tumultuous departments of existence—& on these alone my *recollection* rests with any satisfaction—though not the *best* parts of it.—I wish to know your Joanna & shall be very glad of the opportunity—never mind *ma cousine* I thought Stockton had been your Post town & nearer Seaham.—Mr. Ward & I have talked (I fear it will be only talk as things look undecided in that quarter) of an excursion to Holland—if so—I shall be able to compare a Dutch canal with the Bosphorus.—I never saw a Revolution transacting—or at least completed—but I arrived just after the last Turkish one—& the *effects* were visible—& had all the grandeur of desolation in their aspect— —Streets in ashes—immense barracks (of a very fine construction) in ruins—and above all Sultan Selim's favourite gardens round them in all the wildness of luxurient neglect—his

fountains waterless—& his kiosks defaced but still glittering in
their decay.—They lie between the city & Buyukderé on the hills
above the Bosphorus—& the way to them is through a plain with
the prettiest name in the world—"the Valley of Sweet Waters".—
But I am sending a volume not a letter.

ever yrs. most truly

B

TO LADY MELBOURNE   *Novr. 25th. 1813*

My dear Ly. M[elbourn]e—Thanks by the thousand for yr.
letter.—I have lately been leading a whimsical life—Tuesday I
dined with Ward & met Canning & all the Wits—and yesterday
I dined with the Patrons of Pugilism & some of the professors—
who amused me about as much.— — —I wrote to C[aroline]
a very earnest but not *savage* letter—I believe the obnoxious
sentence was—"if after this you refuse I hope you will forgive
yourself for I fear I cannot["]—all the rest was merely *entreaty*—
The Picture is however—God knows where—*they* have now that
is *four* (the Mussulman *legal* allotment) one picture apiece—and
as many Originals of other people as they please in the interim.—I
had no idea C[aroline] would have restored it but it was very
kind and I am very much obliged to her.—It is strange that Ph's
[Frances Webster's] greatest dread appears to be discovery—&
yet she is perpetually as it were contriving everything to lead to
it—she writes—makes me answer through an address to a 3d.
person—whom she has *not trusted*—of course their curiosity
will not be the least excited by being made an involuntary Post-
office!—Then she would not rest till she had this picture sent—in
the same way—and the odds are—particularly with such a person
as——[Webster] that he has—or will in some manner stumble on
something incontrovertible—& out of which she cant *"conceal"*
herself (as she calls it) that is in other words invent an excuse.—
—To say the truth I am not very unwilling that this should be
the case—as it will hasten a crisis of some kind or other.—His
first impulse will be probably *Martial*—but if I have a *motive* I
don't mind that—it will at least leave her for the Survivor—& the

Survived won't feel the want of her—besides in my case it would be so *dramatic* a conclusion—all the sex would be enamoured of my Memory—all the Wits would have their jest—& the Moralists their sermon—C[aroline] would go wild with *grief* that—*it did not happen* about *her*—Ly. O[xfor]d would say I deserved it for not coming to Cagliari—and— ——[Augusta] poor——[Augusta] she would be really uncomfortable—do you know? I am much afraid that that perverse passion was my deepest after all.—Well—suppose he should not take the angry road—at least with me—it then comes to a point between her & him—"Give him up or part with me"—no one wants spirit—particularly the spirit of contradiction with that they dislike (she swore to me she never would give me up—but that is nothing—) yet I don't know that she would not take him at his word—& send to me; but at all events the superiority this advantage would give him—and the additional distrust & ill agreement between them must increase *soon* so far that *our* union must be the Event.—The 3d. course is her getting the better—& his finding (as he has partly found) that my friendship is not inconvenient—and our all "being happy ever after"—to one of these conclusions we must come sooner or later—& why not now?—We shall have forty other things to think of before Spring—merely from the Irritation of Hope deferred —the most annoying of discordant feelings.—"Have patience" in the mean time—you say—so I will—if I can have nothing else.— — —The Duchess [of Devonshire]'s verses are beautiful—but I don't like *her* a bit the better—I send you in return some, *not* of mine as you will see by the hand—but I am not certain they are *hers* (Ph's) though from the cast of thought—it is very like her.—I hope I am not doing what Lord Grey did—He showed some letters of a woman as the most exquisite &c. &c. till some sagacious person pointed them out either in Rousseau's Eloise—or the Portuguese letters!—I received these this morning—& think them pretty—pray tell me if they are—for seriously I am a very erring Critic—one may write—and yet not be able to judge—and the reverse.—return them on your return to town.—My new Turkish tale will be out directly—I shall of course send you a copy—Frere & Canning & the Hollands have seen & like it—the *public* is another question—but it will for some *reasons interest you* more than anybody—these I leave you to discover—(I mean totally independent of Criticism—for you may not like it a bit the better)—you know me better than most people—and are the only person who can trace & I want to see whether you think my *writings* are *me* or not.—

yrs. ever

B

When I speak of this *tale* & the *author*—I merely mean *feelings*—the characters & the costume & the tale itself (at least are very like it I heard) are Mussulman.—This no one but *you* can tell.—

from Journal
November 14th, 1813–April 19th, 1814
[Thomas Moore's transcription]

If this had been begun ten years ago, and faithfully kept!!!—
heigho! there are too many things I wish never to have remembered,
as it is. Well,—I have had my share of what are called the pleasures of this life, and have seen more of the European and Asiatic
world than I have made a good use of. They say "virtue is its own
reward,"—it certainly should be paid well for its trouble. At five-
and-twenty, when the better part of life is over, one should be
something;—and what am I? nothing but five-and-twenty—and
the odd months. What have I seen? the same man all over the
world,—ay, and woman too. Give *me* a Mussulman who never asks
questions, and a she of the same race who saves one the trouble
of putting them. But for this same plague—yellow fever—and
Newstead delay, I should have been by this time a second time
close to the Euxine. If I can overcome the last, I don't so much
mind your pestilence; and, at any rate, the spring shall see me
there, provided I neither marry myself nor unmarry any one else
in the interval. I wish one was—I don't know what I wish. It is odd
I never set myself seriously to wishing without attaining it—and
repenting. I begin to believe with the good old Magi, that one
should only pray for the nation and not for the individual;—but,
on my principle, this would not be very patriotic.

No more reflections.—Let me see—last night I finished
"Zuleika," my second Turkish Tale. I believe the composition of it
kept me alive—for it was written to drive my thoughts from the
recollection of—

> "Dear sacred name, rest ever unreveal'd"

At least, even here, my hand would tremble to write it. This
afternoon I have burnt the scenes of my commenced comedy.
I have some idea of expectorating a romance, or rather a tale in
prose;—but what romance could equal the events—

"quæque ipse . . . . . . vidi,
Et quorum pars magna fui."

Today Henry Byron called on me with my little cousin Eliza. She will grow up a beauty and a plague; but, in the mean time, it is the prettiest child! dark eyes and eyelashes, black and long as the wing of a raven. I think she is prettier even than my niece, Georgina,—yet I don't like to think so neither; and, though older, she is not so clever.

Dallas called before I was up, so we did not meet. Lewis, too,—who seems out of humour with every thing. What can be the matter? he is not married—has he lost his own mistress, or any other person's wife? Hodgson, too, came. He is going to be married, and he is the kind of man who will be the happier. He has talent, cheerfulness, every thing that can make him a pleasing companion; and his intended is handsome and young, and all that. But I never see any one much improved by matrimony. All my coupled contemporaries are bald and discontented. W[ordsworth] and S[outhey] have both lost their hair and good humour; and the last of the two had a good deal to lose. But it don't much signify what falls *off* a man's temples in that state.

Mem. I must get a toy to-morrow for Eliza, and send the device for the seal of myself and * * * * * [Augusta?] Mem. too, to call on the Staël and Lady Holland to-morrow, and on * * [Dallas?], who has advised me (without seeing it, by the by) not to publish "Zuleika"; I believe he is right, but experience might have taught him that not to print is *physically* impossible. No one has seen it but Hodgson and Mr. Gifford. I never in my life *read* a composition, save to Hodgson, as he pays me in kind. It is a horrible thing to do too frequently;—better print, and they who like may read, and if they don't like, you have the satisfaction of knowing that they have, at least, *purchased* the right of saying so.

I have declined presenting the Debtor's Petition, being sick of parliamentary mummeries. I have spoken thrice; but I doubt my ever becoming an orator. My first was liked; the second and third— I don't know whether they succeeded or not. I have never yet set to it *con amore*;—one must have some excuse to oneself for laziness, or inability, or both, and this is mine. "Company, villanous

company, hath been the spoil of me;"—and then, I "have drunk
medicines," not to make me love others, but certainly enough to
hate myself.

Two nights ago I saw the tigers sup at Exeter 'Change. Except
Veli Pacha's lion in the Morea,—who followed the Arab keeper
like a dog,—the fondness of the hyæna for her keeper amused me
most. Such a conversazione!—There was a "hippopotamus," like
Lord L[iverpoo]l in the face; and the "Ursine Sloth" hath [had] the
very voice and manner of my valet—but the tiger talked too much.
The elephant took and gave me my money again—took off my
hat—opened a door—*trunked* a whip—and behaved so well, that
I wish he was my butler. The handsomest animal on earth is one
of the panthers; but the poor antelopes were dead. I should hate to
see one *here*:—the sight of the *camel* made me pine again for Asia
Minor. "Oh quando te aspiciam?"

* * * * * * * * * * * * * * * *

Nov. 16th

Went last night with Lewis to see the first of Antony and
Cleopatra. It was admirably got up and well acted—a salad of
Shakespeare and Dryden. Cleopatra strikes me as the epitome of
her sex—fond, lively, sad, tender, teasing, humble, haughty, beautiful, the devil!—coquettish to the last, as well with the "asp" as
with Anthony. After doing all she can to persuade him that—but
why do they abuse him for cutting off that poltroon Cicero's head?
Did not Tully tell Brutus it was a pity to have spared Antony? and
did he not speak the Philippics? and are not "*word things*?" and
such "*words*" very pestilent "*things*" too? If he had had a hundred
heads, they deserved (from Antony) a rostrum (his was stuck up
there) apiece—though, after all, he might as well have pardoned
him, for the credit of the thing. But to resume—Cleopatra, after
securing him, says, "yet go"—"it is your interest," etc.—how like
the sex! and the questions about Octavia—it is woman all over.

To-day received Lord Jersey's invitation to Middleton—to
travel sixty miles to meet Madame * * [De Staël]! I once travelled
three thousand to get among silent people; and this same lady

writes octavos, and *talks* folios. I have read her books—like most of them, and delight in the last; so I won't hear it, as well as read.

* * * * * * * * * * * * * * * *

Read Burns to-day. What would he have been, if a patrician? We should have had more polish—less force—just as much verse, but no immortality—a divorce and a duel or two, the which had he survived, as his potations must have been less spirituous, he might have lived as long as Sheridan, and outlived as much as poor Brinsley. What a wreck is that man! and all from bad pilotage; for no one had ever better gales, though now and then a little too squally. Poor dear Sherry! [Sheridan] I shall never forget the day he and Rogers and Moore and I passed together; when *he* talked, and *we* listened, without one yawn, from six till one in the morning.

Got my seals * * * * * *. Have again forgot a plaything for *ma petite cousine* Eliza; but I must send for it to-morrow. I hope Harry will bring her to me. I sent Lord Holland the proofs of the last "*Giaour,*" and "*The Bride of Abydos.*" He won't like the latter, and I don't think that I shall long. It was written in four nights to distract my dreams from * *. Were it not thus, it had never been composed; and had I not done something at that time, I must have gone mad, by eating my own heart,—bitter diet!—Hodgson likes it better than the Giaour, but nobody else will,—and he never liked the Fragment. I am sure, had it not been for Murray, *that* would never have been published, though the circumstances which are the groundwork make it * * * heigho!

Tonight I saw both the sisters of * * [Frances Webster?]; my God! the youngest so like! I thought I should have sprung across the house, and am so glad no one was with me in Lady H.'s box. I hate those likenesses—the mock-bird, but not the nightingale—so like as to remind, so different as to be painful. One quarrels equally with the points of resemblance and of distinction.

Nov. 17th

No letter from * *; but I must not complain. The respectable Job says, "Why should a *living man* complain?" I really don't know, except it be that a *dead man* can't; and he, the said patriarch, *did* complain, nevertheless, till his friends were tired, and his wife recommended that pious prologue. "Curse—and die;" the only time, I suppose, when but little relief is to be found in swearing. I have had a most kind letter from Lord Holland on "The Bride of Abydos," which he likes, and so does Lady H. This is very good-natured in both, from whom I don't deserve any quarter. Yet I *did* think, at the time, that my cause of enmity proceeded from Holland-house, and am glad I was wrong, and wish I had not been in such a hurry with that confounded satire, of which I would suppress even the memory;—but people, now they can't get it, make a fuss, I verily believe, out of contradiction.

George Ellis and Murray have been talking something about Scott and me, George pro Scoto,—and very right too. If they want to depose him, I only wish they would not set me up as a competitor. Even if I had my choice, I would rather be the Earl of Warwick than all the *kings* he ever made! Jeffrey and Gifford I take to be the monarch-makers in poetry and prose. The British Critic, in their Rokeby Review, have presupposed a comparison, which I am sure my friends never thought of, and W. Scott's subjects are injudicious in descending to. I like the man—and admire his works to what Mr. Braham calls *Entusymusy*. All such stuff can only vex him, and do me no good. Many hate his politics—(I hate all politics); and, here, a man's politics are like the Greek *soul*—an εἰδωλον, besides God knows what *other soul*; but their estimate of the two generally go together.

Harry has not brought *ma petite cousine*. I want us to go to the play together;—she has been but once. Another short note from Jersey, inviting Rogers and me on the 23d. I must see my agent to-night. I wonder when that Newstead business will be finished. It cost me more than words to part with it—and to *have* parted with it! What matters it what I do? or what becomes of me?—but let me remember Job's saying, and console myself with being "a living man."

I wish I could settle to reading again,—my life is monotonous, and yet desultory. I take up books, and fling them down again. I began a comedy and burnt it because the scene ran into *reality*;—a novel, for the same reason. In rhyme, I can keep more away from facts; but the thought always runs through, through . . . yes, yes, through. I have had a letter from Lady Melbourne—the best friend I ever had in my life, and the cleverest of women.

Not a word from * * [Lady F. W. Webster]. Have they set out from * *? or has my last precious epistle fallen into the Lion's jaws? If so—and this silence looks suspicious—I must clap on "my musty morion" and "hold out my iron". I am out of practice—but I won't begin again at Manton's now. Besides, I would not return his shot. I was once a famous wafer-splitter; but then the bullies of society made it necessary. Ever since I began to feel that I had a bad cause to support, I have left off the exercise.

What strange tidings from the Anakim of anarchy—Buona-parte! Ever since I defended my bust of him at Harrow against the rascally time-servers, when the war broke out in 1803, he has been a "Héros de Roman" of mine—on the continent; I don't want him here. But I don't like those same flights—leaving of armies, &c. &c. I am sure when I fought for his bust at school, I did not think he would run away from himself. But I should not wonder if he banged them yet. To be beat by men would be something; but by three stupid, legitimate-old-dynasty boobies of regular-bred sovereigns—O-hone-a-rie!—O-hone-a-rie! It must be, as Cobbett says, his marriage with the thick-lipped and thick-headed *Autri-chienne* brood. He had better have kept to her who was kept by Barras. I never knew any good come of your young wife, and legal espousals, to any but your "sober-blooded boy" who "eats fish" and drinketh "no sack." Had he not the whole opera? all Paris? all France? But a mistress is just as perplexing—that is, *one*—two or more are manageable by division.

I have begun, or had begun, a song, and flung it into the fire. It was in remembrance of Mary Duff, my first of flames, before most people begin to burn. I wonder what the devil is the matter with me! I can do nothing, and—fortunately there is nothing to do. It has lately been in my power to make two persons (and their con-nexions) comfortable, *pro tempore*, and one happy, *ex tempore*, —I rejoice in the last particularly, as it is an excellent man. I wish there had been more inconvenience and less gratification to my self-love in it, for then there had been more merit. We are all selfish—and I believe, ye gods of Epicurus! I believe in Rochefoucault about *men*, and in Lucretius (not Busby's translation) about yourselves. Your bard has made you very *nonchalent* and blest; but as he has excused *us* from damnation, I don't envy you your blessedness *much*—a little, to be sure. . . .

I have dined regularly to-day, for the first time since Sunday last—this being Sabbath, too. All the rest, tea and dry biscuits—six *per diem*. I wish to God I had not dined now!—It kills me with heaviness, stupor, and horrible dreams;—and yet it was but a pint of bucellas, and fish. Meat I never touch,—nor much vegetable diet. I wish I were in the country, to take exercise,—instead of being obliged to *cool* by abstinence, in lieu of it. I should not so much mind a little accession of flesh,—my bones can well bear it. But the worst is, the devil always came with it,—till I starve him out,—and I will *not* be the slave of *any* appetite. If I do err, it shall be my heart, at least, that heralds the way. Oh my head—how it aches?—the horrors of digestion! I wonder how Buonaparte's dinner agrees with him? . . .

I remember the effect of the *first* Edinburgh Review on me. I heard of it six weeks before,—read it the day of its denunciation,—dined and drank three bottles of claret, (with S. B. Davies, I think,) neither ate nor slept the less, but, nevertheless, was not easy till I had vented my wrath and my rhyme, in the same pages against every thing and every body. Like George, in the *Vicar of Wakefield*, "the fate of my paradoxes" would allow me to perceive no merit in another. I remembered only the maxim of my boxing-master, which, in my youth, was found useful in all general riots,—"Whoever is not for you is against you—*mill* away right and left," and so I did;— like Ishmael, my hand was against all men, and all men's anent me. I did wonder, to be sure, at my own success—

"And marvels so much wit is all his own." . . .

Rogers is silent,—and, it is said, severe. When he does talk, he talks well; and, on all subjects of taste, his delicacy of expression is pure as his poetry. If you enter his house—his drawing-room—his library—you of yourself say, this is not the dwelling of a common mind. There is not a gem, a coin, a book thrown aside on his chimney-piece, his sofa, his table, that does not bespeak an almost fastidious elegance in the possessor. But this very delicacy must be the misery of his existence. Oh the jarrings his disposition must have encountered through life! . . .

M[oor]e has a peculiarity of talent, or rather talents,—poetry, music, voice, all his own; and an expression in each, which never was, nor will be, possessed by another. But he is capable of still higher flights in poetry. By the by, what humour, what—every thing, in the "Post-Bag!" There is nothing M[oor]e may not do, if he will but seriously set about it. In society, he is gentlemanly, gentle, and, altogether more pleasing than any individual with whom I am acquainted. For his honour, principle, and independence, his conduct to * * * * speaks "trumpet-tongued." He has but one fault—and that one I daily regret—he is not *here*. . . .

Tuesday morning

I awoke from a dream!—well! and have not others dreamed?— Such a dream!—but she did not overtake me. I wish the dead would rest, however. Ugh! how my blood chilled,—and I could not wake—and—and—heigho!

> "Shadows to-night
> Have struck more terror to the soul of Richard,
> Than could the substance of ten thousand * * s,
> Arm'd all in proof, and led by shallow * *."

I do not like this dream,—I hate its "foregone conclusion." And am I to be shaken by shadows? Ay, when they remind us of—no matter—but, if I dream thus again, I will try whether *all* sleep has the like visions. Since I rose, I've been in considerable bodily pain also; but it is gone, and now, like Lord Ogleby, I am wound up for the day.

A note from Mountnorris—I dine with Ward;—Canning is to be there, Frere and Sharpe,—perhaps Gifford. I am to be one of "the five" (or rather six), as Lady * * said a little sneeringly yesterday. They are all good to meet, particularly Canning, and—Ward, when he likes. I wish I may be well enough to listen to these intellectuals.

No letters to-day;—so much the better,—there are no answers. I must not dream again;—it spoils even reality. I will go out of doors, and see what the fog will do for me. Jackson has been here: the boxing world much as usual;—but the Club increases. I shall dine at Crib's to-morrow. I like energy—even animal energy— of all kinds; and I have need of both mental and corporeal. I have not dined out, nor, indeed, *at all*, lately: have heard no music—have seen nobody. Now for a *plunge*—high life and low life. . . .

If I had any views in this country, they would probably be parliamentary. But I have no ambition; at least, if any, it would be "aut Caesar aut nihil." My hopes are limited to the arrangement of my affairs, and settling either in Italy or the East (rather the last), and drinking deep of the languages and literature of both. Past events have unnerved me; and all I can now do is to make life an amusement, and look on, while others play. After all—even the highest game of crowns and sceptres, what is it? *Vide* Napoleon's last twelvemonth. It has completely upset my system of fatalism. I thought, it crushed, he would have fallen, when "*fractus illabitur orbis*," and not have been pared away to gradual insignificance;— that all this was not a mere *jeu* of the gods, but a prelude to greater changes and mightier events. But Men never advance beyond a certain point;—and here we are, retrograding to the dull, stupid old system,—balance of Europe—poising straws upon king's noses, instead of wringing them off! Give me a republic, or a despotism of one, rather than the mixed government of one, two, three. A re- public!—look in the history of the Earth—Rome, Greece, Venice, France, Holland, America, our short (*eheu!*) Commonwealth, and compare it with what they did under masters. The Asiatics are not qualified to be republicans, but they have the liberty of demolishing despots, which is the next thing to it. To be the first man—not the Dictator—not the Sylla, but the Washington or the Aristides—the leader in talent and truth—is next to the Divinity! Franklin, Penn, and, next to these, either Brutus or Cassius—even Mirabeau—or St. Just. I shall never be any thing, or rather always be nothing. The most I can hope is, that some will say, "He might, perhaps, if he would."

12, midnight

Here are two confounded proofs from the printer. I have looked at the one, but, for the soul of me, I can't look over that "Giaour" again,—at least, just now, and at this hour—and yet there is no moon.

Ward talks of going to Holland, and we have partly discussed an *ensemble* expedition. It must be in ten days, if at all, if we wish to be in at the Revolution. And why not? * * is distant, and will be at * *, still more distant, till spring. No one else, except Augusta, cares for me—no ties—no trammels—*andiamo dunque—se torniamo, bene—se non, ch' importa*? Old William of Orange talked of dying in "the last ditch" of his dingy country. It is lucky I can swim, or I suppose I should not well weather the first. But let us see. I have heard hyænas and jackalls in the ruins of Asia; and bull-frogs in the marshes,—besides wolves and angry Mussulmans. Now, I should like to listen to the shout of a free Dutchman.

Alla! Viva! For ever! Hourra! Huzza!—which is the most rational or musical of these cries? "Orange Boven," according to the *Morning Post*.

Wednesday, 24th

No dreams last night of the dead nor the living—so—I am "firm as the marble, founded as the rock"—till the next earthquake. . . .

I am tremendously in arrear with my letters,—except to * *, and to her my thoughts overpower me,—my words never compass them. To Lady Melbourne I write with most pleasure—and her answers, so sensible, so *tactique*—I never met with half her talent. If she had been a few years younger, what a fool she would have made of me, had she thought it worth her while,—and I should have lost a valuable and most agreeable *friend*. Mem. a mistress never is nor can be a friend. While you agree, you are lovers; and, when it is over, any thing but friends.

I have not answered W. Scott's last letter,—but I will. I regret to hear from others, that he has lately been unfortunate in pecuniary involvements. He is undoubtedly the Monarch of Parnassus, and the most *English* of bards. I should place Rogers next in the living list—(I value him more as the last of the *best* school)—Moore and Campbell both *third*—Southey and Wordsworth and Coleridge —the rest ὁι πολλοι —thus:—

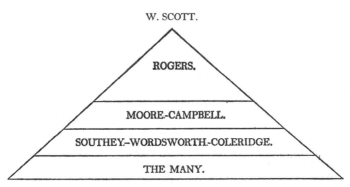

There is a triangular "Gradus ad Parnassum!"—the names are too numerous for the base of the triangle. Poor Thurlow has gone wild about the poetry of Queen Bess's reign—*c'est dommage.* I have ranked the names upon my triangle more upon what I believe popular opinion, than any decided opinion of my own. For, to me, some of M[oor]e's last *Erin* sparks—"As a beam o'er the face of the waters"—"When he who adores thee"—"Oh blame not"—and "Oh breath not his name"—are worth all the Epics that ever were composed.

* * [Rogers] thinks the *Quarterly* will attack me next. Let them. I have been "peppered so highly" in my time, *both* ways, that it must be cayenne or aloes to make me taste. I can sincerely say that I am not very much alive *now* to criticism. But—in tracing this—I rather believe that it proceeds from my not attaching that importance to authorship which many do, and which, when young, I did also. "One gets tired of every thing, my angel," says Valmont. The "angels" are the only things of which I am not a little sick— but I do think the preference of *writers* to *agents*—the mighty stir made about scribbling and scribes, by themselves and others—a sign of effeminacy, degeneracy, and weakness. Who would write, who had any thing better to do? "Action—action—action" said Demosthenes: "Actions—actions," I say, and not writing,—least of all, rhyme. Look at the querulous and monotonous lives of the "genus;"—except Cervantes, Tasso, Dante, Ariosto, Kleist (who were brave and active citizens), Æschylus, Sophocles, and some other of the antiques also—what a worthless, idle brood it is!

12, Mezza Notte.

Just returned from dinner with Jackson (the Emperor of Pugilism) and another of the select, at Crib's the champion's. I drank more than I like, and have brought away some three bottles of very fair claret—for I have no headache. We had Tom [Crib] up after dinner;—very facetious, though somewhat prolix. He don't like his situation—wants to fight again—pray Pollux (or Castor, if he was the *miller*) he may! Tom has been a sailor—a coal-heaver—and some other genteel profession, before he took to the cestus. Tom has been in action at sea, and is now only three-and-thirty. A great man! has a wife and a mistress, and conversations well—bating some sad omissions and misapplications of the aspirate. Tom is an old friend of mine; I have seen some of his best battles in my nonage. He is now a publican, and, I fear, a sinner;—for Mrs. [Crib] is on alimony, and * *'s daughter lives with the champion. This * * told me,—Tom, having an opinion of my morals, passed her off as a legal spouse. Talking of her, he said, "she was the truest of women"—from which I immediately inferred she could *not* be his wife, and so it turned out.

These panegyrics don't belong to matrimony;—for, if "true," a man don't think it necessary to say so; and if not, the less he says the better. [Crib] is the only man except * * * * [Webster?], I ever heard harangue upon his wife's virtue; and I listened to both with great credence and patience, and stuffed my handkerchief into my mouth, when I found yawning irresistible—By the by, I am yawning now—so, good night to thee.—Μπαιρων.

Awoke a little feverish, but no headache—no dreams neither, thanks to stupor! Two letters, one from * * * * [Lady Frances Webster], the other from Lady Melbourne—both excellent in their respective styles. * * * * [Lady Frances]'s contained also a very pretty lyric on "concealed griefs"—if not her own, yet very like her. Why did she not say that the stanzas were, or were not, of her composition? I do not know whether to wish them *hers* or not. I have no great esteem for poetical persons, particularly women; they have so much of the "ideal" in *practics*, as well as *ethics*.

I have been thinking lately a good deal of Mary Duff. How very odd that I should have been so utterly, devotedly fond of that girl, at an age when I could neither feel passion, nor know the meaning of the word. And the effect! My mother used always to rally me about this childish amour; and, at last, many years after, when I was sixteen, she told me one day, "Oh, Byron, I have had a letter from Edinburgh, from Miss Abercromby, and your old sweetheart Mary Duff is married to a Mr. Coe." And what was my answer? I really cannot explain or account for my feelings at that moment; but they nearly threw me into convulsions, and alarmed my mother so much, that after I grew better, she generally avoided the subject—to *me*—and contented herself with telling it to all her acquaintance. Now, what could this be? I had never seen her since her mother's faux pas at Aberdeen had been the cause of her removal to her grandmother's at Banff; we were both the merest children. I had and have been attached fifty times since that period; yet I recollect all we said to each other, all our caresses, her features, my restlessness, sleeplessness, my tormenting my mother's maid to write for me to her, which she at last did, to quiet me. Poor Nancy thought I was wild, and, as I could not write for myself, became my secretary. I remember, too, our walks, and the happiness of sitting by Mary, in the children's apartment, at their house not far from Plainstones at Aberdeen, while her lesser sister Helen played with the doll, and we sat gravely making love, in our way.

How the deuce did all this occur so early? where could it originate? I certainly had no sexual ideas for years afterwards; and yet my misery, my love for that girl were so violent, that I sometimes doubt if I have ever been really attached since. Be that as it may, hearing of her marriage several years after was like a thunder-stroke—it nearly choked me—to the horror of my mother and the astonishment and almost incredulity of every body. And it is a phenomenon in my existence (for I was not eight years old) which has puzzled, and will puzzle me to the latest hour of it; and lately, I know not why, the *recollection* (*not* the attachment) has recurred as forcibly as ever. I wonder if she can have the least remembrance of it or me? or remember her pitying sister Helen for not having an admirer too? How very pretty is the perfect image of her in my memory—her brown, dark hair, and hazel eyes; her very dress! I should be quite grieved to see *her now*; the reality, however beau-tiful, would destroy, or at least confuse, the features of the lovely Peri which then existed in her, and still lives in my imagination, at the distance of more than sixteen years. I am now twenty-five and odd months . . . .

I think my mother told the circumstances (on my hearing of her marriage) to the Parkynses, and certainly to the Pigot family, and probably mentioned it in her answer to Miss A[bercromby], who was well acquainted with my childish *penchant*, and had sent the news on purpose for *me*,—and thanks to her!

Next to the beginning, the conclusion has often occupied my reflections, in the way of investigation. That the facts are thus, others know as well as I, and my memory yet tells me so, in more than a whisper. But, the more I reflect, the more I am bewildered to assign any cause for this precocity of affection. [See page 302 for additional passage.]

Lord Holland invited me to dinner to-day; but three days' dining would destroy me. So, without eating at all since yesterday, I went to my box at Covent Garden.

* * * * * * * * * * * * * * * *

Saw * * * * [Lady Frances Webster's younger sister?] looking very pretty, though quite a different style of beauty from the other two. She has the finest eyes in the world, out of which she pretends *not* to see, and the longest eyelashes I ever saw, since Leila's and Phannio's Moslem curtains of the light. She has much beauty,—just enough,—but is, I think, *méchante*.

* * * * * * * * * * * * * * * *

I have been pondering on the miseries of separation, that—oh how seldom we see those we love! yet we live ages in moments, *when met*. The only thing that consoles me during absence is the reflection that no mental or personal estrangement, from ennui or disagreement, can take place; and when people meet hereafter, even though many changes may have taken place in the mean time, still—unless they are *tired* of each other—they are ready to re-unite, and do not blame each other for the circumstances that severed them. * * * * * * * * * * * *

> *Saturday, 27th* (I believe—or rather am in *doubt,*
> which is the ne plus ultra of mortal faith.)

I have missed a day; and, as the Irishman said, or Joe Miller says for him, "have gained a loss," or *by* the loss. Every thing is settled for Holland, and nothing but a cough, or a caprice of my fellow-traveller's, can stop us. Carriage ordered—funds prepared—and, probably, a gale of wind into the bargain. *N'importe*—I believe with Clym o' the Clow, or Robin Hood, "By our Mary, (dear name!) thou art both Mother and May, I think it never was a man's lot to die before his day." Heigh for Helvoetsluys, and so forth!

To-night I went with young Henry Fox to see "Nourjahad,"—a drama, which the Morning Post hath laid to my charge, but of which I cannot even guess the author. I wonder what they will next inflict upon me. They cannot well sink below a Melodrama; but that is better than a Satire, (at least, a personal one,) with which I stand truly arraigned, and in atonement of which I am resolved to bear silently all criticisms, abuses, and even praises, for bad pantomimes never composed by me, without even a contradictory aspect. I suppose the root of this report is my loan to the manager of my Turkish drawings for his dresses, to which he was more welcome than to my name. I suppose the real author will soon own it, as it has succeeded; if not, Job be my model, and Lethe my beverage!

* * * * [Lady Frances Webster] has received the portrait safe;

and; in answer, the only remark she makes upon it is, "indeed it is like"—and again, "indeed it is like." * * * * With her the likeness "covered a multitude of sins;" for I happen to know that this portrait was not a flatterer, but dark and stern,—even black as the mood in which my mind was scorching last July, when I sat for it. All the others of me—like most portraits whatsoever—are, of course, more agreeable than nature.

Redde the Edinburgh Review of Rogers. He is ranked highly—but where he should be. There is a summary view of us all—*Moore* and *me* among the rest; and both (the *first* justly) praised—though, by implication (justly again) placed beneath our memorable friend. Mackintosh is the writer, and also of the critique on the Staël. His grand essay on Burke, I hear, is for the next number. But I know nothing of the Edinburgh, or of any other Review, but from rumour; and I have long ceased—indeed, I could not, in justice, complain of any, even though I were to rate poetry, in general, and my rhymes in particular, more highly than I really do. To withdraw *myself* from *myself* (oh that cursed selfishness!) has ever been my sole, my entire, my sincere motive in scribbling at all; and publishing is also the continuance of the same object, by the action it affords to the mind, which else recoils upon itself. If I valued fame, I should flatter received opinions, which have gathered strength by time, and will yet wear longer than any living works to the contrary. But, for the soul of me, I cannot and will not give the lie to my own thoughts and doubts, come what may. If I am a fool, it is, at least, a doubting one; and I envy no one the certainty of his self-approved wisdom.

All are inclined to believe what they covet, from a lottery-ticket up to a passport to Paradise,—in which, from description, I see nothing very tempting. My restlessness tells me I have something within that "passeth show." It is for Him, who made it, to prolong that spark of celestial fire which illuminates, yet burns, this frail tenement; but I see no such horror in a "dreamless sleep," and I have no conception of any existence which duration would not render tiresome. How else "fell the angels," even according to your creed? They were immortal, heavenly, and happy, as their *apostate Abdiel* is now by his treachery. Time must decide; and eternity won't be the less agreeable or more horrible because one did not expect it. In the mean time, I am grateful for some good, and tolerably patient under certain evils—grace à Dieu et mon bon tempérament.

Sunday, 28th. Monday, 29th. Tuesday, 30th.

Two days missed in my log-book;—hiatus *haud* deflendus. They were as little worth recollection as the rest; and luckily, laziness or society prevented me from *notching* them.

Sunday, I dined with the Lord Holland in St. James's Square. Large party—among them Sir S. Romilly and Lady Ry.—General Sir Somebody Bentham, a man of science and talent, I am told— . . .

Why does Lady H. always have that damned screen between the whole room and the fire? I, who bear cold no better than an antelope, and never yet found a sun quite *done* to my taste, was absolutely petrified, and could not even shiver. All the rest, too, looked as if they were just unpacked, like salmon from an ice-basket, and set down to table for that day only. When she retired, I watched their looks as I dismissed the screen, and every cheek thawed, and every nose reddened with the anticipated glow

Saturday, I went with Harry Fox to Nourjahad; and, I believe, convinced him, by incessant yawning, that it was not mine. I wish the precious author would own it, and release me from his fame. The dresses are pretty, but not in costume;—Mrs. Horne's, all but the turban, and the want of a small dagger (if she is a sultana), *perfect*. I never saw a Turkish woman with a turban in my life—nor did any one else. The sultanas have a small poniard at the waist. The dialogue is drowsy—the action heavy—the scenery fine—the actors tolerable. I can't say much for their seraglio—Teresa, Phannio, or * * * *, were worth them all.

Sunday, a very handsome note from Mackintosh, who is a rare instance of the union of very transcendent talent and great good-nature. To-day (Tuesday) a very pretty billet from M. la Baronne de Staël Holstein. She is pleased to be much pleased with my mention of her and her last work in my notes. I spoke as I thought. Her works are my delight, and so is she herself, for—half an hour.

I don't like her politics—at least, her *having changed* them; had she been *qualis ab incepto*, it were nothing. But she is a woman by herself, and has done more than all the rest of them together, intellectually;—she ought to have been a man. She *flatters* me very prettily in her note;—but I *know* it. The reason that adulation is not displeasing is, that, though untrue, it shows one to be of consequence enough, in one way or other, to induce people to lie, to make us their friend:—that is their concern.

* * is, I hear, thriving on the repute of a *pun* (which was *mine* at Mackintosh's dinner some time back), on Ward, who was asking, "how much it would take to *re-whig* him?" I answered that, probably, he "must first, before he was *re-whigged*, be re-*warded*." This foolish quibble, before the Staël and Mackintosh, and a number of conversationers, has been mouthed about, and at last settled on the head of * *, where long may it remain!

George is returned from afloat to get a new ship. He looks thin, but better than I expected. I like George much more than most people like their heirs. He is a fine fellow, and every inch a sailor. I would do any thing, *but apostatize*, to get him on in his profession.

Lewis called. It is a good and good-humoured man, but pestilently prolix and paradoxical and *personal*. If he would but talk half, and reduce his visits to an hour, he would add to his popularity. As an author he is very good, and his vanity is *ouverte*, like Erskine's, and yet not offending.

Yesterday, a very pretty letter from Annabella, which I answered. What an odd situation and friendship is ours!—without one spark of love on either side, and produced by circumstances which in general lead to coldness on one side, and aversion on the other. She is a very superior woman, and very little spoiled, which is strange in an heiress—a girl of twenty—a peeress that is to be, in her own right—an only child, and a *savante*, who has always had her own way. She is a poetess—a mathematician—a metaphysician, and yet, withal, very kind, generous, and gentle, with very little pretension. Any other head would be turned with half her acquisitions, and a tenth of her advantages.

Wednesday, December 1st, 1813.

To-day responded to La Baronne de Staël Holstein, and sent to Leigh Hunt (an acquisition to my acquaintance—through Moore—of last summer) a copy of the two Turkish tales. Hunt is an extraordinary character, and not exactly of the present age. He reminds me more of the Pym and Hampden times—much talent, great independence of spirit, and an austere, yet not repulsive, aspect. If he goes on *qualis ab incepto*, I know few men who will deserve more praise or obtain it. I must go and see him again;—the rapid succession of adventure, since last summer, added to some serious uneasiness and business, have interrupted our acquaintance; but he is a man worth knowing; and though, for his own sake, I wish him out of prison, I like to study character in such situations. He has been unshaken, and will continue so. I don't think him deeply versed in life;—he is the bigot of virtue (not religion), and enamoured of the beauty of that "empty name", as the last breath of Brutus pronounced, and every day proves it. He is, perhaps, a little opinionated, as all men who are the *centre* of *circles*, wide or narrow—the Sir Oracles, in whose name two or three are gathered together—must be, and as even Johnson was; but, withal, a valuable man, and less vain than success and even the consciousness of preferring "the right to the expedient" might excuse.

To-morrow there is a party of *purple* at the "blue" Miss * * * [Berry]'s. Shall I go? um!—I don't much affect your blue-bottles;—but one ought to be civil. There will be, "I guess now" (as the Americans say), the Staëls and Mackintoshes—good—the * * * s and * * * s—not so good—the * * * s, &c., &c.—good for nothing. Perhaps that blue-winged Kashmirian butterfly of book-learning, Lady * * * * [Charlemont,] will be there. I hope so; it is a pleasure to look upon that most beautiful of faces. . . .

Last night I supped with Lewis;—and, as usual, though I neither exceeded in solids nor fluids, have been half dead ever since. My stomach is entirely destroyed by long abstinence, and the rest will probably follow. Let it—I only wish the *pain* over. The "leap in the dark" is the least to be dreaded.

The Duke of * * called. I have told them forty times that, except to half-a-dozen old and specified acquaintances, I am invisible. His grace is a good, noble, ducal person; but I am content to think so at a distance, and so—I was not at home.

Galt called.—Mem.—to ask some one to speak to Raymond in favour of his play. We are old fellow-travellers, and, with all his eccentricities, he has much strong sense, experience of the world, and is, as far as I have seen, a good-natured philosophical fellow. I showed him Sligo's letter on the reports of the Turkish girl's *aventure* at Athens soon after it happened. He and Lord Holland, Lewis, and Moore, and Rogers, and Lady Melbourne have seen it. Murray has a copy. I thought it had been *unknown*, and wish it were; but Sligo arrived only some days after, and the *rumours* are the subject of his letter. That I shall preserve,—*it is as well*. Lewis and Galt were both *horrified*; and L. wondered I did not introduce the situation into "the Giaour". He *may* wonder;—he might wonder more at that production's being written at all. But to describe the *feelings* of *that situation* were impossible—it is *icy* even to recollect them.

The Bride of Abydos was published on Thursday the second of December; but how it is liked or disliked, I know not. Whether it succeeds or not is no fault of the public, against whom I can have no complaint. But I am much more indebted to the tale than I can ever be to the most partial reader; as it wrung my thoughts from reality to imagination—from selfish regrets to vivid recollections—and recalled me to a country replete with the *brightest* and *darkest*, but always most *lively* colours of my memory. Sharpe called, but was not let in, which I regret.

* * * * * * * * * * * * * * *

Saw * * [Rogers] yesterday. I have not kept my appointment at Middleton, which has not pleased him, perhaps; and my projected voyage with * * [Ward] will, perhaps, please him less. But I wish to keep well with both. They are instruments that don't do in concert; but, surely, their separate tones are very musical, and I won't give up either.

It is well if I don't jar between these great discords. At present I stand tolerably well with all, but I cannot adopt their *dislikes*;—so many *sets*. Holland's is the first;—every thing *distingué* is welcome there, and certainly the *ton* of his society is the best. Then there is Mde. de Staël's—there I never go, though I might, had I courted it. It is composed of the * * s and the * * family with a strange sprinkling,—orators, dandies, and all kinds of *Blue*, from the regular Grub-street uniform, down to the azure jacket of the *Littérateur*. To see * * and * * sitting together, at dinner, always reminds me of the grave, where all distinctions of friend and foe are levelled; and they—the Reviewer and the Reviewée—the Rhinoceros and Elephant—the Mammoth and Megalonyx—all will lie quietly together. They now *sit* together, as silent, but not so quiet, as if they were already immured.

* * * * * * * * * * * * * * * *

I did not go to the Berrys' the other night. The elder is a woman of much talent, and both are handsome, and must have been beautiful. To-night asked to Lord H.'s—shall I go? um!—perhaps.

Morning, two o'clock.

Went to Lord H.'s—party numerous—*mi*lady in perfect good-humour, and consequently *perfect*. No one more agreeable, or perhaps so much so, when she will. Asked for Wednesday to dine and meet the Staël—asked particularly, I believe, out of mischief to see the first interview after the *note*, with which Corinne professes herself to be so much taken. I don't much like it;—she always talks of *my*self or *her*self, and I am not (except in soliloquy, as now,) much enamoured of either subject—especially one's Works. What the devil shall I say about "De l'Allemagne?" I like it prodigiously; but unless I can twist my admiration into some fantastical expression, she won't believe me; and I know, by experience, I shall be overwhelmed with fine things about rhyme, &c., &c. The lover, Mr. * * [Rocca], was there to-night, and C * * said "it was the only proof *he* had seen of her good taste." Monsieur L'Amant is remarkably handsome; but *I* don't think more so than her book.

C * * [Campbell] looks well,—seems pleased, and dressed to *sprucery*. A blue coat becomes him,—so does his new wig. He really looked as if Apollo had sent him a birthday suit, or a wedding-garment, and was witty and lively. * * * He abused Corinne's book, which I regret; because, firstly, he understands German, and is consequently a fair judge; and, secondly, he is *first-rate*, and, consequently, the best of judges. I reverence and admire him; but I won't give up my opinion—why should I? I read *her* again and again, and there can be no affectation in this. I cannot be mistaken (except in taste) in a book I read and lay down, and take up again; and no book can be totally bad which finds *one*, even *one* reader, who can say as much sincerely.

C[ampbell] talks of lecturing next spring; his last lectures were eminently successful. Moore thought of it, but gave it up,—I don't know why. * * had been prating *dignity* to him, and such stuff; as if a man disgraced himself by instructing and pleasing at the same time.

Introduced to Marquis Buckingham—saw Lord Gower—he is going to Holland;—Sir J. and Lady Mackintosh and Horner, G. Lamb, with I know not how many (R[ichard] Wellesley, one—a clever man), grouped about the room. Little Henry Fox, a very fine boy, and very promising in mind and manner,—he went away to bed, before I had time to talk to him. I am sure I had rather hear him than all the *savans*.

Monday, Dec. 6th.

Murray tells me that C[roke]r asked him why the thing was called the *Bride* of Abydos? It is a cursed awkward question, being unanswerable. *She* is not a *bride*, only about to be one; but for, &c., &c., &c.

I don't wonder at his finding out the *Bull*; but the detection * * * is too late to do any good. I was a great fool to make it, and am ashamed of not being an Irishman. * * * * * * * * *

C[ampbel]l last night seemed a little nettled at something or other—I know not what. We were standing in the ante-saloon, when Lord H. brought out of the other room a vessel of some composition similar to that which is used in catholic churches, and, seeing us, he exclaimed, "Here is some *incense* for you." C[ampbel]l answered—"Carry it to Lord Byron, *he is used to it.*" * * * * * * *

Now, this comes of "bearing no brother near the throne." I,

who have no throne, nor wish to have one *now*—whatever I may
have done—am at perfect peace with all the poetical fraternity;
or, at least, if I dislike any, it is not *poetically* but *personally*. Surely
the field of thought is infinite;—what does it signify who is before
or behind in a race where there is no *goal*? The temple of Fame
is like that of the Persians, the Universe;—our altar, the tops of
mountains. I should be equally content with Mount Caucasus, or
Mount anything; and those who like it, may have Mount Blanc or
Chimborazo, without my envy of their elevation.

I think I may *now* speak thus; for I have just published a Poem,
and am quite ignorant whether it is *likely* to be *liked* or not. I
have hitherto heard little in its commendation, and no one can
downright abuse it to one's face, except in print. It can't be good, or
I should not have stumbled over the threshold, and blundered in
my very title. But I beg[a]n it with my heart full of * * *, and my
head of oriental*ities* (I can't call them *isms*), and wrote on rapidly.

This journal is a relief. When I am tired—as I generally am—
out comes this, and down goes every thing. But I can't read it
over;—and God knows what contradictions it may contain. If I
am sincere with myself (but I fear one lies more to one's self than to
any one else), every page should confute, refute, and utterly abjure
its predecessor.

Another scribble from Martin Baldwin the petitioner: I have
neither head nor nerves to present it. That confounded supper at
Lewis's has spoiled my digestion and my philanthropy. I have no
more charity than a cruet of vinegar. Would I were an ostrich, and
dieted on fire-irons,—or any thing that my gizzard could get the
better of.

To-day saw W[ard]. His uncle is dying, and W. don't much
affect our Dutch determinations. I dine with him on Thursday,
provided *l'oncle* is not dined upon, or peremptorily bespoke by the
posthumous epicures, before that day. I wish he may recover—not
for *our* dinner's sake, but to disappoint the undertaker, and the
rascally reptiles that may well wait, since they *will* dine at last.

Gell called—he of Troy—after I was out. Mem.—to return his
visit. But my Mems. are the very landmarks of forgetfulness;—
something like a lighthouse, with a ship wrecked under the nose
of its lantern. I never look at a Mem. without seeing that I have

remembered to forget. Mem.—I have forgotten to pay Pitt's taxes, and suppose I shall be surcharged. "An I do not turn rebel when thou art king"—oons! I believe my very biscuit is leavened with that imposter's imposts.

Lady M[elbourn]e returns from Jersey's to-morrow;—I must call. A Mr. Thomson has sent a song, which I must applaud. I hate annoying them with censure or silence;—and yet I hate *lettering*.

Saw Lord Glenbervie and his Prospectus, at Murray's, of a new Treatise on Timber. Now here is a man more useful than all the historians and rhymers ever planted. For by preserving our woods and forests, he furnishes materials for all the history of Britain worth reading, and all the odes worth nothing.

Redde a good deal, but desultorily. My head is crammed with the most useless lumber. It is odd that when I do read, I can only bear the chicken broth of—*any thing* but Novels. It is many a year since I looked into one, (though they are sometimes ordered, by way of experiment, but never taken) till I looked yesterday at the worst parts of the Monk. These descriptions ought to have been written by Tiberius at Caprea—they are forced—the *philtred* ideas of a jaded voluptuary. It is to me inconceivable how they could have been composed by a man of only twenty—his age when he wrote them. They have no nature—all the sour cream of cantharides. I should have suspected Buffon of writing them on the deathbed of his detestable dotage. I had never redde this edition and merely looked at them from curiosity and recollection of the noise they made, and the name they have left to Lewis. But they could do no harm, except * * * *.

Called this evening on my agent—my business as usual. Our strange adventures are the only inheritances of our family that have not diminished. * * * *

I shall now smoke two cigars, and get me to bed. The cigars don't keep well here. They get as old as a *donna di quaranti anni* in the sun of Africa. The Havannah are the best;—but neither are so pleasant as a hooka or chibouque. The Turkish tobacco is mild, and their horses entire—two things as they should be. I am so far obliged to this Journal, that it preserves me from verse,—at least from keeping it. I have just thrown a Poem into the fire (which it has relighted to my great comfort), and have smoked out of my head the plan of another. I wish I could as easily get rid of thinking, or, at least, the confusion of thought.

Tuesday, December 7.

Went to bed, and slept dreamlessly, but not refreshingly. Awoke, and up an hour before being called; but dawdled three hours in dressing. When one subtracts from life infancy (which is vegetation),—sleep, eating, and swilling—buttoning and unbuttoning—how much remains of downright existence? The summer of a dormouse. * * * * *

Redde the papers and *tea*-ed and soda-watered, and found out that the fire was badly lighted. Lord Glenbervie wants me to go to Brighton—um!

This morning, a very pretty billet from the Staël about meeting her at Ld. H's to-morrow. She has written, I dare say, twenty such this morning to different people, all equally flattering to each. So much the better for her and those who believe all she wishes them, or they wish to believe. She has been pleased to be pleased with my slight eulogy in the note annexed to the "Bride". This is to be accounted for in several ways:—firstly, all women like all, or any, praise; secondly, this was unexpected, because I have never courted her; and thirdly, as Scrub says, those who have been all their lives regularly praised, by regular critics, like a little variety, and are glad when any one goes out of his way to say a civil thing; and fourthly, she is a very good-natured creature, which is the best reason, after all, and, perhaps, the only one.

A knock—knocks single and double. Bland called.—He says Dutch society (he has been in Holland) is second-hand French; but the women are like women every where else. This is a bore: I should like to see them a little *un*like; but that can't be expected. . . .

Friday, December 10th, 1813.

I am *ennuyé* beyond my usual tense of that yawning verb, which I am always conjugating; and I don't find that society much mends the matter. I am too lazy to shoot myself—and it would annoy Augusta, and perhaps * *; but it would be a good thing for George, on the other side, and no bad one for me; but I won't be tempted.

I have had the kindest letter from M[oor]e. I *do* think that man is the best-hearted, the only *hearted* being I ever encountered; and then, his talents are equal to his feelings. . . .

G[al]t says there is a coincidence between the first part of "the Bride" and some story of his—whether published or not, I know not, never having seen it. He is almost the last person on whom any one would commit literary larceny, and I am not conscious of any *witting* thefts on any of the genus. As to originality, all pretensions are ludicrous,—"there is nothing new under the sun".

Went last night to the play. * * * * Invited out to a party, but did not go;—right. Refused to go to Lady * *'s on Monday;—right again. If I must fritter away my life, I would rather do it alone. I was much tempted;—C * * looked so Turkish with her red turban, and her regular dark and clear features. Not that *she* and *I* ever were, or could be, any thing; but I love any aspect that reminds me of the "children of the sun".

To dine to-day with Rogers and Sharpe, for which I have some appetite, not having tasted food for the preceding forty-eight hours. I wish I could leave off eating altogether. . . .

* * * * * * * * * * * * * * * *

December 14, 15, 16.

Much done, but nothing to record. It is quite enough to set down my thoughts,—my actions will rarely bear retrospection.

December 17, 18.

Lord Holland told me a curious piece of sentimentality in Sheridan. The other night we were all delivering our respective and various opinions on him and other *hommes marquans*, and mine was this. "Whatever Sheridan has done or chosen to do has been, *par excellence*, always the *best* of its kind. He has written the *best* comedy (School for Scandal) the *best* drama (in my mind, far before that St. Giles's lampoon, the Beggar's Opera), the best farce (the *Critic*—it is only too good for a farce), and the best Address (Monologue on Garrick), and, to crown all, delivered the very best Oration (the famous Begum Speech) ever conceived or heard in this country." Somebody told S. this the next day, and on hearing it he burst into tears!

Poor Brinsley! if they were tears of pleasure, I would rather have said these few, but most sincere, words than have written the Iliad or made his own celebrated Philippic. Nay, his own comedy never gratified me more than to hear that he had derived a moment's gratification from any praise of mine, humble as it must appear to "my elders and my betters".

Went to my box at Covent-garden to-night; and my deli-cacy felt a little shocked at seeing S * * *'s mistress (who, to my certain knowledge, was actually educated, from her birth, for her profession) sitting with her mother, "a three-piled b – – d, b – – d-Major to the army," in a private box opposite. I felt rather indignant; but, casting my eyes round the house, in the next box to me, and the next, and the next, were the most distinguished old and young Babylonians of quality;—so I burst out a laughing. It was really odd; Lady * * *divorced*—Lady * * and her daughter, Lady * *, both *divorceable*—Mrs. * *, in the next, the *like*, and still nearer * * * * * *! What an assemblage to *me*, who know all their histories. It was as if the house had been divided between your public and your *understood* courtesans;—but the Intriguantes much out-numbered the regular mercenaries. On the other side were only Pauline and *her* mother, and, next box to her, three of inferior note. Now, where lay the difference between *her* and *mamma*, and Lady * * and daughter? except that the two last may enter Carleton and any *other house*, and the two first are limited to the opera and b – – -house. How I do delight in observing life as it really is!—and myself, after all, the worst of any. But no matter—I must avoid egotism, which, just now, would be no vanity.

I have lately written a wild, rambling, unfinished rhapsody, called "The Devil's Drive," the notion of which I took from Porson's "Devil's Walk."

Redde some Italian, and wrote two Sonnets on * * *. I never

wrote but one sonnet before, and that was not in earnest, and many years ago, as an exercise—and I will never write another. They are the most puling, petrifying, stupidly platonic compositions. I detest the Petrarch so much, that I would not be the man even to have obtained his Laura, which the metaphysical, whining dotard never could.

* * * * * * * * * * * * * * * *

January 16, 1814.

Tomorrow I leave town for a few days. I saw Lewis to-day, who is just returned from Oatlands, where he has been squabbling with Mad. de Staël about himself, Clarissa Harlowe, Mackintosh, and me. My homage has never been paid in that quarter, or we would have agreed still worse. I don't talk—I can't flatter, and won't listen, except to a pretty or a foolish woman. She bored Lewis with praises of himself till he sickened—found out that Clarissa was perfection, and Mackintosh the first man in England. There I agree, at least *one* of the first—but Lewis did not. As to Clarissa, I leave to those who can read it to judge and dispute. I could not do the one, and am, consequently, not qualified for the other. She told Lewis wisely, he being my friend, that I was affected, in the first place, and that, in the next place, I committed the heinous offence of sitting at dinner with my *eyes* shut, or half shut. * * * * I wonder if I really have this trick. I must cure myself of it, if true. One insensibly acquires awkward habits, which should be broken in time. If this is one, I wish I had been told of it before. It would not so much signify if one was always to be checkmated by a plain woman, but one may as well see some of one's neighbours, as well as the plate upon the table.

I should like, of all things, to have heard the Amabæan eclogue between her and Lewis—both obstinate, clever, odd, garrulous, and shrill. In fact, one could have heard nothing else. But they fell out, alas!—and now they will never quarrel again. Could not one reconcile them for the "nonce?" Poor Corinne—she will find that some of her fine sayings won't suit our fine ladies and gentleman.

I am getting rather into admiration of [Lady Juliana Annesley?] the youngest sister of [Lady F. Webster]. A wife would be my salvation. I am sure the wives of my acquaintances have hitherto done me little good. [Juliana?] is beautiful, but very young, and, I think, a fool. But I have not seen enough to judge; besides, I hate an *esprit* in petticoats. That she won't love me is very probable, nor shall I love her. But, on my system, and the modern system in general, that don't signify. The business (if it came to business) would probably be arranged between papa and me. She would have her own way; I am good-humoured to women, and docile; and, if I did not fall in love with her, which I should try to prevent, we should be a very comfortable couple. As to conduct, *that* she must look to. * * * * * * * But *if* I love, I shall be jealous;—and for that reason I will not be in love. Though, after all, I doubt my temper, and fear I should not be so patient as becomes the *bienséance* of a married man in my station. * * * * * Divorce ruins the poor *femme*, and damages are a paltry compensation. I do fear my temper would lead me into some oriental tricks of vengeance, or, at any rate, into a summary appeal to the court of twelve paces. So "I'll none on't," but e'en remain single and solitary;—though I should like to have somebody now and then to yawn with one.

W[ard], and, after him, * *, has stolen one of my buffooneries about Mde. de Staël's Metaphysics and the Fog, and passed it, by speech and letter, as their own. As Gibbet says, "they are the most of a gentleman of any on the road." W. is in sad enmity with the Whigs about this Review of Fox (if he *did* review him);—all the epigrammatists and essayists are at him. I hate *odds*, and wish he may beat them. As for me, by the blessing of indifference, I have simplified my politics into an utter detestation of all existing governments; and, as it is the shortest and most agreeable and summary feeling imaginable, the first moment of an universal republic would convert me into an advocate for single and uncontradicted despotism. The fact is, riches are power, and poverty is slavery all over the earth, and one sort of establishment is no better, nor worse, for a *people* than another. I shall adhere to my party, because it would not be honourable to act otherwise; but, as to *opinions*, I don't think politics *worth* an *opinion*. *Conduct* is another thing:—if you begin with a party, go one with them. I have no consistency, except in politics; and *that* probably arises from my indifference on the subject altogether.

Feb. 18.

Better than a month since I last journalised:—most of it out of London, and at Notts., but a busy one and a pleasant, at least three weeks of it. On my return, I find all the newspapers in hysterics, and town in an uproar, on the avowal and republication of two stanzas on Princess Charlotte's weeping at Regency's speech to Lauderdale in 1812. They are daily at it still;—some of the abuse good, all of it hearty. They talk of a motion in our House upon it—be it so.

Got up—redde the Morning Post containing the battle of Buonaparte, the destruction of the Custom-house, and a paragraph on me as long as my pedigree, and vituperative, as usual. * * * * *

Hobhouse is returned to England. He is my best friend, the most lively, and a man of the most sterling talents extant.

"The Corsair" has been conceived, written, published, &c., since I last took up this Journal. They tell me it has great success; —it was written *con amore*, and much from *existence*. Murray is satisfied with its progress; and if the public are equally so with the perusal, there's an end of the matter.

Nine o'clock.

Been to Hanson's on business. Saw Rogers, and had a note from Lady Melbourne, who says, it is said I am "much out of spirits." I wonder if I really am or not? I have certainly enough of "that perilous stuff which weighs upon the heart," and it is better they should believe it to be result of these attacks than of the real cause; but—ay, ay, always *but*, to the end of the chapter. * * * * * *

Hobhouse has told me ten thousand anecdotes of Napoleon, all good and true. My friend H. is the most entertaining of companions, and a fine fellow to boot.

Redde a little—wrote notes and letters, and am alone, which, Locke says, is bad company. "Be not solitary, be not idle."— Um!—the idleness is troublesome; but I can't see so much to regret in the solitude. The more I see of men, the less I like them. If I could but say so of women too, all would be well. Why can't I? I am now six-and-twenty; my passions have had enough to cool them; my affections more than enough to wither them,—and yet—and yet—always *yet* and *but*—"Excellent well, you are a fishmonger—get thee to a nunnery."—"They fool me to the top of my bent."

Midnight.

Began a letter, which I threw into the fire. Redde—but to little purpose. Did not visit Hobhouse, as I promised and ought. No matter, the loss is mine. Smoked cigars.

Napoleon!—this week will decide his fate. All seems against him; but I believe and hope he will win—at least, beat back the Invaders. What right have we to prescribe sovereigns to France? Oh for a Republic! "Brutus, thou sleepest." Hobhouse abounds in continental anecdotes of this extraordinary man; all in favour of his intellect and courage, but against his *bonhommie.* No wonder;—how should he, who knows mankind well, do other than despise and abhor them?

The greater the equality, the more impartially evil is distributed, and becomes lighter by the division among so many—therefore, a Republic! . . .

Saturday, Feb. 19th.

Just returned from seeing Kean in Richard. By Jove, he is a soul! Life—nature—truth—without exaggeration or diminution. Kemble's Hamlet is perfect;—but Hamlet is not Nature. Richard is a man; and Kean is Richard. Now to my own concerns.

* * * * * * * * * * * * * *

Went to Waite's. Teeth are all right and white; but he says that I grind them in my sleep and chip the edges. That same sleep is no friend of mine, though I court him sometimes for half the 24.

February 20th.

Got up and tore out two leaves of this Journal—I don't know why. Hodgson just called and gone. He has much *bonhommie* with his other good qualities, and more talent than he has yet had credit for beyond his circle.

An invitation to dine at Holland-house to meet Kean. He is worth meeting; and I hope by getting into good society, he will be prevented from falling like Cooke. He is greater now on the stage, and off he should never be less. There is a stupid and under-rating criticism upon him in one of the newspapers. I thought that, last night, though great, he rather under-acted more than the first time. This may be the effect of these cavils; but I hope he has more sense than to mind them. He cannot expect to maintain his present eminence, or to advance still higher, without the envy of his green-room fellows, and the nibbling of their admirers. But, if he don't beat them all, why, then—merit hath no purchase in "these coster-monger days."

I wish that I had a talent for the drama; I would write a tragedy *now*. But no,—it is gone. Hodgson talks of one,—he will do it well;—and I think M[oor]e should try. He has wonderful powers, and much variety; besides, he has lived and felt. To write so as to bring home to the heart, the heart must have been tried,—but, perhaps, ceased to be so. While you are under the influence of passions, you only feel, but cannot describe them,—any more than, when in action, you could turn round and tell the story to your next neighbour! When all is over,—all, all, and irrevocable,—trust to memory—she is then but too faithful.

Went out, and answered some letters, yawned now and then, and redde the Robbers. Fine,—but Fiesco is better; and Alfieri, and Monti's Aristodemo *best*. They are more equal than the Tedeschi dramatists.

Answered—or, rather, acknowledged—the receipt of young Reynolds's Poem, Safie. The lad is clever, but much of his thoughts are borrowed,—*whence*, the Reviewers may find out. I hate discouraging a young one; and I think,—though wild, and more oriental than he would be, had he seen the scenes where he has placed his tale,—that he has much talent, and, certainly, fire enough.

Received a very singular epistle; and the mode of its conveyance, through Lord H.'s hands, as curious as the letter itself. But it
was gratifying and pretty.

Sunday, February 27th.

Here I am, alone, instead of dining at Lord H.'s, where I was
asked,—but not inclined to go any where. Hobhouse says I am
growing a *loup garou,*—a solitary hobgoblin. True;—"I am myself
alone." The last week has passed in reading—seeing plays—now
and then, visitors—sometimes yawning and sometimes sighing,
but no writing,—save of letters. If I could always read, I should
never feel the want of society. Do I regret it?—um!—"Man delights not me," and only one woman—at a time.

There is something to me very softening in the presence of a
woman,—some strange influence, even if one is not in love with
them,—which I cannot at all account for, having no very high
opinion of the sex. But yet,—I always feel in better humour with
myself and every thing else, if there is a woman within ken. Even
Mrs. Mule, my firelighter,—the most ancient and withered of her
kind,—and (except to myself) not the best-tempered—always
makes me laugh,—no difficult task when I am "i' the vein."

Heigho! I would I were in mine island!—I am not well; and
yet I look in good health. At times, I fear, "I am not in my perfect
mind;"—and yet my heart and head have stood many a crash, and
what should ail them now? They prey upon themselves, and I am
sick—sick—"prithee, undo this button—why should a cat, a rat,
a dog have life—and *thou* no life at all?" Six-and-twenty years, as
they call them,—why, I might and should have been a Pasha by
this time. "I 'gin to be a-weary of the sun."

Buonaparte is not yet beaten; but has rebutted Blucher, and
repiqued S[ch]wartzenburg. This it is to have a head. If he again
wins, "vae victis!" . . .

Tuesday, March 15th

Dined yesterday with R[ogers], Mackintosh, and Sharpe. Sheridan could not come. Sharpe told several very amusing anecdotes

of Henderson, the actor. Stayed till late, and came home, having drunk so much *tea*, that I did not get to sleep till six this morning. R. says I am to be in *this* Quarterly—cut up, I presume, as they "hate us youth." *N'importe*. As Sharpe was passing by the doors of some Debating Society (the Westminster Forum), in his way to dinner, he saw rubricked on the walls *Scott's* name and *mine*— "Which was the best poet?" being the question of the evening; and I suppose all the Templars and *would-bes* took our rhymes in vain in the course of the controversy. Which had the greater show of hands, I neither know nor care; but I feel the coupling of the names as a compliment,—though I think Scott deserves better company.

* * * * * * * * * * * * * * * *

. . . Redde the "Quarrels of Authors" (another sort of *sparring*) —a new work, by that most entertaining and researching writer, Israeli. They seem to be an irritable set, and I wish myself well out of it. "I'll not march through Coventry with them, that's flat." What the devil had I to do with scribbling? It is too late to inquire, and all regret is useless. But, an' it were to do again,—I should write again, I suppose. Such is human nature, at least my share of it;—though I shall think better of myself, if I have sense to stop now. If I have a wife, and that wife has a son—by any body—I will bring up mine heir in the most anti-poetical way—make him a lawyer, or a pirate, or—any thing. But if he writes too, I shall be sure he is none of mine, and cut him off with a Bank token. Must write a letter—three o'clock.

Sunday, March 20th.

I intended to go to Lady Hardwicke's, but won't. I always begin the day with a bias towards going to parties; but, as the evening advances, my stimulus fails, and I hardly ever go out—and, when I do, always regret it. This might have been a pleasant one;—at least, the hostess is a very superior woman. Lady Lansdowne's to-morrow—Lady Heathcote's, Wednesday. Um!—I must spur myself into going to some of them, or it will look like rudeness, and it is better to do as other people do—confound them!

Redde Machiavel, parts of Chardin, and Sismondi, and Bandello —by starts. Redde the Edinburgh, 44, just come out. In the beginning of the article on "Edgeworth's Patronage," I have gotten a high compliment, I perceive. Whether this is creditable to me, I know not; but it does honour to the editor, because he once abused me. Many a man will retract praise; none but a high-spirited mind will revoke its censure, or *can* praise the man it has once attacked. I have often, since my return to England, heard Jeffrey most highly commended by those who know him for things independent of his talents. I admire him for *this*—not because he has *praised me* (I have been so praised elsewhere and abused, alternately, that mere habit has rendered me as indifferent to both as a man at twenty-six can be to any thing), but because he is, perhaps, the *only man* who, under the relations in which he and I stand, or stood, with regard to each other, would have had the liberality to act thus; none but a great soul dared hazard it. The height on which he stands has not made him giddy;—a little scribbler would have gone on cavilling to the end of the chapter. As to the justice of his panegyric, that is a matter of taste. There are plenty to question it, and glad, too, of the opportunity.

Lord Erskine called to-day. He means to carry down his reflections on the war—or rather wars—to the present day. I trust that he will. Must send to Mr. Murray to get the binding of my copy of his pamphlet finished, as Lord E. has promised me to correct it, and add some marginal notes to it. Any thing in his handwriting will be a treasure, which will gather compound interest from years. Erskine has high expectations of Mackintosh's promised History. Undoubtedly it must be a classic, when finished.

Sparred with Jackson again yesterday morning, and shall to-morrow. I feel all the better for it, in spirits, though my arms and shoulders are very stiff from it. Mem. to attend the pugilistic dinner—Marquis [Marquess of] Huntley is in the chair.

* * * * * * * * * * * * * * * *

Lord Erskine thinks that ministers must be in peril of going out. So much the better for him. To me it is the same who are in or out;—we want something more than a change of ministers, and some day we will have it.

I remember, in riding from Chrisso to Castri (Delphos), along the sides of Parnassus, I saw six eagles in the air. It is uncommon to see so many together; and it was the number—not the species, which is common enough—that excited my attention.

The last bird I ever fired at was an *eaglet*, on the shore of the Gulf of Lepanto, near Vostitza. It was only wounded, and I tried to save it, the eye was so bright; but it pined, and died in a few days; and I never did since, and never will, attempt the death of another bird. I wonder what put these two things into my head just now? I have been reading Sismondi, and there is nothing there that could induce the recollection. . . .

* * * * * * * * * * * * * * * * *

Tuesday, March 22d.

Last night, *party* at Lansdowne-house. To-night, *party* at Lady Charlotte Greville's—deplorable waste of time, and something of temper. Nothing imparted—nothing acquired—talking without ideas—if any thing like *thought* in my mind, it was not on the subjects on which we were gabbling. Heigho!—and in this way half London pass what is called life. To-morrow there is Lady Heathcote's—shall I go? yes—to punish myself for not having a pursuit.

Let me see—what did I see? The only person who much struck me was Lady S * * d's [Stafford's] eldest daughter, Lady C. L. [Charlotte Leveson]. They say she is *not* pretty. I don't know—everything is pretty that pleases; but there is an air of *soul* about her—and her colour changes—and there is that shyness of the antelope (which I delight in) in her manner so much, that I observed her more than I did any other woman in the rooms, and only looked at any thing else when I thought she might perceive and feel embarrassed by my scrutiny. After all, there may be something of association in this. She is a friend of Augusta's, and whatever she loves I can't help liking.

Her mother, the Marchioness, talked to me a little; and I was twenty times on the point of asking her to introduce me to *sa fille*, but I stopped short. This comes of that affray with the Carlisles.

Earl Grey told me laughingly of a paragraph in the last *Moniteur*, which has stated, among other symptoms of rebellion, some particulars of the *sensation* occasioned in all our government gazettes by the "tear" lines,—*only* amplifying, in its re-statement, an epigram (by the by, no epigram except in the *Greek* acceptation of the word) into a *roman*. I wonder the *Couriers*, &c., &c., have not translated that part of the Moniteur, with additional comments.

The Princess of Wales has requested Fuseli to paint from "the Corsair"—leaving to him the choice of any passage for the subject: so Mr. Locke tells me. Tired—jaded—selfish and supine—must go to bed.

Roman, at least *Romance*, means a song sometimes, as in the Spanish. I suppose this is the Moniteur's meaning, unless he has confused it with "the Corsair."

Albany, March 28.

This night got into my new apartments, rented of Lord Althorpe, on a lease of seven years. Spacious, and room for my books and sabres. *In* the *house*, too, another advantage. The last few days, or whole week, have been very abstemious, regular in exercise, and yet very *un*well.

Yesterday, dined *tête-a-tête* at the Cocoa with Scrope Davies—sat from six till midnight—drank between us one bottle of champagne and six of claret, neither of which wines ever affect me. Offered to take Scrope home in my carriage; but he was tipsy and pious, and I was obliged to leave him on his knees praying to I know not what purpose or pagod. No headache, nor sickness, that night nor to-day. Got up, if any thing, earlier than usual—sparred with Jackson *ad sudorem*, and have been much better in health than for many days. I have heard nothing more from Scrope. Yesterday paid him four thousand eight hundred pounds, a debt of some standing, and which I wished to have paid before. My mind is much relieved by the removal of that *debit*.

Augusta wants me to make it up with Carlisle. I have refused *every* body else, but I can't deny her any thing;—so I must e'en do it, though I had as lief "drink up Eisel—eat a crocodile." Let me see—Ward, the Hollands, the Lambs, Rogers, &c. &c.—every

body, more or less, have been trying for the last two years to accommodate this *couplet* quarrel to no purpose. I shall laugh if Augusta succeeds.

Redde a little of many things—shall get in all my books to-morrow. Luckily this room will hold them—with "ample room and verge, &c. the characters of hell to trace." I must set about some employment soon; my heart begins to eat *itself* again.

April 8th.

Out of town six days. On my return, found my poor little pagod, Napoleon, pushed off his pedestal;—the thieves are in Paris. It is his own fault. Like Milo, he would rend the oak; but it closed again, wedged his hands, and now the beasts—lion, bear, down to the dirtiest jackall—may all tear him. That Muscovite winter *wedged* his arms;—ever since, he has fought with his feet and teeth. The last may still leave their marks; and "I guess now" (as the Yankees say) that he will yet play them a pass. He is in their rear—between them and their homes. Query—will they ever reach them?

Saturday, April 9th, 1814.

I mark this day!

Napoleon Buonaparte has abdicated the throne of the world. "Excellent well." Methinks Sylla did better; for he revenged and resigned in the height of his sway, red with the slaughter of his foes—the finest instance of glorious contempt of the rascals upon record. Dioclesian did well too—Amurath not amis, had he become aught except a dervise—Charles the Fifth but so so—but Napoleon, worst of all. What! wait till they were in his capital, and then talk of his readiness to give up what is already gone!! "What whining monk art thou—what holy cheat?" 'Sdeath!—Dionysius at Corinth was yet a king to this. The "Isle of Elba" to retire to!—Well—if it had been Caprea, I should have marvelled less. "I see men's minds are but a parcel of their fortunes." I am utterly bewildered and confounded.

I don't know—but I think *I*, even *I* (an insect compared with this creature), have set my life on casts not a millionth part of this man's. But, after all, a crown may be not worth dying for. Yet to outlive *Lodi* for this!!! Oh that Juvenal or Johnson could rise from the dead! "Expende—quot libras in duce summo invenies?" I knew they were light in the balance of mortality; but I thought their living dust weighed more *carats*. Alas! this imperial diamond hath a flaw in it, and is now hardly fit to stick in a glazier's pencil:—the pen of the historian won't rate it worth a ducat.

Psha! "something too much of this." But I won't give him up even now; though all his admirers have, "like the Thanes, fallen from him."

April 10th.

I do not know that I am happiest when alone; but this I am sure of, that I never am long in the society even of *her* I love, (God knows too well, and the Devil probably too,) without a yearning for the company of my lamp and my utterly confused and tumbled-over library. Even in the day, I send away my carriage oftener than I use or abuse it. *Per esempio*,—I have not stirred out of these rooms for these four days past: but I have sparred for exercise (windows open) with Jackson an hour daily, to attenuate and keep up the ethereal part of me. The more violent the fatigue, the better my spirits for the rest of the day; and then, my evenings have that calm nothingness of languor, which I most delight in. To-day I have boxed one hour—written an ode to Napoleon Buonaparte—copied it—eaten six biscuits—drunk four bottles of soda water—redde away the rest of my time—besides giving poor * * a world of advice about this mistress of his, who is plaguing him into a phthisic and intolerable tediousness. I am a pretty fellow truly to lecture about "the sect." No matter, my counsels are all thrown away.

April 19th, 1814.

There is ice at both poles, north and south—all extremes are the same—misery belongs to the highest and the lowest only,—to the emperor and the beggar, when unsixpenced and unthroned. There is, to be sure, a damned insipid medium—an equinoctial line—no one knows where, except upon maps and measurement.

> "And all our *yesterdays* have lighted fools
> The way to dusty death."

I will keep no further journal of that same hesternal torch-light; and, to prevent me from returning, like a dog, to the vomit of memory, I tear out the remaining leaves of this volume, and write, in *Ipecacuanha*,—"that the Bourbons are restored!!!"—"Hang up philosophy." To be sure, I have long despised myself and man, but I never spat in the face of my species before—"O fool! I shall go mad."

[The following passage from the 1813–1814 Journal was not printed by Prothero. Moore extracted it from an earlier period and says (Moore, I, 68) that it should come just after the Mary Duff reminiscence (p. 276).]

In all other respects, I differed not at all from other children, being neither tall nor short, dull nor witty, of my age, but rather lively—except in my sullen moods, and then I was always a Devil. They once (in one of my silent rages) wrenched a knife from me, which I had snatched from table at Mrs. B.'s dinner (I always dined earlier), and applied to my breast;—but this was three or four years after, just before the late Lord B.'s decease.

My *ostensible* temper has certainly improved in later years; but I shudder, and must, to my latest hour, regret the consequence of it and my passions combined. One event—but no matter—there are others not much better to think of also—and to them I give the preference. . . .

But I hate dwelling upon incidents. My temper is now under management—rarely *loud*, and *when* loud, never deadly. It is when silent, and I feel my forehead and my cheek *paling*, that I cannot control it; and then . . . but unless there is a woman (and not any or every woman) in the way, I have sunk into tolerable apathy.

TO THOMAS MOORE *2, Albany, April 9th, 1814*

Viscount Althorpe is about to be married, and I have gotten his spacious bachelor apartments in Albany, to which you will, I hope, address a speedy answer to this mine epistle.

I am but just returned to town, from which you may infer that I have been out of it; and I have been boxing, for exercise, with Jackson for this last month daily. I have also been drinking,—and, on one occasion, with three other friends at the Cocoa Tree, from six till four, yea, unto five in the matin. We clareted and champagned till two—then supped, and finished with a kind of regency punch composed of madeira, brandy, and *green* tea, no *real* water being admitted therein. There was a night for you!—without once quitting the table, except to ambulate home, which I did alone, and in utter contempt of a hackney-coach and my own *vis*, both of which were deemed necessary for our conveyance. And so,—I am very well, and they say it will hurt my constitution.

I have also, more or less, been breaking a few of the favourite commandments; but I mean to pull up and marry,—if any one will have me. In the mean time, the other day I nearly killed myself with a collar of brawn, which I swallowed for supper, and *in*digested for I don't know how long;—but that is by the by. All this gourmandize was in honour of Lent; for I am forbidden meat all the rest of the year,—but it is strictly enjoined me during your solemn fast. I have been, and am, in very tolerable love;—but of that hereafter, as it may be.

My dear Moore, say what you will in your Preface; and quiz any thing, or any body,—me, if you like it. Oons! dost thou think me of the *old*, or rather *elderly*, school? If one can't jest with one's friends, with whom can we be facetious? You have nothing to fear from * *, whom I have not seen, being out of town when he called. He will be very correct, smooth, and all that, but I doubt whether there will be any "grace beyond the reach of art;"—and, whether there is or not, how long will you be so d– – – –d modest? As for Jeffrey, it is a very handsome thing of him to speak well of an old antagonist,—and what a mean mind dared not do. Any one will revoke praise; but—were it not partly my own case—I should say that very few have strength of mind to unsay their censure, or follow it up with praise of other things.

What think you of the review of *Levis*? It beats the Bag and my hand-grenade hollow, as an invective, and hath thrown the Court into hysterics, as I hear from very good authority. Have you heard from * * * * * * * *

No more rhyme for—or rather, *from*—me. I have taken my leave of that stage, and henceforth will mountebank it no longer. I have had my day, and there's an end. The utmost I expect, or even wish, is to have it said in the Biographia Britannica, that I might perhaps have been a poet, had I gone on and amended. My great comfort is, that the temporary celebrity I have wrung from the world has been in the very teeth of all opinions and prejudices. I have flattered no ruling powers; I have never concealed a single thought that tempted me. They can't say I have truckled to the times, nor to popular topics (as Johnson, or somebody, said of Cleveland), and whatever I have gained has been at the expenditure of as much *personal* favour as possible; for I do believe never was a bard more unpopular, *quoad homo*, than myself. And now I have done;—"ludite nunc alios." Every body may be d– – – –d, as they seem fond of it, and resolved to stickle lustily for endless brimstone.

Oh—by the by, I had nearly forgot. There is a long Poem, an "Anti-Byron," coming out, to prove that I have formed a conspiracy to overthrow, by *rhyme*, all religion and government, and have already made great progress! It is not very scurrilous, but serious and ethereal. I never felt myself important, till I saw and heard of my being such a little Voltaire as to induce such a production. Murray would not publish it, for which he was a fool, and so I told him; but some one else will, doubtless. "Something too much of this."

Your French scheme is good, but let it be *Italian*; all the Angles will be at Paris. Let it be Rome, Milan, Naples, Florence, Turin, Venice, or Switzerland, and "egad!" (as Bayes saith), I will connubiate and join you; and we will write a new "Inferno" in our Paradise. Pray, think of this—and I will really buy a wife and a ring, and say the ceremony, and settle near you in a summer-house upon the Arno, or the Po, or the Adriatic.

Ah! my poor little pagod, Napoleon, has walked off his pedestal. He has abdicated, they say. This would draw molten brass from the eyes of Zatanai. What! "kiss the ground before young Malcolm's feet, and then be baited by the rabble's curse!" I cannot bear such a crouching catastrophe. I must stick to Sylla, for my modern favourites don't do,—their resignations are of a different kind. All health and prosperity, my dear Moore. Excuse this lengthy letter. Ever, &c.

P.S.—The Quarterly quotes you frequently in an article on America; and every body I know asks perpetually after you and yours. When will you answer them in person?

TO THOMAS MOORE   *Albany, April 20th, 1814*

I *am* very glad to hear that you are to be transient from Mayfield so very soon, and was taken in by the first part of your letter. Indeed, for aught I know, you may be treating me, as Slipslop says, with "ironing" even now. I shall say nothing of the *shock*, which had nothing of *humeur* in it; as I am apt to take even a critic, and still more a friend, at his word, and never to doubt that I have been writing cursed nonsense, if they say so. There was a mental reservation in my pact with the public, in behalf of *anonymes*; and, even had there not, the provocation was such as to make it physically impossible to pass over this damnable epoch of triumphant tameness. 'Tis a cursed business; and, after all, I shall think higher of rhyme and reason, and very humbly of your heroic people, till—Elba becomes a volcano, and sends him out again. I can't think it all over yet.

My departure for the continent depends, in some measure, on the *in*continent. I have two country invitations at home, and don't know what to say or do. In the mean time, I have bought a macaw and a parrot, and have got up my books; and I box and fence daily, and go out very little.

At this present writing, Louis the Gouty is wheeling in triumph into Piccadilly, in all the pomp and rabblement of Royalty. I had an offer of seats to see them pass; but, as I have seen a Sultan going to mosque, and been at *his* reception of an ambassador, the most

Christian King "hath no attractions for me:"—though in some coming year of the Hegira, I should not dislike to see the place where he *had* reigned, shortly after the second revolution, and a happy sovereignty of two months, the last six weeks being civil war.

Pray write, and deem me ever, &c.

She Walks in Beauty, like the Night

She walks in beauty, like the night
Of cloudless climes and starry skies;
And all that's best of dark and bright
Meet in her aspect and her eyes;
Thus mellowed to that tender light
Which heaven to gaudy day denies.

One shade the more, one ray the less,
Had half impaired the nameless grace
Which waves in every raven tress,
Or softly lightens o'er her face;
Where thoughts serenely sweet express,
How pure, how dear their dwelling-place.

And on that cheek, and o'er that brow,
So soft, so calm, yet eloquent,
The smiles that win, the tints that glow,
But tell of days in goodness spent,
A mind at peace with all below,
A heart whose love is innocent!

My dear Hunt—Many thanks for your books of which you already know my opinion.—Their external splendour should not disturb you as inappropriate—they have still more within than without.— —I take leave to differ from you on Wordsworth as freely as I once agreed with you—at that time I gave him credit for promise which is unfulfilled—I still think his capacity warrants all you say of *it* only—but that his performances since "Lyrical Ballads"—are miserably inadequate to the ability which lurks within him:—there is undoubtedly much natural talent spilt over "the Excursion" but it is rain upon rocks where it stands & stagnates—or rain upon sands where it falls without fertilizing—who can understand him?—let those who do make him intelligible.—Jacob Behman—Swedenborg—& Joanna Southcote are mere types of this Arch-Apostle of mystery & mysticism—but I have done:—no I have not done—for I have two petty & perhaps unworthy objections in small matters to make to him—which with his pretension to accurate observation & fury against Pope's false translation of the "Moonlight scene in Homer" I wonder he should have fallen into—these be they.—He says of Greece in the body of his book—that it is a land of

> "*rivers—fertile* plains—& *sounding* shores
> Under a cope of *variegated* sky"

The rivers are dry half the year—the plains are barren—and the shores *still* & *tideless* as the Mediterranean can make them—the Sky is anything but variegated—being for months & months—but "darkly—deeply—beautifully blue."—The next is in his notes— where he talks of our "Monuments crowded together in the busy &c. of a large town"—as compared with the "still seclusion of a Turkish cemetery in some *remote* place"—this is pure stuff—for *one* monument in our Churchyards—there are *ten* in the Turkish—& so crowded that you cannot walk between them—they are always close to the walks of the towns—that is—merely divided by a path or road—and as to "*remote* places"—men never take the trouble in a barbarous country to carry their dead very far—they must have lived near to where they are buried—there are no cemeteries in "remote places"—except such as have the cypress & the tombstone still left

when the olive & the habitation of the living have perished.—These
things I was struck with as coming peculiarly in my own way—and
in both of these he is wrong—yet I should have noticed neither but
for his attack on Pope for a like blunder—and a peevish affectation
about him of despising a popularity which he will never obtain.—I
write in great haste—& I doubt—*not* much to the purpose—but
you have it hot & hot—just as it comes—& so let it go.— —By the
way—both he & you go too far against Pope's "so when the Moon
&c." it is no translation I know—but it is not such *false* description
as asserted—I have read it on the spot—there is a burst—and a light-
ness—and a glow—about the night in the Troad—which makes the
"planets vivid"—& the "pole glowing" the moon is—at least the sky
is clearness itself—and I know no more appropriate expression for
the expansion of such a heaven—over the scene—the plain—the
sea—the sky—Ida—the Hellespont—Simois—Scamander—and
the isles—than that of a "flood of Glory."— —I am getting horribly
lengthy—& must stop—to the whole of your letter I say "ditto to
Mr. Burke" as the Bristol Candidate cried by way of Electioneering
harangue:—you need not speak of morbid feelings—& vexations to
me—I have plenty—for which I must blame partly the times—&
chiefly myself: but let us forget them—*I* shall be very apt to do so—
when I see you next—will you come to the theatre & see our new
Management?—you shall cut it up to your heart's content root &
branch afterwards if you like—but come & see it?—if not I must
come & see you.—

ever yrs very truly & affectly.

BYRON

P.S.—Not a word from Moore for these 2 months.—Pray let
me have the rest of "Rimini["] you have 2 excellent points in that
poem—originality—& Italianism—I will back you as a bard
against half the fellows on whom you throw away much good criticism & eulogy—but don't let your bookseller publish in *Quarto* it
is the worst size possible for circulation—I say this on Bibliopolical
authority—

again—yours ever
[Byron]

ENGLISH TRAVELS

I won't describe,—that is, if I can help
    Description; and I won't reflect,—that is,
If I can stave off thought, which—as a whelp
    Clings to its teat—sticks to me through the abyss
Of this odd labyrinth; or as the kelp
    Holds by the rock; or as a lover's kiss
Drains its first draught of lips:—but, as I said,
I won't philosophise, and will be read.

DON JUAN X, 28

By the time this reaches your dwelling, I shall (God wot) be in town again probably. I have been here renewing my acquaintance with my old friend Ocean; and I find his bosom as pleasant a pillow for an hour in the morning as his daughter's of Paphos could be in the twilight. I have been swimming and eating turbot, and smuggling neat brandies and silk handkerchiefs,—and listening to my friend Hodgson's raptures about a pretty wife-elect of his,—and walking on cliffs, and tumbling down hills, and making the most of the "dolce far-niente" for the last fortnight. I met a son of Lord Erskine's, who says he has been married a year, and is the "happiest of men;" and I have met the aforesaid H[odgson], who is also the "happiest of men;" so, it is worth while being here, if only to witness the superlative felicity of these foxes, who have cut off their tails, and would persuade the rest to part with their brushes to keep them in countenance.

It rejoiceth me that you like "Lara." Jeffrey is out with his 45th Number, which I suppose you have got. He is only too kind to me, in my share of it, and I begin to fancy myself a golden pheasant, upon the strength of the plumage wherewith he hath bedecked me. But then, "surgit amari," &c.—the gentlemen of the Champion, and Perry, have got hold (I know not how) of the condolatory address to Lady J[ersey] on the picture-abduction by our R * * *[Regent]. and have published them—with my name, too, smack—without even asking leave, or inquiring whether or no! D– –n their impudence, and d– –n every thing. It has put me out of patience, and so, I shall say no more about it.

You shall have Lara and Jacque (both with some additions) when out; but I am still demurring and delaying, and in a fuss, and so is R[ogers] in his way.

Newstead is to be mine again. Claughton forfeits twenty-five thousand pounds; but that don't prevent me from being very prettily ruined. I mean to bury myself there—and let my beard grow—and hate you all.

Oh! I have had the most amusing letter from Hogg, the Ettrick minstrel and shepherd. He wants me to recommend him to Murray, and, speaking of his present bookseller, whose "bills" are never "lifted," he adds, *totidem verbis*, "God d– –n him and them both." I laughed, and so would you too, at the way in which this execration is introduced. The said Hogg is a strange being, but of great, though uncouth, powers. I think very highly of him, as a poet; but he, and half of these Scotch and Lake troubadours, are spoilt by living in little circles and petty societies. London and the world is the only place to take the conceit out of a man—in the milling phrase. Scott, he says, is gone to the Orkneys in a gale of wind;—during which wind, he affirms, the said Scott, "he is sure, is not at his ease,—to say the best of it." Lord, Lord, if these home-keeping minstrels had crossed your Atlantic or my Mediterranean, and tasted a little open boating in a white squall—or a gale in "the Gut"—or the "Bay of Biscay," with no gale at all—how it would enliven and introduce them to a few of the sensations!—to say nothing of an illicit amour or two upon shore, in the way of essay upon the Passions, beginning with simple adultery, and com-pounding it as they went along.

I have forwarded your letter to Murray,—by the way, you had addressed it to *Miller*. Pray write to me, and say what art thou doing? "Not finished!"—Oons! how is this?—these "flaws and starts" must be "authorised by your grandam," and are unbecoming of any other author. I was sorry to hear of your discrepancy with the * * s, or rather your abjuration of agreement. I don't want to be impertinent, or buffoon on a serious subject, and am therefore at a loss what to say.

I hope nothing will induce you to abate from the proper price of your poem, as long as there is a prospect of getting it. For my own part, I have, *seriously*, and *not whiningly* (for that is not my way—at least, it used not to be) neither hopes, nor prospects, and scarcely even wishes. I am, in some respects, happy, but not in a manner that can or ought to last,—but enough of that. The worst of it is, I feel quite enervated and indifferent. I really do not know, if Jupiter were to offer me my choice of the contents of his benevolent cask, what I would pick out of it. If I was born, as the nurses say, with a "silver spoon in my mouth," it has stuck in my throat, and spoiled my palate, so that nothing put into it is swallowed with much relish,—unless it be cayenne. However, I have grievances enough to occupy me that way too;—but for fear of adding to yours by this pestilent long diatribe, I postpone the reading them, *sine die*. Ever, dear M., yours, &c.

P.S.—Don't forget my godson. You could not have fixed on a fitter porter for his sins than me, being used to carry double without inconvenience. * * * * * * *

TO LADY MELBOURNE   *Newstead Abbey—Septr. 18th. 1814*

My dear Lady M[elbourn]e.—Miss Milbanke has accepted me:—and her answer was accompanied by a very kind letter from your brother—may I hope for your consent too? without it I should be unhappy— even were it not for many reasons important in other points of view—& with it I shall have nothing to require except your good wishes now—and your friendship always.— —I lose no time in telling you how things are at present—many circumstances may doubtless occur in this as in other cases to prevent it's completion—but I will hope otherwise.—I shall be in town by thursday—& beg one line to Albany to say you will see me at your own day—hour—& place.— — — —In course I mean to reform most thoroughly & become "a good man and true" in all the various senses of these respective & respectable appellations— seriously—I will endeavour to make your niece happy not by "my deserts but what I will deserve"—of my deportment you may reasonably doubt—of her merits you can have none.— —I need not say that this must be a *secret*—do let me find a few words from you in Albany & believe me ever most affectly yrs.

B.

TO ANNABELLA MILBANKE   *Newstead Abbey—Septr. 18th 1814*

Your letter has given me a new existence—it was unexpected—I need not say welcome—but *that* is a poor word to express my present feelings—and yet equal to any other—for express them adequately I cannot.—I have ever regarded you as one of the first of human beings—not merely from my own observation but that of others—as one whom it was as difficult *not* to love—as scarcely possible to deserve;—I know your worth—& revere your virtues as I love yourself and if every proof in my power of my full sense of what is due to you will contribute to *your* happiness—I shall have secured my own.— —It *is* in your power to render me happy—you have made me so already.—I wish to answer your letter immediately—but am at present scarcely collected enough to do it rationally—I was upon the point of leaving England without hope without fear—almost without feeling—but wished to make one effort to discover—not if I could pretend to your present affections—for to these I had given over all presumption—but whether time—and my most sincere endeavour to adopt any mode of conduct—that might lead you to think well of me—might not eventually in securing your approbation awaken your regard.— — These hopes are now dearer to me than ever; dear as they have ever been;—from the moment I became acquainted my attachment has been increasing—& the very follies—give them a harsher name— with which I was beset & bewildered—the conduct to which I had recourse for forgetfulness only made recollection more lively & bitter by the comparisons it forced upon me in spite of Pride— and of Passions which might have destroyed but never deceived me.— — — —I am going to London on some business which once over—I hope to be permitted to visit Seaham;—your father I will answer immediately & in the mean time beg you will present my best thanks & respects to him & Lady Milbanke.—Will you write to me? & permit me to assure you how faithfully I shall ever be

> yr most attached and obliged Sert.
> [Byron]

TO ANNABELLA MILBANKE   *Newstead Abbey. Septr. 19th. 1814*

I wrote to you yesterday—not very intelligibly I fear—and to your father in a more embarrassed manner than I could have wished—but the fact is that I am even now apprehensive of having misunderstood you and of appearing presumptuous when I am only happy—in the hope that you will not repent having made me more so than I ever thought to have been again.— — —Perhaps in some points our dispositions are not so contrasted as at times you have supposed—but even if they were—I am not sure that a perfect sameness of character (a kind of impossibility by the bye) would ensure the happiness of two human beings any more than an union of tempers and pursuits of very dissimilar qualities.—Our *pursuits* at least I think are not unlike—you have no great passion for the *world* as it is called—and both have those intellectual resources which are the best—if not the only preventatives of ennui of oneself or others;—*my* habits I trust are not very anti-domestic—I have no pleasure in what is named Conviviality—nor is Gaming nor Hunting my vice or my amusement—and with regard to other and perhaps far more objectionable faults & levities of former conduct—I know that I cannot exculpate myself to my own satisfaction—far less to yours—yet there have been circumstances which would prove that although "sinning" I have also been "sinned against."—I have long stood alone in life—and my disposition though I think not unaffectionate—was yet never calculated to acquire the friendships which are often *born* to others—the few that chance or circumstances have presented I have been fortunate enough to preserve—& some whom I could little have hoped to number amongst them.— — —I wont go on with this Egotism—will you write to me soon?—I shall be in London on Thursday I think—I do not answer oftener than is least irksome—but permit me to address you occasionally till I can see you—which I wish so much—and yet I feel more temblingly alive to that meeting than I quite like to own to myself—when your letter arrived my sister was sitting near me and grew frightened at the effect of it's contents—which was even painful for a moment—not a long one—nor am I often so shaken.—I have written—yet hardly a word that I intended to say—except that you must pardon me for repeating so soon how entirely I am

> yr. attached & sincere
>
> BYRON

P.S.—Do not forget me to your father & mother—whom I hope to call mine.—

TO ANNABELLA MILBANKE *Newstead Abbey—Septr. 20th. 1814*

There is one point on which—though you have not lately pressed it—I am sure you feel anxious on my behalf—and to this will I speak, I mean—Religion.—When I tell you that I am so convinced of it's importance in fixing the principles—that I could never have had perfect confidence in any woman who was slightly impressed with it's truth—you will hardly believe that I can exact more tolerance than I am willing to grant.—I will not deny that my own impressions are by no means settled—but that they are perverted to the extent which has been imputed to them on the ground of a few passages in works of fiction—I cannot admit to those whose esteem I would secure—although from a secret aversion from explanations & vindications I have hitherto entered into none to those who would never have made the charge but from a wish to condemn rather than convert.—To you—my conduct must be different—as my feelings—I am rather bewildered by the variety of tenets—than inclined to dispute their foundation—in a word—I will read what books you please—hear what arguments you please—and in leaving the choice to your judgment—let it be a proof that my confidence in your understanding & your virtues is equal.—You shall be "my Guide—Philosopher and friend" my whole heart is yours—and if possible let me make it not unworthy of her to whom it is bound—& from whom but one event can divide it.—This is my third letter in three days—I will therefore shorten it—I proceed on my way to London tomorrow.—With every sentiment of respect—and—may I add the word?—Love—

ever yours
BYRON

TO ANNABELLA MILBANKE *Decr. 25th. 1814*

Dearest A—I am thus far on my way and as warm as Love can make one with the thermometer below God knows what—tomorrow I proceed Northward and if the Snow don't come down impossibly hope to reach S[eaham] in tolerable time—the license is in my portfolio—it is a very droll composition—but enables us to marry in the house—so pray let us [.] I am sure we shall catch cold kneeling any where else, to say nothing of being without a cushion.—Hobhouse is "bodkin" and takes up rather more room than "Happiness" who I believe wont join us till the last stage. We have heard of a treasure of a Maid for you—who is I believe past the usual age of indiscretion though there is no saying where that ends.—Col. L[eigh] is opposite to me making so many complaints of illness and calls for medicine—that my attention is called off and the rest of my letter will be like a prescription if I don't leave off.—A[ugusta] is looking very well—and just as usual—in every respect—so that better can't be in my estimation.—She writes to you with this—ever dearest

thine
B

P.S.—My love to Ly. M[ilbank]e & papa—I hope they will acquit me "of these my crimes supposed" since I went at last like Lord Grizzle "in hurry post haste for a license—in hurry ding-dong I come back" with some apprehension of finding you like Huncamunca already "married to Tom Thumb."—I wish you much merriment and minced pye—it is Xmas day.— — —

TO LADY MELBOURNE   *Halnaby, January 3d. 1815*

My dearest Aunt—We were married yesterday at ten upon ye. Clock—so there's an end of that matter and the beginning of many others.—Bell has gone through all the ceremonies with great forti-tude—and I am much as usual and your dutiful nephew. All those who are disposed to make presents may as well send them forth-with and pray let them be handsome—and we wait your congrats. besides—as I am sure your benediction is very essential to all our undertakings.—Lady Mil[bank]e was a little hysterical and fine-feeling—and the kneeling was rather tedious—and the cushions hard—but upon the whole it did vastly well.—The drawing-room at Seaham was the scene of our conjunction—and thus we set off according to approved custom to be shut up by ourselves.— — You would think we had been married these 50 years—Bell is fast asleep on a corner of the Sopha, and I am keeping myself awake with this epistle—she desires her love—and mine you have had

ever since we were acquainted.—Pray—how many of our new relations (at least of mine) mean to own us? I reckon upon George &
you and Lord M and the Countess and Count of the holy Roman
empire— —as for Caro— —and Caro-George— —and *William*
I don't know what to think do you?— —I shall write to you again
anon— —at present receive this as an apology for that silence of
which you were kind enough to complain— —and believe me
ever most affectionately thine

BYRON

TO THOMAS MOORE   *Halnaby, Darlington, January 10th, 1815*

I was married this day week. The parson has pronounced it—
Perry has announced it—and the Morning Post, also, under the
head of "Lord Byron's Marriage"—as if it were a fabrication, or the
puff-direct of a new stay-maker.

Now for thine affairs. I have redde thee upon the Fathers, and
it is excellent well. Positively, you must not leave off reviewing.
You shine in it—you kill in it; and this article has been taken for
Sydney Smith's (as I heard in town), which proves not only your
proficiency in parsonology, but that you have all the airs of a vet-
eran critic at your first onset. So, prithee, go on and prosper.

Scott's "Lord of the Isles" is out—"the mail-coach copy" I have,
by special licence of Murray.

* * * * * * * * * * * * * * *

Now is *your* time;—you will come upon them newly and freshly.
It is impossible to read what you have lately done (verse or prose)
without seeing that you have trained on tenfold. * * has floun-
dered; * * has foundered. *I* have tired the rascals (i.e. the public)
with my Harrys and Larrys, Pilgrims and Pirates. Nobody but
S * * * y [Southey] has done any thing worth a slice of bookseller's
pudding; and *he* has not luck enough to be found out in doing a
good thing. Now, Tom, is thy time—"Oh joyful day!—I would
not take a knighthood for thy fortune." Let me hear from you
soon, and believe me ever, &c.

P.S.—Lady Byron is vastly well. How are Mrs. Moore and Joe
Atkinson's "Graces?" We must present our women to one another.

OFF TO THE CONTINENT

I can't but say it is an awkward sight
    To see one's native land receding through
The growing waters; it unmans one quite,
    Especially when life is rather new:
I recollect Great Britain's coast looks white,
    But almost every other country's blue,
When gazing on them, mystified by distance,
We enter on our nautical existence.

So Juan stood, bewildered on the deck:
    The wind sung, cordage strained, and sailors swore,
And the ship creaked, the town became a speck,
    From which away so fair and fast they bore.
The best of remedies Is a beef-steak
    Against sea-sickness: try it, sir, before
You sneer, and I assure you this is true,
For I have found it answer—so may you.

DON JUAN II, 12–13

I have received a letter from your father proposing a separation between us—to which I cannot give an answer without being more acquainted with your own thoughts & wishes—& from *yourself*:—to vague & general charges & exaggerated statements from others I can give no reply:— —it is to *you* that I look—& with *you*—that I can communicate on this subject,— —when I permit the interference of relatives—it will be as a courtesy to them—& not the admission of a right.— —I feel naturally at a loss how to address you—ignorant as I am—how far the letter I have received—has received your sanction—& in the circumstances into which this precipitation has forced me—whatever I might say would be liable to misconstruction—I am really ignorant to what part of Sir Ralph's letter alludes—will you explain?— —To conclude—I shall eventually abide by your decision—but I request you most earnestly to weigh well the probable consequences—& to pause before you pronounce.— —Whatever may occur—it is but justice to you to say—that you are exempt from all fault whatever—& that neither now nor at any time have I the slightest imputation of any description to charge upon you.— —I cannot sign myself other than

yours ever most affectionately

B

Dearest Bell—No answer from you yet—perhaps it is as well—but do recollect—that all is at stake—the present—the future—& even the colouring of the past:—The whole of my errors—or what harsher name you choose to give them—you know—but I loved you—& will not part from you without your *own* most express & *expressed* refusal to return to or receive me.— —Only say the word—that you are still mine in your heart—and "Kate!—I will buckler thee against a million"—

ever yours dearest most

B

I know not what to say—every step taken appears to bear you further from me—and to widen "the great Gulph between thee and me" if it cannot be crossed I will at least perish in it's depth.— —Two letters have been written by me to you—but I have not sent them—& I know not well why I write this or whether I shall send it or no.— —How far your conduct is reconcileable to your duties & affections as a wife and a mother—must be a question for your own reflection—the trial has not been very long—a year—I grant you—of distress—distemper—and misfortune—but these fall chiefly on me—& bitter as the recollection is to me of what I have felt—it is much more so to have made you a partaker in my desolation.—On the charges to be preferred against me—I have *twice* been refused any information by your father & his advisers:—it is now a fortnight—which has been passed in suspense—in humiliation—in obloquy—exposed to the most black & blighting calumnies of every kind:—without even the power of contradicting conjecture & vulgar assertion as to the accusations —because I am denied the knowledge of all or any particulars, from the only quarter that can afford them—in the mean time I hope your ears are gratified by the general rumours.—I have invited your return—it has been refused—I have entreated to see you—it is refused—I have requested to know with what I am charged—it is refused—is this mercy—or justice—?— —We shall see.— —And now—Bell—dearest Bell—whatever may be the event of this calamitous difference—whether you are restored to—or torn from me—I can only say in the truth of affliction—& without hope—motive—or end in again saying what I have lately but vainly repeated—that I love you:—bad or good—mad or rational—miserable or content—I love you—& shall do to the dregs of my memory & existence.—If I can feel thus for you now—under every possible aggravation & exasperating circumstance that can corrode the heart—& inflame the brain—perhaps you may one day know—or think at least—that I was not all you have persuaded yourself to believe me—but that's nothing—nothing can touch me further.— —I have hitherto avoided naming my child—but as this was a feeling you never doubted in me—I must ask of it's welfare—I have heard of it's beauty—& it's playfulness—and I request—not from you—but through any other channel—Augusta's—if you please—some occasional news of it's well being.— —

I am yours &c. &c.

B

P.S.—If there are any explanations—I can give—pray require them.—From some parts of your letters I am led to believe that you may have heard exaggerated or imaginary reports with regard to me since our last interview—either now or at our meeting I will not shrink from any question which you or yours may think it requisite to ask me—I will not pretend to deserve—but at least I will never deceive you.—

TO LADY BYRON   *Sunday April* [*14*] *1816*

"More last words"—not many—and such as you will attend to—answer I do not expect—nor does it import—but you will hear me.— —I have just parted from Augusta—almost the last being you had left me to part with—& the only unshattered tie of my existence—wherever I may go—& I am going far—you & I can never meet again in this world—nor in the next—let this content or atone.—If any accident occurs to me—be kind to *her*.— —if she is then nothing—to her children:— —some time ago—I informed you that with the knowledge that any child of ours was already provided for by other & better means—I had made my will in favour of her & her children—as prior to my marriage:—this was not done in prejudice to you for we had not then differed—& even this is useless during your life by the settlements—I say therefore—be kind to her & hers—for never has she acted or spoken otherwise towards you—she has ever been your friend—this may seem valueless to one who has now so many:— —be kind to her—however—& recollect that though it may be advantage to you to have lost your husband—it is sorrow to her to have the waters now—or the earth hereafter—between her & her brother.—She is gone—I need hardly add that of this request she

knows nothing—your late compliances have not been so extensive—as to render this an encroachment:—I repeat it—(for deep
resentments have but *half* recollections) that you once did promise
me thus much—do not forget it—nor deem it cancelled it was
not a vow.— —Mr. Wharton has sent me a letter with a question
—& two pieces of intelligence—to the question I answer that
the carriage is yours—& as it has only carried us to Halnaby—&
London—& you to Kirkby—I hope it will take you many a more
propitious journey.— —The receipts can remain—unless troublesome, if so—they can be sent to Augusta—& through her I would
also hear of my little daughter—my address will be left for Mrs.
Leigh.—The ring is of no lapidary value—but it contains the hair
of a king and an ancestor—which I should wish to preserve to
Miss Byron.—To a subsequent letter of Mr. Wharton's I have to
reply that it is the "law's delay" not mine—& that when he & Mr.
H[anson] have adjusted the tenor of the bond—I am ready to sign,

yrs. ever very truly
BYRON

Childe Harold's Pilgrimage III, 1–9

1

Is thy face like thy mother's, my fair child!
Ada! sole daughter of my house and heart?
When last I saw thy young blue eyes they smiled,
And then we parted,—not as now we part,
But with a hope.—
          Awaking with a start,
The waters heave around me; and on high
The winds lift up their voices: I depart,
Whither I know not; but the hour's gone by,
When Albion's lessening shores could grieve or glad
     mine eye.

2

Once more upon the waters! yet once more!
And the waves bound beneath me as a steed
That knows his rider. Welcome, to their roar!
Swift be their guidance, wheresoe'er it lead!
Though the strain'd mast should quiver as a reed,
And the rent canvas fluttering strew the gale,
Still must I on; for I am as a weed,
Flung from the rock, on Ocean's foam, to sail
Where'er the surge may sweep, or tempest's breath
     prevail.

3

In my youth's summer I did sing of One,
The wandering outlaw of his own dark mind;
Again I seize the theme then but begun,
And bear it with me, as the rushing wind
Bears the cloud onwards: in that Tale I find
The furrows of long thought, and dried-up tears,
Which, ebbing, leave a sterile track behind,
O'er which all heavily the journeying years
Plod the last sands of life,—where not a flower appears.

4

Since my young days of passion—joy, or pain,
Perchance my heart and harp have lost a string,
And both may jar: it may be, that in vain
I would essay as I have sung to sing.
Yet, though a dreary strain, to this I cling;
So that it wean me from the weary dream
Of selfish grief or gladness—so it fling
Forgetfulness around me—it shall seem
To me, though to none else, a not ungrateful theme.

5

He, who grown aged in this world of woe,
In deeds, not years, piercing the depths of life,
So that no wonder waits him; nor below
Can love, or sorrow, fame, ambition, strife,
Cut to his heart again with the keen knife
Of silent, sharp endurance: he can tell
Why thought seeks refuge in lone caves, yet rife
With airy images, and shapes which dwell
Still unimpair'd, though old, in the soul's haunted cell.

6

'Tis to create, and in creating live
A being more intense, that we endow
With form our fancy, gaining as we give
The life we image, even as I do now.
What am I? Nothing; but not so art thou,
Soul of my thought! with whom I traverse earth,
Invisible but gazing, as I glow
Mix'd with thy spirit, blended with thy birth,
And feeling still with thee in my crush'd feeling's dearth.

7

Yet must I think less wildly:—I *have* thought
Too long and darkly, till my brain became,
In its own eddy boiling and o'erwrought,
A whirling gulf of phantasy and flame:
And thus, untaught in youth my heart to tame,
My springs of life were poison'd. 'Tis too late!
Yet am I chang'd; though still enough the same
In strength to bear what time can not abate,
And feed on bitter fruits without accusing Fate.

8

Something too much of this:—but now 'tis past,
And the spell closes with its silent seal.
Long absent HAROLD re-appears at last;
He of the breast which fain no more would feel,
Wrung with the wounds which kill not, but ne'er heal;
Yet Time, who changes all, had altered him
In soul and aspect as in age: years steal
Fire from the mind as vigour from the limb;
And life's enchanted cup but sparkles near the brim.

9

His had been quaff'd too quickly, and he found
The dregs were wormwood; but he fill'd again,
And from a purer fount, on holier ground,
And deem'd its spring perpetual; but in vain! . . .

TO AUGUSTA LEIGH   *April* [*24?*] *1816*

My dearest Augusta,—We sail tonight for Ostend, and I seize this moment to say two or three words.

I met last night with an old Schoolfellow (Wildman by name), a Waterloo Aid-de-camp of Lord Uxbridge's. He tells me poor Fred. Howard was *not* mangled, nor in the hands of the French; he was shot through the body charging a party of infantry, and died (*not* on the field) half an hour afterwards at some house not far off, and in no great pain.

I thought this might make his friends easier, as they had heard that he was a sufferer by falling into the enemy's hands. Capt. Wildman was near him at the time, and I believe saw him again shortly before his death, and after his wound.

We left town early yesterday morning, that is, *rose* early and *set* off late, after all the usual bustle and confusion.

Address to me—à Genève *Poste Restante*, and (when you hear) tell me how little *Da* is, and . . .
[The rest of the letter is missing]

TO JOHN CAM HOBHOUSE   *Bruxelles—May 1st. 1816*

My dear H[obhous]e—You will be surprized that we are not more "en avant" and so am I—but Mr. Baxter's wheels and springs have not done their duty—for which I beg that you will abuse him like a pickpocket (that is—*He*—the said Baxter being the *pickpocket*) and say that I expect a deduction—having been obliged to come out of the way to this place—which was not in my route—for repairs—which however I hope to have accomplished so as to put us in motion in a day or two.— —We passed through Ghent— Antwerp—and Mechlin—& thence diverged here—having seen all the sights—pictures—docks—basins—& having climbed up steeples &c. & so forth— —the first thing—after the flatness & fertility of the country which struck me—was the beauty of the towns—Bruges first—where you may tell Douglas Kinnaird—on entering at Sunset—I overtook a crew of beggarly looking gentlemen not unlike Oxberry—headed by a Monarch with a Staff the very facsimile of King Clause in the said D[ouglas] K[innaird]'s

revived drama.— —We lost our way in the dark—or rather twilight—not far from Ghent—by the stupidity of the postilion (*one*
only by the way to 4 horses) which produced an alarm of intended
robbery among the uninitiated—whom I could not convince
—that four or five well-armed people were not immediately to
be plundered and anatomized by a single person fortified with a
horsewhip to be sure—but nevertheless a little encumbered with
large jack boots—and a tight jacket that did not fit him—The way
was found again without loss of life or limb:— —I thought the
learned Fletcher at least would have known better after our Turkish
expeditions—and defiles—and banditti—& guards &c. &c. than
to have been so valourously alert without at least a better pretext
for his superfluous courage. I don't mean to say that they were
frightened but they were vastly suspicious without any cause.—At
Ghent we stared at pictures—& climbed up a steeple 450 steps in
altitude—from which I had a good view & notion of these "paese
bassi."— —Next day we broke down—by a damned wheel (on
which Baxter should be broken) pertinaciously refusing it's stip-
ulated rotation—this becalmed us at Lo-Kristi—(2 leagues from
Ghent)—& obliged us to return for repairs—At Lo-Kristi I came to
anchor in the house of a Flemish Blacksmith (who was ill of a fever
for whlch Dr. Dori physicked him—I dare say he is dead by now)
and saw somewhat of Lo-Kristi—Low-country—low life—which
regaled us much—besides it being a Sunday—all the world were
in their way to Mass—& I had the pleasure of seeing a number of
very ordinary women in extraordinary garments:—we found the
"Contadini" however very goodnatured & obliging though not at
all useful.— —At Antwerp we pictured—churched—and steepled
again—but the principal Street and *bason* pleased me most—poor
dear Bonaparte!!!—and the foundries &c.—as for Rubens—I was
glad to see his tomb on account of that ridiculous description (in
Smollet's P[eregrine] Pickle) of Pallet's absurdity at his monument
—but as for his works—and his superb "tableaux"—he seems
to me (who by the way know nothing of the matter) the most
glaring—flaring—staring—harlotry imposter that ever passed
a trick upon the senses of mankind—it is not nature—it is not
art—with the exception of some linen (which hangs over the cross
in one of his pictures) which to do it justice looked like a very

handsome table cloth—I never saw such an assemblage of florid night-mares as his canvas contains—his portraits seem clothed in pulpit cushions.— —On the way to Mechlin—a wheel—& a *spring* too gave way—that is—the one went—& the other would not go—so we came off here to get into dock—I hope we shall sail shortly.— —On to Geneva.—Will you have the goodness,—to get at my account at Hoares—(my bankers) I believe there must be a balance in my favour—as I did not draw a great deal previously to going:—whatever there may be over the two thousand five hundred—they can send by you to me in a further credit when you come out:—I wish you to enquire (for fear any tricks might be played with my drafts) my bankers books left with you—will show you exactly what I have drawn—and you can let them have the book to make out the remainder of the account. All I have to urge to Hanson—or to our friend Douglas K[innaird]—is to *sell* if possible.— —All kind things to Scrope—and the rest—

ever yrs. most truly & obligedly

B

P.S.—If you hear of my child—let me know any good of her health—& well doing.—Will you bring out παςανιας (Taylor's ditto) when you come—I shall bring to for you at Geneva—don't forget to urge Scrope into our crew—we will buy females and found a colony—provided Scrope does not find those ossified barriers to "the forefended place"—which cost him such a siege at Brighthelmstone—write at your leisure—or "ipse veni".— —

TO AUGUSTA LEIGH   *Bruxelles—May 1st. 1816*

My Heart— —We are detained here for some petty carriage repairs—having come out of our way to the Rhine on purpose—after passing through Ghent—Antwerp—and Mechlin.— —I have written to you twice—once from Ostend—and again from Ghent—I hope most truly that you will receive my letters—not as important in themselves—but because you wish it—& so do I.—It would be difficult for me to write anything amusing—this country has been so frequently described—& has so little for description—though a good deal for observation—that I know not what to say of it—& one don't like talking only of oneself.—We saw at Antwerp the famous basons of Bonaparte for his navy—which are very superb—as all his undertakings were—& as for churches—& pictures—I have stared at them till my brains are like a guide-book:—the last (though it is heresy to say so) don't please me at all—I think Rubens a very great dauber—and prefer Vandyke a hundred times over—(but then I know nothing about the matter) Rubens' women have all red gowns and red shoulders —to say nothing of necks—of which they are more liberal than charming—it may all be very fine—and I suppose it must be Art—for—I'll swear—'tis not Nature.— —As the low Countries did not make part of my plan (except as a route) I feel a little anxious to get out of them—level roads don't suit me—as thou knowest—it must be up hill or down—& then I am more au fait.—Imagine to yourself a succession of avenues with a Dutch Spire at the end of each—and you see the road;—an accompaniment of highly cultivated farms on each side intersected with small canals or ditches—and sprinkled with very neat & clean cottages—a village every two miles—and you see the country— —not a rise from Ostend to Antwerp—a molehill would make the inhabitants think that the Alps had come here on a visit—it is a perpetuity of plain & an eternity of *pavement* (on the *road*) but it is a country of great apparent comfort—and of singular though *tame* beauty—and were it not out of my way—I should like to survey it less cursorily.—The towns are wonderfully fine.— —The approach to Brussels is beautiful—and there is a fine palace to the right in coming . . . .

Childe Harold's Pilgrimage III, 17–18, 21–28

17

Stop!—for thy tread is on an Empire's dust!
An Earthquake's spoil is sepulchred below!
Is the spot mark'd with no colossal bust?
Nor column trophied for triumphal show?
None; but the moral's truth tells simpler so,
As the ground was before, thus let it be;—
How that red rain hath made the harvest grow!
And is this all the world has gained by thee,
Thou first and last of fields! king-making Victory?

18

And Harold stands upon this place of skulls,
The grave of France, the deadly Waterloo!
How in an hour the power which gave annuls
Its gifts, transferring fame as fleeting too!
In "pride of place" here last the eagle flew,
Then tore with bloody talon the rent plain,
Pierced by the shaft of banded nations through;
Ambition's life and labours all were vain;
He wears the shattered links of the world's broken chain.

21

There was a sound of revelry by night,
And Belgium's capital had gathered then
Her Beauty and her Chivalry, and bright
The lamps shone o'er fair women and brave men;
A thousand hearts beat happily; and when
Music arose with its voluptuous swell,
Soft eyes look'd love to eyes which spake again,
And all went merry as a marriage-bell;
But hush! hark! a deep sound strikes like a rising knell!

22

Did ye not hear it?—No; 'twas but the wind,
Or the car rattling o'er the stony street;
On with the dance! let joy be unconfined;
No sleep till morn, when Youth and Pleasure meet
To chase the glowing Hours with flying feet—
But, hark!—that heavy sound breaks in once more,
As if the clouds its echo would repeat;
And nearer, dearer, deadlier than before!
Arm! Arm! and out—it is—the cannon's opening roar!

23

Within a windowed niche of that high hall
Sate Brunswick's fated chieftain; he did hear
That sound the first amidst the festival,
And caught its tone with Death's prophetic ear;
And when they smiled because he deem'd it near,
His heart more truly knew that peal too well
Which stretch'd his father on a bloody bier,
And roused the vengeance blood alone could quell:
He rush'd into the field, and, foremost fighting, fell.

24

Ah! then and there was hurrying to and fro,
And gathering tears, and tremblings of distress,
And cheeks all pale, which but an hour ago
Blush'd at the praise of their own loveliness;
And there were sudden partings, such as press
The life from out young hearts, and choking sighs
Which ne'er might be repeated; who could guess
If ever more should meet those mutual eyes,
Since upon nights so sweet such awful morn could rise?

25

And there was mounting in hot haste: the steed,
The mustering squadron, and the clattering car,
Went pouring forward in impetuous speed,
And swiftly forming in the ranks of war;
And the deep thunder peal on peal afar;
And near, the beat of the alarming drum
Roused up the soldier ere the morning star;
While throng'd the citizens with terror dumb,
Or whispering, with white lips—"The foe! They come!
    they come!"

26

And wild and high the "Cameron's gathering" rose!
The war-note of Lochiel, which Albyn's hills
Have heard, and heard, too, have her Saxon foes:—
How in the noon of night that pibroch thrills,
Savage and shrill! But with the breach which fills
Their mountain-pipe, so fill the mountaineers
With the fierce native daring which instils
The stirring memory of a thousand years,
And Evan's, Donald's fame rings in each clansman's ears!

27

And Ardennes waves above them her green leaves,
Dewy with nature's tear-drops, as they pass,
Grieving, if aught inanimate e'er grieves,
Over the unreturning brave,—alas!
Ere evening to be trodden like the grass
Which now beneath them, but above shall grow
In its next verdure, when this fiery mass
Of living valour, rolling on the foe
And burning with high hope, shall moulder cold and low.

28

Last noon beheld them full of lusty life,
Last eve in Beauty's circle proudly gay,
The midnight brought the signal-sound of strife,
The morn the marshalling in arms,—the day
Battle's magnificently-stern array!
The thunder-clouds close o'er it, which when rent
The earth is covered thick with other clay,
Which her own clay shall cover, heaped and pent,
Rider and horse,—friend, foe,—in one red burial blent!

SWITZERLAND

Above me are the Alps,
The palaces of Nature, whose vast walls
Have pinnacled in clouds their snowy scalps,
And throned Eternity in icy halls
Of cold sublimity, where forms and falls
The avalanche—the thunderbolt of snow!
All which expands the spirit, yet appals,
Gather around these summits, as to show
How Earth may pierce to Heaven, yet leave vain man
below.

CHILDE HAROLD'S PILGRIMAGE III, 61

Sonnet on Chillon

Eternal spirit of the chainless mind!
    Brightest in dungeons, Liberty! thou art,
    For there thy habitation is the heart—
The heart which love of thee alone can bind;
And when thy sons to fetters are consigned—
    To fetters, and the damp vault's dayless gloom,
    Their country conquers with their martyrdom,
And Freedom's fame finds wings on every wind.

Chillon! thy prison is a holy place,
    And thy sad floor an altar—for 'twas trod,
Until his very steps have left a trace
    Worn, as if thy cold pavement were a sod,
By Bonnivard!—May none those marks efface!
    For they appeal from tyranny to God.

Darkness

I had a dream, which was not all a dream.
The bright sun was extinguish'd, and the stars
Did wander darkling in the eternal space,
Rayless, and pathless, and the icy earth
Swung blind and blackening in the moonless air;
Morn came, and went—and came, and brought no day,
And men forgot their passions in the dread
Of this their desolation; and all hearts
Were chill'd into a selfish prayer for light:
And they did live by watchfires—and the thrones,
The palaces of crowned kings—the huts,
The habitations of all things which dwell,
Were burnt for beacons; cities were consumed,
And men were gathered round their blazing homes
To look once more into each other's face;
Happy were those who dwelt within the eye
Of the volcanos, and their mountain-torch:
A fearful hope was all the world contain'd;
Forests were set on fire—but hour by hour
They fell and faded—and the crackling trunks
Extinguish'd with a crash—and all was black.
The brows of men by the despairing light
Wore an unearthly aspect, as by fits
The flashes fell upon them; some lay down
And hid their eyes and wept; and some did rest
Their chins upon their clenched hands, and smiled;
And others hurried to and fro, and fed
Their funeral piles with fuel, and looked up
With mad disquietude on the dull sky,
The pall of a past world; and then again
With curses cast them down upon the dust,
And gnash'd their teeth and howl'd: the wild birds shriek'd,
And, terrified, did flutter on the ground,
And flap their useless wings; the wildest brutes
Came tame and tremulous; and vipers crawl'd

And twined themselves among the multitude,
Hissing, but stingless—they were slain for food:
And War, which for a moment was no more,
Did glut himself again;—a meal was bought
With blood, and each sate sullenly apart
Gorging himself in gloom: no love was left;
All earth was but one thought—and that was death,
Immediate and inglorious; and the pang
Of famine fed upon all entrails—men
Died, and their bones were tombless as their flesh;
The meagre by the meagre were devoured,
Even dogs assail'd their masters, all save one,
And he was faithful to a corse, and kept
The birds and beasts and famish'd men at bay,
Till hunger clung them, or the dropping dead
Lured their lank jaws; himself sought out no food
But with a piteous and perpetual moan
And a quick desolate cry, licking the hand
Which answered not with a caress—he died.
The crowd was famish'd by degrees; but two
Of an enormous city did survive,
And they were enemies: they met beside
The dying embers of an altar-place
Where had been heap'd a mass of holy things
For an unholy usage; they raked up,
And shivering scraped with their cold skeleton hands
The feeble ashes, and their feeble breath
Blew for a little life, and made a flame
Which was a mockery; then they lifted up
Their eyes as it grew lighter, and beheld
Each other's aspects—saw, and shriek'd, and died—
Even of their mutual hideousness they died
Unknowing who he was upon whose brow
Famine had written Fiend. The world was void
The populous and the powerful—was a lump,
Seasonless, herbless, treeless, manless, lifeless—
A lump of death—a chaos of hard clay.
The rivers, lakes, and ocean all stood still,

And nothing stirred within their silent depths;
Ships sailorless lay rotting on the sea,
And their masts fell down piecemeal; as they dropp'd
They slept on the abyss without a surge—
The waves were dead; the tides were in their grave,
The moon their mistress had expired before;
The winds were withered in the stagnant air,
And the clouds perish'd; Darkness had no need
Of aid from them—She was the universe.

Stanzas to Augusta

1

Though the day of my destiny's over,
   And the star of my fate hath declined,
Thy soft heart refused to discover
   The faults which so many could find;
Though thy soul with my grief was acquainted,
   It shrunk not to share it with me,
And the love which my spirit hath painted
   It never hath found but in *thee*.

2

Then when nature around me is smiling
   The last smile which answers to mine,
I do not believe it beguiling
   Because it reminds me of thine;
And when winds are at war with the ocean,
   As the breasts I believed in with me,
If their billows excite an emotion
   It is that they bear me from *thee*.

3

Though the rock of my last hope is shiver'd,
   And its fragments are sunk in the wave,
Though I feel that my soul is deliver'd
   To pain—it shall not be its slave.
There is many a pang to pursue me:
   They may crush, but they shall not contemn—
They may torture, but shall not subdue me—
   'Tis of *thee* that I think—not of them.

4

Though human, thou didst not deceive me,
   Though woman, thou didst not forsake,
Though loved, thou forborest to grieve me,
   Though slander'd, thou never could'st shake,—

Though trusted, thou didst not betray me,
　　Though parted, it was not to fly,
Though watchful, 'twas not to defame me,
　　Nor, mute, that the world might belie.

5

Yet I blame not the world, nor despise it,
　　Nor the war of the many with one—
If my soul was not fitted to prize it
　　'Twas folly not sooner to shun:
And if dearly that error hath cost me,
　　And more than I once could foresee,
I have found that, whatever it lost me,
　　It could not deprive me of *thee*.

6

From the wreck of the past, which hath perish'd,
　　Thus much I at least may recall,
It hath taught me that what I most cherish'd
　　Deserved to be dearest of all:
In the desert a fountain is springing,
　　In the wide waste there still is a tree,
And a bird in the solitude singing,
　　Which speaks to my spirit of *thee*.

Childe Harold's Pilgrimage III, 68–75, 85–90, 92–97

68

Lake Leman woos me with its crystal face,
The mirror where the stars and mountains view
The stillness of their aspect in each trace
Its clear depth yields of their far height and hue:
There is too much of man here, to look through
With a fit mind the might which I behold;
But soon in me shall Loneliness renew
Thoughts hid, but not less cherish'd than of old,
Ere mingling with the herd had penn'd me in their fold.

69

To fly from, need not be to hate, mankind;
All are not fit with them to stir and toil,
Nor is it discontent to keep the mind
Deep in its fountain, lest it overboil
In the hot throng, where we become the spoil
Of our Infection, till too late and long
We may deplore and struggle with the coil,
In wretched interchange of wrong for wrong
'Midst a contentious world, striving where none are strong.

70

There, in a moment, we may plunge our years
In fatal penitence, and in the blight
Of our own soul, turn all our blood to tears,
And colour things to come with hues of Night;
The race of life becomes a hopeless flight
To those that walk in darkness: on the sea,
The boldest steer but where their ports invite,
But there are wanderers o'er Eternity
Whose bark drives on and on, and anchored ne'er shall be.

71

Is it not better, then, to be alone,
And love Earth only for its earthly sake?
By the blue rushing of the arrowy Rhone,
Or the pure bosom of its nursing lake,
Which feeds it as a mother who doth make
A fair but froward infant her own care,
Kissing its cries away as these awake;—
Is it not better thus our lives to wear,
Than join the crushing crowd, doom'd to inflict or bear?

72

I live not in myself, but I become
Portion of that around me; and to me,
High mountains are a feeling, but the hum
Of human cities torture: I can see
Nothing to loathe in nature, save to be
A link reluctant in a fleshly chain,
Class'd among creatures, when the soul can flee,
And with the sky, the peak, the heaving plain
Of ocean, or the stars, mingle, and not in vain.

73

And thus I am absorb'd, and this is life:
I look upon the peopled desert past,
As on a place of agony and strife,
Where, for some sin, to Sorrow I was cast,
To act and suffer, but remount at last
With a fresh pinion; which I feel to spring,
Though young, yet waxing vigorous, as the blast
Which it would cope with, on delighted wing,
Spurning the clay-cold bonds which round our being cling.

74

And when, at length, the mind shall be all free
From what it hates in this degraded form,
Reft of its carnal life, save what shall be
Existent happier in the fly and worm,—
When elements to elements conform,
And dust is as it should be, shall I not
Feel all I see, less dazzling, but more warm?
The bodiless thought? the Spirit of each spot?
Of which, even now, I share at times the immortal lot?

75

Are not the mountains, waves, and skies, a part
Of me and of my soul, as I of them?
Is not the love of these deep in my heart
With a pure passion? should I not contemn
All objects, if compared with these? and stem
A tide of suffering, rather than forego
Such feelings for the hard and worldly phlegm
Of those whose eyes are only turn'd below,
Gazing upon the ground, with thoughts which dare not
    glow?

. . .

85

Clear, placid Leman! thy contrasted lake,
With the wild world I dwelt in, is a thing
Which warns me, with its stillness, to forsake
Earth's troubled waters for a purer spring.
This quiet sail is as a noiseless wing
To waft me from distraction; once I loved
Torn ocean's roar, but thy soft murmuring
Sounds sweet as if a sister's voice reproved,
That I with stern delights should e'er have been
    so moved.

86

It is the hush of night, and all between
Thy margin and the mountains, dusk, yet clear,
Mellowed and mingling, yet distinctly seen,
Save darken'd Jura, whose capt heights appear
Precipitously steep; and drawing near,
There breathes a living fragrance from the shore,
Of flowers yet fresh with childhood; on the ear
Drops the light drip of the suspended oar,
Or chirps the grasshopper one good-night carol more;

87

He is an evening reveller, who makes
His life an infancy, and sings his fill;
At intervals, some bird from out the brakes,
Starts into voice a moment, then is still.
There seems a floating whisper on the hill,
But that is fancy, for the starlight dews
All silently their tears of love instil,
Weeping themselves away, till they infuse
Deep into Nature's breast the spirit of her hues.

88

Ye stars! which are the poetry of heaven!
If in your bright leaves we would read the fate
Of men and empires,—'tis to be forgiven,
That in our aspirations to be great,
Our destinies o'erleap their mortal state,
And claim a kindred with you; for ye are
A beauty and a mystery, and create
In us such love and reverence from afar,
That fortune, fame, power, life, have named themselves
    a star.

89

All heaven and earth are still—though not in sleep,
But breathless, as we grow when feeling most;
And silent, as we stand in thoughts too deep:—
All heaven and earth are still: From the high host
Of stars, to the lull'd lake and mountain-coast,
All is concentered in a life intense,
Where not a beam, nor air, nor leaf is lost,
But hath a part of being, and a sense
Of that which is of all Creator and defence.

90

Then stirs the feeling infinite, so felt
In solitude, where we are *least* alone;
A truth, which through our being then doth melt
And purifies from self: it is a tone,
The soul and source of music, which makes known
Eternal harmony, and sheds a charm,
Like to the fabled Cytherea's zone,
Binding all things with beauty;—'twould disarm
The spectre Death, had he substantial power to harm

. . .

92

The sky is changed!—and such a change! Oh night,
And storm, and darkness, ye are wondrous strong,
Yet lovely in your strength, as is the light
Of a dark eye in woman! Far along,
From peak to peak, the rattling crags among
Leaps the live thunder! Not from one lone cloud,
But every mountain now hath found a tongue,
And Jura answers, through her misty shroud,
Back to the joyous Alps, who call to her aloud!

93

And this is in the night:—Most glorious night!
Thou wert not sent for slumber! let me be
A sharer in thy fierce and far delight,—
A portion of the tempest and of thee!
How the lit lake shines, a phosphoric sea,
And the big rain comes dancing to the earth!
And now again 'tis black,—and now, the glee
Of the loud hills shakes with its mountain-mirth,
As if they did rejoice o'er a young earthquake's birth.

94

Now, where the swift Rhone cleaves his way between
Heights which appear as lovers who have parted
In hate, whose mining depths so intervene,
That they can meet no more, though broken-hearted;
Though in their souls, which thus each other thwarted,
Love was the very root of the fond rage
Which blighted their life's bloom, and then departed:—
Itself expired, but leaving them an age
Of years all winters,—war within themselves to wage.

95

Now, where the quick Rhone thus hath cleft his way,
The mightiest of the storms hath ta'en his stand:
For here, not one, but many, make their play,
And fling their thunder-bolts from hand to hand,
Flashing and cast around: of all the band,
The brightest through these parted hills hath fork'd
His lightnings,—as if he did understand,
That in such gaps as desolation work'd,
There the hot shaft should blast whatever therein lurk'd.

96

Sky, mountains, river, winds, lake, lightnings! ye!
With night, and clouds, and thunder, and a soul
To make these felt and feeling, well may be
Things that have made me watchful; the far roll
Of your departing voices, is the knoll
Of what in me is sleepless,—if I rest.
But where of ye, oh tempests! is the goal?
Are ye like those within the human breast?
Or do ye find, at length, like eagles, some high nest?

97

Could I embody and unbosom now
That which is most within me,—could I wreak
My thoughts upon expression, and thus throw
Soul, heart, mind, passions, feelings, strong or weak,
All that I would have sought, and all I seek,
Bear, know, feel, and yet breathe—into *one* word,
And that one word were Lightning, I would speak;
But as it is, I live and die unheard,
With a most voiceless thought, sheathing it as a sword.

My dear H[obhous]e/—Despite of this date—address as usual
to the Genevese Poste—which awaits your answers as I await your
arrival—with that of Scrope—whose pocket appears (by your late
letter of revolutions at the Union) to have become as "light" as his
"wines"—though I suppose on the whole he is still worth at ieast
50–000 pds—being what is called here a "Millionaire" that is in
Francs & such Lilliputian coinage. I have taken a very pretty villa
in a vineyard—with the Alps behind—& Mt. Jura and the Lake
before—it is called Diodati—from the name of the Proprietor—
who is a descendant of the critical & illustrissimi Diodati—and
has an agreeable house which he lets at a reasonable rate per season
or annum as suits the lessée—when you come out—don't go to
an Inn—not even to Secheron—but come on to head-quarters—
where I have rooms ready for you—and Scrope—and all "appliances
& means to boot".—Bring with you also for me some bottles of
Calcined Magnesia—a new *Sword cane*—procured by Jackson—he
alone knows the sort—(my last tumbled into this lake—) some of
Waite's *red* tooth-powder—& tooth-brushes—a Taylor's *Pawrsa-
nias*—and—I forget the other things.—Tell Murray I have a 3d.
Canto of Childe Harold finished—it is the longest of the three—
being one hundred & eleven Stanzas—I shall send it by the first
plausible conveyance.—At the present writing I am on my way on
a water-tour round the Lake Leman—and am thus far proceeded
in a pretty open boat which I bought & navigate—it is an English
one & was brought lately from Bordeaux—I am on shore for the
Night—and have just had a row with the Syndic of this town who
wanted my passports which I left at Diodati—not thinking they
would be wanted except in grand route—but it seems this is Savoy
and the dominion of his Cagliari Majesty whom we saw at his
own Opera—in his own city—in 1809—however by dint of references to Geneva—& other corroborations—together with being
in a very ill humour—Truth has prevailed—wonderful to relate
they actually take one's word for a fact—although it is credible
and indubitable.—Tomorrow we go to Meillerei—& Clarens—&
Vevey—with Rousseau in hand—to see his scenery—according to
his delineation in his Heloise now before me.—The views have

hitherto been very fine—but I should conceive less so than those of the remainder of the lake.— —All your letters (that is *two*) have arrived—thanks & greetings:—what—& who—the devil is "Glenarvon". I know nothing—nor ever heard of such a person— and what do you mean by a brother in India?—you have none in India—it is *Scrope* who has a brother in India.—my remembrances to Kinnaird—& Mrs. Kinn[air]d—to all & every body—& Hunt in particular—& Scrope—& Mr. Murray—and believe me

yrs ever most truly

B

P.S.—I left the Doctor at Diodati—he sprained his ancle. P.S. Will you particularly remember to bring me a largish bottle of the strongest *Pot Ash*—as before—Mr. Le Man[n] will furnish it—that Child and Childish Dr. Pollydolly contrived to find it broken, or to break it at Carlsruhe—so that I am in a fuss—the Genevese make it badly—it effervesces in the Sulphuric acid, and it ought not—bring me some of a more quiescent character.

TO JOHN MURRAY   *Ouchy nr. Lausanne—June 27th. 1816*

Dear Sir—I am thus far (kept by stress of weather) on my way back to Diodati (near Geneva) from a voyage in my boat round the lake—& I enclose you a sprig of *Gibbon's Acacia* & some rose leaves from his garden—which with part of his house I have just seen—you will find honourable mention in his life made of this "Acacia" when he walked out on the night of concluding his history.—The garden—& *summer house* where he composed are neglected—& the last utterly decayed—but they still show it as his "Cabinet" & seem perfectly aware of his memory.—My route—through Flanders—& by the Rhine to Switzerland was all I expected & more.— —I have traversed all Rousseau's ground— with the Heloise before me—& am struck to a degree with the force & accuracy of his descriptions—& the beauty of their reality:—Meillerie—Clarens—& Vevey—& the Chateau de Chillon are places of which I shall say little—because all I could say must fall short of the impressions they stamp.— —Three days ago—we were most nearly wrecked in a Squall off Meillerie—& driven to shore—I ran no risk being so near the rocks and a good swimmer—but our party were wet—& incommoded a good deal:—the wind was strong enough to blow down some trees as we found at landing—however all is righted & right—& we are thus far on return.— —Dr. Polidori is not here—but at Diodati—left behind in hospital with a sprained ancle acquired in tumbling from a wall—he can't jump.— —I shall be glad to hear you are well—& have received for me certain helms & swords sent from Waterloo—which I rode over with pain & pleasure.— —I have finished a third Canto of Childe Harold (consisting of one hundred & seventeen stanzas (longer than either of the two former)—& in some parts—it may be—better—but of course on that *I* cannot determine.—I shall send it by the first safe-looking opportunity.—

ever very truly yrs.

B

TO JOHN MURRAY   *Diodati.—August 28th. 1816*

Dear Sir—The Manuscript (containing the third Canto of Childe Harold—the Castle of Chillon &c. &c.) is consigned to the care of my friend Mr. Shelley—who will deliver this letter along with it.—Mr. Gifford will perhaps be kind enough to read it over;—I know not well to whom to consign the correction of the proofs—nor indeed who would be good natured enough to overlook it in its progress—as I feel very anxious that it should be published with as few errata as possible.— —Perhaps—my friend Mr. Moore (if in town) would do this.— —If not—Mr. S[helley] will take it upon himself,—and in any case—he is authorized to act for me in treating with you &c. &c. on this subject.— —You talked of a letter—which was to be sent by you to me—but I have received none—before—or since—one by Mr. Browne.—As that Gentleman returned by Brussels—which is the longest route—I declined troubling him with the care of this packet.—Believe me very truly yours.

BYRON

P.S.—There is in the volume—an epistle to Mrs. Leigh—on which I should wish her to have her opinion consulted—before the publication—if she objects—of course—*omit* it.— —I have been very glad to hear you are well—& well-doing—and that you stopped Master Cawthorne in his foolish attempts to republish the E[nglish] B[ards] & S[cotch] R[eviewers].—I wish you all good things.— —

TO JOHN MURRAY   *Diodati. Septr. 30th. 1816*

My dear Sir—I answered your obliging letters yesterday. Today the Monody arrived—with it's *title page*—which is I presume a separate publication.— "The request of a Friend" —

"Obliged by Hunger and request of friends."

I will request you to expunge that same—unless you please to add "by a person of quality—or of wit and honour about town"— merely say—written to be spoken at D[rury] L[ane].—Tomorrow I dine at Coppet—Saturday I strike tents for Italy—this evening on the lake in my boat with Mr. Hobhouse—the pole which sustains the mainsail slipped in tacking & struck me so violently on one of my legs (the *worst* luckily) as to make me do a foolish thing viz. to *faint*—a downright swoon—the thing must have jarred some nerve or other—for the bone is not injured—& hardly painful (it is six hours since) and cost Mr. H[obhouse] some apprehension and much sprinkling of water to recover me;—the sensation was a very odd one—I never had but two such before—one from a cut on the head from a stone several years ago—and once (long ago also) in falling into a great wreath of snow— —a sort of gray giddiness first—then nothingness—and a total loss of memory on beginning to recover—the last part is not disagreeable—if one did not find it again.— —You want the original M.S.S—Mr. Davies has the first fair copy in my own hand—& I have the rough composition here—and will send or save it for you since you wish it.— —With regard to your new literary project—if any thing falls in the way which will—to the best of my judgment—suit you—I will send you what I can.—At present I must lay by a little—having pretty

well exhausted myself in what I have sent you.—Italy or Dalmatia
& another summer may or may not set me off again—I have no
plans—& am nearly as indifferent what may come—as where I
go. I shall take Felicia Hemans' "restoration &c." with me—it is
a good poem—very.— —Pray repeat my best thanks & remembrances to Mr. Gifford for all his trouble & good nature towards
me. Do not fancy me laid up from the beginning of this scrawl—I
tell you the accident for want of better to say;—but it is over—and
I am only wondering what the deuce was the matter with me—
—I have lately been all over the Bernese Alps—& their lakes—I
think many of the scenes—(some of which were not usually frequented by the English—) finer than Chamouni—which I visited
some time before.— —I have been to Clarens again—& crossed
the mountains behind it—of this tour I kept a short journal for
Mrs. Leigh which I sent yesterday in three letters—it is not at all
for perusal—but if you like to hear about the romantic part—she
will I dare say show you what touches upon the rocks &c.—but
it has not—nor can have anything to do with publication.— —
"Christabel"—I won't have you sneer at Christabel—it is a fine
wild poem.—Mr. H[obhouse] tells me you employed the power
of Attorney to some purpose against Cawthorn;—he deserved
no better—& had fair notice—I regret having made anyone
suffer—but it was his own choice. Keep a watch over him still.—
—M[adam]e de Staël wishes to see the Antiquary & I am going
to take it to her tomorrow;—she has made Coppet as agreeable as
society and talent can make any place on earth

yrs. ever

B

TO AUGUSTA LEIGH   [*Diodati—Geneva Sept. 8th. 1816*]

My dearest Augusta—By two opportunities of private conveyance—I have sent answers to your letter delivered by Mr.
H[obhouse].— —S[crope] is on his return to England—& may
probably arrive before this.—He is charged with a few packets of
seals—necklaces—balls &c.—& I know not what—formed of
Chrystals—Agates—and other stones—*all of* & *from Mont Blanc*

bought & brought by me on & from the spot—expressly for you
to divide among yourself and the children—including also your
niece Ada, for whom I selected a ball (of Granite—a soft substance
by the way—but the only one there) wherewithall to roll & play—
when she is old enough—and mischievous enough—and moreover
a Chrystal necklace—and anything else you may like to add for
her—the Love!— —The rest are for you—& the Nursery—but
particularly Georgiana—who has sent me a very nice letter.—I
hope Scrope will carry them all safely—as he promised— —There
are seals & all kinds of fooleries—pray—like them—for they
come from a very curious place (nothing like it hardly in all I ever
saw)—to say nothing of the giver.— —And so—Lady B[yron]
has been "kind to you" you tell me—"very kind"—umph—it is as
well she should be kind to some of us—and I am glad she has the
heart & the discernment to be still *your* friend—you was ever so
to her.—I heard the other day—that she was very unwell—I was
shocked enough—and sorry enough—God knows—but never
mind;—H[obhouse] tells me however that she is *not* ill—that
she *had* been indisposed—but is better & well to do.—this is a
relief.— —As for me I am in good health—& fair—though very
unequal—spirits—but for all that—she—or rather—the Separation—has broken my heart—I feel as if an Elephant had trodden
on it—I am convinced I shall never get over it—but I try.— —I
had enough before I ever knew her and more than enough—but
time & agitation had done something for me; but this last wreck
has affected me very differently,—if it were *acutely*—it would not
signify—but it is not that,—I breathe lead.— —While the storm
lasted & you were all pressing & comforting me with condemna-
tion in Piccadilly—it was bad enough—& violent enough—but it
is worse now.—I have neither strength nor spirits—nor inclination
to carry me through anything which will clear my brain or lighten
my heart.—I mean to cross the Alps at the end of this month—
and go—God knows where—by Dalmatia—up to the Arnauts
again—if nothing better can be done;—I have still a world before
me—this—or the next.— —H[obhouse] has told me all the
strange stories in circulation of me & mine;—*not* true,—I have
been in some danger on the lake—(near Meillerie) but nothing
to speak of; and as to all these "mistresses"—Lord help me—I

have had but one.—Now—don't scold—but what could I do?—a
foolish girl—in spite of all I could say or do—would come after
me—or rather went before me—for I found her here—and I have
had all the plague possible to persuade her to go back again—but
at last she went.—Now—dearest—I do most truly tell thee—that I
could not help this—that I did all I could to prevent it—& have at
last put an end to it.—I am not in love—nor have any love left for
any,—but I could not exactly play the Stoic with a woman—who
had scrambled eight hundred miles to unphilosophize me—besides
I had been regaled of late with so many "two courses and a *desert*"
(Alas!) of aversion—that I was fain to take a little love (if pressed
particularly) by way of novelty.— —And now you know all that
I know of that matter—& it is over. Pray—write—I have heard
nothing since your last—at least a month or five weeks ago.— —I
go out very little—except into the *air*—and on journeys—and
on the water—and to Coppet—where Me. de Stael has been particularly kind & friendly towards me—& (I hear) fought battles
without number in my very indifferent cause.—It has (they say)
made quite as much noise on this as the other side of "La Manche"
—Heaven knows why—but I seem destined to set people by the
ears.— —Don't hate me—but believe me ever

yrs. most affectly.

B

TO AUGUSTA LEIGH   *Ouchy. Sept. 17. 1816*

My dearest Augusta,—I am thus far on my way to the Bernese
Alps & the Grindenwald, and the *Yung frau* (that is the "Wild
woman" being interpreted—as it is so perverse a mountain that no
other sex would suit it), which journey may occupy me eight days
or so, and then it is my intention to return to Geneva, preparatory
to passing the Simplon—

Continue to direct as usual to Geneva. I have lately written to
you several letters (3 or 4 by post and two by hand) and I have received all yours very safely. I rejoice to have heard that you are well.
You have been in London too lately, & H[obhouse] tells me that
at your levée he generally found Ld. F. Bentinck—pray why is that

fool so often a visitor? is he in love with you? I have recently broken through my resolution of not speaking to you of Lady B[yron]—but do not on that account name her to me. It is a relief—a partial relief to me to talk of her sometimes to you—but it would be none to hear of her. *Of* her you are to judge for yourself, but do not altogether forget that she has destroyed your brother. Whatever my faults might or may have been—*She*—was not the person marked out by providence to be their avenger. One day or another her conduct will recoil on her own head; *not* through *me*, for my feelings towards her are not those of Vengeance, but—mark—if she does not end miserably *tot ou tard*. She may think—talk—or act as she will, and by any process of cold reasoning and jargon of "duty & acting for the best" &c., &c., impose upon her own feelings & those of others for a time—but woe unto her—the wretchedness she has brought upon the man to whom she has been everything evil <except in one respect> will flow back into its fountain. I may thank the strength of my constitution that has enabled me to bear all this, but those who bear the longest and the most do not suffer the least. I do not think a human being could endure more mental torture than that woman has directly & indirectly inflicted upon me—within the present year.

She has (for a time at least) separated me from my child—& from you—but I turn from the subject for the present.

To-morrow I repass Clarens & Vevey; if in the new & more extended tour I am making, anything that I think may please you occurs, I will detail it.

Scrope has by this time arrived with my little presents for you and yours & Ada. I still hope to be able to see you next Spring, perhaps you & one or two of the children could be spared some time next year for a little tour *here* or in France with me for a month or two. I think I could make it pleasing to you, & it should be no expense to L[eigh] or to yourself. Pray think of this hint. You have no idea how very beautiful great part of this country is—and *women* and *children* traverse it with ease and expedition. I would return from any distance at any time to see you, and come to England for you; and when you consider the chances against our—but I won't relapse into the dismals and anticipate long absences—

The great obstacle would be that you are so admirably yoked
—and necessary as a housekeeper—and a letter writer—& a place-
hunter to that very helpless gentleman your Cousin, that I suppose
the usual self-love of an elderly person would interfere between
you & any scheme of recreation or relaxation, for however short
a period.

What a fool I was to marry—and *you* not very wise—my dear—
we might have lived so single and so happy—as old maids and
bachelors; I shall never find any one like you—nor you (vain as it
may seem) like me. We are just formed to pass our lives together,
and therefore—we—at least—I—am by a crowd of circumstances
removed from the only being who could ever have loved me, or
whom I can unmixedly feel attached to.

Had you been a Nun—and I a Monk—that we might have
talked through a grate instead of across the sea—no matter—my
voice and my heart are

ever thine—

B

Alpine Journal

TO AUGUSTA LEIGH   *Clarens. Septr. 18th. 1816*

Yesterday September 17th. 1816—I set out (with H[obhouse]) on
an excursion of some days to the Mountains.—I shall keep a short
journal of each day's progress for my Sister Augusta—

Sept. 17th.—

Rose at 5.—left Diodati about seven—in one of the country
carriages—(a Charaban)—our servants on horseback—weather
very fine—the Lake calm and clear—Mont Blanc—and the Ai-
guille of Argentière both very distinct—the borders of the Lake
beautiful—reached Lausanne before Sunset—stopped & slept at
Ouchy.—H[obhouse] went to dine with a Mr. Okeden—I remained at our Caravansera (though invited to the house of H's
friend—too lazy or tired—or something else to go) and wrote a
letter to Augusta—Went to bed at nine—sheets damp—swore and
stripped them off & flung them—Heaven knows where—wrapt

myself up in the blankets—and slept like a Child of a month's existence—till 5 o Clock of

Septr. 18th.

Called by Berger (my Courier who acts as Valet for a day or two—the learned Fletcher being left in charge of Chattels at Diodati) got up—H[obhouse] walked on before—a mile from Lausanne—the road overflowed by the lake—got on horseback & rode—till within a mile of Vevey—the Colt young but went very well—overtook H. & resumed the carriage which is an open one—stopped at Vevey two hours (the second time I have visited it) walked to the Church—view from the Churchyard superb—within it General Ludlow (the Regicide's) monument—black marble—long inscription—Latin—but simple—particularly the latter part—in which his wife (Margaret de Thomas) records her long—her tried—and unshaken affection—he was an Exile *two and thirty years*—one of the King's (Charles's) Judges—a fine fellow.—I remember reading his memoirs in January 1815 (at Halnaby—) the first part of them very amusing—the latter less so,—I little thought at the time of their perusal by me of seeing his tomb—near him Broughton (who read King Charles's sentence to Charles Stuart)—is buried with a *queer* and rather *cunting*   but still a Republican epitaph——Ludlow's house shown—it retains still his inscription "Omne Solum forte patria"—Walked down to the Lake side—servants—Carriage—saddle horses—all set off and left us plantés la by some mistake—and we walked on after them towards Clarens—H[obhouse] ran on before and overtook them at last—arrived the second time (1st time was by water) at Clarens beautiful Clarens!—went to Chillon through Scenery worthy of I know not whom—went over the Castle of Chillon again—on our return met an English party in a carriage—a lady in it fast asleep!—fast asleep in the most anti-narcotic spot in the world—excellent—I remember at Chamouni—in the very eyes of Mont Blanc—hearing another woman—English also—exclaim to her party—"did you ever see any thing more *rural*"—as if it was Highgate or Hampstead—or Brompton—or Hayes.—"*Rural*" quotha!—Rocks—pines—torrents—Glaciers—Clouds—and Summits of eternal snow far above them—and "*Rural!*" I did not know the thus exclaiming fair one—but she was a—very good kind of a woman.— —After a slight & short dinner—we visited the Chateau de Clarens—an English woman has rented it recently—(it was not let when I saw it first) the roses are gone with their Summer—the family out—but the servants desired us to walk over the interior—saw on the table of the saloon—Blair's sermons—and somebody else's (I forgot who's—) sermons—and a set of noisy children—saw all worth seeing and then descended to the "Bosquet de Julie" &c. &c.—our Guide full of *Rousseau*—whom he is eternally confounding with *St. Preux*—and mixing the man and the book—on the steps of a cottage in the village—I saw a young *paysanne*—beautiful as Julie herself—went again as far as Chillon to revisit the little torrent from the hill behind it—Sunset—reflected in the lake—have to get up at 5 tomorrow to cross the mountains on horseback— carriage to be sent round—lodged at my old Cottage—hospitable & comfortable—tired with a longish ride—on the Colt—and the subsequent jolting of the Charaban—and my scramble in the hot sun—shall go to bed—thinking of you dearest Augusta.— — Mem.—The Corporal who showed the wonders of Chillon was as drunk as Blucher—and (to my mind) as great a man.—He was *deaf* also—and thinking every one else so—roared out the legends of the Castle so fearfully that H[obhouse] got out of humour— however we saw all things from the Gallows to the Dungeon (the *Potence* & the *Cachets*) and returned to Clarens with more freedom than belonged to the 15th. Century.— —At Clarens—the only book (except the Bible) a translation of *"Cecilia"* (Miss Burney's *Cecilia*) and the owner of the Cottage had also called her dog (a fat Pug *ten* years old—and hideous as *Tip*) after Cecilia's (or rather Delville's) dog—Fidde—

Septr. 19th.

Rose at 5—ordered the carriage round.—Crossed the mountains to Montbovon on horseback—and on Mules—and by dint of scrambling on foot also,—the whole route beautiful as a *Dream* and now to me almost as indistinct,—I am so tired—for though healthy I have not the strength I possessed but a few years ago.—At Mont Davant we breakfasted—afterwards on a steep ascent— dismounted—tumbled down & cut a finger open—the baggage

also got loose and fell down a ravine, till stopped by a large tree—
swore—recovered baggage—horse tired & dropping—mounted
Mule—at the approach of the summit of Dent Jamant—dismounted again with H. & all the party.—Arrived at a lake in the
very nipple of the bosom of the Mountain.—left our quadrupeds
with a Shepherd—& ascended further—came to some snow in
patches—upon which my forehead's perspiration fell like rain
making the same dints as in a sieve—the chill of the wind & the
snow turned me giddy—but I scrambled on & upwards— *H*. went
to the highest *pinnacle*—I did not—but paused within a few yards
(at an opening of the Cliff)—in coming down the Guide tumbled three times—I fell a laughing & tumbled too—the descent
luckily soft though steep & slippery—H. also fell—but nobody
hurt. The whole of the Mountain superb—the shepherd on a
very steep & high cliff playing upon his *pipe*—very different from
Arcadia—(where I saw the pastors with a long Musquet instead
of a Crook—and pistols in their Girdles)—our Swiss Shepherd's
pipe was sweet—& his time agreeable—saw a cow strayed—told
that they often break their necks on & over the crags—descended
to Montbovon—pretty scraggy village with a wild river—and a
wooden bridge.—H. went to fish—caught one—our carriage
not come—our horses mules &c knocked up—ourselves fatigued—(but so much the better—I shall sleep). The view from the
highest point of today's journey comprized on one side the greatest
part of Lake Leman—on the other—the valleys & mountains of
the Canton Fribourg—and an immense plain with the Lakes
of Neufchatel & Morat—and all which the borders of these and of
the Lake of Geneva inherit—we had both sides of the Jura before
us in one point of view, with Alps in plenty.—In passing a ravine—
the Guide recommended strenuously a quickening of pace—as the
stones fall with great rapidity & occasional damage—the advice
is excellent—but like most good advice impracticable—the road
being so rough in this precise point—that neither mules nor
mankind—nor horses—can make any violent progress.—Passed
without any fractures or menace thereof.—The music of the Cows'
bells (for their wealth like the Patriarchs is cattle) in the pastures
(which reach to a height far above any mountains in Britain—)
and the Shepherds' shouting to us from crag to crag & playing

on their reeds where the steeps appeared almost inaccessible, with the surrounding scenery—realized all that I have ever heard or imagined of a pastoral existence—much more so than Greece or Asia Minor—for there we are a little too much of the sabre & musquet order—and if there is a Crook in one hand, you are sure to see a gun in the other—but this was pure and unmixed—solitary—savage and patriarchal—the effect I cannot describe—as we went they played the "Ranz des Vaches" and other airs by way of farewell.—I have lately repeopled my mind with Nature.

Septr. 20th.

Up at 6—off at 8—the whole of this days journey at an average of between from two thousand seven hundred to three thousand feet above the level of the Sea. This valley the longest—narrowest—& considered one of the finest of the Alps— —little traversed by travellers—saw the Bridge of La Roche—the bed of the river very low & deep between immense rocks & rapid as anger—a man & mule said to have tumbled over without damage—(the mule was lucky at any rate—unless I knew the *man* I should be loth to pronounce *him* fortunate).—The people looked free & happy and *rich* (which last implies neither of the former) the cows superb—a Bull nearly leapt into the Charaban—"agreeable companion in a postchaise"—Goats & Sheep very thriving—a mountain with enormous Glaciers to the right—the Kletsgerberg—further on—the Hockthorn—nice names—so soft—Hockthorn I believe very lofty & craggy—patched with snow only—no Glaciers on it—but some good epaulettes of clouds.—Past the boundaries— out of Vaud—& into Bern Canton—French exchanged for a bad German—the district famous for Cheese—liberty—property—& no taxes.—H. went to fish—caught none—strolled to river—saw a boy [and] a kid—kid followed him like a dog—kid could not get over a fence & bleated piteously—tried myself to help kid— but nearly overset both self & kid into the river.—Arrived here about six in the evening—nine o clock—going to bed—H. in next room—knocked his head against the door—and exclaimed of course against doors—not tired today—but hope to sleep nevertheless—women gabbling below—read a French translation of Schiller—Good Night—Dearest Augusta.— —

Septr. 21st.

Off early—the valley of Simmenthal as before—entrance to the plain of Thoun very narrow—high rocks—wooded to the top—river—new mountains—with fine Glaciers—Lake of Thoun—extensive plain with a girdle of Alps—walked down to the Chateau de Schadau—view along the lake—crossed the river in a boat rowed by women—*women* [went?] right for the first time in my recollection.—Thoun a pretty town—the whole day's journey Alpine & proud.—

Septr. 22d.

Left Thoun in a boat which carried us the length of the lake in three hours—the lake small—but the banks fine—rocks down to the water's edge.—Landed at Neuhause—passed Interlachen—entered upon a range of scenes beyond all description—or previous conception.—Passed a rock—inscription—2 brothers—one murdered the other—just the place fit for it.—After a variety of windings came to an enormous rock—Girl with fruit—very pretty—blue eyes—good teeth—very fair—long but good features—reminded me of Fy. bought some of her pears—and patted her upon the cheek the expression of her face very mild—but good—and not at all coquettish.—Arrived at the foot of the Mountain (the Yung-frau—i.e. the Maiden) Glaciers—torrents—one of these torrents *nine hundred feet* in height of visible descent—lodge at the Curate's—set out to see the Valley—heard an Avalanche fall—like thunder—saw Glacier—enormous—Storm came on—thunder—lightning—hail—all in perfection—and beautiful—I was on horseback—Guide wanted to carry my cane—I was going to give it him when I recollected that it was a Swordstick and I thought that the lightning might be attracted towards him—kept it myself—a good deal encumbered with it & my cloak—as it was too heavy for a whip—and the horse was stupid—& stood still every other peal. Got in—not very wet—the Cloak being staunch—H. wet through—H. took refuge in cottage—sent man—umbrella—& cloak (from the Curate's when I arrived—) after him.—Swiss Curate's house—very good indeed—much better than most English Vicarages—it is immediately opposite the torrent I spoke of—the torrent is in shape curving over the rock—like the *tail* of a white horse streaming in the wind—such as it might be conceived would be that of the "*pale* horse" on which *Death* is mounted in the Apocalypse.—It is neither mist nor water but a something between both—it's immense height (nine hundred feet) gives it a wave—a curve—a spreading here—a condensation there—wonderful—& indescribable.—I think upon the whole—that this day has been better than any of this present excursion.—

Septr. 23d.

Before ascending the mountain—went to the torrent (7 in the morning) again—the Sun upon it forming a *rainbow* of the lower part of all colours—but principally purple and gold—the bow moving as you move—I never saw anything like this—it is only in the Sunshine.— —Ascended the Wengren [sic] Mountain.— —at noon reached a valley near the summit—left the horses—took off my coat & went to the summit—7000 feet (English feet) above the level of the sea—and about 5000 above the valley we left in the morning—on one side our view comprized the *Yung frau* with all her glaciers—then the *Dent d'Argent*—shining like truth— then the *little Giant* (the Kleiner EIgher) & the great Giant (the Grosser EIgher) and last not least—the Wetterhorn.—The height of the Yung frau is 13000 feet above the sea—and 11000 above the valley—she is the highest of this range,—heard the Avalanches falling every five minutes nearly—as if God was pelting the Devil down from Heaven with snow balls—from where we stood on the *Wengren* [sic] Alp—we had all these in view on one side—on the other the clouds rose from the opposite valley curling up perpendicular precipices—like the foam of the Ocean of Hell during a Springtide—it was white & sulphery—and immeasurably deep in appearance—the side we ascended was (of course) not of so precipitous a nature—but on arriving at the summit we looked down the other side upon a boiling sea of cloud—dashing against the crags on which we stood (these crags on one side quite perpendicular);—staid a quarter of an hour—began to descend—quite clear from cloud on that side of the mountain—in passing the masses of snow—I made a snowball & pelted H. with it—got down to our horses again—eat something—remounted—heard the Avalanches

still—came to a morass—H. dismounted—H. got well over—I
tried to pass my horse over—the horse sunk up [to] the chin—&
of course he & I were in the mud together—bemired all over—but
not hurt—laughed & rode on.—Arrived at the Grindenwald—
dined—mounted again & rode to the higher Glacier—twilight
—but distinct—very fine Glacier—like a *frozen hurricane*—Starlight—beautiful—but a devil of a path—never mind—got safe
in—a little lightning—but the whole of the day as fine in point of
weather—as the day on which Paradise was made.—Passed *whole
woods of withered pines—all withered*—trunks stripped & barkless—branches lifeless—done by a single winter—their appearance
reminded me of me & my family.—

Septr. 24th.

Set out at seven—up at five—passed the black Glacier—the
Mountain Wetterhorn on the right—crossed the Scheideck mountain—came to the Rose Glacier—said to be the largest & finest
in Switzerland.—*I* think the Bossons Glacier at Chamouni—as
fine—H. does not—came to the Reichenback waterfall—two
hundred feet high—halted to rest the horses—arrived in the valley
of Oberhasli—rain came on—drenched a little—only 4 hours rain
however lii 8 days came to Lake of Brientz—then to town of Brientz—changed—H. hurt his head against door.—In the evening
four Swiss Peasant Girls of Oberhasli came & sang the airs of their
country—two of the voices beautiful—the tunes also—they sing
too that *Tyrolese air* & song which you love—Augusta—because
I love it—& I love because you love it— they are still singing—
Dearest—you do not know how I should have liked this—were
you with me—the airs are so wild & original & at the same time of
great sweetness.— —The singing is over—but below stairs I hear
the notes of a Fiddle which bode no good to my nights rest.—The
Lord help us!—I shall go down & see the dancing.—

Septr. 25th.

The whole town of Brientz were apparently gathered together in
the rooms below—pretty music—& excellent Waltzing—none but
peasants—the dancing much better than in England—the English
can't Waltz—never could—nor ever will.—One man with his

pipe in his mouth—but danced as well as the others—some other dances in pairs—and in fours—and very good.— —I went to bed but the revelry continued below late & early.—Brientz but a village.— —Rose early.—Embarked on the Lake of Brientz.—Rowed by women in a long boat—one very young & very pretty—seated myself by her—& began to row also—presently we put to shore & another woman jumped in—it seems it is the custom here for the boats to be *manned by women*—for of five men & three women in our bark—all the women took an oar—and but one man.— —Got to Interlachen in three hours—pretty Lake—not so large as that of Thoun.—Dined at Interlachen—Girl gave me some flowers—& made me a speech in German—of which I know nothing—I do not know whether the speech was pretty but as the woman was—I hope so.—Saw another—very pretty too—and *tall* which I prefer—I hate short women—for more reasons than one.—Reembarked on the Lake of Thoun—fell asleep part of the way—sent our horses round—found people on the shore blowing up a rock with gunpowder—they blew it up near our boat—only telling us a minute before—mere stupidity—but they might have broke our noddles.—Got to Thoun in the Evening—the weather has been tolerable the whole day—but as the wild part of our tour is finished, it don't matter to us—in all the desirable part—we have been most lucky in warmth & clearness of Atmosphere—for which "Praise we the Lord."— —

Septr. 26th.

Being out of the mountains my journal must be as flat as my journey.— —From Thoun to Bern good road—hedges—villages—industry—prosperity—and all sorts of tokens of insipid civilization.— —From Bern to Fribourg.—Different Canton—Catholics—passed a field of Battle—Swiss beat the French—in one of the late wars against the French Republic.—Bought a dog—a very ugly dog—but "*tres mechant*". this was his great recommendation in the owner's eyes & mine—for I mean him to watch the carriage—he hath no tail—& is called "Mutz"—which signifies "*Short-tail*"—he is apparently of the Shepherd dog genus!—The greater part of this tour has been on horseback—on foot—and on mule;—the Filly (which is one of two young horses I bought of the

Baron de Vincy) carried me very well—she is young and as quiet as anything of her sex can be—very goodtempered—and perpetually neighing—when she wants any thing—which is every five minutes—I have called her *Biche*—because her manners are not unlike a little dog's—but she is a very tame—pretty childish quadruped.—

Septr. 28th. [27th.]

Saw the tree planted in honour of the battle of Morat—340 years old—a good deal decayed.—Left Fribourg—but first saw the Cathedral—high tower—overtook the baggage of the Nuns of La Trappe who are removing to Normandy from their late abode in the Canton of Fribourg—afterwards a coach with a quantity of Nuns in it—Nuns old—proceeded along the banks of the Lake of Neufchatel—very pleasing & soft—but not so mountainous—at least the Jura not appearing so—after the Bernese Alps—reached Yverdun in the dusk—a long line of large trees on the border of the lake—fine & sombre—the Auberge nearly full—with a German Princess & suite—got rooms—we hope to reach Diodati the day after tomorrow—and I wish for a letter from you my own dearest Sis—May your sleep be soft and your dreams of me.—I am going to bed—good night.—

Septr. 29th. [28th.]

Passed through a fine & flourishing country—but not mountainous—in the evening reached Aubonne (the entrance & bridge something like that of Durham) which commands by far the fairest view of the Lake of Geneva—twilight—the Moon on the Lake—a grove on the height—and of very noble trees.—Here Tavernier (the Eastern traveller) bought (or built) the Chateau because the site resembled and equalled that of *Erivan* (a frontier city of Persia) here he finished his voyages—and I this little excursion—for I am within a few hours of Diodati—& have little more to see—& no more to say.—In the weather for this tour (of 13 days) I have been very fortunate—fortunate in a companion (Mr. H[obhous]e) fortunate in our prospects—and exempt from even the little petty accidents & delays which often render journeys in a less wild country—disappointing.—I was disposed to be pleased—I am a lover of Nature—and an Admirer of Beauty—I

can bear fatigue—& welcome privation—and have seen some of
the noblest views in the world.—But in all this—the recollections
of bitterness—& more especially of recent & more home desolation—which must accompany me through life—have preyed upon
me here—and neither the music of the Shepherd—the crashing of
the Avalanche—nor the torrent—the mountain—the Glacier—
the Forest—nor the Cloud—have for one moment—lightened the
weight upon my heart—nor enabled me to lose my own wretched
identity in the majesty & the power and the Glory—around—
above—& beneath me.—I am past reproaches—and there is a
time for all things—I am past the wish of vengeance—and I know
of none like for what I have suffered—but the hour will come—
when what I feel must be felt—& the— —but enough.— —To
you—dearest Augusta—I send—and *for* you—I have kept this
record of what I have seen & felt.—Love me as you are beloved
by me.— —

Manfred I, ii

The Mountain of the Jungfrau.—Time, Morning.—
MANFRED alone upon the Cliffs.

MAN. The spirits I have raised abandon me—
 The spells which I have studied baffle me—
 The remedy I reck'd of tortured me;
 I lean no more on super-human aid,
 It hath no power upon the past, and for
 The future, till the past be gulf'd in darkness,
 It is not of my search.—My mother Earth!
 And thou fresh breaking Day, and you, ye Mountains,
 Why are ye beautiful? I cannot love ye.
 And thou, the bright eye of the universe,
 That openest over all, and unto all
 Art a delight—thou shin'st not on my heart.
 And you, ye crags, upon whose extreme edge
 I stand, and on the torrent's brink beneath
 Behold the tall pines dwindled as to shrubs
 In dizziness of distance; when a leap,
 A stir, a motion, even a breath, would bring
 My breast upon its rocky bosom's bed
 To rest for ever—wherefore do I pause?
 I feel the impulse—yet I do not plunge;
 I see the peril—yet do not recede;
 And my brain reels—and yet my foot is firm:
 There is a power upon me which withholds
 And makes it my fatality to live;
 If it be life to wear within myself
 This barrenness of spirit, and to be
 My own soul's sepulchre, for I have ceased
 To justify my deeds unto myself—
 The last infirmity of evil. Ay,
 Thou winged and cloud-cleaving minister,

          [An eagle passes
 Whose happy flight is highest into heaven,
 Well may'st thou swoop so near me—I should be

Thy prey, and gorge thine eaglets; thou art gone
Where the eye cannot follow thee; but thine
Yet pierces downward, onward, or above
With a pervading vision.—Beautiful!
How beautiful is all this visible world!
How glorious in its action and itself;
But we, who name ourselves its sovereigns, we,
Half dust, half deity, alike unfit
To sink or soar, with our mix'd essence make
A conflict of its elements, and breathe
The breath of degradation and of pride,
Contending with low wants and lofty will
Till our mortality predominates,
And men are—what they name not to themselves,
And trust not to each other. Hark! the note,

           [*The Shepherd's pipe in the distance is heard*

The natural music of the mountain reed—
For here the patriarchal days are not
A pastoral fable—pipes in the liberal air,
Mix'd with the sweet bells of the sauntering herd;
My soul would drink those echoes.—Oh, that I were
The viewless spirit of a lovely sound,
A living voice, a breathing harmony,
A bodiless enjoyment—born and dying
With the blest tone which made me!

           Enter from below a CHAMOIS HUNTER

CHAMOIS HUNTER.   Even so

This way the chamois leapt: her nimble feet
Have baffled me; my gains to-day will scarce
Repay my break-neck travail.—What is here?
Who seems not of my trade, and yet hath reach'd
A height which none even of our mountaineers,
Save our best hunters, may attain: his garb
Is goodly, his mien manly, and his air
Proud as a free-born peasant's, at this distance.—
I will approach him nearer.

MAN. [*not perceiving the other*]. To be thus—

Grey-hair'd with anguish, like these blasted pines,
Wrecks of a single winter, barkless, branchless,
A blighted trunk upon a cursed root,
Which but supplies a feeling to decay—
And to be thus, eternally but thus,
Having been otherwise! Now furrow'd o'er
With wrinkles, plough'd by moments, not by years;
And hours—all tortured into ages—hours
Which I outlive!—Ye toppling crags of ice!
Ye avalanches, whom a breath draws down
In mountainous o'erwhelming, come and crush me—
I hear ye momently above, beneath,
Crash with a frequent conflict; but ye pass,
And only fall on things which still would live;
On the young flourishing forest, or the hut
And hamlet of the harmless villager.

C. HUN. The mists begin to rise from up the valley;
I'll warn him to descend, or he may chance
To lose at once his way and life together.

MAN. The mists boil up around the glaciers; clouds
Rise curling fast beneath me, white and sulphury,
Like foam from the roused ocean of deep Hell,
Whose every wave breaks on a living shore,
Heaped with the damn'd like pebbles.—I am giddy.

C. HUN. I must approach him cautiously; if near,
A sudden step will startle him, and he
Seems tottering already.

MAN.   Mountains have fallen,
Leaving a gap in the clouds, and with the shock
Rocking their Alpine brethren; filling up
The ripe green valleys with destruction's splinters;
Damming the rivers with a sudden dash,
Which crush'd the waters into mist, and made
Their fountains find another channel—thus,
Thus, in its old age, did Mount Rosenberg—
Why stood I not beneath it?

C. HUN.   Friend! have a care,
Your next step may be fatal!—for the love

Of him who made you, stand not on that brink!

MAN. [*not hearing him*]. Such would have been for me a
    fitting tomb;
My bones had then been quiet in their depth;
They had not then been strewn upon the rocks
For the wind's pastime—as thus—thus they shall be—
In this one plunge.—Farewell, ye opening heavens
Look not upon me thus reproachfully—
Ye were not meant for me—Earth! take these atoms!
      [*As* MANFRED *is in act to spring from the cliff,*
       the CHAMOIS HUNTER *seizes and retains him*
         with a sudden grasp]

C. HUN. Hold, madman!—though aweary of thy life,
Stain not our pure vales with thy guilty blood.—
Away with me—I will not quit my hold.

MAN. I am most sick at heart—nay, grasp me not—
I am all feebleness—the mountains whirl
Spinning around me—I grow blind—What art thou?

C. HUN. I'll answer that anon.—Away with me—
The clouds grow thicker—there—now lean on me—
Place your foot here—here, take this staff, and cling
A moment to that shrub—now give me your hand,
And hold fast by my girdle—softly—well—
The Chalet will be gained within an hour—
Come on, we'll quickly find a surer footing,
And something like a pathway, which the torrent
Hath wash'd since winter.—Come, 'tis bravely done—
You should have been a hunter.—Follow me.
      [*As they descend the rocks with difficulty, the*
        scene closes]

ITALY

and now, fair Italy!
Thou art the garden of the world, the home
Of all Art yields, and Nature can decree;
Even in thy desart, what is like to thee?

CHILDE HAROLD'S PILGRIMAGE IV, 26

Beppo, 41–46

41

With all its sinful doings, I must say,
    That Italy's a pleasant place to me,
Who love to see the Sun shine every day,
    And vines (not nailed to walls) from tree to tree
Festooned, much like the back scene of a play,
    Or melodrame, which people flock to see,
When the first act is ended by a dance
In vineyards copied from the South of France.

42

I like on Autumn evenings to ride out,
    Without being forced to bid my groom be sure
My cloak is round his middle strapped about,
    Because the skies are not the most secure;
I know too that, if stopped upon my route,
    Where the green alleys windingly allure,
Reeling with *grapes* red waggons choke the way,—
In England 'twould be dung, dust, or a dray.

43

I also like to dine on becaficas,
    To see the Sun set, sure he'll rise to-morrow,
Not through a misty morning twinkling weak as
    A drunken man's dead eye in maudlin sorrow,
But with all Heaven t'himself; the day will break as
    Beauteous as cloudless, nor be forced to borrow
That sort of farthing candlelight which glimmers
Where reeking London's smoky cauldron simmers.

44

I love the language, that soft bastard Latin,
    Which melts like kisses from a female mouth,
And sounds as if it should be writ on satin,
    With syllables which breathe of the sweet South,

And gentle liquids gliding all so pat in,
    That not a single accent seems uncouth,
Like our harsh northern whistling, grunting guttural,
Which we're obliged to hiss, and spit, and sputter all.

          45
I like the women too (forgive my folly!),
    From the rich peasant cheek of ruddy bronze,
And large black eyes that flash on you a volley
    Of rays that say a thousand things at once,
To the high Dama's brow, more melancholy,
    But clear, and with a wild and liquid glance,
Heart on her lips, and soul within her eyes,
Soft as her clime, and sunny as her skies.

          46
Eve of the land which still is Paradise!
    Italian Beauty didst thou not inspire
Raphael, who died in thy embrace, and vies
    With all we know of Heaven, or can desire,
In what he hath bequeathed us?—in what guise,
    Though flashing from the fervour of the Lyre,
Would *words* describe thy past and present glow,
While yet Canova can create below?

MILAN

I hate inconstancy—I loathe, detest,
   Abhor, condemn, abjure the mortal made
Of such quicksilver clay that in his breast
   No permanent foundation can be laid;
Love, constant love, has been my constant guest,
   And yet last night, being at a masquerade,
I saw the prettiest creature, fresh from Milan,
Which gave me some sensations like a villain.

But soon Philosophy came to my aid,
   And whispered, "Think of every sacred tie!"
"I will, my dear Philosophy!" I said,
   "But then her teeth, and then, oh, Heaven! her eye!
I'll just inquire if she be wife or maid,
   Or neither—out of curiosity."
"Stop!" cried Philosophy, with air so Grecian
(Though she was masqued then as a fair Venetian)

DON JUAN II, 209–210

My dearest Augusta—You see I have got to Milan.—We came by the Simplon—escaping all perils of precipices and robbers—of which last there was some talk & apprehension—a chain of English carriages having been stopped near Cesto a few weeks ago—& handsomely pilfered of various chattels.—We were not molested— —The Simplon as you know—is the most superb of all possible routes;—so I shall not describe it—I also navigated the Lago Maggiore—and went over the Borromean Islands—the latter are fine but too artificial—the lake itself is beautiful—as indeed is the whole country from Geneva hither—and the Alpine part most magnificent.— —Close to Milan is the beginning of an unfinished triumphal arch—for Napoleon—so beautiful as to make one regret it's non-completion.—As we only reached Milan last night—I can say little about it—but will write again in a few days.—The Jerseys are here—Made. de Stael is gone to Paris (or going) from Coppet.—I was more there than elsewhere during my stay at Diodati—and she has been particularly kind & friendly towards me the whole time.—When you write—address to *Geneva*—still—Poste *restante*—and my banker—(Monsr. Hentsch) will forward your letters,—I have written to you so often lately—that you will not regret the brevity of this.—I hope that you received safely my presents for the children (by Scrope) and that you also have (by the post) a little journal of a journey in & on the Alps which I sent you early this month—having kept it on purpose for *you.*—

ever my own dearest yrs. most

B

My dearest Augusta—I have been at Churches, Theatres, libraries, and picture galleries. The Cathedral is noble, the theatre grand, the library excellent, and the galleries I know nothing about—except as far as liking one picture out of a thousand. What has delighted me most is a manuscript collection (preserved in the

Ambrosian library), of original love-letters and verses of Lucretia
de Borgia & Cardinal Bembo; and a lock of hair—so long—and
fair & beautiful—and the letters so pretty & so loving that it makes
one wretched not to have been born sooner to have at least seen
her. And pray what do you think is one of her *signatures?*—why
this + a Cross—which she says "is to stand for her name &c."
Is not this amusing? I suppose you know that she was a famous
beauty, & famous for the use she made of it; & that she was the
love of this same Cardinal Bembo (besides a story about her papa
Pope Alexander & her brother Cæsar Borgia—which some people
don't believe—& others do), and that after all she ended with
being Duchess of Ferrara, and an excellent mother & wife also; so
good as to be quite an example. All this may or may not be, but
the hair & the letters are so beautiful that I have done nothing but
pore over them, & have made the librarian promise me a copy of
some of them; and I mean to get some of the hair if I can. The
verses are Spanish—the letters Italian—some signed—others with
a cross—but all in her own hand-writing.

I am so hurried, & so sleepy, but so anxious to send you even
a few lines my dearest Augusta, that you will forgive me troubling
you so often; and I shall write again soon; but I have sent you so
much lately, that you will have too many perhaps. *A thousand loves*
to *you* from *me*—which is very generous for I only ask *one* in return

Ever dearest thine

B

TO JOHN MURRAY   *Milan. Novr. 1st. 1816*

Dear Sir—I have recently written to you rather frequently—
but without any late answer.—It is of no great importance.—Mr.
Hobhouse & myself set out for Venice in a few days—but you had
better still address to me at Mr. Hentsch's Banquier Geneva—he
will forward your letters.— —I do not know whether I mentioned
to you some time ago—that I had parted with the Dr. Polidori—a
few weeks previous to my leaving Diodati. I know no great harm
of him—but he had an alacrity of getting into scrapes—& was too
young and heedless—and having enough to attend to in my own

concerns—without time to become his tutor—I thought it much better to give him his Congé.—He arrived at Milan some weeks before Mr. H. & myself.—About a week ago—in consequence of a quarrel at the theatre with an Austrian Officer—in which he was exceedingly in the wrong—he has contrived to get sent out of the territory and is gone to Florence.— —I was not present—the pit having been the scene of altercation—but on being sent for from the Cavalier Brema's box where I was quietly staring at the Ballet—I found the man of medicine begirt with grenadiers—arrested by the guard—conveyed into the guard-room—where there was much swearing in several languages.— —They were going to keep him there for the night—but on my giving my name—and answering for his apparition the next morning—he was permitted to egress.—Next day—he had an order from the government to be gone in 24 hours—and accordingly gone he is some days ago—we did what we could for him—but to no purpose—and indeed he brought it upon himself—as far as I could learn—for I was not present at the squabble itself.—I believe this is the real state of his case—and I tell it you because I believe things sometimes reach you in England—in a false or exaggerated form. We found Milan very polite and hospitable and have the same hopes of Verona & Venice.—I have filled my paper

ever yrs.

BYRON

TO THOMAS MOORE   *Verona, November 6th, 1816*

My Dear Moore,—Your letter, written before my departure from England, and addressed to me in London, only reached me recently. Since that period, I have been over a portion of that part of Europe which I had not already seen. About a month since, I crossed the Alps from Switzerland to Milan, which I left a few days ago, and am thus far on my way to Venice, where I shall probably winter. Yesterday I was on the shores of the Benacus, with his *fluctibus et fremitu*. Catullus's Sirmium has still its name and site, and is remembered for his sake: but the very heavy autumnal rains and mists prevented our quitting our route, (that is, Hobhouse and myself, who are at present voyaging together), as it was better not to see it at all than to a great disadvantage.

I found on the Benacus the same tradition of a city still visible in calm weather below the waters, which you have preserved of Lough Neagh, "When the clear, cold eve's declining." I do not know that it is authorised by records; but they tell you such a story, and say that the city was swallowed up by an earthquake. We moved to-day over the frontier to Verona, by a road suspected of thieves,—"the wise *convey* it call,"—but without molestation. I shall remain here a day or two to gape at the usual marvels,— amphitheatre, paintings, and all that time-tax of travel—though Catullus, Claudian, and Shakespeare have done more for Verona than it ever did for itself. They still pretend to show, I believe, the "tomb of all the Capulets"—we shall see.

Among many things at Milan, one pleased me particularly, viz. the correspondence (in the prettiest love-letters in the world) of Lucretia Borgia with Cardinal Bembo, (who, *you say*, made a very good cardinal,) and a lock of her hair, and some Spanish verses of hers,—the lock very fair and beautiful. I took one single hair of it as a relic, and wished sorely to get a copy of one or two of the letters; but it is prohibited; *that* I don't mind; but it was impracticable; and so I only got some of them by heart. They are kept in the Ambrosian Library, which I often visited to look them over—to the scandal of the librarian, who wanted to enlighten me with sundry valuable MSS., classical, philosophical, and pious. But I stick to the Pope's daughter, and wish myself a cardinal.

I have seen the finest parts of Switzerland, the Rhine, the Rhone, and the Swiss and Italian lakes; for the beauties of which I refer you to the Guide-book. The north of Italy is tolerably free from the English; but the south swarms with them, I am told. Madame de Stael I saw frequently at Copet, which she renders remarkably pleasant. She has been particularly kind to me. I was for some months her neighbour, in a country house called Diodati, which I had on the Lake of Geneva. My plans are very uncertain; but it is probable that you will see me in England in the spring. I have some business there. If you write to me, will you address to the care of Mons. Hentsch, Banquier, Geneva, who receives and forwards my letters. Remember me to Rogers, who wrote to me lately, with a short account of your poem, which, I trust, is near the light. He speaks of it most highly.

My health is very endurable, except that I am subject to casual giddiness and faintnesses, which is so like a fine lady, that I am rather ashamed of the disorder. When I sailed, I had a physician with me, whom, after some months of patience, I found it expedient to part with, before I left Geneva some time. On arriving at Milan, I found this gentleman in very good society, where he prospered for some weeks; but, at length, at the theatre, he quarrelled with an Austrian officer, and was sent out by the government in twenty-four hours. I was not present at his squabble; but, on hearing that he was put under arrest, I went and got him out of his confinement, but could not prevent his being sent off, which, indeed, he partly deserved, being quite in the wrong, and having begun a row for row's sake. I had preceded the Austrian government some weeks myself, in giving him his congé from Geneva. He is not a bad fellow, but very young and hot-headed, and more likely to incur diseases than to cure them. Hobhouse and myself found it useless to intercede for him. This happened some time before we left Milan. He is gone to Florence.

At Milan I saw, and was visited by, Monti, the most celebrated of the living Italian poets. He seems near sixty; in face he is like the late Cooke the actor. His frequent changes in politics have made him very unpopular as a man. I saw many more of their literati; but none whose names are well known in England, except Acerbi. I lived much with the Italians, particularly with the Marquis of Breme's family, who are very able and intelligent men, especially the Abate. There was a famous improvvisatore who held forth while I was there. His fluency astonished me; but, although I understand Italian, and speak it (with more readiness than accuracy), I could only carry off a few very common-place mythological images, and one line about Artemisia, and another about Algiers, with sixty words of an entire tragedy about Eteocles and Polynices. Some of the Italians liked him—others called his performance "seccatura" (a devilish good word, by the way) and all Milan was in controversy about him.

The state of morals in these parts is in some sort lax. A mother and son were pointed out at the theatre, as being pronounced by the Milanese world to be of the Theban dynasty—but this was all. The narrator (one of the first men in Milan) seemed to be not sufficiently scandalised by the taste or the tie. All society in Milan is carried on at the opera: they have private boxes, where they play cards, or talk, or any thing else; but (except at the Cassino) there are no open houses, or balls, &c., &c. *

The peasant girls have all very fine dark eyes, and many of them are beautiful. There are also two dead bodies in fine preservation—one Saint Carlo Boromeo at Milan; the other not a saint, but a chief, named Visconti, at Monza—both of which appeared very agreeable. In one of the Boromean isles (the Isola bella), there is a large laurel—the largest known—on which Buonaparte, staying there just before the battle of Marengo, carved with his knife the word "Battaglia". I saw the letters, now half worn out and partly erased.

Excuse this tedious letter. To be tiresome is the privilege of old age and absence; I avail myself of the latter, and the former I have anticipated. If I do not speak to you of my own affairs, it is not from want of confidence, but to spare you and myself. My day is over—what then?—I have had it. To be sure, I have shortened it; and if I had done as much by this letter, it would have been as well. But you will forgive that, if not the other faults of

Yours ever and most affectionately,

B

VENICE

Oh Venice, Venice, when thy marble walls
    Are level with the waters, there shall be
A cry of nations o'er thy sunken halls
    A loud lament along the sweeping sea!

VENICE: AN ODE, 1–4

Childe Harold's Pilgrimage IV, 1–4, 18–19

1

I stood in Venice, on the Bridge of Sighs;
A palace and a prison on each hand:
I saw from out the wave her structures rise
As from the stroke of the enchanter's wand:
A thousand years their cloudy wings expand
Around me, and a dying Glory smiles
O'er the far times, when many a subject land
Look'd to the winged Lion's marble piles,
Where Venice sate in state, thron'd on her hundred isles!

2

She looks a sea Cybele, fresh from ocean,
Rising with her tiara of proud towers
At airy distance, with majestic motion,
A ruler of the waters and their powers:
And such she was;—her daughters had their dowers
From spoils of nations, and the exhaustless East
Pour'd in her lap all gems in sparkling showers.
In purple was she robed, and of her feast
Monarchs partook, and deem'd their dignity increas'd.

3

In Venice Tasso's echoes are no more,
And silent rows the songless gondolier;
Her palaces are crumbling to the shore,
And music meets not always now the ear:
Those days are gone—but Beauty still is here.
States fall, arts fade—but Nature doth not die,
Nor yet forget how Venice once was dear,
The pleasant place of all festivity,
The revel of the earth, the masque of Italy!

4

But unto us she hath a spell beyond
Her name in story, and her long array
Of mighty shadows, whose dim forms despond
Above the dogeless city's vanish'd sway;
Ours is a trophy which will not decay
With the Rialto; Shylock and the Moor,
And Pierre, can not be swept or worn away—
The keystones of the arch! though all were o'er,
For us repeopled were the solitary shore. . . .

18

I lov'd her from my boyhood—she to me
Was as a fairy city of the heart,
Rising like water-columns from the sea,
Of joy the sojourn, and of wealth the mart;
And Otway, Radcliffe, Schiller, Shakespeare's art,
Had stamp'd her image in me, and even so,
Although I found her thus, we did not part,
Perchance even dearer in her day of woe,
Than when she was a boast, a marvel, and a show.

19

I can repeople with the past—and of
The present there is still for eye and thought,
And meditation chasten'd down, enough;
And more, it may be, than I hoped or sought;
And of the happiest moments which were wrought
Within the web of my existence, some
From thee, fair Venice! have their colours caught:
There are some feelings Time can not benumb,
Nor Torture shake, or mine would now be cold and dumb.

TO THOMAS MOORE   *Venice, November 17th, 1816*

I wrote to you from Verona the other day in my progress hither, which letter I hope you will receive. Some three years ago, or it may be more, I recollect your telling me that you had received a letter from our friend Sam, dated "On board his gondola". *My* gondola is, at this present, waiting for me on the canal; but I prefer writing to you in the house, it being autumn—and rather an English autumn than otherwise. It is my intention to remain at Venice during the winter, probably, as it has always been (next to the East) the greenest island of my imagination. It has not disappointed me; though its evident decay would, perhaps, have that effect upon others. But I have been familiar with ruins too long to dislike desolation. Besides, I have fallen in love, which, next to falling into the canal, (which would be of no use, as I can swim.) is the best or the worst thing I could do. I have got some extremely good apartments in the house of a "Merchant of Venice," who is a good deal occupied with business, and has a wife in her twenty-second year. Marianna (that is her name) is in her appearance altogether like an antelope. She has the large, black, oriental eyes, with that peculiar expression in them which is seen rarely among *Europeans*—even the Italians—and which many of the Turkish women give themselves by tinging the eyelid,—an art not known out of that country, I believe. This expression she has *naturally*,—and something more than this. In short, I cannot describe the effect of this kind of eye,—at least upon me. Her features are regular, and rather aquiline—mouth small—skin clear and soft, with a kind of hectic colour—forehead remarkably good: her hair is of the dark gloss, curl, and colour of Lady J * * 's [Jersey's]: her figure is light and pretty, and she is a famous songstress—scientifically so; her natural voice (in conversation, I mean) is very sweet; and the naiveté of the Venetian dialect is always pleasing in the mouth of a woman.

November 28.

You will perceive that my description, which was proceeding with the minuteness of a passport, has been interrupted for several days. In the meantime *
* *

December 5

Since my former dates, I do not know that I have much to add on the subject, and, luckily, nothing to take away; for I am more pleased than ever with my Venetian, and begin to feel very serious on that point—so much so, that I shall be silent. * * * * * * * * * * * *

By way of divertisement, I am studying daily, at an Armenian monastery, the Armenian language. I found that my mind wanted something craggy to break upon; and this—as the most difficult thing I could discover here for an amusement—I have chosen, to torture me into attention. It is a rich language, however, and would amply repay any one the trouble of learning it. I try, and shall go on;—but I answer for nothing, least of all for my intentions or my success. There are some very curious MSS. in the monastery, as well as books; translations also from Greek originals, now lost, and from Persian and Syriac, &c.; besides works of their own people. Four years ago the French instituted an Armenian professorship. Twenty pupils presented themselves on Monday morning, full of noble ardour, ingenuous youth, and impregnable industry. They persevered, with a courage worthy of the nation and of universal conquest, till Thursday; when *fifteen* of the *twenty* succumbed to the six-and-twentieth letter of the alphabet. It is, to be sure, a Waterloo of an Alphabet—that must be said for them. But it is so like these fellows, to do by it as they did by their sovereigns—abandon both; to parody the old rhymes, "Take a thing and give a thing"—"Take a King and give a King". They are the worst of animals, except their conquerors.

I hear that H[odgso]n is your neighbour, having a living in Derbyshire. You will find him an excellent-hearted fellow, as well as one of the cleverest; a little, perhaps, too much japanned by preferment in the church and the tuition of youth, as well as inoculated with the disease of domestic felicity, besides being over-run with fine feelings about women and *constancy* (that small change of Love, which people exact so rigidly, receive in such counterfeit coin, and repay in baser metal); but, otherwise, a very worthy man, who has lately got a pretty wife, and (I suppose) a child by this time. Pray remember me to him, and say that I know not which to envy most—his neighbourhood, him, or you.

Of Venice I shall say little. You must have seen many

descriptions; and they are most of them like. It is a poetical place; and classical, to us, from Shakespeare and Otway. I have not yet sinned against it in verse, nor do I know that I shall do so, having been tuneless since I crossed the Alps, and feeling, as yet, no renewal of the "estro". By the way, I suppose you have seen "Glenarvon". Madame de Stael lent it me to read from Copet last autumn. It seems to me that, if the authoress had written the *truth*, and nothing but the truth—the whole truth—the romance would not only have been more *romantic*, but more entertaining. As for the likeness, the picture can't be good—I did not sit long enough. When you have leisure, let me hear from and of you, believing me,

Ever and truly yours most affectionately,

B

P.S.—Oh! *your Poem*—is it out? I hope Longman has paid his thousands: but don't you do as H[orace] T[wiss]'s father did, who, having made money by a quarto tour, became a vinegar merchant; when, lo! his vinegar turned sweet (and be damned to it) and ruined him. My last letter to you (from Verona) was enclosed to Murray—

TO AUGUSTA LEIGH   *Venice. Decr. 19th. 1816*

My dearest Augusta—I wrote to you a few days ago.—Your letter of the 1st. is arrived—and you have "a *hope*" for me—it seems—what "hope"—child?—my dearest Sis. I remember a methodist preacher who on perceiving a profane grin on the faces of part of his congregation—exclaimed "no *hopes* for *them* as *laughs*" and thus it is—with us—we laugh too much for hopes—and so even let them go—I am sick of sorrow—& must even content myself as well as I can—so here goes—I won't be woeful again if I can help it.—My letter to my moral Clytemnestra required no answer—& I would rather have none—I was wretched enough when I wrote it—& had been so for many a long day & month—at present I am less so—for reasons explained in my late letter (a few days ago) and as I never pretend to *be* what I am not you may tell her if you please that I am recovering—and the reason also if you like it.—I do not agree with you about Ada—there was *equivocation* in the answer—and it shall be settled one way or the other—I wrote to Hanson to take proper steps to prevent such a removal of my daughter—and even the probability of it—you do not know the woman so well as I do—or you would perceive in her *very negative answer*—that she *does intend* to take Ada with her—if she should go abroad.— —I have heard of Murray's squabble with one of his brethren—who is an impudent impostor—and should be trounced.— —You do not say whether the *true po's* are out—I hope you like them.—You are right in saying that I like Venice—it is very much what you would imagine it—but I have no time just now for description;—the Carnival is to begin in a week—and with it the mummery of masking.— —I have not been out a great deal—but quite as much as I like—I am going out this evening—in my *cloak* & *Gondola*—there are two nice Mrs. Radcliffe words for you—and then there is the place of St. Mark—and conversaziones—and various fooleries—besides many *nau*[ghty]. indeed every body is *nau*. so much so that a lady with only one lover is not reckoned to have overstepped the modesty of marriage—that being a regular thing;—some have two—three— and so on to twenty beyond which they don't account—but they generally begin by one.— —The husbands of course belong to any body's wives—but their own.— —My present beloved—is aged two & twenty—with remarkably fine black eyes—and very regular & pretty features—figure light & pretty—hair dark—a mighty good singer—as they all are—she is married (of course) & has one child—a girl.—Her temper very good—(as you know it had need to be) and lively—she is a Venetian by birth—& was never further from Venice than Milan in her days—her lord is about five years older than me—an exceeding good kind of a man.—That amatory appendage called by us a lover—is here denominated variously—sometimes an "Amoroso" (which is the same thing) and sometimes a Cavaliero servente—which I need not tell you—is a serving Cavalier.— —I told my fair one—at setting out—that as to the love and the Cavaliership—I was quite of accord—*but as to the servitude*—it would not suit me at all—so I begged to hear no more about it.—You may easily suppose I should not at all shine in the ceremonious department—so little so—that instead of handing the Lady as in duty bound into the Gondola—I as nearly as possible conveyed her into the Canal—and this at midnight—to be sure it was as dark as pitch—but if you could have seen the gravity with which I was committing her to the waves—thinking all the time of something or other not to the purpose;—I always forget that the streets are canals—and was going to walk her over the water—if the servants & the Gondoliers had not awakened me.— —So much for love & all that.— —The music here is famous—and there will be a whole tribe of singers & dancers during the Carnival—besides the usual theatres.—The Society here is something like our own—except that the women sit in a semicircle at one end of the room—& the men stand at the other.—I pass my mornings at the Armenian convent studying Armenian. My evenings here & there—tonight I am going to the Countess Albrizzi's—one of the noblesse—I have also been at the Governor's—who is an Austrian—& whose wife the Countess Goetz appeared to me in the little I have seen of her a very amiable & pleasing woman—with remarkably good manners—as many of the German women have.— —There are no English here—except birds of passage—who stay a day & then go on to Florence—or Rome.—I mean to remain here till Spring.—When you write address *directly* here—as in your present letter.—

ever dearest yrs.

B

TO JOHN MURRAY   *Venice Decr. 27th. 1816*

Dear Sir—As the Demon of Silence seems to have possessed you—I am determined to have my revenge in postage.—This is my sixth or seventh letter since summer and Switzerland.—My last was an injunction to contradict & consign to confusion that Cheapside imposter—who (I heard by a letter from your island) had thought proper to append my name to his spurious poesy—of which I know nothing—nor of his pretended purchase or copy-right.— —I hope you have at least received *that* letter. As the news of Venice must be very interesting to you I will regale you with it.— —Yesterday being the feast of St. Stephen—every mouth was put in motion—there was nothing but fiddling and playing on the virginals—and all kinds of conceits and divertisements on every canal of this aquatic city.— —I dined with the Countess Albrizzi and a Paduan and Venetian party—and afterwards went to the Opera—at the Fenice theatre (which opens for the Carnival on that day) the finest by the way I have ever seen—it beats *our* theatres hollow in beauty & scenery—and those of Milan & Brescia bow before it.— —The Opera and its Syrens were much like all other operas & women—but the subject of the said Opera was something edifying—it turned—the plot & conduct thereof—upon a fact narrated by Livy—of a hundred & fifty married ladies having *poisoned* a hundred & fifty husbands in the good old times—the bachelors of Rome believed this extraordinary mortality to be merely the common effect of matrimony or a pestilence—but the surviving Benedicts being all seized with the cholic examined into the matter—and found that "their possets had been drugged" the consequence of which was much scandal and several suits at law.—This is really & truly the subject of the Musical piece at the Fenice—& you can't conceive what pretty things are sung & recitativoed about the "horrenda strage"[;] the conclusion was a Lady's head about to be chopped off by a lictor—but (I am sorry to say) he left it on—and she got up & sung a trio with the two Consuls—the Senate in the background being chorus.—The ballet was distinguished by nothing remarkable—except that the principal she-dancer went into convulsions because she was applauded at her first appearance—and the manager came forward to ask if there was "ever a physician in the theatre"—there was a Greek one in my Box whom I wished very much to volunteer his services—being sure that in this case these would have been the last convulsions which would have troubled the Ballerina—but he would not.— —The crowd was enormous—and in coming out—having a lady under my arm—I was obliged in making way to "beat a Venetian & traduce the state" being compelled to regale a person with an English punch in the guts—which sent him as far back as the squeeze and the passage would admit—he did not ask for another—but with great signs of disapprobation & dismay appealed to his compatriots—who laughed at him.— —I am going on with my Armenian studies in a morning—and assisting & stimulating in the English portion of an English & Armenian grammar now publishing at the Convent of St. Lazarus.— —The Superior of the Friars is a Bishop and a fine old fellow—with the beard of a meteor.—My spiritual preceptor—pastor—and master—Father Paschal—is also a learned & pious soul—he was two years in England— —I am still dreadfully in love with the Adriatic lady I spoke of in a former letter (and *not* in *this*—I add for fear of mistakes—for the only one mentioned in the first part of this epistle is elderly and bookish—two things which I have ceased to admire) and love in this part of the world is no sinecure.—This is also the season when every body make up their intrigues for the ensuing year—and cut for partners for the next deal.— —And now if you don't write—I don't know what I won't say or do—nor what I will.—send me some news—good news—

yrs. very truly &c. &c. &c.

B

P.S.—Remember me to Mr. G[ifford] with all duty.—I hear that the E[dinburgh] R[eview] has cut up Coleridge's Christabel & me for praising it—which omen I think bodes no great good to your forthcome—or coming Canto and Castle (of Chillon)—my run of luck within the last year seems to have taken a turn every way but never mind—I will bring myself through in the end—if not—I can but be where I began—in the mean time I am not displeased to be where I am—I mean—at Venice.—My Adriatic nymph is this moment here—and I must therefore repose from this letter "rocked by the beating of her heart."

TO DOUGLAS KINNAIRD   *Venice—January 20th. 1817*

My dear Kinnaird—Your letter and its contents (viz. the circulars & indication for £500) are safely arrived—thanks— —I have been up all night at the Opera—& at the Ridotto & it's Masquerade—and the devil knows what—so that my head aches a little—but to business.— —My affairs ought to be in a small compass—if Newstead were sold they would be settled without difficulty—and if Newstead & Rochdale both were sold—I should think with ease—but till one or both of these are disposed of—they are in a very unpleasant situation.—It is for this reason I so much urge a sale—even at almost any price.—With regard to Hanson—I know not how to act—& I know not what to think—except that I think he wishes me well—it is certainly not his fault that Claughton could not fulfil the conditions of sale.— —Mr. Riley has reason—but he must really wait till something can be done about the property—if he likes he may proceed against *it*,—but as to the produce of my *brain*—my M.S.—my Night mare is my own personalty,—& by the Lord as I have earned the sum—so will I expend it upon my own proper pleasances—voyagings & what not—so that I request that you will *not* disburse a ducat save to *me* the *owner*.—You do not say a word about the publication itself—from which I infer that it has failed—if so—you may tell me at once—on Murray's account rather than on mine—for I am not to be perturbed by such matters at this time of day—as the fall of the thermometer of a poetical reputation—but I should be sorry for M[urray] who is a very good fellow.— —However—as with one thing or another—he—Murray must have cleared on the whole account—dating from the commencement—I feel less anxious for him than I otherwise should.—Your quotation from Shakespeare—humph—I believe that it is applied by Othello to his *wife*—who by the way was *innocent*—the Moor made a mistake—& so have you.— —My desire that Murray should pay in the agreement will not appear singular—when you recollect that the time has elapsed within a few days when three quarters of the whole were to have been disbursed by him.— —Since my departure from England I have not spent (in nine months) within some hundreds of two thousand pounds so that neither my pleasures nor my perils—when you consider the ground I have gone over & that I had a physician (now gone thank heaven) to fee & feed out of it—a very extravagant silly gentleman he was into the bargain.— —By the way—I should wish to know if Hanson has been able to collect *any rent* at all (but little it can be in these times) from N[ewstead]—if he has & there be any balance—it may also come to me in the shape of circulars—the time is also approaching when—there will be something due from that magnificent father *at* law of mine—Sir R[alph] N[oel]—from whom I expect punctuality—&

am not disposed to remit him any of his remaining duties—let him keep to his time—even in trifles.— —You tell me Shelley's wife has drowned herself—the devil she has—do you mean his *wife*—or his Mistress?—Mary Godwin?—I hope not the last—I am very sorry to hear of anything which can plague poor Shelley—besides I feel uneasy about another of his *menage.*—You know—& I believe saw once that odd-headed girl—who introduced herself to me shortly before I left England—but you do not know—that I found her with Shelley & her sister at Geneva—I never loved nor pretended to love her—but a man is a man—& if a girl of eighteen comes prancing to you at all hours—there is but one way—the suite of all this is that she was with *child*—& returned to England to assist in peopling that desolate island.—Whether this impregnation took place before I left England or since—I do not know—the (carnal) connection had commenced previously to my setting out—but by or about this time she has—or is about to produce.—The next question is is the brat *mine?*—I have reason to think so—for I know as much as one can know such a thing—that she had *not lived* with S[helley] during the time of our acquaint-ance—& that she had a good deal of that same with me.—This comes of "putting it about" (as Jackson calls it) & be damned to it and thus people come into the world.— —So you wish me to come to England—why? for what?—my affairs—I wish they could be settled without—I repeat that your country is no country for me.—I have neither ambition nor taste for your politics—and there is nothing else among you which may not be had better else-where.—Besides—Caroline Lamb—& Lady B[yron]—my "Lucy" & my "Polly" have destroyed my *moral* existence amongst you—& I am rather sick of being the theme of their mutual inventions—in ten years I could unteach myself even to your language—& am very sure that—but I have no time nor space for futher tirade at present—

ever yrs. very truly

B

P.S.—Pray write soon.— —

Venice & I agree very well—in the mornings I study Arme-nian—& in the evenings I go out sometimes—& indulge in coition always.— —I mentioned my liaison to you in a former letter—it still continues—& probably will—It has however kept me here instead of gadabouting the country.—The Carnival is begun—but the zenith of the masking will not arrive for some weeks.—There is a famous Opera—& several theatres—Catalani is to be here on the 20th—Society is like other foreign society—I see as much of it as I wish—& might see more if I liked it.—

ever yrs. most truly

B

P.S.—My respects to *Madame*—pray answer my letters—& mention anything or everything except my—*family*—I will say—for the other word makes me unwell.— —

Beppo, 10–20

10

Of all the places where the Carnival
    Was most facetious in the days of yore,
For dance, and song, and serenade, and ball,
    And masque, and mime, and mystery, and more
Than I have time to tell now, or at all,
    Venice the bell from every city bore,
And at the moment when I fix my story,
That sea-born city was in all her glory.

11

They've pretty faces yet, those same Venetians,
    Black eyes, arched brows, and sweet expressions still,
Such as of old were copied from the Grecians,
    In ancient arts by moderns mimicked ill;
And like so many Venuses of Titian's
    (The best's at Florence—see it, if ye will)
They look when leaning over the balcony,
Or stepped from out a picture by Giorgione,

12

Whose tints are truth and beauty at their best;
    And when you to Manfrini's palace go,
That picture (howsoever fine the rest)
    Is loveliest to my mind of all the show;
It may perhaps be also to *your* zest,
    And that's the cause I rhyme upon it so,
'Tis but a portrait of his son, and wife,
And self; but *such* a woman! love in life!

13

Love in full life and length, not love ideal,
    No, nor ideal beauty, that fine name,
But something better still, so very real,
    That the sweet model must have been the same;

A thing that you would purchase, beg, or steal,
 Wer't not impossible, besides a shame:
The face recals some face, as 'twere with pain,
You once have seen, but ne'er will see again;

14

One of those forms which flit by us, when we
 Are young, and fix our eyes on every face;
And, oh! the loveliness at times we see
 In momentary gliding, the soft grace,
The youth, the bloom, the beauty which agree,
 In many a nameless being we retrace,
Whose course and home we knew not, nor shall know,
Like the lost Pleiad seen no more below.

15

I said that like a picture by Giorgione
 Venetian women were, and so they *are*,
Particularly seen from a balcony,
 (For beauty's sometimes best set off afar)
And there, just like a heroine of Goldoni,
 They peep from out the blind, or o'er the bar;
And, truth to say, they're mostly very pretty,
And rather like to show it, more's the pity!

16

For glances beget ogles, ogles sighs,
 Sighs wishes, wishes words, and words a letter,
Which flies on wings of light-heeled Mercuries,
 Who do such things because they know no better;
And then, God knows, what mischief may arise,
 When love links two young people in one fetter,
Vile assignations, and adulterous beds,
Elopements, broken vows, and hearts, and heads.

17

Shakespeare described the sex in Desdemona
    As very fair, but yet suspect in fame,
And to this day from Venice to Verona
    Such matters may be probably the same,
Except that since those times was never known a
    Husband whom mere suspicion could inflame
To suffocate a wife no more than twenty,
Because she had a "cavalier servente."

18

Their jealousy (if they are ever jealous)
    Is of a fair complexion altogether,
Not like that sooty devil of Othello's
    Which smothers women in a bed of feather,
But worthier of these much more jolly fellows;
    When weary of the matrimonial tether
His head for such a wife no mortal bothers,
But takes at once another, or another's.

19

Did'st ever see a gondola? For fear
    You should not, I'll describe it you exactly:
'Tis a long covered boat that's common here,
    Carved at the prow, built lightly, but compactly,
Rowed by two rowers, each called "Gondolier,"
    It glides along the water looking blackly,
Just like a coffin clapt in a canoe,
Where none can make out what you say or do.

20

And up and down the long canals they go,
    And under the Rialto shoot along,
By night and day, all paces, swift or slow,
    And round the theatres, a sable throng,
They wait in their dusk livery of woe,
    But not to them do woeful things belong,
For sometimes they contain a deal of fun,
Like mourning coaches when the funeral's done.

You will, perhaps, complain as much of the frequency of my letters now, as you were wont to do of their rarity. I think this is the fourth within as many moons. I feel anxious to hear from you, even more than usual, because your last indicated that you were unwell. At present, I am on the invalid regimen myself. The Carnival—that is, the latter part of it—and sitting up late o'nights, had knocked me up a little. But it is over,—and it is now Lent, with all its abstinence and Sacred Music.

The mumming closed with a masked ball at the Fenice, where I went, as also to most of the ridottos, etc., etc.; and, though I did not dissipate much upon the whole, yet I find "the sword wearing out the scabbard," though I have but just turned the corner of twenty-nine.

> So we'll go no more a roving
>> So late into the night,
> Though the heart be still as loving,
>> And the moon be still as bright.
>
> For the sword outwears its sheath,
>> And the soul wears out the breast
> And the heart must pause to breathe,
>> And Love itself have rest.
>
> Though the night was made for loving,
>> And the day returns too soon,
> Yet we'll go no more a roving
>> By the light of the moon.

I have lately had some news of litter*atoor*, as I heard the editor of the Monthly pronounce it once upon a time. I hear that W. W. has been publishing and responding to the attacks of the Quarterly, in the learned Perry's Chronicle. I read his poesies last autumn, and amongst them found an epitaph on his bull-dog, and another on *myself*. But I beg to assure him (like the astrologer Partridge) that I am not only alive now but was alive also at the time he wrote it. * * * * Hobhouse has (I hear, also) expectorated a letter against the Quarterly, addressed to me. I feel awkwardly situated between him and Gifford, both being my friends.

And this is your month of going to press—by the body of Diana! (a Venetian oath,) I feel as anxious—but not fearful for you—as if it were myself coming out in a work of humour, which would, you know, be the antipodes of all my previous publications. I don't think you have any thing to dread but your own reputation. You must keep up to that. As you never showed me a line of your work, I do not even know your measure; but you must send me a copy by Murray forthwith, and then you shall hear what I think. I dare say you are in a pucker. Of all authors, you are the only really *modest* one I ever met with,—which would sound oddly enough to those who recollect your morals when you were young—that is, when you were *extremely* young—I don't mean to stigmatise you either with years or morality.

I believe I told you that the E[dinburgh] R[eview] had attacked me, in an article on Coleridge (I have not seen it)—"*Et tu*, Jeffrey?"—"there is nothing but roguery in villanous man." But I absolve him of all attacks, present and future; for I think he had already pushed his clemency in my behoof to the utmost, and I shall always think well of him. I only wonder he did not begin before, as my domestic destruction was a fine opening for all the world, of which all, who could, did well to avail themselves.

If I live ten years longer, you will see, however, that it is not over with me—I don't mean in literature, for that is nothing; and it may seem odd enough to say, I do not think it my vocation. But you will see that I will do something or other—the times and fortune permitting—that, "like the cosmogony, or creation of the world, will puzzle the philosophers of all ages." But I doubt whether my constitution will hold out. I have, at intervals, ex*or*cised it most devilishly.

I have not yet fixed a time of return, but I think of the spring. I shall have been away a year in April next. You never mention Rogers, nor Hodgson, your clerical neighbour, who has lately got a living near you. Has he also got a child yet?—his desideratum, when I saw him last. * * * * * * * *

Pray let me hear from you, at your time and leisure, believing me ever and truly and affectionately, &c.

I shall continue to write to you while the fit is on me, by way of penance upon you for your former complaints of long silence. I dare say you would blush, if you could, for not answering. Next week I set out for Rome. Having seen Constantinople, I should like to look at t'other fellow. Besides, I want to see the Pope, and shall take care to tell him that I vote for the Catholics and no Veto.

I sha'n't go to Naples. It is but the second best sea-view, and I have seen the first and third, viz. Constantinople and Lisbon (by the way, the last is but a river-view; however, they reckon it after Stamboul and Naples, and before Genoa), and Vesuvius is silent, and I have passed by Ætna. So I shall e'en return to Venice in July; and if you write, I pray you to address to Venice, which is my head, or rather my *heart*-quarters.

My late physician, Dr. Polidori, is here on his way to England, with the present Lord G[uilford] and the widow of the late earl. Dr. Polidori has, just now, no more patients, because his patients are no more. He had lately three, who are now all dead—one embalmed. Horner and a child of Thomas Hope's are interred at Pisa and Rome. Lord G[uilford] died of an inflammation of the bowels: so they took them out, and sent them (on account of their discrepancies), separately from the carcass, to England. Conceive a man going one way, and his intestines another, and his immortal soul a third!—was there ever such a distribution? One certainly has a soul; but how it came to allow itself to be enclosed in a body is more than I can imagine. I only know if once mine gets out, I'll have a bit of a tussle before I let it get in again to that or any other.

And so poor dear Mr. Maturin's second tragedy has been neglected by the discerning public! [Sotheby] will be d——d glad of this, and d——d without being glad, if ever his own plays come upon "any stage."

I wrote to Rogers the other day, with a message for you. I hope that he flourishes. He is the Tithonus of poetry—immortal already.—You and I must wait for it.

I hear nothing—know nothing. You may easily suppose that the English don't seek me, and I avoid them. To be sure, there are but few or none here, save passengers. Florence and Naples are their Margate and Ramsgate, and much the same sort of company too, by all accounts,—which hurts us among the Italians.

I want to hear of Lalla Rookh—are you out? Death and fiends! why don't you tell me where you are, what you are, and how you are? I shall go to Bologna by Ferrara, instead of Mantua: because I would rather see the cell where they caged Tasso, and where he became mad and * *, than his own MSS. at Modena, or the Mantuan birthplace of that harmonious plagiary and miserable flatterer, whose cursed hexameters were drilled into me at Harrow. I saw Verona and Vicenza on my way here—Padua too.

I go *alone*,—but *alone*, because I mean to return here. I only want to see Rome. I have not the least curiosity about Florence, though I must see it for the sake of the Venus, &c., &c.; and I wish also to see the Fall of Terni, I think to return to Venice by Ravenna and Rimini, of both of which I mean to take notes for Leigh Hunt, who will be glad to hear of the scenery of his Poem. There was a devil of a review of him in the Quarterly, a year ago, which he answered. All answers are imprudent: but to be sure, poetical flesh and blood must have the last word—that's certain. I thought, and think, very highly of his Poem; but I warned him of the row his favourite antique phraseology would bring him into.

You have taken a house at Hornsey: I had much rather you had taken one in the Apennines. If you think of coming out for a summer, or so, tell me, that I may be upon the hover for you.

                                            Ever, &c.

FOLIGNO

UMBRIA

I won't describe; description is my forte,
    But every fool describes in these bright days
His wondrous journey to some foreign court,
    And spawns his quarto, and demands your praise—
Death to his publisher, to him 'tis sport;
    While Nature, tortured twenty thousand ways,
Resigns herself with exemplary patience
To guide-books, rhymes, tours, sketches, illustrations.

DON JUAN V, 52

Dear Sir—I wrote to you the other day from Florence—in-closing an M.S.S. entitled the "Lament of Tasso"—it was written in consequence of my having been lately at Ferrara.—In the last section of this M.S. *but one* (that is the penultimate)—I think that I have omitted a line in the copy sent to you from Florence—viz—after the line

> "And woo compassion to a blighted name ["]
> Insert
> "Sealing the sentence which my foes proclaim."

The *context* will show you *the sense*—which is not clear in this quotation—*remember*—*I write this in the supposition that you have received my Florentine packet.*—At Florence I remained but a day—having a hurry for Rome to which I am thus far advanced.—However—I went to the two galleries—from which one returns drunk with beauty—the Venus is more for admiration than love—but there are sculpture and painting—which for the first time at all gave me an idea of what people mean by their *cant* & (what Mr. Braham calls) "entusimusy" (i.e. enthusiasm) about those two most artificial of the arts.—What struck me most were the Mistress of Raphael a portrait the mistress of Titian a portrait a Venus of Titian in the Medici gallery—*the* Venus—Canova's Venus also in the other gallery—Titian's mistress is also in the other gallery (that is, in the Pitti Palace gallery—) the Parcae of Michel Angelo, a picture—and the Antinous—the Alexander—& one or two not very decent groupes in marble—the Genius of Death—a sleeping figure &c. &c.— —I also went to the Medici Chapel—fine frip-pery in great slabs of various expensive stones—to commemorate fifty rotten & forgotten carcases—it is unfinished & will remain so. The church of "Santa Croce" contains much illustrious noth-ing—the tombs of Machiavelli—Michel Angelo—Galileo Galilei and Alfieri—make it the Westminster abbey of Italy.—I did not admire *any* of these tombs—beyond their contents.—That of Al-fieri is heavy—and all of them seem to me overloaded—what is necessary but a bust & a name?—and perhaps a date?—the last for the unchronological—of whom I am one.—But all your Allegory

& eulogy is infernal—& worse than the long wigs of English numskulls upon Roman bodies in the statuary of [the] reign[s] of Charles—William—and Anne.—When you write—write to *Venice* as usual—I mean to return there in a fortnight.—I shall not be in England for a long time.—This afternoon I met Lord and Lady Jersey—& saw them for some time—all well—children grown & healthy—she very pretty but sunburnt—he very sick of travelling—bound for Paris.—There are not many English on the move—& those who are are mostly homewards—I shall not return till business makes me—being much better where I am in health &c. &c.— —For the sake of my personal comfort—I pray send me immediately *to Venice—mind—Venice*—viz—*Waite's tooth powder—red* a quantity—*Calcined Magnesia* of the best quality—a quantity—and all this by safe sure & speedy means—& by the Lord! do it.—I have done nothing at *Manfred's* third act—you must wait—I'll have at it—in a week or two—or so.—

Yours ever,

B

VENICE AGAIN

Her glossy hair was clustered o'er a brow
    Bright with intelligence, and fair, and smooth;
Her eyebrow's shape was like th' aerial bow,
    Her cheek all purple with the beam of youth,
Mounting at times to a transparent glow,
    As if her veins ran lightning; she, in sooth,
Possessed an air and grace by no means common:
Her stature tall—I hate a dumpy woman.

Wedded she was some years, and to a man
    Of fifty, and such husbands are in plenty;
And yet, I think, instead of such a ONE
    'Twere better to have TWO of five-and-twenty,
Especially in countries near the sun:
    And now I think on 't, "mi vien in mente,"
Ladies even of the most uneasy virtue
Prefer a spouse whose age is short of thirty.

'Tis a sad thing, I cannot choose but say,
    And all the fault of that indecent sun,
Who cannot leave alone our helpless clay,
    But will keep baking, broiling, burning on,
That howsoever people fast and pray,
    The flesh is frail, and so the soul undone:
What men call gallantry, and gods adultery,
Is much more common where the climate's sultry.

DON JUAN I, 61–63

Dear Sir—I have received the proofs of ye "Lament of Tasso" which makes me hope that you have also received the reformed third act of Manfred—from Rome—which I sent soon after my arrival there.—My date will apprize you of my return home within these few days.—For me I have received *none* of your packets—except—after long delay—the "Tales of my Landlord" which I before acknowledged.—I do not at all understand the *why nots*—but so it is—no Manuel—no letters—no tooth powder, no *extract* from Moore's Italy concerning Marino Falieri—no *nothing*—as a man hallooed out at one of Burdett's elections—after a long ulu-latus of No Bastille! No Governor Aris! no—God knows who or what—but his ne plus ultra was no nothing!—& my receipts of your packages amount to about his meaning.—I want the extract from *Moore's* Italy very much—& the tooth powder —& the mag-nesia—I don't care so much about the poetry—or the letters—or Mr. Maturin's by-Jasus tragedy.—Most of the things sent by the post have come—I mean proofs & letters—therefore send me Marino Falieri by the post, in a letter.—I was delighted with Rome—& was on horseback all round it many hours daily besides in it the rest of my time—bothering over its marvels.—I excursed and skirred the country round to Alba—Tivoli—Frascati—Licenza—&c. &c. be-sides I visited twice the fall of Terni—which beats every thing.—On my way back, close to the temple by its banks—I got some famous trout out of the river Clitumnus—the prettiest little stream in all poesy—near the first post from Foligno—& Spoleto.—I did not stay at Florence, being anxious to get home to Venice—& having already seen the galleries—& other sights—I left my commenda-tory letters the evening before I went so I saw nobody.—To-day, Pindemonte the celebrated poet of Verona—called on me—he is a little thin man—with acute and pleasing features—his address good & gentle—his appearance altogether very philosophical—his age about sixty—or more—he is one of their best going.—I gave him *Forsyth* as he speaks or reads rather a little English—& will find there a favourable account of himself.—He enquired after his old Cruscan friends Parsons—Greathead—Mrs. Piozzi—and Merry—all of whom he had known in his youth.—I gave him as bad an account of them as I could—answering as the false "Solomon Lob" does to "Totterton" in the farce—that they were "all gone dead,"—& damned by a satire more than twenty years ago—that the name of their extinguisher was Gifford—that they were but a sad set of scribes after all—& no great things in any other way.—He seemed—as was natural—very much pleased with this account of his old acquaintances—and went away greatly gratified with that & Mr. Forsyth's sententious paragraph of applause in his own (Pindemonte's) favour.—After having been a little libertine in his youth—he is grown devout—& takes prayers—& talks to himself—to keep off the Devil—but for all that he is a very nice little old gentleman.—I forgot to tell you that at Bologna—(which is celebrated for producing Popes—Painters—and Sausages) I saw an Anatomical gallery—where there is a deal of waxwork—in which the parts of shame of both sexes are exhibited to the life—all made & moulded by a *female* Professor whose picture & merits are preserved & described to you—I thought the male part of her performance not very favourable to her imagination—or at least to the Italian Originals—being considerably under our Northern notions of things—& standard of dimensions in such matters—more particularly as the feminine display was a little in the other extreme—which however is envy also as far at least as my own experience & observation goes on this side of the Alps—& both sides of the Appennines.—I am sorry to hear of your row with Hunt—but suppose him to be exasperated by the Quarterly—& your refusal to *deal*—& when one is angry—& edites a paper I should think the temptation too strong for literary nature—which is not always human. I can't conceive in what—& for what he abuses you—what have you done? you are not an author—nor a politician—nor a public character—I know no scrape you have tumbled into.—I am the more sorry for this because I introduced you to Hunt—& because I believe him to be a very good man—but till I know the particulars I can give no opinion.—Let me know about *Lallah Rookh*—which must be out by this time.—I restore the proofs—but the *punctuation* should be corrected—I feel too lazy to have at it myself—so beg & pray Mr. Gifford for me.—Address to Venice—in a few days I go to my *Villeggiatura* in a Casino near the Brenta—a few miles only on the main land—I have determined on another year & *many years* of residence if I can compass them.—Marianna is with me—hardly recovered of the fever—which has been attacking all Italy last winter—I am afraid she is a little hectic—but I hope the best.—

ever yours truly,

B

P.S.—Torwaltzen has done a bust of me at Rome for Mr. Hobhouse—which is reckoned very good—he is their best after Canova—& by some preferred to him.—I have had a letter from Mr. Hodgson—maudlin & fine-feeling—he is very happy—has got a living—but not a child—if he had stuck to a Curacy—babes would have come of course because he could not have maintained them.— —Remember me to all your friends, &c. &c. An Austrian officer the other day, being in love with a Venetian—was ordered with his regiment into Hungary—distracted between love & duty he purchased a deadly drug which dividing with his mistress both swallowed—The ensuing pains were terrific but the pills were purgative—& not poisonous—by the contrivance of the unsentimental apothecary—so that so much suicide was all thrown away—you may conceive the previous confusion & the final laughter—but the intention was good on all sides.— —

TO JOHN MURRAY   *Octr. 12th. 1817*

Dear Sir—Mr. Kinnaird & his brother Lord K. have been here—and are now gone again; all your missives came except the tooth-powder—of which I request further supplies at all convenient opportunities—as also of Magnesia & Soda-powders—both great luxuries here—& neither to be had good—or indeed hardly at all of the natives.—In Coleridge's life I perceive an attack upon the then Committee of D[rury] L[ane] Theatre—for acting Bertram—and an attack upon Mathurin's Bertram for being acted—considering all things—this is not very grateful nor graceful on the part of the worthy auto-biographer—and I would answer—if I had *not* obliged him.—Putting my own pains to forward the views of Coleridge out of the question—I know that there was every disposition on the part of the S[ub] C[ommitte]e to bring forward any production of his were it feasible—the play he offered—though poetical—did not appear at all practicable—and Bertram did—and hence this long tirade—which is the last Chapter of his vagabond life.—As for Bertram, Maturin may defend his own begotten—if he likes it well enough—I leave the Irish Clergyman and the new Orator Henley to battle it out between them—satisfied to have done the best I could for *both*—I may say this to *you*—who know it.—Mr. Coleridge may console himself with the "fervour—the almost religious fervour" of his and Wordsworth's disciples as he calls it—if he means that as any proof of their merits—I will find him as much "fervour" in behalf of Richard Brothers and Joanna Southcote—as ever gathered over his pages—or round his fireside. He is a shabby fellow—and I wash my hands of, and after him.— —My answer to your proposition—about the 4th Canto you will have received—and I await yours—perhaps we may not agree. I have since written a poem (of 84 octave Stanzas) humourous, in or after the excellent manner of Mr. Whistlecraft (whom I take to be Frere), on a Venetian anecdote—which amused me—but till I have your answer—I can say nothing more about it.—Mr. Hobhouse does not return to England in Novr. as he intended, but will perhaps winter here—and as he is to convey the poem or poems—for there may perhaps be more than the two mentioned (which by the way I shall not perhaps include in the same publication or agreement) I shall not be able to publish so soon—as expected—but I suppose there is no harm in the delay.—I have *signed* and sent your former *copyrights* by Mr. Kinnaird—but *not* the *receipt*—because the money is not yet paid—Mr. K[innaird] has a power of Attorney to sign for me—and will when necessary.—Many thanks for the Edin[burgh] R[eview] which is very kind about Manfred—and defends it's originality—which I did not know that any body had attacked.—I *never read*—& do not know that I ever saw—the "Faustus of Marlow" and had & have no Dramatic works by me in English—except the recent things you sent me;—but I heard Mr. Lewis translate verbally some scenes of *Goethe's Faust* (which were some good & some bad) last Summer—which is all I know of the history of that magical personage;—and as to the germs

of Manfred—they may be found in the Journal which I sent to
Mrs. Leigh (part of which you saw) when I went over first the
Dent de Jamant & then the Wengeren [sic] or Wengeberg Alp
& Sheideck and made the giro of the Jungfrau Schreckhorn &c.
&c. shortly before I left Switzerland—I have the whole scene of
Manfred before me as if it was but yesterday—& could point it out
spot by spot, torrent and all.— —Of the Prometheus of Æschylus
I was passionately fond as a boy—(it was one of the Greek plays we
read thrice a year at Harrow) indeed that and the "Medea"—were
the only ones—except the "Seven before Thebes" which ever much
pleased me.—As to the "Faustus of Marlow"—I never read—never
saw—nor heard of it—at least thought of it—except that I think
Mr. Gifford mentioned, in a note of his which you sent me—
something about the catastrophe,—but not as having any thing to
do with mine—which may or may not resemble it—for any thing
I know.— —The Prometheus—if not exactly in my plan—has
always been so much in my head—that I can easily conceive its
influence over all or anything that I have written;—but I deny
Marlow & his progeny—& beg that you will do the same.— —If
you can send me the paper in question—which the E[dinburgh]
R[eview] mentions—do—The Review in the Magazine you say
was written by Mr. Wilson—it had all the air of being a poet's, &
was a very good one.—The Edin. Review—I take to be Jeffrey's
own by it's friendliness.—I wonder they thought it worth while
to do so—so soon after the former;—but it was evidently with a
good motive.— —I saw Hoppner the other day—whose country-
house at Este—I have taken for two years—if you come out next
Summer—let me know in time;—love to Gifford.

Yrs. ever truly

B

"Crabbe—Malcolm—Hamilton and Chantrey,
    Are all partakers of my pantry."—
these two lines were omitted in your letter to the Doctor—after
    "All clever men who make their way."

TO JOHN MURRAY   *Ravenna. August 1st. 1819*

Address yr. answer to Venice however

Dear Sir—Don't be alarmed.—You will see me defend myself gaily—that is—if I happen to be in Spirits—and by *Spirits* I don't mean your meaning of the word—but the spirit of a bull-dog when pinched—or a bull when pinned—it is then that they make best sport—and as my Sensations under an attack are probably a happy compound of the united energies of those amiable animals—you may perhaps see what Marrall calls "rare sport"—and some good tossing and goring in the course of the controversy.— But I must be in the right cue first—and I doubt I am almost too far off to be in a sufficient fury for the purpose—and then I have effeminated and enervated myself with love and the summer in these last two months.—I wrote to Mr. Hobhouse the other day— and foretold that Juan would either fall entirely or succeed completely—there will be no medium—appearances are not favourable—but as you write the day after publication—it can hardly be decided what opinion will predominate.—You seem in a fright—and doubtless with cause.—Come what may—I never will flatter the Million's canting in any shape—circumstances may or may not have placed me at times in a situation to lead the public opinion—but the public opinion—never led nor ever shall lead me.—I will not sit on "a degraded throne" so pray put Messrs. Southey—or Sotheby—or Tom Moore—or Horace Twiss upon it—they will all of them be transported with their coronation.— —You have bought Harlow's drawings of Margarita and me rather dear methinks—but since you desire the story of Margarita Cogni—you shall be told it—though it may be lengthy.— —Her face is of the fine Venetian cast of the old Time—and her figure though perhaps too tall not less fine—taken altogether in the national dress.— —In the summer of 1817, Hobhouse and myself were sauntering on horseback along the Brenta one evening— when amongst a group of peasants we remarked two girls as the prettiest we had seen for some time.—About this period there had been great distress in the country—and I had a little relieved some of the people.—Generosity makes a great figure at very little cost in Venetian livres—and mine had probably been exaggerated—as an Englishman's— —Whether they remarked us looking at them or no—I know not—but one of them called out to me in Venetian—"Why do not you who relieve others—think of us also?"—I turned round and answered her—"Cara—tu sei troppo bella e giovane per aver' bisogno del' soccorso mio"—she answered— ["]if you saw my hut and my food—you would not say so["]—All this passed half jestingly—and I saw no more of her for some days—A few evenings after—we met with these two girls again— and they addressed us more seriously—assuring us of the truth of their statement.—They were cousins—Margarita married—the other single.—As I doubted still of the circumstances—I took the business up in a different light—and made an appointment with them for the next evening.—Hobhouse had taken a fancy to the single lady—who was much shorter—in stature—but a very pretty girl also.— —They came attended by a third woman—who was cursedly in the way—and Hobhouse's charmer took fright (I don't mean at Hobhouse but at not being married—for here no woman will do anything under adultery), and flew off—and mine made some bother—at the propositions—and wished to consider of them.—I told her "if you really are in want I will relieve you without any conditions whatever—and you may make love with me or no just as you please—*that* shall make no difference—but if you are not in absolute necessity—this is naturally a rendezvous—and I presumed that you understood this—when you made the appointment".— —She said that she had no objection to make love with me—as she was married—and all married women did it—but that her husband (a baker) was somewhat ferocious—and would do her a mischief.—In short—in a few evenings we arranged our affairs—and for two years—in the course of which I had <almost two> more women than I can count or recount—she was the only one who preserved over me an ascendancy—which was often disputed & never impaired.—As she herself used to say publicly—"It don't matter—he may have five hundred—but he will always come back to me".— —The reasons of this were firstly—her person— very dark—tall—the Venetian face—very fine black eyes—and certain other qualities which need not be mentioned.—She was two & twenty years old—and never having had children—had not spoilt her figure—nor *anything else*—which is I assure you—a great desideration in a hot climate where they grow relaxed and doughy and *flumpity* in a short time after breeding.— —She was besides a thorough Venetian in her dialect—in her thoughts—in her countenance—in every thing—with all their naïveté and Pantaloon humour.—Besides she could neither read nor write—and could not plague me with letters—except twice that she paid sixpence to a public scribe under the piazza—to make a letter for her—upon some occasion when I was ill and could not see her.— —In other respects she was somewhat fierce and "prepotente" that is—overbearing—and used to walk in whenever it suited her— with no very great regard to time, place, nor persons—and if she found any women in her way she knocked them down.—When I first knew her I was in "relazione" (liaison) with la Signora Segati— who was silly enough one evening at Dolo—accompanied by some of her female friends—to threaten her—for the Gossips of the Villeggiatura—had already found out by the neighing of my horse one evening—that I used to "ride late in the night" to meet the Fornarina.— —Margarita threw back her veil (fazziolo) and replied in very explicit Venetian—"*You* are *not* his *wife*: *I* am *not* his *wife*—*you* are his Donna—and *I* am his *donna*—*your* husband is a cuckold—and mine is another;—for the rest, what *right* have you to reproach me?—if he prefers what is mine—to what is yours—is it my fault? if you wish to secure him—tie him to your petticoat-string—but do not think to speak to me without a reply because you happen to be richer than I am."— —Having delivered this pretty piece of eloquence (which I translate as it was related to me by a byestander) she went on her way—leaving a numerous audience with Madame Segati—to ponder at her leisure on the dialogue between them.—When I came to Venice for the Winter she followed:—I never had any regular *liaison* with her—but whenever she came I never allowed any other connection to interfere with her—and as she found herself out to be a favourite she came pretty often.—But She had inordinate Self-love—and was not tolerant of other women—except of the Segati—who was as she said my regular "Amica"—so that I being at that time somewhat promiscuous—there was great confusion—and demolition of head dresses and handkerchiefs—and sometimes my servants in "redding the fray" between her and other feminine persons

—received more knocks than acknowledgements for their peaceful endeavours.— —At the "Cavalchina" the masqued ball on the last night of the Carnival—where all the World goes—she snatched off the mask of Madame Contarini—a lady noble by birth—and decent in conduct—for no other reason but because she happened to be leaning on my arm.—You may suppose what a cursed noise this made—but this is only one of her pranks.—At last she quarrelled with her husband—and one evening ran away to my house.—I told her this would not do—she said she would lie in the street but not go back to him—that he beat her (the gentle tigress) spent her money—and scandalously neglected his Oven. As it was Midnight—I let her stay—and next day there was no moving her at all.— —Her husband came roaring & crying—& entreating her to come back, *not* She!—He then applied to the Police—and they applied to me—I told them and her husband to *take* her—I did not want her—she had come and I could not fling her out of the window—but they might conduct her through that or the door if they chose it— —She went before the Commissary—but was obliged to return with that "becco Ettico" (consumptive cuckold), as she called the *poor* man who had a Ptisick.—In a few days she ran away again.—After a precious piece of work she fixed herself in my house—really & truly without my consent—but owing to my indolence—and not being able to keep my countenance—for if I began in a rage she always finished by making me laugh with some Venetian pantaloonery or other—and the Gipsy knew this well enough—as well as her other powers of persuasion—and exerted them with the usual tact and success of all She-things—high and low—they are all alike for that.—Madame Benzone also took her under her protection—and then her head turned.—She was always in extremes either crying or laughing—and so fierce when angered that she was the terror of men women and children—for she had the strength of an Amazon with the temper of Medea. She was a fine animal—but quite untameable. *I* was the only person that could at all keep her in any order—and when she saw me really angry—(which they tell me is rather a savage sight), she subsided.—But she had a thousand fooleries—in her fazziolo—the dress of the lower orders—she looked beautiful—but alas! she longed for a hat and feathers and all I could say or do (and

I said much) could not prevent this travestie.—I put the first into the fire—but I got tired of burning them before she did of buying them—so that she made herself a figure—for they did not at all become her.—Then she would have her gowns with a *tail*—like a lady forsooth—nothing would serve her—but "l'abito colla *coua*", or *cua*, (that is the Venetian for "la *Coda*" the tail or train) and as her cursed pronunciation of the word made me laugh—there was an end of all controversy—and she dragged this diabolical tail after her every where.— —In the mean time she beat the women—and stopped my letters.—I found her one day pondering over one—she used to try to find out by their shape whether they were feminine or no—and she used to lament her ignorance—and actually studied her Alphabet—on purpose (as she declared) to open all letters addressed to me and read their contents.— —I must not omit to do justice to her housekeeping qualities—after she came into my house as "donna di governo" the expences were reduced to less than half—and every body did their duty better—the apartments were kept in order—and every thing and every body else except herself.— —That she had a sufficient regard for me in her wild way I had many reasons to believe—I will mention one.— —In the autumn one day going to the Lido with my Gondoliers— we were overtaken by a heavy Squall and the Gondola put in peril—hats blown away—boat filling—oar lost—tumbling sea—thunder—rain in torrents—night coming—& wind increasing.—On our return—after a tight struggle: I found her on the open steps of the Mocenigo palace on the Grand Canal—with her great black eyes flashing though her tears and the long dark hair which was streaming drenched with rain over her brows & breast;—she was perfectly exposed to the storm—and the wind blowing her hair & dress about her tall thin figure—and the lightning flashing round her—with the waves rolling at her feet—made her look like Medea alighted from her chariot—or the Sibyl of the tempest that was rolling around her—the only living thing within hail at that moment except ourselves.—On seeing me safe—she did not wait to greet me as might be expected—but calling out to me—"Ah! Can' della Madonna xe esto il tempo per andar' al' Lido?" (ah! Dog of the Virgin!—is this a time to go to Lido?) ran into the house—and solaced herself with scolding the boatmen for not foreseeing the "temporale".—I was told by the servants that she had only been prevented from coming in a boat to look after me—by the refusal of all the Gondoliers of the Canal to put out into the harbour in such a moment and that then she sate down on the steps in all the thickest of the Squall—and would neither be removed nor comforted. Her joy at seeing me again—was moderately mixed with ferocity—and gave me the idea of a tigress over her recovered Cubs.— —But her reign drew near a close.—She became quite ungovernable some months after—and a concurrence of complaints some true and many false—"a favourite has no friend"—determined me to part with her.—I told her quietly that she must return home—(she had acquired a sufficient provision for herself and mother, &c. in my service,) and She refused to quit the house.—I was firm—and she went—threatening knives and revenge.—I told her—that I had seen knives drawn before her time—and that if she chose to begin—there was a knife—and fork also at her service on the table and that intimidation would not do.—The next day while I was at dinner—she walked in, (having broke open a glass door that led from the hall below to the staircase by way of prologue) and advancing strait up to the table snatched the knife from my hand—cutting me slightly in the thumb in the operation.— Whether she meant to use this against herself or me I know not—probably against neither—but Fletcher seized her by the arms—and disarmed her.—I then called my boatmen—and desired them to get the Gondola ready and conduct her to her own house again—seeing carefully that she did herself no mischief by the way.—She seemed quite quiet and walked down stairs.—I resumed my dinner.—We heard a great noise—I went out—and met them on the staircase—carrying her up stairs.—She had thrown herself into the Canal.—That she intended to destroy herself I do not believe—but when we consider the fear women and men who can't swim have of deep or even of shallow water—(and the Venetians in particular though they live on the waves) and that it was also night—and dark—& very cold—it shows that she had a devilish spirit of some sort within her.—They had got her out without much difficulty or damage except the salt water she had swallowed and the wetting she had undergone.—I foresaw her intention to refix herself, and sent for a Surgeon—enquiring how many hours it would require to restore her from her agitation, and he named the time.—I then said—"I give you that time—and more if you require it—but at the expiration of the prescribed period—if *She* does not leave the house—*I* will".— —All my people were consternated—they had always been frightened at her —and were now paralyzed—they wanted me to apply to the police—to guard myself—&c. &c.—like a pack of sniveling servile boobies as they were— —I did nothing of the kind—thinking that I might as well end that way as another—besides—I had been used to savage women and knew their ways.—I had her sent home quietly after her recovery—and never saw her since except twice at the opera—at a distance amongst the audience.—She made many attempts to return—but no more violent ones.—And this is the story of Margharita Cogni—as far as it belongs to me.—I forgot to mention that she was very devout—and would cross herself if she heard the prayer-time strike—sometimes—when that ceremony did not appear to be much in unison with what she was then about.—She was quick in reply—as for instance; —one day when she had made me very angry with beating somebody or other—I called her a *Cow* (*Cow* in Italian is a sad affront and tantamount to the feminine of dog in English) I called her "Vacca" she turned round—curtsied—and answered "Vacca *tua*—'Celenza" (i.e. Eccelenza) *your* Cow—please your Excellency.—In short—she was —as I said before—a very fine Animal—of considerable beauty and energy—with many good & several amusing qualities—but wild as a witch—and fierce as a demon.—She used to boast publicly of her ascendancy over me—contrasting it with that of other women—and assigning for it sundry reasons physical and moral which did more credit to her person than her modesty.— —True it was that they all tried to get her away—and no one succeeded— till her own absurdity helped them.—Whenever there was a competition, and sometimes—one would be shut in one room and one in another—to prevent battle—she had generally the preference.— —

yrs. very truly and affectly

B

P.S.—The Countess G[uiccioli] is much better than she was.—I sent you before leaving Venice—a letter containing the real original sketch—which gave rise to the "Vampire" &c. did you get it?—

TO THOMAS MOORE   *Venice, February 2d, 1818*

Your letter of Dec. 8th arrived but this day, by some delay, common but inexplicable. Your domestic calamity is very grievous, and I feel with you as much as I *dare* feel at all. Throughout life, your loss must be my loss, and your gain my gain; and, though my heart may ebb, there will always be a drop for you among the dregs.

I know how to feel with you, because (selfishness being always the substratum of our damnable clay) I am quite wrapt up in my children. Besides my little legitimate, I have made unto myself an *il*legitimate since (to say nothing of one before), and I look forward to one of these as the pillars of my old age, supposing that I ever reach—which I hope I never shall—that desolating period. I have a great love for my little Ada, though perhaps she may torture me, like * * * * *

* * * * * * * * * * * * * * * *

Your offered address will be as acceptable as you can wish. I don't much care what the wretches of the world think of me—all *that's* past. But I do care a good deal what *you* think of me, and, so, say what you like. You *know* that I am not sullen; and, as to being *savage*, such things depend on circumstances. However, as to being in good-humour in *your* society, there is no great merit in that, because it would be an effort, or an insanity, to be otherwise.

I don't know what Murray may have been saying or quoting. I called Crabbe and Sam the fathers of present Poesy; and said, that I thought—except them—*all* of "*us youth*" were on a wrong tack. But I never said that we did not sail well. Our fame will be hurt by *admiration* and *imitation*. When I say *our*, I mean *all* (Lakers included), except the postscript of the Augustans. The next generation (from the quantity and facility of imitation) will tumble and break their necks off our Pegasus, who runs away with us; but we keep the *saddle*, because we broke the rascal and can ride. But though easy to mount, he is the devil to guide; and the next fellows must go back to the riding-school and the manège, and learn to ride the "great horse."

Talking of horses, by the way, I have transported my own, four in number, to the Lido (*beach* in English), a strip of some ten miles along the Adriatic, a mile or two from the city; so that I not only get a row in my gondola, but a spanking gallop of some miles daily along a firm and solitary beach, from the fortress to Malamocco, the which contributes considerably to my health and spirits.

I have hardly had a wink of sleep this week past. We are in the agonies of the Carnival's last days, and I must be up all night again, as well as to-morrow. I have had some curious masking adventures this Carnival; but, as they are not yet over, I shall not say on. I will work the mine of my youth to the last veins of the ore, and then—good night. I have lived, and am content.

Hobhouse went away before the Carnival began, so that he had little or no fun. Besides, it requires some time to be thoroughgoing with the Venetians; but of all this anon in some other letter. * * * * *

* * * * * * * * * * * * * * * * *

I must dress for the evening. There is an opera and ridotto, and I know not what, besides balls; and so, ever and ever yours,

B

P.S.—I send this without revision, so excuse errors. I delight in the fame and fortune of Lalla, and again congratulate you on your well-merited success.

TO RICHARD BELGRAVE HOPPNER　　*Venice, February 28, 1818*

My Dear Sir,—Our friend, il Conte M., threw me into a cold sweat last night, by telling me of a menaced version of Manfred (in Venetian, I hope, to complete the thing) by some Italian, who had sent it to you for correction, which is the reason why I take the liberty of troubling you on the subject. If you have any means of communication with the man, would you permit me to convey to him the offer of any price he may obtain or think to obtain for his project, provided he will throw his translation into the fire, and promise not to undertake any other of that or any other of *my* things: I will send his money immediately on this condition.

As I did not write *to* the Italians, nor *for* the Italians, nor *of* the Italians, (except in a poem not yet published, where I have said all the good I know or do not know of them, and none of the harm), I confess I wish that they would let me alone, and not drag me into their arena as one of the gladiators, in a silly contest which I neither understand nor have ever interfered with, having kept clear of all their literary parties, both here and at Milan, and elsewhere.—I came into Italy to feel the climate and be quiet, if possible. Mossi's translation I would have prevented, if I had known it, or could have done so; and I trust that I shall yet be in time to stop this new gentleman, of whom I heard yesterday for the first time. He will only hurt himself, and do no good to his party, for in *party* the whole thing originates. Our modes of thinking and writing are so unutterably different, that I can conceive no greater absurdity than attempting to make any approach between the English and Italian poetry of the present day. I like the people very much, and their literature very much, but I am not the least ambitious of being the subject of their discussions literary and personal (which appear to be pretty much the same thing, as is the case in most countries); and if you can aid me in impeding this publication, you will add to much kindness already received from you by yours

Ever and truly,
BYRON

P.S.—How is *the* son, and mamma? Well, I dare say.

From LETTER TO THOMAS MOORE   *June 1st 1818*

. . . But alas poor human nature! Good night—or, rather, morning. It is an hour, and the dawn gleams over the Grand Canal, and unshadows the Rialto. I must to bed; up all night—but, as George Philpot says, "it's life, though, damme it's life!"

Ever yours,

B

Excuse errors—no time for revision. The post goes out at noon, and I shan't be up then. I will write again soon about your *plan* for a publication.

TO JOHN MURRAY   *Venice. June 18th. 1818*

Dear Sir—Business and the utter and inexplicable silence of all my Correspondents renders me impatient & troublesome.—I wrote to Mr. Hanson for a balance which is (or ought to be) in his hands—no answer.—I expected the Messenger with the Newstead papers two months ago—& instead of him—I received a requisition to proceed to Geneva—which (from Hobhouse who knows my wishes & opinions about approaching England) could only be irony or insult.— —I must therefore trouble *you* to pay into my Bankers *immediately* whatever "sum" or sums you can make it convenient to do on our agreement—otherwise I shall be put to the *severest* & most immediate inconvenience—& this at a time when by every rational prospect & calculation I ought to be in the receipt of considerable sums.— —Pray do not neglect this—you have no idea to what inconvenience you will otherwise put me.—Hobhouse had some absurd notion about the disposal of this money in annuity (or God knows what) which I merely listened to when he was here to avoid squabbles & sermons—but I have occasion for the principal—& had never any serious idea of appropriating it otherwise than to answer my personal expences.— Hobhouse's wish is (if possible) to force me back to England—he will not succeed—& if he did I would not stay—I hate the Country—& like this—& all foolish opposition of course merely adds to the feeling.—*Your* silence makes me doubt the success of C[ant]o 4th.—if it has failed I will make such deduction as you think proper & fair from the original agreement—but I could wish whatever is to be paid—were remitted to me without delay through the usual Channel of course by post.—When I tell you that I have not heard a word from England since very early in May—I have made the eulogium of my friends—or the persons who call themselves so—since I have written so often & in the greatest anxiety—thank God—the longer I am absent the less cause I see for regretting the Country or it's living contents.— —

I am yrs. ever & truly
BYRON

P.S.—Tell Mr. Hobhouse that he has greatly offended all his friends at Milan by some part or other of his illustrations—that I hope (as an author) he will be damned—and that I will never forgive him (or any body) the atrocity of their late neglect & silence at a time when I wished particularly to hear (for every reason) from my friends.—

TO JAMES WEDDERBURN WEBSTER   *Venice. Septr. 8th. 1818*

Dear Webster—[12 lines crossed out] It is not agreeable to me to hear that you are still in difficulties—but as every one has to go through a certain portion of sufferance in this world—the earlier it happens perhaps the better—and in all cases one is better able to battle up in one's youth than in the decline of life.— —My own worldly affairs have had leisure to improve during my residence abroad—Newstead has been sold—& well sold I am given to understand—my debts are in the prospect of being paid—and I have still a large Capital from the residue—besides Rochdale—which ought to sell well—& my reversionary prospects which are considerable in the event of the death of Miss Milbanke's mother.—There is (as is usually said) a great advantage in getting the water between a man and his embarrassments—for things with time and a little prudence insensibly reestablish themselves—and I have spent less money—and had more for it—within the two years and a half since my absence from England—than I have ever done within the same time before—and my literary speculations allowed me to do it more easily—leaving my own property to liquidate some of the claims, till the Sale enables me to discharge the whole;—out of England I have no debts whatever.—You ask about Venice;—I tell you as before that I do not think *you* would like it—at least few English do—& still fewer remain there—Florence & Naples are their Lazarettoes where they carry the infection of their society—indeed if there were as many of them in Venice as residents—as Lot begged might be permitted to be the Salvation of Sodom,—it would not be my abode a week longer—for the reverse of the proposition I should be sure that they would be the *damnation* of all pleasant or sensible society;—I never see any of them when I can avoid it—& when occasionally they arrive with letters of recommendation—I do what I can for them—if they are sick—and if they are well I return my card for theirs—but little more.— —Venice is not an expensive residence—(unless a man chooses it) it has theatres—society—and profligacy rather more than enough—I keep four horses on one of the Islands where there is a beach of some miles along the Adriatic—so that I have daily exercise—I have my Gondola—about fourteen servants including the nurse (for a little girl—a natural daughter of mine) and I reside in one of the Mocenigo palaces on the Grand Canal—the rent of the *whole* house which is very *large* & *furnished* with linen &c. &c. inclusive is two hundred a year—(& I gave more than I need have done) in the two years I have been at Venice—I have spent about *five* thousand pounds—& I needed not have spent one *third* of this—had it not been that I have a passion for women which is expensive in it's variety every where but less so in Venice than in other cities.— —You may suppose that in *two years*—with a large establishment—horses—houses—box at the opera—Gondola— journeys—women—and Charity—(for I have not laid out all upon my pleasures—but have bought occasionally a shillings-worth of Salvation) villas in the country—another carriage & horses pur- chased for the country—books bought &c. &c.—in short every thing I wanted—& *more* than I ought to have wanted—that the sum of five thousand pounds sterling is no great deal—particularly when I tell you that more than half was laid out on the Sex—to be sure I have had plenty for the money—that's certain—I think at least two hundred of one sort or another—perhaps more—for I have not lately kept the recount.— —If you are disposed to come this way—you might live very comfortably—and even splendidly for less than a thousand a year—& find a palace for the rent of one hundred—that is to say—an Italian palace—you know that all houses with a particular front are called so—in short an enormous house,—but as I said—I do not think *you* would like it—or rather that Lady Frances would not—it is not so gay as it has been—and there is a monotony to many people in it's Canals & the comparative silence of it's streets—to me who have been always passionate for Venice—and delight in the dialect & naivete of the people—and the romance of it's old history & institutions & appearance all it's disadvantages are more than compensated by the sight of a single Gondola—The view of the Rialto—of the piazza—& the Chaunt of Tasso (though less frequent than of old) are to me worth all the cities on earth—save Rome & Athens.—Good even

> yrs. ever & most truly
>
> B

TO AUGUSTA LEIGH   *Venice. Septr. 21st. 1818*

Dearest Augusta—I particularly beg that you will contrive to get the enclosed letter safely delivered to Lady Frances—& if there Is an answer to let me have it,—You can write to her first—& state that you have such a letter—at my request—for there is no occasion for any concealment at least with *her*—& pray oblige me so far—for many reasons.— —If the Queen dies you are no more a Maid of Honour—is it not so?— —Allegra is well—but her mother (whom the Devil confound) came prancing the other day over the Appenines—to see her *shild*—which threw my Venetian loves (who are none of the quietest) into great combustion—and I was in a pucker till I got her to the Euganean hills where she & the child now are—for the present—I declined seeing her for fear that the consequence might be an addition to the family;—she is to have the child a month with her and then to return herself to Lucca—or Naples where she was with her relatives (she is English you know) & to send Allegra to Venice again.—I lent her my house at Este for her maternal holidays.—As troubles don't come single—here is another confusion.—The chaste wife of a baker—having quarrelled with her tyrannical husband—has run away *to* me—(God knows without being invited) & resists all the tears & penitence & beg-pardons of her disconsolate Lord—and the threats of the police—and the priest of the parish besides—& swears she won't give up her unlawful love (myself) for any body—or anything—I assure you I have begged her in all possible ways too to go back to her husband—promising her all kinds of eternal fidelity into the bargain—but she only flies into a fury—and as she is a very tall and formidable Girl of three and twenty—with the large black eyes and handsome face of a pretty fiend—a correspondent figure—and a carriage as haughty as a Princess—with the violent passions & capacities for mischief of an Italian when they are roused—I am a little embarrassed with my unexpected acquisition;—however she keeps my household in rare order—and has already frightened the learned Fletcher out of his remnant of wits more than once—we have turned her into a housekeeper.— —As the morals of this place are very lax—all the women commend her & say she has done right—especially her own relations.—You need not be alarmed—I know how to manage her—and can deal with anything but a cold blooded animal such as Miss Milbanke.— —The worst is that she won't let a woman come into the house—unless she is as old & frightful as possible—and has sent so many to the right about— that my former female acquaintances are equally frightened & angry.—She is extremely fond of the child—& is very cheerful & good-natured—when not jealous—but Othello himself was a fool to her in that respect—her soubriquet in her family—was *la Mora* from her colour—as she is very dark (though clear of complexion) which literally means *the Moor* so that I have "the Moor of Venice" in propria persona as part of my houshold—she has been here this month.— —I had known her (and fifty others) more than a year—but did not anticipate this escapade which was the fault of her booby husband's treatment—who now runs about repenting & roaring like a bullcalf—I told him to take her in the devil's name—but she would not stir—& made him a long speech in the Venetian dialect which was more entertaining to anybody than to him to whom it was addressed.— —You see Goose—that there is no quiet in this world—so be a good woman—& repent of yr. sins.—

yrs [scrawl for signature]

My dear Hobhouse—I have not derived from the Scriptures of
Rochfoucault that consolation which I expected "in the misfortunes of our best friends".— —I had much at heart your gaining
the Election—but from "the filthy puddle" into which your Patriotism had run you—I had like Croaker my bodings but like old
"Currycomb" you make so "handsome a Corpse"—that my wailing
is changed into admiration.—With the Burdettites divided—and
the Whigs & Tories united—what else could be expected? If I had
guessed at your *opponent*—I would have made one among you
Certes—and have f— —d Caroline Lamb out of her "two hundred
votes" although at the expence of a testicle.— —I think I could
have neutralized her zeal with a little management—but alas! who
could have thought of that Cuckoldy family's <sitting> *standing*
for a *member*—I suppose it is the first time that George Lamb ever
stood for any thing—& William with his "Corni Cazzo da Seno!"
(as we Venetians say—it means—Penis *in earnest*—a sad way of
swearing) but that you who know them should have to con*cur* with
such dogs—well—did I ever—no I never &c. &c. &c.— —I have
sent my second Canto—but I will have no gelding.— —Murray
has my order of the day.—Douglas Kinnaird with more than usual
politeness writes me vivaciously that I Ianson or I willed the *three
per cents* instead of the five—as if I could prefer *three* to *five* per
Cent!—death & fiends!—and then he lifts up his leg against the
publication of Don Juan—et "tu *Brute*" (the *e mute* recollect) I
shall certainly hitch our dear friend into some d— —d story or
other—"my dear Mr. Sneer—Mr. Sneer—my dear"— —I must
write again in a few days—it being now past four in the morning—it is Passion week—& rather dull.—I am dull too for I have
fallen in love with a Romagnuola Countess from Ravenna—who
is nineteen years old & has a Count of fifty—whom She seems
disposed to qualify the first year of marriage being just over.—I
knew her a little last year at her starting, but they always wait a
year—at least generally.—I met her first at the Albrizzi's, and this
Spring at the Benzone's—and I have hopes Sir—hopes—but She
wants me to come to Ravenna—& then to Bologna—now this
would be all very well for certainties—but for mere hopes—if She

should plant me—and I should make a "fiasco" never could I show my face on the Piazza.— —It is nothing that Money can do—for the Conte is awfully rich—& would be so even in England—but he is fifty and odd—has had two wives & children before this his third—(a pretty fair-haired Girl last year out of a Convent—now making her second tour of the Venetian Conversazioni—) and does not seem so jealous this year as he did last—when he stuck close to her side even at the Governor's.— —She is pretty—but has no tact—answers aloud—when she should whisper—talks of age to old ladies who want to pass for young—and this blessed night horrified a correct company at the Benzona's—by calling out to me "Mio Byron" in an audible key during a dead Silence of pause in the other prattlers, who stared & whispered [to] their respective Serventi.—One of her preliminaries is that I must never leave Italy;—I have no desire to leave it—but I should not like to be frittered down into a regular Cicisbeo.—What shall I do! I am in love—and tired of promiscuous concubinage—& have now an opportunity of settling for life.—

[ever yours]

P.S.—We have had a fortnight ago the devil's own row with an Elephant who broke loose—ate up a fruitshop—killed his keeper—broke into a Church—and was at last killed by a Cannon Shot brought from the Arsenal.—I saw him the day he broke open his own house—he was standing in the *Riva* & his keepers trying to persuade him with *peck-loaves* to go on board a sort of Ark they had got.—I went close to him that afternoon in my Gondola—& he amused himself with flinging great beams that flew about over the water in all directions—he was then not *very* angry—but towards midnight he became furious—& displayed the most extraordinary strength—pulling down every thing before him.—All Musquetry proved in vain—& when he charged the Austrians threw down their musquets & ran.—At last they broke a hole & brought a field-piece the first shot missed the second entered behind—& came out *all but* the Skin at his Shoulder.—I saw him dead the next day—a stupendous fellow.—He went mad for want of a She it being the rutting month.—Fletcher is well.—I have got two monkeys, a fox—& two new mastiffs—Mutz is still in high old age.—The Monkeys are charming.—Last month I had a business about a Venetian Girl who wanted to marry me—a circumstance prevented like Dr. Blifil's Espousals not only by my previous marriage—but by Mr. Allworthy's being acquainted with the existence of Mrs. Dr. Blifil.— —I was very honest and gave her no hopes—but there was a scene—I having been found at her window at Midnight and they sent me a Priest and a friend of the family's to talk with me next day both of whom I treated with Coffee.— —

TO JOHN MURRAY   *Venice April 6 1819*

Dear Sir—The Second Canto of Don Juan was sent on Saturday last by post in 4 packets—two of 4—& two of three sheets each—containing in all two hundred & seventeen stanzas octave measure.—But I will permit no curtailments except those mentioned about Castlereagh & the two "*Bobs*" in the introduction.—You sha'n't make *Canticles* of my Cantos. The poem will please if it is lively—if it is stupid it will fail—but I will have none of your damned cutting & slashing.—If you please you may publish *anonymously*[;] it will perhaps be better;—but I will battle my way against them all—like a Porcupine. So you and Mr Foscolo &c. want me to undertake what you call a "great work" an Epic poem I suppose or some such pyramid.—I'll try no such thing—I hate tasks—and then "seven or eight years!" God send us all well this day three months—let alone years—if one's years can't be better employed than in sweating poesy—a man had better be a ditcher.—And works too!—is Childe Harold nothing? you have so many "*divine*" poems, is it nothing to have written a *Human* one? without any of your worn out machinery.—Why—man—I could have spun the thought of the four cantos of that poem into twenty—had I wanted to book-make—& it's passion into as many modern tragedies—since you want *length* you shall have enough of *Juan* for I'll make 50 cantos.—And Foscolo too! why does *he* not do something more than the letters of Ortis—and a tragedy— and pamphlets—he has good fifteen years more at his command than I have—what has he done all that time?—proved his Genius doubtless—but not fixed it's fame—nor done his utmost.—Besides I mean to write my best work in *Italian*—& it will take me nine years more thoroughly to master the language—& then if my fancy exists & I exist too—I will try what I *can* do *really*.—As to the Estimation of the English which you talk of, let them calculate what it is worth—before they insult me with their insolent condescension.—I have not written for their pleasure;—if they are pleased—it is that they chose to be so,—I have never flattered their opinions—nor their pride—nor will I.—Neither will I make "Ladies books" "al dilettar le femine e la plebe"—I have written from the fullness of my mind, from passion—from impulse—from many motives—but not for their "sweet voices."—I know the precise worth of popular applause—for few Scribblers have had more of it—and if I chose to swerve into their paths—I could retain it or resume it—or increase it—but I neither love ye—nor fear ye—and though I buy with ye—and sell with ye—and talk with ye—I will neither eat with ye—drink with ye—nor pray with ye.—They made me without my search a species of popular Idol—they—without reason or judgement beyond the caprice of their Good pleasure—threw down the Image from it's pedestal—it was not broken with the fall—and they would it seems again replace it—but they shall not. You ask about my health—about the beginning of the year—I was in a state of great exhaustion—attended by such debility of Stomach—that nothing remained upon it—and I was obliged to reform my "way of life" which was conducting me from the "yellow leaf" to the Ground with all deliberate speed.—I am better in health and morals—and very much yrs. ever,

[scrawl]

P.S.—Tell Mrs. Leigh I never had "my Sashes" and I want some tooth-powder—the red—by all or any means.—

TO COUNTESS TERESA GUICCIOLI [TRANSLATION]
Venice, April 22nd, 1819

My dearest Love:—Your dearest letter came today and gave me my first moment of happiness since your departure. My feelings correspond only too closely to the sentiments expressed in your letter, but it will be very difficult for me to reply in your beautiful language to your sweet expressions, which deserve an answer in deeds, rather than words. I flatter myself, however, that your heart will be able to suggest to you *what* and *how much* mine would like to say to you. Perhaps if I loved you less it would not cost me so much to express my thoughts, but now I have to overcome the double difficulty of expressing an unbearable suffering in a language foreign to me. Forgive my mistakes, the more barbarous my style, the more will it resemble my Fate away from you. You, who are my only and last love, who are my only joy, the delight of my life—you who are my only hope—you who were—at least for a moment—all mine—you have gone away—and I remain here alone and desolate. There, in a few words, is our story! It is a common experience, which we must bear like so many others, for love is never happy, but we two must suffer more, because your circumstances and mine are equally extraordinary. But I don't want to think of all this, let us love

> . . . let us love now
> When love to love can give an answering vow.

When *Love* is not *Sovereign* in a heart, when everything does not give way to him, when all is not sacrificed to him, then it is Friendship—esteem—what you will—but no longer *Love*.

You vowed to be true to me and I will make no vows to you; let us see which of us will be the more faithful. Remember that, when the time comes that you no longer feel anything for me, you will not have to put up with my reproaches; I shall suffer, it is true, but in silence. I know only too well what a man's heart is like, and also, a little, perhaps, a woman's; I know that Sentiment is not in our control, but is what is most beautiful and fragile in our existence. So, when you feel for another what you have felt for me, tell me so sincerely—I shall cease to annoy you—I shall not see you again—I shall envy the happiness of my rival, but shall trouble you no more. This however I promise you: You sometimes tell me that I have been your *first* real love—and I assure you that you shall be my last Passion. I may well hope not to fall in love again, now that everything has become indifferent to me. Before I knew you—I felt an interest in many women, but never in one only. Now I love *you*, there is no other woman in the world for me.

You talk of tears and of our unhappiness; my sorrow is within; I do not weep. You have fastened on your arm a likeness that does not deserve so highly; but yours is in my heart, it has become part of my life, of my soul; and were there another life after this one, there too you would be mine—without you where would Paradise be? Rather than Heaven without you, I should prefer the Inferno of that Great Man buried in your city, so long as you were with me, as Francesca was with her lover.

My sweetest treasure—I am trembling as I write to you, as I trembled when I saw you—but no longer—with such sweet heartbeats. I have a thousand things to say to you, and know not how to say them, a thousand kisses to send you—and, alas, how many Sighs! Love me—not as I love you—for that would make you too unhappy, love me not as I deserve, for that would be too little—but as your Heart commands. Do not doubt me—I am and always shall be your most tender lover.

BYRON

P.S.—How much happier than I is this letter: which in a few days will be in your hands—and perhaps may even be brought to your lips. With such a hope I am kissing it before it goes. Goodby—my soul.

April 23d., 4 o'clock

At this moment two other letters of yours have come! The irregularity of the post has been a great trouble to us both—but pray—my Love, do not lose faith in me. When you do not get news from me—believe that I am dead, rather than unfaithful or ungrateful. I will answer your dearest letters soon. Now the post is going—I kiss you ten thousand times.

> On the superscription is added, in Byron's hand:
> "Written April 22nd, 1819.
> April 28th, 1820. I have re-read it in Ravenna,
> after a year of most singular events."

Dear Douglas—

> "When that the Captain comed for to know it,
> He very much applauded what she had done,"

and I only want the command "of the gallant Thunder Bomb" to make you my "first Lieutenant".—I meant "five thousand pounds" and never intend to have so much meaning again—in short—I refer you Gentlemen—to my original letter of instructions which by the blessing of God—seems to bear as many constructions as a Delphic Oracle;—I say I refer you to that when you are at a loss how to avoid paying my money away;—I hate paying—& you are quite right to encourage me.—As to Hanson & *Son*—I make no distinctions—it would be a sort of blasphemy—I should as soon think of untwisting the Trinity—what do they mean by separate bills?—With regard to the Rochdale suit—and the "large discretion" or Indiscretion of a thousand pounds—what could I do? I want to gain my suit—but I will be guided by you—if you think "punds Scottish" will do better—let me know—I am docile.— Pray what could make Farebrother say that Seventeen thousand pounds had been bidden for the undisputed part of Rochdale manor?—it may be so—but I never heard of it before—not even from Spooney—if anybody bids—take it—& send it me by post—but don't pay away to those low people of tradesmen—they may survive Lady Noel—or me—and get it from the executors and heirs—but I don't approve of any living liquidations—a damned deal too much has been paid already—the fact is that the villains owe me money —& not I to them.—Damn "*the Vampire*,"—what do I know of Vampires? it must be some bookselling imposture— contradict it in a solemn paragraph.—I sent off on April 3rd. the 2nd. Canto of "Don Juan" addressed to Murray—I hope it is arrived—by the Lord! it is a Capo d'Opera—so "full of pastime and prodigality"—but you shan't decimate nor mutilate—no—"rather than that come Critics into the list—and champion me to the uttermost."—Nor you nor that rugged rhinoceros Murray have ever told me in answer to fifty times the question—if he ever received the additions to Canto *first* entitled "Julia's letter" and also some four stanzas for the beginning.—I have fallen in love within the last month with a Romagnuola Countess from Ravenna—the Spouse of a year of Count Guiccioli—who is sixty—the Girl twenty— he has eighty thousand ducats of rent—and has had two wives before—but he is Sixty—he is the first of Ravenna Nobles—but he is sixty—She is fair as Sunrise—and warm as Noon—we had but ten days—to manage all our little matters in beginning middle and end. & we managed them;—and I have done my duty—with the proper consummation.—But She is young—and was not con- tent with what she had done—unless it was to be turned to the advantage of the public—and so She made an eclat which rather astonished even the Venetians—and electrified the Conversazioni of the Benzone—the Albrizzi—& the Michelli—and made her <Lord> husband look embarrassed.—They have been gone back to Ravenna—some time—but they return in the Winter.—She is the queerest woman I ever met with—for in general they cost one something in one way or other—whereas by an odd combination of circumstances—I have proved an expence to HER—which is not my custom,—but an accident—however it don't matter.—She is a sort of an Italian Caroline Lamb, except that She is much pret- tier, and not so savage.—But She has the same red-hot head—the same noble dis*dain* of public opinion—with the superstructure of all that Italy can add to such natural dispositions.—To be sure they may go much further here with impunity—as her husband's rank ensured their reception at all societies including the Court—and as it was her first outbreak since Marriage—the Sympathizing world was liberal.—She is also of the Ravenna noblesse—educated in a convent—sacrifice to Wealth—filial duty and all that.—I am dam- nably in love—but they are gone—gone—for many months—and nothing but Hope—keeps me alive seriously.

yrs. [scrawl]

TO JOHN MURRAY   *Venice. May 15th. 1819*

Dear Sir—I have received & return by this post under cover— the first proof of "Don Juan."—Before the second can arrive it is probable that I may have left Venice—and the length of my

absence is so uncertain—that you had better proceed to the publication without boring me with more proofs—I sent by last post
an addition—and a new copy of "Julia's letter," perceiving or supposing the former one in Winter did not arrive.—Mr. Hobhouse
is at it again about indelicacy—there is *no indelicacy*—if he wants
that, let him read Swift—his great Idol—but his Imagination must
be a dunghill with a Viper's nest in the middle—to engender such
a supposition about this poem.—For my part I think you are
all crazed.—What does he mean about "G—d damn"—there is
"*damn*" to be sure—but no "G—d" whatever.—And as to what
he calls "a p—ss bucket"—it is nothing but simple water—as I
am a Sinner—pray tell him so—& request him not "to put me
in a phrenzy," as Sir Anthony Absolute says—"though he was not
the indulgent father that I am."—I have got yr. extract, & the
"Vampire". I need not say it is *not mine*—there is a rule to go by—
you are my publisher (till we quarrel) and what is not published
by you is not written by me.—The Story of Shelley's agitation is
true—I can't tell what seized him—for he don't want courage. He
was once with me in a Gale of Wind in a small boat right under the
rocks between Meillerie & St. Gingo—we were five in the boat—a
servant —two boatmen—& ourselves. The Sail was mismanaged
& the boat was filling fast—he can't swim.—I stripped off my
coat—made him strip off his—& take hold of an oar—telling
him that I thought (being myself an expert swimmer) I could save
him if he would not struggle when I took hold of him—unless
we got smashed against the rocks which were high & sharp with
an awkward Surf on them at that minute;—we were then about a
hundred yards from shore—and the boat in peril.—He answered
me with the greatest coolness—"that he had no notion of being
saved—& that I would have enough to do to save myself, and
begged not to trouble me".—Luckily the boat righted & baling
[sic] we got round a point into St. Gingo—where the Inhabitants
came down and embraced the boatmen on their escape—the Wind
having been high enough to tear up some huge trees from the Alps
above us as we saw next day.—And yet the same Shelley who was
as cool as it was possible to be in such circumstances—(of which
I am no judge myself as the chance of swimming naturally gives
self-possession when near shore) certainly had the fit of phantasy

which P[olidori] describes—though *not exactly* as he describes it.
The story of the agreement to write the Ghost-books is true—
but the ladies are *not Sisters*—one is Godwin's daughter by Mary
Wolstonecraft—and the other the *present* Mrs. Godwin's daughter
by a former husband. So much for Scoundrel Southey's Story of
"*incest*"—neither was there *any promiscuous intercourse* whatever—
both are an invention of the execrable villain Southey—whom
I will term so as publicly as he deserves.—Mary Godwin (now
Mrs. Shelley) wrote "Frankenstein"—which you have reviewed
thinking it Shelley's—methinks it is a wonderful work for a Girl of
nineteen—*not* nineteen indeed—at that time.—I enclose you the
beginning of mine—by which you will see how far it resembles Mr.
Colburn's publication.—If you choose to publish it in the Edinburgh Magazine (*Wilsons* & *Blackwoods*) you may—*stating why*, &
with such explanatory proem as you please.—I never went on with
it—as you will perceive by the date.—I began it in an old account-
book of Miss Milbanke's which I kept because it contains the word
"*Household*" written by her twice on the inside blank page of the
Covers—being the only two Scraps I have in the world in her writing, except her name to the deed of Separation.—Her letters I sent
back—except those of the quarrelling correspondence—and those
being documents are placed in possession of a third person (Mr.
Hobhouse) with copies of several of my own,—so that I have no
kind of memorial whatever of her but these *two* words—and her
actions. I have torn the leaves containing the part of the tale out of
the book & enclose them with this sheet.—Next week—I set out
for Romagna—at least in all probability.—You had better go on
with the publications without waiting to hear farther—for I have
other things in my head.—"Mazeppa" & "the Ode"—*separate*—
what think you?—*Juan anonymous without the dedication*—for I
won't be shabby—& attack Southey under Cloud of night.—What
do you mean? first you seem hurt by my letter? & then in your next
you talk of it's "power" & so forth—"this is a d—d blind Story
Beck—but never mind—go on." You may be sure I said nothing
on *purpose* to plague you—but if you will put me "in a phrenzy, I
will never call you *Jack* again."—I remember nothing of the epistle
at present.—What do you mean by Polidori's *diary*?—why—I
defy him to say any thing about me—but he is welcome—I have

nothing to *reproach* me with on his score—and I am much mistaken if that is not his *own* opinion—but why publish the names of the two girls? & in such a manner?—what a blundering piece of exculpation!—*He* asked Pictet &c. to dinner—and of course was left to entertain them.—I went into *Society solely* to present *him* (as I told him) that he might return into good company if he chose—it was the best thing for his youth & circumstances—for myself I had done with Society—& having presented him—withdrew to my own "way of life."—It is true that I returned without entering Lady Dalrymple Hamilton's—because I saw it full.—It is true—that Mrs. Hervey (She writes novels) fainted at my entrance into Coppet—& then came back again;—on her fainting—the Duchesse de Broglie exclaimed: "This is *too much*—at Sixty five years of age!"—I never gave "the English" an opportunity of "avoiding" me—but I trust, that if ever I do, they will seize it.—

I am yrs. very truly

B

TO AUGUSTA LEIGH   *Venice [Monday] May 17th. 1819*

My dearest Love   I have been negligent in not writing, but what can I say[.] Three years absence—& the total change of scene and habit make such a difference—that we have now nothing in common but our affections & our relationship.—

But I have never ceased nor can cease to feel for a moment that perfect & boundless attachment which bound & binds me to you—which renders me utterly incapable of *real* love for any other human being—what could they be to me after *you?* My own XXXX [short word crossed out] we may have been very wrong—but I repent of nothing except that cursed marriage—& your refusing to continue to love me as you had loved me—I can neither forget nor *quite forgive* you for that precious piece of reformation.—but I can never be other than I have been—and whenever I love anything it is because it reminds me in some way or other of yourself—for instance I not long ago attached myself to a Venetian for no earthly reason (although a pretty woman) but because she was called XXXX [short word crossed out] and she often remarked (without knowing the reason) how fond I was of the name.—It is heart-breaking to think of our long Separation—and I am sure more than punishment enough for all our sins—Dante is more humane in his "Hell" for he places his unfortunate lovers (Francesca of Rimini & Paolo whose case fell a good deal short of *ours*—though sufficiently naughty) in company—and though they suffer—it is at least together.—If ever I return to England—it will be to see you—and recollect that in all time—& place—and feelings—I have never ceased to be the same to you in heart— Circumstances may have ruffled my manner—& hardened my spirit—you may have seen me harsh & exasperated with all things around me; grieved & tortured with *your new resolution*,—& the soon after persecution of that infamous fiend who drove me from my Country & conspired against my life—by endeavouring to deprive me of all that could render it precious—but remember that even then *you* were the sole object that cost me a tear? and *what tears*! do you remember *our* parting? I have not spirits now to write to you upon other subjects—I am well in health—and have no cause of grief but the reflection that we are not together—When you write to me speak to me of yourself—& say that you love me—never mind common-place people & topics—which can be in no degree interesting—to me who see nothing in England but the country which holds *you*—or around it but the sea which divides us.—They say absence destroys weak passions—& confirms strong ones—Alas! *mine* for you is the union of all passions & of all affections—Has strengthened itself but will destroy me—I do not speak of *physical* destruction—for I have endured & can endure much—but of the annihilation of all thoughts feelings or hopes—which have not more or less a reference to you & to *our recollections*—

Ever dearest
[Signature erased]

TO JOHN CAM HOBHOUSE *Venice. Octr. 3d. 1819*

Dear Hobhouse—I wrote to Murray last week and begged him to reassure you of my health and sanity—as far as I know at present.—At Bologna I was out of sorts—in health and spirits.

—Here—I have health at least.—My South American project of
which I believe I spoke to you (as you mention it)—was this.—
—I perceived by the inclosed paragraphs that advantageous offers
were—or are to be held out to settlers in the Venezuelan territory.—My affairs in England are nearly settled—or in prospect of
settlement—in Italy I have no debts—and could leave it when I
chose.—The Anglo-Americans are a little too coarse for me—and
their climate too cold—and I should prefer the others.—I could
soon grapple with the Spanish language.— —Ellice or others
could get me letters to Boliver and his government—and if men
of little or of no property are encouraged there—surely with present income—and if I could sell Rochdale—with some capital—I
might be suffered as a landholder there—or at least a tenant—and
if possible and legal—a Citizen.— —I wish you would speak to
Perry of the M[orning] C[hronicle] who is their *Gazetteer*—about
this—and ask like Jeremy Diddler—not for eighteen pence—but
information on the subject.— —I assure you that I am very *serious*
in the idea—and that the notion has been about me for a long time
as you will see by the worn state of the advertisement.—I should
go there with my natural daughter Allegra—now nearly three years
old—and with me here—and pitch my tent for good and all.—I
am not tired of Italy—but a man must be a Cicisbeo and a singer
in duets and a Connoisseur of operas—or nothing here—I have
made some progress in all these accomplishments—but I can't
say that I don't feel the degradation.—Better be a[n] unskilful
planter—an awkward settler—better be a hunter—or anything
than a flatterer of fiddlers—and a fan-carrier of a woman.—I like
women—God he knows—but the more their system here deve-
lopes upon me—the worse it seems—after Turkey too—here the
polygamy is all on the female side.— —I have been an intriguer,
a husband, and now I am a Cavalier Servente.—by the holy!—it
is a strange sensation.—After having belonged in my own and
other countries—to the intriguing—the married—and the keeping—parts of the town—to be sure an honest arrangement is the
best—and I have had that too—and have—but they expect it to
be for *life*—thereby I presume—excluding longevity.—But let us
be serious if possible.— —You must not talk to me of England—
that is out of the question.—I had a house—and lands—and a

wife and child—and a name there—once—but all these things are transmuted or sequestered.—Of the last & best ten years of my life—nearly six have been passed *out* of it.—I feel no love for the soil after the treatment I received before leaving it for the last time—but I do not hate it enough to wish to take a part in it's calamities—as on either side harm must be done before good can accrue—revolutions are not to be made with rose water.— —My taste for revolution is abated—with my other passions.— —Yet I want a country—and a home—and if possible—a free one—I am not yet thirty two years of age—I might still be a decent citizen and found a *house* and a family,—as good—or better than the former.— —I could at all events occupy myself rationally—my hopes are not high—nor my ambition extensive—and when tens of thousands of our Countrymen are colonizing (like the Greeks of old in Sicily and Italy) from as many causes—does my notion seem visionary or irrational?— —There is no freedom in Europe—that's certain—it is besides a worn out portion of the globe.—What I should be glad of is *information* as to the encouragement—the means required—and what is accorded & what would be my probable reception—Perry—or Ellice—or many merchants would be able to tell you this for me.—I won't go there to travel but to settle.— —Do not laugh at me—you will—but I assure you I am quite in earnest if this thing be practicable. I do not want to have anything to do with the war projects—but to go there as a settler—and if as a Citizen—all the better—my own government would not I think refuse me permission—if they know their own interest—such fellows as I am—are no desideratum for Sidmouth at present—I think.—Address to me at Venice.— —I should of course come to Liverpool—or some town on your coast—to take my passage—and receive my credentials—believe me

ever yrs. most truly
BYRON

My dear Douglas—My late expenditure has arisen from living at a distance from Venice and being obliged to keep up two establishments, from frequent journeys—and buying some furniture and books as well as a horse or two—and not from any renewal of the EPICUREAN system as you suspect. I have been faithful to my honest liaison with Countess Guiccioli—and I can assure you that *She* has never cost me directly or indirectly a sixpence—indeed the circumstance of herself and family render this no merit.—I never offered her but one present—a broach of brilliants—and she sent it back to me with her *own hair* in it (I shall *not* say of *what part* but *that* is an Italian custom) and a note to say that she was not in the habit of receiving presents of that value—but hoped that I would not consider her sending it back as an affront—nor the value diminished by the enclosure.—I have not had a whore this half-year—confining myself to the strictest adultery.— —Why should you prevent Hanson from making a *peer* if he likes it—I think the "*Garretting*" would be by far the best parliamentary privilege—I know of.— —Damn your delicacy.—It is a low commercial quality—and very unworthy a man who prefixes "honourable" to his nomenclature. If you say that I must sign the bonds—I suppose that I must but it is very iniquitous to make me pay my debts—you have no idea of the pain it gives one.—Pray do three things—get my property out of the *funds*—get Rochdale sold—get me some information from Perry about *South America*—and 4thly. ask Lady Noel not to live so very long.— —As to Subscribing to Manchester—if I do that—I will write a letter to Burdett—for publication—to accompany the Subscription—which shall be more radical than anything yet rooted—but I feel lazy.—I have thought of this for some time—but alas! the air of this cursed Italy enervates—and disfranchises the thoughts of a man after nearly four years of respiration—to say nothing of emission.—As to "Don Juan"—confess—confess—you dog—and be candid—that it is the sublime of *that there* sort of writing—it may be bawdy—but is it not good English?—it may be profligate—but is it not *life*, is it not *the thing*?—Could any man have written it—who has not lived in the world?—and tooled in a post-chaise? in a hackney coach? in a Gondola? against a wall? in a court carriage? in a vis a vis?—on a table?—and under it?—I have written about a hundred stanzas of a third Canto—but it is damned modest—the outcry has frightened me.—I had such projects for the Don—but the *Cant* is so much stronger than *Cunt*—now a days,—that the benefit of experience in a man who had well weighed the worth of both monosyllables—must be lost to despairing posterity.—After all what stuff this outcry is—Lalla Rookh and Little—are more dangerous than my burlesque poem can be—Moore has been here—we got tipsy together—and were very amicable—he is gone on to Rome—I put my life (in M.S.) into his hands—(*not* for publication) you—or any body else may see it—at his return.—It only comes up to 1816.— —He is a noble fellow—and looks quite fresh and poetical—nine years (the age of a poem's education) my Senior—he looks younger—this comes of marriage and being settled in the Country. I want to go to South America—I have written to Hobhouse all about it.—I wrote to my wife—three months ago—under care to Murray—has she got the letter—or is the letter got into Blackwood's magazine?— —You ask after my Christmas pye—Remit it any how—*Circulars* is the best—you are right about *income*—I must have it all—how the devil do I know that I may live a year or a month?—I wish I knew that I might regulate my spending in more ways than one.—As it is one always thinks that there is but a span.—A man may as well break or be damned for a large sum as a small one—I should be loth to pay the devil or any other creditor more than sixpence in the pound.—

[scrawl for signature]

P.S.—I recollect nothing of "Davies's landlord"—but what ever Davies *says*—I will *swear* to—and *that's* more than *he* would.—So pray pay—has he a landlady too?—perhaps I may owe her something.— —With regard to the bonds I will sign them but—it goes against the grain.— —As to the rest—you *can't* err—so long as you *don't* pay. — —Paying is executor's or executioner's work.— —You may write somewhat oftener—Mr. Galignani's messenger gives the outline of your public affairs—but I see no results—you have no man yet—(always excepting Burdett—& you & H[obhouse] and the Gentlemanly leaven of your two-penny loaf of rebellion) don't forget however my charge of horse—and commission for the Midland Counties and by the holies!—You shall have your account in decimals.—Love to Hobby—but why leave the Whigs?— —

TO DOUGLAS KINNAIRD   *Venice. Novr. 16th. 1819*

Dear Douglas—A few weeks ago I wrote to you to explain in answer to your letter—that my expenditure at Bologna &c. had arisen from various journeys—and some purchases of horses and furniture—as well as the keeping up two establishments for the time being—one at Venice—and the other in Romagna—besides living at hotels.—Your conjecture of my having "been voluptuous" was wrong in *your* sense of the word—I have not for now a year—touched or disbursed a sixpence to any harlotry.—My "honnete arrangement"—answered all purposes much better—and cost me nothing—unless you calculate my expences in changing my residence.—I had every reason to be satisfied with my lot in all respects—but that is all over now—and I now write to apprize you that in a few weeks you will see me probably in England. — —I have for this reason drawn on Siri & Willhalm to pay off my *rents* here and to furnish for my journey.   My daughter will accompany me.— —The causes are these.— —In Septr. Countess Guiccioli—my Sovereign—was ordered to Venice for her health to consult Dr. Aglietti again.—Her husband went to Ravenna on business.—We travelled together—and lived together in the Country till her husband's arrival in Novr.— —On the road, by the way—we were very near going off together—from Padua—for France and America—but as I had more prudence—and more experience—and know that the time would come when both might repent—I paused—& prevailed on her to pause also.— —At last the Cavalier-Conte Guiccioli came to Venice—where he found his wife considerably improved in health, but hating him so cordially—that they quarrelled *violently*.—He had said nothing before—but at last on finding this to be the case—he gave her the alternative—*him*—or *me*—she decided instantly for *me*—not being allowed to have both—and the lover generally having the preference.—But he had also given her a paper of rules to which he wished her to assent—all of them—establishing *his* authority.— —Her friends and relatives of Ravenna were in the meantime in despair—as an *elopement* in Italy is the devil—worse even than with *us*—because it is *super*erogation—and shows a headlong character.— —What could I do?—on one hand to sacrifice a woman whom I loved for life—leaving her destitute and divided from all ties in case of my death—on the other hand to give up an "amicizia" which had been my pleasure my pride and my passion.—At twenty I should have taken her away—at thirty with the experience of *ten such years*!—I sacrificed myself only—and counselled—and persuaded her with the greatest difficulty to return with her husband to Ravenna—not absolutely denying—that I might come there again—else she refused to go.— —But I shall quit Italy—I have done my duty—but the Country has become sad to me,—I feel alone in it—and as I left England on account of my own wife—I now quit Italy for the wife of another.— —I shall make my way to Calais—as I can without going through Paris.—I do not come to England for pleasure—but I know not where to go unless to America—tell *Scrope* Davies—I must see *him* immediately—I shall write to him from Calais—perhaps to join me there—(he will pardon me the trouble) as there is a matter which has been upon my mind these three years (ever since I knew it) that I must settle immediately on my arrival.—He will understand me—and so perhaps may you—but you are both too much men of honour (as well as Hobhouse from whom I have no secrets) to let it go further.—I have been very unwell with an Intermittent fever—which is leaving—but has not yet quite left me—but I trust that it will— as it is better—or rather I am better of it.—I return to England with a heavier heart than when I left it—with no prospects of pleasure or comfort—and indifferent to every thing—but that which it is my duty to do—& which I could wish done with all proper speed.—I shall bring my little daughter Allegra with me— but I know not where to go—I have nobody to receive me—but my sister—and I must conform to my circumstances—and live accordingly,—that is meanly in London & difficultly—on that which affords splendour & ease in Italy.— —But I hope to get out to America—if I don't take a much longer voyage.— —I should prefer Spanish America.—Pray make my remembrances to all our friends and believe me

yrs. ever & truly

B

P.S.—The enclosed papers will explain to you the close of the Ravenna romance—and confirm this letter;—Hobhouse will translate them to you—"A." means "Alessandro" the name of Count Guiccioli—pray—tell Hobhouse to take care of them for me & not lose them—let me find a line poste restante—Calais.— —Novr. 17th. Since I wrote yesterday—I have had another attack of the tertian not violent—but very tiresome.—My daughter and her nurse are also fallen ill—so that I cannot fix any precise day for my setting out;—it would not be just on second thoughts to expect Scrope to take a winter journey to Calais to see me—but I hope to find him in town on my arrival—I will write to you both [whenever?] I am near at hand.— —I write to you chiefly to account for my having drawn on Siri—as my rent for houses & bills & journey require it.—I am not much worse in body for my illness—but in very low spirits—for that and other reasons— —pray excuse incoherencies and scrawling.— —

TO JOHN CAM HOBHOUSE   *Venice. Novr. 20th. 1819*

My dear Hobhouse—A few days ago I wrote to Douglas K[innaird] to apprize him & my friends of my probable arrival near England in no very long period.—The cause I have detailed at some length in my letter to Douglas.—Il Conte Guiccioli at length discovering that his lady was estranged from him—gave her (like Mr. Croaker in the Goodnatured man) "a mutual choice" that is the husband or the lover—him or me—one but not both.—The lady was for leaving him—and eloping—or separating—and so should I had I been twenty instead of thirty and one years of age—for I loved her—but I knew the event would for her be irreparable—and that all her family[,] her sisters particularly and father[,] would be plunged into despair for the reputation of the rest of the girls—and prevailed on her with great difficulty to

return to Ravenna with her husband—who promised forgetfulness
if she would give me up.—He actually came to *me* crying about
it—and I told him "if you abandon your wife—I will take her
undoubtedly—it is my duty—it is also my inclination in case of
such extremity—but if as you say—you are really disposed to live
with & like her as before—I will not only not carry further distur-
bance into your family—but even repass the Alps—for I have no
hesitation in saying that Italy will be now to me insupportable."—
After ten days of such things—during which I had (& have still)
the tertian ague—She agreed to go back with him—but *I* feel so
wretched and low—and lonely—that I will leave the country reluctantly indeed—but I will do it—for otherwise if I formed a new
liaison she would cut the figure of a woman *planted*—and I never
will willingly hurt her Self-love.—I *can have* no other motive for
here nobody fights—and as to assassination—I have risked it many a
good time for *her* at Ravenna—and should hardly shrink now;—I
will say no more—except that it has been as bitter a cut up for
me—as that of leaving England.—Guiccioli's lord intercepted a
letter of her father (Count Ruggiero Gamba Ghiselli—there is the
name at length) giving her some prudent advice to smooth the
husband—& this blew up the whole affair[,] besides some awkward evidence about sleeping together—and doors locked—which
like a Goose had been locked—& then afterwards forgotten to be
re-opened—so that he knocked his horns against the door of his
own drawing room.— —There is packing and preparation going
on—and I mean to plod through the Tyrol with my little "shild"—
Allegrina—who however is not very well—and half the house
have brought the tertian from the Mira—it made me delirious
during one attack.— —A German of the name of Simon—with
your brother's recommendation from Trieste—has asked me to
take him to England—and I will do so—with the permission of
God.—William Bankes is at Trieste and has written to me.

Novr. 21st.

I have a little plague and some [little trouble] with the present state
of my household of whom *five* including myself have the intermittent fever more or less—Dr. Aglietti has this moment informed me
that Allegra has the "doppia terzana" —a febrile doubloon which it

seems renders my departure from hence quite uncertain—(as I will not & can not go without her) it means that the poor child has the fever *daily*—& her nurse has it—besides a cameriere and barcariola—my own has diminished—at first it was violent to a degree of temporary delirium—but has subsided in the third week to a slight attack—but has left my mind very weak—and unintellectual.— All these things put together prevent me from entering upon any of my purposes—and indeed make me postpone from day to day my departure—for the Doctor will say nothing decided of my daughter and I dare not remove her till her journey is pronounced <proper> innocent.— —I had things to say to Scrope.—There are things to say to you—and to Douglas—but Alas! here I am in a gloomy Venetian palace—never *more* alone than when alone—unhappy in the retrospect—& at least as much so in the prospect—and at the moment when I trusted to set out—taken aback by this indisposition of my child—which however—thank God—as far as I can learn, is not dangerous—but very tiresome & tedious.—At present all my plans of revenge first—and emigration afterwards—in case of arriving & surviving near your coasts—are lulled upon the feverish pillow of a sick infant.— —I began this letter yesterday—and within the twenty four hours only was I made aware of the full extent of Allegra's malady.—But my former letter to Kinnaird is neutralized by this event—except in case of her speedy recovery;—in Italy I will not remain a moment longer than enables me to quit it.—I mean or meant to go by the Tyrol &c. &c. &c. and to write to you on my arrival at Calais.— —You have never answered my letter of South American *enquiries*—I must go there, or to [the] Cape—anything but stay near England—that is to say if I accomplish what I ought to do—in approaching it near enough—and if I do not—succeed in my intention—I shall have no further need to accomplish anything.—I allude to more private business—but have no leisure—or rather too much—and too few spirits to explain further—at present.

yours ever & truly

B

My dearest Augusta—Yours of the 11th. came today—many thanks.—I may be wrong—and right or wrong—have lived long enough not to defend opinions—but my doubts of the funds were Douglas Kinnaird's who also told me that at the investment— Lady B[yron] or her agents had demurred—I know nothing of England but through Douglas & Hobhouse who are alarming reformers—and the Paris papers which are full of bank perplexities.—The Stake concerns you and your children who are in part my heirs—and Lady B[yron] and her child who have a jointure and all that to come out of it—She may do as she pleases—I merely suggest—it is all your affair as much as mine.— —Since I wrote to you last I have had with all my household & family a sharp tertian fever—I have got *well* but Allegra is still laid up though convalescent—and her nurse—and half my ragamuffins—Gondoliers, Nurses—cook—footmen &c.—I cured myself without bark—but all the others are taking it like trees.— —I have also had another hot [crater?]—in the shape of a scene with Count Guiccioli who quarrelled with his wife—who refused to go back to him—and wanted to stay with me—and elope—and be as good as married—at last they made it up—but there was a dreadful scene;— —if I had not loved her better than myself—I could not have resisted her wish—but at thirty one years—as I have—and *such years* as they have been—you may be sure—knowing the world that I would rather sacrifice myself ten times over—than the girl—who did not know the extent of the step she was so eager to take.— —He behaved well enough—saying—"take your lover or retain me—but you shan't have both"—the lady would have taken her lover as in duty bound—not to do—but on representing to her the destruction it would bring on her family (five unmarried sisters) and all the probable consequences—she had the reluctant good grace to acquiesce and return with him to Ravenna.— — But this business has rendered Italy hateful to me— and as I left England on account of my own wife—I leave Italy—because of another's.—You need not be frightened there was no fighting— nobody fights here—they sometimes assassinate—but generally by proxy—and as to intrigue, it is the only employment—but elopements and separations are still more serious than even with us—being so uncommon—and indeed needless—as excepting an occasionally jealous old gentleman—every body lets their spouses have a man or two—provided he be taken with decency.—But the Guiccioli was romantic—and had read "*Corinna*"—in short she was a kind of Italian Caroline Lamb—but very pretty and gentle—at least to me—for I never knew so docile a creature as far as we lived together—except that she had a great desire to leave her husband who is sixty years old—and not pleasant. There was the deuce—for her father's family (a very noble one of Ravenna) were furious against the *husband*—(not against me) for his unreasonable ways.— —You must not dislike *her*—for she was a great admirer of *you*—and used to collect and seal up all *your letters* to me as they came that they might not be lost or mixed with other papers— —and she was a very amiable and accomplished woman—with however some of the drawbacks of the Italian character now corrupted for ages.— —All this—and my fever—have made me low and ill—but the moment Allegra is better—we shall set off over the Tyrolese Alps, and find our way to England as we can, to the great solace of Mr. Fletcher—who may perhaps find his family not less increased than his fortune during his absence.— —I cannot fix any day for departure or arrival—so much depending on circumstances—but we are to be in voyage—as soon as it can be undertaken with safety to the child's health.—As to the Countess G[uiccioli] if I had been single—and could have married her [by] getting her divorced—she would [proba]bly have been of the party—but this being out of the question—though *she* was as "all for love or the world well lost"—I who know what "love" and "the world" both are—persuaded her to keep her station in society.— —Pray let Ada's picture be *portable* as I am likely to see more of the portrait than of the original.—Excuse this scrawl—think that within this month I have had a *fever*—an *Italian husband and wife quarrelling;—a sick family*—and *the preparation for a December journey over the mountains of the Tyrol all brewing at once in my cauldron.*—

yrs.
[scrawl]

P.S.—I enclose you *her* last letter to me by which you may judge for yourself—that it was a serious business.—I have felt it such, but it was my duty to do as I did as her husband offered to forgive every thing if she would return with him to Ravenna and give up her liaison.— —I will talk to you of my American scheme when I see you.

TO JOHN MURRAY *Venice. 10th. 10bre. 1819*

Dear Murray—Since I last wrote I have changed my mind & shall not come to England—the more I contemplate—the more I dislike the place & the prospect.— —You may therefore address to me as usual *here*—though—I mean to go to another city.— —I have finished the third Canto of D[on] J[uan]—but the things I have read & heard discourage all further publication—at least for the present.— —You may try the copy question—but you'll lose it—the cry is up—and cant is up—I should have no objection to return the price of the copyright—& have written to Mr. Kin[nair]d by this post on the subject.— —Talk with him.—I have not the patience—nor do I feel interest enough in the question, to contend with the fellows in their own slang,— —but I perceive Mr. Blackwood Magazine and one or two others of your missives—have been hyperbolical in their praise—and diabolical in their abuse.— —I like & admire Wilson—and *he* should not have indulged himself in such outrageous license—it is overdone and defeats itself—what would he say to the grossness without passion—and the misanthropy without feeling of Gulliver's travels?—when he talks of Lady Byron's business—he talks of what he knows nothing about—and you may tell him that no one can more desire a public investigation of that affair than I do.— —I sent home by Moore—(*for* Moore only who has my journal too) my memoir written up to 1816—and I gave him leave to show it to whom he pleased—but *not* to *publish* on any account.—You may read it—and you may let Wilson read it—if he likes—not for his *public* opinion—but his private—for I like the man—and care very little about his magazine.— —And I could wish Lady B[yron] herself to read it—that she may have it in her power to mark anything mistaken or misstated—as it will probably appear after my extinction, and it would be but fair she should see it— that is to say—herself willing.— —Perhaps I may take a journey to you in the Spring—but I *have* been ill—and *am* indolent—and indecisive because few things interest me.— —These fellows first abused me for being gloomy—and now they are wroth but I am or attempted to be facetious.— —I have got such a cold and head-ache that I can hardly see what I scrawl—the winters here are as sharp as needles.—Some time ago I wrote to you rather fully about my Italian <liaisons> affairs—at present I can say no more—except that you shall know further by and bye.—Your Blackwood accuses me of treating women harshly—it may be so—but I have been their martyr.—My whole life has been sacrificed *to* them & *by* them.—I mean to leave Venice in a few days—but you will address your letters *here* as usual.—When I fix elsewhere you shall know.

yrs
[scrawl]

P.S.—Pray let my Sister be informed that I am not coming as I intended—I have not the courage to tell her so myself—[at] least as yet—but I will soon—*with the reasons*—pray tell her so.— —

BOLOGNA

Italia! Oh Italia! Thou who hast
The fatal gift of beauty, which became
A funeral dower of present woes and past,
On thy sweet brow is sorrow plough'd by shame,
And annals graved in characters of flame.
Oh God! That thou wert in thy nakedness
Less lovely or more powerful

CHILDE HAROLD'S PILGRIMAGE IV, 42

Dear Hoppner—I am at length joined to Bologna—where I am settled like a Sausage—and shall be broiled like one if this weather continues.—Will you thank Mengaldo on my part for the Ferrara acquaintance—which was a very agreeable one—I staid two days at Ferrara—& was much pleased with the Count Mosti and the little the shortness of the time permitted me to see of his family.—I went to his Conversazione which is very far superior to anything of the kind at Venice—the women almost all young—several pretty—and the men courteous & cleanly; the Lady of the mansion who is young—lately married—and with child—appeared very pretty by Candle light (I did not see her by day) pleasing in her manners and very lady-like—or thorough-bred as we call it in England a kind of thing which reminds me of a racer—an Antelope—or an Italian Grey-hound— —She seems very fond of her husband who is amiable and accomplished—he has been in England two or three times—and is young.—The Sister—a Countess Somebody—I forget what—they are both Maffei by birth—and Veronese of course—is a lady of more display—she sings & plays divinely—but I thought She was a d—d long time about it— —her likeness to Madame Flahaut—(Miss Mercer that was) is something quite extraordinary—I had but a bird's eye view of these people and shall not probably see them again—but I am very much obliged to Mengaldo for letting me see them at all;— whenever I meet with any-thing agreeable in this world it surprizes me so much—and pleases me so much (when my passions are not interested one way or the other) that I go on wondering for a week to come.—I fell too in great admiration of the Cardinal Legate's red Stockings.— —I found too such a pretty epitaph in the Certosa Cimetery—or rather two—one was

> Martini Luigi
> *Implora pace.*

the other—

> Lucrezia Picini
> "Implora eterna quiete."

that was all—but it appears to me that these two and three words comprize and compress all that can be said on the subject—and then in Italian they are absolute Music.— —They contain doubt—hope—and humility—nothing can be more pathetic than the "implora" and the modesty of the request—they have had enough of life—they want nothing but rest—they implore it—and "eterna quieta"—it is like a Greek inscription in some good old Heathen "City of the dead".—Pray—if I am shovelled into the Lido Church-yard—in your time—let me have the "implora pace" and nothing else for my epitaph—I never met with any antient or modern that pleased me a tenth part so much.— —In about a day or two after you receive this letter I will thank you to desire Edgecombe to prepare for my return—I shall go back to Venice before I village on the Brenta.— —I shall stay but a few days in Bologna, I am just going out to see sights, but shall not present my introductory letters for a day or two till I have run over again the place & pictures— —nor perhaps at all if I find that I have books & sights enough to do without the inhabitants.— —After that I shall return to Venice where you may expect me about the eleventh—or perhaps sooner—pray make my thanks acceptable to Mengaldo—my respects to the Consuless—and to Mr. Scott;—I hope my daughter is well—ever yrs

& truly
BYRON

P.S.—I went over the Ariosto M.S. &c. &c. again at Ferrara—with the Castle—and Cell—and House—&c. &c. &c. One of the Ferrarese asked me if I knew "Lord Byron" an acquaintance of his *now* at Naples—I told him *No*—which was true both ways—for I know not the Impostor—and in the other—no one knows himself.—He stared when told that I was "the real Simon Pure."—Another asked me if I had *not translated* "Tasso".—You see what *fame* is—how *accurate*—how *boundless*;—I don't know how others feel—but I am always the lighter and the better looked on when I have got rid of mine—it *sits* on me like armour on the Lord Mayor's Champion—and I got rid of all the husk of literature—and the attendant babble by answering that I had not translated Tasso.—but a namesake had—and by the blessing of Heaven I looked so little like a poet that every body believed me.— —I am just setting off for Ravenna.—June 8th 1819. I changed my mind this morning & decided to go on— —

To the Po. June 2nd 1819

River! that rollest by the antient walls
 Where dwells the Lady of my Love, when she
Walks by thy brink and there perchance recalls
 A faint and fleeting memory of me,
What if thy deep and ample stream should be
 A mirror of my heart, where she may read
The thousand thoughts I now betray to thee
 Wild as thy wave and headlong as thy speed?
What do I say? "a mirror of my heart"?
 Are not thy waters sweeping, dark, and strong,
Such as my feelings were and are, thou art,
 And such as thou art were my passions long.
Time may have somewhat tamed them, not forever
 Thou overflow'st thy banks, and not for aye
The bosom overboils, congenial River!
 Thy floods subside, and mine have sunk away,
But left long wrecks behind us, yet again
 Borne on our old career unchanged we move,
Thou tendest wildly to the wilder main
 And I to loving one I should not love.
The current I behold will sweep beneath
 Her palace walls, and murmur at her feet,
Her eyes will look on thee, when she shall breathe
 The twilight air unchained from Summer's heat.
She will look on thee,—I have looked on thee
 Full of that thought, and from this moment ne'er
Thy waters could I name, hear named, or see
 Without the inseparable Sigh for her.
Her bright eyes will be imaged in thy Stream—
 Yes, they will meet the wave I gaze on now,
But mine can not even witness in a dream
 That happy wave repass me in its flow.
The wave that bears my tear returns no more
 Will She return by whom that wave shall sweep?

Both tread thy bank, both wander by thy shore,
    I near thy source, and She by the blue deep.
But that which keepeth us apart, is not
    Distance, nor depth of wave, nor space of earth,
But the distractions of a various lot,
    Ah! various as the climates of our birth!
A Stranger loves a lady of the land,
    Born far beyond the Mountains, but his blood
Is all meridian, as if never fanned
    By the bleak wind that chills the Polar flood.
My heart is all meridian, were it not
    I had not suffered now, nor should I be—
Despite of tortures ne'er to be forgot—
    The Slave again, Oh Love! at least of thee!
'Tis vain to struggle, I have struggled long
    To love again no more as once I loved.
Oh! Time! why leave this earliest Passion strong?
    To tear a heart which pants to be unmoved?

TO JOHN MURRAY   *Bologna. August 12th. 1819*

   Dear Sir—I do not know how far I may be able to reply to your
letter—for I am not very well today.—Last night I went to the
representation of Alfieri's Mirra—the two last acts of which threw
me into convulsions.—I do not mean by that word—a lady's
hysterics—but the agony of reluctant tears—and the choaking
shudder which I do not often undergo for fiction.—This is but
the second time for anything under reality, the first was on seeing
Kean's Sir Giles Overreach.—The worst was that the "*dama*" in
whose box I was—went off in the same way—I really believe
more from fright—than any other sympathy—at least with the
players—but she has been ill—and I have been ill and we are all
languid & pathetic this morning—with great expenditure of Sal
Volatile.—But to return to your letter of the 23d. of July.— —You
are right—Gifford is right—Crabbe is right—Hobhouse is right—
you are all right—and I am all wrong—but do pray let me have
that pleasure.—Cut me up root and branch—quarter me in the
Quarterly—send round my "disjecti membra poetae" like those of
the Levite's Concubine—make—if you will—a spectacle to men
and angels—but don't ask me to alter for I can't—I am obstinate
and lazy—and there's the truth.—But nevertheless—I will answer
your friend C. V. who objects to the quick succession of fun and
gravity—as if in that case the gravity did not (in intention at least)
heighten the fun.—His metaphor is that "we are never scorched
and drenched at the same time!"—Blessings on his experience!—
Ask him these questions about "scorching and drenching".—Did
he never play at Cricket or walk a mile in hot weather?—did he
never spill a dish of tea over his testicles in handing the cup to
his charmer to the great shame of his nankeen breeches?—did he
never swim in the sea at Noonday with the Sun in his eyes and
on his head—which all the foam of ocean could not cool? did he
never draw his foot out of a tub of too hot water damning his eyes
& his valet's? did he never inject for a Gonorrhea?—or make water
through an ulcerated Urethra?—was he ever in a Turkish bath—
that marble paradise of sherbet and sodomy?—was he ever in a
cauldron of boiling oil like St. John?—or in the sulphureous waves
of hell? (where he ought to be for his "scorching and drenching at

the same time") did he never tumble into a river or lake fishing—
and sit in his wet cloathes in the boat—or on the bank afterwards
"scorched and drenched" like a true sportsman?— —"Oh for
breath to utter"— —but make him my compliments—he is a
clever fellow for all that—a very clever fellow.— —You ask me for
the plan of Donny Johnny—I *have* no plan—I *had* no plan—but
I had or have materials—though if like Tony Lumpkin—I am "to
be snubbed so when I am in spirits" the poem will be naught—and
the poet turn serious again.—If it don't take I will leave it off where
it is with all due respect to the Public—but if continued it must
be in my own way—you might as well make Hamlet (or Diggory)
"act mad" in a strait waistcoat—as trammel my buffoonery—if I
am to be a buffoon—their gestures and my thoughts would only
be pitiably absurd—and ludicrously constrained.—Why Man the
Soul of such writing is it's licence?—at least the *liberty* of that *licence*
if one likes—*not* that one should abuse it—it is like trial by Jury
and Peerage—and the Habeas Corpus—a very fine thing—but
chiefly in the *reversion*—because no one wishes to be tried for the
mere pleasure of proving his possession of the privilege.— —But a
truce with these reflections;—you are too earnest and eager about
a work never intended to be serious;—do you suppose that I could
have any intention but to giggle and make giggle?—a playful satire
with as little poetry as could be helped—was what I meant—and
as to the indecency—do pray read in Boswell—what *Johnson*
the sullen moralist—says of *Prior* and Paulo Purgante— —Will
you get a favour done for me?—*you* can by your Government
friends—Croker—Canning—or my old Schoolfellow Peel—and
I can't.—Here it is—will you ask them to appoint (*without salary
or emolument*) a noble Italian (whom I will name afterwards)
Consul or Vice Consul for Ravenna.—He is a man of very large
property—noble too—but he wishes to have a British protection
in case of changes—Ravenna is near the Sea—he wants *no emolument* whatever;—that his office might be useful—I know—as I
lately sent off from Ravenna to Trieste—a poor devil of an English
Sailor—who had remained there sick sorry and penniless (having
been set ashore in 1814) from the want of any accredited agent able
or willing to help him homewards.—Will you get this done?—it
will be the greatest favour to me?—if you do—I will then send

his name and condition—subject of course to rejection if *not* approved—when known.— —I know that in the Levant—you make consuls—and Vice Consuls perpetually—of foreigners—this man is a Patrician and has twelve thousand a year.—His motive is a British protection in case of new Invasions.— —Don't you think Croker would do it for us? to be sure *my interest* is rare!!—but perhaps a brother-wit in the Tory line might do a good turn at the request of so harmless and long absent a Whig—particularly as there is no *salary* nor *burthen* of any sort to be annexed to the office.— —I can assure you I should look upon it as a great obligation—but Alas! that very circumstance may very probably operate to the contrary—indeed it ought.—But I have at least been an honest and an open enemy.— —Amongst your many splendid Government Connections—could not you think you? get our Bibulus made a Consul?—Or make me one that I may make him my Vice.—You may be assured that in case of accidents in Italy—he would be no feeble adjunct—as you would think if you knew his property.— —What is all this about Tom Moore? but—why do I ask?—since the state of my own affairs would not permit me to be of use to him—although they are greatly improved since 1816,—and may be—with some more luck—and a little prudence become quite Clear.—It seems his Claimants are *American* merchants.— *There goes Nemesis.*—Moore abused America.—It is always thus in the long run.—Time the Avenger.—You have seen every trampler down in turn from Buonaparte to the simplest individuals.— — You saw how some were avenged even upon my insignificance; and how in turn Romilly paid for his atrocity.—It is an odd World—but the Watch has its mainspring after all.— —So the Prince has been repealing Lord Ed. Fitzgerald's forfeiture—"Ecco un' Sonnetto!"—

> To be the father of the fatherless
> To stretch the hand from the throne's height and raise
> *His* offspring, who expired in other days
> To make thy Sire's Sway by a kingdom less,
> *This* is to be a Monarch, and repress
> Envy into unutterable praise,
> Dismiss thy Guard, and trust thee to such traits,

For who would lift a hand except to bless?—
Were it not easy, Sir, and is't not sweet
To make thyself beloved? and to be
Omnipotent by Mercy's means? for thus
Thy Sovereignty would grow but more complete,
A Despot thou, and yet thy people free,
And by the Heart not Hand enslaving Us

There you dogs—there's a Sonnet for you—you won't have such as that in a hurray from Mr. Fitzgerald.— —You may publish it with my name—an' ye wool—He deserves all praise bad & good—it was a very noble piece of principality.—Would you like an Epigram? <upon a female> a translation.— —

If for silver or for gold—
You could melt ten thousand pimples
Into half a dozen dimples
Then your face we might behold
Looking doubtless much more smugly
Yet even then 'twould be damned ugly.

This was written on some French-woman, by Rulhières—I believe.—"And so good morrow t'ye—good Master lieutenant."
— —

yrs. [scrawl]

TO JOHN MURRAY   *Bologna. August 29th. 1819*

Dear Sir—I have been in a rage these two days and am still bilious therefrom.—You shall hear. A Captain of Dragoons—Ostheid—Hanoverian by birth—in the Papal troops at present—whom I had obliged by a loan when nobody would lend him a Paul—recommended a horse to me on sale by a Lieutenant Rossi—an officer who unites the sale of cattle to the purchase of men.— —I bought it.—The next day on shoeing the horse—we discovered the *thrush*—the animal being warranted sound.—I sent to reclaim the contract, and the money—The Lieutenant desired to speak with me in person.—I consented.—He came.—It was his own particular request.— —He began a story.—I asked him if he would return the money.—He said no—but he would exchange.—He asked an exorbitant price for his other horses.—I told him that he was a thief.—He said he was an *officer* & a man of honour—and pulled out a Parmesan passport signed by General Count Neipperg.—I answered that as he was an officer I would treat him as such—and that as to his being a Gentleman—he might prove it by returning the money—as for his Parmesan passport—I should have valued it more if it had been a Parmesan Cheese.—He answered in high terms—and said that if it were in the *morning* (it was about eight o Clock in the evening) he would have *satisfaction*.—I then lost my temper.—As for *that* I replied you shall have it directly—it will be *mutual* satisfaction I can assure you—you are a thief and as you say an officer—my pistols are in the next room loaded—take one of the candles examine & make your choice of weapons.—He replied that *pistols* were *English weapons*—*he* always fought with the *Sword*—I told him that I was able to accommodate him, having three regimental swords in a drawer near us—and he might take the longest and put himself on guard.—All this passed in presence of a third person.— —He then said *No* but tomorrow morning he would give me the meeting at any time or place.—I answered that it was not usual to appoint meetings in the presence of witnesses—and that we had best speak man to man—& fix time and instruments.—But as the Man present was leaving the room—the Lieutenant Rossi—before he could shut the door after him—ran out roaring "help and murder" most lustily and fell into a sort of hysteric in the arms of about fifty people, who all saw that I had no weapon of any sort or kind about me, and followed him asking what the devil was the matter with him.—Nothing would do—he ran away without his hat, & went to bed ill of the fright.—He then tried his complaint at the police—which dismissed it as frivolous.— —He is I believe gone away or going—the horse was warranted—but I believe so worded that the villain will not be obliged to refund according to law.— —He endeavoured to raise up an indictment of assault and battery—but as it was in a public inn—in a frequented street—there were too many witnesses to the contrary—and as a military man—he has not cut a martial figure even in the opinion of the Priests.—He ran off in such a hurry that

he left his hat and never missed it till he got to his hostel or inn.—
The facts are as I tell you—I can assure you he began by "coming
Captain Grand over me"—or I should never have thought of
trying his "cunning in fence"—but what could I do?—he talked
of "honour and satisfaction—and his commission"—he produced
a military passport—there are severe punishments for *regular duels*
on the continent, and trifling ones for *rencontres*—so that it is best
to fight it out directly—he had robbed—and then wanted to insult
me—what could I do?—my patience was gone—and the weapons
at hand—fair and equal—besides it was just after dinner when
my digestion is bad—& I don't like to be disturbed.—His friend
Ostheid—is at Forlì—we shall meet on my way back to Ravenna
—the Hanoverian seems the greater rogue of the two—and if my
valour does not ooze away like Acres's—"Odds flints and triggers"
if it should be a rainy morning and my stomach in disorder—there
may be something for the obituary.— —Now pray "Sir Lucius do
not you look upon me as a very ill used *Gentleman*?["]— —I send
my Lieutenant to match Hobhouse's *Major Cartwright*—"and so
good morrow to you good Master Lieutenant".—With regard
to other things I will write soon but I have been f – – – – – g
incessantly for the last three months and Quarrelling—and fooling—till I can scribble no more.

yrs. [scrawl]

RAVENNA

"Sir," said the Count, with brow exceeding grave,
    "Your unexpected presence here will make
It necessary for myself to crave
    Its import? But perhaps 'tis a mistake;
I hope it is so; and, at once to waive
    All compliment, I hope so for *your* sake;
You understand my meaning, or you *shall*."
"Sir," (quoth the Turk) "'tis no mistake at all:

"That Lady is *my wife*!" Much wonder paints
    The lady's changing cheek, as well it might;
But where an Englishwoman sometimes faints,
    Italian females don't do so outright;
They only call a little on their Saints,
    And then come to themselves, almost, or quite;
Which saves much hartshorn, salts, and sprinkling faces,
And cutting stays, as usual in such cases.

She said,—what could she say? Why, not a word;
    But the Count courteously invited in
The Stranger, much appeased by what he heard:
    "Such things, perhaps, we'd best discuss within,"
Said he; "don't let us make ourselves absurd
    In public, by a scene, nor raise a din,
For then the chief and only satisfaction
Will be much quizzing on the whole transaction."

BEPPO, 88–90

Dear Sir—The letters have been forwarded from Venice—but I trust that you will not have waited for further alterations—I will make none— —You ask me to spare "*Romilly*"—ask the Worms.— His dust can suffer nothing from the truth being spoken—and if it *could*—how did he behave to *me?*— —You may talk to the Wind—which will <at least> carry the sound—and to the Caves which will echo you—but *not* to me on the subject of a villain who wronged me—whether dead or alive.— —I have no time to return you the proofs—publish without them.—I am glad you think the poesy good—and as to "thinking of the effect"—think *you* of the sale—and leave me to pluck the Porcupines who may point their quills at you.— —I have been here (at *Ravenna*) these four weeks having left Venice a month ago;—I came to see my "amica" the Countess Guiccioli who has been—& still continues very unwell—after her miscarriage which occurred in May last at Pomposa on her way here from Lombardy.— —She is only twenty years old, but not of a strong constitution and I fear that neither the medical remedies—nor some recent steps of our own to repair at least the miscarriage—have done her any great good—she has a perpetual cough—and an intermittent fever—but bears up most *gallantly* in every sense of the word.— —Her husband (this is his third wife) is the richest Noble of Ravenna—& almost of Romagna—he is also *not* the youngest—being upwards of three score—but in good preservation.—All this will appear strange to you who do not understand the Meridian morality—nor our way of life in such respects, and I cannot at present expound the difference.—But you would find it much the same in these parts.—At Faenza—there is Lord Kinnaird with an Opera Girl.—and at the Inn in the same town is a Neapolitan Prince who serves the wife of the Gonfaloniere of that city.— —I am on duty here—so you see "cosi fan tutt*i*" e tutt*e*— —I have my horses here—*saddle* as well as Carriage—and ride or drive every day in the forest—the *Pineta* the scene of Boccaccio's novel and Dryden's fable of Honoria &c. &c. and I see my Dama every day at the proper (and improper) hours—but I feel seriously uneasy about her health which seems very precarious—in losing her I should lose a being who has run great risks on my account—and whom I have every reason to love—but I must not think this possible—I do not know what I *should* do—if She died—but I ought to blow my brains out—and I hope that I should.—Her husband is a very polite personage—but I wish he would not carry me out in his Coach and Six—like Whittington and his Cat.— —You ask me if I mean to continue D[on] J[uan] &c. how should I know? what encouragement do you give me—all of you with your nonsensical prudery?—publish the two Cantos—and then you will see.— —I desired Mr. Kinnaird to speak to you on a little matter of business—either he has not spoken or you have not answered.—You are a pretty pair—but I will be even with you both—I perceive that Mr. Hobhouse has been challenged by Major Cartwright—is the Major "so cunning of fence?"—why did not they fight?—they ought.

> yrs. ever truly
>
> B

Address your answer to *Venice* as usual.—

TO AUGUSTA LEIGH   *Ravenna. July 26th. 1819*

My dearest Augusta—I am at too great a distance to scold you—but I *will* ask you—whether *your* letter of the *1st.* July *is an answer* to the letter I wrote you before I quitted Venice?—What? is it come to *this*?—Have you no memory? or no heart?—You *had* both—and I *have* both—at least for *you*.— —I write this presuming that you received *that* letter—is it that you fear? do not be afraid of the post—the World has it's own affairs without thinking of *ours* and you may write safely—if you do—address as usual to *Venice*.—My house is not in St. Marc's but on the Grand Canal—within sight of the Rialto Bridge.—I do not like at all this pain in your side and always think of your mother's constitution—you must always be to me the first consideration in the World.—Shall I come to *you*?—or would a warm climate do you good?—if so say the word—and I will provide you & your whole family (including that precious baggage your Husband) with the means of making an agreeable journey—you need not fear about *me*—I am much altered—and should be little trouble to you—nor would I give you more of my company than you like.— —I confess after three years and a half—and *such years*! and *such a year* as preceded those three years! it would be a relief to see you again—and if it would be so to you—I will come to you.— —Pray—answer me—and recollect that I will do as you like in everything—even to returning to England—which is *not* the pleasantest of residences were *you* out of it.— —I write from Ravenna—I came here on account of a Countess Guiccioli—a Girl of Twenty married to a very rich old man of Sixty—about a year ago;—with her last Winter I had a *liaison* according to the good old Italian custom—she miscarried in May—and sent for me here—and here I have been these two months.—She is pretty—a great Coquette—extremely vain—excessively affected—clever enough—without the smallest principle—with a good deal of imagination and some passion;— She had set her heart on carrying me off from Venice out of vanity—and succeeded—and having made herself the subject of general conversation has greatly contributed to her recovery.—Her husband is one of the richest Nobles of Ravenna—threescore years of age—this is his third wife.— —You may suppose what *esteem* I entertain for *her*—perhaps it is about equal on both sides.—I have my saddle-horses here and there is good riding in the forest—with these—and my carriage which is here also—and the Sea—and my books—and the lady—the time passes—I am very fond of riding and always *was out* of England—but I hate your Hyde Park—and your turnpike roads—& must have forests—downs—or deserts to expatiate in—I detest *knowing* the road—one is to go,—and being interrupted by your damned fingerposts, or a blackguard roaring for twopence at a turnpike.— —I send you a sonnet which this faithful Lady had made for the nuptials of one of her relations in which she swears the most *alarming constancey* to her husband—is not this good? you may suppose my *face* when she showed it to me—I could not help laughing—one of *our* laughs.— —All this is very absurd—but you see that I have good morals at bottom.— —She is an Equestrian too—but a bore in her rides—for she can't guide her horse—and he runs after mine—and tries to bite him—and then she begins screaming in a high hat and Sky-blue habit—making a most absurd figure—and embarrassing me

and both our grooms—who have the devil's own work to keep
her from tumbling—or having her clothes torn off by the trees
and thickets of the Pine forest.— —I fell a little in love with her
intimate friend—a certain Geltruda—(that is *Gertrude*) who is
very young & seems very well disposed to be perfidious—but
alas!—*her* husband is jealous—and the G. also detected me in an
illicit squeezing of hands, the consequence of which was that the
friend was whisked off to Bologna for a few days—and since her
return I have never been able to see her but twice—with a dragon
of a mother in law—and a barbarous husband by her side—besides my own dear precious *Amica*—who hates all flirting but her
own.—But I have a Priest who befriends me—and the Gertrude
says a good deal with her great black eyes, so that perhaps—but
Alas! I mean to give up these things altogether.— —I have now
given you some account of my present state—the Guide-book will
tell you about Ravenna—I can't tell how long or short may be my
stay—write to me—love me—as ever

yrs. most affectly.

B

P.S.—*This* affair is *not* in the least expensive—being all in the
wealthy line—but troublesome—for the lady is imperious—and
exigeante—however there are hopes that we may quarrel—when
we do you shall hear
[In margin of printed sonnet enclosed]
    Ask Hobhouse to translate this to you—and tell him the
reason.— —

TO THOMAS MOORE   *January 2d, 1820*

My Dear Moore,—

> To-day it is my wedding-day;
>   And all the folks would stare
> If wife should dine at Edmonton,
>   And I should dine at Ware.

Or *thus*:

> Here's a happy new year! but with reason,
>   I beg you'll permit me to say—
> Wish me *many* returns of the *season*,
>   But as *few* as you please of the *day*.

My [sic] this present writing is to direct you that, *if she chooses*, she may see the MS. Memoir in your possession. I wish her to have fair play, in all cases, even though it will not be published until after my decease. For this purpose, it were but just that Lady B. should know what is there said of her and hers, that she may have full power to remark on or respond to any part or parts, as may seem fitting to herself. This is fair dealing, I presume, in all events.

To change the subject, are you in England? I send you an epitaph for Castlereagh:

                  * * * * * * * * * * * * * * *

> [Posterity will ne'er survey
>   A nobler grave than this;
> Here lie the bones of Castlereagh:
>   Stop traveller, * *]

Another for Pitt:—

> With death doom'd to grapple,
>   Beneath this cold slab, he
> Who lied in the Chapel
>   Now lies in the Abbey.

The gods seem to have made me poetical this day:—

> In digging up your bones, Tom Paine,
>   Will. Cobbett has done well:
> You visit him on earth again,
>   He'll visit you in hell.

Or,

> You come to him on earth again,
>   He'll go with you to hell.

Pray let not these versiculi go forth with *my* name, except among the initiated, because my friend H. has foamed into a reformer,

and, I greatly fear, will subside into Newgate; since the Honourable House, according to Galignani's Reports of Parliamentary
Debates, are menacing a prosecution to a pamphlet of his. I shall
be very sorry to hear of any thing but good for him, particularly
in these miserable squabbles; but these are the natural effects of
taking a part in them.

For my own part, I had a sad scene since you went. Count
Gu[iccioli] came for his wife, and *none* of those consequences
which Scott prophesied ensued. There was no damages, as in England, and so Scott lost his wager. But there was a great scene, for
she would not, at first, go back with him—at least [*sic*] [last?] she
did go back with him; but he insisted, reasonably enough, that all
communication should be broken off between her and me. So,
finding Italy very dull, and having a fever tertian, I packed up my
valise, and prepared to cross the Alps; but my daughter fell ill, and
detained me.

After her arrival at Ravenna, the Guiccioli fell ill again too; and,
at last, her father (who had, all along, opposed the liaison most
violently till now) wrote to me to say that she was in such a state
that *he* begged me to come and see her,—and that her husband
had acquiesced, in consequence of her relapse, and that *he* (her
father) would guarantee all this, and that there would be no further
scenes in consequence between them, and that I should not be
compromised in any way. I set out soon after, and have been here
ever since. I found her a good deal altered, but getting better:—*all*
this comes of reading Corinna.

The Carnival is about to begin, and I saw about two or three
hundred people at the Marquis Cavalli's the other evening, with
as much youth, beauty, and diamonds among the women, as ever
averaged in the like number. My appearance in waiting on the
Guiccioli was considered as a thing of course. The Marquis is her
uncle, and naturally considered me as her relation.

The paper is out, and so is the letter. Pray write. Address to
Venice, whence the letters will be forwarded.

Yours, etc.,

B

Ravenna. February 21st. 1820

Dear Murray—The Bulldogs will be very agreeable—I have only those of this country who though good—& ready to fly at any thing—yet have not the tenacity of tooth and Stoicism in endurance of my canine fellow citizens, then pray send them—by the readiest conveyance, perhaps best by Sea.— —Mr. Kinnaird will disburse for them & deduct from the amount on your application or on that of Captain Fyler.—I see the good old King is gone to his place—one can't help being sorry—though blindness—and age and insanity are supposed to be drawbacks—on human felicity—but I am not at all sure that the latter at least—might not render him happier than any of his subjects.— —I have no thoughts of coming to the Coronation—though I should like to see it—and though I have a right to be a puppet in it—but my division with Lady Byron which has drawn an equinoctial line between me and mine in all other things—will operate in this also to prevent my being in the same procession.

— —By Saturday's post—I sent you four packets containing Cantos third and fourth of D[on] J[uan]—recollect that these two cantos reckon only as one with you and me—being in fact the third Canto cut into two—because I found it too long.—Remember this—and don't imagine that there could be any other motive.—The whole is about 225 Stanzas more or less—and a lyric of 96 lines—so that they are no longer than the first *single* cantos—but the truth is—that I made the first too long—and should have cut those down also had I thought better.— —Instead of saying in future for so many cantos—say so many *Stanzas* or pages—it was Jacob Tonson's way—and certainly the best—it prevents mistakes—I might have sent you a dozen cantos of 40 Stanzas each—those of "the Minstrel" (Beatties's) are no longer—and ruined you at once—if you don't suffer as it is;—but recollect you are not *pinned down* to anything you say in a letter and that calculating even these two cantos as *one* only (which they were and are to be reckoned) you are not bound by your offer,—act as may seem fair to all parties.— —I have finished my translation of the first Canto of the "Morgante Maggiore" of Pulci—which I will transcribe and send—it is the parent not only of Whistlecraft—but of all jocose Italian poetry.— —You must print it side by side with the original Italian because I wish the reader to judge of the fidelity—it is stanza for stanza—and often line for line if not word for word.— —

You ask me for a volume of manners &c.—on Italy; perhaps I am in the case to know more of them than most Englishmen— because I have lived among the natives—and in parts of the country—where Englishmen never resided before—(I speak of Romagna and this place particularly) but there are many reasons why I do not choose to touch in print on such a subject—I have lived in their houses and in the heart of their families—sometimes merely as "amico di casa" and sometimes as "Amico di cuore" of the Dama—and in neither case do I feel myself authorized in making a book of them.— —Their moral is not your moral—their life is not your life—you would not understand it—it is not English nor French—nor German—which you would all understand—the Conventual education—the Cavalier Servitude—the habits of thought and living are so entirely different—and the difference becomes so much more striking the more you live intimately with them—that I know not how to make you comprehend a people—who are at once temperate and profligate—serious in their character and buffoons in their amusements—capable of impressions and passions which are at once *sudden* and *durable* (what you find in no other nation) and who *actually* have *no society* (what we would call so) as you may see by their Comedies—they have no real comedy not even in Goldoni—and that is because they have no society to draw it from.— —

Their Conversazioni are not Society at *all*.—They go to the theatre to talk—and into company to hold their tongues—The *women* sit in a circle and the men gather into groupes [sic]—or they play at dreary Faro—or "Lotto reale"—for small sums.—Their Academie are Concerts like our own—with better music—and more form.—Their best things are the Carnival balls—and masquerades—when every body runs mad for six weeks.— —After their dinners and suppers they make extempore verses—and buffoon one another—but it is in a humour which you would not enter into—ye of the North.— —

In their houses it is better—I should know something of the

matter—having had a pretty general experience among their women—[from] the fisherman's wife—up to the Nobil' Donna whom I serve.— —Their system has it's rules—and it's fitnesses—and decorums—so as to be reduced to a kind of discipline—or game at hearts—which admits few deviations unless you wish to lose it.— —They are extremely tenacious—and jealous as furies—not permitting their Lovers even to marry if they can help it—and keeping them always close to them in public as in private whenever they can.— —In short they transfer marriage to adultery—and strike the *not* out of that commandment.—The reason is that they marry for their parents and love for themselves.—They exact fidelity from a lover as a debt of honour—while they pay the husband as a tradesman—that is not at all.— —You hear a person's character—male or female—canvassed—not as depending on their conduct to their husbands or wives—but to their mistress or lover.— —And—and—that's all.—If I wrote a quarto—I don't know that I could do more than amplify what I have here noted.— —

It is to be observed that while they do all this—the greatest outward respect is to be paid to the husbands—and not only by the ladies but by their Serventi—particularly if the husband serves no one himself—(which is not often the case however) so that you would often suppose them relations—the Servente making the figure of one adopted into the family.—Sometimes the ladies run a little restive—and elope—or divide—or make a scene—but this is at starting generally—when they know no better—or when they fall in love with a foreigner—or some such anomaly—and is always reckoned unnecessary and extravagant.— —

You enquire after "Dante's prophecy"—I have not done more than six hundred lines but will vaticinate at leisure.— —Of the Bust I know nothing—no Cameos or Seals are to be cut here or elsewhere that I know of in any good style.—Hobhouse should write himself to Thorwalsen—the bust was made and paid for three years ago.— —Pray tell Mrs. Leigh to request Lady Byron—to urge forward the transfer from the funds—which Hanson is opposing because he has views of investment for some Client of his own—which I can't consent to—I wrote to Lady B. on business this post addressed to the care of Mr. D. Kinnaird.—Somebody has sent me some American abuse of "Mazeppa"—and "the Ode";—in future I will compliment nothing but Canada—and desert to the English.— —

By the king's death—Mr. H[obhouse] I hear will stand for Westminster—I shall be glad to hear of his standing any where except in the pillory—which from the company he must have lately kept—(I always except Burdett—and Douglas K. and the genteel part of the reformers) was perhaps to be apprehended. I was really glad to hear it was for libel instead of larceny—for though impossible in his own person he might have been taken up by mistake for another at a meeting.— —All reflections on his present case and place are so <very> *Nugatory*—that it would be useless to pursue the subject further.— —

I am out of all patience to see my friends sacrifice themselves for a pack of blackguards—who disgust one with their Cause—although I have always been a friend to and a Voter for reform.— —If Hunt had addressed the language to me—which he did to Mr. H[obhouse] last election—I would not have descended to call out such a miscreant who won't fight—but have passed my sword-stick through his body—like a dog's and then thrown myself on my Peers—who would I hope—have weighed the provocation;—at any rate—it would have been as public a Service as Walworth's chastisement of Wat. Tyler.—If we must have a tyrant—let him at least be a gentleman who has been bred to the business, and let us fall by the axe and not by the butcher's cleaver.— —No one can be more sick of—or indifferent to politics than I am—if they let me alone—but if the time comes when a part must be taken one way or the other—I shall pause before I lend myself to the views of such ruffians—although I cannot but approve of a Constitutional amelioration of long abuses.— —Lord George Gordon—and Wilkes—and Burdett—and Horne Tooke—were all men of education—and courteous deportment—so is Hobhouse—but as for these others—I am convinced—that Robespierre was a Child—and Marat a quaker in comparison of what they would be could they throttle their way to power.— —

[scrawl]

Ravenna. March 14th. 1820

Dear Murray—Enclosed is Dante's Prophecy—Vision—or
what not—where I have left more than *one* reading—(which I
have done often) you may adopt that which Gifford & Frere—
Rose—and Hobhouse (is he still in Newgate?) and others of your
Utican *Senate* think the best—or least bad—the preface will explain all that is explicable.—These are but the four first cantos—if
approved I will go on like Isaiah.— —Pray mind in printing—and
let some good Italian Scholar correct the Italian quotations.— —

Four days ago I was overturned in an open carriage between the
river and a steep bank—wheels dashed to pieces slight bruises—
narrow escape—and all that—but no harm done—though
Coachman—footman—horses—and vehicle were all mixed
together like Maccaroni.— —It was [owing] to bad driving—as
I say—but the Coachman swears to a start on the part of the
horses—we went against a post—on the verge of a steep bank—
and capsized.— —I usually go out of the town in a carriage—and
meet the saddle horses at the bridge—it was in going there—that
we boggled—but I got my ride as usual—after the accident.— —
They say here it was all owing to St. Antonio of Padua (serious
I assure you) who does thirteen miracles a day—that worse did
not come of it;—I have no objection to this being his fourteenth
in the four and twenty hours—he presides over overturns—and
all escapes therefrom it seems; and they dedicate pictures &c. to
him as the Sailors once did to Neptune after "the high Roman
Fashion". — —

Yours in haste
[scrawl]

P.S.—Write directly.—I have sent you Don Juan—Translation
of Morgante Maggiore—and now Dante's &c. Acknowledge all.—

Ravenna, March 30th. [*1820*]

I have just received your letter, dated 15th instant, and will send
you fifty pounds, if you will inform me how I can remit that sum;
for I have no correspondence with Paris of any kind; my letters of

credit being for Italy; but perhaps you can get someone to cash you a bill for fifty pounds on me, which I would honour, or you can give me a safe direction for the remission of a bill to that amount. Address to me at Ravenna, not Venice.

With regard to my refusal, some years ago, to comply with a very different request of yours, you mistook, or chose to mistake the motive: it was not that "I held you much too cheap" as you say, but that my compliance with your request to visit you, would just then have been a great wrong to another person: and, whatever you may have heard, or may believe, I have ever acted with good faith in things even where it is rarely observed, as long as good faith is kept with me. I told you afterwards that I had no wish to hurt your self-love, and I tell you so again, when you will be more disposed to believe me.

In answer to your wish that I shall tell you if I was "happy", perhaps it would be a folly in any human being to say so of themselves, particularly a man who has had to pass through the sort of things which I have encountered; but I can at least say that I am not miserable, and am perhaps more tranquil than ever I was in England.

You can answer as soon as you please: and believe me

Yours, etc.,
BYRON

P.S.—Send me a banker's or merchant's address, or any person's in your confidence, and I will get Langle, my banker at Bologna, to remit you the sum I have mentioned.

It is not a very magnificent one; but it is all I can spare just now.

TO JOHN MURRAY   *Ravenna. April 16th. 1820*

Dear Murray—Post after post arrives without bringing any acknowledgement from you of the different packets (excepting the first) which I have sent within the last two months—all of which ought to be arrived long ere now—& as they were announced in other letters—you ought at least to say whether they are come or not.—You are not expected to write frequent or long letters—as your time is much occupied—but when parcels that have cost some pains in the composition, & great trouble in the copying are sent to you I should at least be put out of Suspense by the immediate acknowledgement per return of post addressed *directly* to *Ravenna*.—I am naturally—knowing what continental *posts* are—anxious to hear that they are arrived especially as I loathe the task of copying so much—that if there was a human being that could copy my blotted M.S.S.—he should have all they can ever bring for his trouble.— —All I desire is two lines to say— such a day I received such a packet—there are now at least *six* unacknowledged.— —This is neither kind nor courteous.— —

I have besides another reason for desiring *you* to be speedy— which is—that there is *that* brewing in Italy—which will speedily cut off all security of communication and set all your Anglo-travellers flying in every direction with their usual fortitude in foreign tumults.— —The Spanish & French affairs have set the Italians in a ferment—and no wonder—they have been too long trampled on.—This will make a sad scene for your exquisite traveller—but not for the resident—who naturally wishes a people to redress itself.—I shall if permitted by the natives remain to see what will come of it—and perhaps to take a turn with them—like Dugald Dalgetty and his horse—in case of business—for I shall think it by far the most interesting spectacle and moment in existence—to see the Italians send the Barbarians of all nations back to their own dens.— —I have lived long enough among them—to feel more for them as a nation than for any other people in existence—but they want Union—and they want principle—and I doubt their success—however they will try probably—and if they do—it will be a good cause—no Italian can hate an Austrian more than I do—unless it be the English—the Austrians seem to me the most obnoxious race under the Sky.— —But I doubt—if anything be done—it won't be so quietly as in Spain;—to be sure Revolutions are not to be made with Rose-water—where there are foreigners as Masters.—Write while you can—for it is but the toss up of a Paul—that there will not be a row that will somewhat retard the Mail, by and bye.

yrs.
[scrawl]

Address right to *Ravenna*.

TO JOHN MURRAY   *Ravenna. April 23d. 1820*

Dear Murray—The proofs don't contain the *last* stanzas of
Canto second—but end shortly after the 105th. Stanza.— —I told
you long ago—that the new Cantos were *not* good—and I also *told
you <the> a reason*—recollect I do not oblige you to publish them,
you may suppress them if you like—but I can alter nothing—I
have erased the six stanzas about those two impostors Southey and
Wordsworth—(which I suppose will give you great pleasure) but
I can do no more—I can neither recast—nor replace—but I give
you leave to put it all in the fire if you like—or *not* to publish—and
I think that's sufficient;—I told you that I wrote on with no good
will—that I had been *not* frightened but *hurt*—by the outcry—
and besides that, when I wrote last November—I was ill in body
and in very great distress of mind about some private things of
my own—but *you would* have it—so I sent it to you—& to make
it lighter *cut* it in two—but I can't piece it together again. I can't
cobble; I must "either make a spoon or spoil a horn" and there is
an end—for there is no remeid [sic]; but I leave you free will to
suppress the *whole* if you like it.—

About the *Morgante* Maggiore—I *wont have a line omitted*—it
may circulate or it may not—but all the Criticism on earth shan't
touch a line—unless it be because it is *badly* translated—now you
say—and I say—and others say—that the translation is a good
one—and so it shall go to press as it is.— —Pulci must answer
for his own irreligion—I answer for the translation only.— —I
am glad you have got the *Dante*—and there should be by this
time a translation of his Francesca of Rimini arrived—to append
to it.— —I sent you a quantity of *prose* observations in answer
to Wilson—but I shall not publish them *at present*—keep them
by you—as *documents*.— —Pray let Mr. Hobhouse look to the
Italian next time in the *proofs;—this time* while I am scribbling to
you—they are corrected by one who passes for the prettiest woman
in Romagna and even the Marches as far as Ancona—be the other
who she may.— —I am glad you like my answer to your enquiries
about Italian Society—it is fit you should *like something* and be
damned to you.— —

My love to Scott—I shall think higher of knighthood ever after

for his being dubbed—by the way—he is the first poet titled for
his talent—in Britain—it has happened abroad before now—but
on the continent titles are universal & worthless.— —Why don't
you send me Ivanhoe & the Monastery?— —I have never written to Sir Walter—for I know he has a thousand things & I a
thousand nothings to do—but I hope to see him at Abbotsford
before very long, and I will sweat his Claret for him—though
Italian abstemiousness has made my brain but a skilpit concern
for a Scotch sitting "inter pocula".—I love Scott and Moore—and
all the better brethren—but I hate & abhor that puddle of water-
worms—whom you have taken into your troop in the *history* line
I see.— —I am obliged to end abruptly.

                                                              yrs
                                                         [scrawl]

    P.S.—You say that *one half* is very good, you are *wrong*—for
if it were it would be the finest poem in existence—*where* is the
poetry of which *one half* is good—is it the *Æneid*? is it *Milton's*, is
it *Dryden's*—is it anyone's except *Pope's* and Goldsmith's; of which
all is good—& yet these two last are the poets—your pond poets
would explode.—But if *one half* of the two new Cantos be good
in your opinion —what the devil would you have more?—no—
no—no poetry is *generally* good—only by fits & starts—& you
are lucky to get a sparkle here & there—you might as well want a
Midnight *all stars*—as rhyme all perfect.— —
    We are on the verge of a *row* here—last night they have
overwritten all the city walls—with "up with the Republic["] &
["]death to the Pope &c. &c." this would be nothing in London
where the walls are privileged—& where when Somebody went to
Chancellor Thurlow to tell him as an alarming sign that he had seen
"Death to the king" on <Hyde> the park wall— —old Thurlow
asked him if he had ever seen "C—t" chalked on the same place,
to which the alarmist responding in the affirmative—Thurlow resumed "& so have I for these last 30 years and yet it never made my
p——k stand."— —But here it is a different thing[;] they are not
used to such fierce political inscriptions—and the police is all on
the alert, and the Cardinal glares pale through all his purple.— —

April 24th. 1820 8 o'clock P.M.

The police have been all Noon and after searching for the In-scribers—but have caught none as yet—they must have been all night about it—for the "Live republics—death to popes & priests" are innumerable—and plastered over all the palaces—ours has plenty.— —There is "down with the Nobility" too—they are down enough already for that matter.— —A very heavy rain & wind having come on—I did not get on horseback to go out & "skirr the country" but I shall mount tomorrow & take a canter among the peasantry—who are a savage resolute race—always riding with guns in their hands.— —I wonder they don't suspect the Serenaders—for they play on the guitar all night here as in Spain—to their Mistresses.— —Talking of politics—as Caleb Quotem says—pray look at the *Conclusion* of my Ode on *Waterloo*, written in the year 1815—& comparing it with the Duke de Berri's catastrophe in 1820—tell me if I have not as good a right to the character of "*Vates*" in both senses of the word as Fitzgerald & Coleridge.—

"Crimson tears will follow yet."

and have not they?— —I can't pretend to foresee what will happen among you Englishers at this distance—but I vaticinate a *row* in Italy—& in which case I don't know that I won't have a finger in it.—I dislike the Austrians and think the Italians infamously oppressed, & if they begin—why I will recommend "the erection of a Sconce upon Drumsnab" like Dugald Dalgetty.

TO THOMAS MOORE   *Ravenna, July 13th, 1820*

To remove or increase your Irish anxiety about my being "in a wisp," I answer your letter forthwith; premising that, as I am a "*Will*" of the wisp," I may chance to flit out of it. But, first, a word on the Memoir;—I have no objection, nay, I would rather that *one* correct copy was taken and deposited in honourable hands, in case of accidents happening to the original; for you know that I have none, and have never even *re*-read, nor, indeed, *read* at all what is there written; I only know that I wrote it with the fullest intention to be "faithful and true" in my narrative, but *not* impartial—no, by the Lord! I can't pretend to be that, while I feel. But I wish to give every body concerned the opportunity to contradict or correct me.

I have no objection to any proper person seeing what is there written,—seeing it was written, like every thing else, for the purpose of being read, however much many writings may fail in arriving at that object.

With regard to "the wisp," the Pope has pronounced *their separation*. The decree came yesterday from Babylon,—it was *she* and *her friends* who demanded it, on the grounds of her husband's (the noble Count Cavalier's) extraordinary usage. *He* opposed it with all his might because of the alimony, which has been assigned, with all her goods, chattels, carriage, etc., to be restored by him. In Italy they can't divorce. He insisted on her giving me up, and he would forgive every thing,—even the adultery, which he swears that he can prove by "famous witnesses." But, in this country, the very courts hold such proofs in abhorrence, the Italians being as much more delicate in public than the English, as they are more passionate in private.

The friends and relatives, who are numerous and powerful, reply to him—"*You*, yourself, are either fool or knave,—fool, if you did not see the consequences of the approximation of these two young persons,—knave, if you connive at it. Take your choice,—but don't break out (after twelve months of the closest intimacy, under your own eyes and positive sanction) with a scandal, which can only make you ridiculous and her unhappy."

He swore that he thought our intercourse was purely amicable, and that *I* was more partial to him than to her, till melancholy testimony proved the contrary. To this they answer, that "Will of *this* wisp" was not an unknown person, and that "clamosa Fama" had not proclaimed the purity of my morals;—that *her* brother, a year ago, wrote from Rome to warn him, that his wife would infallibly be led astray by this ignis fatuus, unless he took proper measures, all of which he neglected to take, &c. &c.

Now he says, that he encouraged my return to Ravenna, to see "*in quanti piedi di acqua siamo*," and he has found enough to drown him in. In short,

> "Ce ne fut pas le tout; sa femme se plaignit—
> 　　Procès—La parenté se joint en excuse et dit
> 　Que du *Docteur* venoit tout le mauvais ménage;
> 　Que cet homme étoit fou, que sa femme étoit sage.
> 　　On fit casser le mariage."

It is best to let the women alone, in the way of conflict, for they are sure to win against the field. She returns to her father's house, and I can only see her under great restrictions—such is the custom of the country. The relations behave very well:—I offered any settlement, but they refused to accept it, and swear she *shan't* live with G. (as he has tried to prove her faithless), but that he shall maintain her; and, in fact, a judgment to this effect came yesterday. I am, of course, in an awkward situation enough.

I have heard no more of the carabiniers who protested against my liveries. They are not popular, those same soldiers, and, in a small row, the other night, one was slain, another wounded, and divers put to flight, by some of the Romagnuole youth, who are dexterous, and somewhat liberal of the knife. The perpetrators are not discovered, but I hope and believe that none of my ragamuffins were in it, though they are somewhat savage, and secretly armed, like most of the inhabitants. It is their way, and saves sometimes a good deal of litigation.

There is a revolution at Naples. If so, it will probably leave a card at Ravenna in its way to Lombardy.

Your publishers seem to have used you like mine. M. has shuffled, and almost insinuated that my last productions are *dull*. Dull, sir!—damme, dull! I believe he is right. He begs for the completion of my tragedy of Marino Faliero, none of which is yet gone to England. The fifth act is nearly completed, but it is dreadfully long—40 sheets of long paper of 4 pages each—about 150 when printed; but "so full of pastime and prodigality" that I think it will do.

Pray send and publish your *Pome* upon me; and don't be afraid of praising me too highly. I shall pocket my blushes.

"Not actionable!"—*Chantre d'enfer!*—by * * that's a speech," and I won't put up with it. A pretty title to give a man for doubting if there be any such place!

So my Gail is gone—and Miss Mah*ony* won't take *mo*ney. I am very glad of it—I like to be generous, free of expense. But beg her not to translate me.

Oh, pray tell Galignani that I shall send him a screed of doctrine if he don't be more punctual. Somebody *regularly detains two*, and sometimes *four*, of his Messengers by the way. Do, pray, entreat him to be more precise. News are worth money in this remote kingdom of the Ostrogoths.

Pray, reply. I should like much to share some of your Champagne and La Fitte, but I am too Italian for Paris in general. Make Murray send my letter to you—it is full of *epigrams*.

Yours, &c.

TO COUNTESS TERESA GIUCCIOLI [TRANSLATION]
Ravenna, September 9th, 1820

My Love + + + Fishing and the Fisherwoman! Always something new.—Do you know that the Milanese *Gazette* says that I have *arrived* in London about the Queen's Business!! The veracity of Gazettes! The London papers report this—and my friends believe it, saying that for the present I want to be *incognito*.—One friend writes to me that many of them have been to see him—and went away again still not believing that I had not returned—among them the *Lamb*—without delay. She went away incredulous.—All this I found in yesterday's post.

Nothing from the filthy parents-in-law—Ferdinando is better— —.

On Monday we shall see each other again.— —I am charged *with Sentiment*, but don't know how to express it—or spread it over four pages of words—but I swear that I love you in a way that all the letters of Cicero could not express—even if the *self-love* of that celebrated *Egoist* were converted into love of his neighbour— and expressed with all the eloquence of his profession— —Love me—my p.o.c.

P.S.—Fishing— —what *Fish*? B?

TO RICHARD BELGRAVE HOPPNER   *Ravenna. Septr. 10th. 1820*

My dear Hoppner—Ecco Advocate Fossati's letter.—No paper
has nor will be signed.—Pray—*draw* on me for the Napoleons—
for I have no mode of remitting them—otherwise. Missiaglia
would empower some one here to receive them for you—as it is
not a *piazza bancale*.—I regret that you have such a bad opinion
of Shiloh—you used to have a good one.—Surely he has talent—
honour—but is crazy against religion and morality.—His tragedy
is sad work—but the subject renders it so.—His Islam had much
poetry.—You seem lately to have got some notion against him.—
Clare writes me the most insolent letters about Allegra—see what
a man gets by taking care of natural children!—Were it not for the
poor little child's sake—I am almost tempted to send her back to
her atheistical mother—but that would be too bad;—you cannot
conceive the excess of her insolence and I know not why—for
I have been at great care and expence—taking a house in the
country on purpose for her—she has *two* maids & every possible
attention.—If Clare thinks that she shall ever interfere with the
child's morals or education—she mistakes—she never shall—The
girl shall be a Christian and a married woman—if possible.—As
to seeing her—she may see her—under proper restrictions—but
She is not to throw every thing into confusion with her Bedlam
behaviour.—To express it delicately—I think Madame Clare is a
damned bitch—what think you?

TO AUGUSTA LEIGH   *Ravenna. 8bre.* [18th?] *1820*

My dearest Augusta—I suppose by this time that you will be
out of yr. fidget—& that the dilatory Hanson will have set Colonel L[eigh] at rest upon the subject of the bond &c.— —Ada's
picture is very like her mother—I mean the prints—for I have not
received the picture,—neither has Murray sent it—I presume.—
—She seems stout of her age—which is five years on the 10th. of
10bre.—is it not so?—It is almost as long since I have seen her—all
but a month—what day of January was it when <the Math> Lady
B—marched upon Kirkby?—which was the Signal of war.— —Sir
Walter Scott says in the beginning of "the Abbot" that ["]every *five*

years we find ourselves another and yet the same with a change of views and no less of the light in which we regard them; a change of motives as well as of actions." This I presume applies still more to those who have past their *five* years in foreign countries—for my part I suppose that I am *two* others—for it seems that some fool has been betting that he saw me in London—the other day—in a *Curricle*—if he said a *Canoe* it would have been much more likely.— —

And *you*? what have *your* "*five* years" done?—made your house like a Lying-in Hospital;—there never was such a creature except a rabbit—for increase & multiplication.—In short we are five years older in fact and I at least *ten* in *appearance*—the Lady B—I suppose retains her old starch obstinacy—with a deeper dash of Sternness—from the dint of time—and the effort it has cost her to be "magnanimous" as they called her mischief-making.—People accused somebody of painting her in "Donna *Inez*"—did it strike you so?—I can't say it did me—There might be something of her in the outline but the Spaniard was only a silly woman—and the other is a cut and dry made up character—which is another matter.— —Time and Events will one day or another revenge her past conduct,—without any interference of mine.— —So—Joe Murray is gathered to his Masters—as you say—the very Ghosts have died with him.—Newstead and he went almost together & now the B's must carve them out another inheritance.—If Ada had been a Son—I do not think that I should have parted with it after all—but I dislike George B[yron] for his behaviour in 1816.—and I am unacquainted with the others who may be in the line of the title—and being myself abroad—and at feud with the whole of the Noels—and with most of the B's except yourself—of course—these concurring with other & pressing circumstances—rendered the disposal of the Abbey necessary & not improper. Somebody said the other day—that "Lady Noel had been ill"—she is too troublesome an old woman ever to die while her death can do any good,—but if she ever does march—it is to be presumed that she will take her "water divining rod" with her—it may be a useful twig to her & the devil too—when she gets home again.— —

I can say very little to you of Italy—except that it is a very distracted State.—In England the Queen has been bountiful to

the Scandal-mongers.—She has got the Noel batch of Counsellors—it seems (except Romilly—who cut his throat) you see
who *those* sort of fellows *are*—and how they prey on a cause of
this kind—like crows on carrion.—Her Majesty's innocence is
probably something like another person's guilt.—However she
has been an ill-used woman—that's the truth on't—and in the
nature of things the woman ought to get the better. They generally do—whether they ought or not.— —I did not come over for
fifty reasons—and amongst others—that I do not think it a very
creditable thing to be one of the Judges even, upon such matters. I
have got a flourishing family (besides my daughter Allegra)—here
are two Cats—six dogs—a badger—a falcon, a tame Crow—and a
Monkey.— —The fox died—and a first Cat ran away.—With the
exception of an occasional civil war about provisions—they agree
to admiration—and do not make more noise than a well-behaved
Nursery.— —I have also eight horses—four carriage—and four
saddle—and go prancing away daily—at present up to the middle
in mire—for here have been the Autumnal rains—& drenched
every thing—amongst others myself yesterday—I got soaked
through cloak & all—& the horse through his skin—I believe.—
—I have now written to you a long family letter

ever yrs. [scrawl]

TO THOMAS MOORE (A)   *Ravenna, Dec. 9th, 1820*

Besides this letter, you will receive *three* packets, containing, in
all, 18 more sheets of Memoranda, which, I fear, will cost you more
in postage than they will ever produce by being printed in the next
century. Instead of waiting so long, if you could make any thing of
them *now* in the way of *reversion*, (that is, after *my* death,) I should
be very glad,—as, with all due regard to your progeny, I prefer you
to your grand-children. Would not Longman or Murray advance
you a certain sum *now*, pledging themselves *not* to have them published till after *my* decease, think you?—and what say you?

Over these latter sheets I would leave you a discretionary power;
because they contain, perhaps, a thing or two which is too sincere
for the public. If I consent to your disposing of their reversion

now, where would be the harm? Tastes may change. I would, in your case, make my essay to dispose of them, *not* publish, now; and if *you* (as is most likely) survive me, add what you please from your own knowledge; and, *above all*, *contradict* any thing, if I have *mis*-stated; for my first object is the truth, even at my own expense.

I have some knowledge of your countryman Muley Molock, the lecturer. He wrote to me several letters upon Christianity, to convert me; and, if I had not been a Christian already, I should probably have been now, in consequence. I thought there was something of wild talent in him, mixed with a due leaven of absurdity,—as there must be in all talent, let loose upon the world, without a martingale.

The ministers seem still to persecute the Queen * * *; but they *won't* go out, the sons of b—es. Damn Reform—I want a place— what say you? You must applaud the honesty of the declaration, whatever you may think of the intention.

I have quantities of paper in England, original and translated— tragedy, &c. &c., and am now copying out a Fifth Canto of Don Juan, 149 stanzas. So that there will be near *three thin* Albemarle, or *two thick* volumes of all sorts of my Muses. I mean to plunge thick, too, into the contest upon Pope, and to lay about me like a dragon till I make manure of [Bowles] for the top of Parnassus.

These rogues are right—*we* do laugh at *t'others*—eh?—don't we? You shall see—you shall see what things I'll say, an' it pleases Providence to leave us leisure. But in these parts they are all going to war; and there is to be liberty, and a row, and a constitution— when they can get them. But I won't talk politics—it is low. Let us talk of the Queen, and her bath, and her bottle—that's the only *motley* nowadays.

If there are any acquaintances of mine, salute them. The priests here are trying to persecute me,—but no matter.

Yours, &c.

TO THOMAS MOORE (B)   *Ravenna, Dec. 9th, 1820*

I open my letter to tell you a fact, which will show the state of this country better than I can. The commandant of the troops is *now* lying *dead* in my house. He was shot at a little past eight o'clock, about two hundred paces from my door. I was putting on my great-coat to visit Madame la Contessa G. when I heard the shot. On coming into the hall, I found all my servants on the balcony, exclaiming that a man was murdered. I immediately ran down, calling on Tita (the bravest of them) to follow me. The rest wanted to hinder us from going, as it is the custom for every body here, it seems, to run away from "the stricken deer".

However, down we ran, and found him lying on his back, almost, if not quite, dead, with five wounds, one in the heart, two in the stomach, one in the finger, and the other in the arm. Some soldiers cocked their guns, and wanted to hinder me from passing. However, we passed, and I found Diego, the adjutant, crying over him like a child—a surgeon, who said nothing of his profession—a priest, sobbing a frightened prayer—and the commandant, all this time, on his back, on the hard, cold pavement, without light or assistance, or any thing around him but confusion and dismay.

As nobody could, or would, do any thing but howl and pray, and as no one would stir a finger to move him, for fear of conse-quences, I lost my patience—made my servant and a couple of the mob take up the body—sent off two soldiers to the guard—despatched Diego to the Cardinal with the news, and had the commandant carried upstairs into my own quarter. But it was too late, he was gone—not at all disfigured—bled inwardly—not above an ounce or two came out.

I had him partly stripped—made the surgeon examine him, and examined him myself. He had been shot by cut balls or slugs. I felt one of the slugs, which had gone through him, all but the skin. Everybody conjectures why he was killed, but no one knows how. The gun was found close by him—an old gun, half filed down.

He only said, "O Dio!" and "Gesu!" two or three times, and appeared to have suffered little. Poor fellow! he was a brave of-ficer, but had made himself much disliked by the people. I knew him personally, and had met with him often at conversazioni and elsewhere. My house is full of soldiers, dragoons, doctors, priests, and all kinds of persons,—though I have now cleared it, and clapt sentinels at the doors. Tomorrow the body is to be moved. The town is in the greatest confusion, as you may suppose.

You are to know that, if I had not had the body moved, they would have left him there till morning in the street for fear of consequences. I would not choose to let even a dog die in such a manner, without succour:—and, as for consequences, I care for none in a duty.

Yours, &c.

P.S.—The lieutenant on duty by the body is smoking his pipe with great composure.—A queer people this.

Ravenna Journal
January 4–February 27, 1821
[Thomas Moore's transcription]

Ravenna, January 4th, 1821

"A sudden thought strikes me." Let me begin a Journal once more. The last I kept was in Switzerland, in record of a tour made in the Bernese Alps, which I made to send to my sister in 1816, and I suppose that she has it still, for she wrote to me that she was pleased with it. Another, and longer, I kept in 1813–1814, which I gave to Thomas Moore in the same year.

This morning I gat me up late, as usual—weather bad—bad as England—worse. The snow of last week melting to the sirocco of to-day, so that there were two d—d things at once. Could not even get to ride on horseback in the forest. Stayed at home all the morning—looked at the fire—wondered when the post would come. Post came at the Ave Maria, instead of half-past one o'clock, as it ought. Galignani's Messengers, six in number—a letter from Faenza, but none from England. Very sulky in consequence (for there ought to have been letters), and ate in consequence a copious dinner; for when I am vexed, it makes me swallow quicker—but drank very little.

I was out of spirits—read the papers—thought what *fame* was, on reading, in a case of murder, that "Mr. Wych, grocer, at Tunbridge, sold some bacon, flour, cheese, and, it is believed, some plums, to some gypsy woman accused. He had on his counter (I quote faithfully) a *book*, the Life of *Pamela*, which he was *tearing* for *waste* paper, &c., &c. In the cheese was found, &c., and a *leaf* of *Pamela wrapt round the bacon*." What would Richardson, the vainest and luckiest of *living* authors (i.e. while alive)—he who, with Aaron Hill, used to prophesy and chuckle over the presumed fall of Fielding (the *prose* Homer of human nature) and of Pope (the most beautiful of poets)—what would he have said, could he have traced his pages from their place on the French prince's toilets (see Boswell's Johnson) to the grocer's counter and the gipsy-murderess's bacon!!!

What would he have said? What can anybody say, save what Solomon said long before us? After all, it is but passing from one counter to another, from the bookseller's to the other trades-man's—grocer or pastry-cook. For my part, I have met with most poetry upon trunks; so that I am apt to consider the trunk-maker as the sexton of authorship.

Wrote five letters in about half an hour, short and savage, to all my rascally correspondents. Carriage came. Heard the news of three murders at Faenza and Forli—a carabinier, a smuggler, and an attorney—all last night. The two first in a quarrel, the latter by premeditation.

Three weeks ago—almost a month—the 7th it was—I picked up the Commandant, mortally wounded, out of the street; he died in my house; assassins unknown, but presumed political. His brethren wrote from Rome last night to thank me for having assisted him in his last moments. Poor fellow! it was a pity; he was a good soldier, but imprudent. It was eight in the evening when they killed him. We heard the shot; my servants and I ran out, and found him expiring, with five wounds, two whereof mortal—by slugs they seemed. I examined him, but did not go to the dissec-tion next morning.

Carriage at 8 or so—went to visit La Contessa G.—found her playing on the piano-forte—talked till ten, when the Count, her father, and the no less Count, her brother, came in from the thea-tre. Play, they said, Alfieri's Filippo—well received.

Two days ago the King of Naples passed through Bologna on his way to congress. My servant Luigi brought the news. I had sent him to Bologna for a lamp. How will it end? Time will show.

Came home at eleven, or rather before. If the road and weather are conformable, mean to ride to-morrow. High time—almost a week at this work—snow, sirocco, one day—frost and snow the other—sad climate for Italy. But the two seasons, last and present, are extraordinary. Read a Life of Leonardo da Vinci by Rossi—ruminated—wrote this much, and will go to bed.

January 5th, 1821

Rose late—dull and drooping—the weather dripping and

dense. Snow on the ground, and sirocco above in the sky, like yesterday. Roads up to the horse's belly, so that riding (at least for pleasure) is not very feasible. Added a postscript to my letter to Murray. Read the conclusion, for the fiftieth time (I have read all W. Scott's novels at least fifty times) of the third series of "Tales of my Landlord",—grand work—Scotch Fielding, as well as great English poet—wonderful man! I long to get drunk with him.

Dined versus six o' the clock. Forgot that there was a plum-pudding, (I have added, lately, *eating* to my "family of vices,") and had dined before I knew it. Drank half a bottle of some sort of spirits—probably spirits of wine; for what they call brandy, rum, &c. &c., here is nothing but spirits of wine, coloured accordingly. Did *not* eat two apples, which were placed by way of dessert. Fed the two cats, the hawk, and the tame (but not *tamed*) crow. Read Mitford's History of Greece—Xenophon's Retreat of the Ten Thousand. Up to this present moment writing, 6 minutes before eight o' the clock—French hours, not Italian.

Hear the carriage—order pistols and great coat, as usual—necessary articles. Weather cold—carriage open, and inhabitants somewhat savage—rather treacherous and highly inflamed by politics. Fine fellows, though,—good materials for a nation. Out of chaos God made a world, and out of high passions comes a people.

Clock strikes—going out to make love. Somewhat perilous, but not disagreeable. Memorandum—a new screen put up to-day. It is rather antique, but will do with a little repair.

Thaw continues—hopeful that riding may be practicable to-morrow. Sent the papers to Al[borghett]i.—grand events coming.

11 o' the clock and nine minutes. Visited La Contessa G[uiccioli] Nata G[hiselli] G[amba]. Found her beginning my letter of answer to the thanks of Alessio del Pinto of Rome for assisting his brother the late Commandant in his last moments, as I had begged her to pen my reply for the purer Italian, I being an ultramontane, little skilled in the set phrase of Tuscany. Cut short the letter—finish it another day. Talked of Italy, patriotism, Alfieri, Madame Albany, and other branches of learning. Also Sallust's Conspiracy of Catiline, and the War of Jugurtha. At 9 came in her brother, Il Conte Pietro—at 10, her father, Conte Ruggiero.

Talked of various modes of warfare—of the Hungarian and

Highland modes of broad-sword exercise, in both whereof I was once a moderate "master of fence". Settled that the R[evolution]. will break out on the 7th or 8th of March, in which appointment I should trust, had it not been settled that it was to have broken out in October, 1820. But those Bolognese shirked the Romagnuoles.

"It is all one to Ranger," One must not be particular, but take rebellion when it lies in the way. Came home—read the "Ten Thousand" again, and will go to bed.

Mem.—Ordered Fletcher (at four o'clock this afternoon) to copy out 7 or 8 apophthegms of Bacon, in which I have detected such blunders as a school-boy might detect rather than commit. Such are the sages! What must they be, when such as I can stumble on their mistakes or misstatements? I will go to bed, for I find that I grow cynical.

January 6th, 1821

Mist—thaw—slop—rain. No stirring out on horseback. Read Spence's Anecdotes. Pope a fine fellow—always thought him so. Corrected blunders in *nine* apophthegms of Bacon—all historical—and read Mitford's Greece. Wrote an epigram. Turned to a passage in Guinguené—ditto in Lord Holland's Lope de Vega. Wrote a note on Don Juan.

At eight went out to visit. Heard a little music—like music. Talked with Count Pietro G. of the Italian comedian Vestris, who is now at Rome—have seen him often act in Venice—a good actor—very. Somewhat of a mannerist; but excellent in broad comedy, as well as in the sentimental pathetic. He has made me frequently laugh and cry, neither of which is now a very easy matter—at least, for a player to produce in me.

Thought of the state of women under the ancient Greeks—convenient enough. Present state, a remnant of the barbarism of the chivalry [chivalric?] and feudal ages—artificial and unnatural. They ought to mind home—and be well fed and clothed—but not mixed in society. Well educated, too, in religion—but to read neither poetry nor politics—nothing but books of piety and cookery. Music—drawing—dancing—also a little gardening and ploughing now and then. I have seen them mending the roads in Epirus with good success. Why not, as well as hay-making and milking?

Came home, and read Mitford again, and played with my mastiff—gave him his supper. Made another reading to the epigram, but the turn the same. To-night at the theatre, there being a prince on his throne in the last scene of the comedy,—the audience laughed, and asked him for a *Constitution*. This shows the state of the public mind here, as well as the assassinations. It won't do. There must be an universal republic,—and there ought to be.

The crow is lame of a leg—wonder how it happened—some fool trod upon his toe, I suppose. The falcon pretty brisk—the cats large and noisy—the monkeys I have not looked to since the cold weather, as they suffer by being brought up. Horses must be gay—get a ride as soon as weather serves. Deuced muggy still—an Italian winter is a sad thing, but all the other seasons are charming.

What is the reason that I have been, all my lifetime, more or less *ennuyé*? and that, if any thing, I am rather less so now than I was at twenty, as far as my recollection serves? I do not know how to answer this, but presume that it is constitutional,—as well as the waking in low spirits, which I have invariably done for many years. Temperance and exercise, which I have practiced at times, and for a long time together vigorously and violently, made little or no difference. Violent passions did;—when under their immediate influence—it is odd, but—I was in agitated, but *not* in depressed spirits.

A dose of salts has the effect of a temporary inebriation, like light champagne, upon me. But wine and spirits make me sullen and savage to ferocity—silent, however, and retiring, and not quarrelsome, if not spoken to. Swimming also raises my spirits,—but in general they are low, and get daily lower. That is *hopeless*: for I do not think I am so much *ennuyé* as I was at nineteen. The proof is, that then I must game, or drink, or be in motion of some kind, or I was miserable. At present, I can mope in quietness; and like being alone better than any company—except the lady's whom I serve. But I feel a something, which makes me think that, if I ever reach near to old age, like Swift, "I shall die at top" first. Only I do not dread idiotism or madness so much as he did. On the contrary, I think some quieter stages of both must be preferable to much of what men think the possession of their senses.

January 7th, 1821, Sunday

Still rain—mist—snow—drizzle—and all the incalculable combinations of a climate, where heat and cold struggle for mastery. Read Spence, and turned over Roscoe, to find a passage I have not found. Read the 4th vol. of W. Scott's second series of "Tales of my Landlord". Dined. Read the Lugano Gazette. Read—I forget what. At 8 went to conversazione. Found there the Countess Geltrude, Betti V. and her husband, and others. Pretty black-eyed woman that—*only* twenty-two—same age as Teresa, who is prettier, though.

The Count Pietro G[amba] took me aside to say that the Patriots have had notice from Forli (twenty miles off) that to-night the government and its party mean to strike a stroke—that the Cardinal here has had orders to make several arrests immediately, and that, in consequence, the Liberals are arming, and have posted patroles in the streets, to sound the alarm and give notice to fight for it.

He asked me "what should be done?" I answered, "Fight for it, rather than be taken in detail;" and offered, if any of them are in immediate apprehension of arrest, to receive them in my house (which is defensible), and to defend them, with my servants and themselves (we have arms and ammunition), as long as we can,— or to try to get them away under cloud of night. On going home, I offered him the pistols which I had about me—but he refused, but said he would come off to me in case of accidents.

It wants half an hour of midnight, and rains;—as Gibbet says, "a fine night for their enterprise—dark as hell, and blows like the devil." If the row don't happen *now*, it must soon. I thought that their system of shooting people would soon produce a reaction—and now it seems coming. I will do what I can in the way of combat, though a little out of exercise. The cause is a good one.

Turned over and over half a score of books for the passage in question, and can't find it. Expect to hear the drum and the musquetry momently (for they swear to resist, and are right,)—but I hear nothing, as yet, save the plash of the rain and the gusts of the wind at intervals. Don't like to go to bed, because I hate to be waked, and would rather sit up for the row, if there is to be one.

Mended the fire—have got the arms—and a book or two, which I shall turn over. I know little of their numbers, but think the Carbonari strong enough to beat the troops, even here. With twenty men this house might be defended for twenty-four hours against any force to be brought against it, *now* in this place, for the same time; and, in such a time, the country would have notice, and would rise,—if ever they *will* rise, of which there is some doubt. In the mean time, I may as well read as do any thing else, being alone.

January 8th, 1821, Monday

Rose, and found Count P. G. in my apartments. Sent away the servant. Told me that, according to the best information, the Government had not issued orders for the arrests apprehended; that the attack in Forli had not taken place (as expected) by the Sanfedisti—opponents of the Carbonari or Liberals—and that, as yet, they are still in apprehension only. Asked me for some arms of a better sort, which I gave him. Settled that, in case of a row, the Liberals were to assemble *here* (with me), and that he had given the word to Vincenzo G. and others of the *Chiefs* for that purpose. He himself and father are going to the chase in the forest; but V[incenzo]. G[allina]. is to come to me, and an express to be sent off to him, P.G., if any thing occurs. Concerted operations. They are to seize—but no matter.

I advised them to attack in detail, and in different parties, in different *places* (though at the *same* time), so as to divide the attention of the troops, who, though few, yet being disciplined, would beat any body of people (not trained) in a regular fight—unless dispersed in small parties, and distracted with different assaults. Offered to let them assemble here if they choose. It is a strongish post—narrow street, commanded from within—and tenable walls. * * * * * *

Dined. Tried on a new coat. Letter to Murray, with corrections of Bacon's Apophthegms and an epigram—the *latter not* for publication. At eight went to Teresa, Countess G. * * * * * * At nine and a half came in Il Conte P. and Count P. G. Talked of a certain proclamation lately issued. Count R. G. had been with * * (the * *), to sound him about the arrests. He, * *, is a *trimmer*, and deals, at present, his cards with both hands. If he don't mind, they'll be full. * * pretends (*I* doubt him—*they* don't—we shall see) that there is no such order, and seems staggered by the immense exertions of the Neapolitans, and the fierce spirit of the Liberals here. The truth is, that * * cares for little but his place (which is a good one), and wishes to play pretty with both parties. He has changed his mind thirty times these last three moons, to my knowledge, for he corresponds with me. But he is not a bloody fellow—only an avaricious one.

It seems that, just at this moment (as Lydia Languish says) "there will be no elopement after all." I wish that I had known as much last night—or, rather, this morning—I should have gone to bed two hours earlier. And yet I ought not to complain; for, though it is a sirocco, and heavy rain, I have not *yawned* for these two days.

Came home—read History of Greece—before dinner had read Walter Scott's Rob Roy. Wrote address to the letter in answer to Alessio del Pinto, who has thanked me for helping his brother (the late Commandant, murdered here last month) in his last moments. Have told him I only did a duty of humanity—as is true. The brother lives at Rome.

Mended the fire with some "sgobole" (a Romagnuole word) and gave the falcon some water. Drank some Seltzer-water. Mem.— received to-day a print, or etching, of the story of Ugolino, by an Italian painter—different, of course, from Sir Joshua Reynolds's, and I think (as far as recollection goes) *no worse*, for Reynolds's is not good in history. Tore a button in my new coat.

I wonder what figure these Italians will make in a regular row. I sometimes think that, like the Irishman's gun (somebody had sold him a crooked one), they will only do for "shooting round a corner;" at least, this sort of shooting has been the late tenor of their exploits. And yet, there are materials in this people, and a noble energy, if well directed. But who is to direct them? No matter. Out of such times heroes spring. Difficulties are the hot-beds of high spirits, and Freedom the mother of the few virtues incident to human nature.

Rose—the day fine. Ordered the horses; but Lega (my *secretary*, an Italianism for steward or chief servant) coming to tell me that the painter had finished the work in fresco for the room he has been employed on lately, I went to see it before I set out. The painter has not copied badly the prints from Titian, &c., considering all things.

* * * * * * * * * * * * * * *

Dined. Read Johnson's "Vanity of Human Wishes,"—all the examples and mode of giving them sublime, as well as the latter part, with the exception of an occasional couplet. I do not so much admire the opening. I remember an observation of Sharpe's (the *Conversationist*, as he was called in London, and a very clever man) that the first line of this poem was superfluous, and that Pope (the best of poets, *I* think,) would have begun at once, only changing the punctuation—

"Survey mankind from China to Peru!"

The former line, "Let observation," &c., is certainly heavy and useless. But 'tis a grand poem—and *so true!*—true as the 10th of Juvenal himself. The lapse of ages *changes* all things—time—language—the earth—the bounds of the sea—the stars of the sky, and every thing "about, around, and underneath" man, *except man himself*, who has always been, and always will be, an unlucky rascal. The infinite variety of lives conduct but to death, and the infinity of wishes lead but to disappointment. All the discoveries which have yet been made have multiplied little but existence. An extirpated disease is succeeded by some new pestilence; and a discovered world has brought little to the old one, except the p[ox]—first and freedom afterwards—the *latter* a fine thing, particularly as they gave it to Europe in exchange for slavery. But it is doubtful whether "the Sovereigns" would not think the *first* the best present of the two to their subjects.

At eight went out—heard some news. They say the King of Naples has declared, by couriers from Florence, to the *Powers* (as they call now those wretches with crowns) that his Constitution was compulsive, &c., &c., and that the Austrian barbarians are placed again on *war* pay, and will march. Let them—"they come like sacrifices in their trim," the hounds of hell! Let it still be a hope to see their bones piled like those of the human dogs at Morat, in Switzerland, which I have seen.

Heard some music. At nine the usual visitors—news, *war*, or rumours of war. Consulted with P. G., &c., &c. They mean to *insurrect* here, and are to honour me with a call thereupon. I shall not fall back; though I don't think them in force or heart sufficient to make much of it. But, *onward*!—it is now the time to act, and what signifies *self*, if a single spark of that which would be worthy of the past can be bequeathed unquenchedly to the future? It is not one man, nor a million, but the *spirit* of liberty which must be spread. The waves which dash upon the shore are, one by one, broken, but yet the *ocean* conquers, nevertheless. It overwhelms the Armada, it wears the rock, and, if the *Neptunians* are to be believed, it has not only destroyed, but made a world. In like manner, whatever the sacrifice of individuals, the great cause will gather strength, sweep down what is rugged, and fertilize (for *sea-weed* is *manure*) what is cultivable. And so, the mere selfish calculation ought never to be made on such occasions; and, at present, it shall not be computed by me. I was never a good arithmetician of chances, and shall not commence now.

January 10th, 1821

Day fine—rained only in the morning. Looked over accounts. Read Campbell's Poets—marked errors of Tom (the author) for correction. Dined—went out—music—Tyrolese air, with variations. Sustained the cause of the original simple air against the variations of the Italian school. * * * * * * *

Politics somewhat tempestuous, and cloudier daily. To-morrow being foreign post-day, probably something more will be known.

Came home—read. Corrected Tom Campbell's slips of the pen. A good work, though—style affected—but his defence of Pope is glorious. To be sure, it is his *own cause* too,—but no matter, it is very good, and does him great credit.

Midnight

I have been turning over different *Lives* of the Poets. I rarely read their works, unless an occasional flight over the classical ones, Pope, Dryden, Johnson, Gray, and those who approach them nearest (I leave the *rant* of the rest to the *cant* of the day), and—I had made several reflections, but I feel sleepy, and may as well go to bed.

January 11th, 1821

Read the letters. Corrected the tragedy and the "Hints from Horace". Dined, and got into better spirits.—Went out—re-turned—finished letters, five in number. Read Poets, and an anecdote in Spence.

Al[borghett]i writes to me that the Pope, and Duke of Tuscany, and King of Sardinia, have also been called to Congress; but the Pope will only deal there by proxy. So the interests of millions are in the hands of about twenty coxcombs, at a place called Leibach!

I should almost regret that my own affairs went well, when those of nations are in peril. If the interests of mankind could be essentially bettered (particularly of these oppressed Italians), I should not so much mind my own "sma' peculiar". God grant us all better times, or more philosophy.

In reading, I have just chanced upon an expression of Tom Campbell's;—speaking of Collins, he says that "no reader cares any more about the *characteristic manners* of his Eclogues than about the authenticity of the tale of Troy". 'Tis false—we *do* care about "the authenticity of the tale of Troy". I have stood upon that plain *daily*, for more than a month, in 1810; and, if any thing diminished my pleasure, it was that the blackguard Bryant had impugned its veracity. It is true I read "Homer Travestied" (the first twelve books), because Hobhouse and others bored me with their learned localities, and I love quizzing. But I still venerated the grand original as the truth of *history* (in the material *facts*) and of *place*. Otherwise, it would have given me no delight. Who will persuade me, when I reclined upon a mighty tomb, that it did not contain a hero?—its very magnitude proved this. Men do not labour over the ignoble and petty dead—and why should not the *dead* be *Homer's* dead? The secret of Tom Campbell's defence of *inaccuracy* in costume and description is, that his Gertrude, &c., has no more locality in common with Pennsylvania than with Penmanmaur. It is notoriously full of grossly false scenery, as all Americans declare, though they praise parts of the Poem. It is thus that self-love for ever creeps out, like a snake, to sting anything which happens, even accidentally, to stumble upon it.

January 12th, 1821

The weather still so humid and impracticable, that London, in its most oppressive fogs, were a summer-bower to this mist and sirocco, which now has lasted (but with one day's interval), chequered with snow or heavy rain only, since the 30th of December, 1820. It is so far lucky that I have a literary turn;—but it is very tiresome not to be able to stir out, in comfort, on any horse but Pegasus, for so many days. The roads are even worse than the weather, by the long splashing, and the heavy soil, and the growth of the waters.

Read the Poets—English, that is to say—out of Campbell's edition. There is a good deal of taffeta in some of Tom's prefatory phrases, but his work is good as a whole. I like him best, though, in his own poetry.

Murray writes that they want to act the Tragedy of Marino Faliero;—more fools they, it was written for the closet. I have protested against this piece of usurpation, (which, it seems, is legal for managers over any printed work, against the author's will) and I hope they will not attempt it. Why don't they bring out some of the numberless aspirants for theatrical celebrity, now encumbering their shelves, instead of lugging me out of the library? I have written a fierce protest against any such attempt; but I still would hope that it will not be necessary, and that they will see, at once, that it is not intended for the stage. It is too regular—the time, twenty-four hours—the change of place not frequent—nothing *melo*dramatic—no surprises, no starts, nor trap-doors, nor opportunities "for tossing their heads and kicking their heels"—and no *love*—the grand ingredient of a modern play.

I have found out the seal cut on Murray's letter. It is meant for Walter Scott—or Sir Walter—he is the first poet knighted since *Sir* Richard Blackmore. But it does not do him justice. Scott's—particularly when he recites—is a very intelligent countenance, and this seal says nothing.

Scott is certainly the most wonderful writer of the day. His novels are a new literature in themselves, and his poetry as good as any—if not better (only on an erroneous system)—and only ceased to be so popular, because the vulgar learned were tired of hearing "Aristides called the Just", and Scott the Best, and ostracised him.

I like him, too, for his manliness of character, for the extreme pleasantness of his conversation, and his good-nature towards myself, personally. May he prosper!—for he deserves it. I know no reading to which I fall with such alacrity as a work of W. Scott's. I shall give the seal, with his bust on it, to Madame la Comtesse G. this evening, who will be curious to have the effigies of a man so celebrated.

How strange are my thoughts!—The reading of the song of Milton, "Sabrina fair" has brought back upon me—I know not how or why—the happiest, perhaps, days of my life (always excepting, here and there, a Harrow holiday in the two latter summers of my stay there) when living at Cambridge with Edward Noel Long, afterwards of the Guards,—who, after having served honourably in the expedition to Copenhagen (of which two or three thousand scoundrels yet survive in plight and pay), was drowned early in 1809, on his passage to Lisbon with his regiment in the St. George transport, which was run foul of, in the night, by another transport. We were rival swimmers—fond of riding—reading—and of conviviality. We had been at Harrow together; but—*there*, at least—his was a less boisterous spirit than mine. I was always cricketing—rebelling—fighting—*rowing* (from *row*, not *boat*-rowing, a different practice), and in all manner of mischiefs; while he was more sedate and polished. At Cambridge—both of Trinity—my spirit rather softened, or his roughened, for we became very great friends. The description of Sabrina's seat reminds me of our rival feats in *diving*. Though Cam's is not a very "translucent wave," it was fourteen feet deep, where we used to dive for, and pick up—having thrown them in on purpose—plates, eggs, and even shillings. I remember, in particular, there was the stump of a tree (at least ten or twelve feet deep) in the bed of the river, in a spot where we bathed most commonly, round which I used to cling, and "wonder how the devil I came there".

Our evenings we passed in music (he was musical, and played on more than one instrument, flute and violoncello), in which I was audience; and I think that our chief beverage was soda-water. In the day we rode, bathed, and lounged, reading occasionally. I remember our buying, with vast alacrity, Moore's new quarto (in 1806), and reading it together in the evenings.

We only passed the summer together;—Long had gone into the Guards during the year I passed in Notts, away from college. *His* friendship, and a violent, though *pure*, love and passion—which held me at the same period—were the then romance of the most romantic period of my life.

* * * * * * * * * * * * * * *

I remember that, in the spring of 1809, H[obhouse] laughed at my being distressed at Long's death, and amused himself with making epigrams upon his name, which was susceptible of a pun—*Long, short*, &c. But three years after, he had ample leisure to repent it, when our mutual friend, and his, H[obhouse]'s particular friend, Charles Matthews, was drowned also, and he, himself, was as much affected by a similar calamity. But *I* did not pay him back in puns and epigrams, for I valued Matthews too much, myself, to do so; and, even if I had not, I should have respected his griefs.

Long's father wrote to me to write his son's epitaph. I promised—but I had not the heart to complete it. He was such a good, amiable being as rarely remains long in this world; with talent and accomplishments, too, to make him the more regretted. Yet, although a cheerful companion, he had strange melancholy thoughts sometimes. I remember once that we were going to his uncle's, I think—I went to accompany him to the door merely, in some Upper or Lower Grosvenor or Brook Street, I forget which, but it was in a street leading out of some square,—he told me that, the night before, he "had taken up a pistol—not knowing or examining whether it was loaded or no—and had snapped it at his head, leaving it to chance whether it might not be charged."

The letter, too, which he wrote me on leaving college to join the Guards, was as melancholy in its tenour as it could well be on such an occasion. But he showed nothing of this in his deportment, being mild and gentle;—and yet with much turn for the ludicrous in his disposition. We were both much attached to Harrow, and sometimes made excursions there together from London to revive our schoolboy recollections.

Midnight

Read the Italian translation by Guido Sorelli of the German Grillparzer—a devil of a name, to be sure, for posterity; but they *must* learn to pronounce it. With all the allowance for a *translation*, and above all, an *Italian* translation (they are the very worst of translators, except from the Classics—Annibale Caro, for instance—and *there*, the bastardy of their language helps them, as, by way of *looking legitimate*, they ape their fathers' tongue)—but with every allowance for such a disadvantage, the tragedy of *Sappho* is superb and sublime! There is no denying it. The man has done a great thing in writing that play. And *who is he*? I know him not; but *ages will*. 'Tis a high intellect.

I must premise, however, that I have read *nothing* of Adolph Müllner's (the author of "Guilt"), and much less of Goëthe, and Schiller, and Wieland, than I could wish. I only know them through the medium of English, French, and Italian translations. Of the *real* language I know absolutely nothing,—except oaths learned from postillions and officers in a squabble. I can *swear* in German potently, when I like—"Sacrament—Verfluchter—Hundsfott"— and so forth; but I have little of their less energetic conversation.

I like, however, their women, (I was once *so desperately* in love with a German woman, Constance,) and all that I have read, translated, of their writings, and all that I have seen on the Rhine of their country and people—all, except the Austrians, whom I abhor, loathe, and—I cannot find words for my hate of them, and should be sorry to find deeds correspondent to my hate; for I abhor cruelty more than I abhor the Austrians—except on an impulse, and then I am savage—but not deliberately so.

Grillparzer is grand—antique—*not so simple* as the ancients,

but very simple for a modern—too Madame de Stael-*ish*, now and
then—but altogether a great and goodly writer.

January 13th, 1821, Saturday

Sketched the outline and Drams. Pers. of an intended tragedy
of Sardanapalus, which I have for some time meditated. Took the
names from Diodorus Siculus, (I know the history of Sardanapalus, and have known it since I was twelve years old), and read
over a passage in the ninth vol. octavo of Mitford's Greece, where
he rather vindicates the memory of this last of the Assyrians.

Dined—news come—the *Powers* mean to war with the peoples.
The intelligence seems positive—let it be so—they will be beaten
in the end. The king-times are fast finishing. There will be blood
shed like water, and tears like mist; but the peoples will conquer in
the end. I shall not live to see it, but I foresee it.

I carried Teresa the Italian translation of Grillparzer's Sappho,
which she promises to read. She quarrelled with me, because I said
that love was *not the loftiest* theme for true tragedy; and, having the
advantage of her native language, and natural female eloquence,
she overcame my fewer arguments. I believe she was right. I must
put more love into "Sardanapalus" than I intended. I speak, of
course, *if* the times will allow me leisure. That *if* will hardly be a
peace-maker.

January 14th, 1821

Turned over Seneca's tragedies. Wrote the opening lines of the
intended tragedy of Sardanapalus. Rode out some miles into the
forest. Misty and rainy. Returned—dined—wrote some more of
my tragedy.

Read Diodorus Siculus—turned over Seneca, and some other
books. Wrote some more of the tragedy. Took a glass of grog. After
having ridden hard in rainy weather, and scribbled, and scribbled
again, the spirits (at least mine) need a little exhilaration, and I
don't like laudanum now as I used to do. So I have mixed a glass
of strong waters and single waters, which I shall now proceed to
empty. Therefore and thereunto I conclude this day's diary.

The effect of all wines and spirits upon me is, however, strange. It *settles*, but it makes me gloomy—gloomy at the very moment of their effect, and not gay hardly ever. But it composes for a time, though sullenly.

January 15th, 1821

Weather fine. Received visit. Rode out into the forest—fired pistols. Returned home—dined—dipped into a volume of Mitford's Greece—wrote part of a scene of "Sardanapalus". Went out—heard some music—heard some politics. More ministers from the other Italian powers gone to Congress. War seems certain—in that case, it will be a savage one. Talked over various important matters with one of the initiated. At ten and half returned home.

I have just thought of something odd. In the year 1814, Moore ("the poet", *par excellence*, and he deserves it) and I were going together, in the same carriage, to dine with Earl Grey, the Capo Politico of the remaining whigs. Murray, the magnificent (the illustrious publisher of that name), had just sent me a Java gazette—I know not why, or wherefore. Pulling it out, by way of curiosity, we found it to contain a dispute (the said Java gazette) on Moore's merits and mine. I think, if I had been there, that I could have saved them the trouble of disputing on the subject. But, there is *fame* for you at six and twenty! Alexander had conquered India at the same age; but I doubt if he was disputed about, or his conquests compared with those of Indian Bacchus, at Java.

It was a great fame to be named with Moore; greater to be compared with him; greatest—*pleasure*, at least—to be *with* him; and, surely, an odd coincidence, that we should be dining together while they were quarrelling about us beyond the equinoctial line.

Well, the same evening, I met Lawrence the painter, and heard one of Lord Grey's daughters (a fine, tall, spirit-looking girl, with much of the *patrician, thorough-bred look* of her father, which I dote upon) play on the harp, so modestly and ingenuously, that she *looked music*. Well, I would rather have had my talk with Lawrence (who talked delightfully) and heard the girl, than have had all the fame of Moore and me put together.

The only pleasure of fame is that it paves the way to pleasure; and the more intellectual our pleasure, the better for the pleasure and for us too. It was, however, agreeable to have heard our fame before dinner, and a girl's harp after.

January 16th, 1821

Read—rode—fired pistols—returned—dined—wrote—visited —heard music—talked nonsense—and went home.

Wrote part of a Tragedy—advanced in Act 1st with "all deliberate speed." Bought a blanket. The weather is still muggy as a London May—mist, mizzle, the air replete with Scotticisms, which, though fine in the descriptions of Ossian, are somewhat tiresome in real, prosaic perspective. Politics still mysterious.

January 17th, 1821

Rode i' the forest—fired pistols—dined. Arrived a packet of books from England and Lombardy—English, Italian, French, and Latin. Read till eight—went out.

January 18th, 1821

To-day, the post arriving late, did not ride. Read letters—only two gazettes instead of twelve now due. Made Lega write to that negligent Galignani, and added a postscript. Dined.

At eight proposed to go out. Lega came in with a letter about a bill *unpaid* at Venice which I thought paid months ago. I flew into a paroxysm of rage, which almost made me faint. I have not been well ever since. I deserve it for being such a fool—but it *was* provoking—a set of scoundrels! It is, however, but five and twenty pounds.

January 19th, 1821

Rode. Winter's wind somewhat more unkind than ingratitude itself, though Shakespeare says otherwise. At least, I am so much more accustomed to meet with ingratitude than the north wind, that I thought the latter the sharper of the two. I had met with both in the course of the twenty-four hours, so could judge.

Thought of a plan of education for my daughter Allegra, who ought to begin soon with her studies. Wrote a letter—afterwards a postscript. Rather in low spirits—certainly hippish—liver touched—will take a dose of salts.

I have been reading the Life, by himself and daughter, of Mr. R. L. Edgeworth, the father of *the* Miss Edgeworth. It is altogether a great name. In 1813, I recollect to have met them in the fashionable world of London (of which I then formed an item, a fraction, the segment of a circle, the unit of a million, the nothing of something) in the assemblies of the hour, and at a breakfast of Sir Humphry and Lady Davy's, to which I was invited for the nonce. I had been the lion of 1812: Miss Edgeworth and Madame de Staël, with "the Cossack," towards the end of 1813, were the exhibitions of the succeeding year.

I thought Edgeworth a fine old fellow, of a clarety, elderly, red complexion, but active, brisk, and endless. He was seventy, but did not look fifty—no, nor forty-eight even. I had seen poor Fitz-patrick not very long before—a man of pleasure, wit, eloquence, all things. He tottered—but still talked like a gentleman, though feebly. Edgeworth bounced about, and talked loud and long; but he seemed neither weakly nor decrepit, and hardly old.

He began by telling "that he had given Dr. Parr a dressing, who had taken him for an Irish bogtrotter," &c., &c. Now I, who know Dr. Parr, and who know (*not* by experience—for I never should have presumed so far as to contend with him—but by hearing him *with* others, and *of* others) that it is not so easy a matter to "dress him," thought Mr. Edgeworth an assertor of what was not true. He could not have stood before Parr for an instant. For the rest, he seemed intelligent, vehement, vivacious, and full of life. He bids fair for a hundred years.

He was not much admired in London, and I remember a "ryghte merrie" and conceited jest which was rife among the gallants of the day,—viz. a paper had been presented for the *recall of Mrs. Siddons to the stage*, (she having lately taken leave, to the loss of ages,—for nothing ever was, or can be, like her), to which all men had been called to subscribe. Whereupon, Thomas Moore, of profane and poetical memory, did propose that a similar paper should be *sub*scribed and *circum*scribed "for the recall of Mr. Edgeworth to Ireland."

The fact was—everybody cared more about *her*. She was a nice little unassuming "Jeanie Deans'-looking bodie," as we Scotch say—and, if not handsome, certainly not ill-looking. Her conversation was as quiet as herself. One would never have guessed she could write *her name*; whereas her father talked, *not* as if he could write nothing else, but as if nothing else was worth writing.

As for Mrs. Edgeworth, I forget—except that I think she was the youngest of the party. Altogether, they were an excellent cage of the kind; and succeeded for two months, till the landing of Madame de Staël.

To turn from them to their works, I admire them; but they excite no feeling, and they leave no love—except for some Irish steward or postillion. However, the impression of intellect and prudence is profound—and may be useful.

January 20th, 1821

Rode—fired pistols. Read from Grimm's Correspondence. Dined—went out—heard music—returned—wrote a letter to the Lord Chamberlain to request him to prevent the theatres from representing the Doge, which the Italian papers say that they are going to act. This is pretty work—what! without asking my consent, and even in opposition to it!

January 21st, 1821

Fine, clear frosty day—that is to say, an Italian frost, for their winters hardly get beyond snow; for which reason nobody knows how to skate (or skait)—a Dutch and English accomplishment. Rode out, as usual, and fired pistols. Good shooting—broke four common, and rather small, bottles, in four shots, at fourteen paces, with a common pair of pistols and indifferent powder. Almost as good *wafering* or shooting—considering the difference of powder and pistol,—as when, in 1809, 1810, 1811, 1812, 1813, 1814, it was my luck to split walking-sticks, wafers, half-crowns, shillings, and even the *eye* of a walking-stick, at twelve paces, with a single bullet—and all by *eye* and calculation; for my hand is not steady, and apt to change with the very weather. To the prowess which I here note, Joe Manton and others can bear testimony;—for the former taught, and the latter has seen me do, these feats.

Dined—visited—came home—read. Remarked on an anecdote in Grimm's Correspondence, which says that "Regnard et la plûpart des poètes comiques étaient gens bilieux et mélancoliques; et que M. de Voltaire, qui est très gai, n'a jamais fait que des tragedies—et que la comedie gaie est le seul genre où il n'ait point réussi. C'est que celui qui rit et celui qui fait rire sont deux hommes fort differens."—Vol. VI.

At this moment I feel as bilious as the best comic writer of them all, (even as Regnard himself, the next to Moliere, who has written some of the best comedies in any language, and who is supposed to have committed suicide), and am not in spirits to continue my proposed tragedy of Sardanapalus, which I have, for some days, ceased to compose.

To-morrow is my birthday—that is to say, at twelve o' the clock, midnight, i.e. in twelve minutes, I shall have completed thirty and three years of age!!!—and I go to my bed with a heaviness of heart at having lived so long, and to so little purpose.

It is three minutes past twelve.—"'Tis the middle of the night by the castle clock," and I am now thirty-three!

> "Eheu, fugaces, Posthume, Posthume,
> Labuntur anni;"—

but I don't regret them so much for what I have done, as for what I *might* have done.

> Through life's road, so dim and dirty,
> I have dragg'd to three-and-thirty.
> What have these years left to me?
> Nothing—except thirty-three.

January 22d, 1821

1821.
Here lies
interred in the Eternity
of the Past,
from whence there is no
Resurrection
for the Days—whatever there may be
for the Dust—
the Thirty-Third Year
of an ill-spent Life,
Which, after
a lingering disease of many months
sunk into a lethargy,
and expired,
January 22d, 1821, A. D.
Leaving a successor
Inconsolable
for the very loss which
occasioned its
Existence.

January 23d, 1821

Fine day. Read—Rode—fired pistols, and returned. Dined—read. Went out at eight—made the usual visit. Heard of nothing but war,—"the cry is still, They come." The Car[bonar]i seem to have no plan—nothing fixed among themselves, how, when, or what to do. In that case, they will make nothing of the project, so often postponed, and never put in action.

Came home, and gave some necessary orders, in case of circumstances requiring a change of place. I shall act according to what may seem proper, when I hear decidedly what the Barbarians mean to do. At present, they are building a bridge of boats over the Po, which looks very warlike. A few days will probably show. I think of retiring towards Ancona, nearer the northern frontier; that is to say, if Teresa and her father are obliged to retire, which is most likely, as all the family are Liberals. If not, I shall stay. But my movements will depend upon the lady's wishes—for myself, it is much the same.

I am somewhat puzzled what to do with my little daughter, and my effects, which are of some quantity and value,—and neither of them [will] do in the seat of war, where I think of going. But there is an elderly lady who will take charge of *her*, and T. says that the Marchese C. will undertake to hold the chattels in safe keeping. Half the city are getting their affairs in marching trim. A pretty Carnival! The blackguards might as well have waited till Lent.

January 24th, 1821

Returned—met some masques in the Corso—"Vive la baga-telle!"—the Germans are on the Po, the Barbarians at the gate, and their masters in council at Leybach (or whatever the eructation of the sound may syllable into a human pronunciation), and lo! they dance and sing, and make merry, "for to-morrow they may die." Who can say that the Arlequins are not right? Like the Lady Baussiere, and my old friend Burton—I "rode on."

Dined—(damn this pen!)—beef tough—there is no beef in Italy worth a curse; unless a man could eat an old ox with the hide on, singed in the sun.

The principal persons in the events which may occur in a few days are gone out on a *shooting party*. If it were like a "*highland hunting*," a pretext of the chase for a grand re-union of counsellors and chiefs, it would be all very well. But it is nothing more or less than a real snivelling, popping, small-shot, water-hen waste of powder, ammunition, and shot, for their own special amuse-ment:—a rare set of fellows for "a man to risk his neck with," as "Marishal Wells" says in the Black Dwarf.

If they gather,—"whilk is to be doubted,"—they will not muster a thousand men. The reason of this is, that the populace are not interested,—only the higher and middle orders. I wish that the peasantry *were*; they are a fine savage race of two-legged leopards. But the Bolognese won't—the Romagnuoles can't without them. Or, if they try—what then? They will try, and man can do no more—and, if he *would* but try his utmost, much might be done.

The Dutch, for instance, against the Spaniards—*then*, the tyrants of Europe—since, the slaves—and, lately, the freedmen.

The year 1820 was not a fortunate one for the individual me, whatever it may be for the nations. I lost a lawsuit, after two decisions in my favour. The project of lending money on an Irish mortgage was finally rejected by my wife's trustee after a year's hope and trouble. The Rochdale lawsuit had endured fifteen years, and always prospered till I married; since which, every thing has gone wrong—with me at least.

In the same year, 1820, the Countess T. G. *nata* G[amb]a G[hisell]i, in despite of all I said and did to prevent it, *would* separate from her husband, Il Cavalier Commendatore G[uicciol]i, &c. &c. &c., and all on the account of "P. P. clerk of this parish." The other little petty vexations of the year—overturns in carriages—the murder of people before one's door, and dying in one's beds—the cramp in swimming—colics—indigestions and bilious attacks, &c. &c. &c.—

> "Many small articles make up a sum,
> And hey ho for Caleb Quotem, oh!"

January 25th, 1821

Received a letter from Lord S. O., state secretary of the Seven Islands—a fine fellow—clever—dished in England five years ago, and came abroad to retrench and to renew. He wrote from Ancona, in his way back to Corfu, on some matters of our own. He is son of the late Duke of L[eeds] by a second marriage. He wants me to go to Corfu. Why not?—perhaps I may, next spring.

Answered Murray's letter—read—lounged. Scrawled this additional page of life's log-book. One day more is over of it, and of me;—but "which is best, life or death, the gods only know," as Socrates said to his judges, on the breaking up of the tribunal. Two thousand years since that sage's declaration of ignorance have not enlightened us more upon this important point; for, according to the Christian dispensation, no one can know whether he is *sure* of salvation—even the most righteous—since a single slip of faith may throw him on his back, like a skaiter, while gliding smoothly to his paradise. Now, therefore, whatever the certainty of faith in the facts may be, the certainty of the individual as to his happiness or misery is no greater than it was under Jupiter.

It has been said that the immortality of the soul is a "grand peut-être"—but still it is a *grand* one. Every body clings to it—the stupidest, and dullest, and wickedest of human bipeds is still persuaded that he is immortal.

January 26th, 1821

Fine day—a few mares' tails portending change, but the sky clear, upon the whole. Rode—fired pistols—good shooting. Coming back, met an old man. Charity—purchased a shilling's worth of salvation. If that was to be bought, I have given more to my fellow-creatures in this life—sometimes for *vice*, but, if not more *often*, at least more *considerably*, for virtue—than I now possess. I never in my life gave a mistress so much as I have sometimes given a poor man in honest distress;—but no matter. The scoundrels who have all along persecuted me (with the help of * * who has crowned their efforts) will triumph;—and, when justice is done to me, it will be when this hand that writes is as cold as the hearts which have stung me.

Returning, on the bridge near the mill, met an old woman. I asked her age—she said "Tre croci". I asked my groom (though myself a decent Italian) what the devil *her* three crosses meant. He said, ninety years, and that she had five years more to boot!! I repeated the same three times—not to mistake—ninety-five years!!!—and she was yet rather active—*heard* my question, for she answered it—*saw* me, for she advanced towards me; and did not appear at all decrepit, though certainly touched with years. Told her to come to-morrow, and will examine her myself. I love phenomena. If she *is* ninety-five years old, she must recollect the Cardinal Alberoni, who was legate here.

On dismounting, found Lieutenant E. just arrived from Faenza. Invited him to dine with me to-morrow. Did *not* invite him for to-day, because there was a small *turbot*, (Friday, fast regularly and religiously,) which I wanted to eat all myself. Ate it.

Went out—found T. as usual—music. The gentlemen, who

make revolutions and are gone on a shooting, are not yet returned. They don't return till Sunday—that is to say, they have been out for five days, buffooning, while the interests of a whole country are at stake, and even they themselves compromised.

It is a difficult part to play amongst such a set of assassins and blockheads—but, when the scum is skimmed off, or has boiled over, good may come of it. If this country could but be freed, what would be too great for the accomplishment of that desire? for the extinction of that Sigh of Ages? Let us hope. They have hoped these thousand years. The very revolvement of the chances may bring it—it is upon the dice.

If the Neapolitans have but a single Massaniello amongst them, they will beat the bloody butchers of the crown and sabre. Holland, in worse circumstances, beat the Spains and Philips; America beat the English; Greece beat Xerxes; and France beat Europe, till she took a tyrant; South America beats her old vultures out of their nest; and, if these men are but firm in themselves, there is nothing to shake them from without.

January 28th, 1821

Lugano Gazette did not come. Letters from Venice. It appears that the Austrian brutes have seized my three or four pounds of English powder. The scoundrels!—I hope to pay them in *ball* for that powder. Rode out till twilight.

Pondered the subjects of four tragedies to be written (life and circumstances permitting) to wit, Sardanapalus, already begun, Cain, a metaphysical subject, something in the style of Manfred, but in five *acts*, perhaps, with the chorus; Francesca of Rimini, in five acts; and I am not sure that I would not try Tiberius. I think that I could extract a something, of *my* tragic, at least, out of the gloomy sequestration and old age of the tyrant—and even out of his sojourn at Caprea—by softening the *details*, and exhibiting the despair which must have led to those very vicious pleasures. For none but a powerful and gloomy mind overthrown would have had recourse to such solitary horrors,—being also, at the same time, *old*, and the master of the world.

Memoranda.

What is Poetry?—The feeling of a Former world and Future.

Thought Second.

Why, at the very height of desire and human pleasure,—worldly, social, amorous, ambitious, or even avaricious,—does there mingle a certain sense of doubt and sorrow—a fear of what is to come—a doubt of what *is*—a retrospect to the past, leading to a prognostication of the future? (The best of Prophets of the future is the Past.) Why is this? or these?—I know not, except that on a pinnacle we are most susceptible of giddiness, and that we never fear falling except from a precipice—the higher, the more awful, and the more sublime; and, therefore, I am not sure that Fear is not a pleasurable sensation; at least, *Hope* is; and *what Hope* is there without a deep leaven of Fear? and what sensation is so delightful as Hope? and, if it were not for Hope, where would the Future be?—in hell. It is useless to say *where* the Present is, for most of us know; and as for the Past, *what* predominates in memory?—*Hope baffled.* Ergo, in all human affairs, it is Hope—Hope—Hope. I allow sixteen minutes, though I never counted them, to any given or supposed possession. From whatever place we commence, we know where it all must end. And yet, what good is there in knowing it? It does not make men better or wiser. During the greatest horrors of the greatest plagues, (Athens and Florence, for example—see Thucydides and Machiavelli) men were more cruel and profligate than ever. It is all a mystery. I feel most things, but I know nothing, except

―― ―― ―― ―― ―― ―― ―― ―― ―― ――
―― ―― ―― ―― ―― ―― ―― ―― ―― ――
―― ―― ―― ―― ―― ―― ―― ―― ―― ――

> *Thought for a Speech of Lucifer, in the Tragedy of Cain:*—
> Were *Death* an *evil*, would *I* let thee *live*?
> Fool! live as I live—as thy father lives,
> And thy son's sons shall live for evermore.

Past Midnight. One o' the clock

I have been reading W. F. S. * * (brother to the other of the name) till now, and I can make out nothing. He evidently shows a great power of words, but there is nothing to be taken hold of. He is like Hazlitt, in English, who *talks pimples*—a red and white corruption rising up (in little imitation of mountains upon maps), but containing nothing, and discharging nothing, except their own humours.

I dislike him the worse (that is, S[chlegel],) because he always seems upon the verge of meaning; and, lo, he goes down like sunset, or melts like a rainbow, leaving a rather rich confusion,—to which, however, the above comparisons do too much honour.

Continuing to read Mr. F[rederick] S[chlegel]. He is not such a fool as I took him for, that is to say, when he speaks of the North. But still he speaks of things *all over the world* with a kind of authority that a philosopher would disdain, and a man of common sense, feeling, and knowledge of his own ignorance, would be ashamed of. The man is evidently wanting to make an impression, like his brother,—or like George in the Vicar of Wakefield, who found out that all the good things had been said already on the right side, and therefore "dressed up some paradoxes" upon the wrong side— Ingenious, but false, as he himself says—to which "the learned world said nothing, nothing at all, sir." The "learned world," however, *has* said something to the brothers S[chlegel].

It is high time to think of something else. What they say of the antiquities of the North is best.

January 29th, 1821

Yesterday, the woman of ninety-five years of age was with me. She said her eldest son (if now alive) would have been seventy. She is thin—short, but active—hears, and sees, and talks incessantly. Several teeth left—all in the lower jaw, and single front teeth. She is very deeply wrinkled, and has a sort of scattered grey beard over her chin, at least as long as my mustachios. Her head, in fact, resembles the drawing in crayons of Pope the poet's mother, which is in some editions of his works.

I forgot to ask her if she remembered Alberoni (legate here), but will ask her next time. Gave her a louis—ordered her a new suit of clothes, and put her upon a weekly pension. Till now, she had worked at gathering wood and pine-nuts in the forest—pretty work at ninety-five years old! She had a dozen children, of whom some are alive. Her name is Maria Montanari.

Met a company of the sect (a kind of Liberal Club) called the "Americani" in the forest, all armed, and singing, with all their might, in Romagnuole—"*Sem* tutti soldat' per la liberta" ("we are all soldiers for liberty"). They cheered me as I passed—I returned their salute, and rode on. This may show the spirit of Italy at present.

My to-day's journal consists of what I omitted yesterday. To-day was much as usual. Have rather a better opinion of the writings of the Schlegels than I had four-and-twenty hours ago; and will amend it still farther, if possible.

They say that the Piedmontese have at length risen—*ça ira*!

Read S[chlegel]. Of Dante he says that "at no time has the greatest and most national of all Italian poets ever been much the favourite of his countrymen." 'Tis false! There have been more editors and commentators (and imitators, ultimately) of Dante than of all their poets put together. *Not* a favourite! Why, they talk Dante—write Dante—and think and dream Dante at this moment (1821) to an excess, which would be ridiculous, but that he deserves it.

In the same style this German talks of gondolas on the Arno—a precious fellow to dare to speak of Italy!

He says also that Dante's chief defect is a want, in a word, of gentle feelings. Of gentle feelings! and Francesca of Rimini—and the father's feelings in Ugolino—and Beatrice—and "La Pia!" Why, there is gentleness in Dante beyond all gentleness, when he is tender. It is true that, treating of the Christian Hades, or Hell, there is not much scope or site for gentleness—but who *but* Dante could have introduced any "gentleness" at all into *Hell*? Is there any in Milton's? No—and Dante's Heaven is all love, and glory, and majesty.

1 o'clock

I have found out, however, where the German is right—it is about the Vicar of Wakefield. "Of all romances in miniature (and, perhaps, this is the best shape in which Romance can appear) the *Vicar of Wakefield* is, I think, the most exquisite." He thinks!—he might be sure. But it is very well for a S[chlegel]. I feel sleepy, and may as well get me to bed. To-morrow there will be fine weather.

"Trust on, and think to-morrow will repay."

January 30th, 1821

The Count P. G. this evening (by commission from the C[arbonar]i. transmitted to me the new *words* for the next six months. * * * and * * *. The new sacred word is * * *—the reply * * *—the rejoinder * * *. The former word (now changed) was * * *—there is also * * *—* * *. Things seem fast coming to a crisis—*ça ira*!

We talked over various matters of moment and movement. These I omit;—if they come to any thing, they will speak for themselves. After these, we spoke of Kosciusko. Count R. G. told me that he has seen the Polish officers in the Italian war burst into tears on hearing his name.

Something must be up in Piedmont—all the letters and papers are stopped. Nobody knows anything, and the Germans are concentrating near Mantua. Of the decision of Leybach nothing is known. This state of things cannot last long. The ferment in men's minds at present cannot be conceived without seeing it.

January 31st, 1821

For several days I have not written any thing except a few answers to letters. In momentary expectation of an explosion of some kind, it is not easy to settle down to the desk for the higher kinds of composition. I *could* do it, to be sure, for, last summer, I wrote my drama in the very bustle of Madame la Contessa G's divorce, and all its process of accompaniments. At the same time, I also had the news of the loss of an important lawsuit in England. But these were only private and personal business; the present is of a different nature.

I suppose it is this, but have some suspicion that it may be laziness, which prevents me from writing; especially as Rochefoucault says that "laziness often masters them all"—speaking of the *passions*. If this were true, it could hardly be said that "idleness is the root of all evil," since this is supposed to spring from the passions only: ergo, that which masters all the passions (laziness, to wit) would in so much be a good. Who knows?

Midnight

I have been reading Grimm's Correspondence. He repeats frequently, in speaking of a poet, or of a man of genius in any department, even in music, (Gretry, for instance), that he must have "une ame qui se tourmente, un esprit violent". How far this may be true, I know not; but if it were, I should be a poet "per excellenza;" for I have always had "une ame", which not only tormented itself but every body else in contact with it; and an "esprit violent", which has almost left me without any "esprit" at all. As to defining what a poet *should* be, it is not worth while, for what are *they* worth? what have they done?

Grimm, however, is an excellent critic and literary historian. His Correspondence forms the annals of the literary part of that age of France, with much of her politics, and still more of her "way of life". He is as valuable, and far more entertaining than Muratori or Tiraboschi—I had almost said, than Ginguené—but there we should pause. However, 't is a great man in its line.

Monsieur St. Lambert has,

> "Et lorsqu'à ses regards la lumière est ravie,
> Il n'a plus, en mourant, à perdre que la vie."

This is, word for word, Thomson's

> "And dying, all we can resign is breath,"

without the smallest acknowledgment from the Lorrainer of a poet. M. St. Lambert is dead as a man, and (for any thing I know to the contrary) damned, as a poet, by this time. However, his Seasons have good things, and, it may be, some of his own.

February 2d, 1821

I have been considering what can be the reason why I always wake, at a certain hour in the morning, and always in very bad spirits—I may say, in actual despair and despondency, in all respects—even of that which pleased me over night. In about an hour or two, this goes off, and I compose either to sleep again, or, at least, to quiet. In England, five years ago, I had the same kind of hypochondria, but accompanied with so violent a thirst that I have drank as many as fifteen bottles of soda-water in one night, after going to bed, and been still thirsty—calculating, however, some lost from the bursting out and effervescence and overflowing of the soda-water, in drawing the corks, or striking off the necks of the bottles from mere thirsty impatience. At present, I have *not* the thirst; but the depression of spirits is no less violent.

I read in Edgeworth's Memoirs of something similar (except that his thirst expended itself on *small beer*) in the case of Sir F. B. Delaval;—but then he was, at least, twenty years older. What is it?—liver? In England, Le Man (the apothecary) cured me of the thirst in three days, and it had lasted as many years. I suppose that it is all hypochondria.

What I feel most growing upon me are laziness, and a disrelish more powerful than indifference. If I rouse, it is into fury. I presume that I shall end (if not earlier by accident, or some such termination) like Swift—"dying at top." I confess I do not contemplate this with so much horror as he apparently did for some years before it happened. But Swift had hardly *begun life* at the very period (thirty-three) when I feel quite an *old sort* of feel.

Oh! there is an organ playing in the street—a waltz, too! I must leave off to listen. They are playing a waltz which I have heard ten thousand times at the balls in London, between 1812 and 1815. Music is a strange thing.

February 5th, 1821

At last, "the kiln's in a low." The Germans are ordered to march, and Italy is, for the ten thousandth time to become a field of battle. Last night the news came.

This afternoon—Count P. G. came to me to consult upon divers matters. We rode out together. They have sent off to the C. for orders. To-morrow the decision ought to arrive, and then something will be done. Returned—dined—read—went out—talked over matters. Made a purchase of some arms for the new inrolled Americani, who are all on tiptoe to march. Gave order for some *harness* and portmanteaus necessary for the horses.

Read some of Bowles's dispute about Pope, with all the replies and rejoinders. Perceive that my name has been lugged into the controversy, but have not time to state what I know of the subject. On some "piping day of peace" it is probable that I may resume it.

February 9th, 1821

Before dinner wrote a little; also, before I rode out, Count P. G. called upon me, to let me know the result of the meeting of the C[arbonar]i at F[aenza] and at B[ologna] * * returned late last night. Every thing was combined under the idea that the Barbarians would pass the Po on the 15th inst. Instead of this, from some previous information or otherwise, they have hastened their march and actually passed two days ago; so that all that can be done at present in Romagna is, to stand on the alert and wait for the advance of the Neapolitans. Every thing was ready, and the Neapolitans had sent on their own instructions and intentions, all calculated for the *tenth* and *eleventh*, on which days a general rising was to take place, under the supposition that the Barbarians could not advance before the 15th.

As it is, they have but fifty or sixty thousand troops, a number with which they might as well attempt to conquer the world as secure Italy in its present state. The artillery marches *last*, and alone, and there is an idea of an attempt to cut part of them off. All this will much depend upon the first steps of the Neapolitans.

Here, the public spirit is excellent, provided it be kept up. This will be seen by the event.

It is probable that Italy will be delivered from the Barbarians if the Neapolitans will but stand firm, and are united among themselves. *Here* they appear so.

February 10th, 1821

Day passed as usual—nothing new. Barbarians still in march—not well equipped, and, of course, not well received on their route. There is some talk of a commotion at Paris.

Rode out between four and six—finished my letter to Murray on Bowles's pamphlets—added postscript. Passed the evening as usual—out till eleven—and subsequently at home.

February 11th, 1821

Wrote—had a copy taken of an extract from Petrarch's Letters, with reference to the conspiracy of the Doge, M[arino] Faliero, containing the poet's opinion of the matter. Heard a heavy firing of cannon towards Comacchio—the Barbarians rejoicing for their principal pig's birthday, which is to-morrow—or Saint day—I forget which. Received a ticket for the first ball to-morrow. Shall not go to the first, but intend going to the second, as also to the Veglioni.

February 13th, 1821

To-day read a little in Louis B.'s Hollande, but have written nothing since the completion of the letter on the Pope controversy. Politics are quite misty for the present. The Barbarians still upon their march. It is not easy to divine what the Italians will now do.

Was elected yesterday "Socio" of the Carnival ball society. This is the fifth carnival that I have passed. In the four former, I racketed a good deal. In the present, I have been as sober as Lady Grace herself.

February 14th, 1821

Much as usual. Wrote, before riding out, part of a scene of "Sardanapalus". The first act nearly finished. The rest of the day and evening as before—partly without, in conversazione—partly at home.

Heard the particulars of the late fray at Russi, a town not far from this. It is exactly the fact of Roméo and Giulietta—*not* Romĕo, as the Barbarian writes it. Two families of Contadini (peasants) are at feud. At a ball, the younger part of the families forget their quarrel, and dance together. An old man of one of them enters, and reproves the young men for dancing with the females of the opposite family. The male relatives of the latter resent this. Both parties rush home and arm themselves. They meet directly, by moonlight, in the public way, and fight it out. Three are killed on the spot, and six wounded, most of them dangerously,—pretty well for two families, methinks—and all *fact*, of the last week. Another assassination has taken place at Cesenna,—in all about *forty* in Romagna within the last three months. These people retain much of the middle ages.

February 15th, 1821

Last night finished the first act of Sardanapalus. To-night, or to-morrow, I ought to answer letters.

February 16th, 1821

Last night Il Conte P. G. sent a man with a bag full of bayonets, some muskets, and some hundreds of cartridges to my house, without apprizing me, though I had seen him not half an hour before. About ten days ago, when there was to be a rising here, the Liberals and my brethren C[arbonar]i asked me to purchase some arms for a certain few of our ragamuffins. I did so immediately, and ordered ammunition, etc., and they were armed accordingly. Well—the rising is prevented by the Barbarians marching a week sooner than appointed; and an *order* is issued, and in force, by the Government, "that all persons having arms concealed, &c. &c.,

shall be liable to," &c. &c.—and what do my friends, the patriots, do two days afterwards? Why, they throw back upon my hands, and into my house, these very arms (without a word of warning previously) with which I had furnished them at their own request, and at my own peril and expense.

It was lucky that Lega was at home to receive them. If any of the servants had (except Tita and F[letcher] and Lega) they would have betrayed it immediately. In the mean time, if they are denounced, or discovered, I shall be in a scrape.

At nine went out—at eleven returned. Beat the crow for stealing the falcon's victuals. Read "Tales of my Landlord"—wrote a letter—and mixed a moderate beaker of water with other ingredients.

February 18th, 1821

The news are that the Neapolitans have broken a bridge, and slain four pontifical carabiniers, whilk carabiniers wished to oppose. Besides the disrespect to neutrality, it is a pity that the first blood shed in this German quarrel should be Italian. However, the war seems begun in good earnest: for, if the Neapolitans kill the Pope's carabiniers, they will not be more delicate towards the Barbarians. If it be even so, in a short time "there will be news o' thae craws," as Mrs. Alison Wilson says of Jenny Blane's "unco cockernony" in the *Tales of my Landlord.*

In turning over Grimm's Correspondence to-day, I found a thought of Tom Moore's in a song of Maupertuis to a female Laplander.

> "Et tous les lieux
> Ou sont ses yeux,
> Font la Zone brûlante."

This is Moore's,

> "And those eyes make my climate, wherever I roam."

But I am sure that Moore never saw it; for this was published in Grimm's Correspondence in 1813,—and I knew Moore's by heart in 1812. There is also another, but an antithetical coincidence—

> "Le soleil luit,
> Des jours sans nuit
> Bientôt il nous destine;
> Mais ces longs jours
> Seront trop courts,
> Passés pres de Christine."

This is the *thought reversed*, of the last stanza of the ballad on Charlotte Lynes, given in Miss Seward's Memoirs of Darwin, which is pretty—I quote from memory of these last fifteen years.

> "For my first night I'll go
> To those regions of snow,
> Where the sun for six months never shines;
> And think, even then
> He too soon came again,
> To disturb me with fair Charlotte Lynes."

To-day I have had no communication with my Carbonari cronies; but, in the mean time, my lower apartments are full of their bayonets, fusils, cartridges, and what not. I suppose that they consider me as a depôt, to be sacrificed, in case of accidents. It is no great matter, supposing that Italy could be liberated, who or what is sacrificed. It is a grand object—the very *poetry* of politics. Only think—a free Italy!!! Why, there has been nothing like it since the days of Augustus. I reckon the times of Caesar (Julius) free; because the commotions left every body a side to take, and the parties were pretty equal at the set out. But, afterwards, it was all praetorian and legionary business—and since!—we shall see, or, at least, some will see, what card will turn up. It is best to hope, even of the hopeless. The Dutch did more than these fellows have to do, in the Seventy Years' War.

February 19th, 1821

Came home solus—very high wind—lightning—moonshine—solitary stragglers muffled in cloaks—women in mask—white houses—clouds hurrying over the sky, like spilt milk blown out of the pail—altogether very poetical. It is still blowing hard—the tiles flying, and the house rocking—rain splashing—lightning flashing—quite a fine Swiss Alpine evening, and the sea roaring in the distance.

Visited—conversazione. All the women frightened by the squall: they *won't* go to the masquerade because it lightens—the pious reason!

Still blowing away. A[lborghetti] has sent me some news to-day. The war approaches nearer and nearer. Oh those scoundrel sovereigns! Let us but see them beaten—let the Neapolitans but have the pluck of the Dutch of old, or the Spaniards of now, or of the German protestants, the Scotch presbyterians, the Swiss under Tell, or the Greeks under Themistocles—*all* small and solitary nations (except the Spaniards and German Lutherans), and there is yet a resurrection for Italy, and a hope for the world.

February 20th, 1821

The news of the day are, that the Neapolitans are full of energy. The public spirit *here* is certainly well kept up. The "Americani" (a patriotic society here, an under branch of the "Carbonari") give a dinner in *The Forest* in a few days, and have invited me, as one of the C[arbonar]i. It is to be in *the Forest* of Boccacio's and Dryden's "Huntsman's Ghost"; and, even if I had not the same political feelings, (to say nothing of my old convivial turn, which every now and then revives), I would go as a poet, or, at least, as a lover of poetry. I shall expect to see the spectre of "Ostasio degli Onesti" (Dryden has turned him into Guido Cavalcanti—an essentially different person, as may be found in Dante) come "thundering for his prey" in the midst of the festival. At any rate, whether he does or no, I will get as tipsy and patriotic as possible.

Within these few days I have read, but not written.

February 21st, 1821

As usual, rode—visited, &c. Business begins to thicken. The Pope has printed a declaration against the patriots, who, he says, meditate a rising. The consequence of all this will be, that, in a fortnight, the whole country will be up. The proclamation is not yet published, but printed ready for distribution. * * [Alborghetti] sent me a copy privately—a sign that he does not know what to think. When he wants to be well with the patriots, he sends to me some civil message or other.

For my own part, it seems to me, that nothing but the most decided success of the Barbarians can prevent a general and immediate rise of the whole nation.

February 23d, 1281

Almost ditto with yesterday—rode, &c.—visited—wrote nothing—read Roman History.

Had a curious letter from a fellow, who informs me that the Barbarians are ill-disposed towards me. He is probably a spy, or an imposter. But be it so, even as he says. They cannot bestow their hostility on one who loathes and execrates them more than I do, or who will oppose their views with more zeal, when the opportunity offers.

February 24th, 1821

Rode, &c. as usual. The secret intelligence arrived this morning from the frontier to the C[arbonar]i is as bad as possible. The *plan* has missed—the Chiefs are betrayed, military, as well as civil—and the Neapolitans not only have not moved, but have declared to the P[apal] government, and to the Barbarians, that they know nothing of the matter!!!

Thus the world goes; and thus the Italians are always lost for lack of union among themselves. What is to be done *here*, between the two fires, and cut off from the N[orther]n frontier, is not decided. My opinion was,—better to rise than be taken in detail; but how it will be settled now, I cannot tell. Messengers are despatched to the delegates of the other cities to learn their resolutions.

I always had an idea that it would be *bungled*; but was willing to hope, and am so still. Whatever I can do by money, means, or person, I will venture freely for their freedom; and have so repeated to them (some of the Chiefs here) half an hour ago. I have two thousand five hundred scudi, better than five hundred pounds, in the house, which I offered to begin with.

February 25th, 1821

Came home—my head aches—plenty of news, but too tiresome to set down. I have neither read nor written, nor thought, but led a purely animal life all day. I mean to try to write a page or two before I go to bed. But, as Squire Sullen says, "My head aches consumedly: Scrub, bring me a dram!" Drank some Imola wine, and some punch.

Log-book continued

February 27th, 1821

I have been a day without continuing the log, because I could not find a blank book. At length I recollected this.

Rode, &c.—wrote down an additional stanza for the 5th canto of D[on] J[uan] which I had composed in bed this morning. Visited *l' Amica*. We are invited, on the night of the Veglione (next Domenica) with the Marchesa Clelia Cavalli and the Countess Spinelli Rasponi. I promised to go. Last night there was a row at the ball, of which I am a "socio". The Vice-legate had the imprudent insolence to introduce *three* of his servants in masque—*without tickets*, too! and in spite of remonstrances. The consequence was, that the young men of the ball took it up, and were near throwing the Vice-legate out of the window. His servants, seeing the scene, withdrew, and he after them. His reverence Monsignore ought to know, that these are not times for the predominance of priests over decorum. Two minutes more, two steps farther, and the whole city would have been in arms, and the government driven out of it.

Such is the spirit of the day, and these fellows appear not to perceive it. As far as the simple fact went, the young men were right, servants being prohibited always at these festivals.

Yesterday wrote two notes on the "Bowles and Pope" controversy and sent them off to Murray by the post. The old woman whom I relieved in the forest (she is ninety-four years of age) brought me two bunches of violets. "Nam vita gaudet mortua floribus." I was much pleased with the present. An Englishwoman would have presented a pair of worsted stockings, at least, in the month of February. Both excellent things; but the former are more elegant. The present, at this season, reminds one of Gray's stanza, omitted from his elegy:

> "Here scatter'd oft, the *earliest* of the year,
>   By hands unseen, are showers of violets found;
> The red-breast loves to build and warble here,
>   And little footsteps lightly print the ground."

As fine a stanza as any in his elegy. I wonder that he could have the heart to omit it.

Last night I suffered horribly—from an indigestion, I believe. I *never* sup—that is, never at home. But, last night, I was prevailed upon by the Countess Gamba's persuasion, and the strenuous example of her brother, to swallow, at supper, a quantity of boiled cockles, and to dilute them, *not* reluctantly, with some Imola wine. When I came home, apprehensive of the consequences, I swallowed three or four glasses of spirits, which men (the venders) call brandy, rum, or Hollands, but which Gods would entitle spirits of wine, coloured or sugared. All was pretty well till I got to bed, when I became somewhat swollen, and considerably vertiginous. I got out, and mixing some soda-powders, drank them off. This brought on temporary relief. I returned to bed; but grew sick and sorry once and again. Took more soda-water. At last I fell into a dreary sleep. Woke, and was ill all day, till I had galloped a few miles. Query—was it the cockles, or what I took to correct them, that caused the commotion? I think both. I remarked in my illness the complete inertion, inaction, and destruction of my chief mental faculties. I tried to rouse them, and yet could not—and this is the *Soul*!!! I should believe that it was married to the body, if they did not sympathise so much with each other. If the one rose, when the other fell, it would be a sign that they longed for the natural state of divorce. But as it is, they seem to draw together like post-horses.

Let us hope the best—it is the grand possession.

TO JOHN MURRAY   *Ravenna. February 21st. 1821*

Dear Sir,—In the 44th. page vol 1st. of Turner's travels (which you lately sent me) it is stated that "Lord Byron—when he expressed such confidence of it's practicability seems to have forgotten that Leander swam both ways with and against the tide, whereas *he* (Ld. B.) only performed the easiest part of the task by swimming *with* it from Europe to Asia."—I certainly could not have forgotten what is known to every Schoolboy—that Leander crossed in the Night and returned towards the morning.—My object was to ascertain that the Hellespont could be crossed *at all* by swimming—and in this—Mr. Ekenhead & myself both succeeded—the one in an hour and ten minutes—the other in one hour & five minutes. The *tide* was *not* in our favour—on the contrary the great difficulty was to bear up against the current—which so far from helping us to the Asiatic side—set us down right towards the Archipelago.—Neither Mr. Ekenhead, myself—nor I will venture to add—any person on board the frigate from Captain (now Admiral) Bathurst downwards—had any notion of the difference of the current on the Asiatic side, of which Mr. Turner speaks.—I never heard of it till this moment—or I would have taken the other course. Lieutenant Ekenhead's sole motive—and mine also, for setting out from the European side was—that the little Cape above Sestos was a more prominent starting place—and the frigate which lay below close under the Asiatic castle—formed a better point of view for us to swim towards—and in fact we landed immediately below it.— —

Mr. Turner says—"Whatever is thrown into the Stream on this part of the European bank, *must* arrive at the Asiatic shore."—This is so far from being the case—that it *must* arrive in the Archipelago—if left to the Current—although a strong wind in the Asiatic direction might have such an effect occasionally.— —Mr. Turner attempted the passage from the Asiatic side and failed.— "After five and twenty minutes in which he did not advance a hundred yards he gave it up from complete exhaustion."—This is very possible—and might have occurred to him just as readily on the European side.— —He should have set out a couple of miles higher—and would then have come out below the European castle.—I particularly stated—and Mr. Hobhouse has done so also—that we were obliged to make the real passage of one mile—extend to between *three* and *four*—owing to the force of the stream.— —I can assure Mr. Turner that his Success would have given me great pleasure—as it would have added one more instance—to the proof of the practicability.—It is not quite fair in him to infer—that—because *he* failed—Leander could not succeed.—There are still four instances on record—a Neapolitan—a young Jew—Mr. Ekenhead —& myself—the two last done in the presence of hundreds of *English* Witnesses.— —With regard to the difference of the *current*—I perceived none—it is favourable to the Swimmer on neither side—but may be stemmed by plunging into the Sea—a considerable way above the opposite point of the coast which the Swimmer wishes to make, but still bearing up against it; it is very strong but—if you *calculate* well you may reach land. My own experience & that of others bids me pronounce the passage of Leander perfectly practicable;—any young man in good health—and tolerable skill in swimming might succeed in it from *either* side.— —

I was three hours in swimming across the Tagus—which is much more hazardous, *being two hours* longer than the passage of the Hellespont.—Of what may be done in swimming I will mention one more instance.—In 1818—The Chevalier Mengaldo (a Gentleman of Bassano) a good Swimmer wished to swim <with an English Gentleman> with my friend Mr. Alexander Scott and myself. As he seemed particularly anxious on the subject we indulged him.—We all three started from the Island of the Lido and swam to Venice.—At the entrance of the Grand Canal—Scott and I were a good way ahead—and we saw no more of our foreign friend—which however was of no consequence—as there was a Gondola to hold his cloathes and pick him up.—Scott swam on till past the Rialto—where he got out—less from fatigue than from *chill*—having been *four hours* in the water—without rest or stay—except what is to be obtained by floating on one's back—this being the *condition* of our performance.—I continued my course on to Santa Chiara—comprizing the whole of the Grand Canal (beside the distance from the Lido) and got out where the Laguna once more opens to Fusina.—I had been in the water by my watch without help or rest—and never touching ground or boat *four hours* and *twenty* minutes.—To this Match and during the greater part of its performance Mr. Hoppner the Consul General was witness—and it is well known to many others.—Mr. Turner can easily verify the fact—if he thinks it worth while—by referring to Mr. Hoppner.—The distance we could not *accurately* ascertain—it was of course considerable.— —

I crossed the *Hellespont* in *one* hour and ten minutes only.—I am now ten years older in time and twenty in constitution—than I was when I passed the Dardanelles—and yet two years ago—I was capable of swimming four hours and twenty minutes—and I am sure that I could have continued two hours longer though I had on a pair of trowsers—an accoutrement which by no means assists the performance. My two companions were also *four* hours in the water.— —Mengaldo might be about thirty years of age—Scott about six and twenty.— —With this experience in swimming at different periods of life—not only upon the *Spot*—but elsewhere— of various persons, what is there to make me doubt that Leander's exploit was perfectly practicable?—If three individuals did more than the passage of the Hellespont why should he have done less? But Mr. Turner failed—and naturally seeking a plausible reason for his failure—lays the blame on the *Asiatic* side of the Strait.— —To me the cause is evident.—He tried to swim *directly* across—instead of going higher up to take the vantage.—He might as well have tried to fly over Mount Athos.— —That a young Greek of the heroic times—in love—and with his limbs in full vigour might have *succeeded* in such an attempt is neither wonderful nor doubtful.—Whether he *attempted* it or *not* is another question—because he might have had a small *boat* to save him the trouble.— — I am

yrs. very truly
BYRON

P.S.—Mr. Turner says that the swimming from Europe to Asia—was "the *easiest* part of the task"—I doubt whether Leander found it so—as it was the return—however he had several hours between the intervals. The argument of Mr. T. "that higher up or lower down the strait widens so considerably that he would save little labour by his starting" is only good for indifferent swimmers—a man of any practice or skill—will always consider the

distance far less than the strength of the stream.—If Ekenhead &
myself had thought of crossing at the *narrowest point* instead of
going up to the Cape above it we should have been swept down
to Tenedos.— —The Strait is however not extremely wide—even
where it broadens above and below the forts.—As the frigate was
stationed some time in the Dardenelles waiting for the firman—I
bathed often in the strait subsequently to our traject—and generally on the Asiatic side without perceiving the greater strength of
the opposing Stream by which the diplomatic traveller palliates his
own failure.— —An amusement in the small bay which opens immediately below the Asiatic fort was to *dive* for the LAND tortoises
which we flung in on purpose—as they amphibiously crawled
along the bottom.—*This* does not argue any greater violence of
current than on the European shore. With regard to the modest
insinuation that we chose the European side as "easier" —I appeal
to Mr. Hobhouse and Admiral Bathurst if it be true or no? (poor
Ekenhead being since dead)—had we been aware of any such difference of Current as is asserted—we would at least have proved
it—and were not likely to have given it up in the twenty five
minutes of Mr. T.'s own experiment. The secret of all this is—that
Mr. Turner failed and that we succeeded—and he is consequently
disappointed—and seems not unwilling to overshadow whatever
little merit there might be in our Success.— —why did he not try
the European side?—If he had succeeded there after failing on the
Asiatic his plea would have been more graceful and gracious.—Mr.
T. may find what fault he pleases with my poetry—or my politics—but I recommend him to leave aquatic reflections—till he is
able to swim "five and twenty minutes" without being "*exhausted*"
though I believe he is the first modern Tory who ever swam "*against
the Stream*" for half the time.— —

TO PERCY BYSSHE SHELLEY   *Ravenna, April 26th, 1821*

The child continues doing well, and the accounts are regular
and favourable. It is gratifying to me that you and Mrs. Shelley
do not disapprove of the step which I have taken, which is merely
temporary.

I am very sorry to hear what you say of Keats—is it *actually* true? I did not think criticism had been so killing. Though I differ from you essentially in your estimate of his performances, I so much abhor all unnecessary pain, that I would rather he had been seated on the highest peak of Parnassus than have perished in such a manner. Poor fellow! though with such inordinate self-love he would probably have not been very happy. I read the review of "Endymion" in the Quarterly. It was severe,—but surely not so severe as many reviews in that and other journals upon others.

I recollect the effect on me of the Edinburgh on my first poem; it was rage, and resistance, and redress—but not despondency nor despair. I grant that those are not amiable feelings; but, in this world of bustle and broil, and especially in the career of writing, a man should calculate upon his powers of *resistance* before he goes into the arena.

> "Expect not life from pain nor danger free,
> Nor deem the doom of man reversed for thee."

You know my opinion of that *second-hand* school of poetry. You also know my high opinion of your own poetry,—because it is of *no* school. I read Cenci—but, besides that I think the *subject* essentially *un*dramatic, I am not an admirer of our old dramatists as *models*. I deny that the English have hitherto had a drama at all. Your Cenci, however, was a work of power, and poetry. As to *my* drama, pray revenge yourself upon it, by being as free as I have been with yours.

I have not yet got your Prometheus, which I long to see. I have heard nothing of mine, and do not know that it is yet published. I have published a pamphlet on the Pope controversy, which you will not like. Had I known that Keats was dead—or that he was alive and so sensitive—I should have omitted some remarks upon his poetry, to which I was provoked by his *attack* upon *Pope*, and my disapprobation of *his own* style of writing.

You want me to undertake a great Poem—I have not the inclination nor the power. As I grow older, the indifference—*not* to life, for we love it by instinct—but to the stimuli of life, increases. Besides, this late failure of the Italians has latterly disappointed me for many reasons,—some public, some personal. My respects to Mrs. S.

Yours ever,

B

P.S.—Could not you and I contrive to meet this summer? Could not you take a run *alone*?

TO RICHARD BELGRAVE HOPPNER   *Ravenna May 11th. 1821*

My dear Hoppner—If I had but known yr. notion about Switzerland before—I should have adopted it at once.—As it is—I shall let the child remain in her Convent—where she seems healthy & happy—for the present—but I shall feel much obliged if you will enquire when you are in the Cantons—about the usual & better modes of education there for females—and let me know the result of your opinions.—It is some consolation that both Mr. & Mrs. Shelley—have written to approve entirely my placing the child with the Nuns for the present.— —No one but the amiable Claire disapproves of it in the natural circumstances—in the interim.—As to what might be said by people—as she amiably puts it—I can refer to my whole conduct—as having neither spared care—kindness—nor expence—since the child was sent to me.—The people may say what they please—I must content myself with not deserving (in this instance) that they should speak ill.—The place is a *Country* town—in a good air—where there is a large establishment for education—& many children some of considerable rank placed in it.—As a *country* town—it is less liable to objections of every kind.—It has always appeared to me that the moral defect in Italy does not proceed from a *Conventual* education—because—to my certain knowledge they come out of their convents innocent even to *ignorance* of moral evil—but to the state of Society into which they are directly plunged on coming out of it.— —It is like educating an infant on a mountain top—and then taking him to the Sea—& throwing him into it, & desiring him to swim.— —The evil however—though still too general is partly wearing away—as the women are more permitted to marry from attachment.—This is I believe the case also in France.—And after all—what is the higher society of England?—according to my own experience & to all that I have seen & heard—(and I have lived there in the very highest—& what is called the *best*) no way of life can be more corrupt.— —In Italy however it is—or rather *was* more *systematized*—but *now* they themselves are ashamed of *regular* Serventismo.— —In England the only homage which they pay to Virtue—is hypocrisy.— —I speak of course of the *tone* of high life—the middle ranks may be very virtuous.— —I have not got any copy—(nor have yet had) of the letter on Bowles—of course I should be delighted to send it to you.—How is Mrs. H? well again I hope.—Let me know when you set out—I regret that I cannot meet you in the Bernese Alps this summer—as I once hoped and intended.—With my best respects to Madame—I am

> ever & most truly yr. obliged Sert.
> [scrawl]

P.S.—I gave to a Musician*er* a letter for you some time ago—has he presented himself?—Perhaps you could introduce him to the Ingrams and other dilettanti.—He is simple and unassuming—two strange things in his profession—and he fiddles like Orpheus himself—or Amphion—tis a pity that he can't make Venice dance away from the brutal tyrant who tramples upon it.—

TO JOHN MURRAY   *Ravenna—May 19th. 1821*

Dear Murray—Enclosed is a letter of Valpy's which it is for you to answer.—I have nothing further to do with the mode of publication.—By the papers of Thursday—& two letters from Mr. K[innair]d I perceive that the Italian Gazettes had lied most *Italically*—& that the drama had *not* been hissed—& that my friends *had* interfered to prevent the representation.— —So it seems they continue to act it—in spite of us all.—For this we must "trouble them at '*Size*'"— —let it by all means be brought to a plea—I am determined to try the right—& will *meet* the expences.— —The reason of the Lombard Lie—was that the Austrians who keep up an Inquisition throughout Italy and a *list* of *names* of all who think or speak of any thing but in favour of their despotism—have for five years past abused me in every form in the Gazettes of Milan &c.— —I wrote to you a week ago upon the subject.— —Now— I should be glad to know what compensation Mr. Elliston could make me—not only for dragging my writings on the stage in *five* days—but for being the cause that I was kept for *four* days—(from Sunday to Thursday morning the only post days) in the *belief* that the *tragedy* had been acted & "unanimously hissed" and with the addition—that "*I* had brought it upon the stage"—and consequently that none of my friends had attended to my request to the contrary.— —Suppose that I had burst a blood vessel like John Keats, or blown [out] my brains in a fit of rage—neither of which would have been unlikely a few years ago.— —At present I am luckily calmer than I used to be—& yet I would not pass those four days over again—for—I know not what.—

I wrote to you to keep up yr. spirits.—for reproach is useless always & irritating—but my feelings were very much hurt—to be dragged like a Gladiator to the fate of a Gladiator—by that "*Retiarius*" Mr. Elliston— —As to his defence—& offers of compensation—what is all this to the purpose? It is like Louis the 14th. who insisted upon buying at any price Algernon Sydney's horse —& on refusal—on taking it by force.—Sydney shot his horse.— I could not shoot my tragedy—but I would have flung it into the fire rather than have had it represented.—I have now written nearly *three* acts of another (intending to complete it in five) and am more anxious than ever to be preserved from such a breach of all literary courtesy—& gentlemanly consideration.— —If we succeed—well;—if not—previous to any future publication—we will request a *promise* not to be acted—which I would even pay for—(as money is their object)—or I will not publish—which however you will probably not much regret.— —The Chancellor has behaved nobly.—You have also conducted yourself in the most satisfactory manner—and I have no fault to find with anybody but the Stage-players, & their proprietor.—I was always so civil to Elliston personally—that he ought to have been the last to attempt to injure me.— —

There is a most rattling thunder-storm pelting away at this present writing—so that I write neither by day nor by candle nor torch light—but by *lightning*-light— —the flashes are as brilliant as the most Gaseous glow of the Gaslight company.—My chimney-board has just been thrown down by a gust of wind.—I thought it was the "bold Thunder" and the "brisk Lightning" in person—*three* of us would be too many.—There it goes—*flash* again—but

> "I tax not you ye elements with unkindness
> I never gave ye *franks* nor *called* upon you"

as I had done by & upon Mr. Elliston.— —Why do not you write—you should have at least sent me a line of particulars—I know nothing yet—but by Galignani & the honourable Douglas.— — Hobhouse has been paying back Mr. Canning's assault.—He was right—for Canning had been like Addison "trying to *cuff* down *new-fledged merit*." Hobhouse has in him "something dangerous" if not let alone.—Well—& how does our Pope Controversy go on—& the pamphlet?—It is impossible to write any news the Austrian scoundrels rummage all letters.—

yrs. [scrawl]

P.S.—I could not [*sic*] have sent you a good deal of Gossip—& some *real* information were it not—that all letters pass through the Barbarians' inspection—and I have no wish to inform *them* of anything but my utter abhorrence of them & theirs. They have only conquered by treachery however.—Send me some Soda-powders—some of "Acton's Corn-rubbers"—and W. Scott's romances.—And do pray write—when there is anything to interest—you are always silent.—

TO JOHN MURRAY   *R[avenn]a July 22d. 1821*

Dear Murray/—By this post is expedited a parcel of notes—addressed to J. Barrow Esqre. &c.—Also by ye. former post—the returned proof of S[ardanapalus]—and the M.S.S. of the "two Foscaris."—Acknowledge these.—The printer has done wonders—he has read what I cannot—my own handwriting.— —I *oppose* the "delay till Winter"—I am particularly anxious to print while the *Winter theatres* are *closed*—to gain time in case they try their former piece of politeness.— —Any *loss*—shall be considered in our contract—whether occasioned by the season or other causes—but print away—and publish.—I think they must own that I have more *styles* than one.— —"Sardanapalus" is however almost a comic character—but for that matter—so is Richard the third.—Mind the *Unities*—which are my great object of research. I am glad that Gifford likes it—as for "the Million"—you see I have carefully consulted anything but the *taste* of the day—for extravagant "coups de theatre".—Any probable loss—as I said before—will be allowed for in our accompts.—The reviews (except one or two, Blackwood's for instance) are cold enough—but never mind those fellows— —I shall send them to the right about—if I take it into my head.—Perhaps that in the Monthly is written by Hodgson—as a reward for having paid his debts and travelled all night to beg his mother in law (by his *own* desire) to let him marry her daughter,—though I had never seen her in my life, it succeeded.—But such are mankind—and I have always found the English *baser* in some things than any other nation.—You stare—but it's true—as to *gratitude*;—perhaps—because they are prouder—& proud people hate obligations.— —

The tyranny of the government here is breaking out—they have exiled about a thousand people of the best families all over the Roman States.—As many of my friends are amongst them—I think of moving too—but not till I have had you answers—continue *your address* to me *here* as usual—& quickly.— —What you will *not* be sorry to hear is—that the *poor* of the place—hearing that I mean to go—got together a petition to the Cardinal—to request that *he* would request me to *remain*. I only heard of it a day or two ago—& it is no dishonour to them nor to me—but it will have displeased the higher powers who look upon me as a Chief of the Coalheavers. They arrested a servant of mine for a Street quarrel with an Officer (they drew upon one another knives & pistols) but as *the Officer* was out of uniform—& in the *wrong* besides—on my protesting stoutly—he was released.—<As> I was not present at the affray—which happened by night near my stables.— —My man (an Italian) a very stout—& not over patient personage would have taken a fatal revenge afterwards if I had not prevented him. As it was he drew his stiletto—and—but for passengers—would have carbonadoed the Captain who (I understand) made but a poor figure in the quarrel—except by beginning it.— —He applied to me—and I offered him any satisfaction—either by turning away the man or otherwise, because he had drawn a knife. He answered that a reproof would be sufficient.—I reproved him—and yet—after this—the shabby dog complained to the *Government*—after being quite satisfied as he said.—*This* roused me—and I gave them a remonstrance which had some effect.—If he had not enough—he should have called me *out*—but that is not the Italian line of conduct,—the Captain has been reprimanded—the servant released—& the business at present rests there.—Write & let me know of the arrival of [scrawl]

P.S.—You will of course publish the two tragedies of Sardanapalus & the Foscaris together.—You can afterwards collect them with "Manfred", and "the Doge"—into the works.—Inclosed is an additional note.—

TO COUNTESS TERESA GUICCIOLI [TRANSLATION]
Ravenna August [*16th*] *1821*

My Love—My letters have arrived, so there is little to keep me here. My intention is to take a house in Pisa where there will be apartments for your family—and for me—separate, but near. If that does not please you—tell me—and we will take a separate house for each of us. This letter will be taken to you by the Englishman who is here now, and is leaving tomorrow. He will explain to everyone many things difficult and lengthy to set down in writing, which is not my talent in a language *not* barbarous. When all is decided, I will send a part of the household with the heavier effects, furniture, etc., needed for the house—then I will come with the others.—

Greet Papa and Pietro—I am always

P.S.—If you have found an apartment in Prato—and can find a house for me, it will do as well—but Pisa would be a more agreeable place to stay in—according to what I am told. I am leaving Ravenna so unwillingly—and so persuaded that my departure can

only lead from one evil to a greater one—that I have no heart to
write any more just now.—

TO DOUGLAS KINNAIRD   *R[avenn]a A[gost]o 31st. 1821*

My dear Douglas/—I write only two words to say that the
new Don Juans are so full of gross *misprints*—especially the 5th
Canto—that I must beg you & Hobhouse to go over it with
the M.S. & correct the whole.—Words—added—misplaced—
mispelt—& in short—a frequent disfigurement.—To Mr. Murray
I have written very freely by this post on the topic.— —He has
also taken the liberty to omit some notes—& a stanza (not that
upon the Queen—*that* I *ordered* to be omitted at Hobhouse's
desire)—now—I have told him—& I beg to repeat it through
you—that I will not allow any earthly being to take such liberties
with me—because I am absent—it is a personal insult—& not to
be suffered.— —Will you tell Hobhouse that I will think upon the
literary part of the letter, & believe me yours ever & in haste

                                                        [scrawl]

P.S.—Let the plays be published when the preface arrives.— —

TO AUGUSTA LEIGH   *R[avenn]a. Septr. 13th. 1821*

My dearest A./—From out the enclosed as well as the former
parcel—(a few posts ago) select some of the *best-behaved* curls—
and set them in a golden locket for Ada my daughter.—Round
the locket let there be this Italian inscription—"*Il Sangue non è
mai Acqua.*"—And do not let the engravers blunder.— —It means
"Blood is never water"—and alludes merely to relationship—being
a common proverb.—I should wish her to wear this—that she may
know she has (or had) a father in the world.—Let the bill for the
locket be sent to Mr. Kinnaird—& let him deduct it from my
accounts.— —Do this and prosper!—

                                                        yrs. ever
                                                        [scrawl]

By this post I have sent to Augusta—to make up into a locket for Ada—some of my hair—I suppose that you have no objection—if you have you can state it to Mrs. Leigh—I wish you to send to Mrs. Leigh's some of the child's in return to be forwarded to me in a letter of Augusta's—it will come very safely by the post—I am anxious to see it's *colour*, for the *print*—gives no information of that, and the picture has not yet been sent by Murray.— —You will not forget to let her learn Italian—& be *musical*—that is if she has an ear & a heart for the latter.—The former will not be difficult, and perhaps by the time that she and I may meet (if ever we meet) it will be nearly necessary to converse with me—for I write English now with more facility than I speak it—from hearing it but seldom. It is the reverse with my Italian which I can speak fluently—but write incorrectly—having never studied it & only acquired it by ear.— —I keep up my English as well as I can by scribbling however.—Murray has at present three tragedies of mine in hand (*not* for the stage you may easily suppose) one of them—on the subject of "Cain" is I think poetical enough.—The other two are in a simpler and severer style.—I am trying an experiment—which is to introduce into our language— the *regular* tragedy—without regard to the Stage—which will not admit of it—but merely to the *mental* theatre of the reader.—As yet—I have had no great success—people looking upon it as a treason to the wild old English drama—which however is a separate and distinct thing—and has as little to do with the question—as Tasso with Ariosto— —they are not of the same genus.— —If you see Joanna Baillie—tell her that *Kean* is going at last to act De Montfort—which I urged him to a hundred times in 1815—this I hear by the way—& am very happy—regretting that I cannot see him.—They want me to alter "the Doge" for Kean—which I have refused (to Douglas Kinnaird) [indeed?] the Stage is not my object—and even interferes with it—as long as it is in it's present state.— —Alfieri's "Philip" and "Mirrha" when well acted (as I have seen them) appeared to me much more classical exhibitions than our own wild pantomimes—but this may be prejudice.—

I won't trouble you more about the funds—but give up the

matter in despair— —I have done what I could for the extrication of the property from what I conceive a precarious state—& must now be content to pay the penalties of absence and my own folly in tying up the greater part of my future against the advice of all about me.— —Your Mr. Bland seems a tolerably impracticable gentleman— —but I have no claim upon him—even for common civility.—Believe me

yrs. very [truly?]

BYRON

P.S.—We have had sad work here since the spring—exiles— proscriptions—and all the routine of ill Success.—Most of my friends have been proscribed more or less—and I escaped as they said themselves merely by being too notorious a person as a stranger to be assailed without a regular trial,—and any thing like an *open* proceeding is contrary to the genius of this government and to the disposition of the neighbouring Tiberius of Austria.—I did all I could to forward the views of the patriots—& was prepared to cast in my lot with them—they were within three days of rising—when the cowardice and treachery of the Neapolitans ruined all.— — The Italians never can unite—that is their bane.—as I think I told you last summer.—The reason that I wrote to you so anxiously about Augusta &c. was that we expected business daily;—and it would not then have been a time to be "bothering you about family matters"—as Sir Lucius says.— —At present I am going into Tuscany—and if the Greek business is not settled soon—shall perhaps go up that way.—The Chief of the Athenian Insurgents is Demetrius Zograffo—who was my Servant for a long time—and with me in London—when I first knew you in 1812.—He was a clever but not an enterprising man—but circumstances make men.—But my going will depend upon more certain information than is yet to be obtained—things are so disguised there.—

TO THOMAS MOORE   *Ravenna, September 19th, 1821*

I am in all the sweat, dust, and blasphemy of an universal pack-ing of all my things, furniture, &c. for Pisa, whither I go for the winter. The cause has been the exile of all my fellow Carbonics, and, amongst them, of the whole family of Madame G., who, you know, was divorced from her husband last week [year?], "on account of P. P. clerk of this parish," and who is obliged to join her father and relatives, now in exile there, to avoid being shut up in a monastery, because the Pope's decree of separation required her to reside in *casa paterna*, or else, for decorum's sake, in a convent. As I could not say, with Hamlet, "Get thee to a nunnery," I am preparing to follow them.

It is awful work, this love, and prevents all a man's projects of good or glory. I wanted to go to Greece lately (as every thing seems up here) with her brother, who is a very fine, brave fellow (I have seen him put to the proof), and wild about liberty. But the tears of a woman who has left her husband for a man, and the weakness of one's own heart, are paramount to these projects, and I can hardly indulge them.

We were divided in choice between Switzerland and Tuscany, and I gave my vote for Pisa, as nearer the Mediterranean, which I love for the sake of the shores which it washes, and for my young recollections of 1809. Switzerland is a curst selfish, swinish country of brutes, placed in the most romantic region of the world. I never could bear the inhabitants, and still less their English visitors; for which reason, after writing for some information about houses, upon hearing that there was a colony of English all over the cantons of Geneva, &c., I immediately gave up the thought, and persuaded the Gambas to do the same.

By the last post I sent you "The Irish Avatar,"—what think you? The last line—"a name never spoke but with curses and jeers" —must run either "a name only uttered with curses or jeers," or "a wretch never named but with curses or jeers." *Because as how*, "spoke" is not grammar, except in the House of Commons; and I doubt whether we can say "a name *spoken*," for *mentioned*. I have some doubts, too, about "repay,"—"and for murder repay with a shout and a smile." Should it not be, "and for murder repay him with shouts and a smile," or "*reward* him with shouts and a smile?"

So, pray put your poetical pen through the MS. and take the least bad of the emendations. Also, if there be any further breaking of Priscian's head, will you apply a plaister? I wrote in the greatest hurry and fury, and sent it you the day after; so, doubtless, there will be some awful constructions, and a rather lawless conscription of rhythmus.

With respect to what Anna Seward calls "the liberty of transcript,"—when complaining of Miss Matilda Muggleton, the accomplished daughter of a choral vicar of Worcester Cathedral, who had abused the said "liberty of transcript," by inserting in the Malvern Mercury, Miss Seward's "Elegy on the South Pole," as her *own* production, with her *own* signature, two years after having taken a copy, by permission of the authoress—with regard, I say, to the "liberty of transcript," I by no means oppose an occasional copy to the benevolent few, provided it does not degenerate into such licentiousness of Verb and Noun as may tend to "disparage my parts of speech" by the carelessness of the transcribblers.

I do not think that there is much danger of the "King's Press being abused" upon the occasion, if the publishers of journals have any regard for their remaining liberty of person. It is as pretty a piece of invective as ever put publisher in the way to "Botany." Therefore, if *they* meddle with it, it is at *their* peril. As for myself, I will answer any jontleman—though I by no means recognise a "right of search" into an unpublished production and unavowed poem. The same applies to things published *sans* consent. I hope you like, at least, the concluding lines of the *Pome*?

What are you doing, and where are you? in England? Nail Murray—nail him to his own counter, till he shells out the thirteens. Since I wrote to you, I have sent him another tragedy—"Cain" by name—making three in MS. now in his hands, or in the printer's. It is in the Manfred, metaphysical style, and full of some Titanic declamation;—Lucifer being one of the dram. pers., who takes Cain a voyage among the stars, and, afterwards, to "Hades," where he shows him the phantoms of a former world, and its inhabitants. I have gone upon the notion of Cuvier, that the world has been destroyed three or four times, and was inhabited by mammoths, behemoths, and what not; but *not* by man till the Mosaic period, as, indeed, it proved by the strata of bones found;—those of all unknown animals, and known, being dug out, but none of mankind. I have, therefore, supposed Cain to be shown, in the *rational* Preadamites, beings endowed with a higher intelligence than man, but totally unlike him in form, and with much greater strength of mind and person. You may suppose the small talk which takes place between him and Lucifer upon these matters is not quite canonical.

The consequence is, that Cain comes back and kills Abel in a fit of dissatisfaction, partly with the politics of Paradise, which had driven them all out of it, and partly because (as it is written in Genesis) Abel's sacrifice was the more acceptable to the Deity. I trust that the Rhapsody has arrived—it is in three acts, and entitled "A Mystery," according to the former Christian custom, and in honour of what it probably will remain to the reader.

Yours, &c.

TO JOHN MURRAY   *Ravenna Septr. 24th. 1821*

Dear Murray/—I have been thinking over our late correspondence and wish to propose the following articles for our future.—1stly—That you shall write to me of yourself—of the health wealth and welfare of all friends—but of *me* (*quoad me*) little or nothing.—

2dly—That you shall send me Soda powders—tooth-paste—tooth-brushes—or any such anti-odontalgic or chemical articles as heretofore "ad libitum" upon being re-imbursed for the same.— 3dly—That you shall *not* send me any modern or (as they are called) *new* publications in *English*—*whatsoever*—save and excepting any writing prose or verse of (or reasonably presumed to be of) Walter Scott—Crabbe—Moore—Campbell—Rogers—Gifford—Joanna Baillie—*Irving*—(the American) Hogg—Wilson (Isle of Palms Man) or any especial *single* work of fancy which is thought to be of considerable merit.—*Voyages* and *travels*—provided that they are *neither in Greece Spain Asia Minor Albania nor Italy* will be welcome—having travelled the countries mentioned—I know that what is said of them can convey nothing further which I desire to know about them.—No other *English* works whatsoever.— —
4thly—That you send me *no periodical works* whatsoever —*no* Edinburgh—Quarterly—Monthly—nor any Review— Magazine—Newspaper English or foreign of any description— —

5thly—That you send me *no* opinions whatsoever either *good*—*bad*—or *indifferent*—of yourself or your friends or others— concerning any work or works of mine—past—present—or to come.—

6thly—That all Negotiations in matters of business between you and me pass through the medium of the Hon[oura]ble Douglas Kinnaird—my friend and trustee, or Mr. Hobhouse—as "Alter Ego" and tantamount to myself during my absence.—or presence.— —

Some of these propositions may at first seem strange—but they are founded.—The quantity of trash I have received as books is incalculable, and neither amused nor instructed.—Reviews & Magazines—are at the best but ephemeral & superficial reading— *who thinks* of the *grand article* of *last year* in any *given review*? in the next place—if they regard *myself*—they tend to increase *Egotism*,—if favourable—I do not deny that the praise *elates*—and if unfavourable that the abuse *irritates*—the latter may conduct me to inflict a species of Satire—which would neither do good to you nor to your friends—*they* may smile *now*, and so may *you* but if I took you all in hand—it would not be difficult to cut you up like gourds. I did as much by as powerful people at nineteen years old—& I know little as yet in three & thirty—which should prevent me from making all your ribs—Gridirons for your hearts—if such were my propensity.—But it is *not*.—Therefore let me hear none of your provocations—if anything occurs so very *gross* as to require my notice—I shall hear of it from my personal friends.—For the rest—I merely request to be left in ignorance.—

The same applies to opinions *good*—*bad* or *indifferent* of persons in conversation or correspondence; these do not *interrupt* but they *soil* the *current* of my *Mind*;—I am sensitive enough—but *not* till I am *touched* & *here* I am beyond the touch of the short arms of literary England—except the few feelers of the Polypus that crawl over the Channel in the way of Extract.— —All these precautions *in* England would be useless—the libeller or the flatterer would there reach me in spite of all—but in Italy we know little of literary England & think less except what reaches us through some garbled & brief extract in some miserable Gazette.— —For *two years* (except two or three articles cut out & sent by *you*—by the post) I never read a newspaper—which was not forced upon me by some accident—& know upon the whole as little of England—as you all do of Italy—& God knows—*that* is little enough with all your travels &c. &c. &c.—The English travellers *know Italy* as *you* know Guernsey—how much is *that?*—If any thing occurs so violently gross or personal as to require notice, Mr. D[ougla]s Kinnaird will let me *know*—but of *praise* I desire to hear *nothing.*— —You will say—"to what tends all this?—" I will answer THAT— —to keep my mind *free and* unbiased—by all paltry and personal irritabilities of praise or censure;—To let my Genius take it's natural direction,—while my feelings are like the dead—who know nothing and feel nothing of all or aught that is said or done in their regard.— —If you can observe these conditions you will spare yourself & others some pain—let me not be worked upon to rise up—for if I do—it will not be for a little;—if you can *not* observe these conditions we shall cease to be correspondents,—but *not friends*—for I shall always be

yrs. ever & truly
BYRON

P.S.—I have taken these resolutions not from any irritation against *you* or *yours* but simply upon reflection that all reading either praise or censure of myself has done me harm. When I was in Switzerland and Greece I was out of the way of hearing either—& *how I wrote there!*—In Italy I am out of the way of it too—but latterly partly through my fault—& partly through your kindness in wishing to send me the *newest* & most periodical publications—I have had a crowd of reviews &c. thrust upon me—which have bored me with their jargon of one kind or another—& taken off my attention from greater objects.— —You have also sent me a parcel of trash of poetry for no reason that I can conceive—unless to provoke me to write a new "English Bards"—Now *this* I wish to avoid—for if ever I *do*—it will be a strong production—and I desire peace as long as the fools will keep their nonsense out of my way.— —

TO THOMAS MOORE *September—no—October 1, 1821*

I have written to you lately, both in prose and verse, at great length, to Paris and London. I presume that Mrs. Moore, or whoever is your Paris deputy, will forward my packets to you in London.

I am setting off for Pisa, if a slight incipient intermittent fever do not prevent me. I fear it is not strong enough to give Murray much chance of realising his thirteens again. I hardly should regret it, I think, provided you raised your price upon him—as what Lady Holderness (my sister's grandmother, a Dutchwoman) used to call Augusta, her *Residee Legatoo*—so as to provide for us all: *my* bones with a splendid and larmoyante edition, and you with double what is extractable during my lifetime.

I have a strong presentiment that (bating some out of the way accident) you will survive me. The difference of eight years, or whatever it is, between our ages, is nothing. I do not feel (nor am, indeed, anxious to feel) the principle of life in me tend to longevity. My father and mother died, the one at thirty-five or six, and the other at forty-five; and Dr. Rush, or somebody else, says that nobody lives long, without having *one parent*, at least, an old stager.

I *should*, to be sure, like to see out my eternal mother-in-law, not so much for her heritage, but from my natural antipathy. But the indulgence of this natural desire is too much to expect from the Providence who presides over old women. I bore you with all this about lives, because it has been put in my way by a calculation of insurances which Murray has sent me. I *really think* you should have more, if I evaporate within a reasonable time.

I wonder if my "Cain" has got safe to England. I have written since about sixty stanzas of a poem, in octave stanzas (in the Pulci style, which the fools in England think was invented by Whistlecraft—it is as old as the hills in Italy) called "The Vision of Judgment, by Quevedo Redivivus," with this motto—

> "A Daniel come to *judgment*, yea, a Daniel:
> I thank thee, Jew, for teaching me that word."

In this it is my intent to put the said George's Apotheosis in a Whig point of view, not forgetting the Poet Laureate for his preface and his other demerits.

I am just got to the pass where Saint Peter, hearing that the royal defunct had opposed Catholic Emancipation, rises up and, interrupting Satan's oration, declares *he* will change places with Cerberus sooner than let him into heaven, while *he* has the keys thereof.

I must go and ride, though rather feverish and chilly. It is the ague season; but the agues do me rather good than harm. The feel after the *fit* is as if one had got rid of one's body for good and all.

The gods go with you!—Address to Pisa.

Ever yours.

P.S.—Since I came back I feel better, though I stayed out too late for this malaria season, under the thin crescent of a very young moon, and got off my horse to walk in an avenue with a Signora for an hour. I thought of you and

> "When at eve thou rovest
> By the star thou lovest."

But it was not in a romantic mood, as I should have been once; and yet it was a *new* woman, (that is, new to me,) and, of course, expected to be made love to. But I merely made a few common-place speeches. I feel as your poor friend Curran said, before his death, "a mountain of lead upon my heart," which I believe to be constitutional, and that nothing will remove it but the same remedy.

TO AUGUSTA LEIGH   *Octr. 5th. 1821*

My dearest Augusta—Has there been nothing to make it grey? to be sure the *years* have not.— —Your parcel will not find me here—I am going to *Pisa*—for the winter.—The late political troubles here have occasioned the exile of all my friends & connections—& I am going there to join them.—You know or you do *not* know that Madame La Comtesse G[uiccioli] was separated from her husband last year (on account of P. P. Clerk of this parish)

that the Pope decided in her favour & gave her a separate maintenance & that we lived very quietly & decently—she at her father's
(as the Pope decided) and I at home—till this Summer.—When
her father was exiled—she was obliged either to accompany him
or retire into a Convent—such being the terms of his Holiness's
deed of divorcement.— —They went to Pisa—by my recommendation & there I go to join them.— —So there's a *romance* for
you—I assure you it was not my wish nor fault altogether—her
husband was old—rich—& must have left her a large jointure
in a few years—but he was jealous—& insisted &c. & *she* like
all the rest—*would* have her own way.—You know that all my
loves go crazy—and make scenes—and so—"She is the sixteenth
Mrs. Shuffleton".— —Being very young—very romantic—and
odd—and being contradicted by her husband besides—& being
of a country where morals are no better than in England—(though
elopements and divorces are rare—and this made an uncommon
noise—the first that had occurred at Ravenna for two hundred
years—that is in a *public* way with appeals to the Pope &c.) you
are not to wonder much at it;—she being too a beauty & the great
Belle of the four Legations—and married not quite a year (at our
first acquaintance) to a man *forty years older* than herself—who had
had two wives already—& a little suspected of having poisoned his
first.— —

We have been living hitherto decently & quietly—these
things here do not exclude a woman from all society as in yr.
hypocritical country.— —It is very odd that all my *fairs* are such
romantic people—and always daggering or divorcing—or making
scenes.— —But this is "positively the last time of performance"
(as the play-bills say) or of my getting into such scrapes for the
future.—Indeed—I have had my share.—But this is a finisher—
for you know when a woman is separated from her husband for
her Amant—he is bound both by honour (and inclination at least
I am) to live with her all his days, as long as there is no miscon-
duct.—So you see that I have closed as papa *begun*— —and you
will probably never see me again as long as you live.—Indeed you
don't deserve it—for having behaved so *coldly*—<when I was ready
to have sacrificed every thing for you—and after *you* had taken the
farther . . . always>—It is nearly three years that this "liaison" has

lasted— —I was dreadfully in love—and she blindly so—for she has sacrificed every thing to this headlong passion.—That comes of being romantic—I can say that without being so *furiously* in love as at first—I am more attached to her—than I thought it possible to be to any woman after three years—<except one & who was she *you* can guess> and have not the least wish—nor prospect of separation from her.—She herself—(and it is now a year since her separation a year too of all kinds of vicissitudes &c.) is still more decided—of course the *step* was a decisive one.—If Lady B[yron] would but please to die—and the Countess G[uiccioli]'s husband—(for Catholics can't marry though divorced) we should probably have to marry—though I would rather *not*—thinking it the way to hate each other—for all people whatsoever.— —However—you must not calculate upon seeing me again in a hurry, if ever.— —How have you sent the *parcel*—& how am I to receive it at Pisa?—I am anxious about the Seal—not about Hodgson's nonsense—what is the fool afraid of the *post* for? it is the *safest*— the only *safe* conveyance—they never meddle but with political packets.

yrs. [scrawl]

P.S.—*You* ought to be a great admirer of the *future* Lady B. for *three* reasons. 1stly. She is a grand patroness of the *present* Lady B.—and always says "that she had no doubt that she was exceedingly ill-used by me["]—2dly. She is an admirer of yours—and I have had great difficulty in keeping her from writing to you eleven pages—(for she is a grand Scribe) and 3dly. she having read "Don Juan" in a *French* translation—made me promise to write *no more* of it—declaring that it was abominable &c. &c.—that *Donna Inez* WAS meant for Ly. B.—& in short made me vow *not* to continue it—(*this* occurred lately & since the last cantos were sent to England last year) is not this altogether odd enough?—She has a good deal of *us* too—I mean that turn for ridicule like Aunt Sophy and you and I & all the B's. Desire Georgiana to write me a letter I suppose she can by this time.—Opened by me—and the Seal taken off—so—don't accuse the post-office without cause

B—that's a sign—a written one where the wax was.

PISA

When coldness wraps this suffering clay,
    Ah! whither strays the immortal mind?
It cannot die, it cannot stay,
    But leaves its darken'd dust behind.

WHEN COLDNESS WRAPS THIS SUFFERING CLAY, 1–4

from Detached Thoughts
October 15th, 1821–May 18th, 1822

I have been thinking over the other day on the various comparisons good or evil which I have seen published of myself in different journals English and foreign.—This was suggested to me by my accidentally turning over a foreign one lately—for I have made it a rule latterly never to search for anything of the kind—but not to avoid the perusal if presented by Chance.— —To begin then—I have seen myself compared personally or poetically—in English French *German* (as interpreted to me) Italian and Portuguese within these nine years—to Rousseau—Goethe—Young—Aretine—Timon of Athens—"An Alabaster Vase lighted up within", Satan—Shakespeare—Buonaparte—Tiberius—Æschylus— Sophocles—Euripides—Harlequin—The Clown—Sternhold and Hopkins—to the Phantasmagoria—to Henry the 8th, to Chenier —to Mirabeau—to young R. Dallas (the Schoolboy) to Michael Angelo—to Raphael—to a petit maitre—to Diogenes, to Childe Harold—to Lara—to the Count in Beppo—to Milton—to Pope—to Dryden—to Burns—to Savage—to Chatterton—to "oft have I heard of thee my Lord Biron" in Shakespeare, to Churchill the poet—to Kean the Actor—to Alfieri &c. &c. &c. —the likeness to Alfieri was asserted very seriously by an Italian who had known him in his younger days—it of course related merely to our apparent personal dispositions— —he did not assert it to *me* (for we were not then good friends) but in society.— —

The object of so many contradictory comparisons must probably be like something different from them all, —but what *that* is, is more than *I* know, or any body else.— —My Mother before I was twenty—would have it that I was like Rousseau—and Madame de Stael used to say so too in 1813—and the Edin[burgh] Review has something of ye sort in it's critique on the 4th Canto of Ch[ild]e Ha[rold]e.— —I can't see any point of resemblance—he wrote prose—I verse—he was of the people—I of the Aristocracy—he was a philosopher—I am none—he published his first work at forty—I mine at eighteen,—his first essay brought him universal applause—mine the contrary—he married his housekeeper—I could not keep house with my wife—he thought all the world in a plot against *him*; my little world seems to think *me* in a plot against it—if I may judge by their abuse in print and coterié—he liked Botany—I like flowers and herbs and trees but know nothing of their pedigrees—he wrote Music—I limit my knowledge of it to what I catch by *Ear*—I never could learn any thing by *study*—not even a language—it was all by rote and ear and memory.—He had a bad memory—I *had* at least an excellent one (ask Hodgson the poet—a good judge for he has an astonishing one) he wrote with hesitation and care—I with rapidity—& rarely with pains— — he could never ride nor swim "nor was cunning of fence"— —I was an excellent swimmer—a decent though not at all a dashing rider—(having staved in a rib at eighteen in the course of scamp- ering) & was sufficient of fence—particularly of the Highland broadsword—not a bad boxer—when I could keep my temper— which was difficult—but which I strove to do ever since I knocked down Mr. Purling and put his knee-pan out (with the gloves on) in Angelo's and Jackson's rooms in 1806 during the sparring, and I was besides a very fair Cricketer—one of the Harrow Eleven when we play[ed] against Eton in 1805.— —

Besides Rousseau's way of life—his country—his manners— his whole character—were so very different—that I am at a loss to conceive how such a comparison could have arisen—as it has done three several times and all in rather a remarkable manner. I forgot to say—that *he* was also short-sighted—and that hitherto my eyes have been the contrary to such a degree that in the larg- est theatre of Bologna—I distinguished and read some busts and inscriptions printed near the stage—from a box so distant—& so *darkly* lighted—that none of the company (composed of young and very bright-eyed people some of them in the same box) could make out a letter—and thought it was a trick though I had never been in that theatre before.—Altogether, I think myself justified in thinking the comparison not well founded. I don't say this out of pique—for Rousseau was a great man—and the thing if true were flattering enough—but I have no idea of being pleased with a chimera.— —

. . .

Horne Tooke and Roscoe both are said to have declared that they left Parliament with a higher opinion of it's aggregate integrity and abilities than that with which they had entered it.—The general amount of both in most parliaments is probably about the same—as also the number of *Speakers* and their *talent*—I except *Orators* of course because *they* are things of Ages and not of Septennial or triennial reunions.—Neither house ever struck me with more awe or respect than the same number of Turks in a Divan—or of Methodists in a barn would have done.—Whatever diffidence or nervousness I felt—(& I felt both in a great degree) arose from the number rather than the quality of the assemblage, and the thought rather of the *public without* than the persons within—knowing (as all know) that Cicero himself—and probably the Messiah could never have alter'd the vote of a single Lord of the Bedchamber or Bishop.— —I thought *our* house dull—but the other animating enough upon great days.— —

Sheridan dying was requested to undergo "an operation" he replied that he had already submitted to *two* which were enough for one man's life time.—Being asked what they were he answered "having his hair cut—and sitting for his picture".—

13

Whenever an American requests to see me—(which is *not* unfrequently) I comply—1stly. because I respect a people who acquired their freedom by firmness without excess—and 2dly. because these transatlantic visits "few and far between" make me feel as if talking with Posterity from the other side of the Styx;—in a century or two the new English & Spanish Atlantides will be masters of the old Countries in all probability—as Greece and Europe overcame their Mother Asia in the older or earlier ages as they are called.

14

Sheridan was one day offered a bet by M. G. Lewis— —"I will bet you, Mr. Sheridan, a very large sum—I will bet you what you *owe me* as Manager for my 'Castle Spectre'"— —"I never make *large bets*—said Sheridan—but I will lay you a *very small* one—I will bet you *what it is worth*!["]

15

Lewis, though a kind man—hated Sheridan—and we had some words upon that score when in Switzerland in 1816.—Lewis afterwards sent me the following epigram upon Sheridan from Saint Maurice.—

> "For worst abuse of finest parts
> Was Misophil begotten;
> There might indeed be *blacker* hearts
> But none could be more *rotten*."

16

Lewis at Oatlands was observed one morning to have his eyes red—& his air sentimental—being asked why?—replied—"that when people said any thing *kind* to him—it affected him deeply —and just now the Duchess has said something *so* kind to me that"— —here "tears began to flow" again— —"Never mind, Lewis—said Col. Armstrong to him—never mind—don't cry— *She could not mean it.*"

17

Lewis was a good man—a clever man—but a bore—a damned bore—one may say.—My only revenge or consolation used to be setting him by the ears with some vivacious person who hated Bores especially—Me. de Stael or Hobhouse for example.—But I liked Lewis—he was a Jewel of a Man had he been better set—I don't mean *personally*, but less *tiresome*—for he was tedious—as well as contradictory to every thing and every body.— —Being short-sighted—when we used to ride out together near the Brenta in the twilight in Summer he made me go *before* to pilot him—I am absent at times—especially towards evening—and the consequence of this pilotage was some narrow escapes to the Monk on horseback.— —Once I led him *into* a ditch—over which I had passed as usual forgetting to warn my Convoy—once I led him nearly into the river instead of *on* the *moveable* bridge which *in*commodes passengers—and twice did we both run against the diligence which being heavy and slow did communicate less damage than it received in its leaders who were *terrassé'd* by the charge.—Thrice did I lose him in the gray of the Gloaming and was obliged to bring to to his distant signals of distance and distress.—All the time he went on talking without interruption for he was a man of many words.—Poor fellow—he died a martyr to his new riches—of a second visit to Jamaica—

> "I'd give the lands of Deloraine—
> Dark Musgrave were alive again!"

----

that is

I would give many a Sugar Cane
Monk Lewis were alive again!

18

Lewis said to me—"why do you talk *Venetian* (such as I could talk not very fine to be sure) to the Venetians? & not the usual Italian?" I answered—partly from habit—& partly to be understood—if possible,—"It may be so["]—said Lewis—"but it sounds to me like talking with a *brogue* to an *Irishman*."— —

. . .

29

I liked the Dandies—they were always very civil to *me*—though in general they disliked literary people—and persecuted and mystified Me. de Stael,—Lewis,—Horace Twiss—and the like—damnably.—They persuaded Me. de Stael that Alvanley had a hundred thousand a year &c. &c. till she praised him to his *face* for his *beauty*!—and made a set at him for Albertine—(*Libertine* as Brummell baptized her—though the poor Girl was—& is as correct as maid or wife can be—& very amiable withal—) and a hundred fooleries besides—The truth is—that though I gave up the business early—I had a tinge of Dandyism in my minority—& probably retained enough of it—to conciliate the great ones—at four & twenty.— —I had gamed—& drank—& taken my degrees in most dissipations—and having no pedantry & not being overbearing—we ran quietly together.— —I knew them all more or less—and they made me a Member of Watier's (a superb Club at that time) being I take it—the only literary man (except *two others* both men of the world M.—& S.) in it.—Our Masquerade was a grand one—as was the Dandy Ball—too at the Argyle—but *that* (the latter) was given by the four Chiefs—B. M. A. and P.—if I err not.—

30

I was a member of the Alfred too—being elected—while in Greece.— —It was pleasant—a little too sober & literary—& bored with Sotheby and Sir Francis D'Ivernois—but one met Peel—and Ward—and Valentia—and many other pleasant or known people—and was upon the whole a decent resource on a rainy day—in a dearth of parties—or parliament—or an empty season.—

31

I belonged or belong to the following Clubs or Societies—to the Alfred, to the Cocoa tree—to Watier's—to the Union—to Racket's (at Brighton) to the Pugilistic—to the Owls or "Fly by Night"—to the *Cambridge* Whig Club—to the Harrow Club—Cambridge— and to one or two private Clubs—to the Hampden political Club—and to the Italian Carbonari &c. &c. &c. "though last *not least*"—I got into all these—and never stood for any other—at least—to my own knowledge.— —I declined being proposed to several others though pressed to stand Candidate.— —

32

If the papers lie not (which they generally do) Demetrius Zograffo of Athens is at the head of the Athenian part of the present Greek Insurrection.—He was my Servant in 1809—1810—1811— 1812—at different intervals in those years—(for I left him in Greece when I went to Constantinople) and accompanied me to England in 1811—he returned to Greece—Spring 1812.—He was a clever but not *apparently* an enterprizing man—but Circumstances make men.—His two sons (*then* infants) were named Miltiades—and Alcibiades—May the Omen be happy!— —

33

I have a notion that Gamblers are as happy as most people—being always *excited*;—women—wine—fame—the table—even Ambition—*sate* now & then—but every turn of the card—& cast of the dice—keeps the Gambler alive—besides one can Game ten times longer than one can do any thing else.—I was very fond of it when young—that is to say of "Hazard" for I hate all *Card* Games even Faro—When Macco (or whatever they spell it) was introduced I gave up the whole thing—for I loved and missed the *rattle* and *dash* of the box & dice—and the glorious uncertainty not only of good luck or bad luck—but of *any luck at all*—as one had sometimes to throw *often* to decide at all.— —I have thrown as many as fourteen mains running—and carried off all the cash upon the table occasionally—but I had no coolness or judgement or calculation.—It was the *delight* of the thing that pleased me.— Upon the whole I left off in time without being much a winner or loser.—Since One and twenty years of age—I played but little & then never above a hundred or two—or three.— —

34

As far as Fame goes (that is to say *living* Fame) I have had my share—perhaps—indeed—*certainly* more than my deserts.— — Some odd instances have occurred to my own experience of the wild & strange places to which a name may penetrate, and where it may impress.—Two years ago (almost three—being in August or July 1819) I received at Ravenna a letter in *English* verse from *Drontheim* in Norway—written by a Norwegian—and full of the usual compliments &c. &c.—It is still somewhere amongst my papers.— —In the same month I received an invitation into *Holstein* from a Mr. Jacobsen (I think) of Hamburgh—also (by the same medium) a translation of Medora's song in the "Corsair" by a Westphalian Baroness (*not* "Thundertontronck") with some original verses of hers (very pretty and Klopstockish) and a prose translation annexed to them—on the subject of my wife;—as they concerned *her* more than me—I sent them to her together with Mr. J's letter.—It was odd enough to receive an invitation to pass the *summer* in *Holstein*—while in *Italy*—from people I never knew.—The letter was addressed to Venice.—Mr. J[acobsen] talked to me of the "wild roses growing in the Holstein summer" why then did the Cimbri & Teutones emigrate?

What a strange thing is life and man? were I to present myself at the door of the house where my daughter now is—the door would be shut in my face—unless (as is not impossible—) I knocked down the porter—and if I had gone in that year—(& perhaps now) to Drontheim (the furthest town in Norway) or into Holstein—I should have been received with open arms into the mansions of Strangers & foreigners—attached to me by no tie by [but?] that of mind and rumour. As far as *Fame* goes—I have had my share—it has indeed been leavened by other human contingencies—and this in a greater degree than has occurred to most literary men—of a *decent* rank in life—but on the whole I take it that such equipoise is the condition of humanity.— —I doubt sometimes whether after all a quiet & unagitated life would have suited me—yet I sometimes long for it— —my earliest dreams—(as most boys' dreams are) were martial—but a little later they were all for *love* & retirement—till the hopeless attachment to M[ary] C[haworth] began—and continued (though sedulously concealed) *very* early in my teens—& so upwards—for a time.— —*This* threw me out again "alone on a wide—wide sea".—In the year 1804—I recollect meeting my Sister at General Harcourt's in Portland Place.—I was then *one thing* and *as* she had always till then found me.— — When we met again in 1805—(she tells me since) that my temper and disposition were so completely altered that I was hardly to be recognized.—I was not then sensible of the change—but I can believe it—and account for it.—

. . .

55

I sometimes wish that—I had studied languages with more attention—those which I know, even the classical (Greek and Latin in the usual proportion of a sixth form boy) and a smattering of modern Greek—the Armenian & Arabic Alphabets—a few Turkish & Albanian phrases, oaths, or requests—Italian tolerably—Spanish less than tolerably—French to read with ease—but speak with difficulty—or rather not at all— —all have been acquired by ear or eye—& never by anything like Study:—like

"Edie Ochiltree"— —"I never dowed to bide a hard turn o'wark in my life"— —To be sure—I set in zealously for the Armenian and Arabic—but I fell in love with some absurd womankind both times before I had overcome the Characters and at Malta & Venice left the profitable Orientalists for—for—(no matter what—) notwithstanding that my master the Padre Pasquale Aucher (for whom by the way I compiled the major part of two Armenian & English Grammars) assured me "that the terrestrial Paradise had been certainly in *Armenia*"—I went seeking it—God knows where—did I find it?—Umph!—Now & then—for a minute or two.

56

Of Actors—Cooke was the most natural—Kemble the most supernatural—Kean a medium between the two—but Mrs. Siddons worth them all put together—of those whom I remember to have seen in England.— —

. . .

60

No man would live his life over again—is an old & true saying which all can resolve for themselves.—At the same time there are probably *moments* in most men's lives—which they would live over the rest of life to *regain?*—Else why do we live at all? because Hope recurs to Memory—both false—but—but—but—but—and—this *but* drags on till—What? I do not know—& who does?—"He that died o' Wednesday"—by the way—there is a poor devil to be shot tomorrow here—(Ravenna) for murder;—he hath eaten half a Turkey for his dinner—besides fruit & pudding—and he refuses to confess?—shall I go to see him exhale?—No.—And why?—because it is to take place at *Nine*;—Now—could I *save* him—or a fly even from the same catastrophe—I would out-watch years—but as I cannot—I will not get up earlier to see another man shot—than I would to run the same risk in person.—Besides—I have seen more than one die that death (and other deaths) before to-day.—It is not cruelty which actuates mankind—but excitement—on such occasions—at least I suppose so;—it is detestable to *take* life in that way—unless it be to preserve two lives.— —

. . .

72

When I first went up to College—it was a new and a heavy hearted scene for me.—Firstly—I so much disliked leaving Harrow that though it was time—(I being seventeen) it broke my very rest for the last quarter—with counting the days that remained.—I always *hated* Harrow till the last year and a half—but then I liked it.—2dly. I wished to go to Oxford and not to Cambridge.—3dly. I was so completely alone in this new world that it half broke my Spirits.—My companions were not unsocial but the contrary—lively—hospitable—of rank—& fortune—& gay far beyond my gaiety—I mingled with—and dined—& supped &c. with them—but I know not how—it was one of the deadliest and heaviest feelings of my life to feel that I was no longer a boy.—From that moment I began to grow old in my own esteem—and in my esteem age is not estimable.—I took my gradations in the vices—with great promptitude—but they were not to my taste—for my early passions though violent in the extreme—were concentrated—and hated division or spreading abroad.—I could have left or lost the world with or for that which I loved—but though my temperament was naturally burning—I could not share in the common place libertinism of the place and time—without disgust.— —And yet this very disgust and my heart thrown back upon itself—threw me into excesses perhaps more fatal than those from which I shrunk—as fixing upon one (at a time) the passions which spread amongst many would have hurt only myself.—

73

People have wondered at the Melancholy which runs through my writings.—Others have wondered at my personal gaiety— — but I recollect once after an hour in which I had been sincerely and particularly gay—and rather brilliant in company—my wife replying to me when I said (upon her remarking my high spirits) "and yet Bell—I have been called and mis-called Melancholy—you must have seen how falsely frequently." "No—*B*—(she answered) it is not so—at *heart* you are the most melancholy of mankind, and often when apparently gayest.["]— —

74

If I could explain at length the *real* causes which have contributed to increase this perhaps *natural* temperament of mine—this Melancholy which hath made me a bye-word—nobody would wonder— —but this is impossible without doing much mischief.— —I do not know what other men's lives have been—but I cannot conceive anything more strange than some of the earlier parts of mine— —I have written my memoirs—but omitted *all* the really *consequential* & *important* parts—from deference to the dead—to the living—and to those who must be both.—

75

I sometimes think that I should have written the *whole*—as a *lesson*— —but it might have proved a lesson to be *learnt*—rather than *avoided*—for passion is a whirlpool, which is not to be viewed nearly without attraction from it's Vortex.— —

76

I must not go on with these reflections—or I shall be letting out some secret or other—to paralyze posterity.—

77

One night Scrope Davies at a Gaming house   (before I was of age) being tipsy as he mostly was at the Midnight hour—& having lost monies—was in vain intreated by his friends one degree less intoxicated than himself to come or go home.—In despair—he was left to himself and to the demons of the dice-box.— —Next day—being visited about two of the Clock by some friends just risen with a severe headache and empty pockets—(who had left him losing at four or five in the morning) he was found in a sound sleep—without a nightcap—& not particularly encumbered with bed-cloathes— —a Chamber-pot stood by the bed-side—*brim-full* of—*Bank Notes*!—all won—God knows how—and crammed—Scrope knew not where—but *there* they were—all good legitimate notes—and to the amount of some thousand pounds.—

78

At Brighthelmstone—(I love orthography at length) in the year 1808 Hobhouse, Scrope Davies, Major Cooper—and myself—having dined together with Lord Delvin—Count (I forget the french Emigrant nomenclature) and others—did about the middle of the night—(we *four*) proceed to a house of Gambling—being then *amongst us* possest of about *twenty guineas* of ready cash—with which we had to maintain about as many of your whoreson horses & servants—besides household and whorehold expenditure. We had I say—twenty guineas or so—& we lost them—returning home in bad humour.—Cooper went home.— —Scrope and Hobhouse and I (it being high Summer) did first-ly strip and plunge into the Sea—whence after half an hour's swimming of those of us (Scrope & I) who could swim—we emerged in our dressing-gowns to discuss a bottle or two of Champaigne and Hock (according to choice) at our quarters.—In the course of the discussion—words arose— —Scrope seized H[obhouse] by the throat—H. seized a knife in self-defence and stabbed Scrope in the shoulder to avoid being throttled.— —Scrope fell bathed in blood & wine—for the *bottle* fell with him.—Being infinitely intoxicated—with Gaming—Sea-bathing at two in the morning—and supplementary Champaigne—The skirmish had past before I had time or thought to interfere.—Of course I lectured against quarrelling—

"Pugnare Thracum est"—

and then examined Scrope's wound which proved to be a gash long and broad—but not deep nor dangerous.— —Scrope was furious—first he wanted to fight—then to go away in a post-chaise & then to *shoot himself*—which last intention I offered to forward—provided that he did not use my *pistols*—which in case of suicide would become a deo-dand to the king. At length with many oaths & some difficulty he was gotten to bed—in the morning Cool reflection & a Surgeon came—and by dint of loss of blood—& Sticking plaister—the quarrel (which Scrope had begun) was healed as well as the wound—& we were all friends as for years before and after.

79

My first dash into poetry, was as early as 1800.— —It was the ebullition of a passion for my first Cousin Margaret Parker (daughter and grand-daughter of the two Admirals Parker) one of the most beautiful of Evanescent beings.—I have long forgotten the verses—but it would be difficult for me to forget her— —Her dark eyes!—her long eyelashes! her completely Greek cast of face and figure!—I was then about twelve—She rather older—perhaps a year.— —She died about a year or two afterwards—in consequence of a fall which injured her spine and induced consumption.—Her Sister Augusta—(by some thought still more beautiful) died of the same malady—and it was indeed in attending her that Margaret met with the accident which occasioned her own death.—My Sister told me that when she went to see her shortly before her death—upon accidentally mentioning my name—Margaret coloured through the paleness of mortality to the eyes—to the great astonishment of my Sister—who (residing with her Grandmother Lady Holderness—saw at that time but little of me for family reasons) knew nothing of our attachment—nor could conceive why my name should affect her at such a time.— —I knew nothing of her illness—(being at Harrow and in the country) till she was gone.— —Some years after I made an attempt at an Elegy.—A very dull one.—I do not recollect scarcely anything equal to the *transparent* beauty of my cousin—or to the sweetness of her temper—during the short period of our intimacy— —she looked as if she had been made out of a rainbow—all beauty and peace.—My passion had it's effects upon me—I could not sleep—I could not eat—I could not rest—and although I had reason to know that she loved me—it was the torture of my life—to think of the time which must elapse before we could meet again—being usually about *twelve hours*—of separation!— —But I was a fool then—and am not much wiser now.

80

My passions were developed very early—so early—that few would believe me—if I were to state the period—and the facts which accompanied it.—Perhaps this was one of the reasons which

caused the anticipated melancholy of my thoughts—having anticipated life.—My earlier poems are the thoughts of one at least ten
years older than the age at which they were written,—I don't mean
for their solidity—but their Experience—the two first Cantos of
C[hild]e H[arold]e were completed at twenty two—and they were
written as if by a man—older than I shall probably ever be.—

81 [omitted by Byron]

82

Upon Parnassus going to the fountain of Delphi (Castri) in
1809—I saw a flight of twelve Eagles—(Hobhouse says they are
Vultures—at least in conversation) and I seized the Omen.—On
the day before, I composed the lines to Parnassus—(in Childe
Harold) and on beholding the birds—had a hope—that Apollo
had accepted my homage.— —I have at least had the name and
fame of a Poet—during the poetical period of life (from twenty to
thirty) whether it will last is another matter—but I *have been*—a
votary of the Deity—and the place—and am grateful for what he
has done in my behalf—leaving the future in his hands as I left
the past.—

83

Like Sylla—I have always believed that all things depend
upon Fortune & nothing upon ourselves.—I am not aware
of any one thought or action worthy of being called good to
myself or others—which is not to be attributed to the Good
Goddess—*Fortune!*—

84

Two or three years ago, I thought of going to one of the Americas—English or Spanish.—But the accounts sent from England
in consequence of my enquiries—discouraged me.—After all—I
believe most countries properly balanced are equal to *a Stranger*
(by no means to the *native* though)— —I remembered General
Ludlow's domal inscription—

"Omne solum forti patria"—

And sate down free in a country of Slavery for many centuries.—
—But there is *no* freedom—even for *Masters*—in the midst of
slaves— —it makes my blood boil to see the thing.—I sometimes wish that I was the Owner of Africa—to do at once—what
Wilberforce will do in time—viz—sweep Slavery from her desarts—and look on upon the first dance of their Freedom.— —As
to *political* slavery—so general—it is men's own fault—if they *will*
be slaves let them!— —yet it is but "a word and a blow"—see how
England formerly—France—Spain—Portugal—America—Switzerland—freed themselves!— —there is no one instance of a *long*
contest in which *men* did not triumph over Systems.—If Tyranny
misses her *first* spring she is cowardly as the tiger and retires to be
hunted.— —

. . .

91

My School friendships were with *me passions* (for I was always
violent) but I do not know that there is one which has endured (to
be sure some have been cut short by death) till now—that with
Lord Clare began one of the earliest and lasted longest—being
only interrupted by distance—that I know of.—I never hear the
word "*Clare*" without a beating of the heart—even *now*, & I write
it—with the feelings of 1803–4–5—ad Infinitum.

92

In 1812, at Middleton (Lord Jersey's) amongst a goodly company—of Lords—Ladies—& wits—&c.—there was poor old
Vice Leach the lawyer—attempting to play off the fine gentleman.—His first exhibition—an attempt on horseback I think to
escort the women—God knows where—in the month of November—ended in a fit of the Lumbago—as Lord Ogleby says—"a
grievous enemy to Gallantry and address"—and if he could have
but heard Lady Jersey quizzing him (as I did) the next day for the
cause of his malady— —I don't think that he would have turned a
"Squire of dames" in a hurry again.—He seemed to me the greatest
fool (in that line) I ever saw.— —This was the last I saw of old
Vice Leach—except in town where he was creeping into assemblies
—and trying to look young—& gentlemanly.—

93

Erskine too!—Erskine—was there—good—but intolerable—
he jested—he talked—he did every thing admirably but then he
would be applauded for the same thing twice over—he would read
his own verses—his own paragraph—and tell his own story—
again and again—and then "the trial by Jury!!!"—I almost wished
it abolished, for I sate next him at dinner— —As I had read his
published speeches—there was no occasion to repeat them to
me.—Chester (the fox hunter) surnamed "*Cheeks* Chester"—and
I sweated the Claret—being the only two who did so.—Cheeks
who loves his bottle—and had no notion of meeting with a "bon
vivant" in a scribbler—in making my eulogy to somebody one
evening summed it up in—"by G—d he *drinks like a Man!*"

94

Nobody drank however but Cheeks and I—to be sure there
was little occasion—for we swept off what was on the table (a
most splendid board—as may be supposed at Jersey's) very sufficiently.—However we carried our liquor discreetly—like "the
Baron of Bradwardine".

95

If I had to live over again—I do not know what I would change
in my life—unless it were *for—not to have lived at all*[.] All history
and experience—and the rest—teaches us that the good and evil
are pretty equally balanced in this existence—and that what is
most to be desired is an easy passage out of it.— —What can it
give us but *years*? & those have little of good but their ending.—

96

Of the Immortality of the Soul—it appears to me that there
can be little doubt—if we attend for a moment to the action of
Mind.—It is in perpetual activity;—I used to doubt of it—but
reflection has taught me better.—It acts also so very independent
of body—in dreams for instance incoherently and madly—I grant
you;—but still it is *Mind* & much more *Mind*—than when we
are awake.— —Now—that *this* should not act *separately*—as well
as jointly—who can pronounce?—The Stoics Epictetus & Marcus

Aurelius call the present state "a Soul which drags a Carcase"— —a heavy chain to be sure, but all chains being material may be shaken off.—How far our future life will be *individual*—or rather—how far it will at all resemble our *present* existence is another question— but that the *Mind* is *eternal*—seems as possible as that the body is not so.—Of course—I have venture[d] upon the question without recurring to Revelation—which however is at least as rational a solution of it—as any other.—A *material* resurrection seems strange and even absurd except for purposes of punishment—and all punishment which is to *revenge* rather than *correct*—must be *morally wrong*—and *when* the *World is at an end*—what moral or warning purpose *can* eternal tortures answer?—human passions have probably disfigured the divine doctrines here—but the whole thing is inscrutable.—It is useless to tell one *not* to *reason* but to *believe*— —you might as well tell a man not to wake but *sleep*— and then to *bully* with torments!—and all that!—I cannot help thinking that the *menace* of Hell makes as many devils as the severe penal codes of inhuman humanity make villains.— —Man is born *passionate* of body—but with an innate though secret tendency to the love of Good in his Main-spring of Mind.— —But God help us all!—It is at present a sad jar of atoms.— —

97

Matter is eternal—always changing—but reproduced and as far as we can comprehend Eternity—Eternal—and why not Mind?— Why should not the Mind act with and upon the Universe?—as portions of it act upon and with the congregated dust—called Mankind?—See—how one man acts upon himself and others—or upon multitudes?—The same Agency in a higher and purer degree may act upon the Stars &c. ad infinitum.

98

I have often been inclined to Materialism in philosophy—but could never bear it's introduction into *Christianity*—which appears to me essentially founded upon the *Soul*.—For this reason, Priestley's Christian Materialism—always struck me as deadly.— Believe the resurrection of the *body*—if you will—but *not without* a *Soul*—the devil's in it—if after having had a Soul—(as surely the *Mind* or whatever you call it—*is*)—in this world we must part with it in the next—even for an Immortal Materiality;—I own my partiality for *Spirit*.—

99

I am always most religious upon a sunshiny day—as if there was some association between an internal approach to greater light and purity—and the kindler of this dark lanthorn of our external existence.— —

100

The Night is also a religious concern—and even more so—when I viewed the Moon and Stars through Herschell's telescope—and saw that they were worlds.—

101

If according to some speculations—you could prove the World many thousand years older than the Mosaic Chronology—or if you could knock up Adam & Eve and the Apple and Serpent— still what is to be put up in their stead?—or how is the difficulty removed? things must have had a beginning—and what matters it *when*—or *how*?— —I sometimes think that *Man* may be the relic of some higher material being wrecked in a former world— and degenerated in the hardships and struggle through Chaos into Conformity—or something like it—as we see Laplanders— Esquimaux—&c. inferior in the present state—as the Elements become more inexorable— —but even then this higher pre-Adamite Supposititious Creation must have had an Origin and a *Creator*—for a *Creator* is a more natural imagination than a fortuitous concourse of atoms—all things remount to a fountain—though they may flow to an Ocean.—

102

What a strange thing is the propagation of life!—A bubble of Seed which may be spilt in a whore's lap—or in the Orgasm of a voluptuous dream—might (for aught we know) have formed a Caesar or a Buonaparte—there is nothing remarkable recorded of their Sires—that I know of.— —

103

Lord Kames has said—(if I misquote not) "that a power to call up agreeable ideas at will would be something greater for mortals than all the boons of a fairy tale."— —I have found increasing upon me (without sufficient cause at times) the depression of Spirits (with few intervals) which I have some reason to believe constitutional or inherited.

. . .

112

There is nothing left for Mankind but a Republic—and I think that there are hopes of Such—the two Americas (South and North) have it—Spain and Portugal approach it—all thirst for it—Oh Washington!—

113

Pisa Novr. 5th. 1821

"There is a strange coincidence sometimes in the little things of this world—Sancho" says Sterne in a letter (if I mistake not) and so I have often found it.— —Page 585 article 91 of this collection of scattered things—I had alluded to my friend Lord Clare in terms such as my feelings suggested.—About a week or two afterwards I met him on the road between Imola and Bologna—after not having met for seven or eight years.—He was abroad in 1814—and came home just as I set out in 1816.— —This meeting annihilated for a moment all the years between the present time and the days of *Harrow*—It was a new and inexplicable feeling like rising from the grave to me.—Clare too was much agitated—more—in *appearance*—than even myself—for I could feel his heart beat to the fingers' ends—unless indeed—it was the pulse of my own which made me think so.—He told me that I should find a note from him left at Bologna—I did.—We were obliged to part for our different journeys—he for Rome—I for Pisa—but with the promise to meet again in Spring.—We were but five minutes together—and in the public road—but I hardly recollect an hour of my existence which could be weighed against them.— —He had heard that I was coming on—& had left his letter for me at

B[ologna] because the people with whom he was travelling could not wait longer.— —Of all I have ever known—he has always been the least altered in every thing from the excellent qualities and kind affections which attracted me to him so strongly at School.—I should hardly have thought it possible for Society—(or the World as it is called) to leave a being with so little of the leaven of bad passions.— —I do not speak from personal experience only—but from all I have ever heard of him from others during absence and distance.—

114

I met with Rogers at Bologna—staid a day there—crossed the Appennines with him.—He remained at Florence— —I went to Pisa— 8bre. 29—30th. &c. 1821.

115

I revisited the Florence Gallery &c. my former impressions were confirmed—but there were too many visitors there to allow me to *feel* anything properly. When we were (about thirty or forty) all stuffed into the Cabinet of Gems & knick-nackeries in a corner of one of the Galleries—I told R[ogers] that I "felt like being in the Watch-house." I left him to make his obeisances to some of his acquaintances—& strolled on alone—the only few minutes I could snatch of any feeling for the works around me.—I do not mean to apply this to a tete a tete scrutiny with Rogers—who has an excellent taste & deep feeling for the Arts (indeed much more of both than I possess for of the *former* I have not much) but to the crowd of jostling starers & travelling talkers around me.— —I heard one bold Briton declare to the woman on his arm looking at the Venus of Titian—"well now—this is very fine indeed."—an observation which like that of the landlord in Joseph Andrews—"on the certainty of death"—was (as the landlord's wife observed) "extremely true"— —In the Pitti palace—I did not omit Goldsmith's prescription for a Connoisseur—viz: "that the pictures would have been better if the painter had taken more pains—and to praise the works of Pietro Perugino["].— —

116

I have lately been reading Fielding over again.—They talk of Radicalism—Jacobinism &c. in England (I am told) but they should turn over the pages of "Jonathan Wild the Great".—The inequality of conditions and the littleness of the great—were never set forth in stronger terms—and his contempt for Conquerors and the like is such that had he lived *now* he would have been denounced in the "Courier" as the grand Mouth-piece and Factionary of the revolutionists.—And yet I never recollect to have heard this turn of Fielding's mind noticed though it is obvious in every page.— —

117

The following dialogue passed between me and a very pretty peasant Girl (Rosa Benini married to Domenico Ovioli or Oviuoli the Vetturino) at Ravenna.—

Rosa. "*What* is the Pope?"
I. "Don't *you* know?"
Rosa. "No, I don't know, what or who is he—is he a Saint?"
I. "He is an old man."
Rosa. "What nonsense to make such a fuss about an old man.—have *you ever seen* him?"
I. "Yes—at Rome."—
Rosa. "You English don't believe in the Pope?"
I. "No—we don't—but you do—"
Rosa. "I don't know what I believe—but the priests talk about him—I am sure I did not know what he was."

This dialogue I have translated nearly verbatim—& I don't think that I have either added to or taken away from it.— —The speaker was under eighteen & an old acquaintance of mine.— —It struck me as odd that I should have to instruct her *who* the Pope was—I think they might have found it out without me—by this time.— —The fact is indisputable & occurred but a few weeks ago, before I left Ravenna.—

Pisa Novr. 6th. 1821

. . .

119

My daughter Ada on her recent birthday the other day (the 10th. of December 1821) completed her sixth year.—Since she was a Month old—or rather better—I have not seen her.—But I hear that she is a fine child with a violent temper.—I have been thinking of an odd circumstance.—My *daughter*—my *wife*—my *half sister*—my *mother*—my sister's *mother*—my natural daughter—and *myself* are or were all *only* children.—My sister's Mother (Lady Conyers) had only my half *sister* by that second marriage—(herself too an only child) and my father had only me (an only child) by his second marriage with my Mother (an only child too)[.] Such a complication of *only* children all tending to *one family* is singular enough, & looks like fatality almost.—But the fiercest Animals have the rarest number in their litters—as Lions—tigers—and even Elephants which are mild in comparison.

Dear Sir/—By extracts in the English papers in your holy Ally—Galignani's messenger—I perceive that the "two greatest examples of human vanity—in the present age"—are firstly "the Ex-Emperor Napoleon"—and secondly—"his Lordship the noble poet &c."—meaning your humble Servant—"poor guiltless I".— —Poor Napoleon!—he little dreamed to what "vile comparisons" the turn of the Wheel would reduce him.—I cannot help thinking however that had our learned brother of the Newspaper Office—seen my very moderate answer to the very scurrile epistle of my radical patron John Hobhouse M.P.—he would have thought the thermometer of my "Vanity" reduced to a very decent temperature.—By the way, you do not happen to know whether Mrs. Fry had commenced her reform of the prisoners at the time when Mr. Hobhouse was in Newgate?— —there are some of his phrases—and much of his style (in that same letter) which lead me to suspect that either she had not—or that he had profited less than the others by her instructions.—Last week—I sent back the deed of Mr. Moore signed—and witnessed.—It was inclosed to Mr. Kinnaird with a request to forward it to you.—I have also transmitted to him my opinions upon your proposition &c &c,—but addressed them to himself.— —

I have got here into a famous old feudal palazzo on the Arno—large enough for a garrison—with dungeons below—and cells in the walls—and so full of *Ghosts* that the learned Fletcher (my Valet) has begged leave to change his room—and then refused to occupy his *new* room—because there were more Ghosts there than in the other.—It is quite true;—that there are most extraordinary noises (as in all old buildings) which have terrified the servants so—as to incommode me extremely.— —There is one place where people were evidently *walled up*—for there is but one possible passage—*broken* through the wall—& then meant to be closed again upon the inmate.—The house belonged to the Lanfranchi family—(the same mentioned by Ugolino in his dream as his persecutor with Sismondi) and [has] had a fierce owner or two in it's t[ime]. The Staircase &c. is said to have been b[uilt] by Michel Agnolo.— —It is not yet cold enough for a fire—what a climate!— —I am however bothered about the spectres—(as they say the last occupants were too—) of whom I have as yet seen nothing—nor indeed heard (*myself*)—but all the other ears—have been regaled by all kinds of supernatural sounds.— —The first night I thought I heard an odd voice—but it has not been repeated.— —I have now been here more than a month.—

yrs. & [scrawl]

P.S.—Pray send me two or three dozen of "*Acton's Corn-rubbers*" in a parcel by the post—*packed dry* & well—if you can.—I have received safely the parcel containing the Seal,—the E[dinburgh] Review—and some pamphlets &c. the others are I presume upon their way.— —Are there not designs from *Faust*? send me some— and a translation of it—if such there is—also of Goethe's life if such there be—if not—the original German.— —

TO JOHN MURRAY   *Pisa. April 22d. 1822*

Dear Sir,—You will regret to hear that I have received intelligence of the death of my daughter Allegra of a fever in the Convent at Bagna Cavallo—where she was placed for the last year to commence her education. It is a heavy blow for many reasons, but must be borne, with time.— —It is my present intention to send her remains to England for sepulture in Harrow Church (where I once hoped to have laid my own) and this is my reason for troubling you with this notice— —I wish the funeral to be very private.—The body is embalmed and in lead.— —It will be embarked from Leghorn.—Would you have any objection to give the proper directions on it's arrival[?]

I am yours &c.
N B

P.S.—You are aware that protestants are not allowed holy ground in Catholic countries.— —

TO PERCY BYSSHE SHELLEY   *April 23d, 1822*

The blow was stunning and unexpected; for I thought the danger over, by the long interval between her stated amelioration and the arrival of the express. But I have borne up against it as I best can, and so far successfully, that I can go about the usual business of life with the same appearance of composure, and even greater. There is nothing to prevent your coming to-morrow; but, perhaps, to-day, and yester-evening, it was better not to have met. I do not know that I have any thing to reproach in my conduct, and certainly nothing in my feelings and intentions toward the dead. But it is a moment when we are apt to think that, if this or that had been done, such event might have been prevented,—though every day and hour shows us that they are the most natural and inevitable. I suppose that Time will do his usual work—Death has done his.

Yours ever,

N B

TO SIR WALTER SCOTT   *Pisa, May 4th, 1822*

My Dear Sir Walter,—Your account of your family is very pleasing: would that I "could answer this comfort with the like!" but I have just lost my natural daughter, Allegra, by a fever. The only consolation, save time, is the reflection that she is either at rest or happy; for her few years (only five) prevented her from having incurred any sin, except what we inherit from Adam.

"Whom the gods love die young."

I need not say that your letters are particularly welcome, when they do not tax your time and patience; and now that our correspondence is resumed, I trust it will continue.

I have lately had some anxiety, rather than trouble, about an awkward affair here, which you may perhaps have heard of; but our minister has behaved very handsomely, and the Tuscan Government as well as it is possible for such a government to behave, which is not saying much for the latter. Some other English, and Scots, and myself, had a brawl with a dragoon, who insulted one of the party, and whom we mistook for an officer, as he was medalled and well mounted, &c.; but he turned out to be a sergeant-major. He called out the guard at the gates to arrest us (we being unarmed); upon which I and another (an Italian) rode through the said guard; but they succeeded in detaining others of the party. I rode to my house, and sent my secretary to give an account of the attempted and illegal arrest to the authorities, and then, without dismounting, rode back towards the gates, which are near my present mansion. Half way I met my man, vapouring away, and threatening to draw upon me (who had a cane in my hand, and no other arms). I, still believing him an officer, demanded his name and address, and gave him my hand and glove thereupon. A servant of mine thrust in between us (totally without orders), but let him go on my command. He then rode off at full speed; but about forty paces further was stabbed, and very dangerously (so as to be in peril), by some *callum beg* or other of my people (for I have some rough-handed folks about me), I need hardly say without my direction or approval. The said dragoon had been sabring our unarmed countrymen, however, at the *gate, after they were in arrest*, and held by the guards, and wounded one, Captain Hay, very severely. However, he got his paiks—having acted like an assassin, and being treated like one. *Who* wounded him, though it was done before thousands of people, they have never been able to ascertain, or prove, nor even the *weapon*; some said a *pistol*, an *air-gun*, a stiletto, a sword, a lance, a pitch-fork, and what not. They have arrested and examined servants and people of all descriptions, but can make out nothing. Mr. Dawkins, our minister, assures me that no suspicion is entertained of the man who wounded him having been instigated by me, or any of the party. I enclose you copies of the depositions of those with us, and Dr. Craufurd, a canny Scot (*not* an acquaintance), who saw the latter part of the affair. They are in Italian.

These are the only literary matters in which I have been engaged since the publication and row about "Cain";—but Mr. Murray has several things of mine in his obstetrical hands. Another Mystery—a Vision—a Drama—and the like. But *you won't* tell me what *you* are doing—however, I shall find you out, write what you will. You say that I should like your son-in-law —it would be very difficult for

me to dislike any one connected with you; but I have no doubt
that his own qualities are all that you describe.

I am sorry you don't like Lord Orford's new work. My aristocracy, which is very fierce, makes him a favourite of mine. Recollect
that those "little factions" comprised Lord Chatham and Fox, the
father; and that *we* live in gigantic and exaggerated times, which
make all under Gog and Magog appear pigmean. After having seen
Napoleon begin like Tamerlane and end like Bajazet in our own
time, we have not the same interest in what would otherwise have
appeared important history. But I must conclude.

> Believe me ever and most truly yours,
> NOEL BYRON

TO JOHN MURRAY   *Montenero. May 26th. 1822*
                                        near Leghorn.— —

Dear Sir,—The body is embarked—in what ship—I know
not—neither could I enter into the details; but the Countess
G[amba] G[uiccioli] has had the goodness to give the necessary
orders to Mr. Dunn—who superintends the embarkation—& will
write to you.— —I wish it to be buried in Harrow Church—there
is a spot in the Churchyard near the footpath on the brow of the
hill looking toward Windsor—and a tomb under a large tree (bearing the name of Peachee—or Peachey) where I used to sit for hours
& hours when a boy—this was my favourite spot—but as I wish to
erect a tablet to her memory—the body had better be deposited in
the Church.—Near the door—on the left as you enter—there is a
monument with a tablet containing these words—

> "When Sorrow weeps o'er Virtue's sacred dust,
> Our tears become us, and our Grief is just,
> Such were the tears she shed, who grateful pays
> This last sad tribute to her love, and praise."

I recollect them (after seventeen years) not from any thing remarkable in them—but because—from my seat in the Gallery—I had
generally my eyes turned towards that monument— —as near it as

convenient I would wish Allegra to be buried—and on the wall—a marble tablet placed with these words.—

In memory of
Allegra—
daughter of G. G. Lord Byron—

TO CAPTAIN DANIEL ROBERTS   *Pisa. July 14th. 1822*

My dear Sir,—Your opinion has taken from me the slender hope to which I still clung.—I need hardly say that the Bolivar is quite at your disposition as she would have been on a less melancholy occasion—and that I am always

yr. obliged & faithful friend & Servant
NOEL BYRON

TO EDWARD J. DAWKINS   *July 15th. 1822*

Dear Sir—Up to this moment I had clung to a slender hope that Mr. Shelley had still survived the late Gale of Wind.—I sent orders yesterday to the Bolivar to cruize along the coast in search of intelligence—but it seems all over.— —I have not waited on you in person being unshaven—unshorn—and uncloathed at this present writing after bathing.— —I hope you may do something at Lucca—which has induced me to delay proceeding to Genoa— or addressing Mr. Hill again till this day.—Many thanks.

yrs. ever
N B

TO DOUGLAS KINNAIRD   *Pisa. July 19th. 1822*

My dear Douglas/—Your letter is dated the 5th. but makes no allusion to the dividend from the funds which I expected and expect still about this time. I regret that you have given up your journey, though I could not have received you very cheerfully, for since the beginning of the year one displeasure has followed another in regular succession. Shelley and Capt. Williams were drowned last week going to Spezia in their boat from Leghorn—supposed to have been swamped in a Squall.—A Boatman was also lost with them.—Shelley's body has been found and identified (though with difficulty) two days ago—chiefly by a book in his Jacket pocket—the body itself being totally disfigured & in a state of putrefaction.—Another body supposed Capt. Williams's also found—with various articles belonging to the boat.—You may imagine the state of their wives and children—& also Leigh Hunt's—who was but just arrived from England.— —Yesterday and the day before I made two journeys to the mouth of the Arno and another river (the Serchio) for the purpose of ascertaining the circumstances—and identifications of the bodies—but they were already interred for the present by order of the Sanità or Health Office.

yrs. ever
N B

TO JOHN MURRAY   *Pisa. <July> August 3d. 1822*

Dear Sir/—I have received your scrap—with H[enry] D[rury]'s letter enclosed.—It is just like him—always kind and ready to oblige his old friends.—Will you have the goodness to *send immediately* to Mr. Douglas Kinnaird—and inform him that I have *not* received the *remittances due* to me from the funds a month & more ago—& *promised by him to be sent by every post*—which omission is of great inconvenience to me— —and indeed inexcusable—as well as unintelligible.—As I have written to *him* repeatedly I suppose that *his* or *my* letters have miscarried.—I presume you have heard that Mr. Shelley & Capt. Williams were lost on the 7th Ulto. [actually the 8th.] in their passage from Leghorn to Spezia in their own open boat. You may imagine the state of their families—I never saw such a scene—nor wish to see such another.—You are all brutally mistaken about Shelley who was without exception—the *best* and least selfish man I ever knew.—I never knew one who was not a beast in comparison.—

yrs. ever
N B

You will have heard by this time that Shelley and another gentleman (Captain Williams) were drowned about a month ago (a
month yesterday), in a squall off the Gulf of Spezia. There is thus
another man gone, about whom the world was ill-naturedly, and
ignorantly, and brutally mistaken. It will, perhaps, do him justice
now, when he can be no better for it.

I have not seen the thing you mention, and only heard of it
casually, nor have I any desire. The price is, as I saw in some advertisement, fourteen shillings, which is too much to pay for a libel on
oneself. Some one said in a letter, that it was a Dr. Watkins, who
deals in the life and libel line. It must have diminished your natural
pleasure, as a friend (vide Rochefoucault), to see yourself in it.

With regard to the Blackwood fellows, I never published any
thing against them; nor, indeed, have seen their magazine (except
in Galignani's extracts) for these three years past. I once wrote, a
good while ago, some remarks on their review of Don Juan, but
saying very little about themselves, and these were *not* published. If
you think that I ought to follow your example (and I like to be in
your company when I can) in contradicting their impudence, you
may shape this declaration of mine into a similar paragraph for me.
It is possible that you may have seen the little I *did* write (and never
published) at Murray's:—it contained much more about Southey
than about the Blacks.

If you think that I ought to do any thing about Watkins's
book, I should not care much about publishing *my Memoir now*,
should it be necessary to counteract the fellow. But, in *that* case,
I should like to look over the *press* myself. Let me know what you
think, or whether I had better *not*:—at least, not the second part,
which touches on the actual confines of still existing matters.

I have written three more cantos of Don Juan, and am hovering
on the brink of another (the ninth). The reason I want the stanzas
again which I sent you is, that as these cantos contain a full detail
(like the storm in Canto Second) of the siege and assault of Ismael,
with much of sarcasm on those butchers in large business, your
mercenary soldiery, it is a good opportunity of gracing the poem
with * * *. With these things and these fellows, it is necessary, in

the present clash of philosophy and tyranny, to throw away the scabbard. I know it is against fearful odds; but the battle must be fought; and it will be eventually for the good of mankind, whatever it may be for the individual who risks himself.

What do you think of your Irish bishop? Do you remember Swift's line, "Let me have a *barrack*—a fig for the *clergy?*" This seems to have been his reverence's motto * * * * * * * * *

* * * * * * * * * * * * * * * *

Yours, etc.

TO THOMAS MOORE   *Pisa, August 27th, 1822*

It is boring to trouble you with "such small gear;" but it must be owned that I should be glad if you would inquire whether my Irish subscription ever reached the committee in Paris from Leghorn. My reasons, like Vellum's, "are threefold:"—First, I doubt the accuracy of all almoners, or remitters of benevolent cash; second, I do suspect that the said Committee, having in part served its time to time-serving, may have kept back the acknowledgment of an obnoxious politician's name in their lists; and third, I feel pretty sure that I shall one day be twitted by the government scribes for having been a professor of love for Ireland, and not coming forward with the others in her distresses.

It is not, as you may opine, that I am ambitious of having my name in the papers, as I can have that any day in the week gratis. All I want is to know if the Reverend Thomas Hall did or did not remit my subscription (200 scudi of Tuscany, or about a thousand francs, more of less,) to the Committee at Paris.

The other day at Viareggio, I thought proper to swim off to my schooner (the Bolivar) in the offing, and thence to shore again— about three miles, or better, in all. As it was at mid-day, under a broiling sun, the consequence has been a feverish attack, and my whole skin's coming off, after going through the process of one large continuous blister, raised by the sun and sea together. I have suffered much pain; not being able to lie on my back, or even side; for my shoulders and arms were equally St. Bartholomewed. But it is over,—and I have got a new skin, and am as glossy as a snake in its new suit.

We have been burning the bodies of Shelley and Williams on the sea-shore, to render them fit for removal and regular interment. You can have no idea what an extraordinary effect such a funeral pile has, on a desolate shore, with mountains in the back-ground and the sea before, and the singular appearance the salt and frank-incense gave to the flame. All of Shelley was consumed, except his *heart*, which would not take the flame, and is now preserved in spirits of wine.

Your old acquaintance Londonderry has quietly died at North Cray! and the virtuous De Witt was torn in pieces by the populace! What a lucky * * the Irishman has been in his life and end. In him your Irish Franklin est mort!

Leigh Hunt is sweating articles for his new Journal; and both he and I think it somewhat shabby in *you* not to contribute. Will you become one of the *properrioters*? "Do, and we go snacks." I recommend you to think twice before you respond in the negative.

I have nearly (*quite three*) four new cantos of *Don Juan* ready. I obtained permission from the female Censor Morum of *my* morals to continue it, provided it were immaculate; so I have been as decent as need be. There is a deal of war—a siege, and all that, in the style, graphical and technical, of the shipwreck in Canto Second, which "took" as they say in the Row.

Yours, etc.

P.S.—That * * * Galignani has about ten lies in one paragraph. It was not a Bible that was found in Shelley's pocket, but John Keats's poems. However, it would not have been strange, for he was a great admirer of Scripture as a composition. *I* did not send my bust to the academy of New York; but I sat for my picture to young West, an American artist, at the request of some members of that Academy to *him* that he would take my portrait,—for the Academy, I believe.

I had, and still have, thought of South America, but am fluctuating between it and Greece. I should have gone, long ago, to one of them, but for my liaison with the Countess G[uicciol]i; for love, in these days, is little compatible with glory. *She* would be delighted to go too; but I do not choose to expose her to a long voyage, and a residence in an unsettled country, where I shall probably take a part of some sort.

GENOA and LIVORNO

In the wind's eye I have sailed, and sail; but for
    The stars, I own my telescope is dim:
But at least I have shunned the common shore,
    And leaving land far out of sight, would skim
The ocean of eternity: the roar
    Of breakers has not daunted my slight, trim,
But still sea-worthy skiff; and she may float
Where ships have foundered, as doth many a boat.

DON JUAN X, 4

My dearest Augusta/—I answered your letter the other day.—I have a proposition to make to you & your husband which I think would be for your advantage.—You must find it sad work living in that expensive England with so large a family.—If you would like to come to *Nice* (a hundred miles from hence) I will furnish you for the journey of the *whole* family—free of any expence—and have a home provided for you there &c.—You can have no idea of the *saving* and the extreme difference of expences for a family—and every species of masters &c. for the children are so much better, & cheaper—you know the [area?] of Nice is a french pro[vince].—You would also be *near* me if that would be any allurement.—I assure you that with your income—you might live not only comfortably but almost splendidly—with carriage &c.— —I would remove from Genoa to Nice to be near you—if you would like that—(but I should occupy a separate house) or just as you like.—I advise you & George to think seriously of what I say—as I assure you it is worth your consideration.—I would guarantee the expence of the journey (by *land* too) and it is not so very far.—The gain in point of economy—would be something of which you have little idea.—Pensez.

yrs. ever

N B

P.S.—If you think of it—you should do so *now*—or—if not now—come over when the winter is waning.— —

Novr. 7th.—I send this as written—though I suppose that it is only to produce a civil answer—you may however think it over by *Spring*—the time of touring.

P.S.—If Murray has delivered up the papers in their perfect state the enclosed is unnecessary; if *not* he deserves it.—

My dearest A.—I have yrs. of the 25th.—My Illness is quite gone—it was only at Lerici—on the fourth night, I had got a

little sleep and was so wearied that though there were three slight
shocks of an Earthquake that frightened the whole town into the
Streets— —neither they nor the tumult awakened me.—We have
had a deluge here—which has carried away half the country between this and Genoa—(about two miles or less distant) but being
on a hill we were only nearly knocked down by the lightning and
battered by columns of rain—and our lower floor afloat— —with
the comfortable view of the whole landscape under water—and
people screaming out of their garret windows—*two bridges* swept
down—and our next door neighbours—a Cobbler a Wigmaker—
and a Gingerbread baker delivering up their whole stock to the
elements—which marched away with a quantity of shoes—several
perukes—and Gingerbread in all it's branches.—The whole came
on so suddenly that there was no time to prepare—think only at
the top of a hill—of the road being an impassable cascade—and a
child being drowned a few yards from it's own door (as we heard
say) in a place where Water is in general a rare commodity.— —
Well—after this comes a preaching Friar—and says that the day of
Judgement will take place positively on the *4th*—with all kinds of
tempest and what not—in consequence of which the whole City—
(except some impious Scoffers) sent him presents to avert the wrath
of Heaven by his prayers—and even the *public authorities*—had
warned the Captains of Ships—who to mend the matter—almost
all bought *new Cables* and anchors—by way of weathering the
Gale.—But the fourth turned out a very fine day.—All those who
had paid their money—are exceptionally angry—and insist either
upon having the day of Judgement—or their cash again.—But the
Friar's device seems to be "no money to be returned"—and he says
that he merely made a mistake in the time—for the day of Judgement will certainly come for all that either here or in some other
part of Italy.—This has a little pacified the expectants—you will
think this a fiction—enquire further then—the populace actually
used to kiss the fellow's feet in the Streets. His Sermon however
had small effect upon some—for they gave a ball on the 3d.—and
a tradesman brought me an *over*charge on the same day—upon
which I threatened him with the friar—but he said that that was a
reason for being paid on the 3d.—as he had a sum to make up for
his last account.—There seem to have been all kinds of tempests all

over the Globe—and for my part it would not surprize me—if the earth should get a little tired of the tyrants and slaves who disturb her surface.— —

I have also had a love letter from *Pimlico* from a lady whom I never saw in my life—but who hath fallen in love with me for having written *Don Juan*!—I suppose that she is either mad or *nau*[ghty].—do you remember *Constantia* and *Echo*—and *la Swissesse*—and all my other inamorate—when I was "gentle and juvenile—curly and gay"—and was myself in love with a certain silly person—[line crossed out]?— —But I am grown very good now—and think all such things vanities which is a very proper opinion at thirty four.—I always *say four*—till the five is out.— Since I last wrote—I had written the enclosed letter—which I did not send—thinking it useless—You will please to recollect that you would not be required to know any Italian acquaintance of mine—the Countess G[uiccioli] has a distinct quarter and generally [in a] house with her father and brother—who were exiled on account of politics—and she [was] obliged to go with them or be shut up in a Convent. The Pope gave her a regular separation from her husband like Lady B[yron]'s—three years ago.—We are all in the same house just *now*—only because *our* Ambassador recommended it as safer for *them* in these suspicious times.—As to our *liaison*—you know that *all* foreign ladies & most English have an amitié of the same kind—or not so good perhaps, as *ours* has lasted nearly four years.

TO MARY SHELLEY   [*Nov. 16?*] *1822*

* * * * * * * * * * * * * * * *

I presume that you, at least, know enough of me to be sure that I could have no intention to insult Hunt's poverty. On the contrary, I honour him for it; for, I know what it is, having been as much embarrassed as ever he was, without perceiving aught in it to diminish an honourable man's self-respect. If you mean to say that, had he been a wealthy man, I would have joined in this Journal, I answer in the negative. * * * I engaged in the Journal from good-will towards him, added to respect for his character, literary and personal; and no less for his political courage, as well as regret for his present circumstances: I did this in the hope that he might, with the same aid from literary friends of literary contributions (which is requisite for all journals of a mixed nature), render himself independent.

* * * * * * * * * * * * * * * *

I have always treated him, in our personal intercourse, with such scrupulous delicacy, that I have forborne intruding advice, which I thought might be disagreeable, lest he should impute it to what is called "taking advantage of a man's situation".

As to friendship, it is a propensity in which my genius is very limited. I do not know the *male* human being, except Lord Clare, the friend of my infancy, for whom I feel anything that deserves the name. All my others are men-of-the-world friendships. I did not even feel it for Shelley, however much I admired and esteemed him; so that you see not even vanity could bribe me into it, for, of all men, Shelley thought highest of my talents,—and, perhaps of my disposition.

I will do my duty by my intimates, upon the principle of doing as you would be done by. I have done so, I trust, in most instances. I may be pleased with their conversation—rejoice in their success—be glad to do them service, or to receive their counsel and assistance in return. But as for friends and friendship, I have (as I already said) named the only remaining male for whom I feel any thing of the kind, excepting, perhaps, Thomas Moore. I have had, and may have still, a thousand friends, as they are called, in *life*, who are like one's partners in the waltz of this world—not much remembered when the ball is over, though very pleasant for the time. Habit, business, and companionship in pleasure or in pain, are links of a similar kind, and the same faith in politics is another. * * *

TO JOHN MURRAY   *Genoa. December 25 1822*

I had sent you back "the Quarterly" without perusal—having resolved to read no more reviews good bad or indifferent—but "who can control his fate?" "Galignani to whom my English studies are confined" has forwarded a copy of at least one half of it—in his indefatigable Catch-penny weekly compilation—and as "like Honour it came unlooked for"—I have looked through it.— —I must say that upon the *whole*—that is the whole of the *half* which I have read (for the other half is to be the Segment of Gal[ignani]'s next week's Circular) it is extremely handsome & any thing but unkind or unfair.—As I take the good in good part—I must not nor will not quarrel with the bad—what the Writer says of D[on] J[uan] is harsh—but it is inevitable—He must follow—or at least not directly oppose the opinion of a prevailing & yet not very firmly seated party—a review may and will direct or "turn away" the Currents of opinion—but it must not directly oppose them.—D[on] Juan will be known by and bye for what it is intended a *satire* on *abuses* of the present *states* of Society—and not an eulogy of vice;—it may be now and then voluptuous—I can't help that—Ariosto is worse—Smollett (see Lord Strutwell in vol 2d. of R[oderick] R[andom]) ten times worse—and Fielding no better.— —No Girl will ever be seduced by reading D[on] J[uan]—no—no—she will go to Little's poems—& Rousseau's romans—for that—or even to the immaculate De Stael— —they will encourage her—& not the Don—who laughs at that—and—and—most other things.—But never mind—"Ca ira!" And now to a less agreeable topic, of which "pars magna es"—you Murray of Albemarle St.—and the other Murray of Bridge Street—"Arcades Ambo" ("*Murrays both*") et *cant*-are pares—ye I say—between you are the Causes of the prosecution of John Hunt Esqre, on account of the Vision;—you by sending him an incorrect copy—and the other by his function.— —Egad—but H[unt]'s Counsel will lay it on you with a trowel—for your tergiversifying as to the M.S.S. &c. whereby poor H[unt] (& for anything I know—myself—I am willing enough) is likely to be impounded.— —

Now—do you see what you and your friends do by your injudicious rudeness?—actually cement a sort of connection which you strove to prevent—and which had the H[unt]s *prospered*—would not in all probability have continued.—As it is—I will not quit them in their adversity—though it should cost me—character—fame—money—and the usual et cetera.—My original motives—I already explained (in the letter which you thought proper to show—) they are the *true* ones and I abide by them—as I tell you—and I told L[eig]h H[un]t when he questioned me on the subject of that letter.— —He was violently hurt—& never will forgive me at bottom—but I can't help that,— —I never meant to make a parade of it—but if he chose to question me—I could only answer the plain truth—and I confess I did not see anything in that letter to hurt him—unless I said he was "a *bore*" which I don't remember.—Had their Journal gone on well—and I could have aided to make it better for them—I should then have left them after my safe pilotage off a lee shore—to make a prosperous voyage by themselves.—As it is—I can't & would not if I could—leave them amidst the breakers.—

As to any community of feeling—thought—or opinion between L[eigh] H[unt] & me—there is little or none—we meet rarely—hardly ever—but I think him a good principled & able man—& must do as I would be done by.—I do not know what world he has lived in—but I have lived in three or four—and none of them like his Keats and Kangaroo terra incognita—Alas! poor Shelley!—how he would have laughed—had he lived, and how we used to laugh now & then—at various things—which are grave in the Suburbs.—You are all mistaken about Shelley— —you do not know—how mild—how tolerant—how good he was in Society— and as perfect a Gentleman as ever crossed a drawing room;—when he liked—& where he liked.— —I have some thoughts of taking a run down to Naples—(solus—or at most—*cum sola*) this Spring—and writing (when I have studied the Country) a fifth & sixth Canto of Ch[ild]e Harolde—but this is merely an idea for the present—and I have other excursions—& voyages in my mind.—The busts are finished—are you worthy of them?—

yrs. &c.
N B

P.S.—Mrs. Sh[elle]y is residing with the Hunts at some distance from me—I see them very seldom— —and generally on account of their business.—Mrs. S[helley] I believe will go to England in the Spring.— —Count Gamba's family—the father—& Son— and daughter are residing with me—by Mr. Hill (the minister's) recommendation as a safer asylum from the political persecutions than they could have in another residence—but they occupy one part of a large house—and I the other—and our establishments are quite separate.— —Since I have read the Q[uarterl]y—I shall erase two or three passages in the latter 6 or 7 Cantos in which I had lightly stroked over two or three of your authors—but I will not return evil for good.—I like what I read of the article much.—Mr. J[ohn] Hunt is most likely the publisher of the new Cantos— —with what prospects of success I know not—nor does it very much matter—as far as I am concerned—but I hope that it may be of use to him—for he is a stiff sturdy conscientious man— and I like him—he is such a one—as Prynne—or Pym might be. I bear you no ill will for declining the D[on] J[uan]s—but I cannot commend yr. conduct to the H[unt]s.—Have you aided Madame de Yossy, as I requested?—I sent her 300 francs—recommend her will you—to the literary F[und] or to some benevolence within your Circles.—

TO EDWARD LE MESURIER, R.N.   *Villa Saluzzo. Albaro.*
                                      May 5th. 1823

Sir—I have received with great gratitude yr. present of the New-foundland Dog. Few gifts could have been more gratifying—as I have ever been partial to the breed.— —He shall be taken the greatest care of—and I would not part with him for any consideration;—he is already a chief favourite with the whole house.— —I have the honour to be

                    your much obliged & very faithfl. Servt.
                                      NOEL BYRON

JOHN BOWRING   *Genoa. May 12th. 1823*

Sir,—I have great pleasure in acknowledging your letter and the honour which the Committee have done me.—I shall endeavour to deserve their confidence by every means in my power.—My first wish is to go up into the Levant in person—where I might be enabled to advance—if not the cause—at least the means of obtaining information which the Committee might be desirous of acting upon,—and my former residence in the Country—my familiarity with the Italian language (which is there universally spoken—or at least to the same extent with French in the more polished parts of the Continent) and my *not* total ignorance of the Romaic—would afford me some advantages of experience.—To this project the only objection is of a domestic nature—and I shall try to get over it,—if I fail in this—I must do what I can where I am—but it will be always a source of regret to me—to think—that I might perhaps have done more for the cause on the spot.—Our last information of Capt. Blaquiere—is from Ancona where he embarked with a fair wind for Corfu on the 15th. Ult[i]mo —he is now probably at his destination.—My last letter *from* him personally—was dated Rome—he had been refused a passport through the Neapolitan territory—and returned to strike off through Romagna for Ancona.—Little time however appears to have been lost by the delay.—

The principal material wanted by the Greeks appears to be—1st. a park of field Artillery—light—and fit for Mountain service—2dly. Gunpowder—3dly. hospital or Medical Stores——the readiest mode of transmission is—I hear—by Idra—addressed to Mr. Negri the Minister.—I meant to send up a certain quantity of the two latter—no great deal—but enough for an individual to show his good wishes for the Greek success—but am pausing— because in case I should go myself—I can take them with me.—I do not mean to limit my own contribution to this merely—but— more especially if I can get to Greece myself—I should devote whatever resources I can muster of my own—to advancing the great object.— —I am in correspondence with Signor Nicolas Karvellas (well known to Mr. Hobhouse) who is now at Pisa—but his latest advice merely states—that the Greeks are at present employed in organizing their *internal* government—and the details of it's administration—this would seem to indicate *security*—but the war is however far from being terminated.—The Turks are an obstinate race—as all former wars have proved them—and will return to the charge for years to come—even if beaten—as it is to be hoped that they will be.— —But in no case can the labours of the Committee be said to be in vain—for in the event even of the Greeks being subdued—and dispersed—the funds which could be employed in succouring and gathering together the remnant—so as to alleviate in part their distresses—and enable them to find or make a country (as so many emigrants of other nations have been compelled to do—) would "bless both those who gave and those who took"—as the bounty both of Justice and of Mercy.—

With regard to the formation of a brigade (which Mr. Hobhouse hints at in his short letter of this day's receipt—enclosing the one to which I have the honour to reply) I would presume to suggest but merely as an opinion—resulting rather from the melancholy experience of the brigades embarked in the Columbian Service—than from any experiment yet fairly tried in *Greece*—that the attention of the Committee had better perhaps be directed to the employment of *Officers* of experience—than the enrolment of raw British Soldiers—which latter are apt to be unruly and not very serviceable—in irregular warfare—by the side of foreigners. — —A small body of good officers—especially Artillery—an Engineer—with a quantity (such as the Committee might deem requisite) of stores of the nature which Capt. Blaquiere indicated is most wanted—would I should conceive be a highly useful accession.—Officers who had previously served in the Mediterranean would be preferable—as some knowledge of *Italian* is nearly indispensable.— —It would also be as well that they should be aware—that they are not going "to rough it on a beef steak—and bottle of Port"—but that Greece—never of late years—very plentifully stocked for a *Mess*—is at present the country of all kinds of *privations*,—this remark may seem superfluous—but I have been led to it—by observing that many *foreign* Officers—Italian—French and even German—(but *fewer* of the latter) have returned in disgust—imagining either that they were going up to make a party of pleasure—or to enjoy full pay—speedy promotion and a very moderate degree of duty;—they complain too of having been ill received by the Government or inhabitants, but numbers of these complainants—were mere adventurers—attracted by a hope of command and plunder,—and disappointed of both;—those Greeks that I have seen strenuously deny the charge of inhospitality—and declare that they shared their pittance to the last Crumb with their foreign volunteers.— —

I need not suggest to the Committee the very great advantage which must accrue to Great Britain from the success of the Greeks—and their probable commercial relations with England in consequence—because I feel persuaded that the *first* object of the Committee—is their *emancipation*—<[when the?] fruitful and important [boughs?] of the tree of Liberty have been> without any interested views—but the consideration might weigh with the English people in general—in their present passion for every kind of speculation— —they need not cross the American Seas—for one much better worth their while—and nearer home.—The resources even for an emigrant population—in the Greek Islands alone—are rarely to be paralelled [sic]—and the cheapness of every kind of not *only necessary*—but *luxury*—(that is to say—*luxury* of *Nature*) fruits—wine—oil—&c.—in a state of peace—are far beyond those of the Cape—and Van Dieman's land—and the other places of refuge—which the English population are searching for over the waters.— —I beg that the Committee will command me in any and every way— —if I am favoured with any instructions—I shall endeavour to obey them to the letter—whether conformable to my own private opinion or not— —I beg leave to add personally my respect for the Gentleman whom I have the honour of addressing—and am Sir—

yr. obliged & very obedt. Sert.

NOEL BYRON

P.S.—The best refutation of Gell—will be the active exertions of the Committee;—I am *too warm* a controversialist—and I suspect that if Mr. Hobhouse has taken him in hand—there will be little occasion for me to "encumber him with help".—If I go up into the Country—I will endeavour to transmit as accurate and impartial an account as circumstances will permit.— —I shall write to Mr. Karvellas;—I expect intelligence from Capt. Blaquiere—who has promised me some early intimation from the seat of the provisional Government.—I gave him a letter of introduction to Lord Sydney Osborne at Corfu—but as Lord S. is in the Government Service— of course his reception could only be a *cautious* one—but as he is an old friend of mine—I should hope not an unkind one.— —

Sir,—At present, [now?] that I know to whom I am indebted for a very flattering mention in the "Rome, Naples, and Florence in 1817, by Mons. Stendhal," it is fit that I should return my thanks (however undesired or undesirable) to Mons. Beyle, with whom I had the honour of being acquainted at Milan in 1816. You only did me too much honour in what you were pleased to say in that work; but it has hardly given me less pleasure than the praise itself, to become at length aware (which I have done by mere accident) that I am indebted for it to one of whose good opinion I was really ambitious. So many changes have taken place since that period in the Milan circle, that I hardly dare recur to it;—some dead, some banished, and some in the Austrian dungeons.—Poor Pellico! I trust that, in his iron solitude, his Muse is consoling him in part—one day to delight us again, when both she and her Poet are restored to freedom.

Of your works I have seen only "Rome", etc., the Lives of Haydn and Mozart, and the *brochure* on Racine and Shakespeare. The "Histoire de la Peinture" I have not yet the good fortune to possess.

There is one part of your observations in the pamphlet which I shall venture to remark upon;—it regards Walter Scott. You say that "his character is little worthy of enthusiasm," at the same time that you mention his productions in the manner they deserve. I have known Walter Scott long and well, and in occasional situations which call forth the *real* character—and I can assure you that his character *is* worthy of admiration—that of all men he is the most *open*, the most *honourable*, the most *amiable*. With his politics I have nothing to do: they differ from mine, which renders it difficult for me to speak of them. But he is *perfectly sincere* in them; and Sincerity may be humble, but she cannot be servile. I pray you, therefore, to correct or soften that passage. You may, perhaps, attribute this officiousness of mine to a false affectation of *candour*, as I happen to be a writer also. Attribute it to what motive you please, but *believe* the *truth*. I say that Walter Scott is as nearly a thorough good man as man can be, because I *know* it by experience to be the case.

If you do me the honour of an answer—may I request a speedy one—because it is possible (though not yet decided) that Circumstances may conduct me once more to Greece;—my present address is *Genoa*—where an answer will reach me in a short time, or be forwarded to me wherever I may be.

I beg you to believe me with a lively recollection of our brief acquaintance—and the hope of one day renewing it.—

> your ever obliged and obedt. humble Servt.
> NOEL BYRON

I make no excuse for writing to you in English, as I understand you are well acquainted with that language.

TO EDWARD JOHN TRELAWNY *June 15, 1823*

My dear T.—You must have heard that I am going to Greece. Why do you not come to me? I want your aid, and am exceedingly anxious to see you. Pray come, for I am at last determined to go to Greece; it is the only place I was ever contented in. I am serious, and did not write before, as I might have given you a journey for nothing; they all say I can be of use in Greece. I do not know how, nor do they; but at all events let us go.

> Yours, etc., truly,
> N BYRON

TO COUNTESS TERESA GUICCIOLI *Livorno July 22d. 1823*

[Note added to Pietro's letter to Teresa]

My dearest Teresa—I have but a few moments to say that we are all well—and thus far on our way to the Levant—believe that I always *love* you—and that a thousand words could only express the same idea.

> ever dearest yrs.
> N B

TO JOHANN WOLFGANG VON GOETHE   *Leghorn.*
July 22d. 1823

Illustrious Sir—I cannot thank you as you ought to be thanked
for the lines which my young friend Mr. Sterling sent me of yours,—
and it would but ill become me to pretend to exchange verses with
him who for fifty years has been the undisputed Sovereign of
European literature.—You must therefore accept my most sincere
acknowledgements in prose—and in hasty prose too—for I am at
present on my voyage to Greece once more—and surrounded by
hurry and bustle which hardly allow a moment even to Gratitude
and Admiration to express themselves.— —I sailed from Genoa
some days ago—was driven back by a Gale of Wind—and have
since sailed again—and arrived here (Leghorn) this morning to
receive on board some Greek passengers for their struggling Country.— —*Here* also I found your lines and Mr. Sterling's letter—and
I could not have had a more favourable Omen or more agreeable
surprise than a word from Goethe written by his own hand.— —I
am returning to Greece to see if I can be of any little use there;—if
ever I come back I will pay a visit to Weimar to offer the sincere
homage of one of the many Millions of your admirers.—I have the
honour to be ever & most respectfully

                              yr. obliged adm[iici] & Se[rvant]
                                        NOEL BYRON

Aux Soins de Monsieur Sterling.

CEPHALONIA

O, thou eternal Homer! who couldst charm
    All ears, though long; all ages, though so short,
By merely wielding with poetic arm
    Arms to which men will never more resort,
Unless gunpowder should be found to harm
    Much less than is the hope of every court,
Which now is leagued young Freedom to annoy;
But they will not find Liberty a Troy:—

O, thou eternal Homer! I have now
    To paint a siege, wherein more men were slain,
With deadlier engines and a speedier blow,
    Than in thy Greek gazette of that campaign;
And yet, like all men else, I must allow,
    To vie with thee would be about as vain
As for a brook to cope with ocean's flood;
But still we moderns equal you in blood,

If not in poetry, at least in fact;
    And fact is truth, the grand desideratum!
Of which, howe'er the Muse describes each act,
    There should be ne'ertheless a slight substratum.
But now the town is going to be attacked;
    Great deeds are doing—how shall I relate 'em?
Souls of immortal generals! Phoebus watches
To colour up his rays from your despatches.

DON JUAN VII, 79–81

My dearest T.—We have received yr. letters safely—and I am rejoiced to hear so good an account of yr. health.—We are still in Cephalonia waiting for news of a more accurate description for all is contradiction and division in the reports of the state of the Greeks &c.—I shall fulfil the object of my mission from the committee—and then probably return into Italy—for it does not seem likely that as [an] individual I can be of use to them.— —At least no one other foreigner has yet appeared to be so—nor does it seem likely that any will be at present.— —Pietro will have said more perhaps on this subject.— —Pray, be as cheerful and tranquil as you can—and be assured that there is nothing here that can excite anything but a wish to be with you again—though we are very kindly treated by the English here of all descriptions. Of the Greeks I can't say much good hitherto and I do not like to speak ill of them though they do so of one another.—We are here in a very pretty village—with fine scenery of every description—and we have kept our health—&c.—very well.—Pray—remember me to Costa and his wife—and to Papa and all our acquaintances and allies.— —When we meet again (if it pleases God) I hope to tell you several things that will make you smile.—I kiss your Eyes (*occhi*) and am ever most affectly

a. a. in e. + + + +
N B

My dear Hobhouse—This letter will be delivered by Capt. Scott of the Hercules—who brought me up into these parts—and has behaved very well—he is a fine tough old tar—and has been a great amusement during our voyage—he is moreover brother to two of yr. constituents and as such to be treated with all due respect—also some Grog with which he regularly rounds off most hours of the four and twenty.— —He is a character I assure you as you will perceive at a single glance.

I have received yours and the Committee's letters—to both of which this will serve for present answer.—I will endeavour to do my duty by the Committee and the Cause.—On our arrival here early in August we found the opposite Coast blockaded by the Turkish fleet—all kinds of reports in circulation about divisions amongst the Greeks themselves—the Greek fleet not out (and it is not out yet as far as I know) Blaquiere gone home again or at least on his way there—and no communications for me from the Morea or elsewhere.—Under these circumstances added to the disinclination of Capt. Scott (naturally enough) to risk his vessel among the blockaders or their vicinity without being insured for the full value of his bastimento—I resolved to remain here for a favourable opportunity of passing over—and also to collect if possible something like positive information.— —In the mean time I made a tour over the hills here in our old style—and then crossed over to Ithaca—which as a pendant to the Troad—a former Greek traveller would like to see.—I was much gratified by both—and we have moreover been treated in the kindest manner by all the authorities military and civil—from Colonel Napier the resident (whose name and fame you are aware of) the officers of the 8th. and in short by all our own countrymen.— —Their hospitality both here and in Ithaca was indeed rather oppressive—for dinners kill a weakly stomached Gentleman.—They also insisted on lodging us—but I would not so far abuse their good nature and am here in a very pretty village between the Mountains and the sea—waiting what Napoleon calls the "March of Events".—These Events however keep their march somewhat secret,—but it appears nearly certain that there be divisions—and that Mavrocordato is *out* (some say *in* again) which were a pity—since he is the only civilized person (on dit) amongst the liberators.—The Turkish fleet has sailed leaving fifteen Algerine vessels to cruise in the Gulph.—

Mr. Browne and Mr. Trelawny are since then gone over in a boat to a part of the Coast out of the blockade with letters from me to the Greek Government at Tripolitza—and to collect information.—There is little risk for small boats but it is otherwise with larger vessels which cannot slide in everywhere—as the Mussulmans are not very particular.—Count Gamba—a young man about twenty-three—is here with me—and is very popular amongst the English—and is I assure you a fine fellow in all respects.— —I

have written to apprize the G[reek] Government of the possible
approach of the vessel indicated by the Committee—and to
prepare them to receive it's Contents.—I caused [had someone]
write soon after my arrival to Marco Botzari—in Acarnania and
at a considerable expence sent the letter by a small boat which
ran through the blockade.—He answered desiring me to come
over—and stating that he meant to give battle to the Turks next
day—(after the date of his epistle) which he did and was killed—
but his party gained the victory—and he behaved most gallantly
by all accounts till mortally wounded.— —This was very vexatious
on all accounts as well for the general loss as the individual—for I
was particularly recommended to him (the Chief of the Suliotes)
and I cannot have the same confidence in his successor who is less
known.— —I took forty Suliotes here into pay—got their arms
(through Col. Napier's intercession with General Adam) and sent
them to join their Countrymen a few days ago—when the blockade was partly done away with— —they have cost me a tolerable
number in dollars—and the price of their passage (somewhat high)
&c. but it was thought best that I should wait for direction from
Tripolitza—before I fixed on the place where I ought to proceed
with the approbation of the G[reek] Gov[ernmen]t.— —I have
also spent some hundred dollars in assisting the Greek refugees
in Ithaca—and providing for a Moreote family who were in great
distress.— —

The Turks are in force in Acarnania—but you cannot depend
upon *any accounts*—the report of the day is contradicted on the
morrow.—Great divisions and difficulties exist—and several foreigners have come away in disgust as usual— —it is at present
my intention to remain *here* or *there* as long as I see a prospect of
advantage to the cause—but I must not conceal from you and the
Committee that the Greeks appear in more danger from their own
divisions than from the attacks of the Enemy.—There is a talk of
treachery—and all sorts of parties amongst them—a jealousy of
strangers and a desire of nothing but *money*—all improvements
in tactics—they decline—and are not very kind it is said—to
the foreign officers &c. in their service.— —I give you this as
report—but certainly I cannot say much for those I have seen
here— —the Slave is not yet improved by his Saturnalia.— —As

you are aware what they were before—I need say very little on the subject.—

Of the things sent by Murray (you say) none arrived at Genoa—but the Canteen—and that broken by negligence in packing—*it* is to be sent on—but the other things as I said have not yet been heard of—so my bankers write from Italy.—You will remember me to Douglas K[innair]d from whom I have not yet heard—and to all friends.—I hear that the publisher got an injunction in favour of the new Cantos—I wish him to publish the remainder (four in each volume their [sic] are eight more—i.e. sixteen in all) and tell him to Correct the proofs from the M.S.S. and not be sending his lumbering packets up here—where I have other matters to attend to.— —I have had a letter from Hanson requesting the balance of his bill (£635) which I will not pay—for the present 1stly.—because I wish to know what it is for—2dly. he has had too many thousands of my money already—and ought to be ashamed to dun—having had £500 this very blessed year,—and 3dly. because I wish to have all my ready at present in bank to answer my credits;—please to instruct the Hon[oura]ble Douglas K[innair]d to this effect.— —It is also time that Murray should make some settlement or other for "Werner".—I understand that he behaves infamously—circulating facsimiles of my letters &c.—with other matters which will go nigh to give him a place by Curll and Osborne if he don't mind what he is about.— — As to his losing by Werner—that may be partly ascertained by comparing his account of ye. number sold—and J. Hunt's of *his publications* at the *comparative* prices—M. said at *first* that he had sold 6000—if so—where were the loss?—It is lucky for John of Albemarle that I have other things on hand—or I would have a buff at him for his delinquencies.—Parchment [Hanson] talks of lending money on Mortgage to Ld. Mountnorris—tell Douglas to allow no such thing—with my monies—Ld. M. is a shuffler—and well known for such—in Cash affairs—at least his own friends say so.—Hanson talks too of urging the appeal against Deardon— but I had hoped that Crabtree had come to some arrangement with said Deardon about Rochdale by this time—I would part with it for a trifle to be rid of the bore and the expence.— — Pray write and say how you are—I am better for my voyage and stood the hot Sun on the hills of this island and of Ithaca like a Dial.—

ever yrs. most truly

N B

Septr. 14th. 1823

P.S.—I have sent over to Missolonghi some medical stores for the wounded there.—Metaxa (the Commandant of the town) is very pressing that I should go over there—but I must first have an answer from the Tripolitza Gov[ernmen]t—and also keep a look out for the arrival of the Committee's vessel.—When these things are settled I may as well be in one place as another I suppose—though I have as little cunning in fortifying a besieged town as "honour hath skill in Surgery".— —Col Napier told me yesterday that there is a story in the Islands—Corfu &c.—"that he and I had a quarrel about *arms* on board my vessel—that it was seized—after some resistance or opposition &c. &c. &c." in short a damned lie—which I merely mention that you may contradict and laugh at it—if you hear anything of the kind.—Napier says if his Commission could be saved to him that he would go over too[;] you know he is a famous soldier—one of Sir John Moore's "Well done my Majors!"—left for dead at Corunna and all alive and martial at this moment.—He is besides an excellent fellow—greatly liked—and a thorough Liberal.—He wishes me to state to the Committee *quietly* recollect—his wish to have some communication with them. He would be just the man for a *Chef*—if it could be managed.— —

Journal in Cephalonia

June 19th. 1823

The Dead have been awakened—shall I sleep?
   The World's at war with tyrants—shall I crouch?
   The harvest's ripe—and shall I pause to reap?
    I slumber not—the thorn is in my Couch—
Each day a trumpet soundeth in mine ear—
    It's Echo in my heart— —

Metaxata—Cephalonia—Septr. 28th. 1823

On the sixteenth (I think) of July I sailed from Genoa on the English Brig Hercules—Jno. Scott Master—on the 17th. a Gale of wind occasioning confusion and threatening damage to the horses in the hold—we bore up again for the same port—where we remained four and twenty hours longer and then put to sea—touched at Leghorn—and pursued our voyage by the straits of Messina for Greece—passing within sight of Elba—Corsica—the Lipari islands including Stromboli Sicily Italy &c.—about the 4th of August we anchored off Argostoli, the chief harbour of the Island of Cephalonia.— —

Here I had some expectation of hearing from Capt. B[laquiere] who was on a mission from the G[ree]k Committee in London to the Gr[eek] Provisional Gov[ernmen]t of the Morea—but rather to my surprise learned that he was on his way home—though his latest letters to me from the peninsula—after expressing an anxious wish that I should come up without delay—stated further that he intended to remain in the Country for the present.— —I have since received various letters from him addrest to Genoa—and forwarded to the Islands—partly explaining the cause of his unexpected return—and also (contrary to his former opinion) requesting me not to proceed to Greece *yet*—for sundry reasons, some of importance.—I sent a boat to Corfu in the hope of finding him still there—but he had already sailed for Ancona.—

In the island of Cephalonia Colonel Napier commanded in chief as Resident—and Col. Duffie the 8th. a King's regiment then forming the Garrison. We were received by both those

Gentlemen—and indeed by all the Officers as well as the Civilians with the greatest kindness and hospitality—which if we did not deserve—I still hope that we have done nothing to forfeit—and it has continued unabated—even since the Gloss of new acquaintance has been worn away by frequent intercourse.— —We have learned what has since been fully confirmed—that the Greeks are in a state of political dissention amongst themselves—that Mavrocordato was dismissed or had resigned (L'Un vaut bien l'autre) and that Colocotroni with I know not what or whose party was paramount in the Morea.—The Turks were in force in Acarnania &c. and the Turkish fleet blockaded the coast from Missolonghi to Chiarenza—and subsequently to Navarino— —the Greek Fleet from the want of means or other causes remained in port in Hydra—Ipsara and Spezas[?]—and for aught that is yet certainly known may be there still. As rather contrary to my expectations I had no advices from Peloponnesus—and had also letters to receive from England from the Committee I determined to remain for the interim in the Ionian Islands—especially as it was difficult to land on the opposite coast without risking the confiscation of the Vessel and her Contents—which Capt. Scott naturally enough declined to do—unless I would insure to him the full amount of his possible damage,— —

To pass the time we made a little excursion over the mountains to Saint Eufemia—by worse roads than I ever met in the course of some years of travel in rough places of many countries.—At Saint Euphemia we embarked for Ithaca—and made the tour of that beautiful Island—as a proper pendant to the Troad which I had visited several years before.—The hospitality of Capt. Knox (the resident) and his lady was in no respect inferior to that of our military friends of Cephalonia.—That Gentleman with Mrs. K. and some of their friends conducted us to the fountain of Arethusa—which alone would be worth the voyage—but the rest of the Island is not inferior in attraction to the admirers of Nature;—the arts and tradition I leave to the Antiquaries,—and so well have those Gentlemen contrived to settle such questions—that as the existence of Troy is disputed—so that of Ithaca (as *Homer's Ithaca* i.e.) is not yet admitted.—Though the month was August and we had been cautioned against travelling in the Sun—yet as I had

during my former experience never suffered from the heat as long
as I continued in *motion*—I was unwilling to lose so many hours
of the day on account of a sunbeam more or less—and though our
party was rather numerous no one suffered either illness or inconvenience as far as could be observed, though one of the Servants
(a Negro)—declared that it was as hot as in the West Indies.—I
had left our thermometer on board—so could not ascertain the
precise degree.—We returned to Saint Eufemia and passed over
to the monastery of Samos on the opposite part of the bay and
proceeded next day to Argostoli by a better road than the path to
Saint Eufemia.—The land Journey was made on Mules.— —

Some days after our return, I heard that there were letters for
me at Zante—but a considerable delay took place before the Greek
to whom they were consigned had them properly forwarded—
and I was at length indebted to Col. Napier for obtaining them
for me;—*what* occasioned the demur or delay—was never explained.—I learned by my advices from England—the request of
the Committee that I would act as their representative near the
G[ree]k Gov[ernmen]t and take charge of the proper disposition
and delivery of certain Stores &c. &c. expected by a vessel which
has not yet arrived up to the present date (Septr. 28th)—Soon
after my arrival I took into my own pay a body of forty Suliotes
under the Chiefs Photomara—Giavella—and Drako—and would
probably have increased the number—but I found them not quite
united among themselves in any thing except raising their demands on me—although I had given a dollar per man more each
month—than they could receive from the G[ree]k Gov[ernmen]t
and they were destitute[,] at the time I took them[,] of every
thing.— —I had acceded too to their own demand—and paid
them a month in advance.— —But set on probably by some of
the trafficking shopkeepers with whom they were in the habit of
dealing on credit—they made various attempts at what I thought
extortion—so that I called them together stating my view of the
case—and declining to take them on with me—but I offered
them another month's pay—and the price of their passage to
Acarnania—where they could now easily go as the Turkish fleet
was gone—and the blockade removed.—This part of them accepted—and they went accordingly.—Some difficulty arose about

restoring their arms by the Septinsular Gov[ernmen]t but these were at length obtained—and they are now with their compatriots in Etolia or Acarnania.— —

I also transferred to the resident in Ithaca—the sum of two hundred and fifty dollars for the refugees there—and I had conveyed to Cephalonia—a Moriote family who were in the greatest helplessness—and provided them with a house and decent maintenance under the protection of Messrs. Corgialegno—wealthy merchants of Argostoli—to whom I had been recommended by my Correspondents.— —I had caused a letter to be written to Marco Bozzari the acting Commander of a body of troops in Acarnania—for whom I had letters of recommended [sic];—his answer was probably the last he ever signed or dictated—for he was killed in action the very day after it's date—with the character of a good Soldier—and an honourable man—which are not always found together nor indeed separately.— —I was also invited by Count Metaxa the Governor of Missolonghi to go over there—but it was necessary in the present state of parties that I should have some communication with the existing Gov[ernmen]t on the subject of their opinion *where* I might be—if not *most* useful—at any rate *least* obnoxious.— —

As I did not come here to join a faction but a nation—and to deal with honest men and not with speculators or peculators (charges bandied about daily by the Greeks of each other) it will require much circumspection <for me> to avoid the character of a partizan—and I perceive it to be the more difficult—as I have already received invitations from more than one of the contending parties—always under the pretext that *they* are the "real Simon Pure".— —After all—one should not despair—though all the foreigners that I have hitherto met with from amongst the Greeks—are going or gone back disgusted.—

Whoever goes into Greece at present should do it as Mrs. Fry went into Newgate—not in the expectation of meeting with any especial indication of existing probity—but in the hope that time and better treatment will reclaim the present burglarious and larcenous tendencies which have followed this General Gaol delivery.—When the limbs of the Greeks are a little less stiff from the shackles of four centuries—they will not march so much "as if they had gyves on their legs".— — At present the Chains are broken indeed—but the links are still clanking—and the Saturnalia is still too recent to have converted the Slave into a sober Citizen.—The worst of them is—that (to use a coarse but the only expression that will not fall short of the truth) they are such d – – – – d liars;—there never was such an incapacity for veracity shown since Eve lived in Paradise.—One of them found fault the other day with the English language—because it had so few shades of a Negative—whereas a Greek can so modify a No—to a yes—and vice versa—by the slippery qualities of his language—that prevarication may be carried to any extent and still leave a loop-hole through which perjury may slip without being perceived.— —This was the Gentleman's own talk—and is only to be doubted because in the words of the Syllogism—"Now Epimenides was a Cretan". But they may be mended by and bye.—

Sept. 30th.

After remaining here some time in expectation of hearing from the G[ree]k G[overnmen]t I availed myself of the opportunity of Messrs B[rowne] and T[relawny] proceeding to Tripolitza—subsequently to the departure of the Turkish fleet to write to the acting part of the Legislature. My object was not only to obtain some accurate information so as to enable me to proceed to the Spot where I might be if not most safe at least more serviceable but to have an opportunity of forming a judgement on the real state of their affairs. In the mean time I hear from Mavrocordato—and the Primate of Hydra—the latter inviting me to that island—and the former hinting that he should like to meet me there or elsewhere.

1823
10bre. 17th.

My Journal was discontinued abruptly and has not been resumed sooner—because on the day of it's former date I received a letter from my Sister Augusta—that intimated the illness of my daughter—and I had not then the heart to continue it.— —Subsequently I had heard through the same channel that she was better—and since that she is well—if so—for me all is well. But although I learned this early in 9bre.—I know not why—I have not continued my journal, though many things which would have formed a curious record have since occurred.—I know not why I resume it even now except that standing at the window of my apartment in this beautiful village—the calm though cool serenity of a beautiful and transparent Moonlight—showing the Islands—the Mountains—the Sea—with a distant outline of the Morea traced between the double Azure of the waves and skies —have quieted me enough to be able to write—from [sic] which (however difficult it may seem for one who has written so much publicly—to refrain) is and always has been to me—a task and a painful one— —I could summon testimonies were it necessary—but my handwriting is sufficient—it is that of one who thinks much, rapidly—perhaps deeply—but rarely with pleasure.— —

But—"En Avant!"—The Greeks are advancing in their public progress—but quarrelling amongst themselves.— —I shall probably bon grè mal grè be obliged to join one of the factions—which I have hitherto strenuously avoided in the hope to unite them in one common interest.—Mavrocordato—has appeared at length with the Idriote Squadron in these seas—which apparition would hardly have taken place had I not engaged to pay two hundred thousand piastres (10 piastres per dollar being the present value—on the Greek Continent) in aid of Messolonghi—and has commenced operations somewhat successfully but not very prudently.—Fourteen (some say Seventeen) Greek Ships attacked a Turkish vessel of *12* guns—and took her— —This is not quite an Ocean-Thermopylæ—but n'importe—they (*on dit*) had found on board 50000 dollars—a sum of great service in their present exigencies—if properly applied.—This prize however has been made within the bounds of Neutrality on the Coast of Ithaca—and the Turks were (it is said) pursued on shore—and some slain.—All this may involve a question of right and wrong with the not very Tolerant Thomas Maitland—who is not very capable of distinguishing either. I have advanced the sum above noted to pay the said Squadron—it is not very large—but it is double that with which Napoleon the Emperor of Emperors—began his campaign in Italy, withal—vide—Las Cases—passim vol 1 (tome premier).

The Turks have retired from before Messolonghi—nobody knows why—since they left provisions and ammunition behind them in quantities—and the Garrison made no sallies or none to any purpose—they never invested Messolonghi this year—but bombarded Anatoliko—(a sort of village which I recollect well having passed through the whole of that country with 50 Albanians in 1809 Messolonghi included) near the Achelous—some say that S[irota?] Pacha heard of an insurrection near Scutari—some one thing some another—for my part I have been in correspondence with the Chiefs—and their accounts are not unanimous.—The Suliotes both there—here—and elsewhere—having taken a kind of liking *to*, or at least formed or renewed a sort of acquaintance *with* me—(as I have aided them and their families in all that I could according to circumstances) are apparently anxious that I should put myself forward as their Chief—(If I may so say) I would rather not for the present—because there are too many divisions and Chiefs already—but if it should appear necessary—why—as they are admitted to be the best and bravest of the present combatants—it might—or may—so happen—that I could would—should—or shall take to me the support of such a body of men—with whose aid—I think something might be done both *in* Greece and *out* of it—(for there is a good deal to put to rights in both)[.] I could maintain them out of my own present means (always supposing my present income and means to be permanent) they are not above a thousand—and of those not six hundred *real* Suliotes—but they are allowed to be equal (that seems a bravado though but it is in print recently) *one* to 5 European Moslems—and *ten* Asiatics—be it as it may—they are in high esteem—and my very good friends.— —

A soldier may be maintained on the Mainland—for 25 piastres (rather better than two dollars a month) monthly—and find his rations out of the Country—or for *five dollars*—including his paying for his rations—therefore for between two and three thousand dollars a month—(and the dollar here is to be had for 4 and 2 pence instead of 4 and 6 pence—the price in England) I could maintain between five hundred and a thousand of these warriors for as long as necessary—and I have more means than are—(supposing them to last) [sufficient] to do so—for my own personal wants are very simple (except in horses for I am no great pedestrian) and my income considerable for any country but England—(being equal to the President's of the United States— the English Secretaries' of State's or the French Ambassador's at Vienna and the greater courts—150000 Francs—I believe) and I have hope to have sold a Manor besides for nearly 3000000 francs more—thus I could (with what We should extract according to the usages of war—also) keep on foot a respectable clan or Sept or tribe or horde—for some time—and as I have not any motive for so doing but the well-wishing to Greece I should hope with advantage.—

TO COUNTESS TERESA GUICCIOLI *8bre. 7mo. 1823*

[Added to Pietro Gamba's letter to Teresa]

My dearest T.—Pietro has told you all the gossip of the Island—our earthquakes—our politics—and present abode in a pretty village.—But he has not told you the result of one of his gallantries—which I leave to him to describe.—As his opinions and mine on the Greeks are nearly similar—I need say little on the subject.— —I was a fool to come here but being here I must see what is to be done. If we were not at such a distance I could tell you many things that would make you smile—but I hope to do so at no very long period.—Pray keep well—and love me as you are beloved by yrs. ever

a.a. + + + in e.
N B

TO CHARLES F. BARRY *Oct. 9, 1823*

[Part of letter quoted in auction catalogue]

I have only time to add a postscript to G[amba]'s letter, I have received several of yours duly. The Greeks are marching and have turned out Mavrocordato, who is at Hydra, on board the fleet. I am waiting for a communication from the Greek Government to know how to proceed myself. We have had shocks of earthquake here, but little damage; everybody tolerably well. Various attempts made to extract my monies, but to these I demur, until sure that they are to be applied to the public weal, which is not at present the first consideration of the patriots, according to all accounts. . . .

TO COLONEL JOHN DUFFIE *October 9, 1823*

Dear Colonel,—The pelisse fits as if it had been made for me, excepting that it is a little too short in the sleeves, which is not of any consequence.

I shall therefore, with many acknowledgments, accept and wear it,—somewhat, I fear, in the mode of the ass in the lion's skin in the fable; or, rather in the hope which the Indians entertain when they wear the spoils of a redoubted enemy, viz. that his good qualities may be transferred to the new possessor with his habiliments. But these being the garments of a friend, may, I trust, be still more propitious.

I send you some papers, but I doubt that you have later ones; however, they can serve the mess as duplicates: the 29th and 30th are among them; but the 26th and 27th (28th being Sunday) are not yet arrived. Believe me ever and truly,

Yours affectionately

NOEL BYRON

TO AUGUSTA LEIGH *Cephalonia, 8bre. 12th. 1823*

My dearest Augusta—Your three letters on the subject of Ada's indisposition have made me very anxious to hear further of her amelioration.—I have been subject to the same complaint but not at so early an age—nor in so great a degree.—Besides it never affected my eyes—but rather my hearing and that only partially and slightly and for a short time.—I had dreadful and almost periodical headaches till I was fourteen—and sometimes since— but abstinence and a habit of bathing my head in cold water every morning cured me—I think—at least I have been less molested since that period.—Perhaps she will get quite well—when she arrives at womanhood—but that is some time to look forward to, though if she is of so sanguine a habit—it is probable that she may attain to that period earlier than is usual in our colder climate;—in Italy and the East—it sometimes occurs at twelve— or even earlier—I knew an instance in a noble Italian house—at ten—but this was considered uncommon.—You will excuse me touching on this topic *medically* and "en passant" because I cannot help thinking that the determination of blood to the head so early unassisted—may have some connection with a similar tendency to earlier maturity.—Perhaps it is a phantasy.—At any rate let me know how she is—I need not say how *very* anxious I am (at this distance particularly) to hear of her welfare.— —

You ask me why I came up amongst the Greeks?—it was

stated to me that my so doing might tend to their advantage in some measure in their present struggle for independence—both as an individual—and as a member for the Committee now in England.—How far this may be realized I cannot pretend to anticipate—but I am willing to do what I can.—They have at length found leisure to quarrel among themselves—after repelling their other enemies—and it is no very easy part that I may have to play to avoid appearing partial to one or other of their factions.—They have turned out Mavrocordato—who was the only *Washington* or *Kosciusko* kind of man amongst them—and they have not yet sent their deputies to London to treat for a loan—nor in short done themselves so much good as they might have done.—I have written to Mr. Hobhouse three several times with a budget of documents on the subject—from which he can extract all the present information for the Committee.—I have written to their Gov[ernmen]t at Tripolizza and Salamis—and am waiting for instructions *where* to proceed—for things are in such a state amongst them—that it is difficult to conjecture where one could be useful to them—if at all.—However I have some hopes that they will see their own interest sufficiently not to quarrel till they have secured their national independence—and then they can fight it out among them in a domestic manner—and welcome.—You may suppose that I have something to *think* of at least—for you can have no idea what an intriguing cunning unquiet generation they are—and as emissaries of all parties come to me at present—and I must act impartially— it makes me exclaim as Julian did at his military exercises—"Oh Plato what a task for a Philosopher!"— —

However *you* won't think much of *my philosophy*—nor do I—"entre nous".— —

If you think this epistle or any part of it worth transmitting to Ly B[yron] you can send her a copy—as I suppose—unless she is become I know not what—she cannot be altogether indifferent as to my "whereabouts" and *what*abouts.

I am at present in a very pretty village (Metaxata in Cephalonia) between the mountains and the Sea—with a view of Zante and the Morea—waiting for some more decisive intelligence from the provisional Gov[ernmen]t in Salamis.— —But here come some visitors.

I was interrupted yesterday—by Col. Napier and the Captain of a King's ship—now in the harbour—Col. N. is resident or Governor here and has been extremely kind and hospitable—as indeed have been all the English here.—When their visit was over a Greek arrived on business about this eternal siege of Mesalonghi (on the coast of Acarnania or Etolia) and some convoys of provisions which we want to throw in—and after this was discussed, I got on horseback (I brought up my horses with me on board and troublesome neighbours they were in blowing weather) and rode to Argostoli and back—and then I had one of my *thunder* headaches (*you* know how my head acts like a barometer when there is electricity in the air) and I could not resume till this morning.—Since my arrival in August I made a tour to Ithaca—(which you will take to be Ireland—but if you look into Pope's Odyssey—you will discover to be the antient name of the Isle of Wight) and also over some parts of Cephalonia.— —

We are pretty well in health the Gods be thanked! by the way, who is this Dr. Tipperary or Mayo or whatever his name is? I never heard of anything of the name except an Irish County?—Laurence the Surgeon if he be the man who has been persecuted for his metaphysics—is I have heard an excellent professional man—but I wonder Ly. B[yron] should employ (so tell her) a Papist or a Sceptic.—I thought that like "douce David Deans" she would not have allowed "a Goutte of physic to go through any of the family" unless she was sure that the prescriber was a Cameronian.— —

There is a clever but eccentric man here a Dr. Kennedy—who is very pious and tries in good earnest to make converts—but his Christianity is a queer one—for he says that the priesthood of the Church of England are no more Christians than "Mahmoud or Termagant" are.—He has made some converts I suspect rather to the beauty of his wife (who is pretty as well as pious) than of his theology.—I like what I have seen of him—of *her* I know nothing—nor desire to know—having other things to think about. *He* says that the dozen shocks of an Earthquake we had the other day—are a sign of his doctrine—or a judgement on his audience—but this opinion has not acquired proselytes.—One of the shocks was so prolonged—that though not very heavy—We thought the house would come down—and as we have a staircase to dismount *out* of the house (the buildings here are different from ours), it was judged expedient by the inmates (all *men* please to recollect—as if there had been females we must have helped them out or broken our bones for company) to make an expeditious retreat into the courtyard.—*Who* was first out the door I know not—but when I got to the bottom of the stairs I found several arrived before me—which could only have happened by their jumping out of the windows—or down *over* or from the stairs (which had no balustrade or bannisters) rather than in the regular way of descent.—The Scene was ludicrous enough—but we had several more slight shocks in the night but stuck quietly to our beds—for it would have been of no use moving—as the house would have been down first—had it been to come down at all.—

There was no great damage done in the Island (except an old house or two cracking in the middle), but the soldiers on parade were lifted up as a boat is by the tide—and you could have seen the whole line waving (though no one was in motion) by the heaving of the ground on which they were drawn up.—You can't complain of this being a brief letter.— —

I wish you would obtain from Lady B[yron] some account of Ada's disposition—habits—studies—moral tendencies—and temper—as well as of her personal appearance[,] for except from the miniature drawn four years ago (and she is now double that age nearly) I have no idea of even her aspect.—When I am advised on these points I can form some notion of her character—and what way her dispositions or indispositions ought [to be] treated—and though I will never interfere with or thwart her mother—yet I may perhaps be permitted to suggest—as she (Lady B.) is not obliged to follow my notions unless she likes—which is not very likely.—Is the Girl imaginative?—at *her* present age—I have an idea that I had many feelings and notions—which people would not believe if I stated them *now*—and therefore I may as well keep them to myself.— —Is she social or solitary—taciturn or talkative—fond of reading or otherwise?—and what is her *tic*?—I mean her foible—is she passionate?—I hope that the Gods have made her any thing save *poetical*—it is enough to have one such fool in a family.—You can answer all this at yr. leisure—address to *Genoa* as usual—the letters will be forwarded better by my Correspondents there.—

yrs. ever
N B

P.S.—Tell Douglas K[innair]d I have only just got his letter of August *14th.* and not only approve of his accepting a sum not under ten or twelve thousand pounds for the property in question—but also of his getting as much as can be gotten *above* that price.

TO PRINCE ALEXANDER MAVROCORDATOS [TRANSLATION]

Cephalonia December 2, 1823

Most Excellent Prince—Colonel Stanhope, the son of Major-General Harrington, etc. etc. etc., will present this letter of mine to your Highness. He has come from London in 50 days after having visited all of the Greek committees in Germany—charged by our committee to work together with me for the liberation of Greece. I believe that his name, or his mission, will be enough to recommend him to Your Highness, without the need of any other recommendation from a foreigner, even though he may be someone who respects and admires—together with all of Europe—the courage, the talents, and above all, the probity of Prince Mavrocordato— —

It pains me exceedingly to hear that the internal dissensions of Greece still continue—and at a time when she could triumph everywhere, as she has triumphed in some places.

Greece now faces these three courses—to win her liberty, to become a Colony of the sovereigns of Europe, or to become a Turkish province.— —Now she can choose one of the three—but civil war cannot lead to anything but the last two. If she envies the fate of Wallachia or of the Crimea she can obtain it tomorrow; if that of Italy, the day after tomorrow. But if Greece wants to become forever free, true, and Independent she had better decide now, or never again will she have the chance, never again. Believe me with the utmost esteem and respect.

N B P[eer] of E[ngland]

P.S.—Your highness already knows that I have tried to satisfy the requests of your Government as much as I could. I wish that this fleet, which we have waited for so long in vain, had arrived— and above all that Your Highness, either on board the fleet on a public mission, or in any other way, had come or would now come to these parts. Believe me again

Your devoted Servant
N B P[eer] of E[ngland]

MISSALONGHI

Between two worlds life hovers like a star
'Twixt night and morn upon the horizon's verge,
How little do we know that which we are!
How less what we may be! The eternal surge
Of time and tide rolls on and bears afar
Our bubbles. As the old burst, new emerge,
Lashed from the foam of ages; while the graves
Of empires heave but like some passing waves.

DON JUAN XV, 99

My dear Sydney—Enclosed is a private communication from Prince Mavrocordato to Sir Thomas Maitland—which you will oblige me much by delivering.—Sir Thomas can take as much or as little notice of it—as he pleases—but I hope—and believe that it is rather calculated to conciliate—than to irritate on the subject of the late events near Ithaca and Santa Maura—which there is every disposition on the part of the Govt. here to disavow—and they are also disposed to give any satisfaction in their power.—You must all be aware how difficult it is under existing circumstances for the Greeks to keep up discipline—however well they may be disposed to do so.—I am doing all I can to convince them of the necessity of the strictest observance of the regulations of the Islands—and I trust with some effect.—

I arrived here a few days ago—after all sorts of adventures—one of my boats taken by the Turks—(but since released) the other chaced from Creek to Creek—as far as Dragomestri—and twice driven on the rocks on the passage near Scrophes—by stress of weather—and narrowly escaping complete shipwreck.—I gave up the hole below decks to one of the people who was ill—but notwithstanding all kinds of weather—and sleeping constantly on deck I never was better So much so—that being somewhat *obscured* by five days and nights without ablution or change of cloathes—I thought the shortest way to kill the fleas—was to strip and take a swim—which I did on the evening of the third (I think) contrary to the remonstrance of crew—passengers—and physician—who prognosticated Cramp or fever—but idly enough—for my cold bath set all to rights—and I have been the better for it ever since.—

I was received here with every possible public and private mark of respect &c. &c. I came opportunely enough to pay their Squadron—&c.—and I have engaged to maintain a certain number of troops—with whom it is probable that I shall have to march—when an expedition now projecting takes place.— —If you write to any of our friends—you can say that I am in good health and spirits—and that I shall stick by the cause as long as a man of honour can—without sparing purse—or (I hope—if need be) person.— —With regard to what may occur to myself—I take it a man is as liable to danger in one place as in another upon the whole—but whether it be so or not—in circumstances of this kind—such should be a secondary consideration with his friends as well as himself.

Yrs. ever dear Sydney

N B

TO CHARLES HANCOCK   *Messolonghi. Jy. 13th. 1824*

Dear Sr. H.—Many thanks for yrs. of ye 5th. ditto to Muir for his.—You will have heard that Gamba and my vessel got out of the hands of the Turks safe and intact—nobody knows well how or why—for there is a mystery in the story somewhat melodramatic—Captain Valsamachi—has I take it spun a long yarn by this time in Argostoli;—I attribute their release entirely to Saint Dionysius of Zante—and the Madonna of the Rock near Cephalonia.—The adventures of my separate bark were also not finished at Dragomestre.—We were conveyed out by some Greek Gunboats—and found the Leonidas brig of war at Sea to look after us.—But blowing weather coming on we were driven on the rocks—*twice*—in the passage of the Scrophes—and the dollars had another narrow escape.—Two thirds of the Crew got ashore over the bowsprit—the rocks were rugged enough—but water very deep close in shore—so that she was after much swearing and some exertion got off again—and away we went with a third of our crew leaving the rest on a desolate island—where they might have been now—had not one of the Gunboats taken them off— for we were in no condition to take them off again.—Tell Muir that Dr. Bruno did not show much fight on the occasion—for besides stripping to the flannel waistcoat—and running about like a rat in an emergency—when I was talking to a Greek boy (the brother of the G[ree]k Girls in Argostoli) and telling him the fact that there was no danger for the passengers whatever there might be for the vessel—and assuring him that I could save both him and myself—without difficulty (though he can't swim) as the water though deep was not very rough—the wind *not* blowing *right* on shore—(it was a blunder of the Greeks who missed stays) the Doctor exclaimed—"Save *him* indeed—by G–d—save *me* rather —I'll be first if I can" a piece of Egotism which he pronounced with such emphatic simplicity—as to set all who had leisure to hear him laughing—and in a minute after—the vessel drove off again after striking twice—she sprung a small leak—but nothing further happened except that the Captain was very nervous after-wards.—To be brief—we had bad weather almost always—though not contrary—slept on deck in the wet generally—for seven or eight nights—but never was in better health (I speak personally) so much so that I actually bathed for a quarter of an hour on the evening of the fourth inst. in the sea—(to kill the fleas and others) and was all the better for it.— —We were received at Messolonghi with all kinds of kindness and honours—and the sight of the fleet saluting &c. and the crowds and different costumes was really picturesque.—We think of undertaking an expedition soon—and I expect to be ordered with the Suliotes to join the army—all well at present—we found Gamba already arrived—and every thing in good condition.—Remembrance to all friends—

yrs. ever
N B

P.S.—You will I hope use every exertion to realize the Assetts—for besides what I have already advanced—I have undertaken to maintain the Suliotes for a year—([and] accompany them either as a Chief or [word torn out with seal] whichever is most agreeable to the Government) besides sundries.—I do not quite understand Browne's "*letter of Credit*"—I neither gave nor ordered a letter of Credit that I know of—(and though of course if you have done it—I will be responsible) I was not aware of any thing—except that I would have backed his bills—which you said was unneces-sary.—As to *orders*—I ordered nothing but some *red* cloth—and oil cloth—both of which I am ready to receive—but if Gamba has exceeded my commission the other things must be sent back *for I cannot permit anything of the kind nor will*.—The Servants' journey will of course be paid for—though *that* is exorbitant.—As for Browne's letter—I do not know anything more than I have said—and I really cannot defray the charges of half Greece and

the Frank adventurers besides.— —Mr. Barff must send us some
dollars soon—for the expences fall on me for the present.— —

P.S. 2d.—Jy. 14th. 1824 Will you tell Saint (Jew) Geronimo
Corgialegno—that I mean to draw for the balance of my credit
with Messrs Webb & Co;—I shall draw for two thousand dollars—(that being about the amount more or less—) but to facilitate
the business I shall make the draft payable also at Messrs Ransom
and Co's Pall Mall East London.—I believe I already showed you
my letters (but if not I have them to show) by which besides the
Credits now realizing—you will have perceived that I am not
limited to any particular amount of credit with my bankers—The
Honourable Douglas my friend and trustee is a principal partner
in that house—and having the direction of my affairs—is aware
to what extent my present resources may go—and the letters in
question were from him.—I can merely say that within *the current*
year, 1824, besides the money already advanced to the Greek Govt.
and the credits now in your hands and yr. partner—(Mr. Barff)
which are all from the income of 1823 (I have anticipated nothing
from that of the present year hitherto) I shall—or ought to have
at my disposition upwards of an hundred thousand dollars—(including my income—and the purchase money of a manor recently
sold) and perhaps more—without impinging on my income for
1825—and not including the remaining balance of 1823.—

yrs. ever
N B

P.S.—Many thanks to Colonel Wright and Muir for their
exertions about the vessell.—

TO ANDREAS LONDOS [TRANSLATION]   *Missolonghi—*
30th January—1824

Most esteemed Sir and friend—The sight of your handwriting
gave me the greatest pleasure. Greece has ever been for me, as it
must be for all men of any feeling or education, the promised land
of valour, of the arts, and of liberty throughout all the ages; and
the journeys I made in my youth amongst her ruins certainly had

not diminished my love for the heroes' native land. In addition to this, I am bound to yourself by ties of friendship and gratitude for the hospitality which I experienced from you during my stay in that country, of which you are now become one of the defenders and ornaments. Seeing you again and serving your country at your side and under your eyes, will be one of the happiest moments of my life. In the mean time, I beg you to command me and believe me now as always

your [most devoted] Friend and Servant
NOEL BYRON, Peer of England

TO CHARLES HANCOCK   *Messolonghi. F[ebbrai] 5 1824*

Dear Sir—Dr. Muir's letter and yrs. of the 23d. reached me some days ago,—tell Muir that I am glad of the promotion for his sake—and of his remaining near us for all our sakes,—though I cannot but regret Dr. Kennedy's departure—which accounts for the previous earthquakes and the present English weather in this climate.—With all respect to my medical pastor—I have to announce to him that amongst other firebrands, our firemaster Parry (just landed) has disembarked an elect blacksmith—entrusted with three hundred and twenty two Greek testaments,   I have given him all facilities in my power for his works spiritual and temporal—and if he can settle matters as easily with the Greek Archbishop and hierarchy I trust that neither the heretic nor the supposed Sceptic will be accused of intolerance.— —

By the way—I met with the said Archbishop at Anatoliko (where I went by invitation of the Primates a few days ago—and was received with a heavier cannonade than the Turks probably) for the second time—(I had known him here before) and he and P[rince] Mavrocordato—and the Chiefs and Primates & I all dined together—and I thought the Metropolitan the merriest of the party—and a very good Christian for all that.— —But Gamba (we got wet through on our way back) has been ill with a fever and Cholic—and Luke (not the Evangelist—but a disciple of mine) has been out of sorts too—and so have some others of the people—and I have been very well—except that I caught cold yesterday with swearing too much in the rain at the Greeks—who would not bear a hand in landing the Committee stores and nearly spoiled our combustibles;—but I turned out in person and made such a row as set them in motion—blaspheming at them all from the Government downwards—till they actually did *some* part of what they ought to have done several days before—and this is esteemed as it deserves to be—a wonder.— —

Tell Muir that notwithstanding his remonstrance—which I receive thankfully—it is perhaps best that I should advance with the troops for if we do not do something soon we shall have a third year of defensive operations—and another siege and all that—we hear that the Turks are coming down in force and sooner than usual—and as these fellows do mind me a little—it is the opinion that I should go,—firstly—because they will sooner listen to a foreigner than one of their own people—out of native jealousies—secondly, because the Turks will sooner treat or capitulate (if such occasions should happen) with a Frank than a Greek—and thirdly,—because nobody else seems disposed to take the responsibility—Mavrocordato being very busy here—the foreign military men too young—or not of authority enough to be obeyed by the natives—and the Chiefs—(as aforesaid—) disinclined to obey any one except or rather than one of their own body.— —

As for me—I am willing to do what I am bidden and to follow my instructions—I neither seek nor shun that nor any thing else that they may wish me to attempt—and as for personal safety—besides that it ought not to be a consideration—I take it that a man is on the whole as safe in one place as another—and after all he had better end with a bullet than bark in his body;—if we are not taken off with the sword—we are like to march off with an ague in this mud-basket—and to conclude with a very bad pun—to the ear rather than to the eye—better—*mart*ially— than *marsh*-ally;—the Situation of Messolonghi is not unknown to you;—the Dykes of Holland when broken down are the Desarts of Arabia for dryness in comparison.— —

And now for the sinews of War— —I thank you and Mr. Barff for your ready answer which next to ready money is a pleasant thing.— —Besides the Assets—and balance—and the relics of the Corgialegno correspondence with Leghorn and Genoa (I sold the dog's flour tell him but not at *his* price) I shall request and require from the beginning of March ensuing—about five thousand dollars every two months—i. e. about twenty five thousand within the current year—at regular intervals—independent of the sums now negociating. I can show you documents to prove that these are considerably *within* my supplies for the year in more ways than one—but I do not like to tell the Greeks *exactly—what*—I *could* or would advance on an emergency—because otherwise they will double and triple their demands (a disposition that they have already shown) and though I am willing to do all I can *when* necessary—yet I do not see why *they* should not help a little—for they are not quite so bare as they pretend to be by some accounts.— —

Fy. 7th. 1824

I have been interrupted by the arrival of Parry and afterwards by the return of Hesketh who has not brought an answer to my epistles which rather surprizes me.—You will write soon I suppose. Parry seems a fine rough subject—but will hardly be ready for the field these three weeks;—he and I will (I think) be able to draw together—at least *I* will not interfere with or contradict him in his own department, he complains grievously of the mercantile and en*thusy*mu*sy* (as Braham pronounces enthusiasm) part of the Committee—but greatly praises Gordon and Hume,—Gordon *would* have given three or four thousand pounds and come out himself—but Bowring or somebody else disgusted him—and thus they have spoiled part of their subscription and cramped their operations.— —Parry says Blaquiere is a humbug;—to which I say nothing.—He sorely laments the printing and civilizing expences—and wishes that there was not a Sunday School in the world—or *any* school *here* at present save and except always an academy for Artilleryship.— —He complained also of the Cold—a little to my surprize—firstly because there being no chimneys—I have used myself to do without other warmth than the animal heat and one's Cloak—in these parts—and secondly because I should as soon have expected to hear a Volcano sneeze—as a Fire-master (who is to burn a whole fleet—) exclaim against the atmosphere.—I fully expected that his very approach would have scorched the town like the burning glasses of Archimedes.—Well—it seems that I am to be Commander in Chief—and the post is by no means a sine-cure—for we are not what Major Sturgeon calls "a Set of the most amicable officers" whether we shall have "a boxing bout between Captain Sheers and the Colonel" I cannot tell—but between Suliote Chiefs—German Barons—English Volunteers—and ad-venturers of all Nations—we are likely to form as goodly an allied army—as ever quarrelled beneath the same banner.—

Fy. 8th. 1824

Interrupted again by business—yesterday—and it is time to conclude my letter.—I drew some time since on Mr. Barff for a thousand dollars—to complete some money wanted by the Govt.—The said Government got cash on that bill *here* and at a profit—but the very same fellow who paid it to them—after prom-ising to give me money for other bills on Barff to the amount of thirteen hundred dollars either could not or thought better of it;—I had written to Barff advising him—but had afterwards to write to tell him of the fellow's having not come up to time.— —You must really send me the balance soon—I have the Artillerists—and my Suliotes to pay and heaven knows what besides—and as every thing depends upon punctuality—all our operations will be at a stand still—unless you use dispatch.—I shall send to Mr. Barff or to you—further bills on England for three thousand pounds—to be negociated as speedily as you can— —I have already stated here and formerly—the sums I can command at home—within the year—(without including my credits or the bills already negociated or negociating—or Corgialegno's balance of Messrs Webb's letter) and my letters from my friends (received by Mr. Parry's vessel) confirm what I already stated.—How much I may require in the course of the year I can't tell but I will take care that it shall not exceed the means to supply it.— —

yrs. ever
NB

P.S.—I have had by desire of a Mr. *Gerostati?*—to draw on Demetrius Delladecima (is it our friend "in Ultima Analise") to pay the Committee expences;—I really do not not [sic] understand what the Committee mean by some of their [proceedings?];——Parry and I get on very well *hitherto*—how long this may last Heaven knows—but I hope it will for a good deal for the Greek service depends upon it—but he has already had some *miffs* with Col. S[tanhope]—and I do all I can to keep the peace amongst them—however Parry is a fine fellow—extremely active—and of strong—sound—practical talent by all accounts.— —Enclosed are bills for three thousand pounds—drawn in the mode directed (i.e. parcelled out in smaller bills—) a good opportunity occurring for Cephalonia—to send letters on I avail myself of it.—Remembrances to Stevens and all friends—also my Compliments and everything kind to the Colonels and officers.

Journal

February 15th. 1824

Upon February 15th—(I write on the 17th. of the same month) I had a strong shock of a Convulsive description but whether Epileptic—Paralytic—or Apoplectic is not yet decided by the two medical men who attend me—or whether it be of some other nature (if such there be) it was very painful and had it lasted a moment longer must have extinguished my mortality—if I can judge by sensations.—I was speechless with the features much distorted—but *not* foaming at the mouth—they say—and my struggles so violent that several persons—two of whom—Mr. Parry the Engineer—and my Servant Tita the Chasseur are very strong men—could not hold me—it lasted about ten minutes— and came on immediately after drinking a tumbler of Cider mixed with cold water in Col. Stanhope's apartments.—This is the first attack that I have had of this kind to the best of my belief. I never heard that any of my family were liable to the same—though my mother was subject to *hysterical* affections. Yesterday (the 16th.) Leeches were applied to my temples. I had previously recovered a good deal—but with some feverish and variable symptoms;—I bled profusely— and as they went too near the temporal Artery— there was some difficulty in stopping the blood—even with the Lunar Caustic—this however after some hours was accomplished about eleven o'clock at night—and this day (the 17th.) though weakly I feel tolerably convalescent.— —

With regard to the presumed cause of this attack—as far as I know there might be several—the state of the place and of the weather permits little exercise at present;—I have been violently agitated with more than one passion recently—and a good deal occupied politically as well as privately—and amidst conflicting parties—politics—and (as far as regards public matters) circumstances;—I have also been in an anxious state with regard to things which may be only interesting to my own private feelings—and perhaps not uniformly so temperate as I may generally affirm that I was wont to be—how far any or all of these may have acted on the mind or body of One who had already undergone many previous changes of place and passion during a life of thirty six years I cannot tell—nor— —but I am interrupted by the arrival of a report from a party returned from reconnoitring a Turkish Brig of War just stranded on the Coast—and which is to be attacked the moment we can get some guns to bear upon her.—I shall hear what Parry says about it—here he comes.—

TO MR. MAYER   *[Feb. 21, 1824?]* *[Undated]*

Sir,—Coming to Greece, one of my principal objects was to
alleviate as much as possible the miseries incident to a warfare
so cruel as the present. When the dictates of humanity are in
question, I know no difference between Turks and Greeks. It is
enough that those who want assistance are men, in order to claim
the pity and protection of the meanest pretender to humane feelings. I have found here twenty-four Turks, including women and
children, who have long pined in distress, far from the means of
support and the consolations of their home. The Government has
consigned them to me: I transmit them to Prevesa, whither they
desire to be sent. I hope you will not object to take care that they
may be restored to a place of safety, and that the Governor of your
town may accept of my present. The best recompense I can hope
for would be to find that I had inspired the Ottoman commanders
with the same sentiments towards those unhappy Greeks who may
hereafter fall into their hands. I beg you to believe me, &c.

N BYRON

TO AUGUSTA LEIGH   *Messolonghi. Fy. 23d. 1824*

My dearest Augusta—I received a few days ago your and Lady
B[yron]'s report of Ada's health with other letters from England
for which I ought to be and am (I hope) sufficiently thankful—as
they were of great comfort and I wanted some—having been recently unwell—but am now much better—so that you need not be
alarmed.— —You will have heard of our journeys—and escapes—
and so forth—perhaps with some exaggeration—but it is all very
well now—and I have been some time in Greece which is in as
good a state as could be expected considering circumstances—but
I will not plague you with politics—wars—or *earthquakes*—
though we had another very smart one three nights ago which
produced a scene ridiculous enough as no damage was done except
to those who stuck fast in the scuffle to get first out of the doors or
windows—amongst whom some recent importations fresh from
England—who had been used to quieter elements—were rather

squeezed in the press for precedence.— —I have been obtaining the release of about nine and twenty Turkish prisoners—men women and children—and have sent them at my own expence home to their friends—but one a pretty little girl of nine years of age—named Hato or Hatageé has expressed a strong wish to remain with me—or under my care—and I have nearly determined to adopt her—if I thought that Lady B[yron] would let her come to England as a Companion to Ada (they are about the same age) and we could easily provide for her—if not I can send her to Italy for education.—She is very lively and quick and with great black Oriental eyes—and Asiatic features—all her brothers were killed in the revolution—her mother wishes to return to her husband who is at Prevesa—but says that she would rather entrust the Child to me—in the present state of the Country— —her extreme youth and sex have hitherto saved her life—but there is no saying—what might occur in the course of the *war* (and of *such* a war) and I shall probably commit her to the charge of some English lady in the Islands for the present.—The Child herself has the same wish—and seems to have a decided character for her age;—you can mention this matter if you think it worth while—I merely wish her to be respectably educated and treated—and if my years and all things be considered—I presume it would be difficult to conceive me to have any other views.—

With regard to Ada's health—I am glad to hear that it is so much better—but I think it right that Lady B[yron] should be informed and guard against it accordingly—that her description of much of her disposition and tendencies very nearly resembles that of my *own* at a similar age—except that I was much more impetuous.—Her preference of *prose* (strange as it may now seem) *was* and indeed *is* mine—(for I hate *reading* verse—and always did) and I never invented anything but "*boats—ships*" and generally something relative to the Ocean—I showed the report to Colonel Stanhope—who was struck with the resemblance of *parts* of it to the *paternal* line—even *now*.—But it is also fit—though unpleasant—that I should mention—that my recent attack and a very severe one—had a strong appearance of *Epilepsy*—*why*—I know not—for it is late in life—it's first appearance at thirty-six— and as far as I *know*—it is *not hereditary*—and it is that it may not *become* so—that you should tell Lady B[yron] to take some precautions in the case of Ada;—my attack has not returned—and I am fighting it off with abstinence and exercise and thus far with success—if merely casual it is all very well.

[No signature in MS.]

TO COUNTESS TERESA GUICCIOLI   F[ebbrai] 24 1824

[At end of Pietro Gamba's letter to Teresa]

My dearest T.—Pietro will have told you all the news—but I have not read the whole of his letter. We are all very well *now*—and every thing appears to wear a hopeful aspect.—Of course you may suppose that a country like this is not exactly the place to pass the Carnival in; but it is nevertheless better than could be expected all things considered.— —I am going out on horseback—and Pietro has hardly left me room enough on this paper to add more at present—but I hope to see you this Spring and to talk over these and all other matters,—so be of good cheer and love

ever yrs. most a a in e + + +
N BN

TO JOHN MURRAY   *Messolonghi.—Fy. 25th. 1824*

I have heard from Mr. Douglas K[innair]d that you state "a report of a satire on Mr. Gifford having arrived from Italy—*said* to be written by *me*!—but that *you* do not believe it."—I dare say you do not nor any body else I should think—whoever asserts that I am the author or abettor of anything of the kind on Gifford—lies in his throat.—I always regarded him as my literary father—and myself as his prodigal son; if any such composition exists it is none of mine— —*you* know as well as any body upon *whom* I have or have not written—and *you* also know whether they *do* or did not deserve that same— —and so much for such matters.—You will perhaps be anxious to hear some news from this part of Greece—(which is the most liable to invasion) but you will hear enough through public and private channels on that head.—I will however give you the events of a week—mingling my own private peculiar with the public for we are here jumbled a little together at present. On Sunday (the 15th. I believe) I had a strong and sudden convulsive attack which left me speechless though not motionless—for some strong men could not hold me—but whether it was epilepsy—catalepsy—cachexy—apoplexy—or what other *exy*—or *opsy*—the Doctors have not decided—or whether it was spasmodic or nervous &c.—but it was very unpleasant—and nearly carried me off—and all that—on Monday—they put leeches to my temples—no difficult matter—but the blood could not be stopped till eleven at night (they had gone too near the temporal Artery for my temporal safety) and neither Styptic nor Caustic would cauterize the orifice till after a hundred attempts.—

On Tuesday a Turkish brig of war ran on shore—on Wednesday—great preparations being made to attack her though protected by her Consorts—the Turks burned her and retired to Patras—on thursday a quarrel ensued between the Suliotes and the Frank Guard at the Arsenal— —a Swedish Officer was killed—and a Suliote severely wounded—and a general fight expected—and with some difficulty prevented—on Friday the Officer buried—and Capt. Parry's English Artificers mutinied under pretence that their lives were in danger and are for quitting the country— —they may.—On Saturday we had the smartest shock of an earthquake which I remember (and I have felt thirty slight or smart at different periods—they are common in the Mediterranean) and the whole army discharged their arms—upon the same principle that savages beat drums or howl during an eclipse of the Moon—it was a rare Scene altogether—if you had but seen the English Johnnies who had never been out of a Cockney workshop before! or will again if they can help it—and on Sunday we heard that the Vizir is come down to Larissa with one hundred and odd thousand men.— —

In coming here I had two escapes one from the Turks (one of my vessels was taken—but afterwards released) and the other from shipwreck—we drove twice on the rocks near the Scrophes— (Islands near the Coast). I have obtained from the Greeks the release of eight and twenty Turkish prisoners—men women and children—and sent them to Patras and Prevesa—at my own charges—one little Girl of nine years old—who prefers remaining with me—I shall (if I live) send with her mother probably to Italy or to England—and adopt her.—Her name is Hato—or Hatagée—she is a very pretty lively child—all her brothers were killed by the Greeks—and she herself and her mother merely spared by special favour—and owing to her extreme youth—she was then but five or six years old. My health is now better and [I] ride about again—My office here is no sinecure—so many parties—and difficulties of every kind—but I will do what I can—Prince Mavrocordato is an excellent person and does all in his power—but his situation is perplexing in the extreme—still we have great hopes of the success of the contest.—You will hear however more of public news from plenty of quarters—for I have little time to write—believe me

yrs. &c. &c.

N BN

TO JOHN BOWRING *Messolonghi, March 30th. 1824*

Dear Sir—Signor Zaimi the third Greek Deputy will deliver this letter of introduction—which he has requested—although I told him that it was superfluous as his name and nation were ample recommendation in themselves.—I have received yrs of the 4th. February in which you mention having received mine of the 10th and 12th 9bre. 1823.— As you merely allude to them—and do not state the receipt of several other communications—addrest either to yourself or to Mr. Hobhouse for your perusal—some of them containing documents of considerable importance relative to the Cause or information connected with it—I am to conclude that these have not arrived.— —

Col. Stanhope's and Capt. Parry's reports will have informed the Committee of what is doing or has been done here—and Signor Zaimi will be able to communicate still further—what will render any detail of mine unnecessary.— —I shall observe the Committee's directions with regard to the Officers and Medical men. Mr. Tyndale [sic] had stated to me—that he *had* a claim on the Committee for 35 £Sterling—as passage money—and some others of the Officers foreign or native—have preferred in a slighter degree—similar pretensions.—To Mr. Tyndale I advanced

100 dollars—and to the Germans a smaller sum. — —I am not stating this—as calling upon the Committee to *repay me*—sensible that such advances are at my own risk—but I do wish seriously to impress upon the Committee—either *not* to send out officers of any description—or to provide for their maintenance.— —I am at this moment paying nearly *thirty Officers**, of whom five and twenty would not have bread to eat (in Greece that is) if I did not. — —Even their rations are obtained with difficulty—and their actual pay comes from myself.— —I am called to a meeting at Salona—with Ulysses and other Chiefs—on business in a few days—the weather and the flooding of the rivers has delayed P[rince] Mavrocordato and myself for some time—but appear to be now settling.— —

The News of the Loan have [has] excited much expectation and pleasure amongst the Greeks—the dissensions in the Morea still continue—and hamper them a good deal—but the Opening of the Campaign will probably re-unite the parties—at least—if that do not—nothing will.— —P[rince] Mavrocordato will write to you by this opportunity—I cashed some bills for him (for 550 £Sterling) lately-drawn by him on you—for which—he says that S.S. Orlando and Luriotti have assetts to answer the amount.— This you will know better than I can do.—I have the honour to be

yr. very obedt. and faithful Servt.

NOEL BYRON

P.S.—I shall continue to pursue my former plan of stating to the Committee things as they *really* are—I am an enemy to Cant of all kinds—but it will be seen in time—who are or are not the firmest friends of the Greek Cause—or who will stick by them longest—the Lempriere dictionary quotation Gentlemen—or those who neither dissemble their faults nor their virtues.—"I could mouthe" as well as any of them if I liked it—but I reserved (when I was in the habit of writing) such things for verse—in business—plain

---

* [Byron's marginal note] It is to be observed however that most of these are either German or other foreigners, but very few of the English are better provided—it is true that they do not claim actual pay from the Committee—but they state that hopes were held out to them which the Greek Govt have not realized.— —

prose is best—and simplest—and was so—I take it even amongst
the antient Greeks themselves—if we may judge from their history.
You surprize me by what you say of Baring—I thought that he had
been a wiser man.—It would have been a very good reason for not
lending money to the offender—but I do not see what the Greeks
had to do with the offence.— —They may say what they will of
the work in question—but it will stand—and as high as most
others in time.— —This latter observation is addrest to you—as
an *author*—I have only recently received your translation—from
which I promise myself much pleasure—the Russians are greatly
obliged to you—but I did not know that you so greatly admired
their Czar—their poetry—at least in your version—will be [words
torn off with seal] than [words torn off] princes. Remember me to
any acquaintances or friends of the C[ommitt]ee and to the two
Deputies.

TO THE EARL OF CLARE   *Messolonghi March 31st. 1824*

My dearest Clare—This will be presented to you by a live Greek
Deputy—for whom I desiderate and solicit your countenance and
good will.—I hope that you do not forget that I always regard
you as my dearest friend—and love you as when we were Harrow
boys together—and if I do not repeat this as often as I ought—it
is that I may not tire you with what you so well know.— —I refer
you to Signor Zaimi the Greek Deputy—for all news public and
private.—He will do better than an epistle in this respect.— —I
was sorry to hear that Dick had exported a married woman from
Ireland not only on account of morals but monies—I trust that the
Jury will be considerate. I thought that Richard looked sentimental
when I saw him at Genoa—but little expected what he was to land
in.—Pray who *is* the Lady? the papers merely inform us by dint
of Asterisks that she is Somebody's wife—and has Children—and
that Dick—(as usual) was "the intimate friend of the confiding
husband["]. It is to be hoped that the Jury will be bachelors—pray
take care of *yourself*—Clare—my dear—for in some of your letters
I had a glimpse of a similar intrigue of yours—have a care of an
Eclât—ye Irish Juries lay it on heavy—and then besides you would

be fixed for life—with a *second-hand* Epouse—whereas I wish to see you lead a virgin Heiress from Saville Row to Mount-Shannon.— Let me hear from you at your best leisure—and believe me ever and truly my dearest Clare—

yrs.

NOEL BYRON

P.S.—The Turkish fleet are just bearing down to blockade this port—so how our Deputy is to get by—is a doubt—but the Island-boats frequently evade them.—The Sight is pretty—but much finer for a Limner than a Lodger.—It is the Squadron from the Gulph of Corinth—(Hodie—Gulph of Lepanto); they (the Greeks I mean) are all busy enough as you may suppose—as the Campaign is expected to commence next Month.—But as aforesaid I refer you for news to the Bearer.— —

January 22nd 1824.
Messalonghi.
On this day I complete my thirty sixth year.

1

'T is time this heart should be unmoved
    Since others it hath ceased to move,
Yet though I cannot be beloved
      Still let me love.

2

My days are in the yellow leaf
    The flowers and fruits of love are gone—
The worm, the canker and the grief
      Are mine alone.

3

The fire that on my bosom preys
    Is lone as some Volcanic Isle,
No torch is kindled at its blaze
      A funeral pile!

4

The hope, the fear, the jealous care
    The exalted portion of the pain
And power of Love I cannot share
      But wear the chain.

5

But 't is not *thus*—and 't is not *here*
    Such thoughts should shake my soul, nor *now*
Where glory decks the hero's bier
      Or binds his brow.

6

The Sword—the Banner—and the Field
    Glory and Greece around us see!
The Spartan borne upon his shield
        Was not more free!

7

Awake! (*not* Greece—She *is* awake!)
    Awake my spirit—think through *whom*
Thy Life blood tracks its parent lake
        And then strike home!

8

Tread those reviving passions down
    Unworthy Manhood;—unto thee
Indifferent should the smile or frown
        Of Beauty be.

9

If thou regret'st thy youth, why *live*?
    The Land of honourable Death
Is here— up to the Field! and give
        Away thy Breath.

10

Seek out—less often sought than found,
    A Soldier's Grave—for thee the best,
Then look around and choose thy ground
        And take thy Rest.
                [Messalonghi. January 22nd 1824]

AESCHYLUS
The Oresteia

JOHN JAMES AUDUBON
The Audubon Reader

AUGUSTINE
The Confessions

BABUR
The Babur Nama

JAMES BALDWIN
The Fire Next Time,
Nobody Knows My Name,
No Name in the Street,
The Devil Finds Work
(in 1 vol.)

SIMONE DE BEAUVOIR
The Second Sex

HECTOR BERLIOZ
The Memoirs of Hector Berlioz

WILLIAM BLAKE
Poems and Prophecies

JAMES BOSWELL
The Life of Samuel Johnson
The Journal of a Tour to
the Hebrides

JEAN ANTHELME
BRILLAT-SAVARIN
The Physiology of Taste

EDMUND BURKE
Reflections on the Revolution in
France and Other Writings

GIACOMO CASANOVA
History of My Life

BENVENUTO CELLINI
The Autobiography of
Benvenuto Cellini

GEOFFREY CHAUCER
Canterbury Tales

G. K. CHESTERTON
The Everyman Chesterton

CARL VON CLAUSEWITZ
On War

S. T. COLERIDGE
Poems

CONFUCIUS
The Analects

THOMAS CRANMER
The Book of Common Prayer
(UK only)

DANTE ALIGHIERI
The Divine Comedy

CHARLES DARWIN
The Origin of Species
The Voyage of the Beagle
(in 1 vol.)

JOHN DONNE
The Complete English Poems

JOHN EVELYN
The Diary of John Evelyn
(UK only)

BENJAMIN FRANKLIN
The Autobiography
and Other Writings

EDWARD GIBBON
The Decline and Fall of the
Roman Empire
Vols 1 to 3: The Western Empire
Vols 4 to 6: The Eastern Empire

KAHLIL GIBRAN
The Collected Works

J. W. VON GOETHE
Selected Works

ROBERT GRAVES
Goodbye to All That

GEORGE HERBERT
The Complete English Works

HERODOTUS
The Histories

HINDU SCRIPTURES
(tr. R. C. Zaehner)

HOMER
The Iliad
The Odyssey

ALEXANDER VON
HUMBOLDT
Selected Writings

SAMUEL JOHNSON
A Journey to the Western
Islands of Scotland

JOHN KEATS
The Poems

SØREN KIERKEGAARD
Fear and Trembling and
The Book on Adler

THE KORAN
(tr. Marmaduke Pickthall)

WILLIAM LANGLAND
Piers Plowman
with (anon.) Sir Gawain and the
Green Knight, Pearl, Sir Orfeo
(UK only)

LAO-TZU
Tao Te Ching

NICCOLÒ MACHIAVELLI
The Prince

NADEZHDA MANDELSTAM
Hope Against Hope

MARCUS AURELIUS
Meditations

ANDREW MARVELL
The Complete Poems

JOHN STUART MILL
On Liberty and Utilitarianism

JOHN MILTON
The Complete English Poems

MARY WORTLEY MONTAGU
Letters

MICHEL DE MONTAIGNE
The Complete Works

THOMAS MORE
Utopia

JOHN MUIR
Selected Writings

VLADIMIR NABOKOV
Speak, Memory

THE NEW TESTAMENT
(King James Version)

THE OLD TESTAMENT
(King James Version)

GEORGE ORWELL
Essays

OVID
The Metamorphoses

THOMAS PAINE
Rights of Man
and Common Sense

SAMUEL PEPYS
The Diary of Samuel Pepys

PLATO
The Republic
Symposium and Phaedrus

MARCO POLO
The Travels of Marco Polo

JEAN-JACQUES
ROUSSEAU
Confessions
The Social Contract and
the Discourses

JOHN RUSKIN
Praeterita and Dilecta

OLIVER SACKS
The Man Who Mistook His
Wife for a Hat

WILLIAM SHAKESPEARE
Comedies Vols 1 and 2
Histories Vols 1 and 2
Romances
Sonnets and Narrative Poems
Tragedies Vols 1 and 2

ADAM SMITH
The Wealth of Nations

SOPHOCLES
The Theban Plays

SUN TZU
The Art of War

TACITUS
Annals and Histories

RABINDRANATH TAGORE
The Best of Tagore

HENRY DAVID THOREAU
Walden

ALEXIS DE TOCQUEVILLE
Democracy in America

MARK TWAIN
Collected Non-fiction (in 2 vols)

GIORGIO VASARI
Lives of the Painters, Sculptors and
Architects (in 2 vols)

VIRGIL
The Aeneid

HORACE WALPOLE
Selected Letters

OSCAR WILDE
Plays, Prose Writings and Poems

MARY WOLLSTONECRAFT
A Vindication of the Rights of
Woman

WILLIAM WORDSWORTH
Selected Poems (UK only)

W. B. YEATS
The Poems (UK only)

This book is set in GARAMOND, the first typeface in
the ambitious programme of matrix production
undertaken by the Monotype Corporation
under the guidance of Stanley Morrison
in 1922. Although named after the
great French royal typographer
Claude Garamond (1499–
1561), it owes much to
Jean Jannon of Sedan
(1580–1658).